Cisco CCIE

Fundamentals: Network Design and Case Studies

Cisco Systems, Inc.

Macmillan Technical Publishing
201 West 103rd Street
Indianapolis, IN 46290 USA

Cisco CCIE Fundamentals: Network Design and Case Studies

© 1998 by Cisco Systems, Inc.

Cisco Press logo is a trademark of Cisco Systems, Inc.

Published by:
Macmillan Technical Publishing
201 West 103rd Street
Indianapolis, IN 46290 USA

Printed in the United States of America 3 4 5 6 7 8 9 0

Library of Congress Cataloging-in-Publication: 98-84211

ISBN: 1-57870-066-3

Warning and Disclaimer

This book is designed to provide information about **Network Design**. Every effort has been made to make this book as complete and as accurate as possible, but no warranty or fitness is implied.

The information is provided on an "as is" basis. The authors, Macmillan Technical Publishing, and Cisco Systems, Inc., shall have neither liability nor responsibility to any person or entity with respect to any loss or damages arising from the information contained in this book or from the use of the discs or programs that may accompany it.

The opinions expressed in this book belong to the author and are not necessarily those of Cisco Systems, Inc.

Associate Publisher	Jim LeValley
Executive Editor	Julie Fairweather
Cisco Systems Program Manager	H. Kim Lew
Managing Editor	Caroline Roop
Acquisitions Editor	Tracy Hughes
Development Editor	Kezia Endsley
Project Editor	Dayna Isley
Team Coordinator	Amy Lewis
Manufacturing Coordinator	Brook Farling
Book Designer	Louisa Klucznik
Cover Designer	Karen Ruggles
Director of Production	Larry Klein
Production Team	Deb Kincaid Nicole Ritch Lisa Stumpf
Indexer	Kevin Fulcher

Trademark
Acknowledgments

Acknowledgments

We would like to thank Kevin Downes, Kris Thompson, Syed Ahmed, and Atif Khan for their invaluable contributions and applied expertise in the technical updates to the design materials herein. This book has been significantly enhanced as a result of their supportive and timely efforts.

About the Authors

Andrea Cheek is currently a documentation manager at an Internet startup company and has worked as a project lead and technical writer for more than twelve years in the telecommunication and networking industries. She worked at Cisco Systems for six years and ROLM systems for five years. She holds a B.A. in English Literature from Stanford University.

H. Kim Lew is a program manager for Cisco Press. He has worked as a writer, course developer, marketing manager, and editorial columnist in the internetworking industry for more than a decade. Since 1990, he has worked at Cisco Systems in various program management, management, and information product development roles. He now telecommutes full-time from Redmond, Washington.

Kathleen Wallace is co-founder of Wallace Technical Communications, an Internet service provider (ISP) serving the small businesses and home office professionals in the San Francisco Bay Area. She has worked as a programmer, staff technical writer, and contract writer for a variety of computing and networking firms, including Apple Computer Inc., Cisco Systems, and National Semiconductor Corporation.

About the Reviewers

Kevin Downes is a Senior Network Systems Consultant with International Network Services (INS). His network certifications include the Cisco CCIE, Bay Networks CRS, Certified Network Expert (CNX) Ethernet, Novell CNE, and Banyan Systems CBE. He has published several articles on the subjects of network infrastructure design, network operating systems (NOS), and Internet Protocol (IP). He completed his B.S. in Computer Information Systems from Strayer University in 1993.

Syed P. Ahmed is a Senior Internetworking Consultant at Cisco Systems, Inc. He has been with Cisco for three years. Prior to Cisco, Mr. Ahmed worked at IBM for eight years as an IBM 3745/NCP Software Developer and VTAM/NCP System Engineer. Prior to IBM, Mr. Ahmed worked at Northern Telecom for eight years as a Senior Product Engineer in DMS 100/200 Switching products and DPN100 Data products. Mr. Ahmed holds a M.Sc. (high honor) from N.C. State in Computer Engineering and a B.Sc. (highest honor) from North Eastern University in Electrical Engineering. He has been a professional engineer since 1979 and a CCIE (Cisco Certified Internetwork Engineer) since 1995. He is a regular contributor to *CCIE Forum* and CCIE/NETWORKERS Seminars at Cisco Systems.

Kris Thompson was raised in Kingston, Ontario where he attended Queen's University Faculty of Applied Science - Electrical Engineering 1988. Ontario P. Eng. 1990. Kris has experience with GM, Bell Canada, NorTel, and Apple and is currently at Cisco Systems, Inc. with Global Support Engineering where he specializes in remote access technologies. Kris is living as a telecommuter on Lake Travis outside Austin, Texas in his new Rammed Earth house. Thanks to my wife Cindy Kosarek.

Contents at a Glance

Table of Contents

Foreword

In today's internetworking environment, protocols and services are being added constantly, making it more and more complex to design and implement large-scale networks. The demands for organizations and individuals to maintain and optimally run these networks requires internetworking expertise.

The Cisco Certified Internetwork Expert (CCIE) program has been in the forefront in providing the expertise for the design and implementation of large-scale networks. The basic criteria to design and implement a large-scale network is to have an in-depth knowledge of internetworking protocols and services transported.

Cisco CCIE Fundamentals: Network Design and Case Studies is an excellent CCIE preparation tool that covers in-depth analysis of IP, IBM, IPX, and ISDN protocols. An understanding of all these protocols is required to pass the CCIE exam. The best part about this handbook is that it covers issues such as convergence, route selection, topologies, and design issues. The case studies take these concepts a step further by providing configuration examples.

Please check the CCIE Web page on www.cisco.com for future Cisco Press books.

Imran Qureshi
CCIE Program Manager
Cisco Systems, Inc.

Preface and Acknowledgments

ABOUT THIS BOOK

This publication is directly derived from two existing publications created by Cisco Systems: *Internetwork Design Guide* and *Internetworking Case Studies*. These publications evolved over the course of several years to provide a comprehensive collection of configuration scenarios and design recommendations tailored to the needs of the experienced internetworking specialist. Cisco Press has combined these publications to provide a primer covering many of the technologies and typical implementations encountered by professionals preparing for Cisco Certified Internetwork Expert (CCIE) candidacy.

Although the material provided in this publication was not developed with the *specific* intent of helping professionals achieve CCIE status, it has been used as a foundation guide by many CCIE candidates. It is the first in a series of publications that Cisco Press intends to deliver to prepare IS professionals who are working toward CCIE program completion.

The following discussion provides an author acknowledgment, summarizes the overall objectives, audience, organization, and conventions of *Cisco CCIE Fundamentals: Network Design and Case Studies*, outlines the CCIE program, and introduces plan for Cisco Press support of the CCIE program.

AUTHOR ACKNOWLEDGMENTS

The original Cisco publications *Internetwork Design Guide* and *Internetworking Case Studies* were developed over a period of several years by Andrea Cheek, H. Kim Lew, and Kathleen Wallace. Paula Delay, Donna Kidder, and Diantha Pinner integrated new material into the *Internetwork Design Guide* in the most recent update. An array of subject matter experts and editors contributed to the development of the two source publications during their parallel evolution toward this combined product. Contributors included Rick Fairweather, Bill Kelly, Bill Miskovetz, Morgan Littlewood, Jeff Baher, Jim Grubb, Terri Quinn-Andry, Steve Spanier, Bob Deutsch,

Paulina Knibbe, Adrien Fournier, Kris Thompson, Stuart Hamilton, Phil Byrnes, Bruce Pinsky, Won Lee, George Murickan, Dianna Johansen, and Betsy Fitch. This material was originally assembled to help Cisco network implementers build scalable, reliable, and secure networks. It is with this same intent that Cisco Press brings the combined publication *Cisco CCIE Fundamentals: Network Design and Case Studies* to the general networking community.

DOCUMENT OBJECTIVES

The objective of this publication is to help you identify and implement practical internetworking strategies that are flexible enough to fit a variety of situations and that can also scale as your network requirements change.

Part I, "Internetwork Design," provides a set of general guidelines for planning internetworks and specific suggestions for several key internetworking implementations. Part I focuses on identifying the essential technologies and appropriate implementations for specific environments.

Part II, "Internetworking Case Studies," provides practical examples illustrating how you can implement Cisco Systems software features. Case studies address implementation concerns and show how to apply features. Detailed configuration file examples and network diagrams are included.

This collection of design tips and configuration examples is by no means the final word in internetwork design. Do not try to use this as a step-by-step handbook for designing every facet of your internetwork. Instead, use this publication to help you identify features and capabilities of routers and switches that meet specific internetworking requirements.

AUDIENCE

The design guide portion of this publication is intended to support the network administrator who designs and implements router- or switched-based internetworks. The case study portion of the publication is designed for a similar audience, but focuses on showing practical examples of how to apply Cisco features to meet internetworking needs. Readers should know how to configure a Cisco router and should be familiar with the protocols and media that their routers have been configured to support.

DOCUMENT ORGANIZATION

This document consists of two distinct "parts" and a series of appendixes. Each of these parts and the associated set of appendixes are outlined in the follow descriptions.

Part I: Internetwork Design

Part I, "Internetwork Design," consists of the following 13 chapters, focusing primarily on design strategies and recommendations:

- Chapter 1, "Introduction," provides an overview of the trends and challenges that network designers face today when designing internetworks.

- Chapter 2, "Internetworking Design Basics," provides introductory material that outlines the key issues in designing effective large-scale internetworks, contrasts switching and routing, and describes the three key service layers associated with internetworks: access, distribution, and backbone. The chapter also provides a general mapping of feature capabilities into this hierarchical approach to internetwork design along with a brief overview of the different types of internetworking devices.

- Chapter 3, "Designing Large-Scale IP Internetworks," focuses on routing protocols for large-scale IP internetworks and describes the characteristics of two routing protocols: Enhanced IGRP and Open Shortest Path First (OSPF).

- Chapter 4, "Designing SRB Internetworks," describes the issues that pertain to designing internetworks that use source-route bridging and remote source-route bridging.

- Chapter 5, "Designing SDLC, SDLLC, and QLLC Internetworks," provides information about designing internetworks that use routers in IBM front-end processor (FEP) environments.

- Chapter 6, "Designing APPN Internetworks," describes the issues that pertain to designing internetworks that use APPN.

- Chapter 7, "Designing DLSw+ Internetworks," provides information about designing internetworks that use Data Link Switching Plus (DLSw+).

- Chapter 8, "Designing ATM Internetworks," focuses on the use of Asynchronous Transfer Mode (ATM) technology and LAN Emulation (LANE) in designing WANs.

- Chapter 9, "Designing Packet Service Internetworks," focuses on Frame Relay to describe the implementation of packet-switching services in terms of hierarchical network design, topology, broadcast issues, and performance.

- Chapter 10, "Designing DDR Internetworks," describes the design of dial-on-demand routing (DDR) internetworks. DDR provides connectivity across Public Switched Telephone networks and works with access lists to determine the kinds of packets that initiate a connection.

- Chapter 11, "Designing ISDN Internetworks," describes issues that pertain to designing internetworks that use Integrated Services Digital Network (ISDN) technology. The chapter includes techniques for maximizing performance and minimizing connection costs.

- Chapter 12, "Designing Switched LAN Internetworks," focuses on the operation of LAN switches and compares them with routers. The chapter provides vital information on stability and the use of routers and virtual LANs (VLANs) in switched LAN internetwork designs.

- Chapter 13, "Designing Internetworks for Multimedia," describes the evolution of video and audio capture and compression standards and how these standards affect the way that multimedia applications run in networks today. This chapter shows the transition of a traditional LAN design (capable of handling modest multimedia applications) to switched LAN designs capable of handling bandwidth-intensive multimedia applications.

Part II: Internetworking Case Studies

Part II, "Internetworking Case Studies," consists of 12 chapters, focusing on configuration examples:

- Chapter 14, "RIP and OSPF Redistribution," addresses the issue of integrating Routing Information Protocol (RIP) networks with Open Shortest Path First (OSPF) networks.

- Chapter 15, "Dial-on-Demand Routing," describes Cisco's dial-on-demand (DDR) routing features, which allow you to form wide-area networks (WANs) over existing telephone lines.

- Chapter 16, "Increasing Security on IP Networks," describes Cisco's approach to network security and tells you how to use features of the Cisco IOS software to increase security in Internet Protocol (IP) networks.

- Chapter 17, "Integrating Enhanced IGRP into Existing Networks," describes the use of Enhanced IGRP with three network level protocols: IP, AppleTalk, and Internetwork Packet Exchange (IPX).

- Chapter 18, "Reducing SAP Traffic in Novell IPX Networks," tells you how to use access lists and incremental SAP updates to reduce congestion caused by Service Advertisement Protocol (SAP) updates.

- Chapter 19, "UDP Broadcast Flooding," describes techniques for using directed and flooded UDP broadcasts to deliver incoming data from a few sources to a large number of users in a network that is designed for redundancy.

- Chapter 20, "STUN for Front-End Processors," provides information about configuring serial tunneling (STUN) in traditional Systems Network Architecture (SNA) networks.

- Chapter 21, "Using ISDN Effectively in Multiprotocol Networks," describes the relationship between DDR and ISDN and presents a variety of techniques that can be used to control unnecessary connections in ISDN environments.

- Chapter 22, "Using HSRP for Fault-Tolerant IP Routing," tells you how to use the Hot Standby Routing Protocol (HSRP) to configure a router to assume the IP routing tasks of another router in the event that the other router becomes unavailable.

- Chapter 23, "LAN Switching," describes switching and describes how virtual LANs can be used to control congestion in switched LAN networks.

- Chapter 24, "Multicasting in IP and AppleTalk Networks," provides information about how to configure routers to support multicasting multimedia applications in IP and AppleTalk networks.

- Chapter 25, "Scaling Dial-on-Demand Routing," describes a large asynchronous dial-up network and tells you how to configure it for IP routing.

Appendixes

Cisco CCIE Fundamentals: Network Design and Case Studies concludes with a series of appendixes that support the primary text:

- Appendix A, "Subnetting an IP Address Space," provides a detailed example of subnetting a Class B network.

- Appendix B, "IBM Serial Link Implementation Notes," clarifies some common misconceptions about half-duplex, full-duplex, and multipoint connections.

- Appendix C, "SNA Host Configuration for SRB Networks," describes the configuration of IBM devices, such as FEPs, VTAM-switched major nodes and 3174 cluster controllers, and provides information about configuration values that optimize the device's connection to a router.

- Appendix D, "SNA Host Configuration for SDLC Networks," provides configuration information about FEPs and 3174 cluster controllers in routed SDLC environments.

- Appendix E, "Broadcasts in Switched LANs," presents the results of testing the effect of broadcasts on UNIX, PC, and Macintosh hosts running IP, IPX, and AppleTalk in a flat network topology.

- Appendix F, "References and Recommended Reading," lists books, periodicals, technical publications, and standards that provide additional information that will help you design efficient internetworks.

DOCUMENT CONVENTIONS

This publication uses a number of conventions. Command descriptions use these conventions:

- Examples that contain system prompts denote interactive sessions, indicating that the user enters commands at the prompt. The system prompt indicates the current command mode. For example, the prompt `router(config)#` indicates global configuration mode.

- Commands and keywords are in **boldface** font.

- Arguments for which you supply values are in *italic* font.

- Elements in square brackets ([ ]) are optional.

- Alternative but required keywords are grouped in braces ({ }) and separated by vertical bars (|).

Examples use these conventions:

- Terminal sessions and information the system displays are in `screen` font.

- Modified configurations show new commands in **`boldface`** `screen` font.

- Nonprinting characters, such as passwords, are in angle brackets (< >).

- Default responses to system prompts are in square brackets ([ ]).

- Exclamation points (!) at the beginning of a line indicate a comment line.

CCIE PROGRAM AND CISCO PRESS

Cisco's efforts to facilitate the creation of competent network operations center (NOC) and information systems (IS) staff is exemplified in its Cisco Certified Internetwork Expert (CCIE) program. To support these efforts, Cisco Press is working closely with CCIE program management to create information products that help build the knowledge and expertise of NOC and IS professionals supporting Cisco-based networks. As of this writing, there are three CCIE program certifications:

- CCIE WAN Switching
- CCIE-ISP
- CCIE-Routing and Switching

It is likely that as the networking landscape evolves, the program will evolve to meet the changing needs of networking professionals. It is the intent of Cisco Press to coordinate its efforts to synchronize with changes in the CCIE program. The brief discussions that follow provide an overview of the CCIE program and lab tests and a summary of plans for additional products from Cisco Press that are intended to support CCIE programs.

You can obtain details about the CCIE program directly from Cisco's World Wide Web presence at www.cisco.com.

CCIE Program Description

In becoming the definitive network certification program for Cisco network professionals, the CCIE program provides:

- A definition of "expert-level" technical knowledge and skill
- State-of-the-art methods to evaluate this knowledge and skill
- Enhanced services targeting the needs of these "best in class" engineers

Achieving CCIE status denotes proficiency in supporting diverse internetworks that use routing, bridging, and switching technologies. By passing Cisco's rigorous assessment process, your organization or customers will know that you have passed strict testing and hands-on skill evaluations.

The Cisco Certified Internetwork Expert program certifies individuals, not companies. If you move to another company, your status remains with you as long as you adhere to the program requirements and maintain your certification.

CCIE Certification Laboratory

Internetworking experts agree that written evaluations alone cannot adequately measure an individual's ability to design, implement, or solve problems in a dynamic internetwork.

Proper evaluation of these skills must include hands-on execution that is observed and quantified by an internetworking expert. Cisco has taken this concept to heart by creating the CCIE Certification Lab. Candidates are required to demonstrate competency by:

- Building, configuring, and testing complex internets to provided specifications
- Diagnosing and resolving media, transport, and session problems
- Isolating application-layer problems
- Using packet/frame analysis and Cisco debugging tools
- Documenting and reporting the problem-solving processes used

Candidates are evaluated individually by a senior CCIE internetworking engineer, acting as the lab administrator. Cisco's intent is to make the CCIE Certification Lab as realistic as possible. The lab assessment is currently two full days in length and includes homework.

The CCIE candidate is presented with a complex design to implement from the physical layer, through logical configuration. Candidates are not required to configure any end-user systems, but are responsible for any device residing in the internetwork, including hubs, MAUs, DSU/CSU, and so on. Network specifics, point values, and testing criteria used to assess correctness of the individual configurations are provided.

Upon completion of the implementation, the lab engineer will insert faults in the candidate's internetwork. The candidate must recognize, isolate, document, and resolve each fault. Additionally, the candidate will be required to outline the proper reporting procedures when dealing with the Cisco TAC.

Each configuration scenario and problem has pre-assigned point values. The candidate will strive to gain a minimum aggregate of 80 percent to pass.

Cisco Press CCIE Series

In close coordination with the Cisco CCIE program team, Cisco Press is creating a series of preparation materials aimed at providing up-to-date, accurate information on technologies addressed in the CCIE program. Two basic sets of materials will be developed for distribution via Cisco Press:

- **CCIE Preparation Publication Series**

  Based on CCIE program guidelines from Cisco. This series will be presented as a set of technology-specific volumes.

- **Cisco Certification Courseware Series**

  Based on the Cisco-developed *Introduction to Cisco Router Configuration* (ICRC), *Advanced Cisco Router Configuration* (ACRC), and other key implementation-oriented courses, this series will present course material provided in recommended Cisco-developed, instructor-led classes.

DISCLAIMER

Cisco Systems and Macmillan Computer Publishing make no claims that individual readers will pass any part of CCIE Qualification (Sylvan) tests or CCIE labs. Material presented in Cisco Press publications is not intended to be construed as a replacement for either recommended in-class training or the recommended two years of internetworking field experience. All material is offered as is. Cisco Systems and Macmillan Computer Publishing make no claims as to the effectiveness of information presented.

PART I

Internetwork Design

CHAPTER 1

Introduction

Internetworking—the communication between two or more networks—encompasses every aspect of connecting computers together. Internetworks have grown to support vastly disparate end-system communication requirements. An internetwork requires many protocols and features to permit scalability and manageability without constant manual intervention. Large internetworks can consist of the following three distinct components:

- Campus networks, which consist of locally connected users in a building or group of buildings
- Wide-area networks (WANs), which connect campuses together
- Remote connections, which link branch offices and single users (mobile users and/or tele-commuters) to a local campus or the Internet

Figure 1–1 provides an example of a typical enterprise internetwork.

Figure 1–1

Example of a typical enterprise internetwork.

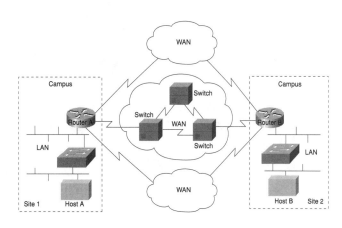

3

Designing an internetwork can be a challenging task. To design reliable, scalable internetworks, network designers must realize that each of the three major components of an internetwork have distinct design requirements. An internetwork that consists of only 50 meshed routing nodes can pose complex problems that lead to unpredictable results. Attempting to optimize internetworks that feature thousands of nodes can pose even more complex problems.

Despite improvements in equipment performance and media capabilities, internetwork design is becoming more difficult. The trend is toward increasingly complex environments involving multiple media, multiple protocols, and interconnection to networks outside any single organization's dominion of control. Carefully designing internetworks can reduce the hardships associated with growth as a networking environment evolves.

This chapter provides an overview of the technologies available today to design internetworks. Discussions are divided into the following general topics:

- Designing Campus Networks
- Designing WANs
- Utilizing Remote Connection Design
- Providing Integrated Solutions
- Determining Your Internetworking Requirements

DESIGNING CAMPUS NETWORKS

A *campus* is a building or group of buildings all connected into one enterprise network that consists of many local area networks (LANs). A campus is generally a portion of a company (or the whole company) constrained to a fixed geographic area, as shown in Figure 1–2.

Figure 1–2

Example of a campus network.

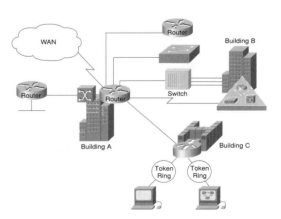

The distinct characteristic of a campus environment is that the company that owns the campus network usually owns the physical wires deployed in the campus. The campus network topology is primarily LAN technology connecting all the end systems within the building. Campus networks generally use LAN technologies, such as Ethernet, Token Ring, Fiber Distributed Data Interface (FDDI), Fast Ethernet, Gigabit Ethernet, and Asynchronous Transfer Mode (ATM).

A large campus with groups of buildings can also use WAN technology to connect the buildings. Although the wiring and protocols of a campus might be based on WAN technology, they do not share the WAN constraint of the high cost of bandwidth. After the wire is installed, bandwidth is inexpensive because the company owns the wires and there is no recurring cost to a service provider. However, upgrading the physical wiring can be expensive.

Consequently, network designers generally deploy a campus design that is optimized for the fastest functional architecture that runs on existing physical wire. They might also upgrade wiring to meet the requirements of emerging applications. For example, higher-speed technologies, such as Fast Ethernet, Gigabit Ethernet, and ATM as a backbone architecture, and Layer 2 switching provide dedicated bandwidth to the desktop.

Trends in Campus Design

In the past, network designers had only a limited number of hardware options—routers or hubs—when purchasing a technology for their campus networks. Consequently, it was rare to make a hardware design mistake. Hubs were for wiring closets and routers were for the data center or main telecommunications operations.

Recently, local-area networking has been revolutionized by the exploding use of LAN switching at Layer 2 (the data link layer) to increase performance and to provide more bandwidth to meet new data networking applications. LAN switches provide this performance benefit by increasing bandwidth and throughput for workgroups and local servers. Network designers are deploying LAN switches out toward the network's edge in wiring closets. As Figure 1–3 shows, these switches are usually installed to replace shared concentrator hubs and give higher bandwidth connections to the end user.

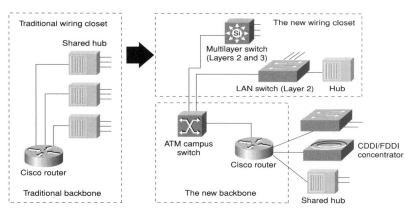

Figure 1–3
Example of trends in campus design.

Layer 3 networking is required in the network to interconnect the switched workgroups and to provide services that include security, quality of service (QoS), and traffic management. Routing integrates these switched networks, and provides the security, stability, and control needed to build functional and scalable networks.

Traditionally, Layer 2 switching has been provided by LAN switches, and Layer 3 networking has been provided by routers. Increasingly, these two networking functions are being integrated into common platforms. For example, multilayer switches that provide Layer 2 and 3 functionality are now appearing in the marketplace.

With the advent of such technologies as Layer 3 switching, LAN switching, and virtual LANs (VLANs), building campus networks is becoming more complex than in the past. Table 1–1 summarizes the various LAN technologies that are required to build successful campus networks. Cisco Systems offers product solutions in all of these technologies.

Table 1–1   *Summary of LAN Technologies*

LAN Technology	Typical Uses
Routing technologies	Routing is a key technology for connecting LANs in a campus network. It can be either Layer 3 switching or more traditional routing with Layer 3 switching and additional router features.
Gigabit Ethernet	Gigabit Ethernet builds on top of the Ethernet protocol, but increases speed ten-fold over Fast Ethernet to 1000 Mbps, or 1 Gbps. Gigabit Ethernet provides high bandwidth capacity for backbone designs while providing backward compatibility for installed media.
LAN switching technologies • Ethernet switching • Token Ring switching	Ethernet switching provides Layer 2 switching, and offers dedicated Ethernet segments for each connection. This is the base fabric of the network. Token Ring switching offers the same functionality as Ethernet switching, but uses Token Ring technology. You can use a Token Ring switch as either a transparent bridge or as a source-route bridge.
ATM switching technologies	ATM switching offers high-speed switching technology for voice, video, and data. Its operation is similar to LAN switching technologies for data operations. ATM, however, offers high bandwidth capacity.

Network designers are now designing campus networks by purchasing separate equipment types (for example, routers, Ethernet switches, and ATM switches) and then linking them together. Although individual purchase decisions might seem harmless, network designers must not forget that the entire network forms an internetwork.

It is possible to separate these technologies and build thoughtful designs using each new technology, but network designers must consider the overall integration of the network. If this overall integration is not considered, the result can be networks that have a much higher risk of network outages, downtime, and congestion than ever before.

DESIGNING WANs

WAN communication occurs between geographically separated areas. In enterprise internetworks, WANs connect campuses together. When a local end station wants to communicate with a remote end station (an end station located at a different site), information must be sent over one or more WAN links. Routers within enterprise internetworks represent the LAN/WAN junction points of an internetwork. These routers determine the most appropriate path through the internetwork for the required data streams.

WAN links are connected by switches, which are devices that relay information through the WAN and dictate the service provided by the WAN. WAN communication is often called a *service* because the network provider often charges users for the services provided by the WAN (called *tariffs*). WAN services are provided through the following three primary switching technologies:

- Circuit switching
- Packet switching
- Cell switching

Each switching technique has advantages and disadvantages. For example, *circuit-switched* networks offer users dedicated bandwidth that cannot be infringed upon by other users. In contrast, *packet-switched* networks have traditionally offered more flexibility and used network bandwidth more efficiently than circuit-switched networks. *Cell switching*, however, combines some aspects of circuit and packet switching to produce networks with low latency and high throughput. Cell switching is rapidly gaining in popularity. ATM is currently the most prominent cell-switched technology. For more information on switching technology for WANs and LANs, see Chapter 2, "Internetworking Design Basics."

Trends in WAN Design

Traditionally, WAN communication has been characterized by relatively low throughput, high delay, and high error rates. WAN connections are mostly characterized by the cost of renting media (wire) from a service provider to connect two or more campuses together. Because the WAN infrastructure is often rented from a service provider, WAN network designs must optimize the cost of bandwidth and bandwidth efficiency. For example, all technologies and features used to connect campuses over a WAN are developed to meet the following design requirements:

- Optimize WAN bandwidth
- Minimize the tariff cost
- Maximize the effective service to the end users

Recently, traditional shared-media networks are being overtaxed because of the following new network requirements:

- Necessity to connect to remote sites
- Growing need for users to have remote access to their networks
- Explosive growth of the corporate intranets
- Increased use of enterprise servers

Network designers are turning to WAN technology to support these new requirements. WAN connections generally handle mission-critical information, and are optimized for price/performance bandwidth. The routers connecting the campuses, for example, generally apply traffic optimization, multiple paths for redundancy, dial backup for disaster recovery, and QoS for critical applications.

Table 1–2 summarizes the various WAN technologies that support such large-scale internetwork requirements.

Table 1–2   *Summary of WAN Technologies*

WAN Technology	Typical Uses
Asymmetric Digital Subscriber Line	A new modem technology. Converts existing twisted-pair telephone lines into access paths for multimedia and high-speed data communica- tions. ADSL transmits more than 6 Mbps to a subscriber, and as much as 640 kbps more in both directions.
Analog modem	Analog modems can be used by telecommuters and mobile users who access the network less than two hours per day, or for backup for another type of link.
Leased line	Leased lines can be used for Point-to-Point Protocol (PPP) networks and hub-and-spoke topologies, or for backup for another type of link.
Integrated Services Digital Network (ISDN)	ISDN can be used for cost-effective remote access to corporate networks. It provides support for voice and video as well as a backup for another type of link.

Table 1–2 *Summary of WAN Technologies, Continued*

Frame Relay	Frame Relay provides a cost-effective, high- speed, low-latency mesh topology between remote sites. It can be used in both private and carrier-provided networks.
Switched Multimegabit Data Service (SMDS)	SMDS provides high-speed, high-performance connections across public data networks. It can also be deployed in metropolitan-area networks (MANs).
X.25	X.25 can provide a reliable WAN circuit or backbone. It also provides support for legacy applications.
WAN ATM	WAN ATM can be used to accelerate bandwidth requirements. It also provides support for multiple QoS classes for differing application requirements for delay and loss.

UTILIZING REMOTE CONNECTION DESIGN

Remote connections link single users (mobile users and/or telecommuters) and branch offices to a local campus or the Internet. Typically, a remote site is a small site that has few users and therefore needs a smaller size WAN connection. The remote requirements of an internetwork, however, usually involve a large number of remote single users or sites, which causes the aggregate WAN charge to be exaggerated.

Because there are so many remote single users or sites, the aggregate WAN bandwidth cost is proportionally more important in remote connections than in WAN connections. Given that the three-year cost of a network is nonequipment expenses, the WAN media rental charge from a service provider is the largest cost component of a remote network. Unlike WAN connections, smaller sites or single users seldom need to connect 24 hours a day.

Consequently, network designers typically choose between dial-up and dedicated WAN options for remote connections. Remote connections generally run at speeds of 128 Kbps or lower. A network designer might also employ bridges in a remote site for their ease of implementation, simple topology, and low traffic requirements.

Trends in Remote Connections

Today, there is a large selection of remote WAN media that include the following:

- Analog modem
- Asymmetric Digital Subscriber Line
- Leased line

- Frame Relay
- X.25
- ISDN

Remote connections also optimize for the appropriate WAN option to provide cost-effective bandwidth, minimize dial-up tariff costs, and maximize effective service to users.

Trends in LAN/WAN Integration

Today, 90 percent of computing power resides on desktops, and that power is growing exponentially. Distributed applications are increasingly bandwidth hungry, and the emergence of the Internet is driving many LAN architectures to the limit. Voice communications have increased significantly with more reliance on centralized voice mail systems for verbal communications. The internetwork is the critical tool for information flow. Internetworks are being pressured to cost less, yet support the emerging applications and higher number of users with increased performance.

To date, local- and wide-area communications have remained logically separate. In the LAN, bandwidth is free and connectivity is limited only by hardware and implementation costs. The LAN has carried data only. In the WAN, bandwidth has been the overriding cost, and such delay-sensitive traffic as voice has remained separate from data. New applications and the economics of supporting them, however, are forcing these conventions to change.

The Internet is the first source of multimedia to the desktop, and immediately breaks the rules. Such Internet applications as voice and real-time video require better, more predictable LAN and WAN performance. These multimedia applications are fast becoming an essential part of the business productivity toolkit. As companies begin to consider implementing new intranet-based, bandwidth-intensive multimedia applications—such as video training, videoconferencing, and voice over IP—the impact of these applications on the existing networking infrastructure is a serious concern. If a company has relied on its corporate network for business-critical SNA traffic, for example, and wants to bring a new video training application on line, the network must be able to provide guaranteed quality of service (QoS) that delivers the multimedia traffic, but does not allow it to interfere with the business-critical traffic. ATM has emerged as one of the technologies for integrating LANs and WANs. The Quality of Service (QoS) features of ATM can support any traffic type in separate or mixed streams, delay sensitive traffic, and nondelay-sensitive traffic, as shown in Figure 1–4.

ATM can also scale from low to high speeds. It has been adopted by all the industry's equipment vendors, from LAN to private branch exchange (PBX).

PROVIDING INTEGRATED SOLUTIONS

The trend in internetworking is to provide network designers greater flexibility in solving multiple internetworking problems without creating multiple networks or writing off existing data communication investments. Routers might be relied upon to provide a reliable, secure network and act as a barrier against inadvertent broadcast storms in the local networks. Switches, which can be divided into two main categories—LAN switches and WAN switches—can be deployed at the workgroup, campus backbone, or WAN level. Remote sites might use low-end routers for connection to the WAN.

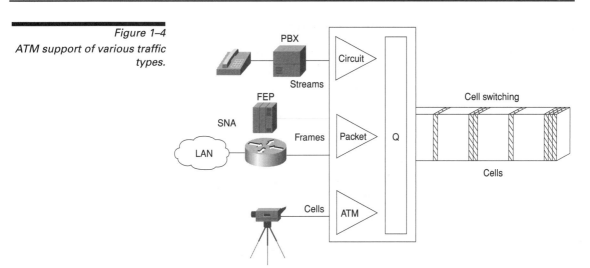

Figure 1–4
ATM support of various traffic types.

Underlying and integrating all Cisco products is the Cisco Internetworking Operating System (Cisco IOS) software. The Cisco IOS software enables disparate groups, diverse devices, and multiple protocols all to be integrated into a highly reliable and scalable network. Cisco IOS software also supports this internetwork with advanced security, quality of service, and traffic services.

DETERMINING YOUR INTERNETWORKING REQUIREMENTS

Designing an internetwork can be a challenging task. Your first step is to understand your internetworking requirements. The rest of this chapter is intended as a guide for helping you determine these requirements. After you have identified these requirements, refer to Chapter 2 for information on selecting internetwork capability and reliability options that meet these requirements.

Internetworking devices must reflect the goals, characteristics, and policies of the organizations in which they operate. Two primary goals drive internetworking design and implementation:

- *Application availability*—Networks carry application information between computers. If the applications are not available to network users, the network is not doing its job.

- *Cost of ownership*—Information system (IS) budgets today often run in the millions of dollars. As large organizations increasingly rely on electronic data for managing business activities, the associated costs of computing resources will continue to rise.

A well-designed internetwork can help to balance these objectives. When properly implemented, the network infrastructure can optimize application availability and allow the cost-effective use of existing network resources.

The Design Problem: Optimizing Availability and Cost

In general, the network design problem consists of the following three general elements:

- *Environmental givens*—Environmental givens include the location of hosts, servers, terminals, and other end nodes; the projected traffic for the environment; and the projected costs for delivering different service levels.

- *Performance constraints*—Performance constraints consist of network reliability, traffic throughput, and host/client computer speeds (for example, network interface cards and hard drive access speeds).

- *Internetworking variables*—Internetworking variables include the network topology, line capacities, and packet flow assignments.

The goal is to minimize cost based on these elements while delivering service that does not compromise established availability requirements. You face two primary concerns: availability and cost. These issues are essentially at odds. Any increase in availability must generally be reflected as an increase in cost. As a result, you must weigh the relative importance of resource availability and overall cost carefully.

As Figure 1–5 shows, designing your network is an iterative activity. The discussions that follow outline several areas that you should carefully consider when planning your internetworking implementation.

Figure 1–5
General network design process.

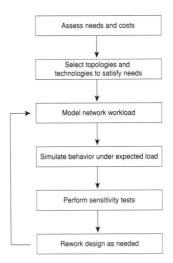

Assessing User Requirements

In general, users primarily want application availability in their networks. The chief components of application availability are *response time*, *throughput*, and *reliability*:

- Response time is the time between entry of a command or keystroke and the host system's execution of the command or delivery of a response. User satisfaction about response time is generally considered to be a *monotonic* function up to some limit, at which point user satisfaction falls off to nearly zero. Applications in which fast response time is considered critical include interactive online services, such as automated tellers and point-of-sale machines.

- Applications that put high-volume traffic onto the network have more effect on throughput than end-to-end connections. Throughput-intensive applications generally involve file-transfer activities. However, throughput-intensive applications also usually have low response-time requirements. Indeed, they can often be scheduled at times when response-time-sensitive traffic is low (for example, after normal work hours).

- Although reliability is always important, some applications have genuine requirements that exceed typical needs. Organizations that require nearly 100 percent up time conduct all activities online or over the telephone. Financial services, securities exchanges, and emergency/police/military operations are a few examples. These situations imply a requirement for a high level of hardware and topological redundancy. Determining the cost of any downtime is essential in determining the relative importance of reliability to your internetwork.

You can assess user requirements in a number of ways. The more involved your users are in the process, the more likely that your evaluation will be accurate. In general, you can use the following methods to obtain this information:

- *User community profiles*—Outline what different user groups require. This is the first step in determining internetwork requirements. Although many users have roughly the same requirements of an electronic mail system, engineering groups using XWindows terminals and Sun workstations in an NFS environment have different needs from PC users sharing print servers in a finance department.

- *Interviews, focus groups, and surveys*—Build a baseline for implementing an internetwork. Understand that some groups might require access to common servers. Others might want to allow external access to specific internal computing resources. Certain organizations might require IS support systems to be managed in a particular way according to some external standard. The least formal method of obtaining information is to conduct interviews with key user groups. Focus groups can also be used to gather information and generate discussion among different organizations with similar (or dissimilar) interests. Finally, formal surveys can be used to get a statistically valid reading of user sentiment regarding a particular service level or proposed internetworking architecture.

- *Human factors tests*—The most expensive, time-consuming, and possibly revealing method is to conduct a test involving representative users in a lab environment. This is most applicable when evaluating response time requirements. As an example, you might set up working systems and have users perform normal remote host activities from the lab network. By evaluating user reactions to variations in host responsiveness, you can create benchmark thresholds for acceptable performance.

Assessing Proprietary and Nonproprietary Solutions

Compatibility, conformance, and interoperability are related to the problem of balancing proprietary functionality and open internetworking flexibility. As a network designer, you might be forced to choose between implementing a multivendor environment and implementing a specific, proprietary capability. For example, the *Interior Gateway Routing Protocol* (IGRP) provides many useful capabilities, such as a number of features that are designed to enhance its stability. These include *hold-downs*, *split horizons*, and *poison reverse updates*.

The negative side is that IGRP is a proprietary routing protocol. In contrast, the integrated *Intermediate System-to Intermediate System* (IS-IS) protocol is an open internetworking alternative that also provides a fast converging routing environment; however, implementing an open routing protocol can potentially result in greater multiple-vendor configuration complexity.

The decisions that you make have far-ranging effects on your overall internetwork design. Assume that you decide to implement integrated IS-IS instead of IGRP. In doing this, you gain a measure of interoperability; however, you lose some functionality. For instance, you cannot load balance traffic over unequal parallel paths. Similarly, some modems provide a high level of proprietary diagnostic capabilities, but require that all modems throughout a network be of the same vendor type to fully exploit proprietary diagnostics.

Previous internetworking (and networking) investments and expectations for future requirements have considerable influence over your choice of implementations. You need to consider installed internetworking and networking equipment; applications running (or to be run) on the network; traffic patterns; physical location of sites, hosts, and users; rate of growth of the user community; and both physical and logical network layout.

Assessing Costs

The internetwork is a strategic element in your overall information system design. As such, the cost of your internetwork is much more than the sum of your equipment purchase orders. View it as a total cost-of-ownership issue. You must consider the entire life cycle of your internetworking environment. A brief list of costs associated with internetworks follows:

- *Equipment hardware and software costs*—Consider what is really being bought when you purchase your systems; costs should include initial purchase and installation, maintenance, and projected upgrade costs.

- *Performance tradeoff costs*—Consider the cost of going from a five-second response time to a half-second response time. Such improvements can cost quite a bit in terms of media selection, network interfaces, internetworking nodes, modems, and WAN services.

- *Installation costs*—Installing a site's physical cable plant can be the most expensive element of a large network. The costs include installation labor, site modification, fees associated with local code conformance, and costs incurred to ensure compliance with environmental restrictions (such as asbestos removal). Other important elements in keeping your costs to a minimum will include developing a well-planned wiring closet layout and implementing color code conventions for cable runs.

- *Expansion costs*—Calculate the cost of ripping out all thick Ethernet, adding additional functionality, or moving to a new location. Projecting your future requirements and accounting for future needs saves time and money.

- *Support costs*—Complicated internetworks cost more to monitor, configure, and maintain. Your internetwork should be no more complicated than necessary. Costs include training, direct labor (network managers and administrators), sparing, and replacement costs. Additional cost that should be included is out-of-band management, SNMP management stations, and power.

- *Cost of downtime*—Evaluate the cost for every minute that a user is unable to access a file server or a centralized database. If this cost is high, you must attribute a high cost to downtime. If the cost is high enough, fully redundant internetworks might be your best option.

- *Opportunity costs*—Every choice you make has an opposing alternative option. Whether that option is a specific hardware platform, topology solution, level of redundancy, or system integration alternative, there are always options. *Opportunity costs* are the costs of *not* picking one of those options. The opportunity costs of not switching to newer technologies and topologies might be lost competitive advantage, lower productivity, and slower overall performance. Any effort to integrate opportunity costs into your analysis can help to make accurate comparisons at the beginning of your project.

- *Sunken costs*—Your investment in existing cable plant, routers, concentrators, switches, hosts, and other equipment and software are your *sunken costs*. If the sunken cost is high, you might need to modify your networks so that your existing internetwork can continue to be utilized. Although comparatively low incremental costs might appear to be more attractive than significant redesign costs, your organization might pay more in the long run by not upgrading systems. Over reliance on sunken costs can cost your organization sales and market share when calculating the cost of internetwork modifications and additions.

Estimating Traffic: Work Load Modeling

Empirical *work-load modeling* consists of instrumenting a working internetwork and monitoring traffic for a given number of users, applications, and network topology. Try to characterize activity throughout a normal work day in terms of the type of traffic passed, level of traffic, response time of hosts, time to execute file transfers, and so on. You can also observe utilization on existing network equipment over the test period.

If the tested internetwork's characteristics are close to the new internetwork, you can try extrapolating to the new internetwork's number of users, applications, and topology. This is a *best-guess* approach to traffic estimation given the unavailability of tools to characterize detailed traffic behavior.

In addition to passive monitoring of an existing network, you can measure activity and traffic generated by a known number of users attached to a representative test network and then extrapolate findings to your anticipated population.

One problem with modeling workloads on networks is that it is difficult to accurately pinpoint traffic load and network device performance as functions of the number of users, type of application, and geographical location. This is especially true without a real network in place. Consider the following factors that influence the dynamics of the network:

- *The time-dependent nature of network access*—Peak periods can vary; measurements must reflect a range of observations that includes peak demand.

- *Differences associated with type of traffic*—Routed and bridged traffic place different demands on internetwork devices and protocols; some protocols are sensitive to dropped packets; some application types require more bandwidth.

- *The random (nondeterministic) nature of network traffic*—Exact arrival time and specific effects of traffic are unpredictable.

Sensitivity Testing

From a practical point of view, sensitivity testing involves breaking stable links and observing what happens. When working with a test network, this is relatively easy. Disturb the network by removing an active interface, and monitor how the change is handled by the internetwork: how traffic is rerouted, the speed of convergence, whether any connectivity is lost, and whether problems arise in handling specific types of traffic. You can also change the level of traffic on a network to determine the effects on the network when traffic levels approach media saturation. This empirical testing is a type of *regression* testing: A series of specific modifications (tests) are repeated on different versions of network configurations. By monitoring the effects on the design variations, you can characterize the relative resilience of the design.

NOTES ——————————————————————————————————

Modeling sensitivity tests using a computer is beyond the scope of this publication. A useful source for more information about computer-based network design and simulation is A.S. Tannenbaum, *Computer Networks*, Upper Saddle River, New Jersey: Prentice Hall, 1996.

SUMMARY

After you have determined your network requirements, you must identify and then select the specific capability that fits your computing environment. For basic information on the different types of internetworking devices along with a description of a hierarchical approach to internetworking, refer to Chapter 2.

Chapters 2–13 in this book are technology chapters that present detailed discussions about specific implementations of large-scale internetworks in the following environments:

- Large-scale Internetwork Protocol (IP) internetworks
  - Enhanced Interior Gateway Routing Protocol (IGRP) design
  - Open Shortest Path First (OSPF) design

- IBM System Network Architecture (SNA) internetworks
  - Source-route bridging (SRB) design
  - Synchronous Data Link Control (SDLC) and serial tunneling (STUN), SDLC Logical Link Control type 2 (SDLLC), and Qualified Logical Link Control (QLLC) design
  - Advanced Peer-to-Peer Networking (APPN) and Data Link Switching (DLSw) design
- ATM internetworks
- Packet service internetworks
  - Frame Relay design
- Dial-on-demand routing (DDR) internetworks
- ISDN internetworks

In addition to these technology chapters there are chapters on designing switched LAN internetworks, campus LANs, and internetworks for multimedia applications. The last 12 chapters of this book include case studies relating to the concepts learned in the previous chapters.

CHAPTER 2

Internetworking Design Basics

Designing an internetwork can be a challenging task. An internetwork that consists of only 50 meshed routing nodes can pose complex problems that lead to unpredictable results. Attempting to optimize internetworks that feature thousands of nodes can pose even more complex problems.

Despite improvements in equipment performance and media capabilities, internetwork design is becoming more difficult. The trend is toward increasingly complex environments involving multiple media, multiple protocols, and interconnection to networks outside any single organization's dominion of control. Carefully designing internetworks can reduce the hardships associated with growth as a networking environment evolves.

This chapter provides an overview of planning and design guidelines. Discussions are divided into the following general topics:

- Understanding Basic Internetworking Concepts
- Identifying and Selecting Internetworking Capabilities
- Identifying and Selecting Internetworking Devices

UNDERSTANDING BASIC INTERNETWORKING CONCEPTS

This section covers the following basic internetworking concepts:

- Overview of Internetworking Devices
- Switching Overview

Overview of Internetworking Devices

Network designers faced with designing an internetwork have four basic types of internetworking devices available to them:

- Hubs (concentrators)
- Bridges
- Switches
- Routers

Table 2–1 summarizes these four internetworking devices.

Table 2–1 *Summary of Internetworking Devices*

Device	Description
Hubs (concentrators)	Hubs (concentrators) are used to connect multiple users to a single physical device, which connects to the network. Hubs and concentrators act as repeaters by regenerating the signal as it passes through them.
Bridges	Bridges are used to logically separate network segments within the same network. They operate at the OSI data link layer (Layer 2) and are independent of higher-layer protocols.
Switches	Switches are similar to bridges but usually have more ports. Switches provide a unique network segment on each port, thereby separating collision domains. Today, network designers are replacing hubs in their wiring closets with switches to increase their network performance and bandwidth while protecting their existing wiring investments.
Routers	Routers separate broadcast domains and are used to connect different networks. Routers direct network traffic based on the destination network layer address (Layer 3) rather than the workstation data link layer or MAC address. Routers are protocol dependent.

Data communications experts generally agree that network designers are moving away from bridges and concentrators and primarily using switches and routers to build internetworks. Consequently, this chapter focuses primarily on the role of switches and routers in internetwork design.

Switching Overview

Today in data communications, all switching and routing equipment perform two basic operations:

- *Switching data frames*—This is generally a store-and-forward operation in which a frame arrives on an input media and is transmitted to an output media.

- *Maintenance of switching operations*—In this operation, switches build and maintain switching tables and search for loops. Routers build and maintain both routing tables and service tables.

There are two methods of switching data frames: Layer 2 and Layer 3 switching.

Layer 2 and Layer 3 Switching

Switching is the process of taking an incoming frame from one interface and delivering it out through another interface. Routers use Layer 3 switching to route a packet, and switches (Layer 2 switches) use Layer 2 switching to forward frames.

The difference between Layer 2 and Layer 3 switching is the type of information inside the frame that is used to determine the correct output interface. With Layer 2 switching, frames are switched based on MAC address information. With Layer 3 switching, frames are switched based on network-layer information.

Layer 2 switching does not look inside a packet for network-layer information as does Layer 3 switching. Layer 2 switching is performed by looking at a destination MAC address within a frame. It looks at the frame's destination address and sends it to the appropriate interface if it knows the destination address location. Layer 2 switching builds and maintains a switching table that keeps track of which MAC addresses belong to each port or interface.

If the Layer 2 switch does not know where to send the frame, it broadcasts the frame out all its ports to the network to learn the correct destination. When the frame's reply is returned, the switch learns the location of the new address and adds the information to the switching table.

Layer 2 addresses are determined by the manufacturer of the data communications equipment used. They are unique addresses that are derived in two parts: the manufacturing (MFG) code and the unique identifier. The MFG code is assigned to each vendor by the IEEE. The vendor assigns a unique identifier to each board it produces. Except for Systems Network Architecture (SNA) networks, users have little or no control over Layer 2 addressing because Layer 2 addresses are fixed with a device, whereas Layer 3 addresses can be changed. In addition, Layer 2 addresses assume a flat address space with universally unique addresses.

Layer 3 switching operates at the network layer. It examines *packet* information and forwards packets based on their network-layer destination addresses. Layer 3 switching also supports router functionality.

For the most part, Layer 3 addresses are determined by the network administrator who installs a hierarchy on the network. Protocols such as IP, IPX, and AppleTalk use Layer 3 addressing. By creating Layer 3 addresses, a network administrator creates local areas that act as single addressing units (similar to streets, cities, states, and countries), and assigns a number to each local entity. If users move to another building, their end stations will obtain new Layer 3 addresses, but their Layer 2 addresses remain the same.

As routers operate at Layer 3 of the OSI model, they can adhere to and formulate a hierarchical addressing structure. Therefore, a routed network can tie a logical addressing structure to a physical infrastructure, for example, through TCP/IP subnets or IPX networks for each segment. Traffic flow in a switched (flat) network is therefore inherently different from traffic flow in a routed (hierarchical) network. Hierarchical networks offer more flexible traffic flow than flat networks because they can use the network hierarchy to determine optimal paths and contain broadcast domains.

Implications of Layer 2 and Layer 3 Switching

The increasing power of desktop processors and the requirements of client-server and multimedia applications have driven the need for greater bandwidth in traditional shared-media environments. These requirements are prompting network designers to replace hubs in wiring closets with switches.

Although Layer 2 switches use microsegmentation to satisfy the demands for more bandwidth and increased performance, network designers are now faced with increasing demands for intersubnet communication. For example, every time a user accesses servers and other resources, which are located on different subnets, the traffic must go through a Layer 3 device. Figure 2–1 shows the route of intersubnet traffic with Layer 2 switches and Layer 3 switches.

Figure 2–1

Flow of intersubnet traffic with Layer 2 switches and routers.

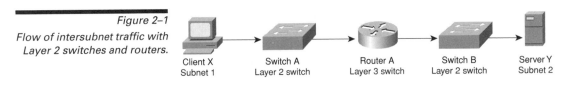

| Client X | Switch A | Router A | Switch B | Server Y |
| Subnet 1 | Layer 2 switch | Layer 3 switch | Layer 2 switch | Subnet 2 |

As Figure 2–1 shows, for Client X to communicate with Server Y, which is on another subnet, it must traverse through the following route: first through Switch A (a Layer 2 switch) and then through Router A (a Layer 3 switch) and finally through Switch B (a Layer 2 switch). Potentially there is a tremendous bottleneck, which can threaten network performance, because the intersubnet traffic must pass from one network to another.

To relieve this bottleneck, network designers can add Layer 3 capabilities throughout the network. They are implementing Layer 3 switching on edge devices to alleviate the burden on centralized routers. Figure 2–2 illustrates how deploying Layer 3 switching throughout the network allows Client X to directly communicate with Server Y without passing through Router A.

IDENTIFYING AND SELECTING INTERNETWORKING CAPABILITIES

After you understand your internetworking requirements, you must identify and then select the specific capabilities that fit your computing environment. The following discussions provide a starting point for making these decisions:

- Identifying and Selecting an Internetworking Model
- Choosing Internetworking Reliability Options

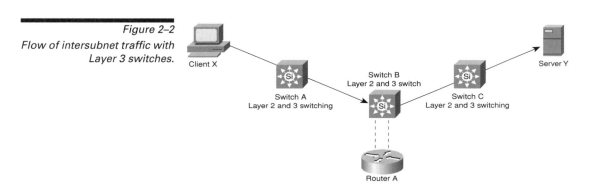

Figure 2–2
Flow of intersubnet traffic with Layer 3 switches.

Identifying and Selecting an Internetworking Model

Hierarchical models for internetwork design allow you to design internetworks in layers. To understand the importance of layering, consider the Open System Interconnection (OSI) reference model, which is a layered model for understanding and implementing computer communications. By using layers, the OSI model simplifies the task required for two computers to communicate. Hierarchical models for internetwork design also uses layers to simplify the task required for internetworking. Each layer can be focused on specific functions, thereby allowing the networking designer to choose the right systems and features for the layer.

Using a hierarchical design can facilitate changes. Modularity in network design allows you to create design elements that can be replicated as the network grows. As each element in the network design requires change, the cost and complexity of making the upgrade is constrained to a small subset of the overall network. In large flat or meshed network architectures, changes tend to impact a large number of systems. Improved fault isolation is also facilitated by modular structuring of the network into small, easy-to-understand elements. Network mangers can easily understand the transition points in the network, which helps identify failure points.

Using the Hierarchical Design Model

A hierarchical network design includes the following three layers:

- The backbone (core) layer that provides optimal transport between sites
- The distribution layer that provides policy-based connectivity
- The local-access layer that provides workgroup/user access to the network

Figure 2–3 shows a high-level view of the various aspects of a hierarchical network design. A hierarchical network design presents three layers—core, distribution, and access—with each layer providing different functionality.

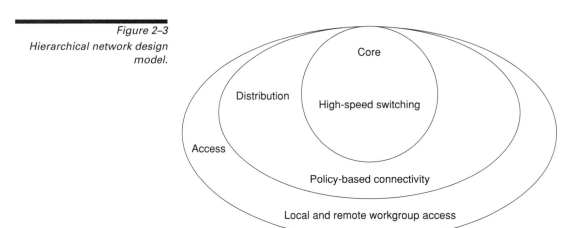

Figure 2–3
Hierarchical network design model.

Function of the Core Layer

The core layer is a high-speed switching backbone and should be designed to switch packets as fast as possible. This layer of the network should not perform any packet manipulation, such as access lists and filtering, that would slow down the switching of packets.

Function of the Distribution Layer

The distribution layer of the network is the demarcation point between the access and core layers and helps to define and differentiate the core. The purpose of this layer is to provide boundary definition and is the place at which packet manipulation can take place. In the campus environment, the distribution layer can include several functions, such as the following:

- Address or area aggregation
- Departmental or workgroup access
- Broadcast/multicast domain definition
- Virtual LAN (VLAN) routing
- Any media transitions that need to occur
- Security

In the non-campus environment, the distribution layer can be a redistribution point between routing domains or the demarcation between static and dynamic routing protocols. It can also be the point at which remote sites access the corporate network. The distribution layer can be summarized as the layer that provides policy-based connectivity.

Function of the Access Layer

The access layer is the point at which local end users are allowed into the network. This layer may also use access lists or filters to further optimize the needs of a particular set of users. In the campus environment, access-layer functions can include the following:

- Shared bandwidth
- Switched bandwidth
- MAC layer filtering
- Microsegmentation

In the non-campus environment, the access layer can give remote sites access to the corporate network via some wide-area technology, such as Frame Relay, ISDN, or leased lines.

It is sometimes mistakenly thought that the three layers (core, distribution, and access) must exist in clear and distinct physical entities, but this does not have to be the case. The layers are defined to aid successful network design and to represent functionality that must exist in a network. The instantiation of each layer can be in distinct routers or switches, can be represented by a physical media, can be combined in a single device, or can be omitted altogether. The way the layers are implemented depends on the needs of the network being designed. Note, however, that for a network to function optimally, hierarchy must be maintained.

The discussions that follow outline the capabilities and services associated with backbone, distribution, and local access internetworking services.

Evaluating Backbone Services

This section addresses internetworking features that support backbone services. The following topics are discussed:

- Path Optimization
- Traffic Prioritization
- Load Balancing
- Alternative Paths
- Switched Access
- Encapsulation (Tunneling)

Path Optimization

One of the primary advantages of a router is its capability to help you implement a logical environment in which optimal paths for traffic are automatically selected. Routers rely on routing protocols that are associated with the various network layer protocols to accomplish this automated path optimization.

Depending on the network protocols implemented, routers permit you to implement routing environments that suit your specific requirements. For example, in an IP internetwork, Cisco routers can support all widely implemented routing protocols, including Open Shortest Path First (OSPF), RIP, IGRP, Border Gateway Protocol (BGP), Exterior Gateway Protocol (EGP), and HELLO. Key built-in capabilities that promote path optimization include rapid and controllable route convergence and tunable routing metrics and timers.

Convergence is the process of agreement, by all routers, on optimal routes. When a network event causes routes to either halt operation or become available, routers distribute routing update messages. Routing update messages permeate networks, stimulating recalculation of optimal routes and eventually causing all routers to agree on these routes. Routing algorithms that converge slowly can cause routing loops or network outages.

Many different metrics are used in routing algorithms. Some sophisticated routing algorithms base route selection on a combination of multiple metrics, resulting in the calculation of a single hybrid metric. IGRP uses one of the most sophisticated distance vector routing algorithms. It combines values for bandwidth, load, and delay to create a composite metric value. Link state routing protocols, such as OSPF and IS-IS, employ a metric that represents the cost associated with a given path.

Traffic Prioritization

Although some network protocols can prioritize internal homogeneous traffic, the router prioritizes the heterogeneous traffic flows. Such traffic prioritization enables policy-based routing and ensures that protocols carrying mission-critical data take precedence over less important traffic.

Priority Queuing

Priority queuing allows the network administrator to prioritize traffic. Traffic can be classified according to various criteria, including protocol and subprotocol type, and then queued on one of four output queues (high, medium, normal, or low priority). For IP traffic, additional fine-tuning is possible. Priority queuing is most useful on low-speed serial links. Figure 2–4 shows how priority queuing can be used to segregate traffic by priority level, speeding the transit of certain packets through the network.

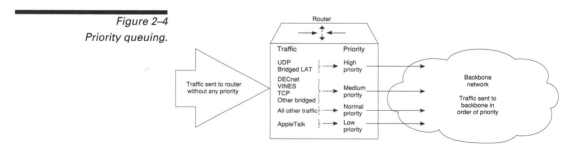

Figure 2–4
Priority queuing.

You can also use intraprotocol traffic prioritization techniques to enhance internetwork performance. IP's type-of-service (TOS) feature and prioritization of IBM logical units (LUs) are intraprotocol prioritization techniques that can be implemented to improve traffic handling over routers. Figure 2–5 illustrates LU prioritization.

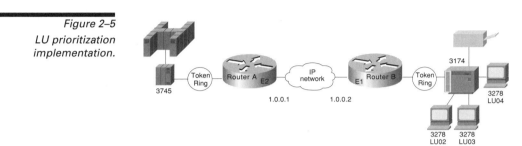

Figure 2–5
LU prioritization
implementation.

In Figure 2–5, the IBM mainframe is channel-attached to a 3745 communications controller, which is connected to a 3174 cluster controller via remote source-route bridging (RSRB). Multiple 3270 terminals and printers, each with a unique local LU address, are attached to the 3174. By applying LU address prioritization, you can assign a priority to each LU associated with a terminal or printer; that is, certain users can have terminals that have better response time than others, and printers can have lowest priority. This function increases application availability for those users running extremely important applications.

Finally, most routed protocols (such as AppleTalk, IPX, and DECnet) employ a cost-based routing protocol to assess the relative merit of the different routes to a destination. By tuning associated parameters, you can force particular kinds of traffic to take particular routes, thereby performing a type of manual traffic prioritization.

Custom Queuing

Priority queuing introduces a fairness problem in that packets classified to lower priority queues might not get serviced in a timely manner, or at all. Custom queuing is designed to address this problem. Custom queuing allows more granularity than priority queuing. In fact, this feature is commonly used in the internetworking environment in which multiple higher-layer protocols are supported. Custom queuing reserves bandwidth for a specific protocol, thus allowing mission-critical traffic to receive a guaranteed minimum amount of bandwidth at any time.

The intent is to reserve bandwidth for a particular type of traffic. For example, in Figure 2–6, SNA has 40 percent of the bandwidth reserved using custom queuing, TCP/IP 20 percent, NetBIOS 20 percent, and the remaining protocols 20 percent. The APPN protocol itself has the concept of class of service (COS), which determines the transmission priority for every message. APPN prioritizes the traffic before sending it to the DLC transmission queue.

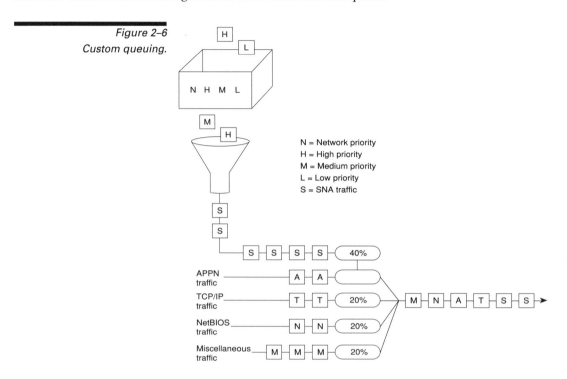

Figure 2–6
Custom queuing.

N = Network priority
H = High priority
M = Medium priority
L = Low priority
S = SNA traffic

Custom queuing prioritizes multiprotocol traffic. A maximum of 16 queues can be built with custom queuing. Each queue is serviced sequentially until the number of bytes sent exceeds the configurable byte count or the queue is empty. One important function of custom queuing is that if SNA traffic uses only 20 percent of the link, the remaining 20 percent allocated to SNA can be shared by the other traffic.

Custom queuing is designed for environments that want to ensure a minimum level of service for all protocols. In today's multiprotocol internetwork environment, this important feature allows protocols of different characteristics to share the media.

Weighted Fair Queuing

Weighted fair queuing is a traffic priority management algorithm that uses the time-division multiplexing (TDM) model to divide the available bandwidth among clients that share the same interface. In time-division multiplexing, each client is allocated a time slice in a round-robin fashion. In weighted fair queuing, the bandwidth is distributed evenly among clients so that each client gets a fair share if every one has the same weighting. You can assign a different set of weights, for example through type-of-service, so that more bandwidth is allocated.

If every client is allocated the same bandwidth independent of the arrival rates, the low volume traffic has effective priority over high volume traffic. The use of weighting allows time-delay-sensitive traffic to obtain additional bandwidth, thus consistent response time is guaranteed under heavy traffic. There are different types of data stream converging on a wire, as shown in Figure 2–7.

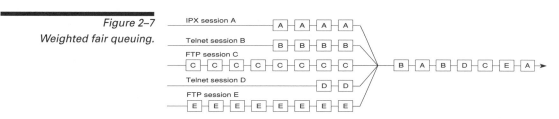

Figure 2–7
Weighted fair queuing.

Both C and E are FTP sessions, and they are high-volume traffic. A, B, and D are interactive sessions and they are low-volume traffic. Every session in this case is termed a *conversation*. If each conversation is serviced in a cyclic manner and gets a slot regardless of its arrival rate, the FTP sessions do not monopolize the bandwidth. Round trip delays for the interactive traffic, therefore, become predictable.

Weighted fair queuing provides an algorithm to identify data streams dynamically using an interface, and sorts them into separate logical queues. The algorithm uses various discriminators based on whatever network layer protocol information is available and sorts among them. For example, for IP traffic, the discriminators are source and destination address, protocol type, socket numbers, and TOS. This is how the two Telnet sessions (Sessions B and D) are assigned to different logical queues, as shown in Figure 2–7.

Ideally, the algorithm would classify every conversation that is sharing the wire so that each conversation receives its fair share of the bandwidth. Unfortunately, with such protocols as SNA, you cannot distinguish one SNA session from another. For example, in DLSw+, SNA traffic is multiplexed onto a single TCP session. Similarly in APPN, SNA sessions are multiplexed onto a single LLC2 session.

The weighted fair queuing algorithm treats these sessions as a single conversation. If you have many TCP sessions, the TCP sessions get the majority of the bandwidth and the SNA traffic gets the minimum. For this reason, this algorithm is not recommended for SNA using DLSw+ TCP/IP encapsulation and APPN.

Weighted fair queuing, however, has many advantages over priority queuing and custom queuing. Priority queuing and custom queuing require the installation of access lists; the bandwidth has to be pre-allocated and priorities have to be predefined. This is clearly a burden. Sometimes, network administrators cannot identify and prioritize network traffic in real time. Weighted fair queuing sorts among individual traffic streams without the administrative burden associated with the other two types of queuing.

Load Balancing

The easiest way to add bandwidth in a backbone network is to implement additional links. Routers provide built-in load balancing for multiple links and paths. You can use up to four paths to a destination network. In some cases, the paths need not be of equal cost.

Within IP, routers provide load balancing on both a per-packet and a per-destination basis. For per-destination load balancing, each router uses its route cache to determine the output interface. If IGRP or Enhanced IGRP routing is used, unequal-cost load balancing is possible. The router uses metrics to determine which paths the packets will take; the amount of load balancing can be adjusted by the user.

Load balancing bridged traffic over serial lines is also supported. Serial lines can be assigned to circuit groups. If one of the serial links in the circuit group is in the spanning tree for a network, any of the serial links in the circuit group can be used for load balancing. Data ordering problems are avoided by assigning each destination to a serial link. Reassignment is done dynamically if interfaces go down or come up.

Alternative Paths

Many internetwork backbones carry mission-critical information. Organizations running such backbones are usually interested in protecting the integrity of this information at virtually any cost. Routers must offer sufficient reliability so that they are not the weak link in the internetwork chain. The key is to provide alternative paths that can come on line whenever link failures occur along active networks.

End-to-end reliability is not ensured simply by making the backbone fault tolerant. If communication on a local segment within any building is disrupted for any reason, that information will not reach the backbone. End-to-end reliability is only possible when redundancy is employed throughout the internetwork. Because this is usually cost prohibitive, most companies prefer to employ redundant paths only on those segments that carry mission-critical information.

What does it take to make the backbone reliable? Routers hold the key to reliable internetworking. Depending on the definition of reliability, this can mean duplicating every major system on each router and possibly every component. However, hardware component duplication is not the entire solution because extra circuitry is necessary to link the duplicate components to allow them to communicate. This solution is usually very expensive, but more importantly, it does not completely address the problem. Even assuming all routers in your network are completely reliable systems, link problems between nodes within a backbone can still defeat a redundant hardware solution.

To really address the problem of network reliability, *links* must be redundant. Further, it is not enough to simply duplicate all links. Dual links must terminate at multiple routers unless all backbone routers are completely fault tolerant (no single points of failure). Otherwise, backbone routers that are not fault tolerant become single points of failure. The inevitable conclusion is that a completely redundant router is not the most effective solution to the reliability problem because it is expensive and still does not address link reliability.

Most network designers do not implement a completely redundant network. Instead, network designers implement partially redundant internetworks. The section, "Choosing Internetworking Reliability Options," later in this chapter, addresses several hypothetical networks that represent commonly implemented points along the reliability continuum.

Switched Access

Switched access provides the capability to enable a WAN link on an as-needed basis via automated router controls. One model for a reliable backbone consists of dual, dedicated links and one switched link for idle hot backup. Under normal operational conditions, you can load balance over the dual links, but the switched link is not operational until one of the dedicated links fails.

Traditionally, WAN connections over the Public Switched Telephone Network (PSTN) have used dedicated lines. This can be very expensive when an application requires only low-volume, periodic connections. To reduce the need for dedicated circuits, a feature called *dial-on-demand routing* (DDR) is available. Figure 2–8 illustrates a DDR connection.

Figure 2–8
The Dial-on-demand routing environment.

Using DDR, low-volume, periodic network connections can be made over the PSTN. A router activates the DDR feature when it receives a bridged or routed IP packet destined for a location on the other side of the dial-up line. After the router dials the destination phone number and establishes the connection, packets of any supported protocol can be transmitted. When the transmission is complete, the line is automatically disconnected. By terminating unneeded connections, DDR reduces cost of ownership.

Encapsulation (Tunneling)

Encapsulation takes packets or frames from one network system and places them inside frames from another network system. This method is sometimes called *tunneling*. Tunneling provides a means for encapsulating packets inside a routable protocol via virtual interfaces. Synchronous Data Link Control (SDLC) transport is also an encapsulation of packets in a routable protocol. In addition, transport provides enhancements to tunneling, such as local data-link layer termination, broadcast avoidance, media conversion, and other scalability optimizations.

Cisco routers support the following encapsulation and tunneling techniques:

- The IBM technology feature set provides these methods:
  - Serial tunneling (STUN) or Synchronous Data Link Control (SDLC) Transport
  - SRB with direct encapsulation
  - SRB with Fast Sequenced Transport (FST) encapsulation
  - SRB with Transmission Control Protocol/Internet Protocol (TCP/IP) encapsulation
  - Data Link Switching Plus (DLSw+) with direct encapsulation
  - DLSw+ with TCP/IP encapsulation
  - DLSw+ with Fast Sequenced Transport/Internet Protocol (FST/IP) encapsulation
  - DLSw+ with DLSw Lite (Logical Link Control Type 2 [LLC2]) encapsulation
- Generic Routing Encapsulation (GRE)

  Cisco supports encapsulating Novell Internetwork Packet Exchange (IPX), Internet Protocol (IP), Connectionless Network Protocol (CLNP), AppleTalk, DECnet Phase IV, Xerox Network Systems (XNS), Banyan Virtual Network System (VINES), and Apollo packets for transport over IP

- Single-protocol tunneling techniques: Cayman (AppleTalk over IP), AURP (AppleTalk over IP), EON (CLNP over IP), and NOS (IP over IP)

The following discussion focuses on IBM encapsulations and the multiprotocol GRE tunneling feature.

IBM Features

STUN allows two devices that are normally connected by a direct serial link, using protocols compliant with SDLC or High-level Data Link Control (HDLC), to be connected through one or more routers. The routers can be connected via a multiprotocol network of arbitrary topology. STUN allows integration of System Network Architecture (SNA) networks and non-SNA networks using routers and existing network links. Transport across the multiprotocol network that connects the routers can use TCP/IP. This type of transport offers reliability and intelligent routing via any supported IP routing protocol. A STUN configuration is shown in Figure 2–9.

SDLC Transport is a variation of STUN that allows sessions using SDLC protocols and TCP/IP encapsulation to be locally terminated. SDLC Transport permits participation in SDLC windowing and retransmission activities.

When connecting remote devices that use SRB over a slow-speed serial link, most network designers choose RSRB with direct HDLC encapsulation. In this case, SRB frames are encapsulated in an HDLC-compliant header. This solution adds little overhead, preserving valuable serial link bandwidth. Direct HDLC encapsulation is not restricted to serial links (it can also be used over Ethernet, Token Ring, and FDDI links), but is most useful in situations in which additional control overhead on the encapsulating network is not tolerable.

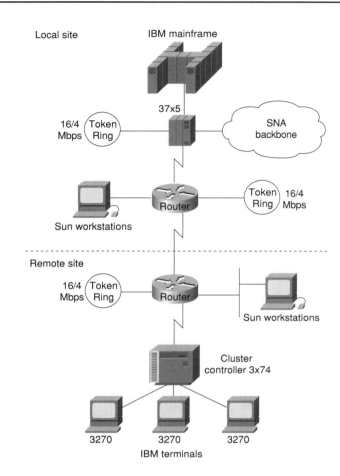

Figure 2–9
STUN configuration.

When more overhead can be tolerated, frame sequencing is important, but extremely reliable delivery is not needed, and SRB packets can be sent over serial, Token Ring, Ethernet, and FDDI networks using FST encapsulation. FST is similar to TCP in that it provides packet sequencing. However, unlike TCP, FST does not provide packet-delivery acknowledgment.

For extremely reliable delivery in environments in which moderate overhead can be tolerated, you can choose to encapsulate SRB frames in TCP/IP packets. This solution is not only reliable, it can also take advantage of routing features that include handling via routing protocols, packet filtering, and multipath routing.

Generic Routing Encapsulation (GRE)

Cisco's Generic Routing Encapsulation (GRE) multiprotocol carrier protocol encapsulates IP, CLNP, IPX, AppleTalk, DECnet Phase IV, XNS, VINES, and Apollo packets inside IP tunnels. With GRE tunneling, a Cisco router at each site encapsulates protocol-specific packets in an IP header, creating a virtual point-to-point link to Cisco routers at other ends of an IP cloud, where the IP header is stripped off. By connecting multiprotocol subnetworks in a single-protocol backbone environment, IP tunneling allows network expansion across a single-protocol backbone environment. GRE tunneling involves three types of protocols:

- *Passenger*—The protocol is encapsulated (IP, CLNP, IPX, AppleTalk, DECnet Phase IV, XNS, VINES and Apollo).
- *Carrier*—GRE protocol provides carrier services.
- *Transport*—IP carries the encapsulated protocol.

GRE tunneling allows desktop protocols to take advantage of the enhanced route selection capabilities of IP. Many local-area network (LAN) protocols, including AppleTalk and Novell IPX, are optimized for local use. They have limited route selection metrics and hop count limitations. In contrast, IP routing protocols allow more flexible route selection and scale better over large internetworks. Figure 2–10 illustrates GRE tunneling across a single IP backbone between sites. Regardless of how many routers and paths may be associated with the IP cloud, the tunnel is seen as a single hop.

Figure 2–10

Using a single protocol backbone.

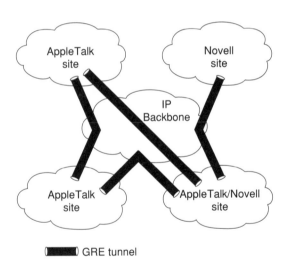

GRE provides key capabilities that other encapsulation protocols lack: sequencing and the capability to carry tunneled data at high speeds. Some higher-level protocols require that packets are delivered in correct order. The GRE sequencing option provides this capability. GRE also has an optional key feature that allows you to avoid configuration errors by requiring the same key to be entered at each tunnel endpoint before the tunneled data is processed. IP tunneling also allows network designers to implement policies, such as which types of traffic can use which routes or assignment of priority or security levels to particular traffic. Capabilities like these are lacking in many native LAN protocols.

IP tunneling provides communication between subnetworks that have invalid or discontiguous network addresses. With tunneling, virtual network addresses are assigned to subnetworks, making discontiguous subnetworks reachable. Figure 2–11 illustrates that with GRE tunneling, it is possible for the two subnetworks of network 131.108.0.0 to talk to each other even though they are separated by another network.

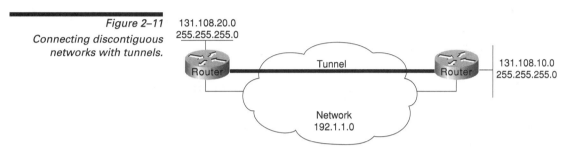

Figure 2–11
Connecting discontiguous
networks with tunnels.

Because encapsulation requires handling of the packets, it is generally faster to route protocols natively than to use tunnels. Tunneled traffic is switched at approximately half the typical process switching rates. This means approximately 1,000 packets per second (pps) aggregate for each router. Tunneling is CPU intensive, and as such, should be turned on cautiously. Routing updates, SAP updates, and other administrative traffic may be sent over each tunnel interface. It is easy to saturate a physical link with routing information if several tunnels are configured over it. Performance depends on the passenger protocol, broadcasts, routing updates, and bandwidth of the physical interfaces. It is also difficult to debug the physical link if problems occur. This problem can be mitigated in several ways. In IPX environments, route filters and SAP filters cut down on the size of the updates that travel over tunnels. In AppleTalk networks, keeping zones small and using route filters can limit excess bandwidth requirements.

Tunneling can disguise the nature of a link, making it look slower, faster, or more or less costly than it may actually be in reality. This can cause unexpected or undesirable route selection. Routing protocols that make decisions based only on hop count will usually prefer a tunnel to a real interface. This may not always be the best routing decision because an IP cloud can comprise several different media with very disparate qualities; for example, traffic may be forwarded across both 100-Mbps Ethernet lines and 9.6-Kbps serial lines. When using tunneling, pay attention to the media over which virtual tunnel traffic passes and the metrics used by each protocol.

If a network has sites that use protocol-based packet filters as part of a firewall security scheme, be aware that because tunnels encapsulate unchecked passenger protocols, you must establish filtering on the firewall router so that only authorized tunnels are allowed to pass. If tunnels are accepted from unsecured networks, it is a good idea to establish filtering at the tunnel destination or to place the tunnel destination outside the secure area of your network so that the current firewall scheme will remain secure.

When tunneling IP over IP, you must be careful to avoid inadvertently configuring a recursive routing loop. A routing loop occurs when the passenger protocol and the transport protocol are identical. The routing loop occurs because the best path to the tunnel destination is via the tunnel interface. A routing loop can occur when tunneling IP over IP, as follows:

1. The packet is placed in the output queue of the tunnel interface.

2. The tunnel interface includes a GRE header and enqueues the packet to the transport protocol (IP) for the destination address of the tunnel interface.

3. IP looks up the route to the tunnel destination address and learns that the path is the tunnel interface.

4. Once again, the packet is placed in the output queue of the tunnel interface, as described in Step 1, hence, the routing loop.

When a router detects a recursive routing loop, it shuts down the tunnel interface for 1 to 2 minutes and issues a warning message before it goes into the recursive loop. Another indication that a recursive route loop has been detected is if the tunnel interface is up and the line protocol is down.

To avoid recursive loops, keep passenger and transport routing information in separate locations by implementing the following procedures:

- Use separate routing protocol identifiers (for example, igrp 1 and igrp 2).

- Use different routing protocols.

- Assign the tunnel interface a very low bandwidth so that routing protocols, such as IGRP, will recognize a very high metric for the tunnel interface and will, therefore, choose the correct next hop (that is, choose the best physical interface instead of the tunnel).

- Keep the two IP address ranges distinct; that is, use a major address for your tunnel network that is different from your actual IP network. Keeping the address ranges distinct also aids in debugging because it is easy to identify an address as the tunnel network instead of the physical network and vice versa.

Evaluating Distribution Services

This section addresses internetworking features that support distribution services. The following topics are discussed:

- Backbone Bandwidth Management

- Area and Service Filtering

- Policy-Based Distribution

- Gateway Service

- Interprotocol Route Redistribution

- Media Translation

Backbone Bandwidth Management

To optimize backbone network operations, routers offer several performance tuning features. Examples include priority queuing, routing protocol metrics, and local session termination.

You can adjust the output queue length on priority queues. If a priority queue overflows, excess packets are discarded and quench messages that halt packet flow are sent, if appropriate, for that protocol. You can also adjust routing metrics to increase control over the paths that the traffic takes through the internetwork.

Local session termination allows routers to act as proxies for remote systems that represent session endpoints. (A *proxy* is a device that acts on behalf of another device.) Figure 2–12 illustrates an example of local session termination in an IBM environment.

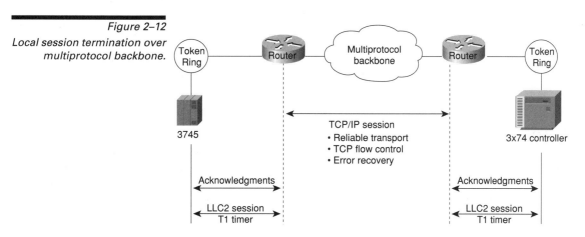

Figure 2–12
Local session termination over multiprotocol backbone.

In Figure 2–12, the routers locally terminate Logical Link Control type 2 (LLC2) data-link control sessions. Instead of end-to-end sessions, during which all session control information is passed over the multiprotocol backbone, the routers take responsibility for acknowledging packets that come from hosts on directly attached LANs. Local acknowledgment saves WAN bandwidth (and, therefore, WAN utilization costs), solves session timeout problems, and provides faster response to users.

Area and Service Filtering

Traffic filters based on *area* or *service* type are the primary distribution service tools used to provide policy-based access control into backbone services. Both area and service filtering are implemented using *access lists*. An access list is a sequence of statements, each of which either permits or denies certain conditions or addresses. Access lists can be used to permit or deny messages from particular network nodes and messages sent using particular protocols and services.

Area or network access filters are used to enforce the selective transmission of traffic based on network address. You can apply these on incoming or outgoing ports. Service filters use access lists applied to protocols (such as IP's UDP), applications such as the Simple Mail Transfer Protocol (SMTP), and specific protocols.

Suppose you have a network connected to the Internet, and you want any host on an Ethernet to be able to form TCP connections to any host on the Internet. However, you do not want Internet hosts to be able to form TCP connections to hosts on the Ethernet except to the SMTP port of a dedicated mail host.

SMTP uses TCP port 25 on one end of the connection and a random port number on the other end. The same two port numbers are used throughout the life of the connection. Mail packets coming in from the Internet will have a destination port of 25. Outbound packets will have the port numbers reversed. The fact that the secure system behind the router always accepts mail connections on port 25 is what makes it possible to separately control incoming and outgoing services. The access list can be configured on either the outbound or inbound interface.

In the following example, the Ethernet network is a Class B network with the address 128.88.0.0, and the mail host's address is 128.88.1.2. The keyword **established** is used only for the TCP protocol to indicate an established connection. A match occurs if the TCP datagram has the ACK or RST bits set, which indicate that the packet belongs to an existing connection.

```
access-list 102 permit tcp 0.0.0.0 255.255.255.255 128.88.0.0 0.0.255.255 established
access-list 102 permit tcp 0.0.0.0 255.255.255.255 128.88.1.2 0.0.0.0 eq 25
interface ethernet 0
ip access-group 102
```

Policy-Based Distribution

Policy-based distribution is based on the premise that different departments within a common organization might have different policies regarding traffic dispersion through the organization-wide internetwork. Policy-based distribution aims to meet the differing requirements without compromising performance and information integrity.

A *policy* within this internetworking context is a rule or set of rules that governs end-to-end distribution of traffic to (and subsequently through) a backbone network. One department might send traffic representing three different protocols to the backbone, but might want to expedite one particular protocol's transit through the backbone because it carries mission-critical application information. To minimize already excessive internal traffic, another department might want to exclude all backbone traffic except electronic mail and one key custom application from entering its network segment.

These examples reflect policies specific to a single department. However, policies can reflect overall organizational goals. For example, an organization might want to regulate backbone traffic to a maximum of 10 percent average bandwidth during the work day and 1-minute peaks of 30 percent utilization. Another corporate policy might be to ensure that communication between two remote departments can freely occur, despite differences in technology.

Different policies frequently require different workgroup and department technologies. Therefore, support for policy-based distribution implies support for the wide range of technologies currently used to implement these policies. This in turn allows you to implement solutions that support a wide range of policies, which helps to increase organizational flexibility and application availability.

In addition to support for internetworking technologies, there must be a means both to keep separate and integrate these technologies, as appropriate. The different technologies should be able to coexist or combine intelligently, as the situation warrants.

Consider the situation depicted in Figure 2–13. Assume that a corporate policy limits unnecessary backbone traffic. One way to do this is to restrict the transmission of Service Advertisement Protocol (SAP) messages. SAP messages allow NetWare servers to advertise services to clients. The organization might have another policy stating that all NetWare services should be provided locally. If this is the case, there should be no reason for services to be advertised remotely. SAP filters prevent SAP traffic from leaving a router interface, thereby fulfilling this policy.

Figure 2–13
Policy-based distributation:
SAP filtering.

Gateway Service

Protocol gateway capabilities are part of each router's standard software. For example, DECnet is currently in Phase V. DECnet Phase V addresses are different than DECnet Phase IV addresses. For those networks that require both type of hosts to coexist, two-way Phase IV/Phase V translation conforms to Digital-specified guidelines. The routers interoperate with Digital routers, and Digital hosts do not differentiate between the different devices.

The connection of multiple independent DECnet networks can lead to addressing problems. Nothing precludes two independent DECnet administrators from assigning node address 10 to one of the nodes in their respective networks. When the two networks are connected at some later time, conflicts result. DECnet address translation gateways (ATGs) address this problem. The ATG solution provides router-based translation between addresses in two different DECnet networks connected by a router. Figure 2–14 illustrates an example of this operation.

In Network 0, the router is configured at address 19.4 and is a Level 1 router. In Network 1, the router is configured at address 50.5 and is an area router. At this point, no routing information is exchanged between the two networks. The router maintains a separate routing table for each network. By establishing a translation map, packets in Network 0 sent to address 19.5 will be routed to Network 1, and the destination address will be translated to 50.1. Similarly, packets sent to address 19.6 in Network 0 will be routed to Network 1 as 19.1; packets sent to address 47.1 in Network 1 will be routed to Network 0 as 19.1; and packets sent to 47.2 in Network 1 will be sent to Network 0 as 19.3.

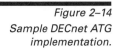

Figure 2–14

Sample DECnet ATG implementation.

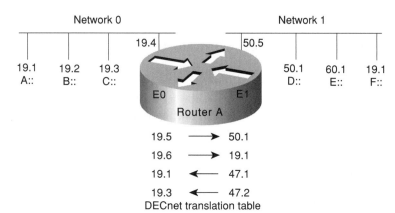

DECnet translation table

AppleTalk is another protocol with multiple revisions, each with somewhat different addressing characteristics. AppleTalk Phase 1 addresses are simple local forms; AppleTalk Phase 2 uses extended (multinetwork) addressing. Normally, information sent from a Phase 2 node cannot be understood by a Phase 1 node if Phase 2 extended addressing is used. Routers support routing between Phase 1 and Phase 2 nodes on the same cable by using transitional routing.

You can accomplish transitional routing by attaching two router ports to the same physical cable. Configure one port to support nonextended AppleTalk and the other to support extended Apple-Talk. Both ports must have unique network numbers. Packets are translated and sent out the other port as necessary.

Interprotocol Route Redistribution

The preceding section, "Gateway Service," discussed how *routed* protocol gateways (such as one that translates between AppleTalk Phase 1 and Phase 2) allow two end nodes with different implementations to communicate. Routers can also act as gateways for *routing* protocols. Information derived from one routing protocol, such as the IGRP, can be passed to, and used by, another routing protocol, such as RIP. This is useful when running multiple routing protocols in the same internetwork.

Routing information can be exchanged between any supported IP routing protocols. These include RIP, IGRP, OSPF, HELLO, EGP, and BGP. Similarly, route redistribution is supported by ISO CLNS for route redistribution between ISO IGRP and IS-IS. Static route information can also be redistributed. Defaults can be assigned so that one routing protocol can use the same metric for all redistributed routes, thereby simplifying the routing redistribution mechanism.

Media Translation

Media translation techniques translate frames from one network system into frames of another. Such translations are rarely 100 percent effective because one system might have attributes with no corollary to the other. For example, Token Ring networks support a built-in priority and reservation system, whereas Ethernet networks do not. Translations between Token Ring and Ethernet networks must somehow account for this discrepancy. It is possible for two vendors to make different decisions about how this discrepancy will be handled, which can prevent multivendor interoperation.

For those situations in which communication between end stations on different media is required, routers can translate between Ethernet and Token Ring frames. For direct bridging between Ethernet and Token Ring environments, use either source-route translational bridging or source-route transparent bridging (SRT). Source-route translational bridging translates between Token Ring and Ethernet frame formats; SRT allows routers to use both SRB and the transparent bridging algorithm used in standard Ethernet bridging.

When bridging from the SRB domain to the transparent bridging domain, the SRB fields of the frames are removed. RIFs are cached for use by subsequent return traffic. When bridging in the opposite direction, the router checks the packet to determine whether it has a multicast or broadcast destination or a unicast destination. If it has a multicast or broadcast destination, the packet is sent as a spanning-tree explorer. If it has a unicast destination, the router looks up the path to the destination in the RIF cache. If a path is found, it will be used; otherwise, the router will send the packet as a spanning-tree explorer. A simple example of this topology is shown in Figure 2–15.

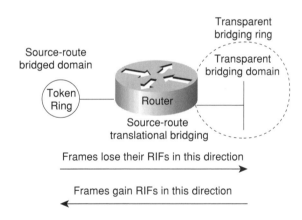

Figure 2–15
Source-route translational
bridging topology.

Routers support SRT through implementation of both transparent bridging and SRB algorithms on each SRT interface. If an interface notes the presence of a RIF field, it uses the SRB algorithm; if not, it uses the transparent bridging algorithm.

Translation between serial links running the SDLC protocol and Token Rings running LLC2 is also available. This is referred to as SDLLC frame translation. SDLLC frame translation allows connections between serial lines and Token Rings. This is useful for consolidating traditionally disparate SNA/SDLC networks into a LAN-based, multiprotocol, multimedia backbone network. Using SDLLC, routers terminate SDLC sessions, translate SDLC frames to LLC2 frames, and then forward the LLC2 frames using RSRB over a point-to-point or IP network. Because a router-based IP network can use arbitrary media, such as FDDI, Frame Relay, X.25, or leased lines, routers support SDLLC over all such media through IP encapsulation.

A complex SDLLC configuration is shown in Figure 2–16.

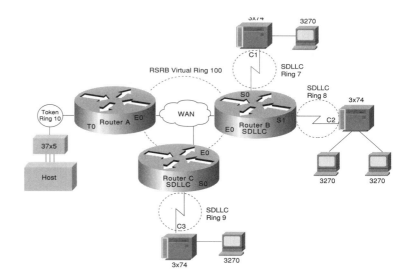

Figure 2–16
Complex SDLLC configuration.

Evaluating Local-Access Services

The following discussion addresses internetworking features that support local-access services. Local-access service topics outlined here include the following:

- Value-Added Network Addressing
- Network Segmentation
- Broadcast and Multicast Capabilities
- Naming, Proxy, and Local Cache Capabilities
- Media Access Security
- Router Discovery

Value-Added Network Addressing

Address schemes for LAN-based networks, such as NetWare and others, do not always adapt perfectly to use over multisegment LANs or WANs. One tool routers implement to ensure operation of such protocols is protocol-specific *helper addressing*. Helper addressing is a mechanism to assist the movement of specific traffic through a network when that traffic might not otherwise transit the network.

The use of *helper addressing* is best illustrated with an example. Consider the use of helper addresses in Novell IPX internetworks. Novell clients send broadcast messages when looking for a server. If the server is not local, broadcast traffic must be sent through routers. Helper addresses and access lists can be used together to allow broadcasts from certain nodes on one network to be directed specifically to certain servers on another network. Multiple helper addresses on each interface are supported, so broadcast packets can be forwarded to multiple hosts. Figure 2–17 illustrates the use of NetWare-based helper addressing.

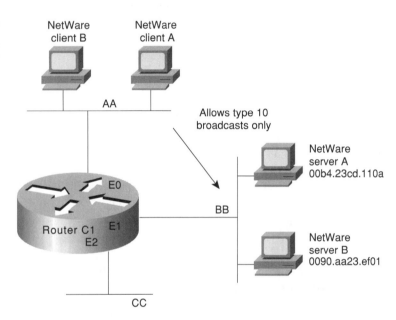

Figure 2–17

Sample network map illustrating helper address broadcast control.

NetWare clients on Network AA are allowed to broadcast to any server on Network BB. An applicable access list would specify that broadcasts of type 10 will be permitted from all nodes on Network AA. A configuration-specified helper address identifies the addresses on Network BB to which these broadcasts are directed. No other nodes on Network BB receive the broadcasts. No other broadcasts other than type 10 broadcasts are routed.

Any downstream networks beyond Network AA (for example, some Network AA1) are not allowed to broadcast to Network BB through Router C1, unless the routers partitioning Networks AA and AA1 are configured to forward broadcasts with a series of configuration entries. These entries must be applied to the input interfaces and be set to forward broadcasts between directly connected networks. In this way, traffic is passed along in a directed manner from network to network.

Network Segmentation

The splitting of networks into more manageable pieces is an essential role played by local-access routers. In particular, local-access routers implement local policies and limit unnecessary traffic. Examples of capabilities that allow network designers to use local-access routers to segment networks include IP subnets, DECnet area addressing, and AppleTalk zones.

You can use local-access routers to implement local policies by placing the routers in strategic locations and by configuring specific segmenting policies. For example, you can set up a series of LAN segments with different subnet addresses; routers would be configured with suitable interface addresses and subnet masks. In general, traffic on a given segment is limited to local broadcasts, traffic intended for a specific end station on that segment, or traffic intended for another specific router. By distributing hosts and clients carefully, you can use this simple method of dividing up a network to reduce overall network congestion.

Broadcast and Multicast Capabilities

Many protocols use *broadcast* and *multicast* capabilities. Broadcasts are messages that are sent out to all network destinations. Multicasts are messages sent to a specific subset of network destinations. Routers inherently reduce broadcast proliferation by default. However, routers can be configured to relay broadcast traffic if necessary. Under certain circumstances, passing along broadcast information is desirable and possibly necessary. The key is controlling broadcasts and multicasts using routers.

In the IP world, as with many other technologies, broadcast requests are very common. Unless broadcasts are controlled, network bandwidth can be seriously reduced. Routers offer various broadcast-limiting functions that reduce network traffic and minimize broadcast storms. For example, directed broadcasting allows for broadcasts to a specific network or a series of networks, rather than to the entire internetwork. When flooded broadcasts (broadcasts sent through the entire internetwork) are necessary, Cisco routers support a technique by which these broadcasts are sent over a spanning tree of the network. The spanning tree ensures complete coverage without excessive traffic because only one packet is sent over each network segment.

As discussed previously in the section "Value-Added Network Addressing," broadcast assistance is accommodated with the *helper address* mechanisms. You can allow a router or series of routers to relay broadcasts that would otherwise be blocked by using helper addresses. For example, you can permit retransmission of SAP broadcasts using helper addresses, thereby notifying clients on different network segments of certain NetWare services available from specific remote servers.

The Cisco IP multicast feature allows IP traffic to be propagated from one source to any number of destinations. Rather than sending one packet to each destination, one packet is sent to a multicast group identified by a single IP destination group address. IP multicast provides excellent support for such applications as video and audio conferencing, resource discovery, and stock market traffic distribution.

For full support of IP multicast, IP hosts must run the Internet Group Management Protocol (IGMP). IGMP is used by IP hosts to report their multicast group memberships to an immediately neighboring multicast router. The membership of a multicast group is dynamic. Multicast routers send IGMP query messages on their attached local networks. Host members of a multicast group respond to a query by sending IGMP reports for multicast groups to which they belong. Reports sent by the first host in a multicast group suppress the sending of identical reports from other hosts of the same group.

The multicast router attached to the local network takes responsibility for forwarding multicast datagrams from one multicast group to all other networks that have members in the group. Routers build multicast group distribution trees (routing tables) so that multicast packets have loop-free paths to all multicast group members so that multicast packets are not duplicated. If no reports are received from a multicast group after a set number of IGMP queries, the multicast routers assume the group has no local members and stop forwarding multicasts intended for that group.

Cisco routers also support Protocol Independent Multicast (PIM). For more information on this topic, see Chapter 13, "Designing Internetworks for Multimedia."

Naming, Proxy, and Local Cache Capabilities

Three key router capabilities help reduce network traffic and promote efficient internetworking operation: name service support, proxy services, and local caching of network information.

Network applications and connection services provided over segmented internetworks require a rational way to resolve names to addresses. Various facilities accommodate this requirement. Any router you select must support the name services implemented for different end-system environments. Examples of supported name services include NetBIOS, IP's Domain Name System (DNS) and IEN-116, and AppleTalk Name Binding Protocol (NBP).

A router can also act as a *proxy* for a name server. The router's support of NetBIOS name caching is one example of this kind of capability. NetBIOS name caching allows the router to maintain a cache of NetBIOS names, which avoids the overhead of transmitting all of the broadcasts between client and server NetBIOS PCs (IBM PCs or PS/2s) in an SRB environment. When NetBIOS name caching is enabled, the router does the following:

- Notices when any host sends a series of duplicate query frames and limits retransmission to one frame per period. The time period is a configuration parameter.

- Keeps a cache of mappings between NetBIOS server and client names and their MAC addresses. As a result, broadcast requests sent by clients to find servers (and by servers in response to their clients) can be sent directly to their destinations, rather than being broadcast across the entire bridged network.

When NetBIOS name caching is enabled and default parameters are set on the router, the NetBIOS name server, and the NetBIOS name client, approximately 20 broadcast packets per login are kept on the local ring where they are generated.

In most cases, the NetBIOS name cache is best used when large amounts of NetBIOS broadcast traffic might create bottlenecks on a WAN that connects local internetworks to distant locations.

The router can also save bandwidth (or handle nonconforming name resolution protocols) by using a variety of other proxy facilities. By using routers to act on behalf of other devices to perform various functions, you can more easily scale networks. Instead of being forced to add bandwidth when a new workgroup is added to a location, you can use a router to manage address resolution and control message services. Examples of this kind of capability include the proxy explorer feature of SRB and the proxy polling feature of STUN implementations.

Sometimes portions of networks cannot participate in routing activity or do not implement software that conforms to generally implemented address-resolution protocols. Proxy implementations on routers allow network designers to support these networks or hosts without reconfiguring an internetwork. Examples of these kinds of capabilities include proxy ARP address resolution for IP internetworks and NBP proxy in AppleTalk internetworks.

Local caches store previously learned information about the network so that new information requests do not need to be issued each time the same piece of information is desired. A router's ARP cache stores physical address and network address mappings so that it does not need to broadcast ARP requests more than once within a given time period for the same address. Address caches are maintained for many other protocols as well, including DECnet, Novell IPX, and SRB, where RIF information is cached.

Media Access Security

If all corporate information is readily available to all employees, security violations and inappropriate file access can occur. To prevent this, routers must do the following:

- Keep local traffic from inappropriately reaching the backbone
- Keep backbone traffic from exiting the backbone into an inappropriate department or workgroup network

These two functions require packet filtering. Packet filtering capabilities should be tailored to support a variety of corporate policies. Packet filtering methods can reduce traffic levels on a network, thereby allowing a company to continue using its current technology rather than investing in more network hardware. In addition, packet filters can improve security by keeping unauthorized users from accessing information and can minimize network problems caused by excessive congestion.

Routers support many filtering schemes designed to provide control over network traffic that reaches the backbone. Perhaps the most powerful of these filtering mechanisms is the access list. Each of the following possible local-access services can be provided through access lists:

- You have an Ethernet-to-Internet routing network and you want any host on the Ethernet to be able to form TCP connections to any host on the Internet. However, you do not want Internet hosts to be able to form TCP connections into the Ethernet except to the SMTP port of a dedicated mail host.
- You want to advertise only one network through a RIP routing process.

- You want to prevent packets that originated on any Sun workstation from being bridged on a particular Ethernet segment.

- You want to keep a particular protocol based on Novell IPX from establishing a connection between a source network or source port combination and a destination network or destination port combination.

Access lists logically prevent certain packets from traversing a particular router interface, thereby providing a general tool for implementing network security. In addition to this method, several specific security systems already exist to help increase network security. For example, the U.S. government has specified the use of an optional field within the IP packet header to implement a hierarchical packet security system called the Internet Protocol Security Option (IPSO).

IPSO support on routers addresses both the basic and extended security options described in a draft of the IPSO circulated by the Defense Communications Agency. This draft document is an early version of Request for Comments (RFC) 1108. IPSO defines security levels (for example, TOP SECRET, SECRET, and others) on a per-interface basis and accepts or rejects messages based on whether they include adequate authorization.

Some security systems are designed to keep remote users from accessing the network unless they have adequate authorization. For example, the Terminal Access Controller Access Control System (TACACS) is a means of protecting modem access into a network. The Defense Data Network (DDN) developed TACACS to control access to its TAC terminal servers.

The router's TACACS support is patterned after the DDN application. When a user attempts to start an EXEC command interpreter on a password-protected line, TACACS prompts for a password. If the user fails to enter the correct password, access is denied. Router administrators can control various TACACS parameters, such as the number of retries allowed, the timeout interval, and the enabling of TACACS accounting.

The Challenge Handshake Authentication Protocol (CHAP) is another way to keep unauthorized remote users from accessing a network. It is also commonly used to control router-to-router communications. When CHAP is enabled, a remote device (for example, a PC, workstation, router, or communication server) attempting to connect to a local router is "challenged" to provide an appropriate response. If the correct response is not provided, network access is denied.

CHAP is becoming popular because it does not require a secret password to be sent over the network. CHAP is supported on all router serial lines using Point-to-Point Protocol (PPP) encapsulation.

Router Discovery

Hosts must be able to locate routers when they need access to devices external to the local network. When more than one router is attached to a host's local segment, the host must be able to locate the router that represents the optimal path to the destination. This process of finding routers is called *router discovery*.

The following are router discovery protocols:

- *End System-to-Intermediate System (ES-IS)*—This protocol is defined by the ISO OSI protocol suite. It is dedicated to the exchange of information between intermediate systems (routers) and end systems (hosts). ESs send "ES hello" messages to all ISs on the local subnetwork. In turn, "IS hello" messages are sent from all ISs to all ESs on the local subnetwork. Both types of messages convey the subnetwork and network-layer addresses of the systems that generate them. Using this protocol, end systems and intermediate systems can locate one another.

- *ICMP Router Discovery Protocol (IRDP)*—Although the issue is currently under study, there is currently no single standardized manner for end stations to locate routers in the IP world. In many cases, stations are simply configured manually with the address of a local router. However, RFC 1256 outlines a router discovery protocol using the Internet Control Message Protocol (ICMP). This protocol is commonly referred to as IRDP.

- *Proxy Address Resolution Protocol (ARP)*—ARP uses broadcast messages to determine the MAC-layer address that corresponds to a particular internetwork address. ARP is sufficiently generic to allow use of IP with virtually any type of underlying media-access mechanism. A router that has proxy ARP enabled responds to ARP requests for those hosts for which it has a route, which allows hosts to assume that all other hosts are actually on their network.

- *RIP*—RIP is a routing protocol that is commonly available on IP hosts. Many hosts use RIP to find the address of the routers on a LAN or, when there are multiple routers, to pick the best router to use for a given internetwork address.

Cisco routers support all the router discovery protocols listed. You can choose the router discovery mechanism that works best in your particular environment.

Choosing Internetworking Reliability Options

One of the first concerns of most network designers is to determine the required level of application availability. In general, this key consideration is balanced against implementation cost. For most organizations, the cost of making a network completely fault tolerant is prohibitive. Determining the appropriate level of fault tolerance to be included in a network and where redundancy should be used is not trivial.

The nonredundant internetwork design in Figure 2–18 illustrates the considerations involved with increasing levels of internetwork fault tolerance.

The internetwork shown in Figure 2–18 has two levels of hierarchy: a corporate office and remote offices. Assume the corporate office has eight Ethernet segments, to which approximately 400 users (an average of 50 per segment) are connected. Each Ethernet segment is connected to a router. In the remote offices, two Ethernet segments are connected to the corporate office through a router. The router in each remote office is connected to the router in the corporate office through a T1 link.

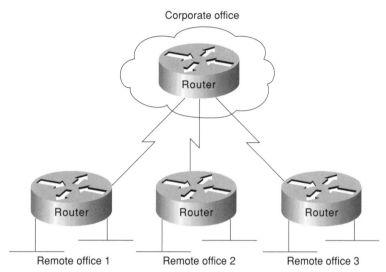

Figure 2–18
Typical nonredundant
internetwork design.

The following sections address various approaches to creating redundant internetworks, provide some context for each approach, and contrast their relative merits and drawbacks. The following four sections are provided:

- Redundant Links Versus Meshed Topologies
- Redundant Power Systems
- Fault-Tolerant Media Implementations
- Backup Hardware

Redundant Links Versus Meshed Topologies

Typically, WAN links are the least reliable components in an internetwork, usually because of problems in the local loop. In addition to being relatively unreliable, these links are often an order of magnitude slower than the LANs they connect. However, because they are capable of connecting geographically diverse sites, WAN links often make up the backbone network, and are therefore critical to corporate operations. The combination of potentially suspect reliability, lack of speed, and high importance makes the WAN link a good candidate for redundancy.

As a first step in making the example internetwork more fault tolerant, you might add a WAN link between each remote office and the corporate office. This results in the topology shown in Figure 2–19. The new topology has several advantages. First, it provides a backup link that can be used if a primary link connecting any remote office and the corporate office fails. Second, if the routers support load balancing, link bandwidth has now been increased, lowering response times for users and increasing application availability.

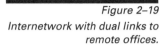

Figure 2–19

Internetwork with dual links to remote offices.

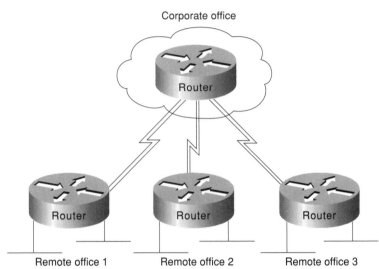

Load balancing in transparent bridging and IGRP environments is another tool for increasing fault tolerance. Routers also support load balancing on either a per-packet or a per-destination basis in all IP environments. Per-packet load balancing is recommended if the WAN links are relatively slow (for example, less than 56 Kbps). If WAN links are faster than 56 Kbps, enabling fast switching on the routers is recommended. When fast switching is enabled, load balancing occurs on a per-destination basis.

Routers can automatically compensate for failed WAN links through routing algorithms of protocols, such as IGRP, OSPF, and IS-IS. If one link fails, the routing software recalculates the routing algorithm and begins sending all traffic through another link. This allows applications to proceed in the face of WAN link failure, improving application availability.

The primary disadvantage of duplicating WAN links to each remote office is cost. In the example outlined in Figure 2–19, three new WAN links are required. In large star networks with more remote offices, 10 or 20 new WAN links might be needed, as well as new equipment (including new WAN router interfaces). A lower cost alternative that is becoming increasingly popular links the remote offices using a meshed topology, as shown in Figure 2–20.

In the "before" portion of Figure 2–20, any failure associated with either Link A or B blocks access to a remote site. The failure might involve the link connection equipment, such as a data service unit (DSU) or a channel service unit (CSU), the router (either the entire router or a single router port), or the link itself. Adding Link C as shown in the "after" portion of the figure, offsets the effect of a failure in any single link. If Link A or B fails, the affected remote site can still access the corporate office through Link C and the other site's link to the corporate office. Note also that if Link C fails, the two remote sites can communicate through their connections to the corporate office.

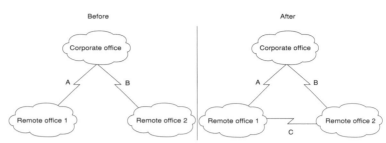

Figure 2–20
Evolution from a star to a
meshed topology.

A meshed topology has three distinct advantages over a redundant star topology:

- A meshed topology is usually slightly less expensive (at least by the cost of one WAN link).

- A meshed topology provides more direct (and potentially faster) communication between remote sites, which translates to greater application availability. This can be useful if direct traffic volumes between remote sites are relatively high.

- A meshed topology promotes distributed operation, preventing bottlenecks on the corporate router and further increasing application availability.

A redundant star is a reasonable solution under the following conditions:

- Relatively little traffic must travel between remote offices.

- Traffic moving between corporate and remote offices is delay sensitive and mission critical. The delay and potential reliability problems associated with making an extra hop when a link between a remote office and the corporate office fails might not be tolerable.

Redundant Power Systems

Power faults are common in large-scale networks. Because they can strike across a very local or a very wide scale, power faults are difficult to preempt. Simple power problems include dislodged power cords, tripped circuit breakers, and local power supply failures. More extensive power problems include large-scale outages caused by natural phenomena (such as lightning strikes) or brown-outs. Each organization must assess its needs and the probability of each type of power outage before determining which preventative actions to take.

You can take many precautions to try to ensure that problems, such as dislodged power cords, do not occur frequently. These fall outside the scope of this publication and will not be discussed here. This chapter focuses on issues addressable by internetworking devices.

From the standpoint of internetworking devices, dual power systems can prevent otherwise debilitating failures. Imagine a situation where the so-called *backbone-in-a-box* configuration is being used. This configuration calls for the connection of many networks to a router being used as a *connectivity hub*. Benefits include a high-speed backbone (essentially the router's backplane) and cost efficiency (less media). Unfortunately, if the router's power system becomes faulty, each network connected to that router loses its capability to communicate with all other networks connected to that router.

Some backbone-in-a-box routers can address this requirement by providing redundant power systems. In addition, many sites connect one power system to the local power grid and the other to an uninterruptable power supply. If router power fails, the router can continue to provide connectivity to each connected network.

General power outages are usually more common than failures in a router's power system. Consider the effect of a site-wide power failure on redundant star and meshed topologies. If the power fails in the corporate office, the organization might be seriously inconvenienced. Key network applications are likely to be placed at a centralized, corporate location. The organization could easily lose revenue for every minute its network is down. The meshed network configuration is superior in this case because links between the remote offices would still be able to communicate with each other.

If power fails at a remote site, all connections to that remote site will be terminated unless otherwise protected. Neither the redundant star nor the meshed topology is superior. In both cases, all other remote offices will still be able to communicate with the corporate office. Generally, power failures in a remote office are more serious when network services are widely distributed.

To protect against local and site-wide power outages, some companies have negotiated an arrangement with local power companies to use multiple power grids within their organization. Failure within one power grid will not affect the network if all critical components have access to multiple power grids. Unfortunately, this arrangement is very expensive and should only be considered by companies with substantial resources, extremely mission-critical operations, and a relatively high likelihood of power failures.

The effect of highly localized power failures can be minimized with prudent network planning. Wherever possible, redundant components should use power supplied by different circuits. Further, these redundant components should not be physically colocated. For example, if redundant routers are employed for all stations on a given floor, these routers can be physically stationed in wiring closets on different floors. This prevents local wiring closet power problems from affecting the capability of all stations on a given floor to communicate. Figure 2–21 shows such a configuration.

For some organizations, the need for fault tolerance is so great that potential power failures are protected against with a duplicate corporate data center. Organizations with these requirements often locate a redundant data center in another city, or in a part of the same city that is some distance from the primary data center. All backend services are duplicated, and transactions coming in from remote offices are sent to both data centers. This configuration requires duplicate WAN links from all remote offices, duplicate network hardware, duplicate servers and server resources, and leasing another building. Because this approach is so costly, it is typically the last step taken by companies desiring the ultimate in fault tolerance.

Partial duplication of the data center is also a possibility. Several key servers and links to those servers can be duplicated. This is a common compromise to the problem presented by power failures.

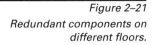

Figure 2–21
Redundant components on
different floors.

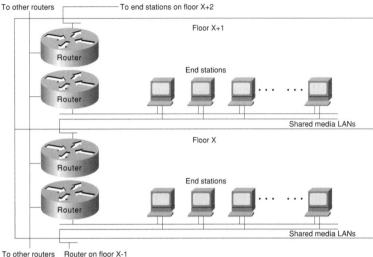

Fault-Tolerant Media Implementations

Media failure is another possible network fault. Included in this category are all problems associated with the media and its link to each individual end station. Under this definition, media components include network interface controller failures, lobe or attachment unit interface (AUI) cable failures, transceiver failures, hub failures, and all failures associated with media components (for example, the cable itself, terminators, and other parts). Many media failures are caused by operator negligence and cannot easily be eliminated.

One way to reduce the havoc caused by failed media is to divide existing media into smaller segments and support each segment with different hardware. This minimizes the effect of a failure on a particular segment. For example, if you have 100 stations attached to a single switch, move some of them to other switches. This reduces the effect of a hub failure and of certain subnetwork failures. If you place an internetworking device (such as a router) between segments, you protect against additional problems and cut subnetwork traffic.

As shown in Figure 2–21, redundancy can be employed to help minimize media failures. Each station in this figure is attached to two different media segments. NICs, hub ports, and interface cables are all redundant. This approach doubles the cost of network connectivity for each end station as well as the port usage on all internetworking devices, and is therefore only recommended in situations where complete redundancy is required. It also assumes that end station software, including both the network and the application subsystems, can handle and effectively use the redundant components. The application software or the networking software or both must be able to detect network failures and initiate use of the other network.

Certain media access protocols have some fault-tolerant features built in. Token Ring multistation access units (MAUs) can detect certain media connection failures and bypass the failure internally.

FDDI dual rings can wrap traffic onto the backup ring to avoid portions of the network with problems.

From a router's standpoint, many media failures can be bypassed so long as alternative paths are available. Using various hardware detection techniques, routers can sense certain media-level problems. If routing updates or routing keepalive messages have not been received from devices that would normally be reached through a particular router port, the router will soon declare that route down and will look for alternative routes. Meshed networks provide these alternative paths, allowing the router to compensate for media failures.

Backup Hardware

Like all complex devices, routers, switches, and other internetworking devices develop hardware problems. When serious failures occur, the use of dual devices can effectively reduce the adverse effects of a hardware failure. After a failure, discovery protocols help end stations choose new paths with which to communicate across the network. If each network connected to the failed device has an alternative path out of the local area, complete connectivity will still be possible.

For example, when backup routers are used, routing metrics can be set to ensure that the backup routers will not be used unless the primary routers are not functioning. Switchover is automatic and rapid. For example, consider the situation shown in Figure 2–22. In this network, dual routers are used at all sites with dual WAN links. If Router R1 fails, the routers on FDDI 1 will detect the failure by the absence of messages from Router R1. Using any of several dynamic routing protocols, Router A, Router B, and Router C will designate Router R3 as the new next hop on the way to remote resources accessible via Router R4.

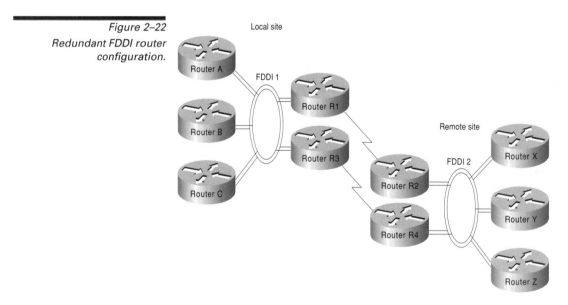

Figure 2–22
Redundant FDDI router
configuration.

Many networks are designed with multiple routers connecting particular LANs in order to provide redundancy. In the past, the effectiveness of this design was limited by the speed at which the hosts on those LANs detected a topology update and changed routers. In particular, IP hosts tend to be configured with a default gateway or configured to use Proxy ARP in order to find a router on their LAN. Convincing an IP host to change its router usually required manual intervention to clear the ARP cache or to change the default gateway.

The Hot Standby Router Protocol (HSRP) is a solution that allows network topology changes to be transparent to the host. HSRP typically allows hosts to reroute in approximately 10 seconds. HSRP is supported on Ethernet, Token Ring, FDDI, Fast Ethernet, and ATM.

An HSRP group can be defined on each LAN. All members of the group know the standby IP address and the standby MAC address. One member of the group is elected the leader. The lead router services all packets sent to the HSRP group address. The other routers monitor the leader and act as HSRP routers. If the lead router becomes unavailable, the HSRP router elects a new leader who inherits the HSRP MAC address and IP address.

High-end routers (Cisco 4500, 7000, and 7500 families) can support multiple MAC addresses on the same Ethernet or FDDI interface, allowing the routers to simultaneously handle both traffic that is sent to the standby MAC address and the private MAC address. The commands for enabling HSRP and configuring an HSRP group are **standby ip** and **standby group**.

IDENTIFYING AND SELECTING INTERNETWORKING DEVICES

Network designers have four basic types of internetworking devices available to them:

- Hubs (concentrators)
- Bridges
- Switches
- Routers

For a summary of these four internetworking devices, see Table 2–1 earlier in this chapter. Data communications experts generally agree that network designers are moving away from bridges and primarily using switches and routers to build internetworks. Consequently, this section focuses on the role of switches and routers in designing internetworks.

Switches can be functionally divided into two main groups: Layer 2 switches and multilayer switches that provide Layer 2 and Layer 3 switching capabilities. Today, network designers are replacing hubs in their wiring closets with switches to increase their network performance and protect their existing wiring investments.

Routers segment network traffic based on the destination network layer address (Layer 3) rather than the workstation data link layer or MAC address. Consequently, routers are protocol dependent.

Benefits of Switches (Layer 2 Services)

An individual Layer 2 switch might offer some or all of the following benefits:

- *Bandwidth*—LAN switches provide excellent performance for individual users by allocating dedicated bandwidth to each switch port. Each switch port represents a different network segment. This technique is known as *microsegmenting*.

- *VLANs*—LAN switches can group individual ports into switched logical workgroups called VLANs, thereby restricting the broadcast domain to designated VLAN member ports. VLANs are also known as switched domains and autonomous switching domains. Communication between VLANs requires a router.

- *Automated packet recognition and translation*—This capability allows the switch to translate frame formats automatically, such as Ethernet MAC to FDDI SNAP.

Benefits of Routers (Layer 3 Services)

Because routers use Layer 3 addresses, which typically have structure, routers can use techniques (such as address summarization) to build networks that maintain performance and responsiveness as they grow in size. By imposing structure (usually hierarchical) on a network, routers can effectively use redundant paths and determine optimal routes even in a dynamically changing network.

Routers are necessary to ensure scalability as the network grows and expands. They provide the following capabilities that are vital in network designs:

- Broadcast and multicast control

- Broadcast segmentation

- Security

- Quality of service (QoS)

- Multimedia

Backbone Routing Options

In an ideal world, the perfect enterprise-wide internetwork would feature a single, bullet-proof network protocol capable of transporting all manner of data communications seamlessly, error free, and with sufficient resilience to accommodate any unforeseen connectivity disruption. However, in the real world, there are many protocols with varying levels of resilience.

In designing a backbone for your organization, you might consider several options. These options are typically split into the following two primary categories:

- Multiprotocol routing backbone

- Single-protocol backbone

The following discussions outline the characteristics and properties of these two strategies.

Multiprotocol Routing Backbone

When multiple network layer protocols are routed throughout a common backbone without encapsulation (also referred to as *native* mode routing), the environment is referred to as a multiprotocol routing backbone. A multiprotocol backbone environment can adopt one of two routing strategies, or both, depending on the routed protocol involved. The two strategies are generally referred to as the following:

- *Integrated routing*—Integrated routing involves the use of a single routing protocol (for example, a link state protocol) that determines the least cost path for different routed protocols.

- *Ships in the night*—The ships-in-the-night approach involves the use of a different routing protocol for each network protocol. For instance, some large-scale networks might feature multiple protocols in which Novell IPX traffic is routed using a proprietary version of the Routing Information Protocol (RIP), IP is routed with IGRP, and DECnet Phase V traffic is routed via ISO CLNS-compliant IS-IS.

Each of these network layer protocols is routed independently, with separate routing processes handling their traffic and separate paths calculated. Mixing routers within an internetwork that supports different combinations of multiple protocols can create a confusing situation, particularly for integrated routing. In general, integrated routing is easier to manage if all the routers attached to the integrated routing backbone support the same integrated routing scheme. Routes for other protocols can be calculated separately. As an alternative, you can use encapsulation to transmit traffic over routers that do not support a particular protocol.

Single-Protocol Backbone

With a single-protocol backbone, all routers are assumed to support a single routing protocol for a single network protocol. In this kind of routing environment, all other routing protocols are ignored. If multiple protocols are to be passed over the internetwork, unsupported protocols must be encapsulated within the supported protocol or they will be ignored by the routing nodes.

Why implement a single-protocol backbone? If relatively few other protocols are supported at a limited number of isolated locations, it is reasonable to implement a single protocol backbone. However, encapsulation does add overhead to traffic on the network. If multiple protocols are supported widely throughout a large internetwork, a multiprotocol backbone approach is likely to work better.

In general, you should support all the network layer protocols in an internetwork with a native routing solution and implement as few network layer protocols as possible.

Types of Switches

Switches can be categorized as follows:

- *LAN switches*—The switches within this category can be further divided into Layer 2 switches and multilayer switches.

- *ATM switches*—ATM switching and ATM routers offer greater backbone bandwidth required by high-throughput data services.

Network managers are adding LAN switches to their wiring closets to augment bandwidth and reduce congestion in existing shared-media hubs while using new backbone technologies, such as Fast Ethernet and ATM.

LAN Switches

Today's cost-effective, high-performance LAN switches offer network managers the following benefits:

- Superior microsegmentation
- Increased aggregate data forwarding
- Increased bandwidth across the corporate backbone

LAN switches address end users' bandwidth needs for wiring closet applications. By deploying switches rather than traditional shared hubs, network designers can increase performance and leverage the current investments in existing LAN media and adapters. These switches also offer functionality not previously available, such as VLANs, that provide the flexibility to use software to move, add, and change users across the network.

LAN switches are also suited to provide segment switching and scalable bandwidth within network data centers by delivering switched links to interconnect existing hubs in wiring closets, LAN switches, and server farms. Cisco provides the Catalyst family of multilayer switches for connecting multiple wiring closet switches or shared hubs into a backbone configuration.

ATM Switches

Even though all ATM switches perform cell relay, ATM switches differ markedly in the following capabilities:

- Variety of interfaces and services that are supported
- Redundancy
- Depth of ATM internetworking software
- Sophistication of traffic management mechanism

Just as there are routers and LAN switches available at various price/performance points with different levels of functionality, ATM switches can be segmented into the following four distinct types that reflect the needs of particular applications and markets:

- Workgroup ATM switches
- Campus ATM switches
- Enterprise ATM switches
- Multiservice access switches

Cisco offers a complete range of ATM switches.

Workgroup and Campus ATM Switches

Workgroup ATM switches have Ethernet switch ports and an ATM uplink to connect to a campus ATM switch. An example of a workgroup ATM switch is the Cisco Catalyst 5000.

Campus ATM switches are generally used for small-scale ATM backbones (for example, to link ATM routers or LAN switches). This use of ATM switches can alleviate current backbone congestion and enable the deployment of such new services as VLANs. Campus switches need to support a wide variety of both local backbone and WAN types, but be price/performance optimized for the local backbone function. In this class of switches, ATM routing capabilities that allow multiple switches to be tied together is very important. Congestion control mechanisms for optimizing backbone performance is also important. The LightStream 1010 family of ATM switches is an example of a campus ATM switch. For more information on deploying workgroup and campus ATM switches in your internetwork, see Chapter 12, "Designing Switched LAN Internetworks."

Enterprise ATM Switches

Enterprise ATM switches are sophisticated multiservice devices that are designed to form the core backbones of large, enterprise networks. They are intended to complement the role played by today's high-end multiprotocol routers. Enterprise ATM switches are used to interconnect campus ATM switches. Enterprise-class switches, however, can act not only as ATM backbones but can serve as the single point of integration for all of the disparate services and technology found in enterprise backbones today. By integrating all of these services onto a common platform and a common ATM transport infrastructure, network designers can gain greater manageability and eliminate the need for multiple overlay networks.

Cisco's BPX/AXIS is a powerful broadband ATM switch designed to meet the demanding, high-traffic needs of a large private enterprise or public service provider. For more information on deploying enterprise ATM switches in your internetwork, see Chapter 8, "Designing ATM Internetworks."

Multiservice Access Switches

Beyond private networks, ATM platforms will also be widely deployed by service providers both as customer premises equipment (CPE) and within public networks. Such equipment will be used to support multiple MAN and WAN services—for example, Frame Relay switching, LAN interconnect, or public ATM services—on a common ATM infrastructure. Enterprise ATM switches will often be used in these public network applications because of their emphasis on high availability and redundancy, their support of multiple interfaces, and capability to integrate voice and data.

Switches and Routers Compared

To highlight the differences between switches and routers, the following sections examine the different roles of these devices in the following situations:

* Implementation of VLANs
* Implementation of switched internetworks

Role of Switches and Routers in VLANs

VLANs address the following two problems:

- Scalability issues of a flat network topology
- Simplification of network management by facilitating network reconfigurations (moves and changes)

A VLAN consists of a single broadcast domain and solves the scalability problems of large flat networks by breaking a single broadcast domain into several smaller broadcast domains or VLANs. Virtual LANs offer easier moves and changes in a network design than traditional networks. LAN switches can be used to segment networks into logically defined virtual workgroups. This logical segmentation, commonly referred to as VLAN communication, offers a fundamental change in how LANs are designed, administered, and managed. Although logical segmentation provides substantial benefits in LAN administration, security, and management of network broadcast across the enterprise, there are many components of VLAN solutions that network designers should consider prior to large scale VLAN deployment.

Switches and routers each play an important role in VLAN design. Switches are the core device that controls individual VLANs while routers provide interVLAN communication, as shown in Figure 2–23.

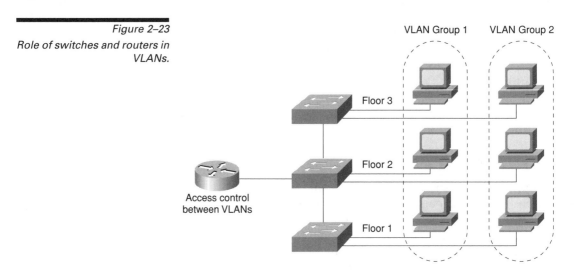

Figure 2–23
Role of switches and routers in VLANs.

Switches remove the physical constraints imposed by a shared-hub architecture because they logically group users and ports across the enterprise. As a replacement for shared hubs, switches remove the physical barriers imposed within each wiring closet. Additionally, the role of the router evolves beyond the more traditional role of firewalls and broadcast suppression to policy-based control, broadcast management, and route processing and distribution. Equally as important, routers remain vital for switched architectures configured as VLANs because they provide the communication between VLANs. Routers also provide VLAN access to shared resources, such as servers and hosts. For more information on deploying VLANs, see Chapter 12, "Designing Switched LAN Internetworks."

Examples of Campus Switched Internetwork Designs

A successful campus switched internetworking solution must combine the benefits of both routers and switches in every part of the network, as well as offer a flexible evolution path from shared-media networking to switched internetworks.

For example, incorporating switches in campus network designs will generally result in the following benefits:

- High bandwidth
- Improved performance
- Low cost
- Easy configuration

If you need advanced internetworking services, however, routers are necessary. Routers offer the following services:

- Broadcast firewalling
- Hierarchical addressing
- Communication between dissimilar LANs
- Fast convergence
- Policy routing
- QoS routing
- Security
- Redundancy and load balancing
- Traffic flow management
- Multimedia group membership

Some of these router services will be offered by switches in the future. For example, support for multimedia often requires a protocol, such as Internet Group Management Protocol (IGMP), that allows workstations to join a group that receives multimedia multicast packets. In the future, Cisco will allow switches to participate in this process by using the Cisco Group Management Protocol (CGMP). One router will still be necessary, but you will not need a router in each department because CGMP switches can communicate with the router to determine if any of their attached users are part of a multicast group.

Switching and bridging sometimes can result in non-optimal routing of packets. This is because every packet must go through the root bridge of the spanning tree. When routers are used, the routing of packets can be controlled and designed for optimal paths. Cisco now provides support for improved routing and redundancy in switched environments by supporting one instance of the spanning tree per VLAN.

The following figures illustrate how network designers can use switches and routers to evolve their shared-media networks to switching internetworks. Typically, this evolution to a campus switched internetwork architecture will extend over four phases.

Phase 1 is the microsegmentation phase in which network designers retain their hubs and routers, but insert a LAN switch to enhance performance. Figure 2–24 shows an example of how a LAN switch can be used to segment a network.

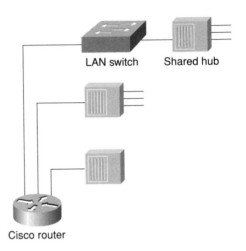

Figure 2–24

Using switches for microsegmentation.

LAN switch   Shared hub

Cisco router

Phase 2 is the addition of high-speed backbone technology and routing between switches. LAN switches perform switch processing and provide dedicated bandwidth to the desktop and to shared-media hubs. Backbone routers are attached to either Fast Ethernet or ATM switches. The increase in backbone bandwidth matches the increase bandwidth in the wiring closet. Figure 2–25 shows an example of how you can add high-speed backbone technology and routing between existing switches in your network.

In Phase 3, routers are distributed between the LAN switches in the wiring closet and the high-speed core switch. The network backbone is now strictly a high-speed transport mechanism with all other devices, such as the distributed routers, at the periphery. Figure 2–26 illustrates such a network.

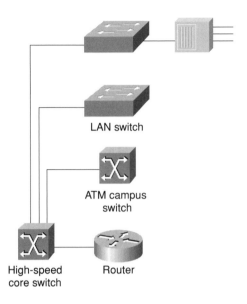

Figure 2–25
Adding high-speed backbone technology and routing between switches.

LAN switch

ATM campus switch

High-speed core switch

Router

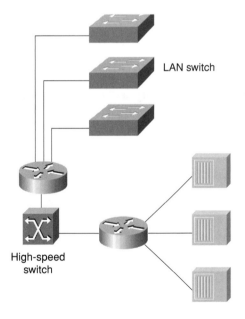

Figure 2–26
Distributing routers between high-speed core and LAN switches.

LAN switch

High-speed switch

Phase 4 is the final phase—the end point. It involves end-to-end switching with integral VLANs and multilayer switching capability. By this point, Layer 2 and Layer 3 integrated switching is distributed across the network and is connected to the high-speed core. Figure 2–27 shows an example of this final phase.

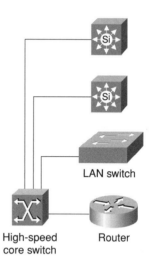

Figure 2–27

End-to-end switching with VLAN and multilayer switching capability.

LAN switch

High-speed   Router
core switch

SUMMARY

Now that the basic internetworking devices and general design principles have been examined, the remaining chapters in this part focus on the different technologies available when designing an internetwork.

CHAPTER 3

Designing Large-Scale IP Internetworks

This chapter focuses on the following design implications of the Enhanced Interior Gateway Routing Protocol (IGRP), Open Shortest Path First (OSPF) protocols, and the Border Gateway Protocol (BGP):

- Network Topology
- Addressing and Route Summarization
- Route Selection
- Convergence
- Network Scalability
- Security

Enhanced IGRP, OSPF, and BGP are routing protocols for the Internet Protocol (IP). An introductory discussion outlines general routing protocol issues; subsequent discussions focus on design guidelines for the specific IP protocols.

IMPLEMENTING ROUTING PROTOCOLS

The following discussion provides an overview of the key decisions you must make when selecting and deploying routing protocols. This discussion lays the foundation for subsequent discussions regarding specific routing protocols.

Network Topology

The physical topology of an internetwork is described by the complete set of routers and the networks that connect them. Networks also have a logical topology. Different routing protocols establish the logical topology in different ways.

Some routing protocols do not use a logical hierarchy. Such protocols use addressing to segregate specific areas or domains within a given internetworking environment and to establish a logical topology. For such nonhierarchical, or *flat*, protocols, no manual topology creation is required.

Other protocols require the creation of an explicit hierarchical topology through establishment of a backbone and logical areas. The OSPF and Intermediate System-to-Intermediate System (IS-IS) protocols are examples of routing protocols that use a hierarchical structure. A general hierarchical network scheme is illustrated in Figure 3–1. The explicit topology in a hierarchical scheme takes precedence over the topology created through addressing.

Figure 3–1
Hierarchical network.

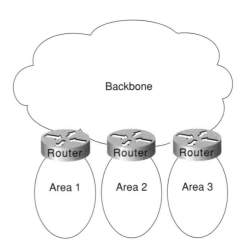

If a hierarchical routing protocol is used, the addressing topology should be assigned to reflect the hierarchy. If a flat routing protocol is used, the addressing implicitly creates the topology. There are two recommended ways to assign addresses in a hierarchical network. The simplest way is to give each area (including the backbone) a unique network address. An alternative is to assign address ranges to each area.

Areas are logical collections of contiguous networks and hosts. Areas also include all the routers having interfaces on any one of the included networks. Each area runs a separate copy of the basic routing algorithm. Therefore, each area has its own topological database.

Addressing and Route Summarization

Route summarization procedures condense routing information. Without summarization, each router in a network must retain a route to every subnet in the network. With summarization, routers can reduce some sets of routes to a single advertisement, reducing both the load on the router and the perceived complexity of the network. The importance of route summarization increases with network size.

Figure 3–2 illustrates an example of route summarization. In this environment, Router R2 maintains one route for all destination networks beginning with B, and Router R4 maintains one route for all destination networks beginning with A. This is the essence of route summarization. Router R1 tracks all routes because it exists on the boundary between A and B.

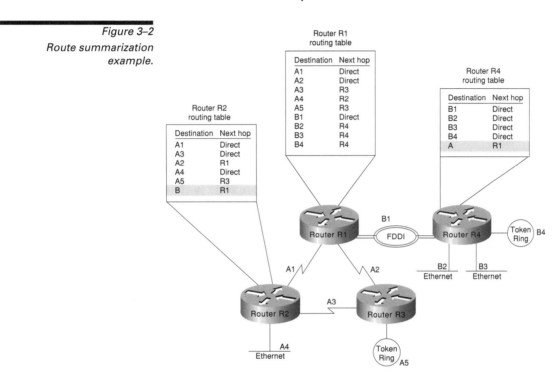

Figure 3–2
Route summarization example.

The reduction in route propagation and routing information overhead can be significant. Figure 3–3 illustrates the potential savings. The vertical axis of Figure 3–3 shows the number of routing table entries. The horizontal axis measures the number of subnets. Without summarization, each router in a network with 1,000 subnets must contain 1,000 routes. With summarization, the picture changes considerably. If you assume a Class B network with eight bits of subnet address space, each router needs to know all of the routes for each subnet in its network number (250 routes, assuming that 1,000 subnets fall into four major networks of 250 routers each) plus one route for each of the other networks (three) for a total of 253 routes. This represents a nearly 75-percent reduction in the size of the routing table.

The preceding example shows the simplest type of route summarization: collapsing all the subnet routes into a single network route. Some routing protocols also support route summarization at any bit boundary (rather than just at major network number boundaries) in a network address. A routing protocol can summarize on a bit boundary only if it supports *variable-length subnet masks* (VLSMs).

Some routing protocols summarize automatically. Other routing protocols require manual configuration to support route summarization, as shown in Figure 3–3.

Figure 3–3

Route summarization benefits.

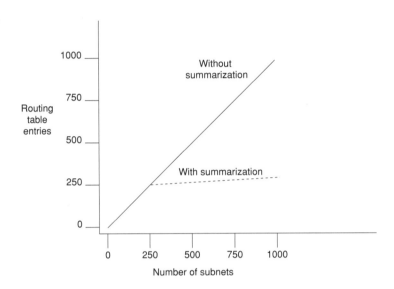

Route Selection

Route selection is trivial when only a single path to the destination exists. However, if any part of that path should fail, there is no way to recover. Therefore, most networks are designed with multiple paths so there are alternatives in case a failure occurs.

Routing protocols compare route metrics to select the best route from a group of possible routes. Route metrics are computed by assigning a characteristic or set of characteristics to each physical network. The metric for the route is an aggregation of the characteristics of each physical network in the route. Figure 3–4 shows a typical meshed network with metrics assigned to each link and the best route from source to destination identified.

Figure 3–4

Routing metrics and route selection.

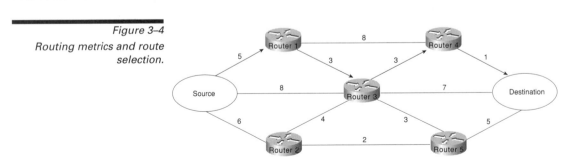

Routing protocols use different techniques for assigning metrics to individual networks. Further, each routing protocol forms a metric aggregation in a different way. Most routing protocols can use multiple paths if the paths have an equal cost. Some routing protocols can even use multiple paths when paths have an unequal cost. In either case, load balancing can improve overall allocation of network bandwidth.

When multiple paths are used, there are several ways to distribute the packets. The two most common mechanisms are *per-packet load balancing* and *per-destination load balancing*. Per-packet load balancing distributes the packets across the possible routes in a manner proportional to the route metrics. With equal-cost routes, this is equivalent to a round-robin scheme. One packet or destination (depending on switching mode) is distributed to each possible path. Per-destination load balancing distributes packets across the possible routes based on destination. Each new destination is assigned the next available route. This technique tends to preserve packet order.

NOTES ——————————————————————————————————————

Most TCP implementations can accommodate out-of-order packets. However, out-of-order packets may cause performance degradation.

When fast switching is enabled on a router (default condition), route selection is done on a per-destination basis. When fast switching is disabled, route selection is done on a per-packet basis. For line speeds of 56 Kbps and faster, fast switching is recommended.

Convergence

When *network* topology changes, network traffic must reroute quickly. The phrase "convergence time" describes the time it takes a router to start using a new route after a topology changes. Routers must do three things after a topology changes:

- Detect the change
- Select a new route
- Propagate the changed route information

Some changes are immediately detectable. For example, serial line failures that involve carrier loss are immediately detectable by a router. Other failures are harder to detect. For example, if a serial line becomes unreliable but the carrier is not lost, the unreliable link is not immediately detectable. In addition, some media (Ethernet, for example) do not provide physical indications such as carrier loss. When a router is reset, other routers do not detect this immediately. In general, failure detection is dependent on the media involved and the routing protocol used.

Once a failure has been detected, the routing protocol must select a new route. The mechanisms used to do this are protocol-dependent. All routing protocols must propagate the changed route. The mechanisms used to do this are also protocol-dependent.

Network Scalability

The capability to extend your internetwork is determined, in part, by the scaling characteristics of the routing protocols used and the quality of the network design.

Network scalability is limited by two factors: operational issues and technical issues. Typically, operational issues are more significant than technical issues. Operational scaling concerns encourage the use of large areas or protocols that do not require hierarchical structures. When hierarchical protocols are required, technical scaling concerns promote the use of small areas. Finding the right balance is the art of network design.

From a technical standpoint, routing protocols scale well if their resource use grows less than linearly with the growth of the network. Three critical resources are used by routing protocols: memory, central processing unit (CPU), and bandwidth.

Memory

Routing protocols use memory to store routing tables and topology information. Route summarization cuts memory consumption for all routing protocols. Keeping areas small reduces the memory consumption for hierarchical routing protocols.

CPU

CPU usage is protocol-dependent. Some protocols use CPU cycles to compare new routes to existing routes. Other protocols use CPU cycles to regenerate routing tables after a topology change. In most cases, the latter technique will use more CPU cycles than the former. For link-state protocols, keeping areas small and using summarization reduces CPU requirements by reducing the effect of a topology change and by decreasing the number of routes that must be recomputed after a topology change.

Bandwidth

Bandwidth usage is also protocol-dependent. Three key issues determine the amount of bandwidth a routing protocol consumes:

- *When routing information is sent*—Periodic updates are sent at regular intervals. Flash updates are sent only when a change occurs.

- *What routing information is sent*—Complete updates contain all routing information. Partial updates contain only changed information.

- *Where routing information is sent*—Flooded updates are sent to all routers. Bounded updates are sent only to routers that are affected by a change.

NOTES

These three issues also affect CPU usage.

Distance vector protocols such as Routing Information Protocol (RIP), Interior Gateway Routing Protocol (IGRP), Internetwork Packet Exchange (IPX) RIP, IPX Service Advertisement Protocol (SAP), and Routing Table Maintenance Protocol (RTMP), broadcast their complete routing table periodically, regardless of whether the routing table has changed. This periodic advertisement varies from every 10 seconds for RTMP to every 90 seconds for IGRP. When the network is stable, distance vector protocols behave well but waste bandwidth because of the periodic sending of routing table updates, even when no change has occurred. When a failure occurs in the network, distance vector protocols do not add excessive load to the network, but they take a long time to reconverge to an alternative path or to flush a bad path from the network.

Link-state routing protocols, such as Open Shortest Path First (OSPF), Intermediate System-to-Intermediate System (IS-IS), and NetWare Link Services Protocol (NLSP), were designed to address the limitations of distance vector routing protocols (slow convergence and unnecessary bandwidth usage). Link-state protocols are more complex than distance vector protocols, and running them adds to the router's overhead. The additional overhead (in the form of memory utilization and bandwidth consumption when link-state protocols first start up) constrains the number of neighbors that a router can support and the number of neighbors that can be in an area.

When the network is stable, link-state protocols minimize bandwidth usage by sending updates only when a change occurs. A hello mechanism ascertains reachability of neighbors. When a failure occurs in the network, link-state protocols flood link-state advertisements (LSAs) throughout an area. LSAs cause every router within the failed area to recalculate routes. The fact that LSAs need to be flooded throughout the area in failure mode and the fact that all routers recalculate routing tables constrain the number of neighbors that can be in an area.

Enhanced IGRP is an advanced distance vector protocol that has some of the properties of link-state protocols. Enhanced IGRP addresses the limitations of conventional distance vector routing protocols (slow convergence and high bandwidth consumption in a steady state network). When the network is stable, Enhanced IGRP sends updates only when a change in the network occurs. Like link-state protocols, Enhanced IGRP uses a hello mechanism to determine the reachability of neighbors. When a failure occurs in the network, Enhanced IGRP looks for feasible successors by sending messages to its neighbors. The search for feasible successors can be aggressive in terms of the traffic it generates (updates, queries, and replies) to achieve convergence. This behavior constrains the number of neighbors that is possible.

In WANs, consideration of bandwidth is especially critical. For example, Frame Relay, which statistically multiplexes many logical data connections (virtual circuits) over a single physical link, allows the creation of networks that share bandwidth. Public Frame Relay networks use bandwidth sharing at all levels within the network. That is, bandwidth sharing may occur within the Frame Relay network of Corporation X, as well as between the networks of Corporation X and Corporation Y.

Two factors have a substantial effect on the design of public Frame Relay networks:

- Users are charged for each permanent virtual circuit (PVC), which encourages network designers to minimize the number of PVCs.

- Public carrier networks sometimes provide incentives to avoid the use of committed information rate (CIR) circuits. Although service providers try to ensure sufficient bandwidth, packets can be dropped.

Overall, WANs can lose packets because of lack of bandwidth. For Frame Relay networks, this possibility is compounded because Frame Relay does not have a broadcast replication facility, so for every broadcast packet that is sent out a Frame Relay interface, the router must replicate it for each PVC on the interface. This requirement limits the number of PVCs that a router can handle effectively.

In addition to bandwidth, network designers must consider the size of routing tables that need to be propagated. Clearly, the design considerations for an interface with 50 neighbors and 100 routes to propagate are very different from the considerations for an interface with 50 neighbors and 10,000 routes to propagate. Table 3–1 gives a rough estimate of the number of WAN neighbors that a routing protocol can handle effectively.

Table 3–1   *Routing Protocols and Number of WAN Neighbors*

Routing Protocol	Number of Neighbors per Router
Distance vector	50
Link state	30
Advanced distance vector	30

Security

Controlling access to network resources is a primary concern. Some routing protocols provide techniques that can be used as part of a security strategy. With some routing protocols, you can insert a filter on the routes being advertised so that certain routes are not advertised in some parts of the network.

Some routing protocols can authenticate routers that run the same protocol. Authentication mechanisms are protocol specific and generally weak. In spite of this, it is worthwhile to take advantage of the techniques that exist. Authentication can increase network stability by preventing unauthorized routers or hosts from participating in the routing protocol, whether those devices are attempting to participate accidentally or deliberately.

ENHANCED IGRP INTERNETWORK DESIGN GUIDELINES

The Enhanced Interior Gateway Routing Protocol (Enhanced IGRP) is a routing protocol developed by Cisco Systems and introduced with Software Release 9.21 and Cisco Internetworking

Operating System (Cisco IOS) Software Release 10.0. Enhanced IGRP combines the advantages of distance vector protocols, such as IGRP, with the advantages of link-state protocols, such as Open Shortest Path First (OSPF). Enhanced IGRP uses the Diffusing Update ALgorithm (DUAL) to achieve convergence quickly.

Enhanced IGRP includes support for IP, Novell NetWare, and AppleTalk. The discussion on Enhanced IGRP covers the following topics:

- Enhanced IGRP Network Topology
- Enhanced IGRP Addressing
- Enhanced IGRP Route Summarization
- Enhanced IGRP Route Selection
- Enhanced IGRP Convergence
- Enhanced IGRP Network Scalability
- Enhanced IGRP Security

NOTES

Although the general discussion in this section is applicable to IP, IPX, and AppleTalk Enhanced IGRP, IP issues are highlighted here. For case studies on how to integrate Enhanced IGRP into IP, IPX, and AppleTalk networks, including detailed configuration examples and protocol-specific issues, see Chapter 17, "Integrating Enhanced IGRP into Existing Networks."

CAUTION

If you are using *candidate default route* in IP Enhanced IGRP and have installed multiple releases of Cisco router software within your internetwork that include any versions prior to September 1994, contact your Cisco technical support representative for version compatibility and software upgrade information. Refer to your software release notes for details.

Enhanced IGRP Network Topology

Enhanced IGRP uses a nonhierarchical (or flat) topology by default. Enhanced IGRP automatically summarizes subnet routes of directly connected networks at a network number boundary. This automatic summarization is sufficient for most IP networks. See the section "Enhanced IGRP Route Summarization" later in this chapter for more details.

Enhanced IGRP Addressing

The first step in designing an Enhanced IGRP network is to decide on how to address the network. In many cases, a company is assigned a single NIC address (such as a Class B network address) to be allocated in a corporate internetwork. Bit-wise subnetting and variable-length subnetwork masks (VLSMs) can be used in combination to save address space. Enhanced IGRP for IP supports the use of VLSMs.

Consider a hypothetical network where a Class B address is divided into subnetworks, and contiguous groups of these subnetworks are summarized by Enhanced IGRP. The Class B network 156.77.0.0 might be subdivided as illustrated in Figure 3–5.

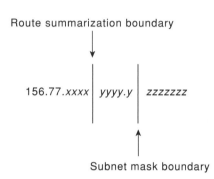

Figure 3–5
Variable-length subnet masks (VLSMs) and route summarization boundaries.

In Figure 3–5, the letters x, y, and z represent bits of the last two octets of the Class B network as follows:

- The four *x* bits represent the route summarization boundary.
- The five *y* bits represent up to 32 subnets per summary route.
- The seven *z* bits allow for 126 (128-2) hosts per subnet.

Appendix A, "Subnetting an IP Address Space," provides a complete example illustrating assignment for the Class B address 150.100.0.0.

Enhanced IGRP Route Summarization

With Enhanced IGRP, subnet routes of directly connected networks are automatically summarized at network number boundaries. In addition, a network administrator can configure route summarization at any interface with any bit boundary, allowing ranges of networks to be summarized arbitrarily.

Enhanced IGRP Route Selection

Routing protocols compare route metrics to select the best route from a group of possible routes. The following factors are important to understand when designing an Enhanced IGRP internetwork. Enhanced IGRP uses the same vector of metrics as IGRP. Separate metric values are assigned for bandwidth, delay, reliability, and load. By default, Enhanced IGRP computes the metric for a route by using the minimum bandwidth of each hop in the path and adding a media-specific delay for each hop. The metrics used by Enhanced IGRP are as follows:

- *Bandwidth*—Bandwidth is deduced from the interface type. Bandwidth can be modified with the **bandwidth** command.

- *Delay*—Each media type has a propagation delay associated with it. Modifying delay is very useful to optimize routing in network with satellite links. Delay can be modified with the **delay** command.

- *Reliability*—Reliability is dynamically computed as a rolling weighted average over five seconds.

- *Load*—Load is dynamically computed as a rolling weighted average over five seconds.

When Enhanced IGRP summarizes a group of routes, it uses the metric of the best route in the summary as the metric for the summary.

NOTES

For information on Enhanced IGRP load sharing, see the section "IP Routing Protocol Selection for SRB Networks" in Chapter 4, "Designing SRB Internetworks."

Enhanced IGRP Convergence

Enhanced IGRP implements a new convergence algorithm known as DUAL (Diffusing Update ALgorithm). DUAL uses two techniques that allow Enhanced IGRP to converge very quickly. First, each Enhanced IGRP router stores its neighbors' routing tables. This allows the router to use a new route to a destination instantly if another *feasible* route is known. If no feasible route is known based upon the routing information previously learned from its neighbors, a router running Enhanced IGRP becomes *active* for that destination and sends a query to each of its neighbors, asking for an alternative route to the destination. These queries propagate until an alternative route is found. Routers that are not affected by a topology change remain *passive* and do not need to be involved in the query and response.

A router using Enhanced IGRP receives full routing tables from its neighbors when it first communicates with the neighbors. Thereafter, only *changes* to the routing tables are sent and only to *routers* that are *affected* by the change. A *successor* is a neighboring router that is currently being used for packet forwarding, provides the *least cost* route to the destination, and is not part of a routing loop. Information in the routing table is based on *feasible successors*. Feasible successor routes can be used in case the existing route fails. Feasible successors provide the *next least-cost* path without introducing routing loops.

The routing table keeps a list of the computed costs of reaching networks. The topology table keeps a list of all routes advertised by neighbors. For each network, the router keeps the real cost of getting to that network and also keeps the advertised cost from its neighbor. In the event of a failure, convergence is instant if a feasible successor can be found. A neighbor is a feasible successor if it meets the feasibility condition set by DUAL. DUAL finds feasible successors by the performing the following computations:

- Determines membership of V_1. V_1 is the set of all neighbors whose advertised distance to network x is less than FD. (FD is the feasible distance and is defined as the best metric during an active-to-passive transition.)

- Calculates D_{min}. D_{min} is the minimum computed cost to network x.

- Determines membership of V_2. V_2 is the set of neighbors that are in V1 whose computed cost to network x equals D_{min}.

The feasibility condition is met when V_2 has one or more members. The concept of feasible successors is illustrated in Figure 3–6. Consider Router A's topology table entries for Network 7. Router B is the *successor* with a computed cost of 31 to reach Network 7, compared to the computed costs of Router D (230) and Router H (40).

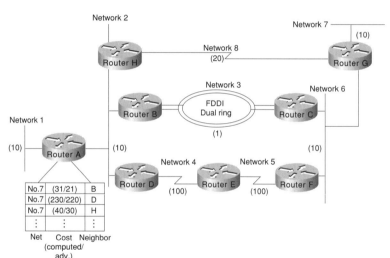

Figure 3–6
DUAL feasible successor.

If Router B becomes unavailable, Router A will go through the following three-step process to find a feasible successor for Network 7:

Step 1   Determining which neighbors have an advertised distance to Network 7 that is less than Router A's feasible distance (FD) to Network 7. The FD is 31 and Router H meets this condition. Therefore, Router H is a member of V_1.

Step 2   Calculating the minimum computed cost to Network 7. Router H provides a cost of 40, and Router D provides a cost of 230. D_{min} is, therefore, 40.

Step 3   Determining the set of neighbors that are in V_1 whose computed cost to Network 7 equals D_{min} (40). Router H meets this condition.

The feasible successor is Router H which provides a least cost route of 40 from Router A to Network 7. If Router H now also becomes unavailable, Router A performs the following computations:

Step 1   Determines which neighbors have an advertised distance to Network 7 that is less than the FD for Network 7. Because both Router B and H have become unavailable, only Router D remains. However, the advertised cost of Router D to Network 7 is 220, which is greater than Router A's FD (31) to Network 7. Router D, therefore, cannot be a member of V_1. The FD remains at 31—the FD can only change during an active-to-passive transition, and this did not occur. There was no transition to active state for Network 7; this is known as a *local computation.*

Step 2   Because there are no members of V1, there can be no feasible successors. Router A, therefore, transitions from passive to active state for Network 7 and queries its neighbors about Network 7. There was a transition to active; this is known as a *diffusing computation.*

NOTES

For more details on Enhanced IGRP convergence, see Appendix F, "References and Recommended Reading," for a list of reference papers and materials.

The following example and graphics further illustrate how Enhanced IGRP supports virtually instantaneous convergence in a changing internetwork environment. In Figure 3–7, all routers can access one another and Network N. The computed cost to reach other routers and Network N is shown. For example, the cost from Router E to Router B is 10. The cost from Router E to Network N is 25 (cumulative of 10 + 10 + 5 = 25).

Figure 3–7
DUAL example (part 1): initial network connectivity.

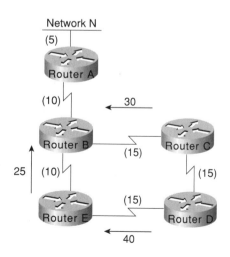

In Figure 3–8, the connection between Router B and Router E fails. Router E sends a multicast query to all of its neighbors and puts Network N into an active state.

Figure 3–8
DUAL example (part 2):
sending queries.

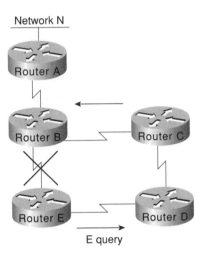

Next, as illustrated in Figure 3–9, Router D determines that it has a feasible successor. It changes its successor from Router E to Router C and sends a reply to Router E.

Figure 3–9
DUAL example (part 3):
switching to a feasible
successor.

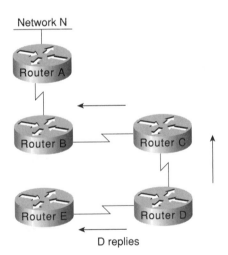

In Figure 3–10, Router E has received replies from all neighbors and therefore brings Network N out of active state. Router E puts Network N into its routing table at a distance of 60.

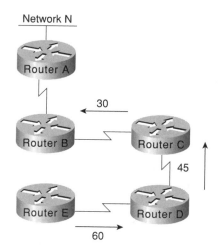

Figure 3–10
Flow of intersubnet traffic with
layer 3 switches.

Network N

Router A

30

Router B   Router C

45

Router E   Router D

60

NOTES

Router A, Router B, and Router C were not involved in route recomputation. Router D recomputed its path to Network N without first needing to learn new routing information from its downstream neighbors.

Enhanced IGRP Network Scalability

Network scalability is limited by two factors: operational issues and technical issues. Operationally, Enhanced IGRP provides easy configuration and growth. Technically, Enhanced IGRP uses resources at less than a linear rate with the growth of a network.

Memory

A router running Enhanced IGRP stores all routes advertised by neighbors so that it can adapt quickly to alternative routes. The more neighbors a router has, the more memory a router uses. Enhanced IGRP automatic route aggregation bounds the routing table growth naturally. Additional bounding is possible with manual route aggregation.

CPU

Enhanced IGRP uses the DUAL algorithm to provide fast convergence. DUAL recomputes only routes which are affected by a topology change. DUAL is not computationally complex, so it does not require a lot of CPU.

Bandwidth

Enhanced IGRP uses partial updates. Partial updates are generated only when a change occurs; only the changed information is sent, and this changed information is sent only to the routers affected. Because of this, Enhanced IGRP is very efficient in its usage of bandwidth. Some additional bandwidth is used by Enhanced IGRP's HELLO protocol to maintain adjacencies between neighboring routers.

Enhanced IGRP Security

Enhanced IGRP is available only on Cisco routers. This prevents accidental or malicious routing disruption caused by hosts in a network. In addition, route filters can be set up on any interface to prevent learning or propagating routing information inappropriately.

OSPF Internetwork Design Guidelines

OSPF is an Interior Gateway Protocol (IGP) developed for use in Internet Protocol (IP)-based internetworks. As an IGP, OSPF distributes routing information between routers belonging to a single autonomous system (AS). An AS is a group of routers exchanging routing information via a common routing protocol. The OSPF protocol is based on shortest-path-first, or link-state, technology.

The OSPF protocol was developed by the OSPF working group of the Internet Engineering Task Force (IETF). It was designed expressly for the Internet Protocol (IP) environment, including explicit support for IP subnetting and the tagging of externally derived routing information. OSPF Version 2 is documented in Request for Comments (RFC) 1247.

Whether you are building an OSPF internetwork from the ground up or converting your internetwork to OSPF, the following design guidelines provide a foundation from which you can construct a reliable, scalable OSPF-based environment.

Two design activities are critically important to a successful OSPF implementation:

- Definition of area boundaries
- Address assignment

Ensuring that these activities are properly planned and executed will make all the difference in your OSPF implementation. Each is addressed in more detail with the discussions that follow. These discussions are divided into nine sections:

- OSPF Network Topology
- OSPF Addressing and Route Summarization
- OSPF Route Selection
- OSPF Convergence
- OSPF Network Scalability
- OSPF Security
- OSPF NSSA (Not-So-Stubby Area) Capabilities

- OSPF On Demand Circuit Protocol Issues
- OSPF over Non-Broadcast Networks

NOTES ──

For a detailed case study on how to set up and configure RIP and OSPF redistribution, see Chapter 14, "RIP and OSPF Redistribution."

OSPF Network Topology

OSPF works best in a hierarchical routing environment. The first and most important decision when designing an OSPF network is to determine which routers and links are to be included in the backbone and which are to be included in each area. There are several important guidelines to consider when designing an OSPF topology:

- *The number of routers in an area*—OSPF uses a CPU-intensive algorithm. The number of calculations that must be performed given n link-state packets is proportional to $n \log n$. As a result, the larger and more unstable the area, the greater the likelihood for performance problems associated with routing protocol recalculation. Generally, an area should have no more than 50 routers. Areas with unstable links should be smaller.

- *The number of neighbors for any one router*—OSPF floods all link-state changes to all routers in an area. Routers with many neighbors have the most work to do when link-state changes occur. In general, any one router should have no more than 60 neighbors.

- *The number of areas supported by any one router*—A router must run the link-state algorithm for each link-state change that occurs for every area in which the router resides. Every area border router is in at least two areas (the backbone and one area). In general, to maximize stability, one router should not be in more than three areas.

- *Designated router selection*—In general, the designated router and backup designated router on a local-area network (LAN) have the most OSPF work to do. It is a good idea to select routers that are not already heavily loaded with CPU-intensive activities to be the designated router and backup designated router. In addition, it is generally not a good idea to select the same router to be designated router on many LANs simultaneously.

The discussions that follow address topology issues that are specifically related to the backbone and the areas.

Backbone Considerations

Stability and *redundancy* are the most important criteria for the backbone. Stability is increased by keeping the size of the backbone reasonable. This is caused by the fact that every router in the backbone needs to recompute its routes after every link-state change. Keeping the backbone small reduces the likelihood of a change and reduces the amount of CPU cycles required to recompute routes. As a general rule, each area (including the backbone) should contain no more than 50 routers. If link quality is high and the number of routes is small, the number of routers can be increased. Redundancy is important in the backbone to prevent partition when a link fails. Good backbones are designed so that no single link failure can cause a partition.

OSPF backbones must be contiguous. All routers in the backbone should be directly connected to other backbone routers. OSPF includes the concept of virtual links. A virtual link creates a path between two area border routers (an area border router is a router connects an area to the backbone) that are not directly connected. A virtual link can be used to heal a partitioned backbone. However, it is not a good idea to design an OSPF network to require the use of virtual links. The stability of a virtual link is determined by the stability of the underlying area. This dependency can make troubleshooting more difficult. In addition, virtual links cannot run across stub areas. See the section "Backbone-to-Area Route Advertisement" later in this chapter for a detailed discussion of stub areas.

Avoid placing hosts (such as workstations, file servers, or other shared resources) in the backbone area. Keeping hosts out of the backbone area simplifies internetwork expansion and creates a more stable environment.

Area Considerations

Individual areas must be contiguous. In this context, a contiguous area is one in which a continuous path can be traced from any router in an area to any other router in the same area. This does not mean that all routers must share common network media. It is not possible to use virtual links to connect a partitioned area. Ideally, areas should be richly connected internally to prevent partitioning. The two most critical aspects of area design follow:

- Determining how the area is addressed
- Determining how the area is connected to the backbone

Areas should have a contiguous set of network and/or subnet addresses. Without a contiguous address space, it is not possible to implement route summarization. The routers that connect an area to the backbone are called *area border routers*. Areas can have a single area border router or they can have multiple area border routers. In general, it is desirable to have more than one area border router per area to minimize the chance of the area becoming disconnected from the backbone.

When creating large-scale OSPF internetworks, the definition of areas and assignment of resources within areas must be done with a pragmatic view of your internetwork. The following are general rules that help ensure that your internetwork remains flexible and provides the kind of performance needed to deliver reliable resource access:

- *Consider physical proximity when defining areas*—If a particular location is densely connected, create an area specifically for nodes at that location.
- *Reduce the maximum size of areas if links are unstable*—If your internetwork includes unstable links, consider implementing smaller areas to reduce the effects of route flapping. Whenever a route is lost or comes online, each affected area must converge on a new topology. The Dykstra algorithm will run on all the affected routers. By segmenting your

internetwork into smaller areas, you can isolate unstable links and deliver more reliable overall service.

OSPF Addressing and Route Summarization

Address assignment and route summarization are inextricably linked when designing OSPF internetworks. To create a scalable OSPF internetwork, you should implement route summarization. To create an environment capable of supporting route summarization, you must implement an effective hierarchical addressing scheme. The addressing structure that you implement can have a profound impact on the performance and scalability of your OSPF internetwork. The following sections discuss OSPF route summarization and three addressing options:

- Separate network numbers for each area

- Network Information Center (NIC)-authorized address areas created using bit-wise subnetting and VLSM

- Private addressing, with a *demilitarized zone* (DMZ) buffer to the official Internet world

---

NOTES

You should keep your addressing scheme as simple as possible, but be wary of oversimplifying your address assignment scheme. Although simplicity in addressing saves time later when operating and troubleshooting your network, taking shortcuts can have certain severe consequences. In building a scalable addressing environment, use a structured approach. If necessary, use bit-wise subnetting— but make sure that route summarization can be accomplished at the area border routers.

OSPF Route Summarization

Route summarization is extremely desirable for a reliable and scalable OSPF internetwork. The effectiveness of route summarization, and your OSPF implementation in general, hinges on the addressing scheme that you adopt. Summarization in an OSPF internetwork occurs between each area and the backbone area. Summarization must be configured manually in OSPF. When planning your OSPF internetwork, consider the following issues:

- Be sure that your network addressing scheme is configured so that the range of subnets assigned within an area is contiguous.

- Create an address space that will permit you to split areas easily as your network grows. If possible, assign subnets according to simple octet boundaries. If you cannot assign addresses in an easy-to-remember and easy-to-divide manner, be sure to have a thoroughly defined addressing structure. If you know how your entire address space is assigned (or will be assigned), you can plan for changes more effectively.

- Plan ahead for the addition of new routers to your OSPF environment. Be sure that new routers are inserted appropriately as area, backbone, or border routers. Because the addition of new routers creates a new topology, inserting new routers can cause unexpected routing changes (and possibly performance changes) when your OSPF topology is recomputed.

Separate Address Structures for Each Area

One of the simplest ways to allocate addresses in OSPF is to assign a separate network number for each area. With this scheme, you create a backbone and multiple areas, and assign a separate IP network number to each area. Figure 3–11 illustrates this kind of area allocation.

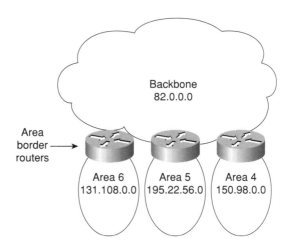

Figure 3–11
Assignment of NIC addresses example.

The following are the basic steps for creating such a network:

Step 1   Define your structure (identify areas and allocate nodes to areas).

Step 2   Assign addresses to networks, subnets, and end stations.

In the network illustrated in Figure 3–11, each area has its own unique NIC-assigned address. These can be Class A (the backbone in Figure 3–11), Class B (areas 4 and 6), or Class C (Area 5). The following are some clear benefits of assigning separate address structures to each area:

- Address assignment is relatively easy to remember.

- Configuration of routers is relatively easy and mistakes are less likely.

- Network operations are streamlined because each area has a simple, unique network number.

In the example illustrated in Figure 3–11, the route summarization configuration at the area border routers is greatly simplified. Routes from Area 4 injecting into the backbone can be summarized as follows: *All routes starting with 150.98 are found in Area 4.*

The main drawback of this approach to address assignment is that it wastes address space. If you decide to adopt this approach, be sure that area border routers are configured to do route summarization. Summarization must be explicitly set; it is disabled by default in OSPF.

Bit-Wise Subnetting and VLSM

Bit-wise subnetting and variable-length subnetwork masks (VLSMs) can be used in combination to save address space. Consider a hypothetical network where a Class B address is subdivided using an area mask and distributed among 16 areas. The Class B network, 156.77.0.0, might be subdivided as illustrated in Figure 3–12.

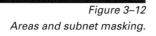

Figure 3–12
Areas and subnet masking.

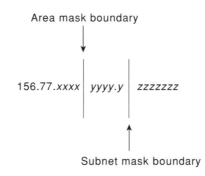

In Figure 3–12, the letters *x*, *y*, and *z* represent bits of the last two octets of the Class B network as follows:

- The four *x* bits are used to identify 16 areas.
- The five *y* bits represent up to 32 subnets per area.
- The seven *z* bits allow for 126 (128-2) hosts per subnet.

Appendix A, "Subnetting an IP Address Space," provides a complete example illustrating assignment for the Class B address 150.100.0.0. It illustrates both the concept of *area masks* and the breakdown of large subnets into smaller ones using VLSMs.

Private Addressing

Private addressing is another option often cited as simpler than developing an area scheme using bit-wise subnetting. Although private address schemes provide an excellent level of flexibility and do not limit the growth of your OSPF internetwork, they have certain disadvantages. For instance, developing a large-scale internetwork of privately addressed IP nodes limits total access to the Internet, and mandates the implementation of what is referred to as a *demilitarized zone* (DMZ). If you need to connect to the Internet, Figure 3–13 illustrates the way in which a DMZ provides a buffer of valid NIC nodes between a privately addressed network and the Internet.

All nodes (end systems and routers) on the network in the DMZ must have NIC-assigned IP addresses. The NIC might, for example, assign a single Class C network number to you. The DMZ shown in Figure 3–13 has two routers and a single application gateway host (Garp). Router A provides the interface between the DMZ and the Internet, and Router B provides the firewall between the DMZ and the private address environment. All applications that need to run over the Internet must access the Internet through the application gateway.

Figure 3–13

Connecting to the Internet from a privately addressed network.

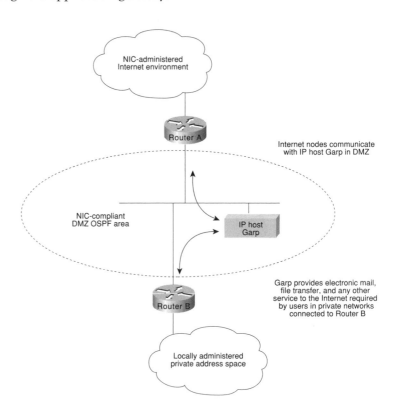

NOTES

For a case study on network security that includes information on how to set up firewall routers and communication servers, see Chapter 16, "Increasing Security on IP Networks."

Route Summarization Techniques

Route summarization is particularly important in an OSPF environment because it increases the stability of the network. If route summarization is being used, routes within an area that change do not need to be changed in the backbone or in other areas. Route summarization addresses two important questions of route information distribution:

- What information does the backbone need to know about each area? The answer to this question focuses attention on area-to-backbone routing information.

- What information does each area need to know about the backbone and other areas? The answer to this question focuses attention on backbone-to-area routing information.

Area-to-Backbone Route Advertisement

There are several key considerations when setting up your OSPF areas for proper summarization:

- OSPF route summarization occurs in the area border routers.

- OSPF supports VLSM, so it is possible to summarize on any bit boundary in a network or subnet address.

- OSPF requires manual summarization. As you design the areas, you need to determine summarization at each area border router.

Backbone-to-Area Route Advertisement

There are four potential types of routing information in an area:

- *Default*—If an explicit route cannot be found for a given IP network or subnetwork, the router will forward the packet to the destination specified in the default route.

- *Intra-area routes*—Explicit network or subnet routes must be carried for all networks or subnets inside an area.

- *Interarea routes*—Areas may carry explicit network or subnet routes for networks or subnets that are in this AS but not in this area.

- *External routes*—When different ASs exchange routing information, the routes they exchange are referred to as external routes.

In general, it is desirable to restrict routing information in any area to the minimal set that the area needs. There are three types of areas, and they are defined in accordance with the routing information that is used in them:

- *Nonstub areas*—Nonstub areas carry a default route, static routes, intra-area routes, interarea routes, and external routes. An area must be a nonstub area when it contains a router that uses both OSPF and any other protocol, such as the Routing Information Protocol (RIP). Such a router is known as an autonomous system border router (ASBR). An area must also be a nonstub area when a virtual link is configured across the area. Nonstub areas are the most resource-intensive type of area.

- *Stub areas*—Stub areas carry a default route, intra-area routes and interarea routes, but they do not carry external routes. Stub areas are recommended for areas that have only one area border router and they are often useful in areas with multiple area border routers. See "Controlling Interarea Traffic" later in this chapter for a detailed discussion of the design trade-offs in areas with multiple area border routers. There are two restrictions on the use of stub areas: Virtual links cannot be configured across them and they cannot contain an ASBR.

- *Stub areas without summaries*—Software releases 9.1(11), 9.21(2), and 10.0(1) and later support stub areas without summaries, allowing you to create areas that carry only a default route and intra-area routes. Stub areas without summaries do not carry interarea routes or external routes. This type of area is recommended for simple configurations in which a single router connects an area to the backbone.

Table 3–2 shows the different types of areas according to the routing information that they use.

Table 3–2   *Routing Information Used in OSPF Areas*

Area Type	Default Route	Intra-area Routes	Interarea Routes	External Routes
Nonstub	Yes	Yes	Yes	Yes
Stub	Yes	Yes	Yes	No
Stub without summaries	Yes	Yes	No	No

— **NOTES** ——————————————————————————

Stub areas are configured using the **area** *area-id* **stub** router configuration command. Routes are summarized using the **area** *area-id* **range** *address mask* router configuration command. Refer to your *Router Products Configuration Guide* and *Router Products Command Reference* publications for more information regarding the use of these commands.

OSPF Route Selection

When designing an OSPF internetwork for efficient route selection, consider three important topics:

- Tuning OSPF Metrics
- Controlling Interarea Traffic
- Load Balancing in OSPF Internetworks

Tuning OSPF Metrics

The default value for OSPF metrics is based on bandwidth. The following characteristics show how OSPF metrics are generated:

- Each link is given a metric value based on its bandwidth. The metric for a specific link is the inverse of the bandwidth for that link. Link metrics are normalized to give FDDI a metric of 1. The metric for a route is the sum of the metrics for all the links in the route.

NOTES

In some cases, your network might implement a media type that is faster than the fastest default media configurable for OSPF (FDDI). An example of a faster media is ATM. By default, a faster media will be assigned a cost equal to the cost of an FDDI link—a link-state metric cost of 1. Given an environment with both FDDI and a faster media type, you must manually configure link costs to configure the faster link with a lower metric. Configure any FDDI link with a cost greater than 1, and the faster link with a cost less than the assigned FDDI link cost. Use the **ip ospf cost** interface configuration command to modify link-state cost.

- When route summarization is enabled, OSPF uses the metric of the best route in the summary.
- There are two forms of external metrics: type 1 and type 2. Using an external type 1 metric results in routes adding the internal OSPF metric to the external route metric. External type 2 metrics do not add the internal metric to external routes. The external type 1 metric is generally preferred. If you have more than one external connection, either metric can affect how multiple paths are used.

Controlling Interarea Traffic

When an area has only a single area border router, all traffic that does not belong in the area will be sent to the area border router. In areas that have multiple area border routers, two choices are available for traffic that needs to leave the area:

- Use the area border router closest to the originator of the traffic. (Traffic leaves the area as soon as possible.)
- Use the area border router closest to the destination of the traffic. (Traffic leaves the area as late as possible.)

If the area border routers inject only the default route, the traffic goes to the area border router that is closest to the source of the traffic. Generally, this behavior is desirable because the backbone typically has higher bandwidth lines available. However, if you want the traffic to use the area border router that is nearest the destination (so that traffic leaves the area as late as possible), the area border routers should inject summaries into the area instead of just injecting the default route.

Most network designers prefer to avoid asymmetric routing (that is, using a different path for packets that are going from A to B than for those packets that are going from B to A). It is important to understand how routing occurs between areas to avoid asymmetric routing.

Load Balancing in OSPF Internetworks

Internetwork topologies are typically designed to provide redundant routes in order to prevent a partitioned network. Redundancy is also useful to provide additional bandwidth for high traffic areas. If equal-cost paths between nodes exist, Cisco routers automatically load balance in an OSPF environment.

Cisco routers can use up to four equal-cost paths for a given destination. Packets might be distributed either on a per-destination (when fast switching) or a per-packet basis. Per-destination load balancing is the default behavior. Per-packet load balancing can be enabled by turning off fast switching using the **no ip route-cache** interface configuration command. For line speeds of 56 Kbps and faster, it is recommended that you enable fast switching.

OSPF Convergence

One of the most attractive features about OSPF is the capability to quickly adapt to topology changes. There are two components to routing convergence:

- *Detection of topology changes*—OSPF uses two mechanisms to detect topology changes. Interface status changes (such as carrier failure on a serial link) is the first mechanism. The second mechanism is failure of OSPF to receive a hello packet from its neighbor within a timing window called a *dead timer*. After this timer expires, the router assumes the neighbor is down. The dead timer is configured using the **ip ospf dead-interval** interface configuration command. The default value of the dead timer is four times the value of the Hello interval. That results in a dead timer default of 40 seconds for broadcast networks and two minutes for nonbroadcast networks.

- *Recalculation of routes*—After a failure has been detected, the router that detected the failure sends a link-state packet with the change information to all routers in the area. All the routers recalculate all of their routes using the Dykstra (or SPF) algorithm. The time required to run the algorithm depends on a combination of the size of the area and the number of routes in the database.

OSPF Network Scalability

Your ability to scale an OSPF internetwork depends on your overall network structure and addressing scheme. As outlined in the preceding discussions concerning network topology and route summarization, adopting a hierarchical addressing environment and a structured address assignment will be the most important factors in determining the scalability of your internetwork. Network scalability is affected by operational and technical considerations:

- Operationally, OSPF networks should be designed so that areas do not need to be split to accommodate growth. Address space should be reserved to permit the addition of new areas.

- Technically, scaling is determined by the utilization of three resources: memory, CPU, and bandwidth, all discussed in the following sections.

Memory

An OSPF router stores all of the link states for all of the areas that it is in. In addition, it can store summaries and externals. Careful use of summarization and stub areas can reduce memory use substantially.

CPU

An OSPF router uses CPU cycles whenever a link-state change occurs. Keeping areas small and using summarization dramatically reduces CPU use and creates a more stable environment for OSPF.

Bandwidth

OSPF sends partial updates when a link-state change occurs. The updates are flooded to all routers in the area. In a quiet network, OSPF is a quiet protocol. In a network with substantial topology changes, OSPF minimizes the amount of bandwidth used.

OSPF Security

Two kinds of security are applicable to routing protocols:

- *Controlling the routers that participate in an OSPF network*

    OSPF contains an optional authentication field. All routers within an area must agree on the value of the authentication field. Because OSPF is a standard protocol available on many platforms, including some hosts, using the authentication field prevents the inadvertent startup of OSPF in an uncontrolled platform on your network and reduces the potential for instability.

- *Controlling the routing information that routers exchange*

    All routers must have the same data within an OSPF area. As a result, it is not possible to use route filters in an OSPF network to provide security.

OSPF NSSA (Not-So-Stubby Area) Overview

Prior to NSSA, to disable an area from receiving external (Type 5) link-state advertisements (LSAs), the area needed to be defined as a stub area. Area Border Routers (ABRs) that connect stub areas do not flood any external routes they receive into the stub areas. To return packets to destinations outside of the stub area, a default route through the ABR is used.

RFC 1587 defines a hybrid area called the Not-So-Stubby Area (NSSA). An OSPF NSSA is similar to an OSPF stub area but allows for the following capabilities:

- Importing (redistribution) of external routes as Type 7 LSAs into NSSAs by NSSA Autonomous System Boundary Routers (ASBRs).

- Translation of specific Type 7 LSAs routes into Type 5 LSAs by NSSA ABRs.

Using OSPF NSSA

Use OSPF NSSA in the following scenarios:

- When you want to summarize or filter Type 5 LSAs before they are forwarded into an OSPF area. The OSPF Specification (RFC 1583) prohibits the summarizing or filtering of Type 5 LSAs. It is an OSPF requirement that Type 5 LSAs always be flooding throughout a routing domain. When you define an NSSA, you can import specific external routes as Type 7 LSAs into the NSSA. In addition, when translating Type 7 LSAs to be imported into nonstub areas, you can summarize or filter the LSAs before importing them as Type 5 LSAs.

- If you are an Internet service provider (ISP) or a network administrator that has to connect a central site using OSPF to a remote site that is using a different protocol, such as RIP or EIGRP, you can use NSSA to simplify the administration of this kind of topology. Prior to NSSA, the connection between the corporate site ABR and the remote router used RIP or EIGRP. This meant maintaining two routing protocols. Now, with NSSA, you can extend OSPF to cover the remote connection by defining the area between the corporate router and the remote router as an NSSA, as shown in Figure 3–14. You cannot expand the normal OSPF area to the remote site because the Type 5 external will overwhelm both the slow link and the remote router.

In Figure 3–14, the central site and branch office are interconnected through a slow WAN link. The branch office is not using OSPF, but the central site is. Rather than define an RIP domain to connect the sites, you can define an NSSA.

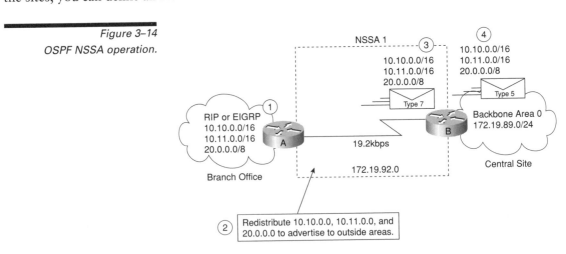

Figure 3–14

OSPF NSSA operation.

In this scenario, Router A is defined as an ASBR (autonomous system border router). It is configured to redistribute any routes within the RIP/EIGRP domain to the NSSA. The following lists what happens when the area between the connecting routers is defined as an NSSA:

1. Router A receives RIP or EGRP routes for networks 10.10.0.0/16, 10.11.0.0/16, and 20.0.0.0/8.

2. Because Router A is also connected to an NSSA, it redistributes the RIP or EIGRP routers as Type 7 LSAs into the NSSA.

3. Router B, an ABR between the NSSA and the backbone Area 0, receives the Type 7 LSAs.

4. After the SPF calculation on the forwarding database, Router B translates the Type 7 LSAs into Type 5 LSAs and then floods them throughout Backbone Area 0. It is at this point that router B could have summarized routes 10.10.0.0/16 and 10.11.0.0/16 as 10.0.0.0/8, or could have filtered one or more of the routes.

Type 7 LSA Characteristics

Type 7 LSAs have the following characteristics:

- They are originated only by ASBRs that are connected between the NSSA and autonomous system domain.

- They include a forwarding address field. This field is retained when a Type 7 LSA is translated as a Type 5 LSA.

- They are advertised only within an NSSA.

- They are not flooded beyond an NSSA. The ABR that connects to another nonstub area reconverts the Type 7 LSA into a Type 5 LSA before flooding it.

- NSSA ABRs can be configured to summarize or filter Type 7 LSAs into Type 5 LSAs.

- NSSA ABRs can advertise a Type 7 default route into the NSSA.

- Type 7 LSAs have a lower priority than Type 5 LSAs, so when a route is learned with a Type 5 LSA and Type 7 LSA, the route defined in the Type 5 LSA will be selected first.

Configuring OSPF NSSA

The steps used to configure OSPF NSSA are as follows:

Step 1   Configure standard OSPF operation on one or more interfaces that will be attached to NSSAs.

Step 2   Configure an area as NSSA using the following commands:

```
router(config)#area area-id nssa
```

Step 3   (Optional) Control the summarization or filtering during the translation. Figure 3–15 shows how Router will summarize routes using the following command:

```
router(config)#summary-address prefix mask [not-advertise] [tag tag]
```

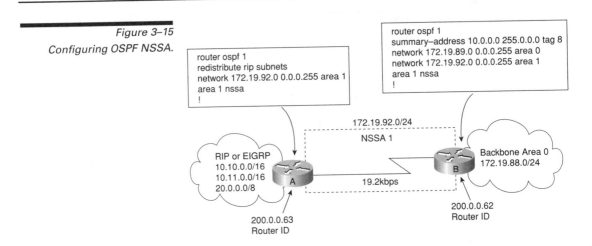

Figure 3–15
Configuring OSPF NSSA.

NSSA Implementation Considerations

Be sure to evaluate these considerations before implementing NSSA. As shown in Figure 3-15, you can set a Type 7 default route that can be used to reach external destinations. The command to issue a Type 7 default route is as follows:

```
router(config)#area area-id nssa [default-information-originate]
```

When configured, the router generates a Type 7 default into the NSSA by the NSSA ABR. Every router within the same area must agree that the area is NSSA; otherwise, the routers will not be able to communicate with one another.

If possible, avoid doing explicit redistribution on NSSA ABR because you could get confused about which packets are being translated by which router.

OSPF On Demand Circuit

OSPF On Demand Circuit is an enhancement to the OSPF protocol that allows efficient operation over on-demand circuits such as ISDN, X.25 SVCs, and dial-up lines. This feature supports RFC 1793, OSPF Over On Demand Circuits. This RFC is useful in understanding the operation of this feature. It has good examples and explains the operation of OSPF in this type of environment.

Prior to this feature, OSPF periodic Hello and link-state advertisement (LSA) updates would be exchanged between routers that connected the on-demand link even when there were no changes in the Hello or LSA information.

With OSPF On Demand Circuit, periodic Hellos are suppressed and periodic refreshes of LSAs are not flooded over demand circuits. These packets bring up the links only when they are exchanged for the first time, or when there is a change in the information they contain. This operation allows the underlying data link layer to be closed when the network topology is stable, thus keeping the cost of the demand circuit to a minimum.

This feature is a standards-based mechanism that is similar to the Cisco Snapshot feature used for distance vector protocols such as RIP.

Why Use OSPF On Demand Circuit?

This feature is useful when you want to have an OSPF backbone at the central site and you want to connect telecommuters or branch offices to the central site. In this case, OSPF On Demand Circuit allows the benefits of OSPF over the entire domain without excessive connection costs. Periodic refreshes of Hello updates and LSA updates and other protocol overhead are prevented from enabling the on-demand circuit when there is no "real" data to transmit.

Overhead protocols such as Hellos and LSAs are transferred over the on-demand circuit only upon initial setup and when they reflect a change in the topology. This means that topology-critical changes that require new shortest path first (SPF) calculations are transmitted in order to maintain network topology integrity, but periodic refreshes that do not include changes are not transmitted across the link.

OSPF On Demand Circuit Operation

Figure 3–16 illustrates general OSPF operation over on-demand circuits.

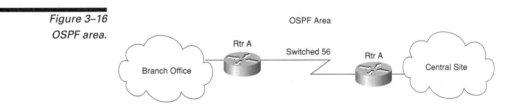

Figure 3–16
OSPF area.

The following steps describe the procedure shown in Figure 3–16:

1. Upon initialization, Router A brings up the on demand circuit to exchange Hellos and synchronize LSA databases with Router B. Because both routers are configured for OSPF On Demand Circuit, each router's Hello packets and database description packets have the demand circuit (DC) bit set. As a result, both routers know to suppress periodic Hello packet updates. When each router floods LSAs over the network, the LSAs will have the DoNotAge (DNA) bit set. This means that the LSAs will not age. They can be updated if a new LSA is received with changed information, but no periodic LSA refreshes will be issued over the demand circuit.

2. When Router A receives refreshed LSAs for existing entries in its database, it will determine whether the LSAs include changed information. If not, Router A will update the existing LSA entries, but it will not flood the information to Router B. Therefore, both routers will have the same entries, but the entry sequence numbers may not be identical.

3. When Router A does receive an LSA for a new route or an LSA that includes changed information, it will update its LSA database, bring up the on-demand circuit, and flood the information to Router B. At this point, both routers will have identical sequence numbers for this LSA entry.

4. If there is no data to transfer while the link is up for the updates, the link is terminated.

5. When a host on either side needs to transfer data to another host at the remote site, the link will be brought up.

Configuring OSPF On Demand Circuit

The steps used to configure OSPF On Demand Circuit are summarized as follows:

Step 1   Configure your on-demand circuit. For example:
```
interface bri 0
ip address 10.1.1.1 255.255.255.0
encapsulation ppp
dialer idle-timeout 3600
dialer map ip name rtra 10.1.1.2 broadcast 1234
dialer group 1
ppp authentication chap
dialer list 1 protocol ip permit
```

Step 2   Enable OSPF operation, as follows:
```
router(config)#router ospf process-id
```

Step 3   Configure OSPF on an on-demand circuit using the following interface command:
```
interface bri 0
ip ospf demand-circuit
```

If the router is part of a point-to-point topology, only one end of the demand circuit needs to be configured with this command, but both routers need to have this feature loaded. All routers that are part of a point-to-multipoint topology need to be configured with this command.

Implementation Considerations for OSPF On Demand Circuit

Evaluate the following considerations before implementing OSPF On Demand Circuit:

1. Because LSAs indicating topology changes are flooded over an on-demand circuit, you are advised to put demand circuits within OSPF stub areas or within NSSAs to isolate the demand circuits from as many topology changes as possible.

2. To take advantage of the on-demand circuit functionality within a stub area or NSSA, every router in the area must have this feature loaded. If this feature is deployed within a regular area, all other regular areas must also support this feature before the demand circuit functionality can take effect. This is because external LSAs are flooded throughout all areas.

3. Do not enable this feature on a broadcast-based network topology because Hellos cannot be successfully suppressed, which means the link will remain up.

OSPF Over Non-Broadcast Networks

NBMA networks are those networks that support many (more than two) routers, but have no broadcast capability. Neighboring routers are maintained on these nets using OSPF's Hello Protocol. However, due to the lack of broadcast capability, some configuration information may be necessary to aid in the discovery of neighbors. On non-broadcast networks, OSPF protocol packets that are normally multicast need to be sent to each neighboring router, in turn. An X.25 Public Data Network (PDN) is an example of a non-broadcast network. Note the following:

- *OSPF runs in one of two modes over non-broadcast networks.* The first mode, called non-broadcast multiaccess or NBMA, simulates the operation of OSPF on a broadcast network. The second mode, called point-to-multipoint, treats the non-broadcast network as a collection of point-to-point links. Non-broadcast networks are referred to as NBMA networks or point-to-multipoint networks, depending on OSPF's mode of operation over the network.

- *In NBMA mode, OSPF emulates operation over a broadcast network.* A Designated Router is elected for the NBMA network, and the Designated Router originates an LSA for the network. The graph representation for broadcast networks and NBMA networks is identical.

NBMA Mode

NBMA mode is the most efficient way to run OSPF over non-broadcast networks, both in terms of link-state database size and in terms of the amount of routing protocol traffic. However, it has one significant restriction: It requires all routers attached to the NBMA network to be able to communicate directly. This restriction may be met on some non-broadcast networks, such as an ATM subnet utilizing SVCs. But it is often not met on other non-broadcast networks, such as PVC-only Frame Relay networks.

On non-broadcast networks in which not all routers can communicate directly, you can break the non-broadcast network into logical subnets, with the routers on each subnet being able to communicate directly. Then each separate subnet can be run as an NBMA network or a point-to-point network if each virtual circuit is defined as a separate logical subnet. This setup, however, requires quite a bit of administrative overhead, and is prone to misconfiguration. It is probably better to run such a non-broadcast network in Point-to-MultiPoint mode.

Point-to-MultiPoint Mode

Point-to-MultiPoint networks have been designed to work simply and naturally when faced with partial mesh connectivity. In Point-to-MultiPoint mode, OSPF treats all router-to-router connections over the non-broadcast network as if they were point-to-point links. No Designated Router is elected for the network, nor is there an LSA generated for the network. It may be necessary to configure the set of neighbors that are directly reachable over the Point-to-MultiPoint network. Each neighbor is identified by its IP address on the Point-to-MultiPoint network. Because no

Designated Routers are elected on Point-to-MultiPoint networks, the Designated Router eligibility of configured neighbors is undefined.

Alternatively, neighbors on Point-to-MultiPoint networks may be dynamically discovered by lower-level protocols such as Inverse ARP. In contrast to NBMA networks, Point-to-MultiPoint networks have the following properties:

1. Adjacencies are established between all neighboring routers. There is no Designated Router or Backup Designated Router for a Point-to-MultiPoint network. No network-LSA is originated for Point-to-MultiPoint networks. Router Priority is not configured for Point-to-MultiPoint interfaces, nor for neighbors on Point-to-MultiPoint networks.

2. When originating a router-LSA, Point-to-MultiPoint interface is reported as a collection of "point-to-point links" to all of the interface's adjacent neighbors, together with a single stub link advertising the interface's IP address with a cost of 0.

3. When flooding out a non-broadcast interface (when either in NBMA or Point-to-MultiPoint mode) the Link State Update or Link State Acknowledgment packet must be replicated in order to be sent to each of the interface's neighbors.

The following is an example of point-to-multipoint configuration on a NBMA (Frame Relay in this case) network. Attached is the resulting routing table and Router Link state along with other pertinent information:

```
interface Ethernet0
 ip address 130.10.6.1 255.255.255.0
!
interface Serial0
 no ip address
 encapsulation frame-relay
 frame-relay lmi-type ansi
!
interface Serial0.1 multipoint
 ip address 130.10.10.3 255.255.255.0
 ip ospf network point-to-multipoint
 ip ospf priority 10
 frame-relay map ip 130.10.10.1 140 broadcast
 frame-relay map ip 130.10.10.2 150 broadcast
!
router ospf 2
 network 130.10.10.0 0.0.0.255 area 0
 network 130.10.6.0 0.0.0.255 area 1

R6#sh ip ospf int s 0.1
Serial0.1 is up, line protocol is up
Internet Address 130.10.10.3/24, Area 0
Process ID 2, Router ID 140.10.1.1, Network Type POINT_TO_MULTIPOINT, Cost: 6,
Timer intervals configured, Hello 30, Dead 120, Wait 120, Retransmit 5
Hello due in 00:00:18
Neighbor Count is 2, Adjacent neighbor count is 2
Adjacent with neighbor 130.10.10.2
Adjacent with neighbor 130.10.5.129
```

```
R6#sh ip ospf ne

Neighbor ID PriStateDead Time  Address        Interface
130.10.10.20FULL/  00:01:37130.10.10.2    Serial0.1
130.10.5.129 0FULL/  -00:01:53    130.10.10.1     Serial0.1
R6#

R6#sh ip ro
Codes: C - connected, S - static, I - IGRP, R - RIP, M - mobile, B - BGP
       D - EIGRP, EX - EIGRP external, O - OSPF, IA - OSPF inter area
       E1 - OSPF external type 1, E2 - OSPF external type 2, E - EGP
       i - IS-IS, L1 - IS-IS level-1, L2 - IS-IS level-2, * - candidate default
       U - per-user static route

Gateway of last resort is not set

130.10.0.0/16 is variably subnetted, 9 subnets, 3 masks
O130.10.10.2/32 [110/64] via 130.10.10.2, 00:03:28, Serial0.1
C130.10.10.0/24 is directly connected, Serial0.1
O130.10.10.1/32 [110/64] via 130.10.10.1, 00:03:28, Serial0.1
O IA130.10.0.0/22 [110/74] via 130.10.10.1, 00:03:28, Serial0.1
O130.10.4.0/24 [110/74] via 130.10.10.2, 00:03:28, Serial0.1
C130.10.6.0/24 is directly connected, Ethernet0

R6#sh ip ospf data router 140.10.1.1

  OSPF Router with ID (140.10.1.1) (Process ID 2)

Router Link States (Area 0)

  LS age: 806
  Options: (No TOS-capability)
  LS Type: Router Links
  Link State ID: 140.10.1.1
  Advertising Router: 140.10.1.1
  LS Seq Number: 80000009
  Checksum: 0x42C1
  Length: 60
  Area Border Router
   Number of Links: 3

    Link connected to: another Router (point-to-point)
     (Link ID) Neighboring Router ID: 130.10.10.2
     (Link Data) Router Interface address: 130.10.10.3
      Number of TOS metrics: 0
       TOS 0 Metrics: 64

    Link connected to: another Router (point-to-point)
     (Link ID) Neighboring Router ID: 130.10.5.129
     (Link Data) Router Interface address: 130.10.10.3
      Number of TOS metrics: 0
       TOS 0 Metrics: 64
```

```
Link connected to: a Stub Network
 (Link ID) Network/subnet number: 130.10.10.3
 (Link Data) Network Mask: 255.255.255.255
  Number of TOS metrics: 0
   TOS 0 Metrics: 0
```

BGP INTERNETWORK DESIGN GUIDELINES

The Border Gateway Protocol (BGP) is an interautonomous system routing protocol. The primary function of a BGP speaking system is to exchange network reachability information with other BGP systems. This network reachability information includes information on the list of Autonomous Systems (ASs) that reachability information traverses. BGP-4 provides a new set of mechanisms for supporting classless interdomain routing. These mechanisms include support for advertising an IP prefix and eliminate the concept of network *class* within BGP. BGP-4 also introduces mechanisms that allow aggregation of routes, including aggregation of AS paths. These changes provide support for the proposed supernetting scheme. This section describes how BGP works and it can be used to participate in routing with other networks that run BGP. The following topics are covered:

- BGP operation
- BGP attributes
- BGP path selection criteria
- Understanding and defining BGP routing policies

BGP Operation

This section presents fundamental information about BGP, including the following topics:

- Internal BGP
- External BGP
- BGP and Route Maps
- Advertising Networks

Routers that belong to the same AS and exchange BGP updates are said to be running internal BGP (IBGP). Routers that belong to different ASs and exchange BGP updates are said to be running external BGP (EBGP).

With the exception of the neighbor **ebgp-multihop** router configuration command (described in the section "External BGP" later in this chapter), the commands for configuring EBGP and IBGP are the same. This chapter uses the terms EBGP and IBGP as a reminder that, for any particular context, routing updates are being exchanged between ASs (EBGP) or within an AS (IBGP). Figure 3–17 shows a network that demonstrates the difference between EBGP and IBGP.

Before it exchanges information with an external AS, BGP ensures that networks within the AS are reachable. This is done by a combination of internal BGP peering among routers within the AS and by redistributing BGP routing information to Interior Gateway Protocols (IGPs) that run within the AS, such as Interior Gateway Routing Protocol (IGRP), Intermediate System-to-Intermediate System (IS-IS), Routing Information Protocol (RIP), and Open Shortest Path First (OSPF).

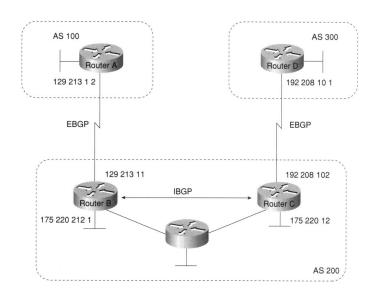

Figure 3–17
EBGP, IBGP, and multiple ASs.

BGP uses the Transmission Control Protocol (TCP) as its transport protocol (specifically, port 179). Any two routers that have opened a TCP connection to each other for the purpose of exchanging routing information are known as peers or neighbors. In Figure 3–17, Routers A and B are BGP peers, as are Routers B and C, and Routers C and D. The routing information consists of a series of AS numbers that describe the full path to the destination network. BGP uses this information to construct a loop-free map of ASs. Note that within an AS, BGP peers do not have to be directly connected.

BGP peers initially exchange their full BGP routing tables. Thereafter, BGP peers send incremental updates only. BGP peers also exchange keepalive messages (to ensure that the connection is up) and notification messages (in response to errors or special conditions).

NOTES

Routers A and B are running EBGP, and Routers B and C are running IBGP, as shown in Figure 3–17. Note that the EBGP peers are directly connected and that the IBGP peers are not. As long as there is an IGP running that allows the two neighbors to reach each other, IBGP peers do not have to be directly connected.

All BGP speakers within an AS must establish a peer relationship with one another. That is, the BGP speakers within an AS must be fully meshed logically. BGP-4 provides two techniques that alleviate the requirement for a logical full mesh: confederations and route reflectors. For information about these techniques, see the sections "Confederations" and "Route Reflectors" later in this chapter.

AS 200 is a transit AS for AS 100 and AS 300. That is, AS 200 is used to transfer packets between AS 100 and AS 300.

Internal BGP

Internal BGP (IBGP) is the form of BGP that exchanges BGP updates within an AS. Instead of IBGP, the routes learned via EBGP could be redistributed into IGP within the AS and then redistributed again into another AS. However, IBGP is more flexible, more scalable, and provides more efficient ways of controlling the exchange of information within the AS. It also presents a consistent view of the AS to external neighbors. For example, IBGP provides ways to control the exit point from an AS. Figure 3–18 shows a topology that demonstrates IBGP.

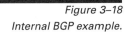

Figure 3–18
Internal BGP example.

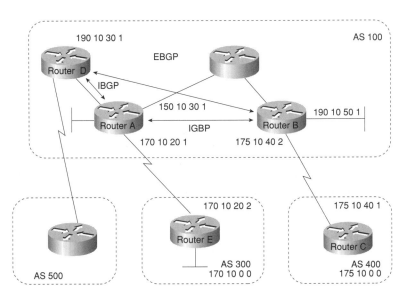

When a BGP speaker receives an update from other BGP speakers in its own AS (that is, via IBGP), the receiving BGP speaker uses EBGP to forward the update to external BGP speakers only. This behavior of IBGP is why it is necessary for BGP speakers within an AS to be fully meshed.

For example, in Figure 3–18, if there were no IBGP session between Routers B and D, Router A would send updates from Router B to Router E but not to Router D. If you want Router D to receive updates from Router B, Router B must be configured so that Router D is a BGP peer.

Loopback Interfaces. Loopback interfaces are often used by IBGP peers. The advantage of using loopback interfaces is that they eliminate a dependency that would otherwise occur when you use the IP address of a physical interface to configure BGP. Figure 3–19 shows a network in which using the loopback interface is advantageous.

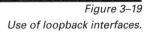

Figure 3–19
Use of loopback interfaces.

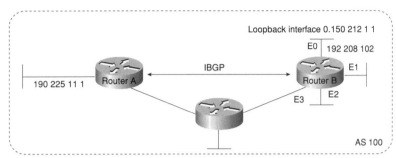

In Figure 3–19, Routers A and B are running IBGP within AS 100. If Router A were to specify the IP address of Ethernet interface 0, 1, 2, or 3 in the **neighbor remote-as** router configuration command, and if the specified interface were to become unavailable, Router A would not be able to establish a TCP connection with Router B. Instead, Router A specifies the IP address of the loopback interface that Router B defines. When the loopback interface is used, BGP does not have to rely on the availability of a particular interface for making TCP connections.

NOTES

Loopback interfaces are rarely used between EBGP peers because EBGP peers are usually directly connected and, therefore, depend on a particular physical interface for connectivity.

External BGP (EBGP)

When two BGP speakers that are not in the same AS run BGP to exchange routing information, they are said to be running EBGP.

Synchronization

When an AS provides transit service to other ASs when there are non-BGP routers in the AS, transit traffic might be dropped if the intermediate non-BGP routers have not learned routes for that traffic via an IGP. The BGP synchronization rule states that if an AS provides transit service to another AS, BGP should not advertise a route until all of the routers within the AS have learned about the route via an IGP. The topology shown in Figure 3–20 demonstrates this synchronization rule.

In Figure 3–20, Router C sends updates about network 170.10.0.0 to Router A. Routers A and B are running IBGP, so Router B receives updates about network 170.10.0.0 via IBGP. If Router B wants to reach network 170.10.0.0, it sends traffic to Router E. If Router A does not redistribute network 170.10.0.0 into an IGP, Router E has no way of knowing that network 170.10.0.0 exists and will drop the packets.

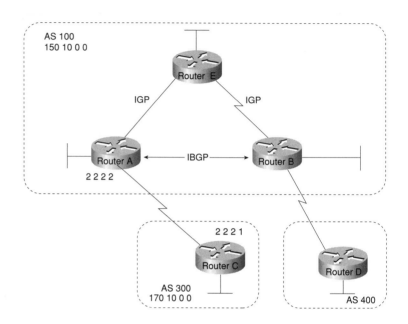

Figure 3–20
EBGP synchronization rule.

If Router B advertises to AS 400 that it can reach 170.10.0.0 before Router E learns about the network via IGP, traffic coming from Router D to Router B with a destination of 170.10.0.0 will flow to Router E and be dropped.

This situation is handled by the synchronization rule of BGP. It states that if an AS (such as AS 100 in Figure 3–20) passes traffic from one AS to another AS, BGP does not advertise a route before all routers within the AS (in this case, AS 100) have learned about the route via an IGP. In this case, Router B waits to hear about network 170.10.0.0 via an IGP before it sends an update to Router D.

Disabling Synchronization

In some cases, you might want to disable synchronization. Disabling synchronization allows BGP to converge more quickly, but it might result in dropped transit packets. You can disable synchronization if one of the following conditions is true:

- Your AS does not pass traffic from one AS to another AS.
- All the transit routers in your AS run BGP.

BGP and Route Maps

Route maps are used with BGP to control and modify routing information and to define the conditions by which routes are redistributed between routing domains. The format of a route map is as follows:

```
route-map map-tag [[permit ¦ deny] ¦ [sequence-number]]
```

The map-tag is a name that identifies the route map, and the sequence-number indicates the position that an instance of the route map is to have in relation to other instances of the same route map. (Instances are ordered sequentially.) For example, you might use the following commands to define a route map named MYMAP:

```
route-map MYMAP permit 10
! First set of conditions goes here.
route-map MYMAP permit 20
! Second set of conditions goes here.
```

When BGP applies MYMAP to routing updates, it applies the lowest instance first (in this case, instance 10). If the first set of conditions is not met, the second instance is applied, and so on, until either a set of conditions has been met, or there are no more sets of conditions to apply.

The **match** and **set route map** configuration commands are used to define the condition portion of a route map. The **match** command specifies a criteria that must be matched, and the **set** command specifies an action that is to be taken if the routing update meets the condition defined by the **match** command. The following is an example of a simple route map:

```
route-map MYMAP permit 10
match ip address 1.1.1.1
set metric 5
```

When an update matches the IP address 1.1.1.1, BGP sets the metric for the update to 5, sends the update (because of the **permit** keyword), and breaks out of the list of route-map instances. When an update does not meet the criteria of an instance, BGP applies the next instance of the route map to the update, and so on, until an action is taken, or until there are no more route map instances to apply. If the update does not meet any criteria, the update is not redistributed or controlled.

When an update meets the match criteria, and the route map specifies the **deny** keyword, BGP breaks out of the list of instances, and the update is not redistributed or controlled. Figure 3–21 shows a topology that demonstrates the use of route maps.

Figure 3–21
Route map example.

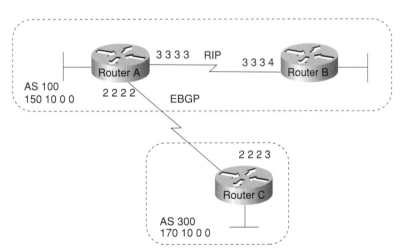

In Figure 3–21, Routers A and B run RIP with each other, and Routers A and C run BGP with each other. If you want Router A to redistribute routes from 170.10.0.0 with a metric of 2 and to redistribute all other routes with a metric of 5, use the following commands for Router A:

```
!Router A
router rip
network 3.0.0.0
network 2.0.0.0
network 150.10.0.0
passive-interface serial 0
redistribute bgp 100 route-map SETMETRIC
!
router bgp 100
neighbor 2.2.2.3 remote-as 300
network 150.10.0.0
!
route-map SETMETRIC permit 10
match ip-address 1
set metric 2
!
route-map SETMETRIC permit 20
set metric 5
!
access-list 1 permit 170.10.0.0 0.0.255.255
```

When a route matches the IP address 170.10.0.0, it is redistributed with a metric of 2. When a route does not match the IP address 170.10.0.0, its metric is set to 5, and the route is redistributed.

Assume that on Router C you want to set to 300 the community attribute of outgoing updates for network 170.10.0.0. The following commands apply a route map to outgoing updates on Router C:

```
!Router C
router bgp 300
network 170.10.0.0
neighbor 2.2.2.2 remote-as 100
neighbor 2.2.2.2 route-map SETCOMMUNITY out
!
route-map SETCOMMUNITY permit 10
match ip address 1
set community 300
!
access-list 1 permit 0.0.0.0 255.255.255.255
```

Access list 1 denies any update for network 170.10.0.0 and permits updates for any other network.

Advertising Networks

A network that resides within an AS is said to originate from that network. To inform other ASs about its networks, the AS advertises them. BGP provides three ways for an AS to advertise the networks that it originates:

- Redistributing Static Routes
- Redistributing Dynamic Routes
- Using the **network** Command

This section uses the topology shown in Figure 3–22 to demonstrate how networks that originate from an AS can be advertised.

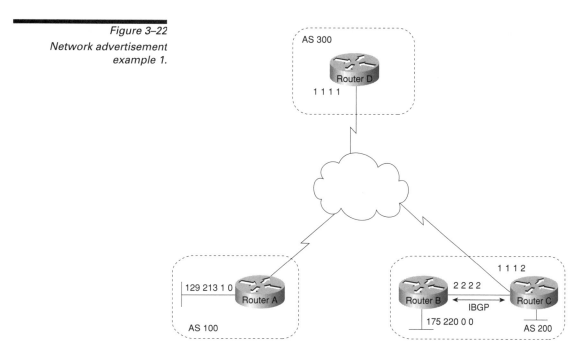

Figure 3–22
Network advertisement example 1.

Redistributing Static Routes

One way to advertise that a network or a subnet originates from an AS is to redistribute static routes into BGP. The only difference between advertising a static route and advertising a dynamic route is that when you redistribute a static route, BGP sets the origin attribute of updates for the route to Incomplete. (For a discussion of other values that can be assigned to the origin attribute, see the section "Origin Attribute" later in this chapter.) To configure Router C in Figure 3–22 to originate network 175.220.0.0 into BGP, use these commands:

```
!Router C
router bgp 200
neighbor 1.1.1.1 remote-as 300
redistribute static
!
ip route 175.220.0.0 0.0.255.255 null 0
```

The **redistribute router** configuration command and the **static** keyword cause all static routes to be redistributed into BGP. The **ip route** global configuration command establishes a static route for network 175.220.0.0. In theory, the specification of the null 0 interface would cause a packet destined for network 175.220.0.0 to be discarded. In practice, there will be a more specific match for the packet than 175.220.0.0, and the router will send it out the appropriate interface. Redistributing a static route is the best way to advertise a supernet because it prevents the route from flapping.

NOTES ───

Regardless of route type (static or dynamic), the **redistribute router** configuration command is the only way to inject BGP routes into an IGP.

Redistributing Dynamic Routes

Another way to advertise networks is to redistribute dynamic routes. Typically, you redistribute IGP routes (such as Enhanced IGRP, IGRP, IS-IS, OSPF, and RIP routes) into BGP. Some of your IGP routes might have been learned from BGP, so you need to use access lists to prevent the redistribution of routes back into BGP. Assume that in Figure 3–22, Routers B and C are running IBGP, that Router C is learning 129.213.1.0 via BGP, and that Router B is redistributing 129.213.1.0 back into Enhanced IGRP. The following commands configure Router C:

```
!Router C
router eigrp 10
network 175.220.0.0
redistribute bgp 200
redistributed connected
default-metric 1000 100 250 100 1500
!
router bgp 200
neighbor 1.1.1.1 remote-as 300
neighbor 2.2.2.2 remote-as 200
neighbor 1.1.1.1 distribute-list 1 out
redistribute eigrp 10
!
access-list 1 permit 175.220.0.0 0.0.255.255
```

The **redistribute router** configuration command with the **eigrp** keyword redistributes Enhanced IGRP routes for process ID 10 into BGP. (Normally, distributing BGP into IGP should be avoided because too many routes would be injected into the AS.) The **neighbor distribute-list router** configuration command applies access list 1 to outgoing advertisements to the neighbor whose IP address is 1.1.1.1 (that is, Router D). Access list 1 specifies that network 175.220.0.0 is to be advertised. All other networks, such as network 129.213.1.0, are implicitly prevented from being advertised. The access list prevents network 129.213.1.0 from being injected back into BGP as if it originated from AS 200, and allows BGP to advertise network 175.220.0.0 as originating from AS 200.

Using the **network** Command

Another way to advertise networks is to use the **network router** configuration command. When used with BGP, the **network** command specifies the networks that the AS originates. (By way of contrast, when used with an IGP such as RIP, the **network** command identifies the interfaces on which the IGP is to run.) The **network** command works for networks that the router learns dynamically or that are configured as static routes. The origin attribute of routes that are injected into BGP by means of the **network** command is set to IGP. The following commands configure Router C to advertise network 175.220.0.0:

```
!Router C
router bgp 200
neighbor 1.1.1.1 remote-as 300
network 175.220.0.0
```

The **network router** configuration command causes Router C to generate an entry in the BGP routing table for network 175.220.0.0. Figure 3–23 shows another topology that demonstrates the effects of the **network** command.

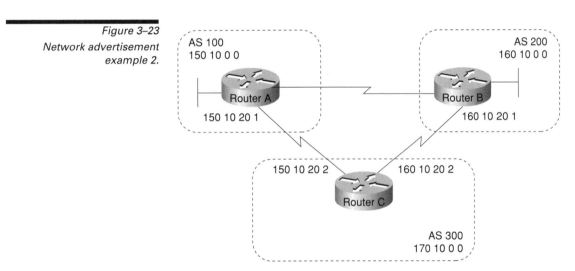

Figure 3–23
Network advertisement example 2.

The following configurations use the **network** command to configure the routers shown in Figure 3–23:

```
!Router A
router bgp 100
neighbor 150.10.20.2 remote-as 300
network 150.10.0.0
!Router B
router bgp 200
neighbor 160.10.20.2 remote-as 300
network 160.10.0.0
!Router C
router bgp 300
neighbor 150.10.20.1 remote-as 100
neighbor 160.10.20.1 remote-as 200
network 170.10.0.0
```

To ensure a loop-free interdomain topology, BGP does not accept updates that originated from its own AS. For example, in Figure 3–23, if Router A generates an update for network 150.10.0.0 with the origin set to AS 100 and sends it to Router C, Router C will pass the update to Router B with the origin still set to AS 100. Router B will send the update (with the origin still set to AS 100) to Router A, which will recognize that the update originated from its own AS and will ignore it.

BGP Attributes

When a BGP speaker receives updates from multiple ASs that describe different paths to the same destination, it must choose the single best path for reaching that destination. Once chosen, BGP propagates the best path to its neighbors. The decision is based on the value of attributes (such as next hop, administrative weights, local preference, the origin of the route, and path length) that the update contains and other BGP-configurable factors. This section describes the following attributes and factors that BGP uses in the decision-making process:

- AS_path Attribute
- Origin Attribute
- Next Hop Attribute
- Weight Attribute
- Local Preference Attribute
- Multi-Exit Discriminator Attribute
- Community Attribute

AS_path Attribute

Whenever an update passes through an AS, BGP prepends its AS number to the update. The AS_path attribute is the list of AS numbers that an update has traversed in order to reach a destination. An AS-SET is a mathematical set of all the ASs that have been traversed. Consider the network shown in Figure 3–24.

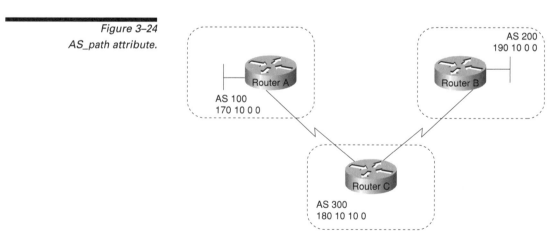

Figure 3–24
AS_path attribute.

Origin Attribute

The origin attribute provides information about the origin of the route. The origin of a route can be one of three values:

- **IGP**—The route is interior to the originating AS. This value is set when the **network router** configuration command is used to inject the route into BGP. The IGP origin type is represented by the letter *i* in the output of the **show ip bgp** EXEC command.

- **EGP**—The route is learned via the Exterior Gateway Protocol (EGP). The EGP origin type is represented by the letter *e* in the output of the **show ip bgp** EXEC command.

- **Incomplete**—The origin of the route is unknown or learned in some other way. An origin of Incomplete occurs when a route is redistributed into BGP. The Incomplete origin type is represented by the *?* symbol in the output of the **show ip bgp** EXEC command.

Figure 3–25 shows a network that demonstrates the value of the origin attribute.

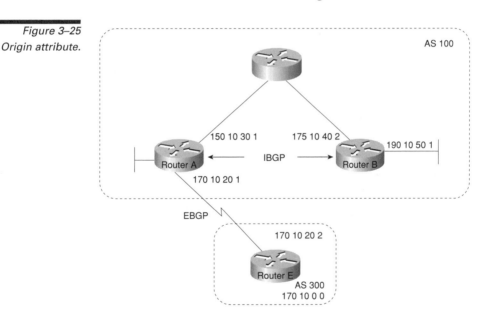

Figure 3–25
Origin attribute.

Next Hop Attribute

The BGP next hop attribute is the IP address of the next hop that is going to be used to reach a certain destination. For EBGP, the next hop is usually the IP address of the neighbor specified by the **neighbor remote-as router** configuration command. (The exception is when the next hop is on a multiaccess media, in which case, the next hop could be the IP address of the router in the same subnet.) Consider the network shown in Figure 3–26.

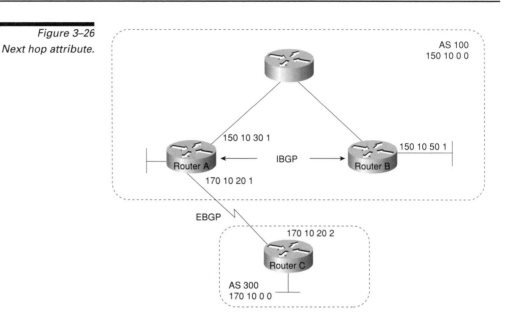

Figure 3–26
Next hop attribute.

In Figure 3–26, Router C advertises network 170.10.0.0 to Router A with a next hop attribute of 170.10.20.2, and Router A advertises network 150.10.0.0 to Router C with a next hop attribute of 170.10.20.1.

BGP specifies that the next hop of EBGP-learned routes should be carried without modification into IBGP. Because of that rule, Router A advertises 170.10.0.0 to its IBGP peer (Router B) with a next hop attribute of 170.10.20.2. As a result, according to Router B, the next hop to reach 170.10.0.0 is 170.10.20.2, instead of 150.10.30.1. For that reason, the configuration must ensure that Router B can reach 170.10.20.2 via an IGP. Otherwise, Router B will drop packets destined for 170.10.0.0 because the next hop address is inaccessible.

For example, if Router B runs IGRP, Router A should run IGRP on network 170.10.0.0. You might want to make IGRP passive on the link to Router C so that only BGP updates are exchanged.

Next Hop Attribute and Multiaccess Media

BGP might set the value of the next hop attribute differently on multiaccess media, such as Ethernet. Consider the network shown in Figure 3–27.

In Figure 3–27, Routers C and D in AS 300 are running OSPF. Router C is running BGP with Router A. Router C can reach network 180.20.0.0 via 170.10.20.3. When Router C sends a BGP update to Router A regarding 180.20.0.0, it sets the next hop attribute to 170.10.20.3, instead of its own IP address (170.10.20.2). This is because Routers A, B, and C are in the same subnet, and it makes more sense for Router A to use Router D as the next hop rather than taking an extra hop via Router C.

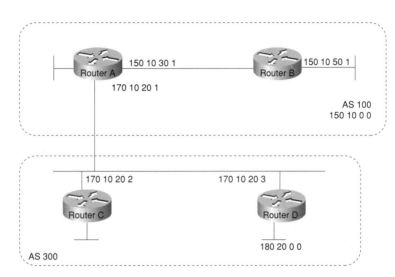

Figure 3–27
Multiaccess media network.

Next Hop Attribute and Nonbroadcast Media Access

In Figure 3–28, three networks are connected by a nonbroadcast media access (NBMA) cloud, such as Frame Relay.

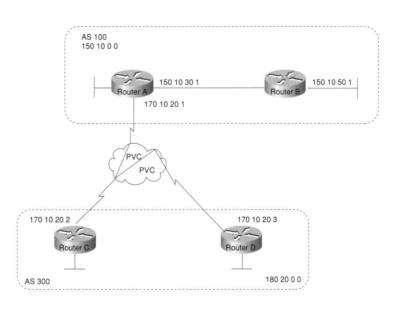

Figure 3–28
Next Hop attritbute and
nonbroadcast media access.

If Routers A, C, and D use a common media such as Frame Relay (or any NBMA cloud), Router C advertises 180.20.0.0 to Router A with a next hop of 170.10.20.3, just as it would do if the common media were Ethernet. The problem is that Router A does not have a direct permanent virtual connection (PVC) to Router D and cannot reach the next hop, so routing will fail. To remedy this situation, use the **neighbor next-hop-self router** configuration command, as shown in the following configuration for Router C:

```
!Router C
router bgp 300
neighbor 170.10.20.1 remote-as 100
neighbor 170.10.20.1 next-hop-self
```

The **neighbor next-hop-self** command causes Router C to advertise 180.20.0.0 with the next hop attribute set to 170.10.20.2.

Weight Attribute

The weight attribute is a special Cisco attribute that is used in the path selection process when there is more than one route to the same destination. The weight attribute is local to the router on which it is assigned, and it is not propagated in routing updates. By default, the weight attribute is 32768 for paths that the router originates and zero for other paths. Routes with a higher weight are preferred when there are multiple routes to the same destination. Consider the network shown in Figure 3–29.

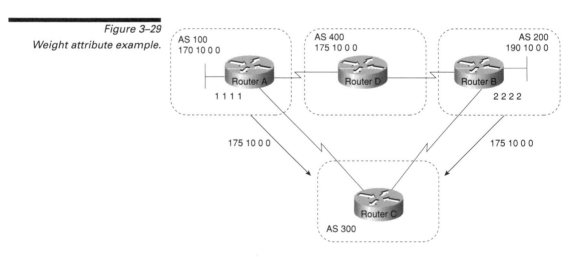

Figure 3–29
Weight attribute example.

In Figure 3–29, Routers A and B learn about network 175.10.0.0 from AS 400, and each propagates the update to Router C. Router C has two routes for reaching 175.10.0.0 and has to decide which route to use. If, on Router C, you set the weight of the updates coming in from Router A to be higher than the updates coming in from Router B, Router C will use Router A as the next hop to reach network 175.10.0.0. There are three ways to set the weight for updates coming in from Router A:

- Using an Access List to Set the Weight Attribute
- Using a Route Map to Set the Weight Attribute
- Using the **neighbor weight** Command to Set the Weight Attribute

Using an Access List to Set the Weight Attribute

The following commands on Router C use access lists and the value of the AS_path attribute to assign a weight to route updates:

```
!Router C
router bgp 300
neighbor 1.1.1.1 remote-as 100
neighbor 1.1.1.1 filter-list 5 weight 2000
neighbor 2.2.2.2 remote-as 200
neighbor 2.2.2.2 filter-list 6 weight 1000
!
ip as-path access-list 5 permit ^100$
ip as-path access-list 6 permit ^200$
```

In this example, 2000 is assigned to the weight attribute of updates from the neighbor at IP address 1.1.1.1 that are permitted by access list 5. Access list 5 permits updates whose AS_path attribute starts with 100 (as specified by ^) and ends with 100 (as specified by $). (The ^ and $ symbols are used to form regular expressions.) This example also assigns 1000 to the weight attribute of updates from the neighbor at IP address 2.2.2.2 that are permitted by access list 6. Access list 6 permits updates whose AS_path attribute starts with 200 and ends with 200.

In effect, this configuration assigns 2000 to the weight attribute of all route updates received from AS 100 and assigns 1000 to the weight attribute of all route updates from AS 200.

Using a Route Map to Set the Weight Attribute

The following commands on Router C use a route map to assign a weight to route updates:

```
!Router C
router bgp 300
neighbor 1.1.1.1 remote-as 100
neighbor 1.1.1.1 route-map SETWEIGHTIN in
neighbor 2.2.2.2 remote-as 200
neighbor 2.2.2.2 route-map SETWEIGHTIN in
!
ip as-path access-list 5 permit ^100$
!
route-map SETWEIGHTIN permit 10
match as-path 5
set weight 2000
route-map SETWEIGHTIN permit 20
set weight 1000
```

This first instance of the **setweightin** route map assigns 2000 to any route update from AS 100, and the second instance of the **setweightin** route map assigns 1000 to route updates from any other AS.

Using the *neighbor weight* Command to Set the Weight Attribute

The following configuration for Router C uses the **neighbor weight router** configuration command:

```
!Router C
router bgp 300
neighbor 1.1.1.1 remote-as 100
neighbor 1.1.1.1 weight 2000
neighbor 2.2.2.2 remote-as 200
neighbor 2.2.2.2 weight 1000
```

This configuration sets the weight of all route updates from AS 100 to 2000, and the weight of all route updates coming from AS 200 to 1000. The higher weight assigned to route updates from AS 100 causes Router C to send traffic through Router A.

Local Preference Attribute

When there are multiple paths to the same destination, the local preference attribute indicates the preferred path. The path with the higher preference is preferred (the default value of the local preference attribute is 100). Unlike the weight attribute, which is relevant only to the local router, the local preference attribute is part of the routing update and is exchanged among routers in the same AS. The network shown in Figure 3–30 demonstrates the local preference attribute.

Figure 3–30

Local preference.

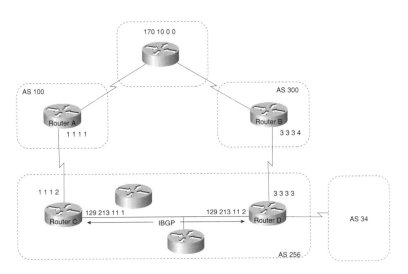

In Figure 3–30, AS 256 receives route updates for network 170.10.0.0 from AS 100 and AS 300. There are two ways to set local preference:

- Using the **bgp default local-preference** Command
- Using a Route Map to Set Local Preference

Using the *bgp default local-preference* Command

The following configurations use the **bgp default local-preference** router configuration command to set the local preference attribute on Routers C and D:

```
!Router C
router bgp 256
neighbor 1.1.1.1 remote-as 100
neighbor 128.213.11.2 remote-as 256
bgp default local-preference 150
!Router D
router bgp 256
neighbor 3.3.3.4 remote-as 300
neighbor 128.213.11.1 remote-as 256
bgp default local-preference 200
```

The configuration for Router C causes it to set the local preference of all updates from AS 300 to 150, and the configuration for Router D causes it to set the local preference for all updates from AS 100 to 200. Because local preference is exchanged within the AS, both Routers C and D determine that updates regarding network 170.10.0.0 have a higher local preference when they come from AS 300 than when they come from AS 100. As a result, all traffic in AS 256 destined for network 170.10.0.0 is sent to Router D as the exit point.

Using a Route Map to Set Local Preference

Route maps provide more flexibility than the **bgp default local-preference** router configuration command. When the **bgp default local-preference** command is used on Router D in Figure 3–30, the local preference attribute of all updates received by Router D will be set to 200, including updates from AS 34.

The following configuration uses a route map to set the local preference attribute on Router D specifically for updates regarding AS 300:

```
!Router D
router bgp 256
neighbor 3.3.3.4 remote-as 300
route-map SETLOCALIN in
neighbor 128.213.11.1 remote-as 256
!
ip as-path 7 permit ^300$
route-map SETLOCALIN permit 10
match as-path 7
set local-preference 200
!
route-map SETLOCALIN permit 20
```

With this configuration, the local preference attribute of any update coming from AS 300 is set to 200. Instance 20 of the SETLOCALIN route map accepts all other routes.

Multi-Exit Discriminator Attribute

The multi-exit discriminator (MED) attribute is a hint to external neighbors about the preferred path into an AS when there are multiple entry points into the AS. A lower MED value is preferred over a higher MED value. The default value of the MED attribute is 0.

NOTES

In BGP Version 3, MED is known as Inter-AS_Metric.

Unlike local preference, the MED attribute is exchanged between ASs, but a MED attribute that comes into an AS does not leave the AS. When an update enters the AS with a certain MED value, that value is used for decision making within the AS. When BGP sends that update to another AS, the MED is reset to 0.

Unless otherwise specified, the router compares MED attributes for paths from external neighbors that are in the same AS. If you want MED attributes from neighbors in other ASs to be compared, you must configure the **bgp always-compare-med** command. The network shown in Figure 3–31 demonstrates the use of the MED attribute.

Figure 3–31
MED example.

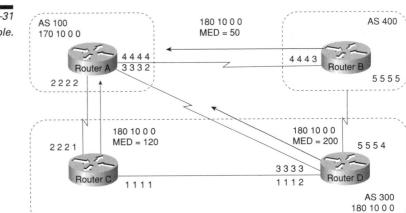

In Figure 3–31, AS 100 receives updates regarding network 180.10.0.0 from Routers B, C, and D. Routers C and D are in AS 300, and Router B is in AS 400. The following commands configure Routers A, B, C, and D:

```
!Router A
router bgp 100
neighbor 2.2.2.1 remote-as 300
neighbor 3.3.3.3 remote-as 300
neighbor 4.4.4.3 remote-as 400
```

```
!Router B
router bgp 400
neighbor 4.4.4.4 remote-as 100
neighbor 4.4.4.4 route-map SETMEDOUT out
neighbor 5.5.5.4 remote-as 300
!
route-map SETMEDOUT permit 10
set metric 50
!Router C
router bgp 300
neighbor 2.2.2.2 remote-as 100
neighbor 2.2.2.2 route-map SETMEDOUT out
neighbor 5.5.5.5 remote-as 400
neighbor 1.1.1.2 remote-as 300
!
route-map SETMEDOUT permit 10
set metric 120
!Router D
router bgp 300
neighbor 3.3.3.2 remote-as 100
neighbor 3.3.3.2 route map SETMEDOUT out
neighbor 1.1.1.1 remote-as 300
route-map SETMEDOUT permit 10
set metric 200
```

By default, BGP compares the MED attributes of routes coming from neighbors in the same external AS (such as AS 300 in Figure 3–31). Router A can only compare the MED attribute coming from Router C (120) to the MED attribute coming from Router D (200) even though the update coming from Router B has the lowest MED value.

Router A will choose Router C as the best path for reaching network 180.10.0.0. To force Router A to include updates for network 180.10.0.0 from Router B in the comparison, use the **bgp always-compare-med router** configuration command, as in the following modified configuration for Router A:

```
!Router A
router bgp 100
neighbor 2.2.2.1 remote-as 300
neighbor 3.3.3.3 remote-as 300
neighbor 4.4.4.3 remote-as 400
bgp always-compare-med
```

Router A will choose Router B as the best next hop for reaching network 180.10.0.0 (assuming that all other attributes are the same).

You can also set the MED attribute when you configure the redistribution of routes into BGP. For example, on Router B you can inject the static route into BGP with a MED of 50 as in the following configuration:

```
!Router B
router bgp 400
redistribute static
default-metric 50
!
ip route 160.10.0.0 255.255.0.0 null 0
```

The preceding configuration causes Router B to send out updates for 160.10.0.0 with a MED attribute of 50.

Community Attribute

The community attribute provides a way of grouping destinations (called communities) to which routing decisions (such as acceptance, preference, and redistribution) can be applied. Route maps are used to set the community attribute. A few predefined communities are listed in Table 3–3.

Table 3–3 *Predefined Communities*

Community	Meaning
no-export	Do not advertise this route to EBGP peers.
no-advertised	Do not advertise this route to any peer.
internet	Advertise this route to the Internet community; all routers in the network belong to it.

The following route maps set the value of the community attribute:

```
route-map COMMUNITYMAP
match ip address 1
set community no-advertise
!
route-map SETCOMMUNITY
match as-path 1
set community 200 additive
```

If you specify the **additive** keyword, the specified community value is added to the existing value of the community attribute. Otherwise, the specified community value replaces any community value that was set previously. To send the community attribute to a neighbor, you must use the **neighbor send-community router** configuration command, as in the following example:

```
router bgp 100
neighbor 3.3.3.3 remote-as 300
neighbor 3.3.3.3 send-community
neighbor 3.3.3.3 route-map setcommunity out
```

For examples of how the community attribute is used to filter updates, see the section "Community Filtering" later in this chapter.

BGP Path Selection Criteria

BGP selects only one path as the best path. When the path is selected, BGP puts the selected path in its routing table and propagates the path to its neighbors. BGP uses the following criteria, in the order presented, to select a path for a destination:

1. If the path specifies a next hop that is inaccessible, drop the update.

2. Prefer the path with the largest weight.

3. If the weights are the same, prefer the path with the largest local preference.

4. If the local preferences are the same, prefer the path that was originated by BGP running on this router.

5. If no route was originated, prefer the route that has the shortest AS_path.

6. If all paths have the same AS_path length, prefer the path with the lowest origin type (where IGP is lower than EGP, and EGP is lower than Incomplete).

7. If the origin codes are the same, prefer the path with the lowest MED attribute.

8. If the paths have the same MED, prefer the external path over the internal path.

9. If the paths are still the same, prefer the path through the closest IGP neighbor.

10. Prefer the path with the lowest IP address, as specified by the BGP router ID.

Understanding and Defining BGP Routing Policies

This section describes how to understand and define BGP Policies to control the flow of BGP updates. The techniques include the following:

- Administrative Distance
- BGP Filtering
- BGP Peer Groups
- CIDR and Aggregate Addresses
- Confederations
- Route Reflectors
- Route Flap Dampening

Administrative Distance

Normally, a route could be learned via more than one protocol. Administrative distance is used to discriminate between routes learned from more than one protocol. The route with the lowest administrative distance is installed in the IP routing table. By default, BGP uses the administrative distances shown in Table 3–4.

Table 3–4   *BGP Administrative Distances*

Distance	Default Value	Function
External	20	Applied to routes learned from EBGP
Internal	200	Applied to routes learned from IBGP
Local	200	Applied to routes originated by the router

NOTES

Distance does not influence the BGP path selection algorithm, but it does influence whether BGP-learned routes are installed in the IP routing table.

BGP Filtering

You can control the sending and receiving of updates by using the following filtering methods:

- Prefix Filtering
- AS_path Filtering
- Route Map Filtering
- Community Filtering

Each method can be used to achieve the same result—the choice of method depends on the specific network configuration.

Prefix Filtering

To restrict the routing information that the router learns or advertises, you can filter based on routing updates to or from a particular neighbor. The filter consists of an access list that is applied to updates to or from a neighbor. The network shown in Figure 3–32 demonstrates the usefulness of prefix filtering.

In Figure 3–32, Router B is originating network 160.10.0.0 and sending it to Router C. If you want to prevent Router C from propagating updates for network 160.10.0.0 to AS 100, you can apply an access list to filter those updates when Router C exchanges updates with Router A, as demonstrated by the following configuration for Router C:

```
!Router C
router bgp 300
network 170.10.0.0
neighbor 3.3.3.3 remote-as 200
neighbor 2.2.2.2 remote-as 100
neighbor 2.2.2.2 distribute-list 1 out
!
access-list 1 deny 160.10.0.0 0.0.255.255
access-list 1 permit 0.0.0.0 255.255.255.255
```

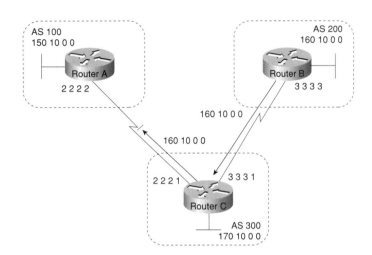

Figure 3–32
Prefix route filtering.

In the preceding configuration, the combination of the **neighbor distribute-list** router configuration command and access list 1 prevents Router C from propagating routes for network 160.10.0.0 when it sends routing updates to neighbor 2.2.2.2 (Router A).

Using access lists to filter supernets is a bit trickier. Assume, for example, that Router B in Figure 3–32 has different subnets of 160.10.x.x, and you want to advertise 160.0.0.0/8 only. The following access list would permit 160.0.0.0/8, 160.0.0.0/9, and so on:

```
access-list 1 permit 160.0.0.0 0.255.255.255
```

To restrict the update to 160.0.0.0/8 only, you have to use an extended access list, such as the following:

```
access-list 101 permit ip 160.0.0.0 0.255.255.255 255.0.0.0 0.255.255.255
```

AS_path Filtering

You can specify an access list on both incoming and outgoing updates based on the value of the AS_path attribute. The network shown in Figure 3–33 demonstrates the usefulness of AS_path filters.

```
!Router C
neighbor 3.3.3.3 remote-as 200
neighbor 2.2.2.2 remote-as 100
neighbor 2.2.2.2 filter-list 1 out
!
ip as-path access-list 1 deny ^200$
ip as-path access-list 1 permit .*
```

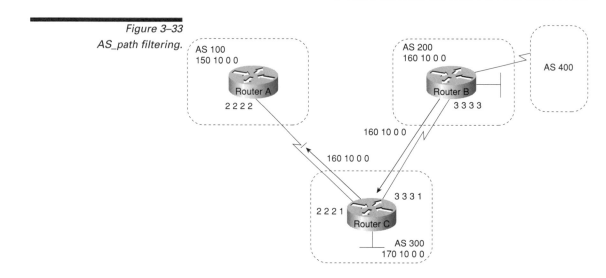

Figure 3–33
AS_path filtering.

In this example, access list 1 denies any update whose AS_path attribute starts with 200 (as specified by ^) and ends with 200 (as specified by $). Because Router B sends updates about 160.10.0.0 whose AS_path attributes start with 200 and end with 200, such updates will match the access list and will be denied. By specifying that the update must also end with 200, the access list permits updates from AS 400 (whose AS_path attribute is 200, 400). If the access list specified ^200 as the regular expression, updates from AS 400 would be denied.

In the second access-list statement, the period (.) symbol means any character, and the asterisk (*) symbol means a repetition of that character. Together, .* matches any value of the AS_path attribute, which in effect permits any update that has not been denied by the previous access-list statement. If you want to verify that your regular expressions work as intended, use the following EXEC command:

```
show ip bgp regexp regular-expression
```

The router displays all of the paths that match the specified regular expression.

Route Map Filtering

The **neighbor route-map** router configuration command can be used to apply a route map to incoming and outgoing routes. The network shown in Figure 3–34 demonstrates using route maps to filter BGP updates.

Assume that in Figure 3–34, you want Router C to learn about networks that are local to AS 200 only. (That is, you do not want Router C to learn about AS 100, AS 400, or AS 600 from AS 200.) Also, on those routes that Router C accepts from AS 200, you want the weight attribute to be set to 20. The following configuration for Router C accomplishes this goal:

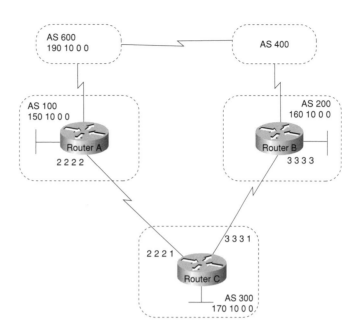

Figure 3–34
BGP route map filtering.

```
!Router C
router bgp 300
network 170.10.0.0
neighbor 3.3.3.3 remote-as 200
neighbor 3.3.3.3 route-map STAMP in
!
route-map STAMP permit 10
match as-path 1
set weight 20
!
ip as-path access-list 1 permit ^200$
```

In the preceding configuration, access list 1 permits any update whose AS_path attribute begins with 200 and ends with 200 (that is, access list 1 permits updates that originate in AS 200). The weight attribute of the permitted updates is set to 20. All other updates are denied and dropped.

Community Filtering

The network shown in Figure 3–35 demonstrates the usefulness of community filters.

Assume that you do not want Router C to propagate routes learned from Router B to Router A. You can do this by setting the community attribute on updates that Router B sends to Router C, as in the following configuration for Router B:

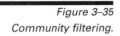

Figure 3–35
Community filtering.

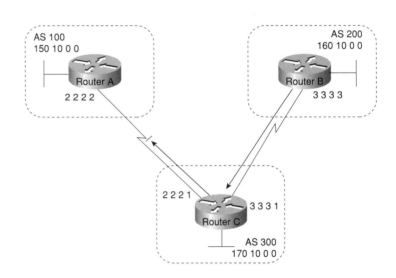

```
!Router B
router bgp 200
network 160.10.0.0
neighbor 3.3.3.1 remote-as 300
neighbor 3.3.3.1 send-community
neighbor 3.3.3.1 route-map SETCOMMUNITY out
!
route-map SETCOMMUNITY permit 10
match ip address 1
set community no-export
!
route-map SETCOMMUNITY permit 20
!
access list 1 permit 0.0.0.0 255.255.255.255
```

For routes that are sent to the neighbor at IP address 3.3.3.1 (Router C), Router B applies the route map named setcommunity. The setcommunity route map sets the community attribute of any update (by means of access list 1) destined for 3.3.3.1 to no-export. The **neighbor send-community router** configuration command is required to include the community attribute in updates sent to the neighbor at IP address 3.3.3.1. When Router C receives the updates from Router B, it does not propagate them to Router A because the value of the community attribute is no-export.

Another way to filter updates based on the value of the community attribute is to use the **ip community-list** global configuration command. Assume that Router B has been configured as follows:

```
!Router B
router bgp 200
network 160.10.0.0
neighbor 3.3.3.1 remote-as 300
neighbor 3.3.3.1 send-community
neighbor 3.3.3.1 route-map SETCOMMUNITY out
!
```

```
route-map SETCOMMUNITY permit 10
match ip address 2
set community 100 200 additive
route-map SETCOMMUNITY permit 20
!
access list 2 permit 0.0.0.0 255.255.255.255
```

In the preceding configuration, Router B adds 100 and 200 to the community value of any update destined for the neighbor at IP address 3.3.3.1. To configure Router C to use the **ip community-list** global configuration command to set the value of the weight attribute. Based on whether the community attribute contains 100 or 200, use the following configuration:

```
!Router C
router bgp 300
neighbor 3.3.3.3 remote-as 200
neighbor 3.3.3.3 route-map check-community in
!
route-map check-community permit 10
match community 1
set weight 20
!
route-map check-community permit 20
match community 2 exact
set weight 10
!
route-map check-community permit 30
match community 3
!
ip community-list 1 permit 100
ip community-list 2 permit 200
ip community-list 3 permit internet
```

In the preceding configuration, any route that has 100 in its community attribute matches community list 1 and has its weight set to 20. Any route whose community attribute is only 200 (by virtue of the exact keyword) matches community list 2 and has its weight set to 10. In the last community list (list 3), the use of the **internet** keyword permits all other updates without changing the value of an attribute. (The **internet** keyword specifies all routes because all routes are members of the Internet community.)

BGP Peer Groups

A *BGP peer group* is a group of BGP neighbors that share the same update policies. Update policies are usually set by route maps, distribution lists, and filter lists. Instead of defining the same policies for each individual neighbor, you define a peer group name and assign policies to the peer group.

Members of a peer group inherit all of the configuration options of the peer group. Peer group members can also be configured to override configuration options if the options do not affect outgoing updates. That is, you can override options that are set only for incoming updates. The use of BGP peer groups is demonstrated by the network shown in Figure 3–36.

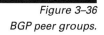

Figure 3–36
BGP peer groups.

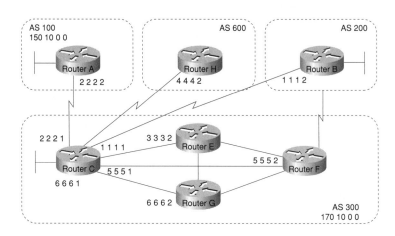

The following commands configure a BGP peer group named internalmap on Router C and apply it to the other routers in AS 300:

```
!Router C
router bgp 300
neighbor INTERNALMAP peer-group
neighbor INTERNALMAP remote-as 300
neighbor INTERNALMAP route-map INTERNAL out
neighbor INTERNALMAP filter-list 1 out
neighbor INTERNALMAP filter-list 2 in
neighbor 5.5.5.2 peer-group INTERNALMAP
neighbor 6.6.6.2 peer-group INTERNALMAP
neighbor 3.3.3.2 peer-group INTERNALMAP
neighbor 3.3.3.2 filter-list 3 in
```

The preceding configuration defines the following policies for the internalmap peer group:

```
A route map named INTERNAL
A filter list for outgoing updates (filter list 1)
A filter list for incoming updates (filter list 2)
```

The configuration applies the peer group to all internal neighbors—Routers E, F, and G. The configuration also defines a filter list for incoming updates from the neighbor at IP address 3.3.3.2 (Router E). This filter list can be used only to override options that affect incoming updates.

The following commands configure a BGP peer group named externalmap on Router C and apply it to routers in AS 100, 200, and 600:

```
!Router C
router bgp 300
neighbor EXTERNALMAP peer-group
neighbor EXTERNALMAP route-map SETMED
neighbor EXTERNALMAP filter-list 1 out
neighbor EXTERNALMAP filter-list 2 in
neighbor 2.2.2.2 remote-as 100
neighbor 2.2.2.2 peer-group EXTERNALMAP
neighbor 4.4.4.2 remote-as 600
```

```
neighbor 4.4.4.2 peer-group EXTERNALMAP
neighbor 1.1.1.2 remote-as 200
neighbor 1.1.1.2 peer-group EXTERNALMAP
neighbor 1.1.1.2 filter-list 3 in
```

In the preceding configuration, the **neighbor remote-as router** configuration commands are placed outside of the **neighbor peer-group router** configuration commands because different external ASs have to be defined. Also note that this configuration defines filter list 3, which can be used to override configuration options for incoming updates from the neighbor at IP address 1.1.1.2 (Router B).

CIDR and Aggregate Addresses

BGP4 supports classless interdomain routing (CIDR). CIDR is a new way of looking at IP addresses that eliminates the concept of classes (Class A, Class B, and so on). For example, network 192.213.0.0, which is an illegal Class C network number, is a legal supernet when it is represented in CIDR notation as 192.213.0.0/16. The /16 indicates that the subnet mask consists of 16 bits (counting from the left). Therefore, 192.213.0.0/16 is similar to 192.213.0.0 255.255.0.0.

CIDR makes it easy to aggregate routes. Aggregation is the process of combining several different routes in such a way that a single route can be advertised, which minimizes the size of routing tables. Consider the network shown in Figure 3–37.

Figure 3–37
Aggregation example.

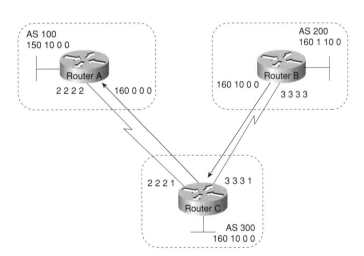

In Figure 3–37, Router B in AS 200 is originating network 160.11.0.0 and advertising it to Router C in AS 300. To configure Router C to propagate the aggregate address 160.0.0.0 to Router A, use the following commands:

```
!Router C
router bgp 300
neighbor 3.3.3.3 remote-as 200
```

```
neighbor 2.2.2.2 remote-as 100
network 160.10.0.0
aggregate-address 160.0.0.0 255.0.0.0
```

The **aggregate-address router** configuration command advertises the prefix route (in this case, 160.0.0.0/8) and all of the more specific routes. If you want Router C to propagate the prefix route only, and you do not want it to propagate a more specific route, use the following command:

```
aggregate-address 160.0.0.0 255.0.0.0 summary-only
```

This command propagates the prefix (160.0.0.0/8) and suppresses any more specific routes that the router may have in its BGP routing table. If you want to suppress specific routes when aggregating routes, you can define a route map and apply it to the aggregate. If, for example, you want Router C in Figure 3-37 to aggregate 160.0.0.0 and suppress the specific route 160.20.0.0, but propagate route 160.10.0.0, use the following commands:

```
!Router C
router bgp 300
neighbor 3.3.3.3 remote-as 200
neighbor 2.2.2.2 remote-as 100
network 160.10.0.0
aggregate-address 160.0.0.0 255.0.0.0 suppress-map CHECK
!
route-map CHECK permit 10
match ip address 1
!
access-list 1 deny 160.20.0.0 0.0.255.255
access-list 1 permit 0.0.0.0 255.255.255.255
```

If you want the router to set the value of an attribute when it propagates the aggregate route, use an attribute map, as demonstrated by the following commands:

```
route-map SETORIGIN permit 10
set origin igp
!
aggregate-address 160.0.0.0 255.0.0.0 attribute-map SETORIGIN
```

NOTES

Aggregation and AS-SET. When aggregates are generated from more specific routes, the AS_path attributes of the more specific routes are combined to form a set called the AS-SET. This set is useful for preventing routing information loops.

Confederations

A *confederation* is a technique for reducing the IBGP mesh inside the AS. Consider the network shown in Figure 3–38.

In Figure 3–38, AS 500 consists of nine BGP speakers (although there might be other routers that are not configured for BGP). Without confederations, BGP would require that the routers in AS 500 be fully meshed. That is, each router would need to run IBGP with each of the other eight routers, and each router would need to connect to an external AS and run EBGP, for a total of nine peers for each router.

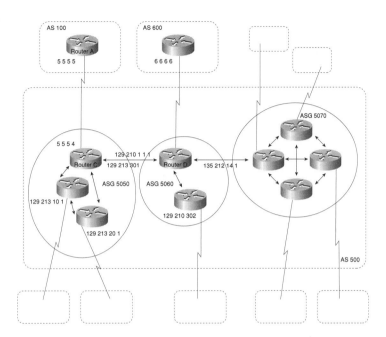

Figure 3–38
Example of confederations.

Confederations reduce the number of peers within the AS, as shown in Figure 3–38. You use confederations to divide the AS into multiple mini-ASs and assign the mini-ASs to a confederation. Each mini-AS is fully meshed, and IBGP is run among its members. Each mini-AS has a connection to the other mini-ASs within the confederation. Even though the mini-ASs have EBGP peers to ASs within the confederation, they exchange routing updates as if they were using IBGP. That is, the next hop, MED, and local preference information is preserved. To the outside world, the confederation looks like a single AS. The following commands configure Router C:

```
!Router C
router bgp 65050
bgp confederation identifier 500
bgp confederation peers 65060 65070
neighbor 128.213.10.1 remote-as 65050
neighbor 128.213.20.1 remote-as 65050
neighbor 128.210.11.1 remote-as 65060
neighbor 135.212.14.1 remote-as 65070
neighbor 5.5.5.5 remote-as 100
```

The **router bgp** global configuration command specifies that Router C belongs to AS 50.

The **bgp confederation identifier** router configuration command specifies that Router C belongs to confederation 500. The first two **neighbor remote-as router** configuration commands establish IBGP connections to the other two routers within AS 65050. The second two **neighbor remote-as commands** establish BGP connections with confederation peers 65060 and 65070. The last

neighbor remote-as command establishes an EBGP connection with external AS 100. The following commands configure Router D:

```
!Router D
router bgp 65060
bgp confederation identifier 500
bgp confederation peers 65050 65070
neighbor 129.210.30.2 remote-as 65060
neighbor 128.213.30.1 remote-as 65050
neighbor 135.212.14.1 remote-as 65070
neighbor 6.6.6.6 remote-as 600
```

The **router bgp** global configuration command specifies that Router D belongs to AS 65060. The **bgp confederation identifier** router configuration command specifies that Router D belongs to confederation 500.

The first **neighbor remote-as router** configuration command establishes an IBGP connection to the other router within AS 65060. The second two **neighbor remote-as** commands establish BGP connections with confederation peers 65050 and 65070. The last **neighbor remote-as** command establishes an EBGP connection with AS 600. The following commands configure Router A:

```
!Router A
router bgp 100
neighbor 5.5.5.4 remote-as 500
```

The **neighbor remote-as** command establishes an EBGP connection with Router C. Router A is unaware of AS 65050, AS 65060, or AS 65070. Router A only has knowledge of AS 500.

Route Reflectors

Route reflectors are another solution for the explosion of IBGP peering within an AS. As described earlier in the section "Synchronization," a BGP speaker does not advertise a route learned from another IBGP speaker to a third IBGP speaker. Route reflectors ease this limitation and allow a router to advertise (reflect) IBGP-learned routes to other IBGP speakers, thereby reducing the number of IBGP peers within an AS. The network shown in Figure 3–39 demonstrates how route reflectors work.

Without a route reflector, the network shown in Figure 3–39 would require a full IBGP mesh (that is, Router A would have to be a peer of Router B). If Router C is configured as a route reflector, IBGP peering between Routers A and B is not required because Router C will reflect updates from Router A to Router B and from Router B to Router A. To configure Router C as a route reflector, use the following commands:

```
!Router C
router bgp 100
neighbor 1.1.1.1 remote-as 100
neighbor 1.1.1.1 route-reflector-client
neighbor 2.2.2.2 remote-as 100
neighbor 2.2.2.2 route-reflector-client
```

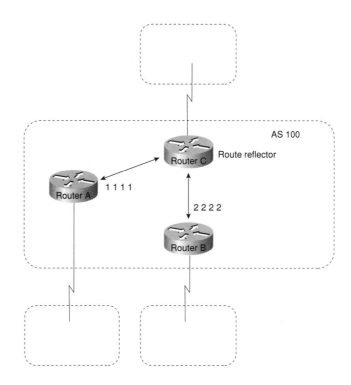

Figure 3–39
Simple route reflector
example.

The router whose configuration includes **neighbor route-reflector-client** router configuration commands is the route reflector. The routers identified by the **neighbor route-reflector-client** commands are clients of the route reflector. When considered as a whole, the route reflector and its clients are called a *cluster*. Other IBGP peers of the route reflector that are not clients are called nonclients.

An AS can have more than one route reflector. When an AS has more than one route reflector, each route reflector treats other route reflectors as normal IBGP speakers. There can be more than one route reflector in a cluster, and there can be more than one cluster in an AS.

Route Flap Dampening

Route flap dampening (introduced in Cisco IOS Release 11.0) is a mechanism for minimizing the instability caused by route flapping. The following terms are used to describe route flap dampening:

- *Penalty*—A numeric value that is assigned to a route when it flaps.

- *Half-life time*—A configurable numeric value that describes the time required to reduce the penalty by one half.

- *Suppress limit*—A numeric value that is compared with the penalty. If the penalty is greater than the suppress limit, the route is suppressed.

- *Suppressed*—A route that is not advertised even though it is up. A route is suppressed if the penalty is more than the suppressed limit.

- *Reuse limit*—A configurable numeric value that is compared with the penalty. If the penalty is less than the reuse limit, a suppressed route that is up will no longer be suppressed.

- *History entry*—An entry that is used to store flap information about a route that is down.

A route that is flapping receives a penalty of 1000 for each flap. When the accumulated penalty reaches a configurable limit, BGP suppresses advertisement of the route even if the route is up. The accumulated penalty is decremented by the half-life time. When the accumulated penalty is less than the reuse limit, the route is advertised again (if it is still up).

Summary of BGP

The primary function of a BGP system is to exchange network reachability information with other BGP systems. This information is used to construct a graph of AS connectivity from which routing loops are pruned and with which AS-level policy decisions are enforced. BGP provides a number of techniques for controlling the flow of BGP updates, such as route, path, and community filtering. It also provides techniques for consolidating routing information, such as CIDR aggregation, confederations, and route reflectors. BGP is a powerful tool for providing loop-free interdomain routing within and between ASs.

SUMMARY

Recall the following design implications of the Enhanced Interior Gateway Routing Protocol (IGRP), Open Shortest Path First (OSPF) protocols, and the BGP protocol:

- Network topology
- Addressing and route summarization
- Route selection
- Convergence
- Network scalability
- Security

This chapter outlined these general routing protocol issues and focused on design guidelines for the specific IP protocols.

CHAPTER 4

Designing SRB Internetworks

This chapter discusses source-route bridging (SRB) and remote source-route bridging (RSRB). SRB is evaluated within two contexts: Systems Network Architecture (SNA) and NetBIOS.

When IBM developed SRB technology in the mid-eighties, it was viewed as a local technology that would interconnect a few rings and terminate at a remote 3745. The challenge for any SRB internetwork occurs when the scale exceeds what was originally intended by IBM. This technology encounters problems when non-IBM protocols are required to coexist with native Token Ring traffic. Source-route bridges were intended to be the primary internetworking tool for creating a corporate-wide Token Ring internetwork. These bridges were never meant to scale to the level that many customers require. This chapter addresses the challenges of this environment and aims to help network designers successfully implement SRB within a large, multiprotocol topology. This chapter is grouped into the following topics:

- SRB technology and implementation overview
- Internet Protocol (IP) routing protocol selection and implementation
- SRB network design recommendations and guidelines

NOTES

For information concerning IBM serial line connections, refer to Appendix B, "IBM Serial Link Implementation Notes."

SRB TECHNOLOGY OVERVIEW AND IMPLEMENTATION ISSUES

The following discussions address SRB-related technology, features provided to support SRB requirements, and implementation issues that can affect large-scale, router-based SRB networks. Specific topics include the following:

- Typical SRB Environments
- Multiport Bridging
- Explorer Packets and Propagation
- NetBIOS Broadcast Handling
- LAN Framing
- WAN Framing
- WAN Parallelism
- WAN Frame Sizes
- SNA Host Configuration Considerations for SRB

NOTES

If you have eight or fewer routers operating as SRBs, you can skip this chapter. You probably do not need to tune your network.

Typical SRB Environments

SRB is used in three types of user environments:

- *Many end stations to few end stations (hierarchical)*—In a hierarchical SNA network, end users from multiple access sites need connectivity to a host site through a limited number of front-end processors (FEPs).

- *Many end stations to several end stations (distributed)*—Many users need to access a limited number of servers or a limited number of devices, such as an AS/400.

- *Any-to-any (flat)*—End users at one site need to access end stations at another site.

The following discussions evaluate SRB environment design issues in relation to these user environments.

Multiport Bridging

The fundamental design of an SRB, as initially created by IBM, was a two-port, ring-to-bridge- to-ring combination. IBM also created a half-bridge configuration that consisted of a ring-to-wide-area-network (WAN) combination followed by a second WAN-to-ring half-bridge combination.

To support more than two rings, multiport routers adopt an implementation that allows SRBs to include multiple rings on a single internetworking node. This is accomplished via the *virtual ring* capability. A virtual ring is a conceptual entity that connects two or more physical rings together, locally or remotely.

Figure 4–1 illustrates the concept of multiport bridges and a virtual ring.

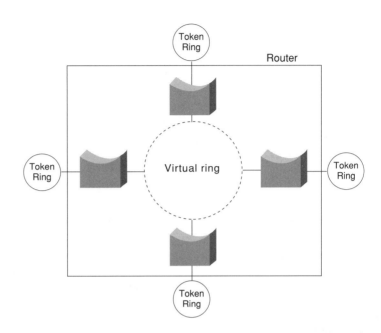

Figure 4–1
Multiport bridge using virtual
ring concept to permit multiple
ring interconnection.

The concept of virtual rings can be expanded across router boundaries. A large virtual ring can connect several access points to a central router with an FEP. Figure 4–2 illustrates this expansion.

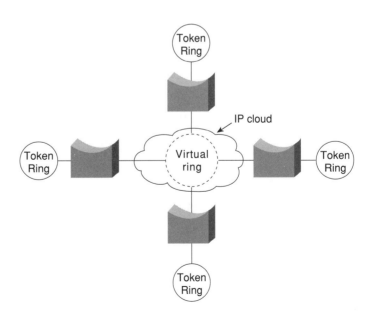

Figure 4–2
Virtual rings expanded across
an IP cloud.

Routers support simple bridging, multiport bridging, and connections to both local and remote virtual rings. A virtual ring configuration is required to communicate with remote rings. The half-bridge configuration is not supported. The IBM half bridge does not use the concept of virtual rings; two IBM half bridges use two rings. The virtual ring advantage is in a topology that features many SRBs. In such an arrangement, only a single unit is required at a central site.

Remote virtual rings have a property not found in physical ring topologies: The logical connectivity is determined by the network administrator. Two options are available: partially meshed topologies (sometimes called *redundant star topologies*) or fully meshed topologies. In a partially meshed topology, a single central location (such as an FEP Token Ring) is connected to all access locations. Each access location is logically connected to the central FEP rings and is not connected to any other ring. Partially meshed topologies using virtual rings do not permit *direct* communication between remote rings. However, communication is allowed from the central ring to the remote rings, which also allows communication among remote rings through the central ring.

In a fully meshed virtual ring topology, any ring can communicate with any other ring. Figure 4–3 and Figure 4–4 illustrate partially meshed and fully meshed topologies. In the partially meshed topology depicted in Figure 4–3, all rings are logically bridged to Token Ring 10. The access rings are not bridged together. In the fully meshed topology illustrated in Figure 4–4, all rings are bridged to all other rings.

Figure 4–3
Typical hierarchical topology.

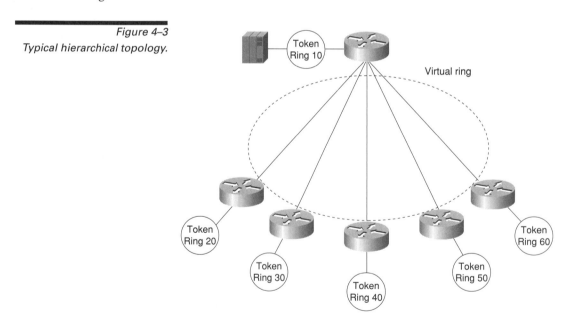

In the topology illustrated in Figure 4–3, each of the access routers is a peer to the FEP router. They are not peers to one another. Thus, SRB is enabled between all rings and Token Ring 10 and is not enabled between token rings 20, 30, 40, 50 and 60.

Assuming this is only a hierarchical SNA environment, users connected to these rings do not have SRB connectivity. Broadcasts are not forwarded across the lower layer rings (token rings 20 through 60); broadcasts are sent only from Token Ring 10 to or from the other rings.

In the topology illustrated in Figure 4–4, each router is a peer to each other router. All rings are logically bridged to all other rings. The actual physical topology is less important than the logical topology. In Figure 4–4, the same logical topology can exist even if there are no physical connections between the access routers.

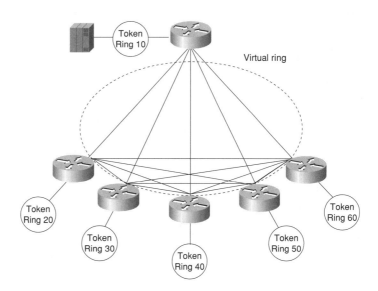

Figure 4–4
Typical fully meshed (flat)
topology.

Explorer Packets and Propagation

Once you build a network of ring and bridge combinations, you must have a method for the end stations to find other end stations in the network.

An IBM bridge uses a system of *explorer packet marking* to propagate routing information through an SRB internetwork. The explorer packet is produced by the source end station and is marked (updated) by each bridge that it traverses. The marked field is called the Routing Information Field (RIF). Two important transactions occur in the explorer packet handling exchange: the transmission of the explorer packet and the reply by the end station to the explorer packets that it receives.

In this environment, the source end stations must know the Token Ring Media Access Control (MAC) address of the destination end stations. Once the MAC address is understood, the source end station produces an explorer packet.

The source-route bridge updates the explorer packet to include its bridge-ring combination in the explorer packet's RIF in the MAC frame. By accumulating this information, the explorer packet gathers a hop-by-hop description of a path through the SRB network. In addition, the bridge forwards the explorer to each destination ring it encounters, therefore creating a complete topological map for each end station trying to find its way through the network.

Explorer Packet Types

There are three types of explorer packets: *local explorer packets*, *spanning explorer packets*, and *all-routes explorer packets*. Note that all-routes explorer packets are also known as *all-rings explorer packets*, and spanning explorer packets are also known as *single-route* and *limited-route explorer packets*. Single router explorers are explorers that pass through a predetermined path constructed by a spanning tree algorithm in the bridge. A station should receive only one single router explorer from the network.

A local explorer packet is generated by some end systems (either NetBIOS or SNA) to find a host connected to the local ring. After this event has occurred without finding a local host, the end station produces either a spanning explorer or an all-routes explorer packet. This behavior depends on the type of end station. SNA end stations generally produce an all-routes explorer packet. NetBIOS end stations produce a spanning explorer packet.

--- **NOTES** --

As of Cisco IOS Software Release 10.2, auto spanning tree (AST) for SRB is supported. The implementation of AST in Cisco IOS Software Release10.2 is based on the IEEE 802.1 standard and is fully compatible with IBM PC bridging. New global and interface configuration commands are required to configure a router for AST. Once configured, AST can be enabled and disabled through LAN Network Manager (LNM). The following discussion of spanning tree explorer packets applies to the manual spanning tree functionality available in software releases prior to Cisco IOS Software Release 10.2.

To pass a spanning explorer packet on a router, the configuration for the router's Token Ring interface must have the **source-bridge spanning** interface configuration command for the specific ring. If this interface command is not included, spanning explorer packets are discarded.

In contrast, an all-routes explorer packet can find any valid SRB ring. No specific router configuration other than specification of SRB is required to pass all-routes explorer packets.

Explorer packet processing works as illustrated in Figure 4–5. If End station X sends an all-routes explorer packet, Bridge B1 and Bridge B2 both forward the explorer packet. End station Y receives two all-routes explorer packets in this configuration. End station Y responds to each of the all-routes explorer packets by sending a directed, nonbroadcast packet. In the example illustrated in Figure 4–5, four packets are generated:

- Two all-routes explorer packets inbound (to End station Y)
- Two nonbroadcast packets outbound (from End station Y)

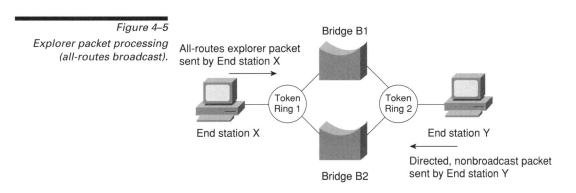

Figure 4–5
Explorer packet processing (all-routes broadcast).

Figure 4–6 illustrates an end station sending a spanning explorer packet. Bridge B1 and Bridge B2 make their respective forwarding decisions based on whether or not spanning is enabled. Assume Bridge B1 has spanning enabled and Bridge B2 does not have spanning enabled. Bridge B1 forwards the spanning explorer packet, and Bridge B2 does not. End station Y receives one spanning explorer packet and returns an all-routes explorer packet for each single route received. As before, Bridge B1 and Bridge B2 forward the all-routes explorer packet. In this example, the following packets are generated:

- One spanning explorer packet inbound (to End station Y)
- Two all-routes explorer packets outbound (to End station X)

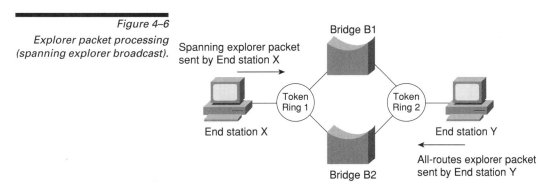

Figure 4–6
Explorer packet processing (spanning explorer broadcast).

If spanning were enabled on Bridge B2, it would also forward the spanning explorer packet. The following packets would be generated:

- Two spanning explorer packets inbound (to End station Y)
- Four all-routes explorer packets outbound (to End station X)

In general, there should be only a single path through the network for spanning explorer packets. If redundancy is required, a trade-off should be made between automatic redundancy and tolerance for additional explorer packet traffic. When redundancy is required, AST should be used.

Redundancy can be achieved in many instances within the router-based cloud as a result of encapsulation in either TCP or IP, the latter called *Fast Sequenced Transport* (FST). To contrast redundancy provided by a pure SRB environment and an internetwork that combines routing capabilities with SRBs, consider the networks illustrated in Figure 4–7, Figure 4–8, and Figure 4–9. Figure 4–7 illustrates a pure bridged network. Figure 4–8 and Figure 4–9 illustrate an SRB network running over routers.

Figure 4–7
Redundancy in a pure SRB network.

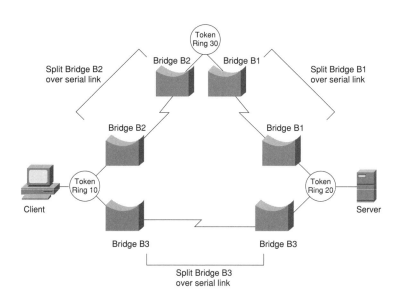

In Figure 4–7, there are two SRB paths between Token Ring 10 and Token Ring 20:

- Token Ring 10 to split Bridge B3 to Token Ring 20
- Token Ring 10 to split Bridge B2 to Token Ring 30 to split Bridge B1 to Token Ring 20

If spanning is enabled on both paths, the traffic resulting from a spanning explorer broadcast from the server is as follows:

- Two spanning explorer packets inbound (to the server)
- Four all-routes explorer packets outbound (to the client)

In router-based networks, the same type of redundancy is achieved in a different, more efficient manner, as illustrated in Figure 4–8 and Figure 4–9.

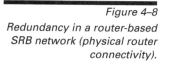

Figure 4–8
Redundancy in a router-based SRB network (physical router connectivity).

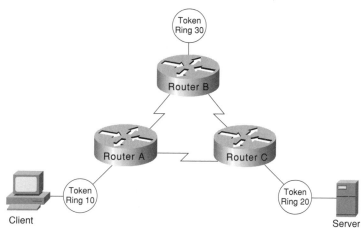

Figure 4–9
Redundancy in a router-based SRB network (logical SRB connectivity).

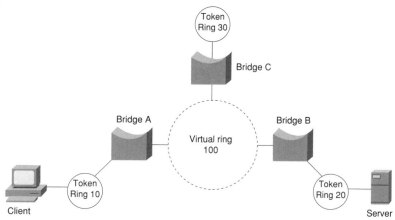

In Figure 4–9, there is only one SRB path between Token Ring 10 and Token Ring 20. The path is Token Ring 10 to Bridge A to Virtual ring 100 to Bridge B to Token Ring 20. When the client sends a spanning explorer packet, the following occurs:

- One spanning explorer packet goes inbound (to the server).
- Two all-routes broadcasts go outbound—one to the client on Token Ring 10 and one to Token Ring 30.

These broadcast rules are valid even when spanning is enabled on all the routers. In this example, spanning does not affect the traffic. The redundancy is a result of router-to-router traffic handling.

Each explorer packet is modified and copied at each destination ring when a multiring bridge is connected to more than two rings or to a virtual ring with multiple remote destinations. The virtual ring in these cases operates indistinguishably from a physical ring. The RIFs are modified exactly as if the virtual ring were a physical ring. All source-route bridges are designed to forward packets, so frame copying can be a limiting factor in both large-scale bridges and topologies with many token rings. In these topologies, your most important job as a network designer is to prevent excessive forwarding of explorer packets, which can disable an entire network.

Most source-route bridges do not propagate an explorer packet onto a ring from which it has just arrived. As a result, explorer packets are not copied from a virtual ring back to the same virtual ring, even in the presence of valid remote peers.

Figure 4–10 illustrates a situation in which incoming explorer packets arriving on virtual ring 1A are transmitted to Bridge 1 but are not copied back to Virtual ring 1A, even in the presence of multiple remote peer statements pointing to Virtual ring 1A. This is desirable behavior. Bridge 2 does not forward frames that originated from Bridge 1 because the frame has been on Virtual ring 1A.

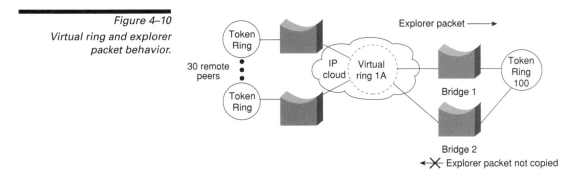

Figure 4–10

Virtual ring and explorer packet behavior.

In contrast, Figure 4–11 illustrates a topology that can result in a storm of explorer packets. In this topology, two virtual rings are separated by physical Token Ring 2.

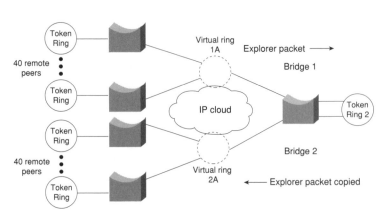

Figure 4–11

Virtual ring topology resulting in explorer packet storms.

An incoming explorer packet arriving on Virtual ring 1A is propagated to physical Token Ring 2 through Bridge 1. This explorer packet is then propagated into Bridge 2 and copied 40 times for each remote peer statement. Because the SRB protocol does not scale effectively, it results in this kind of explorer packet explosion that causes performance problems in Token Ring environments. The bridge must modify and copy the explorer packet in the CPU, causing inefficient use of the CPU and system bus for copying and modifying each explorer packet bound for a new destination.

You can reduce the number of forwarded explorer packets by enabling the explorer packet processing queue. The queue is used to divide traffic into data frames and explorer packets, as illustrated in Figure 4–12.

Figure 4–12

Queuing process resulting in the division of frames between real data and explorer packets.

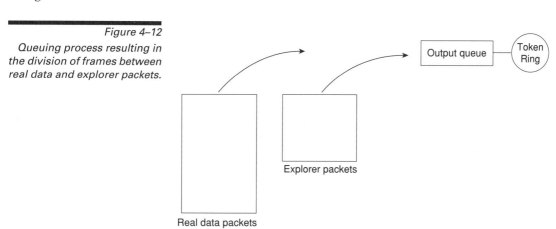

Reduce the number of forwarded explorer packets and improve overall efficiency by allowing the CPU to spend more cycles transmitting frames for routing and bridging and less time copying, modifying, and forwarding explorer packets. To enable the explorer packet processing queue, use the following global configuration command (available with Software Release 9.1.8(5) and subsequent releases):

    source-bridge explorerq-depth *number*

The value of *number* specifies the queue depth. The default value of *number* is 30 queue entries. The disadvantage of enabling the explorer packet processing queue is the potential for suboptimal paths. For most SRB networks that are plagued by excessive explorer packet, this potential is an acceptable trade-off.

Limiting the copying of explorer packets is an important factor in designing SRB networks. Poorly designed SRB networks can collapse under high explorer packet copying loads and the resulting volume of explorer packet traffic. Although good internetwork design, such as a single unified virtual ring, can eliminate large-scale explorer packet copying, this solution does not scale infinitely. For very large internetworks, contact your technical support representative for more information about specific limitations. Also, refer to the section "SRB Network Design" later in this chapter for more information about how different topologies scale.

Proxy Explorer

Another way of limiting explorer packet traffic is to use the *proxy explorer* feature. The function of the *proxy explorer* feature is to create an explorer packet reply cache, the entries of which are reused when subsequent explorer packets need to find the same host. The proxy explorer feature allows the SRB network designer to minimize exploding explorer packet traffic throughout the network. Routers cache the explorer packet reply and reuse it for subsequent explorer packets that are searching for the same MAC address.

Proxy explorer functionality is very useful in traditional SNA configurations because most explorer packets are destined for a single FEP on a single ring. However, if the host to be reached is an FEP on two rings (with a single locally administered address duplicated on both rings), this feature will select a single path without the possibility of redundant paths from a single router. Different routers can use different paths.

If your configuration does not involve duplicate FEPs with the same locally administered address, you can use the proxy explorer function in any SNA environment. Use the following interface configuration command:

    source-bridge proxy-explorer

NetBIOS Broadcast Handling

NetBIOS stations issue broadcasts for several reasons: to verify at startup that a station name is unique to the network, to find the route to a particular server, and to provide a heartbeat function to maintain connectivity between servers and requesters. These broadcasts are addressed either to a specific name, or to the NetBIOS functional address (such as C000 0000 0080). Station requests, such as a NAME QUERY frame, are sent as a spanning explorer broadcast to a unique NetBIOS name, and the corresponding response is returned as a broadcast of all-routes explorer packets.

NetBIOS is a broadcast-intensive protocol that can quickly consume lower bandwidth bridge paths. To address this problem, the router provides four different methods of preventing single and all-routes broadcast traffic from consuming your network:

- NetBIOS Name Caching
- NetBIOS Datagram Broadcast Handling
- NetBIOS Broadcast Throttling
- NetBIOS Broadcast Damping

NetBIOS Name Caching

NetBIOS name caching allows the router to maintain a cache of NetBIOS names that it uses to avoid the high overhead of transmitting many of the broadcasts used between client and server PCs in an SRB environment.

Name caching allows the router to detect when any host sends a series of duplicate query frames and to limit the host to one frame per configurable time period. The name cache includes a cache of mappings between NetBIOS server and client names and their MAC addresses. The name cache allows the router to send broadcast requests from clients to find servers and from servers in response to their clients directly to their destinations. It does this rather than sending the broadcast across the entire bridged network.

In most cases, the NetBIOS name cache is best used in situations in which large amounts of broadcast traffic creates bottlenecks on the WAN media. However, the traffic savings of NetBIOS name caching is probably not worth the router processor overhead when two local-area network (LAN) segments are interconnected.

As NetBIOS broadcasts traverse the router, the router caches the NetBIOS name in the NAME-QUERY and NAME-RECOGNIZED broadcast frames along with the station MAC address, RIF, and the physical port from which the broadcast was received. Because the router has the NetBIOS name as well as the route to the station, it can respond locally to broadcasts and eliminate the overhead of propagating broadcast frames throughout the network.

NetBIOS name caching can be enabled on each interface by using the following interface configuration commands:

> **source-bridge proxy-explorer**
> **netbios enable-name-cache**

The **source-bridge proxy-explorer** command is a prerequisite for NetBIOS name caching. To limit proxy-explorer to NetBIOS only, use the following configuration command:

> **source-bridge proxy-netbios-only**

NetBIOS Name Caching Operation

Figure 4–13 illustrates the NetBIOS name-caching process. Workstation A issues a NAME-QUERY frame looking for Server C. The single-route broadcast is propagated to all rings in the network and Server C responds with a NAME-RECOGNIZED response as a broadcast of all-routes explorer packets. The all-routes broadcast propagates throughout the network, and generates two duplicate NAME-RECOGNIZED responses to Workstation A, each with different routes reflected in the MAC header. Workstation A and Server C are now cached in routers 1, 2, and 3.

Workstation B now broadcasts a NAME-QUERY frame also looking for Server C. The broadcast is received by Router 1, which finds Server C in its cache. To verify that Server C and the cached route are still available, the router converts the broadcast frame to a directed frame using the cached RIF information, forwards the NAME-QUERY frame, and starts the RIF validate-age timer. When Server C receives the NAME-QUERY frame, it responds with a NAME-RECOGNIZED (all-routes) broadcast. If the router receives Server C's response before the validate-age timer expires, it keeps the RIF information; if not, the router deletes the RIF information from the cache.

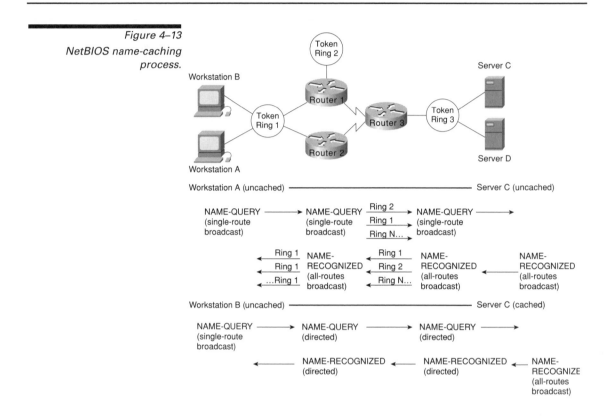

Figure 4–13
NetBIOS name-caching process.

Router 3 copies the NAME-RECOGNIZED broadcast and checks its cache for Workstation B. If an entry exists, the all-routes broadcast is converted to a directed frame and is forwarded to Workstation B. This example demonstrates that once a station name is broadcast into the network and its name is cached, no further broadcasts traverse the network. Without name caching, the broadcast activity in a network with 100 fully meshed ring segments can become a serious issue. NetBIOS name caching significantly reduces the bandwidth consumed by nonproductive broadcast traffic.

Each NetBIOS name cache entry is aged out of the table if activity does not occur within a configurable period of time. Aging ensures the information in the cache is current and that the cache is kept to a minimum size to maintain optimal performance.

The following global configuration command controls the name-caching age timer:

netbios name-cache timeout *minutes*

The default is 15 minutes.

NetBIOS Datagram Broadcast Handling

The router also checks the NetBIOS name cache when it receives NetBIOS datagram broadcasts (addressed to unique names), which allows the router to handle NetBIOS datagram broadcasts locally in a way that is similar to NAME-QUERY and NAME-RECOGNIZED broadcast handling. The difference is that datagram broadcasts are generally one-way flows with no corresponding reply. If datagram broadcasts represent a small percentage of overall broadcast traffic, you can disable datagram handling and avoid expending additional router overhead for relatively minor effect. This decision can be made only with an understanding of your broadcast traffic patterns.

NetBIOS Broadcast Throttling

NetBIOS applications broadcast by issuing multiple successive copies of the broadcast frame into the network. For example, IBM's OS/2 LAN Requester sends six successive copies of a NAME-QUERY frame, with a pause of a half second between each repeated transmission. Some applications allow you to tune this behavior, but tuning NetBIOS broadcasts is difficult to maintain if the number of NetBIOS workstations in your network is high.

As illustrated in Figure 4–14, when NetBIOS name caching is enabled, the router forwards the first of these six broadcasts, and drops the duplicate five broadcasts. The duplicate broadcasts (which originated from the same station), continue to be dropped until the dead timer expires. Two global configuration commands control relevant timers:

netbios name-cache query-timeout *seconds*

The default is 6 seconds.

netbios name-cache recognized-timeout *seconds*

The default is 1 second.

NetBIOS Broadcast Damping

The router remembers the physical port from which a NetBIOS station's route was cached. As a result, the router can remember where a cached station resides relative to the router. If the router receives a broadcast frame that is addressed to a cached NetBIOS name and if the router knows that the route to that station exists off of the same interface, the router does not need to forward the broadcast to find the target station. Instead, the router drops the broadcast and prevents unnecessary broadcast traffic from traversing the network.

As illustrated in Figure 4–15, a NetBIOS broadcast addressed to Server D is received by Router 1 on interface T0. Router 1 finds a cached entry for Server D, which indicates that the route to Server D is via interface T0. Because the broadcast was received on T0 and because the route to Server D is via T0, the broadcast is prevented from continuing on the network, and the requester finds Server D via the local SRB topology.

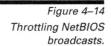

Figure 4–14
Throttling NetBIOS
broadcasts.

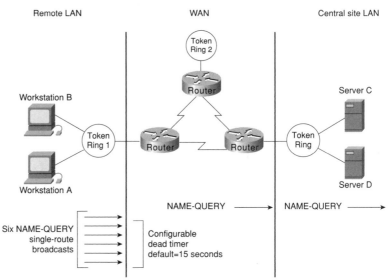

Figure 4–15
NetBIOS broadcast damping.

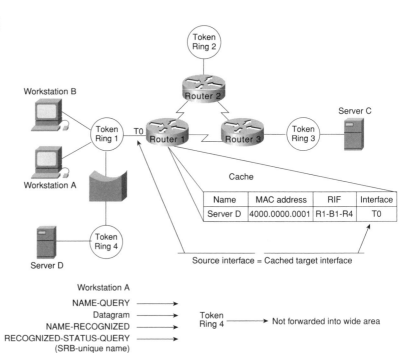

LAN Framing

Framing for SRB networks is straightforward. Using a basic IEEE 802.5 frame with Logical Link Control type 2 (LLC2) 802.2 framing, a RIF field follows the source MAC field in the IEEE 802.5 frame. The presence of a RIF field is indicated by setting the Routing Information Identifier (RII), which is the high-order bit of the source MAC field, as shown in Figure 4–16.

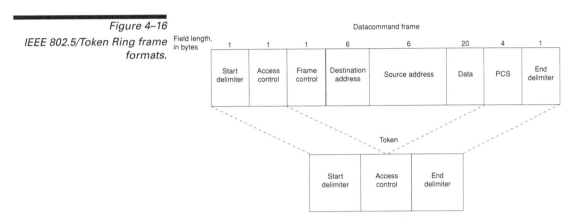

Figure 4–16
IEEE 802.5/Token Ring frame formats.

An SRB-configured router evaluates incoming frames based on IEEE 802.5 values, which is mostly a Subnetwork Access Protocol (SNAP) evaluation. Once the router determines whether the packet is to be routed, it evaluates whether to use SRB based on the value of the RII bit. If the bit is set and the router is not configured to route a specific protocol, the router sends the frame using SRB. Figure 4–17 illustrates this process.

IBM's original Token Ring bridging designs use a Routing Information Field (RIF) in the Token Ring frame header. This information stored the path that the frame took to get across multiple Token Ring segments (allowing the response to be sent along the same path). The fields of the RIF are as follows:

- The *routing control* filed, which consists of the following subfields:
  - The *type* subfield in the RIF indicates whether the frame should be routed to a single node, a group of nodes that make up a spanning tree of the internetwork, or all nodes. The first type is called a *specifically routed* frame; the second type is called a *spanning-tree explorer;* and the third type is called an *all paths explorer*. The spanning-tree explorer can be used as a transit mechanism for multicast frames. It can also be used as a replacement for all-paths explorer in outbound route queries. In this case, the destination responds with an all-paths explorer.
  - The *length* subfield indicates the total length (in bytes) of the RIF.
  - The *D* bit indicates the direction of the frame (forward or reverse).
  - The *largest* field indicates the largest frame that can be handled along this route.

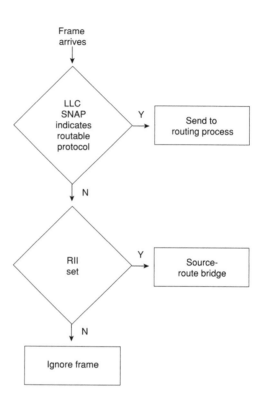

Figure 4–17

Process for identifying routable versus SRB packets.

- The *route descriptor* field, of which there can be more than one. Each router descriptor field carries a ring number-bridge number pair that specifies a portion of a route. Routes, then, are simply alternating sequences of LAN and bridge numbers that start and end with LAN numbers.

Routers provide a feature called *multiring,* which provides several benefits when SRB networks are mixed with multiprotocol routers. The first benefit is realized when connecting a multiprotocol router to an existing pure SRB network to support routable protocols (such as Novell's IPX). In this case, the multiring feature allows you to connect IPX and SRB networks seamlessly by routing IPX even in the presence of SRB framing. IPX stations can be linked via SRB networks or locally connected to a Token Ring with SRB framing. A router will route to the IPX station by first searching for the station and then framing each Token Ring frame with RII and a RIF.

The second benefit of multiring is that all outgoing packets for a specific routable protocol are framed in an SRB frame. The router creates a valid SRB frame by transmitting an explorer packet to create a valid RIF entry for the SRB frame of a routable network packet.

The third benefit of multiring is that it allows a smooth transition from a previously framed SRB network to a routed network. For example, a locally connected Token Ring can either use an IPX frame or an SRB frame depending on what is currently in use. To leverage existing IPX servers with

SRB drivers, configure the multiring for that specific Token Ring. A typical **multiring** interface configuration example might be as follows:

```
interface tokenring 0
source-bridge 10 1 100
multiring ipx spanning
```

WAN Framing

Routers recognize two forms of SRB. The first is *local* SRB, which is characterized by either the standard single ring-to-bridge-to-ring combination, or a flexible form using a multiple ring-to-bridge-to-virtual ring arrangement. The second form of SRB involves WAN connections and is called *remote* SRB (RSRB).

The framing that occurs to support WAN activities is twofold. First, the SRB frame is encapsulated in one of three ways: Transmission Control Protocol/Internet Protocol (TCP/IP) encapsulation, Fast Sequence Transport (FST) encapsulation, or direct High-Level Data Link Control (HDLC) encapsulation. Next, the frame is placed in the WAN frame for the appropriate WAN media, such as HDLC, Frame Relay, or Switched Multimegabit Data Service (SMDS).

If you select direct encapsulation for a WAN serial link, you avoid the overhead of encapsulating into either IP or TCP. The datagram is framed directly into HDLC. Direct encapsulation for WAN frames works only for HDLC. Over a multiaccess media, such as Ethernet or Fiber Distributed Data Interface (FDDI), direct encapsulation can be used to transmit data from one router to another.

Selection of encapsulation is critical to the performance of the underlying network and affects the degree to which the topology can scale to very large networks of token rings. Each encapsulation form is addressed in the following sections.

TCP/IP Encapsulation

TCP/IP encapsulation is the most common encapsulation format. Figure 4–18 illustrates a TCP/IP-encapsulated SRB frame. The chief benefit of TCP/IP encapsulation is a robust set of capabilities that ensures reliable transport.

Figure 4–18
SRB frame encapsulated in
TCP/IP with HDLC header.

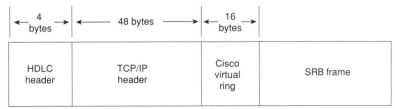

Because many tasks are involved in TCP/IP encapsulation, such as packet reordering, running timers for retransmission, and sending acknowledgments, TCP/IP encapsulation is costly in terms of CPU overhead. For both LANs and WANs, TCP/IP encapsulation incurs additional CPU overhead because all framing occurs in the CPU and the resulting IP frame is then process switched, which incurs additional overhead. (Process switching and its associated costs are discussed in "Process Switching" later in this chapter.)

Because of the high overhead associated with TCP/IP encapsulation, there is a significant upper boundary to maximum traffic forwarding. Performance is not the only constraint for using TCP/IP; fewer connections to other SRB rings can be supported using TCP/IP than any other encapsulation because of the processor overhead required to maintain the TCP structure. In general, you should limit the maximum number of remote peers connected to a single Cisco CSC/4 or RP card using TCP/IP encapsulation. Issues that can affect the acceptable number of remote peers include link speed, traffic load, number of supported protocols, routing platform implemented, and the level of other non-SRB activity occurring in the router.

Fast Sequenced Transport (FST) Encapsulation

Fast Sequenced Transport (FST) encapsulation is an alternative to TCP/IP encapsulation. FST encapsulation creates an IP frame with a sequence number; this frame is transmitted to an IP destination. At arrival, FST encapsulation strips the IP frame. If the sequence number of the arriving frame is greater than the sequence number of the last frame that arrived, FST encapsulation places the frame on the destination ring. If the sequence number of the arriving frame is less than the last frame transmitted by FST encapsulation, the frame is discarded, and the router relies on the transport mechanism of LLC2 to request the discarded or out-of-order frames to be retransmitted.

FST encapsulation is configured on a per-remote-ring basis. A typical example of using the **fst** keyword with the **source-bridge remote-peer** global configuration command follows:

```
source-bridge remote-peer 10 fst 131.108.3.2
```

The benefit of FST encapsulation is sustained end-to-end performance across multiple hops. FST is fast because the IP encapsulation happens on the interface card (AGS+, Cisco 7000, MGS, and CGS) or the system memory (IGS, Cisco 2000, Cisco 2500, Cisco 3000, and Cisco 4000) while the processor is in interrupt mode. For WAN transmissions, once the framing occurs, you can select an IP switching mechanism, either process switching or fast switching, depending on the result you want. Figure 4–19 illustrates the frame format of FST encapsulation.

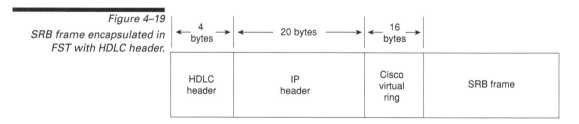

Figure 4–19
SRB frame encapsulated in FST with HDLC header.

← 4 bytes →	← 20 bytes →	← 16 bytes →	
HDLC header	IP header	Cisco virtual ring	SRB frame

There is a cost to implementing FST encapsulation. Because the packet discard feature associated with FST encapsulation does not guarantee delivery, FST encapsulation cannot be used in conjunction with the router's local acknowledgment feature.

Direct HDLC Encapsulation

Direct HDLC encapsulation is the fastest SRB encapsulation, but has the most restrictions. Direct HDLC encapsulation allows the network designer to configure two token rings separated by a single Ethernet, FDDI ring, Token Ring, or serial link.

For multiaccess media such as Ethernet or FDDI, you must know the destination MAC address of the neighbor. For HDLC on a WAN link, you need only to know the serial interface over which you intend to transmit traffic. As with FST, direct HDLC encapsulation occurs at processor interrupt level and is very fast. Figure 4–20 illustrates the format.

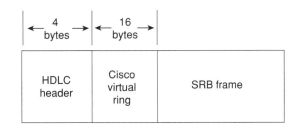

Figure 4–20
SRB frame encapsulated in direct HDLC.

The following is an example of a global configuration command that configures direct HDLC encapsulation on a serial interface:

```
source-bridge remote-peer 10 interface Serial0
```

The following is an example of a global configuration command that configures direct HDLC encapsulation on an FDDI interface:

```
source-bridge remote-peer 10 interface Fddi0 00c0.3456.768a
```

When connected to parallel WAN links, direct HDLC encapsulation can operate over only one of the links. Contact your technical support representative for specific information regarding likely performance characteristics, given your specific network configuration and type of encapsulation.

WAN Parallelism

Parallelism implies that multiple paths exist between two points that are parallel to each other. These paths might be of equal or unequal cost. Parallel links present a number of potential problems to network designers. Parallelism is not specifically a WAN issue. However, because WAN links are expensive, parallelism becomes an important design factor. For that reason, this chapter explores some of the considerations for implementing parallel links.

Problems with parallel links in an SRB environment result from the tandem objectives of minimizing session loss when links fail and maximizing traffic across a WAN infrastructure. Pure SRB networks maximize the WAN infrastructure but cause session losses at each link failure. IP-routed SRB networks minimize session loss but leave the challenge of maximizing WAN links to network designers. The goal of this section is to explore the issues that affect your efforts to balance these objectives.

Setting up parallel links between either two routers (see Figure 4–21) or several routers (see Figure 4–22) can pose challenges in an SRB environment. First, consider environments running NetBIOS and SNA over SRB environments. When an SNA or NetBIOS frame is delivered out of sequence, the end station might declare a protocol violation and terminate the session. Session loss is probably the worst possible outcome for a user or a network administrator.

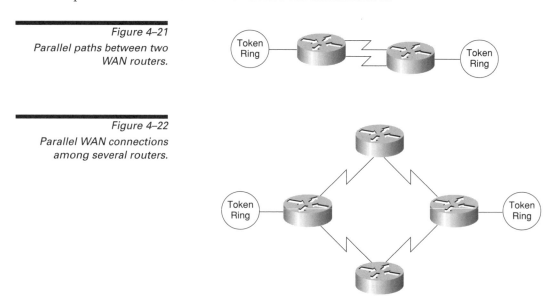

Figure 4–21
Parallel paths between two WAN routers.

Figure 4–22
Parallel WAN connections among several routers.

Delivering frames in sequence is the key objective of any SRB delivery mechanism. When you create parallel WAN links, you expect parallel delivery. In an SRB universe, this might not be achievable because timing differences on WAN links alone can cause packet resequencing. If the router uses parallel links and starts one frame header ahead of a second frame header, the frames might not arrive with the same sequencing. The second frame might arrive before the first frame because of WAN link delays. This is particularly true of packet-switched WANs.

When selecting or applying an encapsulation strategy with parallel WAN links, other factors influence the encapsulation that is used. These factors include the WAN switching technology and the IP routing protocols. A discussion of these factors follows. Some choices are predetermined. For example, direct HDLC encapsulation voids all parallel connections across a single virtual ring. In a multiprotocol environment, you can place SRB traffic on a single parallel link, whereas other protocols are load balanced on parallel links. As an alternative, you can configure the second link exclusively for multiprotocol (non-SRB) traffic.

WAN technologies can use two primary switching types: *process switching* and *fast switching*. Process switching provides full route evaluation and per-packet load balancing across parallel WAN links. Fast switching associates an IP host destination to a single interface to avoid out of order frames. The fact that the destination of a remote peer is a single IP destination can impact SRB decisions.

Process-switching and fast-switching techniques provide different features and performance characteristics. Each technique must be applied in situations that can optimize its respective capabilities. These switching strategies are addressed in detail in the following sections, "Process Switching" and "Fast Switching." Later in this chapter, "IP Routing Protocols with Parallel Links" addresses routing and switching in the context of SRB framing options.

Process Switching

Process switching is the most expensive switching operation that the CPU can perform. Process switching involves transmitting entire frames to the router CPU. Frames are then repackaged for delivery to or from a WAN interface, and the router makes a route selection for each packet. TCP/IP framing must be process switched because switching must occur when the rings are encapsulating or unencapsulating data, which occurs at processor level. FST framing can be process switched or fast switched.

Process switching begins when a frame arrives on a Token Ring interface and causes an interrupt to be transmitted to the CPU. The CPU then determines that the frame must be process switched and schedules the switch in noninterrupt mode. The frame is then transferred to the CPU and placed on an input queue, whose depth is viewable with the **show interfaces** EXEC command. Once the entire frame is transferred across the system bus, the frame is reworked for appropriate TCP headers and header compression.

Next, the IP route for the destination is examined. If multiple paths exist, the frame pointer is updated to use the next path for the next frame that arrives. After a route is selected, the frame is transmitted across the system bus to the output interface queue of the specific interface card from which the frame will exit. The queue entry is placed on the specific exit interface and the SCI card dequeues and transmits the frame down the WAN link.

Fast Switching

Fast switching maximizes the volume of traffic that the router can handle by streamlining the router's queuing mechanisms. Fast switching deals with incoming frames in *processor interrupt mode* and minimizes the number of decisions that must be applied.

Fast switching precaches routes. Once an IP destination is process switched, its route is cached and associated with a specific interface. When an IP destination is precached, it is tied to a specific path. For either FST or TCP/IP encapsulations, a single IP destination carries all of the SRB traffic to an FEP destination. If fast switching is used with multiple IP paths, a single path exists for each ring destination. You must use process switching to load-balance traffic across multiple paths.

Two of the SRB framing techniques are capable of being fast switched: direct HDLC encapsulation and FST encapsulation. Direct HDLC encapsulation is by definition fast switched; it cannot be process switched. FST can be fast switched or process switched.

Two IBM SRB WAN options do not allow fast switching of a frame: TCP header compression and priority or custom queuing. If either of these features is invoked, the frame cannot be fast switched. The reason for these caveats is that certain frame components are modified when using fast switching in AGS+, MGS, CGS, or Cisco 7000 interface memory and not in the CPU memory. If the frame needs to be extensively modified, it must be done in CPU system buffers and not in buffers associated with individual interface cards.

In addition, fast switching uses only interface buffers that are not generally reported using monitoring EXEC commands, such as **show interfaces**. The buffers reported in the **show interfaces** EXEC command are CPU buffers for input and output that are only used during process switching. Fast switching uses preconfigured interface buffers. You can view the allocation of buffers using the **show controllers** EXEC command.

For direct HDLC encapsulation, SRB frames are directly linked to an output serial port (such as interface serial 0). When an SRB frame enters the 2R or CTR card, an interrupt is transmitted to the CPU. The CPU verifies that the frame is an SRB frame and that the buffer on either the 2R card or the ciscoBus controller is modified to create an HDLC header. The new frame is transmitted two bytes at a time through the CPU from either the 2R card or the ciscoBus controller across the system bus to the SCI card or SIP card.

A similar process occurs for FST encapsulation; however, SRB frames are directly linked to a destination IP address. When an SRB frame enters the 2R or CTR card, an interrupt is transmitted to the CPU. The CPU verifies that the frame is an SRB frame and the buffer on either the 2R card or the ciscoBus controller is modified to create an IP datagram with appropriate WAN framing for the destination. The new frame is transmitted two bytes at a time through the CPU from either the 2R card or the ciscoBus controller across the system bus to the SCI card or SIP card.

Use the EXEC command **show ip route cache** to determine whether an IP destination is being fast switched. This command lists IP destinations as well as the relevant MAC frame and destination interface that the specific IP address uses. If the entry is fast switched, the destination IP address is present. If the destination IP address is not present, the router is using process switching to reach the destination. By default, HDLC WAN links are fast switched for IP. If the router is configured for direct HDLC encapsulation, the only status indication is the output for the **show source-bridge** EXEC command. The bridge indicates it is using a direct serial interface and not an IP address.

IP Routing Protocols with Parallel Links

IP routing protocols play a part in the parallel SRB WAN decisions because they can create wider parallelism than two routers with parallel links. Given the parallel links shown in Figure 4–23, load balancing makes three critical assumptions: equal-cost paths, routing protocol support for equal-cost load balancing, and process switching for a single IP destination.

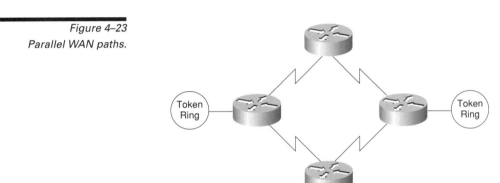

Figure 4–23
Parallel WAN paths.

Process switching is discussed extensively in the section "Process Switching" earlier in this chapter. Issues relating to equal-cost path IP routing and unequal-cost path routing are discussed in the sections that follow, "IP Routing over Equal-Cost Paths" and "IP Routing over Unequal-Cost Paths Using Variance."

IP Routing over Equal-Cost Paths

An *equal-cost path* is *metrically* equivalent to another parallel path between two points. In RIP, equivalence is parallel WAN paths of equal hops. In Interior Gateway Routing Protocol (IGRP) and Open Shortest Path First (OSPF), metric equivalence translates into WAN paths of equal bandwidth, where the bandwidth is declared by the network administrator. IGRP also adds the concept of delay to determine metrically equivalent links. To create parallel links for equal-cost paths and to actively use these paths, the router must use process switching because all frames sent from one ring to another have the same IP destination.

The following list outlines the capability of supported IP routing technologies to create equal-cost paths:

- *Static routes*—For Cisco software releases prior to Software Release 9.1, static routes cannot be created in parallel; only a single path can be selected. As of Software Release 9.1, static routes can be created in parallel.

- *IGRP and Enhanced Interior Gateway Routing Protocol (Enhanced IGRP)*—Can use up to four equal-cost paths in parallel. Ensure that the bandwidth command is correctly configured on all links.

- *OSPF*—If paths are of equal declared metrics, OSPF can use up to four equal-cost paths in parallel.

- *RIP*—RIP can use four equal-cost paths in parallel. Remember that this will not take into account anything but hops, so even unequal bandwidth links will be evaluated as having equivalent cost.

IGRP, Enhanced IGRP, and OSPF can route traffic across equal-cost paths and split SRB traffic across equal-cost links if the router is process switching. RIP will route across equal-cost paths and it will assume that all WAN links are the same speed regardless of reality. Static routes allow parallel paths and are a tool for the advanced network designer.

A router's capability to use parallel paths is determined in part by the encapsulation method. If TCP/IP encapsulation is used, parallel paths are used. If FST encapsulation is used under normal operational conditions, all traffic must use only one of the parallel links. This is because all the RSRB traffic sent to another FST peer goes to a single IP destination address. When using fast switching, the router might alternate some traffic across parallel links based on destination address. However, because all traffic to a peer router uses only one destination IP address, all RSRB traffic flows across one link.

IP Routing over Unequal-Cost Paths Using Variance

The only routing protocols that can handle intentional unequal-cost path balancing are IGRP and Enhanced IGRP. Using a feature called *variance*, the router can load balance over unequal-cost paths. Figure 4–24 illustrates one such configuration from A to B. In this figure, load balancing the link from C to B is assumed to be faster than the link from A to B.

Figure 4–24

Unequal-cost load balancing with IGRP.

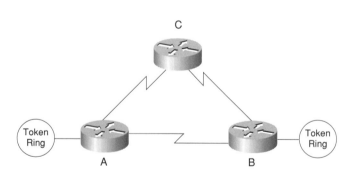

Variance has two rules that apply in this or any unequal-cost load balancing situation:

- *Rule 1*—Parallelism must exist in the topology.
- *Rule 2*—Packets must make *forward progress* on any parallel link toward an intended destination. In other words, a router will not forward traffic to another router that has the same (or greater) relative distance metric to a destination. This rule prevents loops. The rule of forward progress is straightforward. If the next-hop router is closer to the destination (than some other router) a path through it will be used as a valid alternative path.

If these rules are met and the network administrator adds variance to the IGRP configuration, the router will load balance over parallel paths for a single IP destination when it is process switching. Figure 4–25 illustrates a case in which variance might be used.

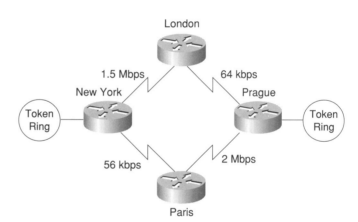

Figure 4–25
Environmental illustrating variance applications.

Consider a set of routers connected via WAN links in a circle, where each WAN link is the same speed, as illustrated in Figure 4–26. Assume that a data center is at location A and that all the link speeds are the same. Consider parallelism from B to A. A parallel link exists from A to B and A to C to D to E to B; however, routing protocols are not intuitive. This topology satisfies the first rule because parallelism clearly exists; however, this topology fails the forward progress rule.

The way to evaluate the forward progress rule is to examine the obvious short path separately from the long variant path, subtracting the first hop. Is C to D to E to B a better path than A to B? The answer is *no*; variance will have no effect in this topology for the problem as described.

Now evaluate the problem from the perspective of A to E. Using the forward progress rule, compare A to B to E with C to D to E. In this topology, these paths are equal and they fail the forward progress rule. If these paths are to pass data in parallel, router A must have two paths: one to C and one to B. If C had variance configured, it would have two paths: one to A and one to D. This leaves the possibility of C routing to A and A routing to C in a loop. Thus, the variance rule is that the metric of the next-hop router must be less than the metric through the shortest path. In a five-router topology with equal-cost WAN links, parallelism cannot be achieved.

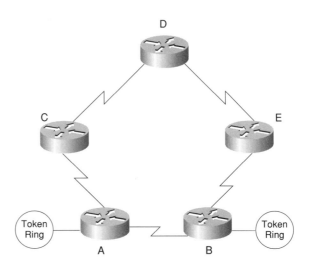

Figure 4–26

ıl-cost path and
,e implementation
example.

By default, variance is not configured. If it is, it must be configured as an integer multiple of the allowable metric variance. Consider the following use of the **variance** router configuration command:

```
router igrp 1343
variance 2
```

Using this particular instance of the **variance** command results in a load-balanced topology with a 2:1 ratio of bandwidth. For all practical topologies, this should be an upper maximum because you should not load balance an overly high variance of WAN links such as E1 and 64 Kbps.

Use variance carefully. Because IP fast switching links an IP destination to an interface or next hop, a single IP destination can be stuck on a 64-Kbps link while most other IP destinations are wired to a fast link such as an E1. This situation will cause users to call their network administrators to determine why transmission is slow one day when it was fast the day before. If SRB is fast switched, all users of a destination ring can be linked to the slower path using variance.

Variance has another major benefit: If a link fails for any reason, the router immediately switches all traffic to the parallel link without any convergence overhead. The router can do this because the parallel link is a known valid path and the router does not need to wait for the routing protocols to converge.

Local Acknowledgment Recommendations

If you configure your remote source-route bridge to use IP encapsulation over a TCP connection, you also can enable LLC2 Local Acknowledgment. The following explains how this feature can be useful.

LLC2, or Logical Link Control-Type 2, an ISO standard data link level protocol used in Token Ring networks, was designed to ensure reliable transmission of data across LAN media with minimal or predictable time delays. With the advent of remote source route bridging (RSRB) and wide area network (WAN) backbones, LANs are now separated by wide, geographic distances spanning countries and continents. As a result, these LANs have time delays that are longer than LLC2 allows for bidirectional communication between hosts. The Local Acknowledgment capability in router/bridges supporting remote source-route bridging addresses the problem of unpredictable time delays, multiple retransmissions, and many user sessions.

In a typical LLC2 session, when host A sends a frame to host B, the sending host A expects host B to respond positively or negatively in a certain amount of predefined time commonly called the T1 time. If host A does not receive an acknowledgment of the frame it sent to host B within the T1 time, it will retry a few number of times (normally 8 to 10). If there is still no response from host B, host A will drop the session.

Figure 4–27 shows how Local Acknowledgment operates in an SRB environment. With Local Acknowledgment for LLC2 enabled in both routers, Router A acknowledges frames received from the 37x5. The 37x5 still thinks that the acknowledgments it receives are from the 3x74. The 3x74 thinks that the acknowledgments it receives are from the 37x5. Router B looks like the 3x74 to 37x5. Because the frames no longer have to travel the WAN backbone networks to be acknowledged, but instead are locally acknowledged by routers, the end machines do not time out, resulting in no loss of sessions.

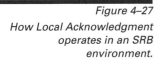

Figure 4–27

How Local Acknowledgment operates in an SRB environment.

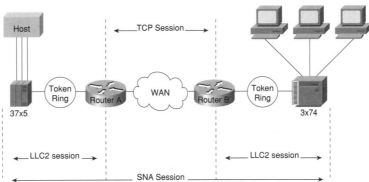

The following recommendations apply to the implementation of local acknowledgment. Use local acknowledgment under the following conditions:

- When the WAN implementation must accommodate long network delays
- When the internetwork includes slow links, heavily used links, or poor quality links
- When the internetwork requires that sessions remain active during router convergence
- When WAN traffic must be minimized
- When the amount of LLC traffic on backbone needs to be reduced (when more than 50 percent of packets are LLC packets)
- When WAN costs must be reduced

- When network integrity must be improved, assuming TCP/IP encapsulation is used
- When unreliable WAN links exist that are causing frequent session loss
- When end station timer or retry modifications are difficult or costly
- When bandwidth constraints require the elimination of acknowledgment traffic

Parallel Link Recommendations

The following recommendations apply to parallel WAN link configuration:

- Do not combine multiple CTR cards with multiple WAN links; create a separate router primarily with WAN links. For example, do not create an 8-T1/E1 process-switched WAN solution on top of a 75-kilopackets-per-second (Kpps) Token Ring engine. You will run out of CPU bandwidth.
- Use FST encapsulation whenever possible.
- Use TCP/IP encapsulation when local acknowledgment or prioritization is required.
- Maximize fast switching.

When link speeds are primarily 64 Kbps and slower and local acknowledgment or prioritization is a requirement, use TCP/IP encapsulation with IGRP variance in meshed topologies when the topology can take advantage of these features.

When link speeds are primarily greater than 64 Kbps and local acknowledgment is a requirement, follow this recommendation:

- Use TCP/IP encapsulation only on those links that have a history of session loss (local acknowledgment).
- Use FST encapsulation on the remaining links.

SNA Host Configuration Considerations for SRB

When designing SRB-based internets that feature routers and IBM SNA entities, you must carefully consider the configuration of SNA nodes, as well as routing nodes. Appendix C, "SNA Host Configuration for SRB Networks," provides examples of SNA host configurations that focus on three specific SNA devices:

- Front-end processors
- VTAM-switched major nodes
- 3174 cluster controllers

IP ROUTING PROTOCOL SELECTION FOR SRB NETWORKS

When designing large SRB networks, the goal is to optimize the underlying IP network so it can carry SNA and NetBIOS traffic more efficiently. To do this, select your IP routing protocol carefully. You should consider the following parameters when selecting your routing protocol:

- Time to converge
- Maintainability of the internetwork routing environment

If you select a protocol using only one criterion, you might build a network that cannot be expanded and that might eventually break.

Three interior gateway routing protocols work best in an SRB environment: IGRP, Enhanced IGRP, and OSPF. In general, IGRP, Enhanced IGRP, and OSPF are the only options for building an IP SNA network. You can also consider RIP. However, because RIP does not provide any consistent WAN bandwidth sensitivity, it is not a good choice for redundancy or meshed topologies.

The following discussion focuses on network topology and convergence considerations.

Convergence Considerations

Convergence is the time it takes a router to start using a new route when an active link fails in a network where alternative routes are available.

Rapid convergence is critical for SNA environments, particularly when local acknowledgment is not used. Consider a 3174 failure recovery scenario—an SNA device can lose its session with the host in 13 seconds. The result is session loss and route rediscovery for all affected units. If the 3174 had not just sent data to the host, the session would not be lost for somewhere between 13 and 42 seconds, depending on the value of the T1 Timer Inactivity parameter when the link failed. If local acknowledgment is used, the SNA session does not fail while the routers are converging.

Convergence becomes an issue when installing large meshed networks with multiple valid alternative paths. Distance vector protocols such as RIP or IGRP cannot determine the source of a learned route. A route could be learned by Router A from a neighbor that had originally learned the route from Router A. If Router A and its neighbor both use this route, they create a *routing loop*. Routing loops imply *broadcast storms* and, as a result, are widely viewed as undesirable events.

Enhanced IGRP provides superior convergence properties and operating efficiencies. It uses a convergence algorithm that eliminates routing loops throughout a route computation. More importantly, convergence time with Enhanced IGRP is reduced to a level below the threshold for session loss.

OSPF was also designed to minimize convergence time. It is good at convergence, but has side effects that will be discussed in the next section. For routers, total convergence time has two primary components:

- Link failure detection time
- IP routing protocol convergence time

Link failure detection time is the minimum, maximum, or average time it takes the router to detect that no frames are crossing the link. IP routing protocol convergence time is the time it takes the routing protocol to detect a failure and switch to alternative links.

Link Failure Effects on Convergence

Links fail in a hierarchical order of occurrence. Serial links are the most unreliable. FDDI networks, Token Ring networks, and Ethernet networks are about equal in reliability and rarely fail.

The following sections describe the significance of media-failure detection mechanisms with respect to recovery from media failure and the effects of different media failures on convergence in an IBM internetwork.

Keepalives and Convergence

Routers institute *keepalives* to verify the stability of a link. A router transmits a packet every 10 seconds by default, and when three keepalives sequentially fail to cross the link, the router declares the link to be down. To recover, the router retransmits the packet every few seconds.

For IBM IP networks, keepalives should be active only on serial and Ethernet links. Ethernet link keepalives are acceptable because the failure rate is low, but serial links (especially those faster than 64 Kbps) should be set to three seconds. Use the **keepalive** interface configuration command to adjust the keepalive timer for a specific interface. For example:

```
interface serial 0
keepalive 3
```

This configuration reduces the maximum failure detection for the serial interface from 30 seconds to nine seconds. (The interface is declared down after three consecutive update intervals pass with no keepalives detected.) Media-related keepalive specifics are provided in the sections that follow.

Enhanced IGRP uses small hello packets to verify link stability. Hello packets are transmitted by default every five seconds. When three hello packets fail to cross the link, the router immediately converges. Hello packets originate from the network layer and are protocol dependent. Use the **ip hello-interval eigrp** interface configuration command to configure a different hello packet interval for IP. For example:

```
ip hello-interval eigrp 109 3
```

This example configures a hello packet interval of three seconds for the IP protocol on Enhanced IGRP autonomous system number 109.

Serial Link Failure Effects

Serial links are inherently unreliable because they usually extend over long distances and because they are subject to a variety of failures.

In general, if a router detects loss of the carrier signal, it immediately disables the link. Unfortunately, carrier loss is not a guaranteed way of detecting a failed link, so the router must also use keepalives or hello packets to determine whether an interface is connected to an operational medium.

When the carrier signal is lost, the router detects the failure immediately. For any other serial failure, given the default keepalive timer of 10 seconds and the rule that three keepalives must be missed before the router declares that the interface is down, failure detection takes at least 21 seconds and could take as long as 30 seconds, with an average detection time of 25.5 seconds. When the keepalive timer is three seconds, the failure is detected within seven to nine seconds.

Token Ring Failure Effects

Token Ring media, whether twisted-pair or IBM media attachment units (MAUs), rarely encounter failures. When media failures occur, the Token Ring protocol fails, causing the ring to transition, beacon, and reinitialize.

Token Ring has built-in reliability that allows the interface to determine whether the ring is up or down: The returning token indicates an active ring. Keepalives, which provide a fail-safe mechanism in case the Token Ring protocol itself fails, are also available but can be disabled in most networks to prevent unnecessary network traffic. Any keepalive failure usually indicates that the Token Ring interface is under tremendous load or may have already failed. The failure detection time for Token Ring is immediate.

FDDI Failure Effects

Like Token Ring, FDDI rings are reliable media. Users who turn their devices off, which causes the FDDI ring to "wrap," are the most common cause of failure in dual-attached FDDI networks. Keepalives are available, but are not particularly useful. Enabling keepalives with FDDI can cause problems in high-load environments because the keepalives add to the traffic. Because the router disables the interface when it is experiencing intolerably heavy traffic loads, detection of a keepalive loss is usually a false error indication. The failure detection time for FDDI rings is immediate.

Ethernet Failure Effects

Ethernet media is generally reliable but lacks a failure-detection protocol. Therefore, keepalives play a critical role in determining the availability of the media. The keepalive must fail three times before the router disables the interface. There is no indication of the location or source of the failure, whether it is from router to MAU or across the physical media.

Given the default keepalive timer of 10 seconds and the rule that three keepalives must be missed before the router declares that the interface is down, failure detection takes at least 21 seconds and could take as long as 30 seconds, with an average detection time of 25.5 seconds.

Routing Protocol Convergence

When analyzing routing convergence, it is assumed that a link has failed or router keepalives have not been detected. The router waits for a link failure detection period to expire. After this waiting period passes, the router incurs a *routing protocol convergence time*. The following discussions address convergence for IGRP, Enhanced IGRP, and OSPF.

IGRP Convergence

IGRP convergence is controlled by a single factor: whether *holddown* is enabled (the default). This discussion focuses on determining when it is appropriate to disable holddown.

Because a router learns about routes from its neighbors, a distance vector routing protocol never actually understands the topologies to which it is connected; instead, it approximates the topologies. When enabled, holddown, which is a property of distance vector routing protocols, specifies that alternative paths are not used until the paths in question are determined to be actual alternative routes. When a failure occurs and alternative paths exists, the router holds down any routing protocol changes until the holddown timer expires to determine that the network is now completely known.

IGRP allows you to configure the protocol so that it will *not* hold down a link. The danger of administratively disabling holddown is that the routers might loop packets to each other for networks that are unreachable, which would cause the receipt of high volumes of errant traffic that could dominate low-bandwidth links. Any errant datagram would loop up to 254 times before the "counting to infinity" process causes the datagram to be dropped. The length of time associated with "counting to infinity" can be modified using the **metric maximum-hops** *hops* router configuration command. The default *hops* value is 100; the maximum is 255.

Generally, meshed WAN bandwidth that consists of fractional T1/E1 or greater can converge faster than parallel WAN bandwidth that is 64 Kbps. Network topologies with high WAN bandwidth can support disabling holddown, so you can safely disable holddown on all routers in any network with a high WAN bandwidth.

If convergence time is worth trading off against potential bandwidth for sites with lower-speed links, you can disable holddown on these sites. However, if a loop occurs when a link is lost, the network performance for end systems connected to affected sites might be poor until "counting to infinity" ends. If you require faster convergence and can live with congestion for a brief period, you can disable holddown in any case. To disable holddown, enter the following router configuration commands for all routers in the network:

> **router igrp** *autonomous-system*
> **network** *network-number*
> **no metric holddown**

Including the **no metric holddown** router configuration command changes the convergence of IP to 50 percent of neighbor update time (on average) assuming a neighbor is using this other valid route. Consider a topology as illustrated in Figure 4–28.

Assume that all links illustrated in Figure 4–28 are of equal speed and that the link from A to B fails. If C is using A to get to B, the IGRP Flash update tells C that its route to B is probably down. When D sends the next IGRP update, C uses D to get to B. A knows its route to B is down, and waits for two updates from C (on average) to get a new route to B. Most topologies converge with a single neighbor update.

If variance is active and there are two separate paths to a destination network, the network converges immediately to the remaining path when the router receives a Flash update.

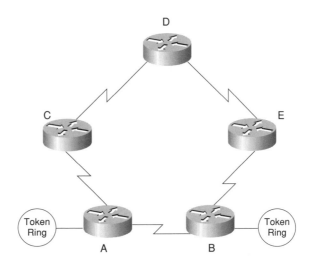

Figure 4–28
Convergence topology.

Also note that the default values for IGRP timers are appropriate for general IP networks, not for IBM IP networks. It is necessary to change a few timer defaults for an IBM IP environment. The basic neighbor update timer is set to 90 seconds. For IBM IP networks, use 20 seconds, which results in an average IBM IP convergence for IGRP of 10 seconds with a Flash update. To make this change, modify the IGRP configuration of each router. The router configuration commands are as follows:

router igrp *autonomous-system*
network *network-number*
timers basic *update invalid holddown flush* [*sleeptime*]

Consider the following configuration for the **timers basic** router configuration command:

```
timers basic 20 60 60 120
```

These values optimize IGRP convergence in an IBM IP environment. If holddown is enabled, the worst-case convergence is three update periods of 20 seconds each, for a total of 60 seconds. Although these values optimize convergence, the worst-case convergence time can break IBM sessions. Try using local acknowledgment to keep sessions up while IGRP converges.

Enhanced IGRP Convergence

Enhanced IGRP is an advanced version of IGRP. The same distance vector technology found in IGRP is used in Enhanced IGRP, and the underlying distance information remains unchanged. Enhanced IGRP implements a new convergence algorithm that permits loop-free operation throughout a route computation, which improves Enhanced IGRP convergence properties and operating efficiency. Enhanced IGRP allows all routers involved in a topology change to synchronize at the same time. Routers that are not affected by topology changes are not involved in the recomputation. The result is very fast convergence time.

OSPF Convergence

OSPF uses two mechanisms for detecting failure. The first mechanism consists of interface status changes, such as carrier loss on a serial link or keepalive loss. The second mechanism is failure of OSPF to transmit and receive a hello packet within a timing window called a *dead timer*. Once the dead timer expires, the router assumes the link is dead. Once a router running OSPF assumes a link is dead, it produces an area-wide broadcast that causes all nodes to recompute their topology maps.

When OSPF receives an active multicast with link down information, the convergence time is less than one second. Suboptimal OSPF convergence occurs when a link is down but the router receives no forward indication. In this failure situation, the router must wait for the dead timer to expire. By default, the OSPF dead timer is set to 40 seconds. In most IP networks, you can set the dead timer equal to at least three OSPF hello packets.

In the IBM IP environment, the default values of the OSPF timers are too high for the session layer convergence that SNA and NetBIOS require; therefore, you should change the dead timer to 18 seconds and the hello timer to six seconds for each interface in your network. For example:

```
interface tokenring 0
ip ospf dead-interval 18
ip ospf hello-interval 6
```

Convergence Summary

If you followed all the recommendations in this section, the behavior of the two routing protocols is as follows:

- IGRP provides instant convergence with carrier loss and active variant paths. Assuming that *serial keepalive* = 3 and *update* = 20, convergence delays are as follows:

  - Seven- to nine-second convergence (eight-second convergence on average) with serial keepalive loss and active variant paths. This assumes that three keepalives have expired, there was no holddown, and no routing update was required.

  - One- to 20-second convergence (10.5-second convergence on average) with carrier loss, Flash update, and no holddown. This assumes failure detection is immediate; therefore time for routing update is the only factor.

  - Ten- to 29-second convergence with keepalive loss, Flash update, and no holddown. This assumes a nine-second keepalive loss, the Flash update was immediate, and one to 20 seconds for the routing update.

  - Sixty-nine-second convergence worst-case scenario (nine-second keepalive loss, three updates of 20 seconds each).

- Enhanced IGRP provides instant convergence with carrier loss and presence of a feasible successor. Convergence delays are as follows:

  - Eleven- to 15-second convergence by default for Hello packet loss in all cases.

- OSPF provides instant convergence with carrier loss and active broadcasts. Convergence delays are as follows:

○ Nine-second convergence with serial keepalive loss and active broadcasts.

○ Eighteen-second convergence, worst-case scenario.

NOTES

Assuming that OSPF is configured with realistic timer settings, the total convergence time is the sum of the time it takes the interface to change its state from up to down, combined with the time it takes the routing protocol to converge.

Routing Protocol Design and Maintenance Issues

You must consider two key design and maintenance factors when creating networks based on IGRP, Enhanced IGRP, or OSPF for primarily SNA traffic:

- Routing Protocol Network Design
- Routing Protocol Scalability

Routing Protocol Network Design

Some routing protocols do not require an additional topological structure to build a successful internetwork. Other routing protocols require a separate topological structure outside of the existing addressing structure that must be maintained and well understood. IGRP, Enhanced IGRP, and OSPF show how different routing protocols handle network design issues.

IGRP Routing Protocol Network Design

IGRP has no implicit network design requirements. IGRP networks can scale as nonhierarchical topologies to thousands of networks and hundreds of routers.

However, implementing hundreds of IGRP routers in the same autonomous system results in the transmission of an extremely large routing update every 90 seconds (by default). The impact of routing update transmission is dampened by a feature of IGRP called *route summarization*, which summarizes unconnected network numbers into a single routing table entry.

For example, if 1000 subnets of TCP/IP are distributed evenly across 10 IP networks, a single router with route summarization would see the 100 subnets of its locally connected network and nine summary routes to all other networks. Route summarization reduces the routing table of large networks, but can result in suboptimal routing at the border points.

Enhanced IGRP Routing Protocol Network Design

Enhanced IGRP, like IGRP, has no implicit network design requirements. Unlike IGRP, Enhanced IGRP does not make large routing table updates in a single large autonomous system, which makes the use of Enhanced IGRP even more scalable. Only routers that are directly involved in a topology change are involved in route recomputation, which saves processor overhead and results in minimal bandwidth utilization for routing updates.

Enhanced IGRP uses an automatic redistribution mechanism so IGRP routes are imported into Enhanced IGRP and vice versa, for compatibility and seamless interoperation with IGRP routers. The compatibility feature allows you to take advantage of the benefits of both protocols while migrating from IGRP to Enhanced IGRP and allows Enhanced IGRP to be enabled in strategic locations carefully without disrupting IGRP performance. By default, IGRP routes take precedence over Enhanced IGRP routes, but a configuration command that does not require routing processes to restart can change the default.

OSPF Routing Protocol Network Design

OSPF has a network structure that must be maintained separately from the addressing structure of IP. The concept in OSPF is that a single backbone of routers will communicate with several leaf areas. Consider the general environment illustrated in Figure 4–29.

Figure 4–29
OSPF backbone communicating with several leaf areas.

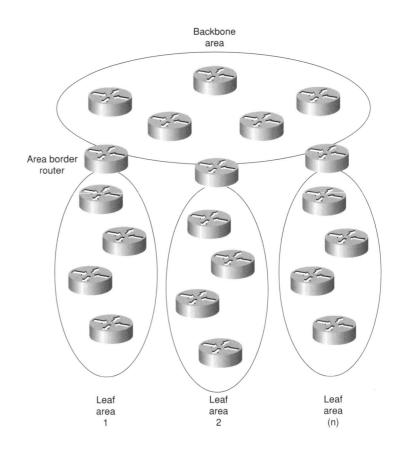

Communication between areas occurs through the backbone only. There is no interarea communication except through the backbone, which is not an overwhelming constraint for most SNA networks because they are already hierarchical in nature. NetBIOS networks, however, are not hierarchical in nature, which poses a potential design challenge.

A hierarchical structure limits the extent of link-state broadcasts that indicate link failures. In each router, OSPF builds a full area topological database that describes each router and each link. When any link changes state, each router within an area recomputes the entire database and builds a new routing table. Traffic associated with this recomputation process occurs across all links in the area. With a typical large installation (for example, 400 routers), you might expect several link updates per second. However, link updates can occur more often, flooding the network and forcing the routers to use all active cycles maintaining routing tables instead of forwarding traffic.

To avoid these problems, create a *structure* of leaf areas and a unique backbone. To create this structure, take the square root of the number of routers and subtract one for the backbone. For example, 100 routers would optimally be allocated with 10 routers in the backbone and nine areas each with 10 routers. Each area must touch the backbone, so the selection of the backbone routers is critical.

Modifying an existing topology to add an additional 10 routers to a geographically remote location poses a greater challenge. You must decide whether to create an unbalanced area that connects the remote location to the backbone, or to rebalance the topology by adding an OSPF backbone router at the remote location.

After you create the topology, you must impose IP addressing on it. If you do not assign a separate network to each leaf area, the boundaries between the leaf areas and the backbone are meaningless and link status changes will propagate throughout the entire network. Each backbone router that bounds an area (called an *area border router*) must summarize the routes imported to and from the backbone. Route summarization does not occur by default, so for most IP networks you must include a common set of commands at each area border router. The following is a typical configuration for area border routers:

```
router ospf 10
network 192.30.0.0 0.0.0.255 area 0
network 131.108.0.0 0.0.255.255 area 0.0.0.1
area 0.0.0.1 range 131.108.0.0 255.255.0.0
```

In this example, the importation of routes into the backbone of network 131.108.0.0 is limited. Unfortunately, it specifies only a single point of entry for network 131.108.0.0. If several area border routers are connected to leaf area 1 using network 131.108.0.0, the router uses the nearest area border router with connectivity to 131.108.0.0.

The techniques used for addressing an OSPF using multiple areas are discussed in the "Addressing and Route Summarization" section in Chapter 3, "Designing Large-Scale IP Internetworks."

Routing Protocol Scalability

Only one significant design challenge exists for large scalable IBM networks using IGRP as the routing protocol: low-speed links individually connected as leaf networks in which IGRP transmits large routing tables. To prevent potential problems, configure the router to transmit IGRP information in a single direction—toward the backbone. The leaf router uses default routing to find the backbone and all other valid routes. The leaf router will transmit IGRP information about its routes to the backbone. The backbone router does not transmit any IGRP information to the leaf. The following examples illustrate configurations for leaf and backbone routers:

```
! Leaf router configuration
router igrp 109
network 131.108.0.0
ip route 0.0.0.0 Serial0
ip route 131.108.0.0 Serial0

! Backbone router configuration
router igrp 109
network 131.108.0.0
passive-interface Serial0
```

Figure 4–30 illustrates what happens when the preceding leaf and backbone router configurations are used. This configuration does not send routing information to the lower-speed leaf routers, while the backbone retains all valid routes in the network.

Figure 4–30

Effects of using the passive-interface router configuration command.

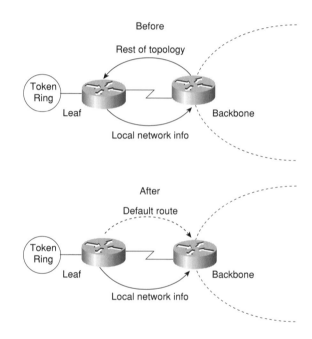

NOTES

When designing large branch networks based on OSPF routing, OSPF has a natural limit. When link instability raises broadcast traffic and route recomputation to an unacceptable level, the network is at its limit. Always contact your router technical support representative when designing large OSPF-based internetworks.

SRB NETWORK DESIGN

The key to building predictable and scalable SRB networks is to follow the network design guidelines in this chapter. Ultimately, there is a limit to the maximum diameter of a single meshed virtual ring, so before you begin designing a network, consider four critical questions. Answering these questions helps you assess the available options.

- *How many routers are required?* This question assesses the capability to build a simple SRB network. If you are implementing a large internetwork, contact your technical support representative for specific information about virtual ring limitations.

- *Are there any T1/T3, E1/E3, fractional T1/T3, or fractional E1/E3 links?* This question assesses SRB WAN traffic that may reduce a meshed topology to a smaller radius. If you are using T1/T3 or E1/E3 technology, you can take advantage of their increased bandwidth capabilities by increasing traffic loads to and from the rings, which allows you to reduce the number of routers.

- *Is the design for an SNA network, a NetBIOS network, or both?* This question helps you determine whether a partially meshed topology can be used when an FEP-connected ring is a peer of each Token Ring in the network. The remote token rings are allowed to be peers only of the FEP rings, not of one another. This topology is called a partially meshed network because certain points can connect only to certain points. Partially meshed SRB networks are much more scalable than fully meshed networks, in which all rings can reach all rings. Fully meshed topologies are often required in NetBIOS environments.

- *Is the network a multiprotocol environment?* This question implicitly raises the topic of *prioritization.* When dealing with a multiprotocol internetwork, you must consider your options for prioritizing traffic to ensure acceptable response time for interactive traffic, while maintaining adequate internetworking resources to handle other types of traffic, such as file transfers.

In general, it is best to design a router network in a hierarchical fashion; there are typically three logical service layers: the backbone (or core) service layer, the distribution service layer, and the access service layer. Figure 4–31 illustrates these basic service layers.

When designing a router network for SRB, consideration should be given to the design of virtual rings. Two key issues affect the design of virtual rings:

- The type of SRB connectivity required (hierarchical, distributed, or flat)
- The corporate organizational structure

The remainder of this section focuses on network design approaches that help create scalable networks. The following topics are discussed:

- Hierarchical Design for SNA Environments
- Hierarchical Design for NetBIOS Environments
- Queuing and Prioritization Schemes

Figure 4–31

Backbone, distribution, and access service layers in an SRB environment.

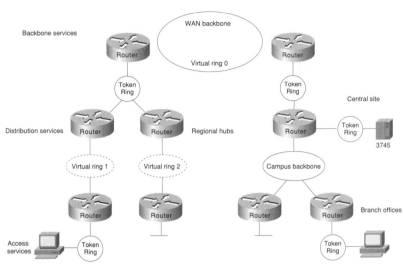

Hierarchical Design for SNA Environments

In SNA-only networks, all processing is hierarchical, where a single FEP or a few FEPs (one primary and one secondary) are the target of all remote rings. The SRB topology is focused from all remote rings to a single or a few redundant rings. A topology featuring a single FEP is illustrated in Figure 4–32.

Figure 4–32

Hierarchical topology featuring a single FEP.

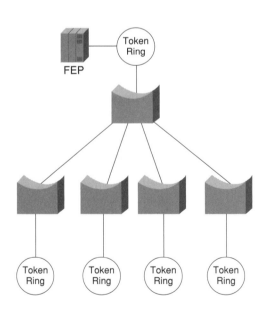

A topology featuring duplicate FEPs on duplicate rings is illustrated in Figure 4–33.

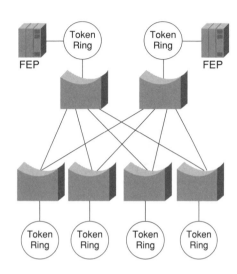

Figure 4–33
Duplicate FEPs on duplicate
rings.

The topology in Figure 4–33 is a partially meshed topology because the remote nodes cannot reach each other; they can reach only the core of the network where the FEPs are located.

When you are designing a partially meshed topology, several options are available. SNA traffic can be generalized as having few explorer packets and having the requirement to connect many remote sites. The suggested topology for a partially meshed topology depends on whether the link speed to the core is greater than 64 Kbps. Contact your technical support representative for specific limitations and capabilities regarding the maximum number of peers for the various encapsulation implementations and your specific network attributes.

To scale a partially meshed network to diameters of greater than 15 to 100 remote rings, you can take two approaches: Build a hierarchical structure of virtual rings, or build a scalable partially meshed structure using a single virtual ring.

Proceed with caution to avoid uncontrolled growth in virtual rings, especially in parallel, because parallel virtual rings replicate explorer packets, which results in unnecessary explorer packet traffic.

Scalable Partially Meshed Rings

With a partially meshed ring topology, the objective is to leverage the advantage of a network that does not require *any-to-any* connectivity. You can use a single virtual ring to connect a series of routers at the FEP sites. For each additional 15 to 100 remote peers, you must add a router to the central site. Figure 4–34 illustrates this kind of environment. Contact your technical support representative for more information about specific limitations and recommendations that might apply to your network specifications.

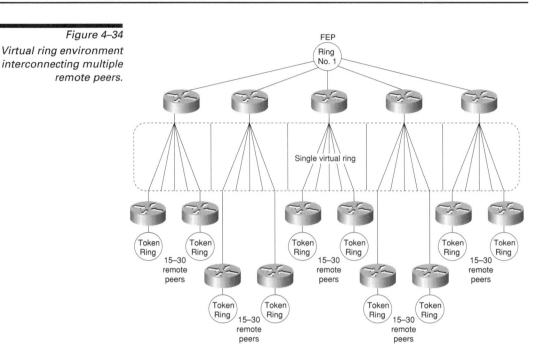

Figure 4–34

Virtual ring environment interconnecting multiple remote peers.

The network illustrated in Figure 4–34 will work for local acknowledgment because all traffic exists on a single virtual ring. A potential problem with this topology is that the number of routers is related to the number of virtual rings, not to the LAN or WAN connectivity at the FEP site. A site with two WAN links and a Token Ring can require several routers if it is the main FEP site.

Hierarchical Virtual Rings

Using *hierarchical* virtual rings, you can use physical token rings and virtual rings to create a hierarchy of virtual rings. Figure 4–35 illustrates such a hierarchy.

Because the destination of all explorer packets is to the core virtual ring, you can use filters to eliminate explorer packet traffic crossing between local-access virtual rings at the point where rings meet. The filters would also filter out FEP traffic. As an alternative, you can use the same virtual ring number for each virtual ring to filter out FEP traffic that might otherwise traverse the local-access virtual rings.

This design is limited in that the hop count might limit Token Ring SRB connectivity. Because the connectivity from access point to FEP uses four hops, additional local bridges at the access points or at the central site might not be reachable from the entire network.

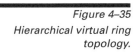

Figure 4–35
Hierarchical virtual ring
topology.

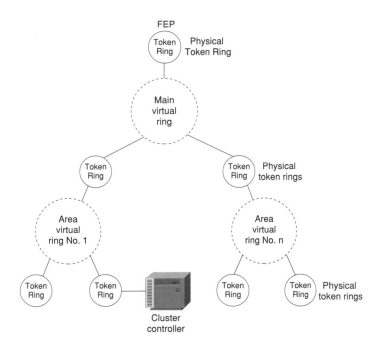

Combined Designs

Networks can be built from hierarchical designs and from scalable partially meshed designs as long as you prevent explorer packet traffic from reexploring access points. To fulfill this requirement, write access lists to prevent explorer packet traffic from entering a ring if that traffic did not originate from the ring that has an FEP.

Hierarchical Design for NetBIOS Environments

The challenge of NetBIOS is that applications might require unrestricted ring-to-ring connectivity. The SRB protocol was not designed to scale, and network designers often demand that routers help scale beyond the original design of the protocol.

Limitations on the maximum number of peers mandates that your only topological option for a NetBIOS SRB network is the hierarchical environment illustrated in Figure 4–35. This design poses certain challenges because of increased explorer packet traffic. It is imperative that you create a single-stream, spanning connection through the network to minimize explorer packets. To succeed, a hierarchical NetBIOS network needs three elements:

- Proxy explorer
- Aggressive explorer packet caching
- NetBIOS name caching

These features allow switching of valid NetBIOS traffic even under the worst conditions of high explorer packet load. You might not be able to use the partially meshed network design if you have to maintain unrestricted ring-to-ring connectivity. Contact your technical support representative to determine any specific limitations for your network topology and design implementation. Refer to the "Explorer Packets and Propagation" and "NetBIOS Broadcast Handling" sections earlier in this chapter for additional details concerning these topics.

Queuing and Prioritization Schemes

The following information focuses on current prioritization mechanisms. Prioritization tools discussed include:

- Priority Queuing
- Custom Queuing
- SAP Prioritization
- Enhanced LU Address Prioritization
- SAP Filters on WAN Links

— **NOTES**

The queuing and prioritization schemes described in this section rely on process switching. If the router is configured for fast switching or for autonomous switching, the configuration of a queuing or prioritization scheme will increase processor utilization. However, increased processor utilization is usually not a problem when the router is sending traffic over low-speed WAN links.

Priority Queuing

Priority queuing (introduced in Software Release 9.1) allows packets to be prioritized. When priority queuing is enabled on an interface, the router maintains up to four output queues for that interface. During congestion, the packets are placed in one of the four queues according to their priority. The router services all packets on the highest priority queue before moving on to the next highest priority queue. In other words, the queuing delay of a packet on a lower priority queue is nondeterministic: An RSRB session set to normal priority might time out if, for example, IPX packet traffic is heavy and is configured for the highest priority queue.

This scheme introduces a problem in that packets configured for lower priority queues might not be serviced in a timely manner, or at all, depending on the bandwidth used by packets sent from the higher priority queues. Priority queuing does not provide bandwidth allocation.

Priority queuing can be used when there is sufficient bandwidth to accommodate all packets destined for a particular interface, but where packets from certain protocols such as file transfers cause other protocols such as Telnet sessions to suffer from poor response.

If there is insufficient bandwidth on an output interface to pass data from various sources, priority queuing cannot solve the limited bandwidth condition. If there is not enough bandwidth to pass all of the data destined for an interface, protocols assigned to the lower priority queues suffer packet loss.

Priority queuing introduces processor overhead that might be acceptable for slow interfaces, but might be unacceptable for higher speed interfaces such as Ethernet, Token Ring, or FDDI. If you are currently fast switching packets, be aware that priority queuing requires that these packets be process switched, which would negatively impact performance.

Use the **priority-list** global configuration command to define priority lists and the **priority-group** interface command to assign a list to an interface. Priority queuing can be configured instead of, but not in addition to, custom queuing.

NOTES

Priority queuing does not operate over X.25.

Custom Queuing

Custom queuing (introduced in Software Release 9.21 and enhanced in Cisco IOS Software Release 11.0) allows you to allocate a percentage of bandwidth to a particular kind of traffic when the available bandwidth is unable to accommodate the aggregate traffic queued.

When custom queuing is enabled on an interface, the router maintains 16 output queues (numbered from 0 to 15) for that interface that can be used to modify queuing behavior. The router cycles through queue numbers 1 to 15 in a sequential fashion, delivering packets in the current queue before moving on to the next. Associated with each output queue is a configurable byte count, which specifies how many bytes of data should be delivered from the current queue by the router before the router moves on to the next queue. When a particular queue is being processed, packets are sent until the number of bytes sent exceeds the queue byte count or the queue is empty.

Queue number 0 is a system queue; its queue is emptied before any of the queues numbered 1 to 15 are processed. The router queues high priority packets to this queue, such as interface keepalive packets. Routing protocol packets are not automatically placed in the system queue.

The custom queuing implementation should not impact the performance of existing packet queuing code. The queuing algorithm implementation is time-critical because it affects packet delivery time when custom queuing is in use.

When custom queuing (or priority queuing) is enabled, it should take much longer for the router to switch packets because each packet has to be classified by the processor card.

Use the **queue-list** global configuration command to define custom queue lists and the **custom-queue-list** interface configuration command to assign a custom queue list to an interface. Custom queuing can be configured instead of, but not in addition to, priority queuing.

Figure 4–36 describes the syntax of the **priority-list** and **queue-list** commands.

NOTES

Custom queuing does not operate over X.25.

Figure 4–36
Priority and custom queuing command syntax.

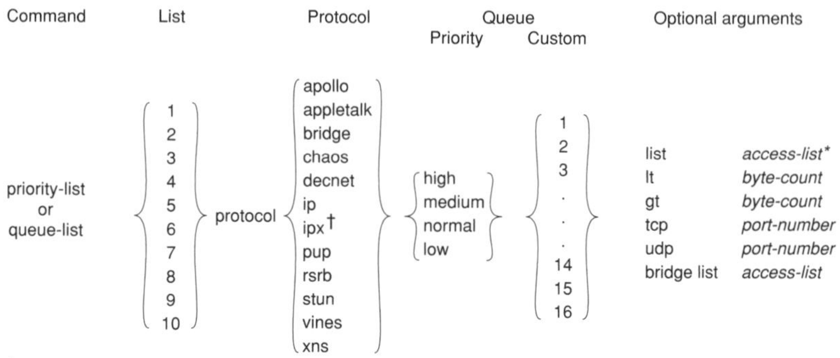

Command	List	Protocol	Queue Priority	Queue Custom	Optional arguments	
priority-list or queue-list	1 2 3 4 5 6 7 8 9 10	protocol	apollo appletalk bridge chaos decnet ip ipx† pup rsrb stun vines xns	high medium normal low	1 2 3 . . . 14 15 16	list lt gt tcp udp bridge list	access-list* byte-count byte-count port-number port-number access-list

† In releases prior to Cisco IOS 10.0, the protocol argument is "novell".

*Applies only to AppleTalk, bridging, IP, IPX, VINES, and XNS.

SAP Prioritization

The purpose of the SAP prioritization feature is to allow you to specify the priority (precedence and bandwidth) of a protocol over another protocol across the RSRB/SDLLC WAN. The prioritization is based on the destination service access point (DSAP) address and source service access point (SSAP) address.

SAP prioritization can be built based on priority queuing or on custom queuing. The actual SAP classification code can be developed regardless of the underlying prioritization mechanism. The priority queuing mechanism addresses only the *precedence* criteria. The custom queuing mechanism provides *precedence* and guarantees *bandwidth*. This section describes SAP prioritization using priority queuing.

To provide a fine granularity in the prioritization of packets, the **sap priority-list** global configuration command (available in Software Release 9.1[9]) allows you to specify any combination of DSAP, SSAP, destination MAC (DMAC) address, and source MAC (SMAC) address.

For example, if you want to prioritize all SNA traffic (SAP 04) over NetBIOS traffic (SAP F0), only the DSAP or SSAP must be configured. In contrast, if you want to give precedence to traffic on a particular LLC2 session, you must specify four parameters: DSAP address, SSAP address, DMAC address, and SMAC address. Use the **sap-priority** *list* interface configuration command (available in Software Release 9.1[9]) to tie the priority list to a particular input interface.

You must also specify the **priority** option in the **source-bridge remote-peer** global configuration command to enable SAP prioritization. In addition, you must configure the **priority-list** global configuration command for the appropriate interfaces and use the **priority-group** interface configuration command on the output interface.

Enhanced LU Address Prioritization

The enhanced logical unit (LU) address-prioritization feature allows you to specify the physical unit (PU) on which an LU resides. This is important because multiple PUs on a Token Ring or on a multidropped SDLC line might have LUs with the same LU address. For example, Figure 4–37 illustrates a situation in which LU02 on 3174-2 is a 3287 printer, and LU02 on 3174-1 is a 3278 terminal. It is undesirable to assign the same priority to the printer and the terminal.

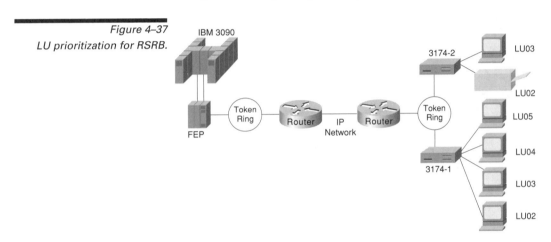

Figure 4–37
LU prioritization for RSRB.

As of Software Release 9.1(9), the LU address prioritization for both RSRB and serial tunneling (STUN) allow you to prioritize the following addresses in addition to the LU address:

- In the RSRB case, you can specify the MAC and SAP address, which together uniquely identify a PU.

- In the STUN case, you can specify the SDLC address to identify a PU on a multidropped SDLC line.

SAP Filters on WAN Links

SAP filters, which are currently available for serial, Token Ring, and Ethernet interfaces, can be used to prevent local NetBIOS and other broadcasts from traversing the RSRB/SDLLC WAN. To implement SAP filter logic on the RSRB/SDLLC WAN interface, it is desirable to place the code at the RSRB level independent from the encapsulation type on the interface. The same filter code should work for direct HDLC encapsulation, TCP/IP encapsulation, and FST encapsulation. In addition to filtering by SAP address, SAP filters can also be used to filter packets by NetBIOS name.

The commands, which are available in Software Release 9.1.(9), are the same as those used for SRB on the Token Ring interface:

- The **access-list** *list* global configuration command builds the access list.

- The **rsrb remote-peer** *ring-group* interface configuration command filters by Local Service Access Point (LSAP) address or by NetBIOS station name on the RSRB WAN interface.

- The **netbios access-list** *host* global configuration command builds a NetBIOS access filter by host name.

SRB Design Checklist

Before implementing a source-route bridging (SRB) network, be sure to familiarize yourself with the technical reference material in the *Router Products Configuration Guide* and the *Router Products Command Reference* publications that deals with SRB internetworking.

Next, read the "Multiport Bridging" through "WAN Framing" sections earlier in this chapter. Depending on your implementation, you should review the "IP Routing Protocol Selection for SRB Networks" and "SRB Network Design" sections earlier in this chapter. If you require more than eight routers, continue as follows:

Step 1   Evaluate the following requirements:

- Determine which protocols are to be used. Relevant options are hierarchical Systems Network Architecture (SNA) and NetBIOS. If you are running hierarchical SNA, determine the link speeds to the core front end processor (FEP) sites.

- Determine whether parallel paths exist in the network either between individual routers or in the general network. If they do, refer to the "WAN Parallelism" section earlier in this chapter.

- Determine whether the network requires greater than 2-kilobyte frames to be sent across WAN links. If so, refer to the "WAN Frame Sizes" section earlier in this chapter.

Step 2   If the access ring and the FEP-connected sites exceed 15 token rings, you must address the following issues:

- Determine whether local acknowledgment is a requirement. Refer to the "Local Acknowledgment Recommendations" section earlier in this chapter.

- Select an encapsulation method. Refer to the "WAN Framing" section.

- Design a network topology incorporating the rules outlined in the "SRB Network Design" section.

- Select a routing protocol described in the "WAN Parallelism" and "IP Routing Protocol Selection for SRB Networks" sections.

Step 3   If performance is important for your internetwork, review the "IP Routing Protocol Selection for SRB Networks" section.

Step 4   Prepare each router's configuration for the following:

- SRB (Refer to the "Explorer Packets and Propagation" and "WAN Framing" sections.)

- IP route tuning (Refer to the "IP Routing Protocol Selection for SRB Networks" section.)

Step 5   Turn on proxy explorer as needed. Refer to the "Explorer Packets and Propagation" section.

Step 6   If the network requires NetBIOS, proceed as follows:

- Turn on NetBIOS name caching.

- Limit the explorer packet processing queue to 20 entries. Refer to the "Explorer Packets and Propagation" section.

Step 7   If you expect to exceed 250 Token Rings, contact your technical support representative for additional information.

SUMMARY

This chapter discussed source-route bridging (SRB) and remote source-route bridging (RSRB). It addressed the challenges of this environment and helped network designers successfully implement SRB within a large, multiprotocol topology, including covering the following areas:

- SRB technology and implementation overview

- Internet Protocol (IP) routing protocol selection and implementation

- SRB network design recommendations and guidelines

CHAPTER 5

Designing SDLC, SDLLC, and QLLC Internetworks

This chapter addresses some of the special requirements for implementing routing technology within IBM System Network Architecture (SNA) environments. Internetworking within an SNA environment often involves making special accommodations for devices that were not originally designed for connection to meshed internetworks.

This chapter describes three techniques designed to enable internetworking capabilities for SNA-based network architectures:

- SDLC via STUN
- SDLLC Implementation
- QLLC Conversion

The sections that describe serial tunneling (STUN), Synchronous Data Link Control (SDLC) over the Logical Link Control, type 2 (LLC) protocol (SDLLC), and Qualified Logical Link Control (QLLC) focus on the following topics:

- Technology overview and issues
- Router technology options, implementation guidelines, and configuration examples

---

NOTES

For information about IBM serial lines, refer to Appendix B, "IBM Serial Link Implementation Notes."

SDLC VIA STUN

SDLC via serial tunneling (STUN) encapsulates SDLC frames into Internet Protocol (IP) packets and routes the encapsulated packets over IP-supported network media. The SDLC frame is transmitted without modification, and the information within the frame is transparent to the network.

187

All SNA physical unit (PU) types are supported. This section focuses on the SDLC data-link protocol and its various configurations and then explains how to implement STUN.

NOTES

For a case study on how to configure STUN for FEPs, see Chapter 20, "STUN for Front-End Processors."

Figure 5–1 illustrates elements of STUN configuration in an environment that includes front-end processors (FEPs) and cluster controllers.

Figure 5–1

Sample STUN network configuration.

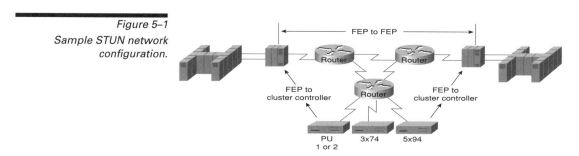

SDLC Data Link

SDLC is the synchronous, bit-oriented protocol used by the SNA data-link control layer. As formally defined by IBM, SDLC is a line discipline for managing synchronous, code-transparent, serially transmitted bit information over a data link. Transmission exchanges can be full duplex or half duplex and can occur over switched or nonswitched links. The configuration of the link connection can be point-to-point, multidrop, or loop.

Common physical link-layer implementations are V.24 (EIA/TIA-232, formerly RS-232), V.35, and X.21. This section describes SDLC as it applies to STUN.

The SDLC data link allows a reliable exchange of information over a communication facility between SNA devices. The protocol synchronizes receivers and transmitters and detects transmission errors. It accomplishes these functions by acknowledging frame receipt and by performing a cyclic redundancy check (CRC) on the data.

Supported Data-Link Configurations

This section provides information related to router-specific hardware implementation. Table 5–1 provides a matrix of SDLC support for V.24.

Table 5–1 *SDLC Support for V.24 (EIA/TIA-232)*

Product Type	NRZ/NRZI	DTE/DCE	Full Duplex	Half Duplex	Maximum MTU
Cisco 7000	Both	Both	Yes	Yes	4 KB
Cisco 7010	Both	Both	Yes	Yes	4 KB
AGS+	Both	Both	Yes	Yes	4 KB
MGS	Both	Both	Yes	Yes	4 KB
Cisco 2500	Both	Both	Yes	Yes	8 KB
Cisco 4000	Both	Both	Yes	4T card only	8 KB
Cisco 4500	Both	Both	Yes	4T card only	8 KB
Cisco 3104	Both	Both	Yes	Dual serial card only	8 KB
Cisco 3204	Both	Both	Yes	Dual serial card only	8 KB

The following notes apply to the entries in Table 5–1:

- For the Cisco 7000, Cisco 4000, Cisco 4500, and Cisco 3000 products, support of data terminal equipment (DTE) or data communications equipment (DCE) functionality depends on which cable is used.

- For the AGS+ and MGS, if you are using a nonreturn to zero inverted (NRZI) applique, the systems support DCE natively. A special cable is required to support DTE mode operation. Prior to the availability of the NRZI applique, customers specifically ordered a DCE or DTE applique.

- Half-duplex support is available for the AGS+ and MGS with Software Release 9.1(7) or later. The NRZI applique, three-port SCI card, and Software Release 9.1(7) or later are all required for half-duplex support.

- Prior to software releases 8.3(6), 9.0(3), or 9.1(2), only 2-KB frame sizes were supported. When increasing maximum transmission unit (MTU) size, consider interface card buffer memory size constraints.

SDLC Frame Format

The SDLC frame format is illustrated in Figure 5–2.

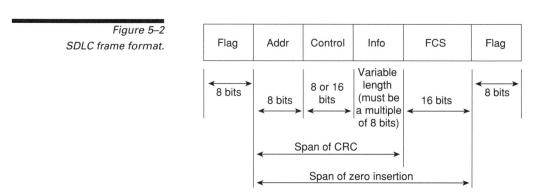

Figure 5–2
SDLC frame format.

The *Flag* field starts and ends the frame and initiates and terminates error checking. When the link is idle, the router sends streaming flags to maintain link synchronization, but this is not necessary to keep the link up.

The *Addr* field contains the SDLC address of the secondary station regardless of whether the frame is coming from the primary or secondary station. The Addr field can contain a specific address, a group address, or a broadcast address. Routers support specific addresses and support broadcast addressing on a limited basis.

The *Control* field is a 1-byte field (for modulo 8 frames) or a 2-byte field (for modulo 128 frames). The extra byte is required for modulo 128 frames to accommodate larger send and receive *frame count fields*. The value of the Control field identifies three different frame formats, as shown in Table 5–2.

Table 5–2 *Components of the Control Field*

Format	Binary Configuration	Hex Equivalent [P/F off]	(P/F on)	Command Name	Acronym
Unnumbered	000 P*/F† 0011	03	13	Unnumbered Info	UI
	000 F 0111	07	17	Request Initialization Mode	RIM
	000 P 0111	07	17	Set Initialization Mode	SIM
	000 F 1111	0F	1F	Disconnect Mode	DM
	010 F 0011	43	53	Request Disconnect	RD
	010 P 0111	43	53	Disconnect	DISC
	011 F 0011	63	73	Unnumbered Ack	UA
	100 P 0011	83	93	Set Normal Response.	SNRM
	110 P 1111	CF	DF	Set Normal Response. Mode Ex.	SNRME
	100 F 0111	87	97	Frame REJECT	FRMR
	101 P/F 1111	AF	BF	Exchange ID	XID
	111 P/F 0011	E3	F3	Test	TEST
Supervisory	RRR‡ P/F 0001	x1**	x1	Receive Ready	RR
	RRR P/F 0101	x5	x5	Receive Not Ready	RNR
	RRR P/F 1101	x9	x9	Reject	REJ
Information	RRR P/F SSS0††	xx	xx	Numbered Info Present	Transfer

* P = Poll bit
† F = Final bit
‡ RRR = Nr (receive count)
** x = Any single digit hexadecimal value
†† SSS = Ns (send count)

The *Info* field is a variable-length field containing a path information unit (PIU) or exchange identification (XID) information. Table 5–3 lists supported PIUs.

Table 5–3 *PIU Support*

PIU Type	Router Support
PIU FID0-bisync and start/stop (non-SNA)	Not supported
PIU FID1-host channel to FEP to remote FEP	Supported via STUN
PIU FID2-FEP to cluster controller (PU 2)	Supported via STUN and SDLLC
PIU FID3-FEP to SNA terminal (PU 1)	Supported via STUN
PIU FID4-FEP to FEP using virtual route	Supported via STUN
PIU FIDF-FEP to FEP (VR SNF overflow sweep)	Supported via STUN
XID 2-Contains PU parameters for PU types 1, 2, 4, and 5	PU types 2 and 4 supported via STUN and SDLLC
XID 3-APPN variable format for PU 2 and PU 2.1	Not supported

The *frame check sequence (FCS)* field is a 2-byte field that, for transmitted data, contains the result of a CRC performed on the first bit after the Flag field through the last bit of the Info field. If the frame format is unnumbered or supervisory, the CRC is performed through the last bit of the Control field. As the remote device receives the data, it performs the same CRC computation and compares the result with the contents of the FCS field. If the comparison fails to find a match, the frame is discarded and recovery procedures take place.

STUN Configuration for SDLC

The following sections provide design and implementation information for a variety of STUN-related configuration topics:

- Local Acknowledgment
- Virtual Multidrop
- SDLC Address Prioritization
- SDLC Two-Way Simultaneous Mode
- LU Address Prioritization
- Flow Control
- Transmission Groups and Class of Service Capabilities
- SNA Host Configuration Considerations for STUN

Local Acknowledgment

Local termination of SDLC sessions allows frames to be locally acknowledged by the receiving router. By locally terminating SDLC sessions, acknowledgment and keepalive traffic is prevented from traversing the backbone, and SNA sessions are preserved if the network fails.

Local acknowledgment locally terminates supervisory frames, which include receiver-ready, receiver-not-ready, and reject frames. Figure 5–3 illustrates the operation of SDLC local acknowledgment.

Figure 5–3
STUN-to-SDLC local acknowledgment.

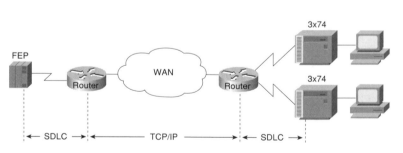

NOTES

Local acknowledgment requires that TCP/IP sessions be maintained between the routers to provide reliable transport.

Virtual Multidrop

Virtual multidrop exploits SDLC address mapping to allow an FEP to communicate with multiple cluster controllers. With a virtual multidrop configuration, the address of each SDLC frame is checked individually. Only addresses that match the configuration are forwarded to the specified destination, which allows an FEP to communicate with multiple 3174s from a single serial link—a multidrop link. You can also use SDLC address mapping as a security feature to restrict access based on SDLC address, as shown in Figure 5–4.

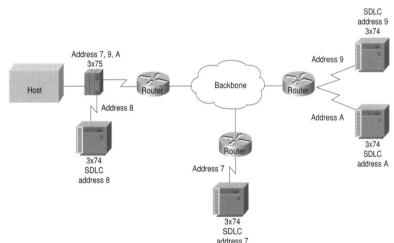

Figure 5–4
SDLCtransport in virtual multidrop environment.

The following steps are required to establish the network configuration illustrated in Figure 5–4:

Step 1   Include a LINE definition in the Network Control Program (NCP) running in the FEP, followed by PU definitions for SDLC address 7, 9, and A. The NCP interprets these definitions as a multidrop link.

Step 2   Use the **stun route address tcp** global configuration command to specify how to forward frames.

Step 3   Determine whether priority queuing is required. If so, local acknowledgment is required.

SDLC Broadcast Across Virtual Multidrop Lines

The SDLC broadcast feature (introduced in Cisco IOS Software Release 10.2) allows SDLC broadcast address 0xFF to be replicated for each of the STUN peers, so that each end station receives the broadcast frame.

In Figure 5–5, the FEP views the end stations as if they were on an SDLC multidrop link. Router A duplicates any broadcast frames sent by the FEP and sends them to any downstream routers (in this example, routers B and C).

Figure 5–5
SDLC broadcast in virtual
multidrop line environment.

The **sdlc virtual-multidrop** interface configuration command enables SDLC broadcast and should be used only on the router that is configured as the secondary station on the SDLC link. In addition, the **stun route address tcp** command for SDLC address 0xFF must be configured on the secondary station (in this example, Router A) for each STUN peer. A sample configuration follows:

```
stun peername xxx.xxx.xxx.xxx
stun protocol-group 1 sdlc
!
interface serial 1
encapsulation stun
stun group 1
stun sdlc-role secondary
sdlc virtual-multidrop
sdlc address 01
sdlc address 02
sdlc address 03
stun route address 01 tcp yyy.yyy.yyy.yyy local-ack
stun route address 02 tcp zzz.zzz.zzz.zzz local-ack
stun route address 03 tcp zzz.zzz.zzz.zzz local-ack
stun route address FF tcp yyy.yyy.yyy.yyy
stun route address FF tcp zzz.zzz.zzz.zzz
```

SDLC Address Prioritization

For STUN prioritization of SDLC addresses over simple serial transport connections, use the **priority-list** or the **queue-list** global configuration command and the **priority-group** interface configuration command or the **custom-queue-list** interface configuration command, respectively, on the interface that connects to the remote router (the output interface).

For STUN prioritization of SDLC addresses over TCP/IP transport connections, you must configure the **priority-list** global configuration command and use the **priority-group** interface configuration command on the interfaces that connect to the end devices (the input interfaces). Also, you must specify the **local-ack** and **priority** keywords of the **stun route address tcp** global configuration command.

SDLC Two-Way Simultaneous Mode

Two-way simultaneous mode (introduced in Cisco IOS Software Release 10.2) allows a router that is configured as a primary SDLC station to utilize a full-duplex serial line more efficiently. When two-way simultaneous mode is enabled in a multidrop environment, the router can poll a secondary station and receive data from that station while it sends data to, or receives data from, a different secondary station on the same serial line. (See Figure 5–6.)

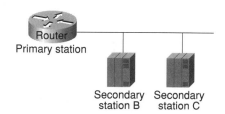

Figure 5–6
Two-way simultaneous mode
in a multidrop environment.

The **sdlc simultaneous** command enables two-way simultaneous mode in a multidrop environment. When two-way simultaneous mode is enabled for a point-to-point connection to a secondary station, the router can send data to the secondary station even if there is an outstanding poll, as long as the window size limit is not reached. The **sdlc simultaneous** command with the **single** keyword enables two-way simultaneous mode in a point-to-point link environment.

LU Address Prioritization

To prioritize logical units, use the **locaddr-priority-list** global configuration command on each router. For example:

```
locaddr-priority-list 1 02 high
locaddr-priority-list 1 03 high
locaddr-priority-list 1 04 low
```

You must also assign a priority list to the STUN priority ports using the **priority-list** global command. For example:

```
priority-list 1 protocol ip high tcp 1994
priority-list 1 protocol ip medium tcp 1990
priority-list 1 protocol ip low tcp 1991
```

The serial interfaces attached to the end systems (input interfaces) must be associated with priority lists using the **locaddr-priority** and **priority-group** interface configuration commands. The **locaddr-priority** command links the interface to a local LU priority list (specified with the **locaddr-priority-list** global configuration command). The **priority-group** command links the interface to a TCP priority list (specified with a **priority-list** global configuration command). For example:

```
interface serial 1
locaddr-priority 1
priority-group 1
```

In addition, you must specify the **local-ack** and **priority** keyword options of the **stun route address tcp** global configuration command.

The LU address prioritization feature has been enhanced to allow you to specify the PU on which an LU resides. This enhancement is important because there might be multiple PUs on a multi-dropped SDLC line that have the same LU address. For example, in Figure 5–7, LU02 on 3174-2 is a 3287 printer, and LU02 on 3174-1 is a 3278 terminal. Do not assign the same priority to the printer and the terminal.

Figure 5–7
LU prioritization for STUN.

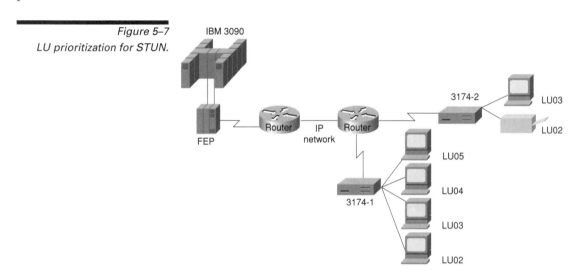

As of Software Release 9.1(9), LU address prioritization for both remote source-route bridging (RSRB) and STUN solved this problem. In addition to the LU address, you can specify the SDLC address to identify a PU in a multidropped SDLC line. The syntax of the **locaddr-priority** global configuration command follows:

> **locaddr-priority** *list lu-address* **sdlc** *secondary*

The keyword **sdlc** indicates the next byte (in hexadecimal), and *secondary* is the secondary SDLC address.

Flow Control

SDLC-level flow control is also offered with local termination. When the router detects that the TCP queue is 90 percent full, it blocks further SDLC frames until the TCP queue recedes to 80 percent full. This is accomplished by transmitting receiver-not-ready frames.

There is also a flow control protocol between STUN peers. When SDLC output queues become congested, a router can request the remotely attached router to exert back-pressure on the SDLC link.

Transmission Groups and Class of Service Capabilities

This section describes the transmission group and class of service (CoS) support that NCP-to-NCP communications provide, including the following topics:

- Typical NCP-to-NCP Communications
- NCP-to-NCP Communications over a Routed Network
- Transmission Group and CoS Support
- Transmission Group and CoS Design Guidelines and Notes

Typical NCP-to-NCP Communications

In a typical NCP-to-NCP communications arrangement, a host is channel-attached to an FEP acting as an NCP. In Figure 5–8, NCP A is the primary SDLC station, and NCP B (remote NCP) is a secondary SDLC station. The NCPs dynamically determine their relationship; the NCP with the higher subarea number becomes the primary SDLC station. NCP V5R4 and later allows you to determine which NCP is the primary and which NCP is the secondary station.

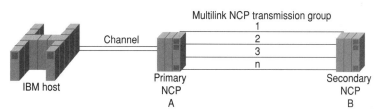

Figure 5–8
Typical NCP-to-NCP multilink transmission group communication configuration.

A *transmission group* is defined as one or more parallel SDLC links connecting adjacent PU Type 4 (NCP) nodes. Transmission groups are used to increase the reliability of the logical link connection between NCPs and to provide additional bandwidth capacity. When one link fails or is congested, data is routed on one of the other links in the group. The transmission group function is implemented at the path control (PC) layer of the NCP architectural model. The PC layer encapsulates request/response units in PIUs and sends them to the data-link control (DLC) layer for transmission.

The PC layer uses the transmission header of the PIU to route messages through the network. SNA defines different transmission header formats and identifies the different formats by Format Identification (FID) type. A transmission header of type FID 4 is used to route data between type 4 nodes that support explicit and virtual routes.

The NCP assigns a sequence order number to each link in a transmission group. In later versions of NCP, you can specify the sequence order in which an NCP should use the transmission group links; otherwise, this order is determined by the order of link activation. Deactivation and reactivation of a link cause it to become the last activated link in the transmission group, and PIU traffic will be sent on the last activated link only if all other links fail or are busy.

Traditionally, the PC layer communicates directly with the DLC layer to transmit PIUs. When sending PIUs over a multilink transmission group, a transmission group layer exists between the PC and DLC layers. The transmission group layer contains a transmit queue. When the transmission group layer gets a frame to send, it checks for the availability of a link in the transmission group in priority (activation default) order. If the transmission group layer finds an available link (that is, a link that is not down and is not busy), it assigns the PIU the next NCP sequence number and sends the frame on that link. NCP sequence numbers range from 0 to 4,095 and wrap on overflow.

When all links in the transmission group are busy, PIUs are placed in the transmission group transmit queue to await transmission. PIUs accumulate in the queue until a link becomes available. When an SDLC link becomes available, a CoS algorithm is performed on the PIUs in the transmit queue. The PIU with the highest priority is dequeued, assigned the next NCP sequence number, and sent on the available link. Sequence numbering must occur when PIUs are removed from the transmit queue because PIUs can overtake each other on the transmit queue when CoS priority processing is performed. PIUs are never preempted by other PIUs on the same SDLC link queue.

There are several reasons why PIUs might arrive at the receiving NCP out of transmission group sequence: links that operate at different speeds, PIUs on different links that have different lengths, and SDLC link transmission errors that cause retransmission. Because PIUs can arrive out of order, the receiving FEP performs resequencing by queuing incoming PIUs if their sequence number is larger than the next expected sequence number. The algorithm is not important, but the rule is that the receiving FEP propagates PIUs by sequence number order. PIUs with a lower sequence number than expected are considered duplicates and are discarded.

Later versions of NCP deviate from the SDLC standard in their use of SDLC echo addressing. The SDLC secondary NCP sets the high-order bit of the SDLC address when sending a response. For example, the primary NCP sends frames with address 01, and the secondary NCP sends frames with address 81. This addressing scheme limits the range of SDLC addresses from 01 to 7F. Additionally, SDLC address FF is used on frames preceding and during the NCP's XID exchange. The XID and DM frames use the broadcast address.

Another deviation from the SDLC standard occurs in NCP-to-NCP communication when a host NCP loads a remote NCP. Normally, numbered information frames can be sent only after an SNRM (or SNRME), which resets the station counts to ensure that the two stations start with consistent counts. When a host NCP loads a remote NCP, the host sends a Set Initialization Mode (SIM), and the remote NCP responds with a Request Initialization Mode (RIM), which allows numbered information frames to flow. NCPs are allowed to violate the SDLC standard because these violations (echo addressing, broadcast addressing, and sending numbered information frames before SNMRE) occur only when an NCP communicates with another NCP.

NCP-to-NCP Communications over a Routed Network

There are several reasons for routers to carry NCP-to-NCP traffic. Routers allow other protocols to share high-cost bandwidth (such as leased lines) that is set aside for SNA traffic. In the traditional NCP-to-NCP communications, a leased line is required for each line in a transmission group. However, routers enable a number of leased lines to be collapsed into one leased line. In addition, routing capabilities enable routers to dynamically determine wide-area network paths, which can result in a more reliable network.

Figure 5–9 illustrates NCP-to-NCP communications in a router-based internetwork.

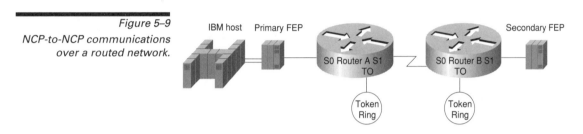

Figure 5–9
NCP-to-NCP communications over a routed network.

Changing from STUN pass-through to STUN local acknowledgment has the following benefits:

- Keeps SDLC poll (RR) traffic off of an overutilized WAN
- Prevents NCP timers from expiring due to network delay
- Collapses multiple WAN leased lines into one leased line
- Reduces store-and-forward delays through the router network

Consider the situation illustrated in Figure 5–9. Notice that the router attached to the SDLC primary NCP (Router A) acts as an SDLC secondary station, and vice versa for the other router (Router B). For this discussion, assume that all serial links between NCPs and routers are in the same transmission group. This means that the NCP considers the lines to be in transmission group X, and the router considers the lines to be in transmission group Y. There is no relationship between X and Y. X is used in the NCP system generation, and Y is used in the router configuration.

Transmission Group and CoS Support

The following features facilitate the support of transmission groups and CoS in Cisco routers:

- SDLC address violation allowances

   Two specific instances are exempt from SDLC addressing restrictions:

   ○ Echo addressing
   ○ Broadcast addressing
- Remote NCP load sequence

   During the load sequence, the remote NCP performs minimal SDLC functions. It cannot go into Normal Response Mode (NRM) until it is loaded. The load sequence for a remote

NCP starts with a SIM/RIM exchange between NCPs, which initializes each NCP's SDLC frame count to zero. After the SIM/RIM exchange, the NCPs pass numbered information frames; this event normally does not occur until after a SNRM/UA sequence. The router's SDLC transmission group local-acknowledgment support allows loading of remote NCPs when the routers pass through all frames after a SIM/RIM sequence and before a SNRM/UA sequence. After the SNRM/UA exchange, normal local acknowledgment occurs.

- Rerouting in multilink transmission groups

  When a router acknowledges an Information frame, it must ensure delivery of that frame to the receiving NCP. If, after the frame is locally acknowledged, the corresponding link in the receiving transmission group is lost, the receiving router reroutes the frame onto another SDLC link in the same transmission group.

- CoS

  The sending NCP performs CoS. Each PIU is assigned a sequence number. The best service the routers can perform is to try to preserve the CoS as assigned by the sending NCP via sequence numbers. Therefore, all SNA data PIUs are treated equally with the goal to preserve PIU order. However, virtual route-pacing responses flow at SNA network priority level and do not have sequence numbers (that is, they have a sequence number of 0). The router prioritizes all SNA network priority PIUs higher than SNA data to achieve more efficient virtual route pacing.

NOTES

The router cannot use the PIU to determine whether traffic is interactive or batch. Even if the router could make this determination, prioritizing one type of traffic over another would cause the receiving NCP to waste CPU time resequencing the PIUs. This would also degrade throughput because the receiving NCP would hold PIUs longer when resequencing.

- Flow control tuning for better CoS operation

  The **tcp-queue-max** keyword of the **stun route address tcp** global configuration command allows you to tune the size of the outbound TCP queue so that when the WAN becomes congested, frames generated by an NCP can be stored in the router as well as in the NCP. When the size of the outbound TCP queue is small, back-pressure via SDLC RNRs is applied to sending NCPs sooner, causing the NCP to hold more frames. The more frames that are held by the NCP, the more frames to which the NCP's CoS algorithm is applied. The size of the outbound TCP queue should be configured to 70 or above.

Transmission Group and CoS Design Guidelines and Notes

The following guidelines should be considered when implementing transmission groups and CS:

1. Bandwidth of the WAN should be greater than, or equal to, the aggregate bandwidth of all the serial lines. If other protocols are also using the WAN, bandwidth of the WAN should be greater than the aggregate bandwidth of all the serial lines.

2. If the network delay associated with one line of an NCP transmission group is different from the network delay associated with another line in the same NCP transmission group, the receiving NCP spends additional time resequencing PIUs. This happens when one or more of the NCP transmission group lines is routed and one or more lines is directly connected between NCPs.

3. The Software Release 9.1 prioritizing algorithm ensures that only the highest priority traffic is guaranteed to get through. Software Release 9.21 prioritization is enhanced by the addition of *custom queuing*. Custom queuing can be used to guarantee specific bandwidth allocated to protocols with respect to bandwidth allocated to other protocols.

   If you are using Software Release 9.1 and an SNA WAN as a multiprotocol backbone, give SNA traffic the highest priority and assign the next highest priority to other mission-critical protocols. In addition, make sure that your WAN bandwidth is significantly greater than your aggregate SNA serial line bandwidth so that your SNA traffic does not monopolize the WAN.

   Table 5–4 lists equivalent commands for configuring priority queuing and custom queuing.

Table 5–4 *Comparison of Priority Queuing and Custom Queuing Configuration Commands*

Priority Queuing	Custom Queuing
priority-list 4 protocol ip high tcp 1994	queue-list 2 protocol ip 1 tcp 1994
priority-list 4 protocol ip medium tcp 1992	queue-list 2 protocol ip 2 tcp 1992
priority-list 4 protocol ip normal tcp 1991	queue-list 2 protocol ip 3 tcp 1991
priority-list 4 protocol ip low tcp 1990	queue-list 2 protocol ip 4 tcp 1990

4. When NCPs are directly connected, their poll-and-pause timers should be configured for maximum throughput using the NCP PAUSE statement. Configuration of this parameter depends on whether the NCP is acting as a primary or secondary SDLC station. Table 5–5 outlines the defaults and recommendations as specified in the IBM publication *Tuning and Problem Analysis for NCP SDLC Devices*.

   Adding routers with local acknowledgment creates two SDLC sessions instead of one. The result is that the two SDLC sessions do not preserve the original characteristics of the original NCP-to-NCP SDLC session. To adapt a secondary NCP to the router environment, change its system generation PAUSE statement to a value between 0.0 and 0.1 seconds, inclusive.

Table 5–5   *NCP PAUSE Parameter Guidelines*

Pause Statement Parameter	IBM Guideline
NCP primary PAUSE	Specifies the time the NCP will wait between sending polls if it has no data to send. (Default is 0.2 seconds; 0 is recommended.)
NCP secondary PAUSE	Specifies the time that the secondary NCP will wait before returning a frame with the final bit set. (Default is 0.2 seconds; recommended to be high –0.2 to 1.0 seconds.)

SNA Host Configuration Considerations for STUN

When designing STUN-based internetworks featuring routers and IBM SNA entities, you must carefully consider the configuration of SNA nodes and routing nodes. Appendix D, "SNA Host Configuration for SDLC Networks," provides examples of SNA host configurations that focus on two specific SNA devices:

- FEP configuration for SDLC links
- 3174 SDLC configuration example

STUN Implementation Checklist

Before implementing a serial tunneling (STUN) internetwork, make sure you are familiar with Synchronous Data Link control (SDLC). Depending on your implementation, you may need to review the "SDLC via STUN" section at the beginning of this chapter.

Use the following steps as a checklist when implementing SDLC STUN in your internetwork:

Step 1   Evaluate your current environment by answering the following questions:

- What host-attached cluster controllers or front end processors (FEPs) are being used (such as 37x5, 3172, and 3174)? The host site might be referred to as a local, core, or backbone site, or as a data center.
- Through what media is the network connected to the host site?
  - STUN: Serial connection at both ends.

○ SDLLC: Token Ring at primary station and SDLC at secondary station, or Ethernet at primary stations and SDLC at secondary station.

○ Reverse SDLLC: SDLC at primary station and Token Ring or Ethernet at secondary station.

- What are the link speeds for local and remote end systems?

- What are the current SDLC line utilization measurements of those links that will attach to the router? This information will be helpful in determining the site requirements.

- What interface types are to be used (for example, V.24 [EIA/TIA-232, formerly RS-232], V.35, X.21)?

- What modems, data service units (DSUs), channel service units (CSUs), or modem-sharing or line-sharing devices are to be used?

- What remote end system types are involved (for example: 3174, 3274, or AS/400)?

- What kind of emulation requirements are involved (for example: half or full duplex, NRZ or NRZI)?

- What are the current transaction response times? Consider peak load periods and characterize traffic patterns.

- How many PUs are in place? How many are planned? This information is important for router utilization sizing.

- How many LUs are in place? How many are planned? Many busy LUs attached to a PU will increase link utilization.

Step 2   Determine current host configurations. Important information includes the following:

- If the FEP is a 3745, 3725, or 3720, the Network Control Program (NCP) definition listing, especially the GROUP, LINE, PU, and LU definition statements.

- Remote controller configuration worksheets for 3x74, 5x94.

- OS/2 Communication Manager configuration files.

- Network topology diagram.

Step 3   Determine what router-based IBM features will best suit your requirements:

- If remote devices are SDLC-attached PU type 2 devices, consider using SDLLC. See the following section, "SDLLC Implementation."

- Depending on the specific situation, STUN can be used in many instances and supports all PU types.

Step 4   Determine what FEP-to-NCP conversion changes are required:

- Are FEP lines multidrop? Is virtual multidrop required? Refer to the "Virtual Multidrop" section earlier in this chapter.

- Do PU addresses require changing if SDLC address prioritization is used? Refer to the "SDLC Address Prioritization" section earlier in this chapter.

- Does the reply timeout T1 timer need to be increased to accommodate network delays if local acknowledgment is not used?

- Does the "Retries" parameter need to be adjusted for longer elapsed retry sequences?

Step 5   Determine how end-station controllers are configured and, if possible, configure the router to accommodate them:

- Addresses might need to be changed if you use virtual multidrop. Refer to the "Virtual Multidrop" section earlier in this chapter.

- NRZ support might be required depending on router platform and interface used. Refer to the "Supported Data-Link Configurations" section earlier in this chapter.

- If the controller toggles RTS (assumes half-duplex mode), refer to the "Supported Data-Link Configurations" section earlier in this chapter.

SDLLC IMPLEMENTATION

The SDLLC function allows serial-attached devices using the SDLC protocol to communicate with LAN-attached devices using the LLC2 protocol. The basic purpose of the SDLLC function is to consolidate the traditionally disparate SNA/SDLC networks onto a LAN-based, multiprotocol, multimedia backbone network.

Routers use the SDLLC feature to terminate SDLC sessions, to translate SDLC to the LLC2 protocol, and to forward the LLC2 traffic through remote source-route bridging (RSRB) over a point-to-point or IP network. Because a router-based IP network can use any arbitrary media, such as FDDI, Frame Relay, X.25, or leased lines, routers support SDLLC over all such media through IP encapsulation. Figure 5–10 illustrates a general SDLLC media translation internetwork arrangement.

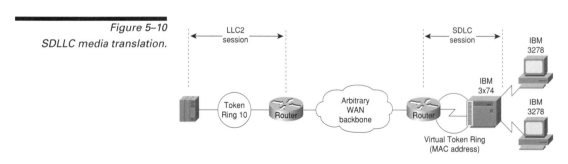

Figure 5–10
SDLLC media translation.

NOTES

In Figure 5–10, the Token Ring connection (Token Ring 10) could also be an Ethernet segment that connects the FEP or 3172 and router.

SDLLC Configuration

The following sections provide design and implementation information for the following SDLLC-related configuration topics:

- Local Acknowledgment
- Multidrop Access
- Router Configuration
- Encapsulation Overhead

Local Acknowledgment

Local acknowledgment of LLC2 sessions allows frames to be locally terminated by the Token Ring-attached router, which guarantees delivery to the ultimate destination through the reliable transport services of TCP/IP. Locally terminating LLC2 sessions enables packet reception to be locally acknowledged, prevents acknowledgment and keepalive traffic from traversing the backbone, and preserves SNA sessions if the network fails. The router that is performing the media translation always acknowledges the SDLC session in an SDLLC environment.

Local acknowledgment locally terminates supervisory frames, which include receiver-ready, receiver-not-ready, and reject frames. Figure 5–11 illustrates the operation of local acknowledgment.

Figure 5–11
Local acknowledgment operation.

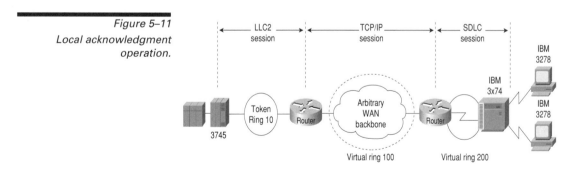

NOTES

Local acknowledgment requires that TCP sessions be maintained between the routers. It is not uncommon to see high router CPU utilization at idle traffic times and then decreased utilization as traffic increases. Polling overhead in the router may increase processor use.

Multidrop Access

There are two ways to configure multidrop operation for the SDLC link in an SDLLC environment. The first way is to use a line-sharing device or a modem-sharing device (MSD) to connect multiple controllers at a single site to a single SDLC port on the router. The second way is to connect multiple controllers at different sites through a multidrop service provided by a telephone company. For more information about multidrop connections, refer to Appendix B, "IBM Serial Link Implementation Notes."

Consider line speed, link utilization, and the number of controllers that will share a single line when designing a multidrop environment. In addition, consider the number of attached LUs associated with individual PUs, and determine if these LUs are being heavily used. If so, increase the bandwidth of the attached serial line. When implementing multidrop environments featuring large numbers of PUs and LUs, contact your technical support representative for specific capabilities.

Router Configuration

To configure a router for SDLLC, you need certain virtual telecommunications access method (VTAM) and NCP definition statements. Figure 5–12 illustrates the required configuration information.

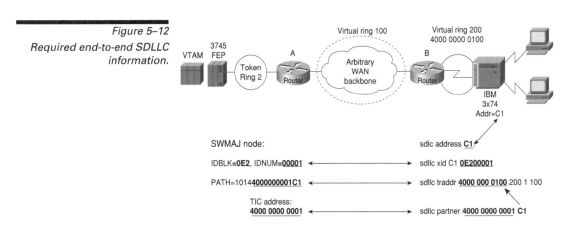

Figure 5–12

Required end-to-end SDLLC information.

Consider an example of two routers that implement the SDLLC functionality in an environment that interconnects a remote site to a host channel attached to a 3174 Token Ring gateway, as shown in Figure 5–13.

NOTES

Routers also support SDLLC implementations in environments with a 3745 Token Ring gateway.

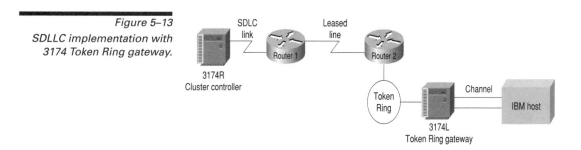

Figure 5–13
SDLLC implementation with 3174 Token Ring gateway.

The following conditions apply to the sample network illustrated in Figure 5–13:

- The SDLC address of the 3174R is C1.

- The device called 3174L is a 3174 Token Ring that is channel attached to an IBM mainframe.

The 3174R must be defined in the configuration of the 3174L using the virtual Token Ring MAC address. This address is created in the router configuration; it includes the SDLC address as the last byte. This virtual MAC address is mapped to a host subchannel address. One host subchannel address is assigned for each downstream physical unit at host system generation time. PU and LU functions are defined to VTAM within the switched major node function. The following configuration commands are required on Router 1:

- The **sdllc traddr** interface configuration command with a virtual ring address for the 3174R. Note that the last byte must be 00 and that you must specify the appropriate SDLC address (in this case, C1) for the same last byte during the 3174L customization.

- The **sdllc partner** interface configuration command with the MAC address of the 3174L gateway and the SDLC address of the 3174R.

- The following version of the **sdllc xid** interface configuration command:

```
sdllc xid c1 00000000
```

The **sdllc xid** interface configuration command is specified with all zeros in the IDBLK/IDNUM field to establish the LLC session between Router 1 and the 3174L. All zeros in the node ID field of the XID command indicate that there is no unique node identifier in this field.

Encapsulation Overhead

Cisco routers provide several types of encapsulation solutions. Because encapsulation always incurs a certain amount of overhead, you need to assess the advantages and performance trade-offs of each encapsulation solution within the constraints of your environment.

TCP/IP encapsulation is recommended most frequently because it is very robust, provides a high quality of service, and is media independent. If SDLLC local acknowledgment is required, TCP/IP encapsulation is required. If SDLLC local acknowledgment is not required, Fast-Sequenced Transport (FST) encapsulation is highly recommended because it is less CPU intensive.

Direct High-Level Data Link Control (HDLC) encapsulation can be used only in point-to-point environments. FST and direct HDLC encapsulation are comparable in performance, but FST has more overhead, which may be an issue on low-speed serial links. TCP/IP encapsulation has the most overhead in terms of processor utilization and the WAN connection. If TCP/IP encapsulation with header compression is a requirement, use it only on link speeds of 64 Kbps or less.

Table 5–6 outlines encapsulation overhead for SDLLC and RSRB implementations.

Table 5–6 *SDLLC and RSRB Encapsulation Overhead*

TCP/IP	FST	TCP/IP with Header Compression	HDLC
CPU intensive	Less CPU intensive	Very CPU intensive	Least CPU intensive
4 bytes for HDLC	4 bytes for HDLC	4 bytes for HDLC	4 bytes for HDLC
20 bytes for IP	20 bytes for IP	3–8 bytes for TCP/IP	16 bytes for virtual ring
20–24 bytes for TCP	16 bytes for virtual ring	16 bytes for virtual ring	
16 bytes for virtual ring			
Total: 60–64 bytes	Total: 40 bytes	Total: 23–28 bytes	Total: 20 bytes

SDLLC Guidelines and Recommendations

The following suggestions can help improve resource response time and network performance:

- *Token Ring frame size*—Allow the Token Ring Interface Coupler (TIC) FEP to send the largest possible frame, and let the router segment the frame into multiple SDLC Information frames.

- *MAXOUT (window size)*—Change the MAXOUT value in the VTAM-switched major node for the 3174 PU. MAXOUT is IBM's terminology for *window size*. IBM recommends setting window sizes on LAN-attached devices to 1 because their tests found no performance benefit with a larger window size. The *red books*, which are published by the IBM International Systems Center, show examples with MAXOUT=1. Because the remote device is an SDLC-attached 3x74, not a Token Ring-attached device, changing MAXOUT to 7 can improve performance dramatically.

- *SDLC line speed*—Increase the line speed of the 3x74 to 19.2 Kbps (older units) or 64 Kbps (newer units) when the controller is directly attached (as opposed to being attached through a modem) to the router. Modem and communication facilities are frequently the limiting factors in determining the line speed in the prerouter configuration.

- *SDLC frame size*—Set the largest SDLC frame size to 521 on newer 3274 models (not 265, which is required for older 3274 models). *See the note that follows.*

- *Request To Send (RTS) control*—Set the 3174 for permanent RTS if the device is not connected via a multidrop service through modem-sharing devices or line-sharing devices. Modem-sharing and line-sharing connections require that RTS be toggled when the device is transmitting. Setting permanent RTS cuts down online turnaround delays and can improve link utilization by 10 percent. (However, setting permanent RTS is unlikely to achieve any perceptible response time improvements.)

NOTES

Changing configurations of end devices, such as terminal controllers, is not recommended. The high number of devices requiring changes and the cost and unavailability associated with these changes can make these modifications onerous. Modify SDLC maximum frame size and RTS control with discretion.

SDLLC Implementation Scenarios

The following case study shows how an internetwork can evolve from a SNA-specific SDLC environment featuring 3x74 controllers and 3270 terminals to a network of PCs with client-server applications. The most important requirement for this evolution is the protection of existing SNA investment.

Assume that the original network consisted of hundreds of SDLC 3x74 controllers connected to a number of 37x5 FEPs in the data center. A disaster recovery center maintains the "mirror-image" of the data center. Many 3x74s are multidrop-connected to the host via 9.6- or 19.2-Kbps leased lines. The challenges facing the corporate MIS organization for this internetwork include the following:

- *Reliability*—When an SDLC line goes down, all the downstream users are affected. There is no network redundancy.

- *Leased line charges*—Providing lines to multiple remote SDLC devices results in excessive service charges and must be minimized.

- *FEP CPU use*—CPU use is higher for SDLC-supported sessions than for LAN-supported sessions.

- *Maintaining VTAM and NCP*—Every move and change requires system programmers to regenerate VTAM/NCP, which increases the cost of maintaining a statistically defined network.

- *Supporting LAN-based applications*—There is a growing need to support LAN-based interconnection, both PC-to-host and PC-to-PC.

- *Availability and up time*—To maintain a competitive advantage, the organization needs to keep SNA sessions alive even if the network fails.

A phased strategy aimed at addressing these challenges would consist of three phases. Each of these phases is discussed in the following implementation examples.

Phase 1: Redundant Backbone Using STUN and Virtual Multidrop

Build a redundant backbone network with routers and high-speed E1 or T1 links in each regional office, as shown in Figure 5–14. Connect multiple SDLC devices to a router via SDLC transport with virtual multidrop. The resulting network increases reliability and minimizes leased-line charges.

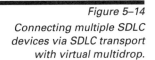

Figure 5–14
Connecting multiple SDLC devices via SDLC transport with virtual multidrop.

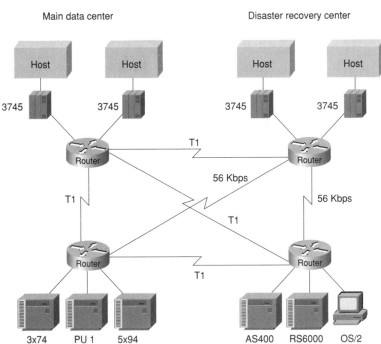

Phase 2: Fault-Tolerant Host FEP Token Ring and SDLLC Implementation

Implement a fault-tolerant host FEP Token Ring, as shown in Figure 5–15. Connecting existing SDLC devices to the host Token Ring via SDLLC improves response time. Because SDLC devices appear as Token Ring-attached devices to the host, you do not need to regenerate NCP and reload when you are adding or changing PUs and LUs. This can be done dynamically through VTAM-switched major nodes. This implementation also reduces FEP CPU utilization.

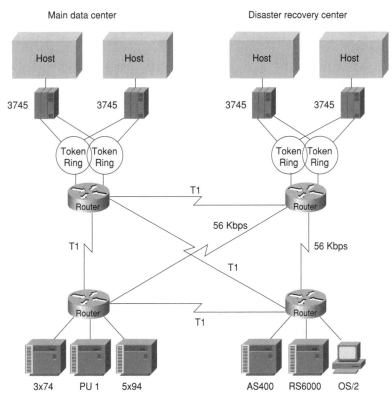

Figure 5–15
Fault-tolerant TICs and SDLLC
implementation.

Phase 3: Strategic LAN-to-WAN Implementation

Implement LAN (both Token Ring and Ethernet) internetworks in selected locations along with alternative WAN technologies, such as Frame Relay, as shown in Figure 5–16. Connect LAN-based and remote SDLC devices to host FEP Token Ring via SDLLC, RSRB, and translational bridging, and to host FEP SDLC via reverse SDLLC (SDLC side primary). SNA session integrity is maintained through local termination of both LLC2 and SDLC traffic. These solutions provide needed support of LAN-based applications and improve availability and up time for SNA network devices.

SDLLC Implementation Checklist

Before implementing an SDLLC-based internetwork, make sure you are familiar with the information that deals with SDLC. Depending on your implementation, you might need to review the "SDLLC Configuration" and "SDLLC Implementation Scenarios" sections earlier in this chapter. In general, the following guidelines help you create a working, manageable network:

- Use a phased approach to implement your router network.

- Establish a test environment to initially bring up the routers.

- Plan a gradual cutover of end devices into the production environment.

- During the cutover period, observe the router's behavior by using **show** commands.

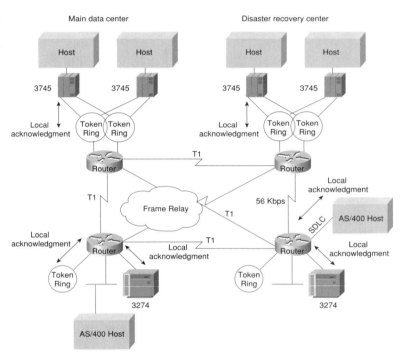

Figure 5–16

Implementing alternative LAN-to-WAN technologies for an integrated solution.

Strive to create a network that has predictable behavior early in the development cycle. This strategy can prevent problems as more devices are brought online. The following is a specific SDLLC implementation checklist that you can use to identify technologies, implementations, and possible solutions for your internetwork:

Step 1   Evaluate the customer requirements for SDLLC support:

- Identify all host-attached controllers. Examples include 37x5, 3172, and 3174 devices. The host sites might be referred to as local, core, backbone, or data center sites.

- How are the host site controllers connected to the network?

- Is Token Ring already in place? Ethernet?

- What are the link speeds for remote end systems?

- What are the current line utilization measurements? Network Performance Monitor, which makes historical data available, is typically installed in the larger SNA shops.

- What interface type is required (for example: V.24 (EIA/TIA-232, formerly RS-232), V.35, or X.21)?

- What modems, data service units, channel service units, modem-sharing devices or line-sharing devices will be used?

- Is Link Problem Determination Aid (LPDA) support required? LPDA is a feature of IBM modems and data service units that reports line quality and statistics to NetView. LPDA Version 1 is not compatible with STUN and SDLLC; LAPD Version 2 may be compatible with STUN.

- What remote end-system types are expected? Examples include 3174, 3274, and AS/400.

- Will there be end-system emulation?

- What is the current transaction response time? Is subsecond response required?

- How many PUs are there? (This information will be important for router utilization sizing.)

- How many LUs are there? (Many busy LUs attached to a PU increases link utilization.)

Step 2   Determine current configuration. Important information includes the following:

- NCP system generation for 3745, 3725, and 3720 devices; in particular, note the LINE, PU, and LU definition statements.

- Local controller current worksheets for 3174 and 3172 devices.

- Remote controller configuration worksheets for 3x74 and 5x94 devices.

- OS/2 Communication Manager configuration files.

- Network topology diagram.

Step 3   Determine the SDLLC features that best suit your requirements.

Confirm that devices to be attached are SDLC PU type 2 devices. Select specific feature requirements, such as local acknowledgment and virtual multidrop.

Step 4   Determine what host conversion changes are required:

- Switched major node definitions for VTAM.

- FEP/NCP changes for Token Ring addition and SDLC link reduction.

QLLC CONVERSION

QLLC is a data-link protocol defined by IBM that allows SNA data to be transported across X.25 networks. With QLLC, each SDLC physical link is replaced by a single virtual circuit. Figure 5–17 illustrates a typical QLLC topology. In this topology, both ends of the connection over the X.25 network must be configured for QLLC.

Figure 5–17

Typical QLLC topology.

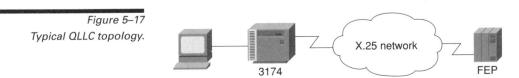

QLLC conversion is a feature of Cisco IOS Software Release 10.2 that causes the router to perform all of the translation required to send SNA data over an X.25 network so that IBM devices that are connected to a router do *not* have to be configured for QLLC.

QLLC conversion allows a device (typically a FEP or an AS/400) that is attached either directly to the router or through a Token Ring to communicate with a device (typically a 3174 terminal controller) that is attached to an X.25 network, as shown in Figure 5–18. In this example, only the terminal controller must be configured for QLLC and must have an X.25 interface.

Figure 5–18

Simple topology for QLLC conversion.

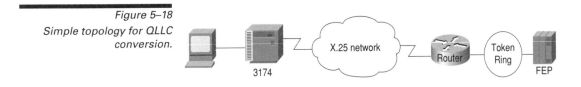

In some topologies, one router interface uses SDLC to communicate with the terminal controller, and another router interface uses X.25 to communicate with the remote device over the X.25 network. In Figure 5–19, the router, configured for QLLC conversion, handles SNA traffic between the terminal controller and the FEP.

Figure 5–19

Topology that uses SDLC and QLLC conversion.

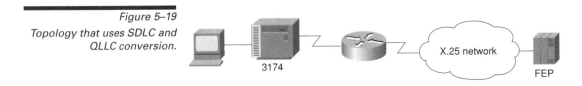

QLLC conversion also supports multiple SDLC connections coming through an MSD, as shown in Figure 5–20.

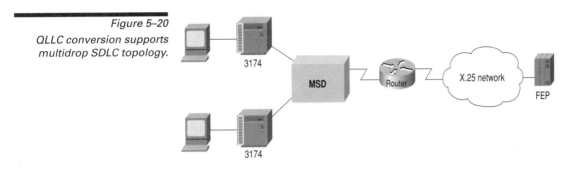

Figure 5–20
QLLC conversion supports multidrop SDLC topology.

The router that is configured for QLLC conversion does not need to be on the same Token Ring as the FEP. In Figure 5–21, Router A is configured for QLLC and remote source-route bridging (RSRB), and Router B is configured for RSRB only. RSRB allows the FEP to connect to Router A. If a Token Ring connected to the X.25 network communicates with the Token Ring attached to the FEP by a protocol other than SRB, RSRB can provide connectivity.

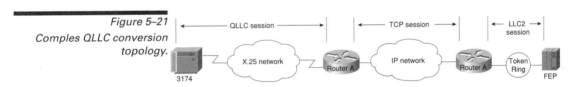

Figure 5–21
Comples QLLC conversion topology.

Figure 5–21 shows an example using local acknowledgment, which causes the LLC2 session from the Token Ring-attached SNA device (the FEP) to be terminated at the adjacent router (Router B). A TCP session transports the data from Router B to the router attached to the X.25 network (Router A). Only Router A is configured for QLLC conversion. When enabled, local acknowledgment applies to all QLLC connections. The **source-bridge qllc-local-ack** global configuration command enables local acknowledgment and applies to all QLLC connections.

In pass-through mode, local acknowledgment is not used. Instead, the LLC2 session from the Token Ring-attached SNA device (the FEP) is terminated at the router connected to the X.25 network (Router A).

QLLC conversion also supports a configuration in which SNA end stations (3174 or equivalent) that are connected to a Token Ring reach the FEP through an X.25 connection, as shown in Figure 5–22. In this case, IBM Network Packet Switching Interface (NPSI) software is installed on the FEP.

Figure 5–22

QLLC conversion supports SNA end-station connections over Token Ring and X.25 networks.

SUMMARY

This chapter addresses some of the special requirements for implementing routing technology within IBM System Network Architecture (SNA) environments. It describes the three techniques designed to enable internetworking capabilities for SNA-based network architectures, as follows:

- SDLC via STUN
- SDLLC Implementation
- QLLC Conversion

CHAPTER 6

Designing APPN Internetworks

Advanced peer-to-peer networking (APPN) is a second generation of the Systems Network Architecture (SNA) from IBM. It moves SNA from a hierarchical, mainframe-centric environment to a peer-to-peer environment. It provides capabilities similar to other LAN protocols, such as dynamic resource definition and route discovery.

This chapter focuses on developing the network design and planning a successful migration to APPN. It covers the following topics:

- Evolution of SNA
- When to Use APPN as Part of a Network Design
- When to Use APPN Versus Alternative Methods of SNA Transport
- Overview of APPN
- Scalability Issues
- Backup Techniques in an APPN Network
- APPN in a Multiprotocol Environment
- Network Management
- Configuration Examples

NOTES

Although this chapter does discuss using APPN with DLSw+, for detailed information on using DLSw+, refer to Chapter 7, "Designing DLSw+ Internetworks."

EVOLUTION OF SNA

Introduced in 1974, subarea SNA made the mainframe computer running Advanced Communications Function/Virtual Telecommunication Access Method (ACF/VTAM) the hub of the network. The mainframe was responsible for establishing all sessions (a connection between two resources over which data can be sent), activating resources, and deactivating resources. The design point of subarea SNA was reliable delivery of information across low-speed analog lines. Resources were explicitly predefined. This eliminated the need for broadcast traffic and minimized header overhead.

Many enterprises today maintain two networks: a traditional, hierarchical SNA subarea network and an interconnected LAN network that is based on connectionless, dynamic protocols. The advantage of the subarea SNA network is that it is manageable and provides predictable response time. The disadvantages are that it requires extensive system definition and does not take advantage of the capabilities of intelligent devices (for example, the PCs and workstations).

Role of APPN

With APPN, you can consolidate the two networks (an SNA subarea network and an interconnected LAN network) because APPN has many of the characteristics of the LAN networks and still offers the advantages of an SNA network. The major benefits of using APPN include the following:

- Connections are peer-to-peer, allowing any end user to initiate a connection with any other end user without the mainframe (VTAM) involvement.

- APPN supports subarea applications as well as newer peer-to-peer applications over a single network.

- APPN provides an effective routing protocol to allow SNA traffic to flow natively and concurrently with other protocols in a single network.

- Traditional SNA class of service (COS)/transmission priority can be maintained.

As SNA has evolved, one feature has remained critical to many users: COS. This feature provides traffic prioritization on an SNA session basis on the backbone. This, in turn, allows a single user to have sessions with multiple applications, each with a different COS. In APPN, this feature offers more granularity and extends this capability all the way to the end node rather than just between communication controllers.

Types of APPN Nodes

An APPN network has three types of nodes: LEN nodes, end nodes (EN), and network nodes (NN), as shown in Figure 6–1.

NOTES

Throughout the rest of this chapter, the abbreviations EN and NN are used in the illustrations. The full terms (end node and network node) are used within the text for clarity.

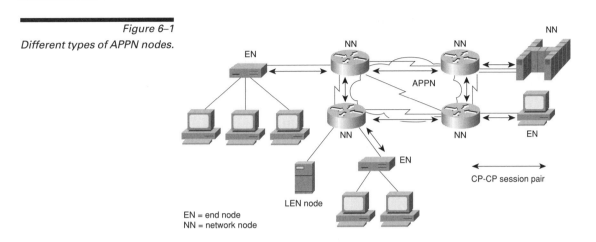

Figure 6–1
Different types of APPN nodes.

Table 6–1 describes these different types of APPN nodes. The control point (CP), which is responsible for managing a node's resources and adjacent node communication in APPN, is key to an APPN node. The APPN Control Point is the APPN equivalent of the SSCP.

Table 6–1 *Different Types of APPN Nodes*

Type of APPN Node	Description
Local Entry Networking (LEN) nodes	LEN nodes are pre-APPN, peer-to-peer nodes. They can participate in an APPN network by using the services provided by an adjacent network node. The CP of the LEN node manages the local resources but does not establish a CP-CP session with the adjacent network node. Session partners must be predefined to the LEN node, and the LEN node must be predefined to the adjacent network node. LEN nodes are also referred to as SNA node type 2.1, physical unit (PU) type 2.1, or PU2.1.

Table 6–1 *Different Types of APPN Nodes, Continued*

End nodes	End nodes contain a subset of full APPN functionality. They access the network through an adjacent network node and use the adjacent network node's routing services. An end node establishes a CP-CP session with an adjacent network node, and then uses that session to register resources, request directory services, and request routing information.
Network nodes	Network nodes contain full APPN functionality. The CP in a network node is responsible for managing the resources of the network node along with the attached end nodes and LEN nodes. The CP establishes CP-CP sessions with adjacent end nodes and network nodes. It also maintains network topology and directory databases, which are created and updated by dynamically gathering information from adjacent network nodes and end nodes over CP-CP sessions. In an APPN environment, network nodes are connected by transmission groups (TGs), which in the current APPN architecture refers to a single link. Consequently, the network topology is a combination of network nodes and transmission groups.

For more background information on APPN, refer to the section "Overview of APPN" later in this chapter.

WHEN TO USE APPN AS PART OF A NETWORK DESIGN

APPN has two key advantages over other protocols:

- Native SNA routing
- COS for guaranteed service delivery

APPN, like Transmission Control Protocol/Internet Protocol (TCP/IP), is a routable protocol in which routing decisions are made at the network nodes. Although only the network node adjacent to the originator of the session selects the session path, every network node contributes to the process by keeping every other network node informed about the network topology. The network node adjacent to the destination also participates by providing detailed information about the destination. Only routers that are running as APPN network nodes can make routing decisions.

You need APPN in your network when a routing decision (for example, which data center or path) must be made. Figure 6–2 helps to illustrate the criteria you use to determine where APPN should be used in a network.

In Figure 6–2, a single link connects the branch office to the backbone. Therefore, a routing decision does not need to be made at the branch office. Consequently, an APPN network node might not be necessary at those sites.

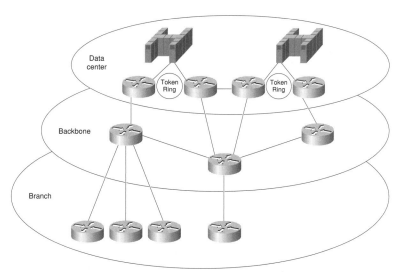

Figure 6–2
Determining where to use
APPN in a network.

Because there are two data centers, however, the routing decision about which data center to send the message to must be made. This routing decision can be made either at the data center or at the backbone routers. If you want this routing decision made at the data center, all messages are sent to a single data center using DLSw+, for example, and then routed to the correct data center using APPN only in the routers in the data center. If you want the routing decision to be made at the backbone routers, place the APPN network node in the backbone routers, where alternative paths are available for routing decisions outside of the data center. In this example, this latter approach is preferred because it isolates the function at the data centers routers to channel attachment, reduces the number of hops to the second data center, and provides a path to a backup data center if something catastrophic occurs.

Because APPN requires more memory and additional software, it is generally a more expensive solution. The advantages of direct APPN routing and COS, however, often offset the added expense. In this case, the added expense to add APPN to the backbone and data center routers might be justifiable, whereas added expense at the branch might not be justifiable.

APPN at Every Branch

There are two cases for which adding an APPN network node at every branch can be cost justified:

- When COS Is Required
- When Branch-to-Branch Routing Is Required

When COS Is Required

COS implies that the user accesses multiple applications and must be able to prioritize traffic at an application level. Although other priority schemes, such as custom queuing, might be able to prioritize by end user, they cannot prioritize between applications for an individual user. If this capability is critical, APPN network nodes must be placed in the individual branches to consolidate the traffic between multiple users using COS. For instance, COS can ensure that credit card verification always gets priority over batch receipts to a retail company's central site.

It is important to understand where COS is used in the network today. If the network is a subarea SNA network, COS is used only between front-end processors (FEPs) and ACF/VTAM on the mainframe. Unless there is already an FEP at the branch office, they do not have traffic prioritization from the branch, although traffic can be prioritized from the FEP out. In this case, adding an APPN network node at the branch office would prioritize the traffic destined for the data center sooner rather than waiting until it reaches the FEP—adding function over what is available today.

When Branch-to-Branch Routing Is Required

If branch-to-branch traffic is required, you can send all traffic to the central site and let those APPN network nodes route to the appropriate branch office. This is the obvious solution when both data center and branch-to-branch traffic are required and the branch is connected to the backbone over a single link. However, if a separate direct link to another branch is cost-justifiable, routing all traffic to the data center is unacceptable. In this case, making the routing decision at the branch is necessary. Using an APPN network node at the branch, data center traffic is sent over the data center link and branch-to-branch traffic is sent over the direct link.

In the example in Figure 6–3, each branch has two links to alternative routers at the data center. This is a case where APPN network nodes might be required at the branches so that the appropriate link can be selected. This can also be the design for branch-to-branch routing, adding a single hop rather than creating a full mesh of lines. This provides more direct routing than sending everything through the data center.

Figure 6–3

Sample network for which branch-to-branch routing is required.

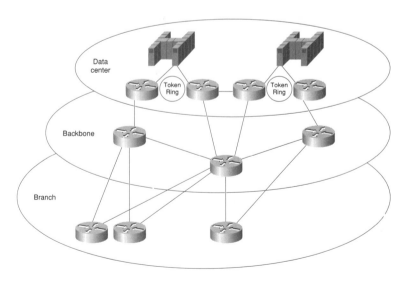

As you also learn in this chapter, scalability issues make it advantageous to keep the number of network nodes as small as possible. Understanding where native routing and COS is needed is key in minimizing the number of network nodes.

In summary, choosing where to implement APPN must be decided based on cost, scalability, and where native routing and COS are needed. Implementing APPN everywhere in your network might seem to be an obvious solution, even when not necessary. It must be understood, however, that if you were to deploy APPN everywhere in your network it probably would be a more costly solution than necessary and may potentially lead to scalability problems. Consequently, the best solution is to deploy APPN only where it is truly needed in your network.

WHEN TO USE APPN VERSUS ALTERNATIVE METHODS OF SNA TRANSPORT

APPN and boundary network node (BNN)/boundary access node (BAN) over Frame Relay using RFC 1490 are the two methods of native SNA transport, where SNA is not encapsulated in another protocol. BAN and BNN allow direct connection to an FEP, using the Frame Relay network to switch messages, rather than providing direct SNA routing.

Although *native* might seem to be the appropriate strategy, APPN comes at the price of cost and network scalability, as indicated in the preceding section. With BNN/BAN additional cost is required to provide multiprotocol networking because the FEP does not handle multiple protocols. This implies that additional routers are required in the data center for other protocols and separate virtual circuits are required to guarantee service delivery for the SNA or APPN traffic.

DLSw+ provides encapsulation of SNA, where the entire APPN message is carried as data inside a TCP/IP message. There is often concern about the extra 40 bytes of header associated with TCP/IP. However, because Cisco offers alternatives such as Data Link Switching Lite, Fast Sequenced Transport (FST), and Direct Transport, which have shorter headers, header length is deemed noncritical to this discussion.

DLSw+ is attractive for those networks in which the end stations and data center will remain SNA-centric, but the backbone will be TCP/IP. This allows a single protocol across the backbone, while maintaining access to all SNA applications. DLSw+ does not provide native APPN routing, nor does it provide native COS. Consequently, DLSw+ is preferable for networks, in which cost is a key criterion, that have the following characteristics:

- A single data center or mainframe
- Single links from the branches

In general, DLSw+ is a lower-cost solution that requires less memory and software. In the vast majority of networks, DLSw+ will be combined with APPN—using APPN only where routing decisions are critical. With TCP/IP encapsulation, the TCP layer provides the same reliable delivery as SNA/APPN, but does not provide the native routing and COS.

TN3270 transports 3270 data stream inside a TCP/IP packet without SNA headers. Therefore, this solution assumes that the end station has only a TCP/IP protocol stack and no SNA. Therefore, TN3270 is not an alternative to APPN because APPN assumes the end station has an SNA protocol stack. APPN, like DLSw+, may still be required in the network to route between TN3270 servers and multiple mainframes or data centers.

In summary, APPN will frequently be used with DLSw+ in networks when a single backbone protocol is desired. BAN/BNN provides direct connectivity to the FEP but lacks the multiprotocol capabilities of other solutions. TN3270 is used only for TCP/IP end stations.

OVERVIEW OF APPN

This section provides an overview of APPN and covers the following topics:

- Defining Nodes
- Establishing APPN Sessions
- Understanding Intermediate Session Routing
- Using Dependent Logical Unit Requester/Server

Defining Nodes

Nodes, such as ACF/VTAM, OS/400 and Communications Server/2 (CS/2), can be defined as either network nodes or end nodes. When you have a choice, consider the following issues:

- *Network size*—How large is the network? Building large APPN networks can introduce scalability issues. Reducing the number of network nodes is one solution for avoiding scalability problems. For more information on reducing the number of network nodes, see the section "Reducing the Number of Network Nodes" later in this chapter.
- *Role of the node*—Is it preferable to have this node performing routing functions as well as application processing? A separate network node can reduce processing cycles and memory requirements in an application processor.

Generally, you should define a network node whenever a routing decision needs to be made.

APPN Node Identifiers

An APPN node is identified by its network-qualified CP name, which has the format netid.name. The network identifier (netid) is an eight-character name that identifies the network or subnetwork in which the resource is located. The network identifier and name must be a combination of uppercase letters (A through Z), digits (0 through 9), and special characters ($,#,or @) but cannot have a digit as the first character.

Establishing APPN Sessions

In order for an APPN session to be established, the following must occur:

1. The end user requests a session with an application, which causes the end node to begin the process of session establishment by sending a LOCATE message to its network node server. For session initiation, the network node server provides the path to the destination end node, which allows the originating end node to send messages directly to the destination.

2. The network node uses directory services to locate the destination by first checking its internal directories. If the destination is not included in the internal directory, the network node sends a LOCATE request to the central directory server if one is available. If a central directory server is not available, the network node sends a LOCATE broadcast to the adjacent network nodes that in turn propagate the LOCATE throughout the network. The network node server of the destination returns a reply that indicates the location of the destination.

3. Based on the location of the destination, the COS requested by the originator of the session, the topology database, and the COS tables, the network node server of the originator selects the least expensive path that provides the appropriate level of service.

4. The originating network node server sends a LOCATE reply to the originating end node. The LOCATE reply provides the path to the destination.

5. The originating end node is then responsible for initiating the session. A BIND is sent from the originating end node to the destination end node, requesting a session. After the destination replies to the BIND, session traffic can flow.

Understanding Intermediate Session Routing

Session connectors are used in place of routing tables in APPN. The unique session identifier and port from one side of the node are mapped to the unique session identifier and port on the other side. As data traffic passes through the node, the unique session identifier in the header is swapped for the outgoing identifier and sent out on the appropriate port, as shown in Figure 6–4.

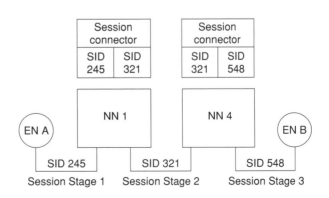

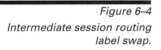

Figure 6–4
Intermediate session routing label swap.

This routing algorithm is called *intermediate session routing* (ISR). It supports dynamic route definition and incorporates the following legacy features:

- *Node-to-node error and flow control processing*—This reflects the 1970s method of packet switching in which many line errors dictated error and flow control at each node. Given the current high-quality digital facilities in many locations, this redundant processing is unnecessary and significantly reduces end-to-end throughput. End-to-end processing provides better performance and still delivers the necessary reliability.

- *Disruptive session switching around network failures*—Whenever a network outage occurs, all sessions using the path fail and have to be restarted to use an alternative path.

Because these features are undesirable in most high-speed networks today, a newer routing algorithm—High Performance Routing (HPR)—has been added to APPN that supports nondisruptive rerouting around failures and end-to-end error control, flow control, and segmentation. Cisco routers support both ISR and HPR.

Using Dependent Logical Unit Requester/Server

Dependent Logical Unit Requester/Server (DLUR/DLUS) is an APPN feature that allows legacy traffic to flow on an APPN network. Prior to the introduction of this feature, the APPN architecture assumed that all nodes in a network could initiate peer-to-peer traffic (for example, sending the BIND to start the session). Many legacy terminals that are referred to as Dependent Logical Units (DLUs) cannot do this and require VTAM to notify the application, which then sends the BIND.

Getting the legacy sessions initiated requires a client-server relationship between ACF/VTAM (Dependent LU server—DLUS) and the Cisco router (Dependent LU Requester—DLUR). A pair of logical unit (LU) type 6.2 sessions are established between the DLUR and DLUS—one session is established by each end point. These sessions are used to transport the legacy control messages that must flow to activate the legacy resources and initiate their logical unit to logical unit (LU-LU) sessions. An LU-LU session is the connection that is formed when the five steps described earlier in the section "Establishing APPN Sessions" are completed.

For example, an activate logical unit (ACTLU) message must be sent to the LU to activate a legacy LU. Because this message is not recognized in an APPN environment, it is carried as encapsulated data on the LU 6.2 session. DLUR then deencapsulates it, and passes it to the legacy LU. Likewise, the DLU session request is passed to the ACF/VTAM DLUS, where it is processed as legacy traffic. DLUS then sends a message to the application host, which is responsible for sending the BIND. After the legacy LU-LU session is established, the legacy data flows natively with the APPN traffic, as shown in Figure 6–5.

CISCO IMPLEMENTATION OF APPN

This section provides an overview of Cisco's implementation of APPN and discusses where APPN resides in the Cisco IOS software. Cisco licensed the APPN source code from IBM and then ported it to the Cisco IOS software using network services from the data-link controls (DLCs).

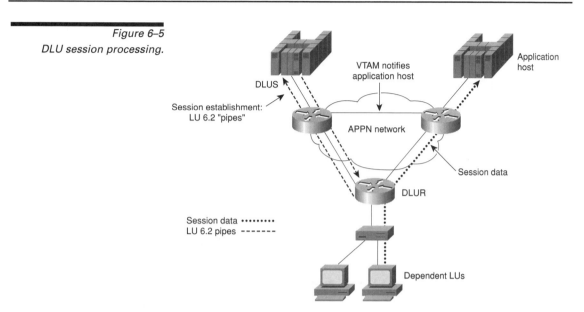

Figure 6–5
DLU session processing.

Applications use APPN to provide network transport. APPN runs on top of the Cisco IOS software. APPN is a higher-layer protocol stack that requires network services from DLC. Cisco's APPN implementation is compliant with the APPN Architecture of record. When used with other features in the Cisco IOS software, APPN provides the following unique features:

- APPN can use DLSw+ or RSRB as a network transport, thereby supporting APPN over a native TCP/IP network.

- APPN can be used with downstream physical unit concentration (DSPU) to reduce the number of downstream PUs visible to VTAM. This reduces VTAM definition and network restart times.

- In addition to COS, priority queuing, custom queuing, and weighted fair queuing can be used with COS to ensure traffic prioritization and/or bandwidth reservation between protocols.

- Network management options are supported that include native SNA management services using Native Service Point (NSP) in the Cisco router, and Simple Network Management Protocol (SNMP) management using CiscoWorks Blue applications.

- Using Channel Interface Processor (CIP) or Channel Port Adapter (CPA), the Cisco APPN network node can interface directly with ACF/VTAM across the channel. VTAM can be defined either as an end node or network node.

SCALABILITY ISSUES

As a single-network link state architecture, the network topology is updated as changes occur. This results in significant network traffic if instability occurs, and significant memory and processing to maintain the large topology databases and COS tables. Similarly, in large networks, dynamic discovery of resources can consume significant bandwidth and processing. For these reasons, scalability becomes a concern as network size increases. The number of nodes that are too large depends on the following:

- Amount of traffic

- Network stability

- The number of the techniques, which are described in this section, that are being used to control traffic and processing

Essentially, to allow growth of APPN networks, the network design must focus on reducing the number of topology database updates (TDUs) and LOCATE search requests.

Topology Database Update Reduction

APPN is a link-state protocol. Like other link-state-based algorithms, it maintains a database of the entire topology information of the network. Every APPN network node in the network sends out TDU packets that describe the current state of all its links to its adjacent network nodes. The TDU contains information that identifies the following:

- The characteristics of the sending node

- The node and link characteristics of the various resources in the network

- The sequence number of the most recent update for each described resource

A network node that receives a TDU packet propagates this information to its adjacent network nodes using a flow reduction technique. Each APPN network node maintains full knowledge of the network and how the network is interconnected. Once a network node detects a change to the network (either a change to the link, or the node), it floods TDUs throughout the network to ensure rapid convergence. If there is an unstable link in the network, it can potentially cause many TDU flows in a network.

As the number of network nodes and links increases, so does the number of TDU flows in your network. This type of distributing topology can consume significant CPU cycles, memory, and bandwidth. Maintaining routes and a large, complete topology subnet can require a significant amount of dynamic memory.

You can use the following techniques to reduce the amount of TDU flows in the network:

- Reduce the number of links

- Reduce the number of CP-CP sessions

- Reduce the number of network nodes in the network

Reducing the Number of Links

The first technique for reducing the amount of TDU flows in the network is to reduce the number of links in your network. In some configurations, it might be possible to use the concept of *connection network* to reduce the number of predefined links in your network. Because network nodes exchange information about their links, the fewer links you define, the fewer TDU flows can occur.

Figure 6–6 shows the physical view of an APPN network. In this network NN1, NN2, and NN3 are routers attached to an FDDI LAN.

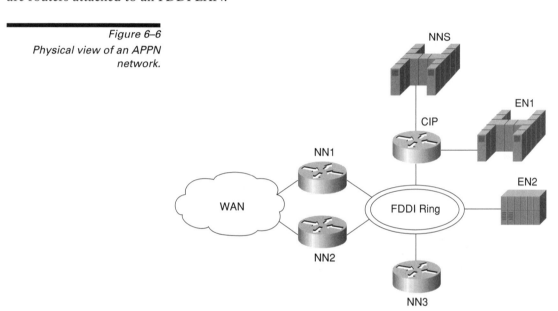

Figure 6–6
Physical view of an APPN network.

The network-node server (NNS), EN1, and EN2 hosts are attached to the same FDDI LAN via a CIP router or a cluster controller. These nodes on the FDDI LAN have any-to-any connectivity. To reflect any-to-any connectivity in APPN, NN1 needs to define a link to NN2, NN3, NNS (VTAM host), EN1 (VTAM data host), and EN2 (EN data host). The transmission groups connecting network nodes are contained in the network topology database. For every link that is defined to the network node, TDUs are broadcast.

NOTES

Throughout the rest of this chapter, the abbreviation NNS is used in the illustrations. When the text refers to an NNS icon in an illustration, the abbreviation is also used; otherwise, the full term (network-node server) is used within the text for clarity.

Figure 6–7 shows the logical view of the APPN network, shown earlier in Figure 6–6. When NN1 first joins the network, NN1 activates the links to NN2, NN3, NNS, EN1, and EN2. CP-CP sessions are established with the adjacent network nodes. Each adjacent network node sends a copy of the current topology database to NN1. Similarly, NN1 creates a TDU about itself and its links to other network nodes and sends this information over the CP-CP sessions to NN2, NN3 and NNS. When NN2 receives the TDU from NN1, it forwards the TDU to its adjacent network nodes, which are NN3 and NNS. Similarly, NN3 and NNS receive the TDU from NN1 and broadcast this TDU to their adjacent network nodes. The result is that multiple copies of the TDU are received by every network node.

Figure 6–7

Logical view of an APPN network without connection network deployed.

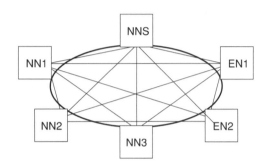

The transmission groups that connect the end nodes are not contained in the network topology database. Consequently, no TDUs are broadcast for the two links to EN1 and EN2. If the number of transmission groups connecting network nodes can be reduced, the number of TDU flows can also be reduced.

By using the concept of connection networks, you can eliminate the transmission group definitions, and therefore reduce TDU flows. A connection network is a single virtual routing node (VRN), which provides any-to-any connectivity for any of its attached nodes. The VRN is not a physical node, it is a logical entity that indicates that nodes are using a connection network and a direct routing path can be selected.

Figure 6–8 shows the APPN network shown in Figure 6–6 with connection network deployed.

Figure 6–8

Logical view of an APPN network with connection network deployed.

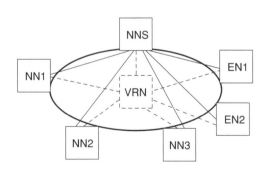

NN1, NN2, and NN3 define a link to the network-node server (NNS) and a link to the VRN. When the link between NN1 and NNS is activated, NNS sends a copy of the current network topology database to NN1. NN1 creates a TDU about itself, its link to NNS, and its link to the VRN. It then sends this information to NNS. NN1 does not have a link defined to NN2 and NN3, therefore, there are no TDUs sent to NN2 and NN3 from NN1. When NNS receives the TDU information from NN1, NNS forwards it to NN2 and NN3. Neither NN2 nor NN3 forwards the TDU information because they only have a connection to NNS. This significantly reduces the number of TDU flows in the network.

When a session is activated between resources on the connection network, the network-node server recognizes that this is a connection network and selects a direct route rather than routing through its own network nodes. Cisco recommends that you apply the concept of connection networks whenever possible. Not only does it reduce the number of TDU flows in the network, it also greatly reduces system definitions.

As shown in the example, a LAN (Ethernet, Token Ring, or FDDI) can be defined as a connection network. With ATM LAN Emulation (LANE) services, you can interconnect ATM networks with traditional LANs. From APPN's perspective, because an ATM-emulated LAN is just another LAN, connection network can be applied. In addition to LANs, the concept of connection networks can apply to X.25, Frame Relay, and ATM networks. It should also be noted that technologies such as RSRB and DLSw appear as LANs to APPN. You can also use connection network in these environments. APPN, in conjunction with DLSw+ or RSRB, provides a synergy between routing and bridging for SNA traffic.

Reducing the Number of CP-CP Sessions

The second technique for reducing the amount of TDU flows in the network is to reduce the number of CP-CP sessions in your network. Network nodes exchange topology updates over CP-CP sessions. The number of CP-CP sessions has a direct impact on the number of TDU flows in the network.

For example, in Figure 6–9, NN2, NN3, NN4, and NN5 are in a fully meshed network. Every network node establishes CP-CP sessions with its adjacent network nodes. This means that NN2 establishes CP-CP sessions with NN3, NN4, and NN5. NN3 establishes CP-CP sessions with NN2, NN4, NN5, and so forth.

If the link fails between NN1 and NN2, TDU updates are broadcast from NN2 to NN3, NN4, and NN5. When NN3 receives the TDU update, it resends this information to NN4 and NN5. Similarly, when NN5 receives the TDU update, it resends this information to NN3 and NN4. This means that NN4 receives the same information three times. It is recommended that the number of CP-CP sessions are kept to a minimum so that duplicate TDU information will not be received.

In Figure 6–10, CP-CP sessions exist only between NN2 and NN3, NN2 and NN4, and NN2 and NN5; no other CP-CP sessions exist. When the link fails between NN1 and NN2, NN2 broadcasts transmission group updates to NN3, NN4, and NN5. None of the three NNs forwards this information to the rest of the network because CP-CP sessions do not exist. Although this minimizes the TDU flows, if the link between NN2 and NN3 fails, this becomes a disjointed APPN network and NN3 is isolated.

Figure 6–9
Fully meshed CP-CP sessions.

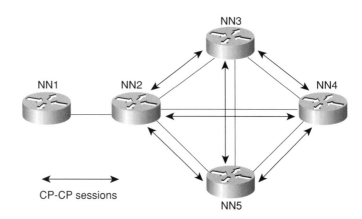

Figure 6–9
Fully meshed CP-CP sessions.

CP-CP sessions

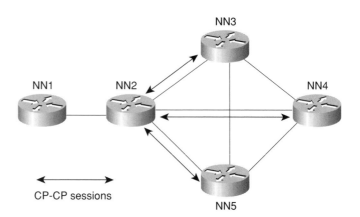

Figure 6–10
Single pair of CP-CP sessions.

CP-CP sessions

Figure 6–11 shows a more efficient design that also provides redundancy. Every network node has CP-CP sessions with two adjacent network nodes. NN2 has CP-CP sessions with NN3 and NN5. If the link between NN2 and NN3 fails, TDU updates will be sent via NN5 and NN4.

For redundancy purposes, it is recommended that each network node has CP-CP sessions to two other network nodes if possible.

Reducing the Number of Network Nodes

The third technique for reducing the amount of TDU flows in the network is to reduce the number of network nodes by defining APPN nodes only at the edges of the network. Minimizing the number of network nodes also reduces the size of the network topology. The following are some technologies for reducing the number of network nodes:

- APPN over DLSw+
- APPN over Frame Relay Access Server (FRAS)/BNN or BAN
- APPN over RSRB

Figure 6–11
Dual pair of CP-CP sessions.

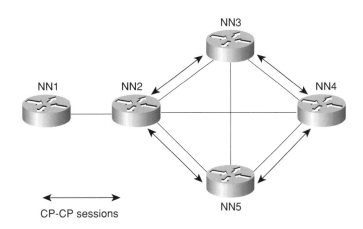

CP-CP sessions

APPN over DLSw+

Data link switching is one way to reduce the number of network nodes in the network. DLSw+ is a means of transporting APPN traffic across a WAN, where APPN network nodes and/or end nodes are defined only at the edges of the network. Intermediate routing is through DLSw+ and not via native SNA.

DLSw+ defines a standard to integrate SNA/APPN and LAN internetworks by encapsulating these protocols within IP. Cisco's implementation of DLSw, known as DLSw+, is a superset of the current DLSw architecture. DLSw+ has many value-added features that are not available in other vendors' DLSw implementations. APPN, when used with DLSw, can benefit from the many scalability enhancements that are implemented in DLSw+, such as border peer, on-demand peers, caching algorithms, and explorer firewalls.

In Figure 6–12, sessions between end-node workstations and the host are transported over the DLSw+ network.

VTAM acts as the network-node server for remote end-node workstations. Optionally, if multiple VTAMs or data centers exist, APPN on the channel-attached router(s) or on other routers in the data center can offload VTAM by providing the SNA routing capability, as shown in Figure 6–13.

Figure 6–12
APPN with DLSw+.

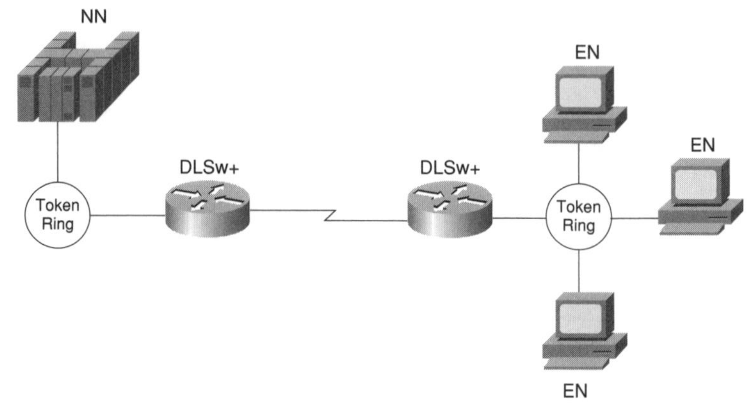

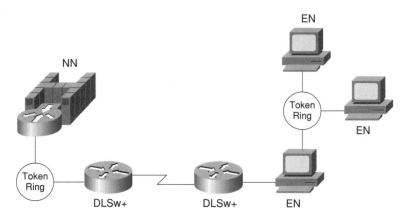

Figure 6–13
APPN with DLSw+ using a
channel-attached router.

DLSw+ also brings nondisruptive rerouting in the event of a WAN failure. Using DLSw+ as a transport reduces the number of network nodes in the network. A disadvantage is that remote end-node workstations require WAN connections for NNS services. Another disadvantage is that without APPN in the routers, APPN transmission priority is lost when traffic enters the DLSw+ network.

For detailed information on DLSw and DLSw+, refer to Chapter 7, "Designing DLSw+ Internetworks."

APPN over FRAS BNN/BAN

If the APPN network is based on a Frame Relay network, one option is to use the FRAS/BNN or the Frame Relay BAN function for host access. Both BNN and BAN allow a Cisco router to attach directly to an FEP. When you use FRAS/BNN, you are assuming that the Frame Relay network is performing the switching and that native routing is not used within the Frame Relay network. For an example of how APPN with FRAS BNN/BAN can be used in your network design, see the section "Example of APPN with FRAS BNN" later in this chapter.

APPN over RSRB

Using RSRB, the SNA traffic can be bridged from a remote site to a data center. The use of RSRB significantly reduces the total number of network nodes in the network, thus reducing the number of TDU flows in the network. Another advantage of using RSRB is that it provides nondisruptive routing in the event of a link failure. For more information on using RSRB, refer to Chapter 4, "Designing SRB Internetworks."

LOCATE Search Reduction

This section describes the broadcast traffic in an APPN network and how LOCATE searches can become a scalability issue in an APPN network. The impact of LOCATE searches in an APPN network varies from one network to the other. This section first identifies some of the causes of an excessive number of LOCATE searches, and then discusses the following four techniques you can use to minimize them:

- Safe-Store of Directory Cache
- Partial Directory Entries
- Central Directory Server (CDS)/Client
- Central Resource Registration

An APPN network node provides dynamic location of network resources. Every network node maintains dynamic knowledge of the resources in its own directory database. The distributed directory database contains a list of all the resources in the network. The LOCATE search request allows one network node to search the directory database of all other network nodes in the network.

When an end-node resource requests a session with a target resource that it has no knowledge of, it uses the distributed search capabilities of its network-node server to locate the target resource. If the network node does not have any knowledge of the target resource, the network node forwards the locate search request to all its adjacent network nodes requesting these nodes to assist the network-node server to locate the resource. These adjacent network nodes propagate these locate search requests to their adjacent network nodes. This search process is known as *broadcast search*.

Although several mechanisms are put into place to reduce the LOCATE broadcast searches (for example, resource registration, and resource caching), there might still be an excessive amount of LOCATE flows in a network for such reasons as the network resources no longer exist, there is a mixture of subarea networks and APPN networks, or the resources are temporarily unavailable.

Safe-Store of Directory Cache

The first technique that you can use to minimize the LOCATE flows in your APPN network is the Safe-Store of Directory Cache, which is supported by the Cisco network-node implementation. Cache entries in a network node's directory database can be periodically written to a permanent storage medium: a tftp host. This speeds recovery after a network-node outage or initial power loss. Resources do not have to be relearned through a LOCATE broadcast search after a router failure. This reduces spikes of broadcasts that might otherwise occur when the APPN network is restarted.

Partial Directory Entries

The second technique that you can use to minimize the LOCATE flows in your APPN network is to define the resources in the local directory database by identifying the end node or network node where the particular resource is located.

The following is a sample configuration:

```
appn partner-lu-location CISCO.LU21
owning-cp CISCO.CP2
complete
```

The preceding example defines the location of an LU named CISCO.LU21 that is located with end node or network node CISCO.CP2. This command improves network performance by allowing directed Locate, instead of a broadcast. The disadvantage is that definitions must be created. To alleviate this definition problem, it may be possible to use partially specified names to define multiple resources.

The following is a sample configuration:

```
Sample configuration:
appn partner-lu-location CISCO.LU
owning-cp CISCO.CP2
wildcard
complete
```

The preceding example defines the location of all the LUs prefixed with the characters LU. Obviously, a naming convention is essential to the success of this type of node definition.

Central Directory Server (CDS)/Client

The third technique that you can use to minimize the LOCATE flows in your APPN network is to use the CDS/client function. The APPN architecture specifies a CDS that allows a designated network node to act as a focal point for locating network resources. In current APPN networks, every network node can potentially perform a broadcast search for a resource. This is because the directory services database is not replicated on every network node.

The CDS function allows a network node, with central directory client support, to send a directed LOCATE search to a CDS. If the CDS has no knowledge of the resource, it performs one broadcast search to find the resource. After the resource is found, the CDS caches the results in its directory. Subsequently, the CDS can provide the location of the resource to other network nodes without performing another broadcast search. The Cisco network-node implementation supports the central directory client function. VTAM is the only product that currently implements the CDS function.

Using the CDS means that there is a maximum of one broadcast search per resource in the network. This significantly reduces the amount of network traffic used for resource broadcast searching. You can define multiple CDSs in an APPN network. A network node learns the existence of a CDS via

TDU exchange. If more than one CDS exists, the nearest one is used based on the number of hop counts. If a CDS fails, the route to the nearest alternative CDS is calculated automatically.

Central Resource Registration

The fourth technique that you can use to minimize the LOCATE flows in your APPN network is to use the central resource registration function. An end node registers its local resources at its network-node server. If every resource is registered, all network nodes can query the CDS, which eliminates the need for broadcast searches.

BACKUP TECHNIQUES IN AN APPN NETWORK

This section provides an overview of the various backup techniques in APPN network. The backup and recovery scenarios are representative of common environments and requirements. The following three backup scenarios are discussed:

- A secondary WAN link as a backup to a primary WAN link
- Dual WAN links and dual routers providing full redundancy
- APPN DLUR backup support using a Cisco CIP router

Link Backup

The first backup technique that you can use in your APPN network is to use a secondary WAN link as a backup to your primary WAN link. By using the concept of auto-activation on demand, you can back up a primary WAN link with a secondary WAN link by using any supported protocols (for example, Point-to-Point [PPP], Switched Multimegabit Data Service [SMDS], and X.25), as shown in Figure 6–14.

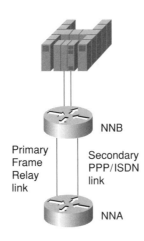

Figure 6–14
Link backup.

NNB

Primary
Frame
Relay
link

Secondary
PPP/ISDN
link

NNA

In Figure 6–14, the Frame Relay link is the primary link and the ISDN dial link is the backup link. The requirement is that the ISDN link provides instantaneous backup for the primary link and it remains inactive until the primary link goes down. No manual intervention is needed. To support this, NNA needs to define two parallel transmission groups to NNB.

The primary link is defined using the following configuration command:

```
appn link-station PRIMARY
port FRAME_RELAY
fr-dest-address 35
retry-limit infinite
complete
```

The secondary link is defined as supporting auto-activation using the following configuration command:

```
appn link-station SECONDARY
port PPP
no connect-at-startup
adjacent-cp-name NETA.NNB
activate-on-demand
complete
```

By specifying **no connect-at-startup**, the secondary link is not activated upon APPN node startup. To indicate auto-activation support, specify **adjacent-cp-name** and **activate-on-demand**.

When the primary link fails, APPN detects the link failure and CP-CP sessions failure, which is disruptive to any existing LU-LU sessions. Because there are multiple links from NNA to NNB, NNA attempts to re-establish the CP-CP sessions over the secondary link. The CP-CP sessions request will activate the secondary dial link automatically.

To ensure that the Frame Relay link is used as primary and the dial PPP link is used as the backup, define the transmission group characteristics to reflect that. For example, use the **cost-per-connect-time** parameter to define the relative cost of using the dial PPP/ISDN link.

```
cost-per-connect-time 5
```

This will make the primary Frame Relay link a lower cost route. Therefore, it is a more desirable route than the secondary dial link because the default cost-per-connect-time is zero. When the primary link becomes active, there is no mechanism in place to automatically switch the sessions back to the primary link. Manual intervention is required.

Full Redundancy

The second backup technique that you can use in your APPN network is dual WAN links and dual routers for full redundancy. In some cases, for example, complete fault tolerance is required for mission-critical applications across the network. You can have dual routers and dual links installed to provide protection against any kind of communications failure.

Figure 6–15 shows how you can use duplicate virtual MAC addresses via RSRB to provide full redundancy and load sharing.

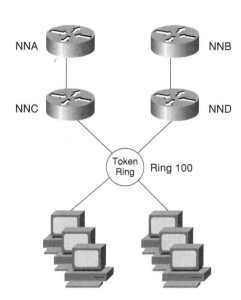

Figure 6–15
Full redundancy.

The router configuration for NNC is as follows:

```
source-bridge ring-group 200
!
interface TokenRing0
 ring-speed 16
 source 100 1 200
!
appn control-point NETA.NNC
  complete
!
appn port RSRB rsrb
  rsrb-virtual-station 4000.1000.2000 50 2 200
  complete
```

The router configuration for NND is as follows:

```
source-bridge ring-group 300
!
interface TokenRing0
 ring-speed 16
 source 100 5 300
!
appn control-point NETA.NND
  complete
!
appn port RSRB rsrb
  rsrb-virtual-station 4000.1000.2000 60 3 300
  complete
```

Both NNC and NND define an RSRB port with the same virtual MAC address. Every workstation will define the RSRB virtual MAC address as its destination MAC address of its network-node server. Essentially, a workstation can use either NNC or NND as its network-node server, depending on which node answers the test explorer frame first. The route to NNC consists of the following routing information:

```
Ring 100 -> Bridge 1 -> Ring 200 -> Bridge 2 -> Ring 50
```

Route to NND will consist of the following routing information:

```
Ring 100 -> Bridge 5 -> Ring 300 -> Bridge 3 -> Ring 60
```

When NND fails, sessions on NND can be re-established over NNC instantaneously. This is analogous to the duplicate Token Ring interface coupler (TIC) support on the FEP except that no hardware is required. In Cisco's RSRB implementation, as shown in Figure 6–15, Segment 20 and Bridge 1, and Segment 30 and Bridge 2 are virtual. Duplicate MAC address can be supported without the hardware in place.

SSCP Takeover

The third backup technique is to use APPN DLUR with a Cisco CIP router to support transfer of resource ownership from one System Services Control Point (SSCP) (VTAM) to another when a failure occurs. This includes maintaining existing sessions over the failure. DLUS/DLUR can provide the capability to transfer SSCP ownership from the primary SSCP to the backup SSCP. It then examines how DLUR can provide the capability to obtain SSCP services from the backup SSCP without terminating LU-LU sessions that are in progress.

Figure 6–16 illustrates how the FEP can be replaced with a CIP router running CIP SNA (CSNA).

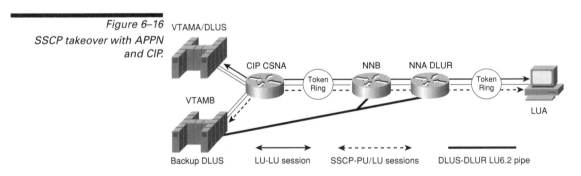

Figure 6–16
SSCP takeover with APPN and CIP.

In this example, VTAMA is the primary DLUS, VTAMB is the backup DLUS, and CIP router is configured as the DLUR. Assume that LUA requests to log on to an application that is residing on VTAMB. When VTAMA and the DLUS to DLUR connections fail, the DLUR node attempts to establish a session with VTAMB, which is configured as backup DLUS. When the control sessions to the DLUS are active, the DLUR node notifies VTAMB about all the active downstream physical and logical units. VTAMB sends active physical unit (ACTPU) and active logical unit (ACTLU) commands to these downstream devices. This transfers the resource ownership from VTAMA to VTAMB.

After the SSCP-PU and SSCP-LU sessions are re-established with VTAMB, new LU-LU sessions are possible. In addition, the DLUR node notifies VTAMB about all the dependent logical units that have active sessions.

The LU-LU path between VTAMB and LUA would be VTAMB -> NNB -> NNA -> LUA. When VTAMA fails, LU-LU sessions are not disrupted because VTAMA is not part of the LU-LU session path. In fact, LUA has no knowledge that the owning SSCP (VTAMA) failed and a new SSCP became the new owner. This process is transparent to LUA.

APPN in a Multiprotocol Environment

The trend in internetworking is to provide network designers with greater flexibility in building multiprotocol networks. Cisco provides the following two mechanisms to transport SNA traffic over an internetwork:

- Encapsulation
- Natively via APPN

The key to building multiprotocol internetworks is to implement some kind of traffic priority or bandwidth reservation to ensure acceptable response time for mission-critical traffic while maintaining some internetworking resource for less delay-sensitive traffic.

Bandwidth Management and Queuing

The following are some Cisco bandwidth management and queuing features that can enhance the overall performance of your network:

- Priority queuing
- Custom queuing
- Weighted fair queuing
- APPN buffer and memory management

For many years, the mainframe has been the dominant environment for processing business-critical applications. Increasingly powerful intelligent workstations, the creation of client-server computing environments, and higher bandwidth applications are changing network topologies. With the proliferation of LAN-based client-server applications, many corporate networks are migrating from purely hierarchical SNA-based networks to all-purpose multiprotocol internetworks that can accommodate the rapidly changing network requirements. This is not an easy transition. Network designers must understand how well the different protocols use shared network resources without causing excessive contentions among them.

Cisco has for many years provided technologies that encapsulate SNA traffic and allow consolidation of SNA with multiprotocol networks. APPN on the Cisco router provides an additional option in multiprotocol internetworks where SNA traffic can now flow natively and concurrently with other protocols. Regardless of the technology used in a multiprotocol environment, network performance is the key consideration.

Some of the major factors affecting network performance in a multiprotocol environment are as follows:

- *Media access speed*—The time it takes for a frame to be sent over a link. The capacity requirement of the network must be understood. Insufficient network capacity is the primary contributor to poor performance. Whether you have a single protocol network or a multiprotocol network, sufficient bandwidth is required.

- *Congestion control*—The router must have sufficient buffering capacity to handle instantaneous bursts of data. In order to support a multiprotocol environment, buffer management plays an important role to ensure that one protocol does not monopolize the buffer memory.

- *Latency in the intermediate routers*—This includes packet processing time while traversing a router and queuing delay. The former constitutes a minor part of the total delay. The latter is the major factor because client-server traffic is bursty.

Typically, subarea SNA traffic is highly predictable and has low bandwidth requirements. Compared to SNA traffic, client-server traffic tends to be bursty in nature and has high bandwidth requirements. Unless there is a mechanism in place to protect mission-critical SNA traffic, network performance could be impacted.

Cisco provides many internetworking solutions to enterprise networks by allowing the two types of traffic with different characteristics to coexist and share bandwidth; at the same time providing protection for mission-critical SNA data against less delay-sensitive client-server data. This is achieved through the use of several priority queuing and/or bandwidth reservation mechanisms.

For example, interface priority output queuing provides a way to prioritize packets transmitted on a per interface basis. The four possible queues associated with priority queuing—high, medium, normal and low—are shown in Figure 6–17. Priorities can be established based upon the protocol type, particular interface, SDLC address, and so forth.

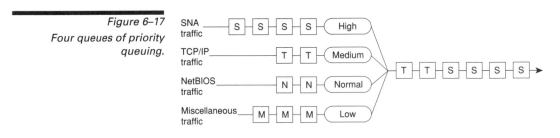

Figure 6–17
Four queues of priority queuing.

In Figure 6–18, SNA, TCP/IP, NetBIOS and other miscellaneous traffic are sharing the media. The SNA traffic is prioritized ahead of all other traffic, followed by TCP/IP, and then NetBIOS, and finally other miscellaneous traffic. There is no aging algorithm associated with this type of queuing. Packets that are queued to the high priority queue are always serviced prior to the medium queue, the medium queue is always serviced before the normal queue, and so forth.

Priority queuing, however, introduces a fairness problem in that packets classified to lower priority queues might not get serviced in a timely manner, or at all. Custom queuing is designed to address this problem. Custom queuing allows more granularity than priority queuing. In fact, this feature is commonly used in the internetworking environment in which multiple higher-layer protocols are supported. Custom queuing reserves bandwidth for a specific protocol, thus allowing mission-critical traffic to receive a guaranteed minimum amount of bandwidth at any time.

The intent is to reserve bandwidth for a particular type of traffic. For example, in Figure 6–18, SNA has 40 percent of the bandwidth reserved using custom queuing, TCP/IP 20 percent, NetBIOS 20 percent, and the remaining protocols 20 percent. The APPN protocol itself has the concept of COS that determines the transmission priority for every message. APPN prioritizes the traffic before sending it to the DLC transmission queue.

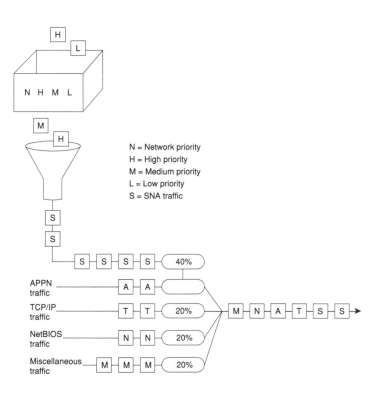

Figure 6–18
Example of custom queuing.

Custom queuing prioritizes multiprotocol traffic. A maximum of 16 queues can be built with custom queuing. Each queue is serviced sequentially until the number of bytes sent exceeds the configurable byte count or the queue is empty. One important function of custom queuing is that if SNA traffic uses only 20 percent of the link, the remaining 20 percent allocated to SNA can be shared by the other traffic.

Custom queuing is designed for environments that want to ensure a minimum level of service for all protocols. In today's multiprotocol internetwork environment, this important feature allows protocols of different characteristics to share the media. For an overview of how to use the other types of queuing to allow multiple protocols to coexist within a router, review Chapter 2, "Internetworking Design Basics."

Other Considerations with a Multiprotocol Environment

The memory requirement to support APPN is considerably higher than other protocols because of its large COS tables, network topology databases, and directory databases. To ensure that APPN will coexist with other network protocols when operating in a multiprotocol environment, users can define the maximum amount of memory available to APPN. The following is the sample configuration command.

```
appn control-point CISCONET.EARTH
  maximum-memory 16
  complete
```

The preceding command specifies that APPN will not use more than 16 megabytes (MB) of memory. The memory is then managed locally by APPN. You can also specify the amount of memory reserved for APPN by using the following command:

```
appn control-point CISCONET.EARTH
  mimimum-memory 32
  complete
```

— **NOTES**

Memory that is dedicated to APPN is not available for other processing. Use this command with caution.

Although memory determines factors such as the number of sessions that APPN can support, buffer memory is required to regulate traffic sent to and from the router. To ensure that APPN has adequate buffers to support the traffic flows, you can define the percentage of buffer memory that is reserved for use by APPN. This prevents APPN from monopolizing the buffer memory available in the router.

The following is the sample configuration command.

```
appn control-point CISCONET.EARTH
  buffer-percent 60
  complete
```

APPN uses a statistical buffering algorithm to manage the buffer usage. When buffer memory is constrained, APPN uses various flow control mechanisms to protect itself from severe congestion or deadlock conditions as a result of buffer shortage.

NETWORK MANAGEMENT

As networks grow in size and complexity, there are many ways to provide network management for an enterprise. Table 6–2 summarizes Cisco's management products.

Table 6–2 *Network Management Tools Available for APPN Networks*

Application	Description
Show commands	A common challenge in APPN networks is to understand the topology and status of the resources in the network. Show commands take advantage of the fact that all network nodes in a network (or subnetwork) have a fully replicated network topology database. Only a single network node is required to get a view of the APPN subnet, and it should not matter which network node is chosen. In order to obtain more detailed information, such as attached end nodes and LEN nodes, and local ports and link stations, additional network nodes should be checked.
	The Cisco router supports the RFC1593, APPN MIB, which is used by the IBM 6611 router, so it can be an agent for SNMP APPN applications. Most APPN nodes can show much of this information in tabular form. In the Cisco router, the **show appn topo** command displays the topology database in tabular form. The **show appn?** command lists all of the options available.
CiscoWorks Blue Maps	A CiscoWorks application that shows logical maps of APPN, RSRB, and DLSw+ networks. It runs on the HP/UX, SunOS, and AIX operating systems. The APPN map is a manager for APPN SNMP agents, and displays the APPN network. The application can handle only a single network topology agent. If there are multiple subnets, the application can be started multiple times.

Table 6–2   *Network Management Tools Available for APPN Networks, Continued*

Native Service Point (NSP)	In SNA, a session between an SSCP and a PU is referred to as an SSCP-PU session. SSCPs use SSCP-PU sessions to send requests and receive status information from individual nodes. This information is then used to control the network configuration.
	NSP in the router can be used to send alerts and respond to requests from NetView on the mainframe computer. A service point allows NetView to establish a session to the router with the help of Cisco's applications that run on NetView. These applications cause commands to be sent to the router, and the router returns the reply. Currently, this is supported only over the SSCP-PU session, but DLUR can be used to accomplish this over an APPN network.
Alerts and Traps	NetView is the primary destination of alerts. It supports receiving alerts from both APPN and on the SSCP-PU session used by NSP. The Cisco router can send alerts on each session. At this time, two sessions are required: one for APPN-unique alerts and one for all other alerts. The new APPN MIB allows for APPN alerts to be sent as traps as well, with the Alert ID and affected resource included in the trap.
	To send alerts to NetView, the following command must be entered at NetView:
| | ```
FOCALPT CHANGE, FPCAT=ALERT, TARGET=NETA.ROUTER
``` |

CONFIGURATION EXAMPLES

This section provides the following APPN network configuration examples:

- Simple APPN network
- APPN network with end stations
- APPN over DLSw+

It also provides the following examples of using APPN when designing your network:

- Subarea to APPN migration
- APPPN/CIP in a Sysplex environment
- APPN with FRAS BNN

As the following examples show, the minimal configuration for an APPN node includes an APPN control-point statement for the node and a port statement for each interface.
```

Simple APPN Network Configuration

Figure 6–19 shows an example of a simple APPN network that consists of four network nodes: Routers A, B, C, and D. Router A is responsible for initiating the connections to Routers B, C, and D. Consequently, it needs to define APPN logical links specifying the FDDI address of Router C, the ATM address of Router D, and so forth. For Routers B, C, and D, they can dynamically create the link-station definitions when Router A connects.

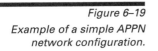

Figure 6–19

Example of a simple APPN network configuration.

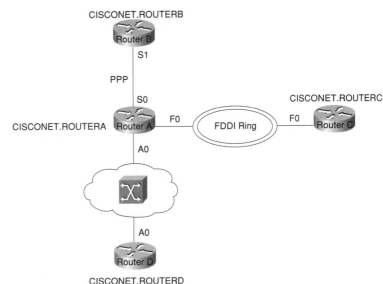

Sample Configurations

This section provides sample configurations for each of these four network nodes (Routers A, B, C, and D) shown in Figure 6–19.

Router A Configuration

The following is a sample configuration for Router A shown in Figure 6–19. Note that all link stations are defined in Router A and dynamically discovered by the other routers. A link station connects two resources and must be defined with the destination address in one of the resources:

```
!
hostname routera
!
interface Serial0
 ip address 10.11.1.1 255.255.255.0
 encapsulation ppp
 no keepalive
 no fair-queue
```

```
    clockrate 4000000
 !
 interface Fddi0
  no ip address
  no keepalive
 !
 interface ATM0
  no ip address
  atm clock INTERNAL
  atm pvc 1 1 32 aal5nlpid
 !
 appn control-point CISCONET.ROUTERA
   complete
 !
 appn port PPP Serial0
   complete
 !
 appn port FDDI Fddi0
   desired-max-send-btu-size 3849
   max-rcv-btu-size 3849
   complete
 !
 appn port ATM ATM0
   complete
 !
 appn link-station LINKTOB
   port PPP
   complete
 !
 appn link-station LINKTOC
   port FDDI
   lan-dest-address 0000.6f85.a8a5
   no connect-at-startup
   retry-limit infinite 5
   complete
 !
 appn link-station LINKTOD
   port ATM
   atm-dest-address 1
   no connect-at-startup
   retry-limit infinite 5
   complete
 !
```

Router B Configuration

The following is a sample configuration for Router B shown in Figure 6–19:

```
 !
 hostname routerb
 !
 interface Serial1
  ip address 10.11.1.2 255.255.255.0
  encapsulation ppp
  no keepalive
```

```
  no fair-queue
!
appn control-point CISCONET.ROUTERB
  complete
!
appn port PPP Serial1
  complete
!
appn routing
!
end
```

Router C Configuration

The following is a sample configuration for Router C shown in Figure 6–19:

```
!
hostname routerc
!
interface Fddi0
 no ip address
 no keepalive
!
appn control-point CISCONET.ROUTERC
  complete
!
appn port FDDI Fddi0
  desired-max-send-btu-size 3849
  max-rcv-btu-size 3849
  complete
!
appn routing
!
end
```

Router D Configuration

The following is a sample configuration for Router D shown in Figure 6–19:

```
!
hostname routerd
!
interface ATM0
 ip address 100.39.15.3 255.255.255.0
 atm pvc 1 1 32 aal5nlpid
!
appn control-point CISCONET.ROUTERD
  complete
!
appn port ATM ATM0
  complete
!
appn routing
!
end
```

APPN Network Configuration with End Stations

Figure 6–20 shows an example of an APPN network with end stations. At the remote location, Router B initiates the APPN connection to Router A at the data center.

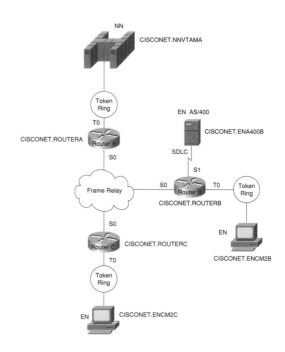

Figure 6–20

Example of an APPN network with end stations.

Sample Configurations

This section provides sample configurations for Routers A, B, and C shown in Figure 6–20.

Sample Configuration for Router A

The following is a sample configuration for Router A in Figure 6–20, which is responsible for initiating the APPN connection to the VTAM host:

```
hostname routera
!
interface TokenRing0
 no ip address
 mac-address 4000.1000.1000
 ring-speed 16
!
interface Serial0
 mtu 4096
 encapsulation frame-relay IETF
 keepalive 12
```

```
 frame-relay lmi-type ansi
 frame-relay map llc2  35
!
appn control-point CISCONET.ROUTERA
  complete
!
appn port FR0 Serial0
  complete
!
appn port TR0 TokenRing0
  complete
!
appn link-station TOVTAM
  port TR0
  lan-dest-address 4000.3745.0000
  complete
!
end
```

Sample Configuration for Router B

The following is a sample configuration for Router B shown in Figure 6–20. At the remote location, Router B initiates the APPN connection to Router A at the data center and EN AS/400. Because a link station is not defined in Router B for CISCONET.ENCM2B, a link station must be defined in ENCM2B for Router B:

```
!hostname routerb
!
interface TokenRing0
 mac-address 4000.1000.2000
 no ip address
 ring-speed 16
!
interface Serial0
 mtu 4096
 encapsulation frame-relay IETF
 keepalive 12
 frame-relay lmi-type ansi
 frame-relay map llc2  35
!
interface Serial2/7
 no ip address
 encapsulation sdlc
 no keepalive
 clockrate 19200
 sdlc role prim-xid-poll
 sdlc address 01
!
appn control-point CISCONET.ROUTERB
  complete
!
appn port FR0 Serial0
  complete
!
```

```
appn port SDLC Serial1
  sdlc-sec-addr 1
  complete
!
appn port TR0 TokenRing0
  complete
!
appn link-station AS400
  port SDLC
  role primary
  sdlc-dest-address 1
  complete
!
appn link-station ROUTERA
  port FR0
  fr-dest-address 35
  complete
!
end
```

Sample Configuration for Router C

The following is a sample configuration for Router C shown in Figure 6–20. Router C initiates an APPN connection to Router A. Because there is not a link station for CISCONET.ENCMC2C, one must be defined in the configuration for ENCM2C:

```
hostname routerc
!
interface TokenRing0
 mac-address 4000.1000.3000
 no ip address
 ring-speed 16
!
interface Serial0
 mtu 4096
 encapsulation frame-relay IETF
 keepalive 12
 frame-relay lmi-type ansi
 frame-relay map llc2 36
!
appn control-point CISCONET.ROUTERC
  complete
!
appn port FR0 Serial0
  complete
!
appn port TR0 TokenRing0
  complete
!
appn link-station TORTRA
  port FR0
  fr-dest-address 36
  complete
!
end
```

APPN over DLSw+ Configuration Example

Figure 6–21 shows an example of APPN with DLSw+. ROUTER A is a DLSw+ router with no APPN functions and ROUTERB is running DLSw+ and APPN.

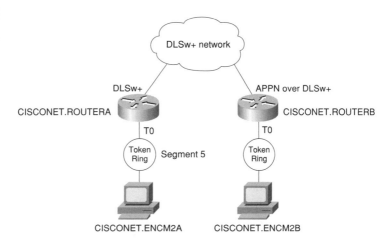

Figure 6–21
Example of APPN with DLSw+.

Sample Configurations of DLSw+ Router A

The following section provides sample configurations for ROUTERA and ROUTERB and the two workstations shown in Figure 6–21.

Sample Configuration of DLSw+ ROUTERA

The following is a sample configuration for the DLSw+ ROUTERA shown in Figure 6–21:

```
hostname routera
!
source-bridge ring-group 100
dlsw local-peer peer-id 10.4.21.3
dlsw remote-peer 0 tcp 10.4.21.1
!
interface Serial0
 mtu 4096
 ip address 10.4.21.3 255.255.255.0
 encapsulation frame-relay IETF
 keepalive 12
 no fair-queue
 frame-relay lmi-type ansi
 frame-relay map llc2  56
!
interface TokenRing0
 ip address 10.4.22.2 255.255.255.0
 ring-speed 16
 multiring all
 source-bridge 5 1 100
!
```

Sample Configuration for Workstation Attached to ROUTERA

The following is a sample CS/2 configuration for the OS/2 workstation named CISCO-NET.ENCM2A shown in Figure 6–21. This workstation is attached to the DLSw+ router named ROUTERA. The workstation is configured as an end node and it uses ROUTERB as the network-node server. The destination MAC address configured on this workstation is the virtual MAC address configured in ROUTERB on the **appn port** statement. A sample of the DLSw+ ROUTERB configuration is provided in the next section.

```
        DEFINE_LOCAL_CP   FQ_CP_NAME(CISCONET.ENCM2A)
                          CP_ALIAS(ENCM2C)
                          NAU_ADDRESS(INDEPENDENT_LU)
                          NODE_TYPE(EN)
                          NODE_ID(X'05D00000')
                          NW_FP_SUPPORT(NONE)
                          HOST_FP_SUPPORT(YES)
                          MAX_COMP_LEVEL(NONE)

                          MAX_COMP_TOKENS(0);
     DEFINE_LOGICAL_LINK   LINK_NAME(TORTRB)
                          ADJACENT_NODE_TYPE(LEARN)
                          PREFERRED_NN_SERVER(YES)
                          DLC_NAME(IBMTRNET)
                          ADAPTER_NUMBER(0)
                          DESTINATION_ADDRESS(X'400010001112')
                          ETHERNET_FORMAT(NO)
                          CP_CP_SESSION_SUPPORT(YES)
                          SOLICIT_SSCP_SESSION(YES)
                          NODE_ID(X'05D00000')
                          ACTIVATE_AT_STARTUP(YES)
                          USE_PUNAME_AS_CPNAME(NO)
                          LIMITED_RESOURCE(NO)
                          LINK_STATION_ROLE(USE_ADAPTER_DEFINITION)
                          MAX_ACTIVATION_ATTEMPTS(USE_ADAPTER_DEFINITION)
                          EFFECTIVE_CAPACITY(USE_ADAPTER_DEFINITION)
                          COST_PER_CONNECT_TIME(USE_ADAPTER_DEFINITION)
                          COST_PER_BYTE(USE_ADAPTER_DEFINITION)
                          SECURITY(USE_ADAPTER_DEFINITION)
                          PROPAGATION_DELAY(USE_ADAPTER_DEFINITION)
                          USER_DEFINED_1(USE_ADAPTER_DEFINITION)
                          USER_DEFINED_2(USE_ADAPTER_DEFINITION)
                          USER_DEFINED_3(USE_ADAPTER_DEFINITION);

        DEFINE_DEFAULTS   IMPLICIT_INBOUND_PLU_SUPPORT(YES)
                          DEFAULT_MODE_NAME(BLANK)
                          MAX_MC_LL_SEND_SIZE(32767)
                          DIRECTORY_FOR_INBOUND_ATTACHES(*)
                          DEFAULT_TP_OPERATION(NONQUEUED_AM_STARTED)
                          DEFAULT_TP_PROGRAM_TYPE(BACKGROUND)
```

```
                      DEFAULT_TP_CONV_SECURITY_RQD(NO)
                      MAX_HELD_ALERTS(10);

      START_ATTACH_MANAGER;
```

Sample Configuration for DLSw+ ROUTERB

ROUTERB, shown in Figure 6–21, is an APPN router that uses the APPN over DLSw+ feature. The VDLC operand on the port statement indicates that APPN is carried over DLSw+. The following is a sample configuration for this router:

```
hostname routerb
!
source-bridge ring-group 100
dlsw local-peer peer-id 10.4.21.1
dlsw remote-peer 0 tcp 10.4.21.3
!
interface Serial2/0
 mtu 4096
 ip address 10.4.21.1 255.255.255.0
 encapsulation frame-relay IETF
 keepalive 12
 no fair-queue
 frame-relay map llc2  35
!
interface TokenRing0
 no ip address
 ring-speed 16
 mac-address 4000.5000.6000
!
appn control-point CISCONET.ROUTERB
  complete
!
appn port VDLC vdlc
  vdlc 100 vmac 4000.1000.1112
  complete
!
```

Sample Configuration for Workstation Attached to ROUTERB

The following is a sample CS/2 configuration for the OS/2 workstation named CISCO-NET.ENCM2B shown in Figure 6–21. This workstation is attached to the DLSw+ router named ROUTERB:

```
DEFINE_LOCAL_CP   FQ_CP_NAME(CISCONET.ENCM2B)
                  CP_ALIAS(ENCM2C)
                  NAU_ADDRESS(INDEPENDENT_LU)
                  NODE_TYPE(EN)
                  NODE_ID(X'05D00000')
                  NW_FP_SUPPORT(NONE)
                  HOST_FP_SUPPORT(YES)
                  MAX_COMP_LEVEL(NONE)
                  MAX_COMP_TOKENS(0);
```

```
DEFINE_LOGICAL_LINK   LINK_NAME(TORTRB)
                      ADJACENT_NODE_TYPE(LEARN)
                      PREFERRED_NN_SERVER(YES)
                      DLC_NAME(IBMTRNET)
                      ADAPTER_NUMBER(0)
                      DESTINATION_ADDRESS(X'400050006000')
                      ETHERNET_FORMAT(NO)
                      CP_CP_SESSION_SUPPORT(YES)
                      SOLICIT_SSCP_SESSION(YES)
                      NODE_ID(X'05D00000')
                      ACTIVATE_AT_STARTUP(YES)
                      USE_PUNAME_AS_CPNAME(NO)
                      LIMITED_RESOURCE(NO)
                      LINK_STATION_ROLE(USE_ADAPTER_DEFINITION)
                      MAX_ACTIVATION_ATTEMPTS(USE_ADAPTER_DEFINITION)
                      EFFECTIVE_CAPACITY(USE_ADAPTER_DEFINITION)
                      COST_PER_CONNECT_TIME(USE_ADAPTER_DEFINITION)
                      COST_PER_BYTE(USE_ADAPTER_DEFINITION)
                      SECURITY(USE_ADAPTER_DEFINITION)
                      PROPAGATION_DELAY(USE_ADAPTER_DEFINITION)
                      USER_DEFINED_1(USE_ADAPTER_DEFINITION)
                      USER_DEFINED_2(USE_ADAPTER_DEFINITION)
                      USER_DEFINED_3(USE_ADAPTER_DEFINITION);

DEFINE_DEFAULTS   IMPLICIT_INBOUND_PLU_SUPPORT(YES)
                  DEFAULT_MODE_NAME(BLANK)
                  MAX_MC_LL_SEND_SIZE(32767)
                  DIRECTORY_FOR_INBOUND_ATTACHES(*)
                  DEFAULT_TP_OPERATION(NONQUEUED_AM_STARTED)
                  DEFAULT_TP_PROGRAM_TYPE(BACKGROUND)
                  DEFAULT_TP_CONV_SECURITY_RQD(NO)
                  MAX_HELD_ALERTS(10);

START_ATTACH_MANAGER;
```

NOTES

For more information on DLSw+, see Chapter 7, "Designing DLSw+ Internetworks."

Example of Subarea to APPN Migration

This section provides an overview of the implementation and conversion of the SNA network from subarea FEP-based to APPN router-based. It explores the use of DLSw+ as a migration technology from traditional SNA to APPN, and covers the migration steps. The example involves a large insurance company in Europe. The company plans to replace the FEPs with Cisco routers, migrating from subarea to APPN routing.

Figure 6–22 shows the company's current SNA network. The network consists of two mainframe sites running four VTAM images with a Communications Management Complex (CMC) host in each data center, as shown in Figure 6–22. In every data center, four NCR Comten FEPs (IBM

3745-compatible) support traffic from multiple regional offices. There are also two NCR Comten FEPs that provide SNA Network Interconnect (SNI) support.

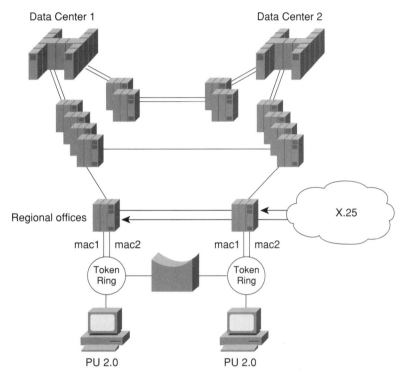

Figure 6–22
SNA FEP-based network.

There are 22 regional offices across the country. Every regional office has two NCR Comten FEPs installed, one connecting to Data Center 1 and the other connecting to Data Center 2. The remote FEPs have dual Token Rings that are connected via a bridge; duplicate TIC address support is implemented for backup and redundancy. This means that a PU2.0 station can connect to the host through any one of the two FEPs. If one FEP fails, PU2.0 stations can access the host via the other FEP.

In addition to the Token-Ring-attached devices (approximately 15 per regional office), the two FEPs also run NCP Packet-Switching Interface (NPSI), supporting over 200 remotely attached devices via the public X.25 network. The total number of LUs supported per regional office is approximately 1800, with 1500 active LU-LU sessions at any one time. The estimated traffic rate is 15 transactions per second.

The first migration step is to implement Cisco CIP routers at one of the data centers, replacing the channel-attached FEPs. A remote router is then installed in one of the regional offices. The two routers are connected using DLSw+, as shown in Figure 6–23.

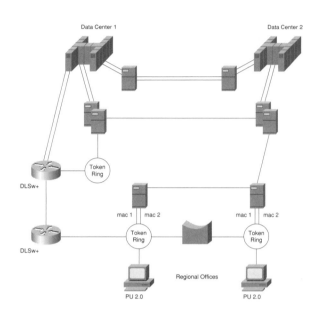

Figure 6–23
Subarea to APPN
migration—phase one.

As Figure 6–23 shows, the FEPs at the regional office continue to provide boundary functions to the Token Ring and X.25-attached devices. The two DLSw+ routers handle the traffic between the FEP at Data Center 1 and the FEP at the regional office. SNA COS is preserved in this environment.

After stability of the routers is ensured, the network designer proceeds to the next phase. As Figure 6–24 shows, this phase involves installation of a second router in Data Center 2 and the regional office. At this point, FEP-to-FEP communications between regional offices and data centers are handled by the routers via DLSw+.

Continuing with the migration plan, the network designer's next step is to install an additional CIP router in each data center to support traffic between the two data centers. As shown in Figure 6–25, the links that are connecting the FEPs in Data Center 1 and Data Center 2 are moved one by one to the routers.

APPN will be enabled to support the traffic between Data Center 1 and Data Center 2. Eventually, the FEP-based network will become a router-based network. The NCR Comten processors will become obsolete. Two of the NCR Comten processors will be kept to provide SNI support to external organizations. Figure 6–26 illustrates the new router-based network.

The communication links that formerly connected the FEPs in the two data centers are now moved to the routers. The FEPs at the data centers can be eliminated. The FEPs at the regional offices are merely providing the boundary functions for dependent LU devices, thus allowing SNA COS to be maintained. The next phase is to migrate the SNA boundary functions support from the FEP to the remote router at the regional office by enabling APPN and DLUR. After this is complete, all the FEPs can be eliminated.

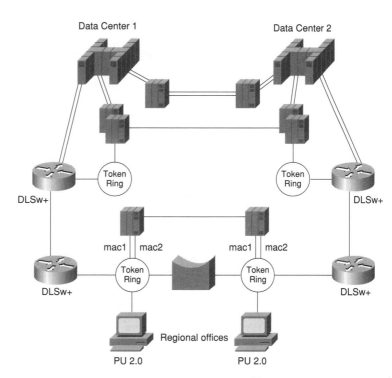

Figure 6–24
Subarea to APPN
migration—phase two.

The next step is to migrate from DLSw+ to APPN between the data center routers and the regional office routers. This is done region by region until stability of the network is ensured. As shown in Figure 6–27, DLUR is enabled to support the dependent PU devices in the regional offices. X.25 attached dependent PU2.0 devices that are formerly connected to the FEPs using NPSI are supported via Qualified Logical Link Control (QLLC) in the router. QLLC is the standard for SNA encapsulation for X.25.

Example of APPN/CIP in a Sysplex Environment

This section examines APPN and the CIP routers in a Sysplex (system complex) environment. It provides an overview of the Sysplex environment and its relationship with APPN along with a description of how to use the following three approaches to support the Sysplex environment:

- Sysplex with APPN Using Subarea Routing—Option One
- Sysplex Using Subarea/APPN Routing—Option Two
- Sysplex Using APPN Routing—Option Three

It also describes how APPN provides fault tolerance and load sharing capabilities in the data center.

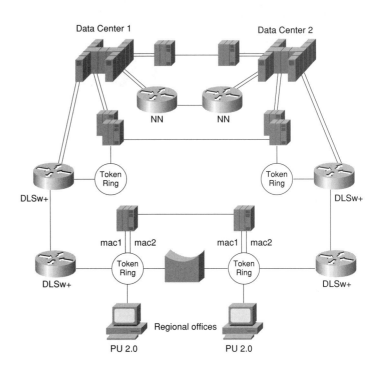

Figure 6–25

Subarea to APPN migration—phase three.

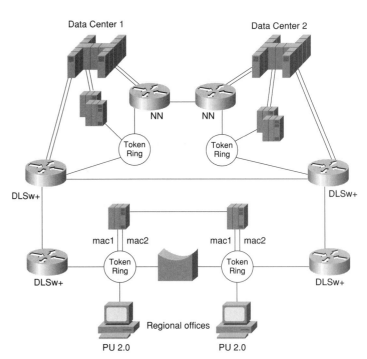

Figure 6–26

Subarea to APPN migration—phase four.

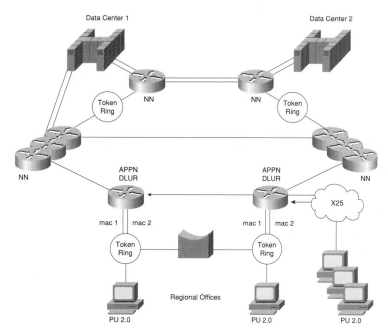

Figure 6–27
Subarea to APPN
migration—phase five.

Sysplex Overview

Sysplex provides a means to centrally operate and manage a group of multiple virtual storage (MVS) systems by coupling hardware elements and software services. Many data processing centers have multiple MVS systems to support their business, and these systems often share data and applications. Sysplex is designed to provide a cost-effective solution to meet a company's expanding requirements by allowing MVS systems to be added and managed efficiently.

A Sysplex environment consists of multiple 9672 CMOS processors, and each CMOS processor presents a VTAM domain. The concept of multiprocessors introduces a problem. Today, users are accustomed to single images. For example, IMS (Information Management System) running on the mainframe can serve the entire organization on a single host image. With the multiprocessor concept, you would not want to instruct User A to establish the session with IMS on System A and User B to establish the session with IMS on System B because IMS might run on either system.

To resolve this, a function called *generic resource* was created. The generic resource function enables multiple application programs, which provide the same function, to be known and accessed by a single generic name. This means that User A might sometimes get IMS on System A, and sometimes get IMS on System B. Because both systems have access to the same shared data in the Sysplex, this switching of systems is transparent to the users. VTAM is responsible for resolving the generic name and determining which application program is used to establish the session. This function enables VTAM to provide workload balancing by distributing incoming session initiations among a number of identical application programs that are running on different processors.

Generic resource runs only on VTAM with APPN support. In order to achieve session load balancing across the different processors, users must migrate VTAM from subarea SNA to APPN. The rest of this section examines three options for supporting the Sysplex environment.

Sysplex with APPN Using Subarea Routing—Option One

The first option to support the Sysplex environment is to convert the CMC host to a composite network node. Traditionally, the CMC host was the VTAM that owned all of the network's SNA resources. With this approach, the composite network node is used to describe the combination of VTAM and Network Control Program (NCP). This means that VTAM and NCP function together as a single network node. In Figure 6–28, the CMC host and the FEPs are configured as the composite network node.

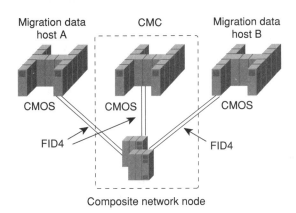

Figure 6–28

CMC composite network node with subarea routing—option one.

The VTAM CMC host owns the FEPs. Each FEP is connected to the 9672 CMOS processors through a parallel channel. Each 9672 CMOS processsor is configured as a migration data host and maintains both an APPN and subarea appearance.

Each migration data host establishes subarea connections to the FEPs using Virtual Route Transmission Group (VRTG), which allows APPN to be transported over traditional subarea routing. CP-CP sessions between the CMC host and the 9672 migration data hosts are established using VRTG. Generic resource function is performed in APPN, but all routing is subarea routing. This is the most conservative way to migrate to a Sysplex.

The disadvantage of this approach is that using subarea routing does not provide dynamic implementation of topology changes in APPN, which is available with APPN connection. If you need to add a CMOS processor, subarea PATH changes to every subarea node are required. Another drawback of this approach is that running APPN over subarea routing introduces complexity to your network.

Sysplex Using Subarea/APPN Routing—Option Two

The second option to support the Sysplex environment is to use subarea/APPN routing. This approach is similar to Option One, which was described in the preceding section. With this second approach, the CMC host and the FEPs are converted to a composite network node, as shown in Figure 6–29.

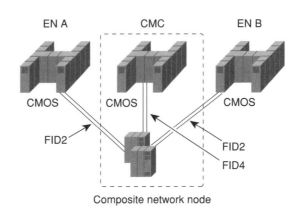

Figure 6–29
CMC composite network node with APPN routing— option two.

As shown in Figure 6–29, the two 9672 CMOS processors are converted to pure end nodes (EN A and EN B). APPN connections are established between the 9672s and the FEPs. Sessions come into the CMC in the usual way and the CMC does subarea/APPN interchange function. This means that sessions are converted from subarea routing to APPN routing on the links between the FEPs and the 9672s.

A disadvantage of this second approach is that it performs poorly because the FEPs must perform an extra conversion. This approach also requires more NCP cycles and memory. Although this is very easy to configure and it does not require any changes to the basic subarea routing, the cost of the NCP upgrades can be expensive.

Sysplex Using APPN Routing—Option Three

The third option to support the Sysplex environment is to use APPN routing. With this approach, you use DLUR as a front end to the CMC-owned logical units. Figure 6–30 illustrates this configuration.

As shown in Figure 6–30, this is a pure APPN network with APPN routing only. Each CMOS end-node processor is attached to the DLUR routers through APPN. Note that the DLUR routers could be remote and not directly next to the mainframe computers (for example, there could be intervening routers).

This is the preferred approach for implementing the Sysplex environment for the company used in this sample scenario. The following section provides more details on this sample implementation.

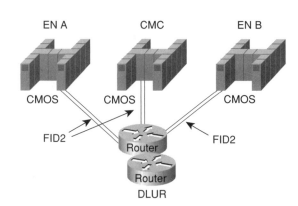

Figure 6–30
Sysplex with DLUR using
CIP—option three.

The Company's Network

The company used in this example has a very large IP backbone and a very large SNA network. Today, its multiprotocol and SNA network are separate. The company's goal is to consolidate the traffic across the multiprotocol Internet. The company has chosen IP as its strategic backbone protocol of choice. To transport the SNA traffic, DLSw+ is used.

In the data center, the company plans to support five different IBM Sysplex environments. Its objective is to have the highest degree of redundancy and fault tolerance. The administrators decided not to run APPN throughout their existing multiprotocol network but chose APPN in the data center to provide the required level of redundancy.

Figure 6–31 shows the configuration of the company's data center. The diagram on the top right in this figure is a logical view of one Sysplex environment and how it is connected to the multiprotocol network through the CIP/CSNA routers and the APPN routers. Each CIP/CSNA router has two parallel channel adapters to each Sysplex host (Sysplex 1 and Sysplex 2) through separate ESCON Directors. To meet the company's high availability requirement, this configuration has no single points of failure.

In each Sysplex environment, there are a minimum of two network nodes per Sysplex acting as a DLUS. VTAM NNA is designated as the primary DLUS node. NNB is designated the backup DLUS. The remaining hosts are data hosts configured as end nodes. These end node data hosts use NNA as the network-node server.

There are two CIP routers to support every Sysplex environment and at least two APPN routers running DLUR to provide boundary functions support for remote devices. The traffic is expected to load share across the two CIP routers. Consequently, APPN provides load balancing and redundancy in this environment.

Figure 6–31
Example of APPN in the data center.

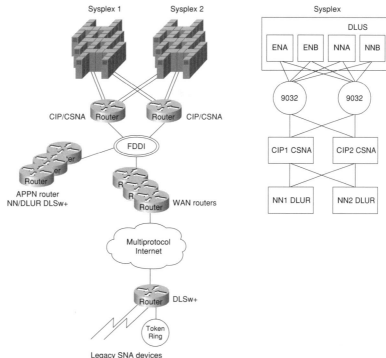

Legend labels: Sysplex 1, Sysplex 2, Sysplex, DLUS, ENA, ENB, NNA, NNB, 9032, 9032, CIP/CSNA, Router, Router, CIP/CSNA, FDDI, CIP1 CSNA, CIP2 CSNA, NN1 DLUR, NN2 DLUR, Router, Router, APPN router NN/DLUR DLSw+, Router, WAN routers, Multiprotocol Internet, Router DLSw+, Token Ring, Legacy SNA devices

Sample Configuration

From an APPN standpoint, NNA in Figure 6–31 can be configured as the primary DLUS. NNB can be configured as the backup DLUS. The following is a configuration example for NN1. NN2 would be configured similarly.

```
!
appn control-point CISCONET.NN1
  dlus CISCONET.NNA
  backup-dlus CISCONET.NNB
  dlur
  complete
```

When the primary DLUS host goes out of service for any reason, the DLUR node is disconnected from its serving DLUS. The DLUR node retries the DLUS/DLUR pipe with NNA. If unsuccessful, it tries its backup DLUS.

To achieve load balancing, every DLUR router defines two parallel APPN transmission groups with equal weights to every VTAM host using the following configuration:

```
!
! Link to VTAM ENA via CIP router 1
!
appn link-station LINK1ENA
  port FDDI0
```

```
    lan-dest-address 4000.3000.1001
    complete
!
! Link to VTAM ENA via CIP router 2
!
appn link-station LINK2ENA
    port FDDI0
    lan-dest-address 4000.3000.2001
    complete
!
! Link to VTAM ENB via CIP router 1
!
appn link-station LINK1ENB
    port FDDI0
    lan-dest-address 4000.3000.1002
    complete
!
! Link to VTAM ENB via CIP router 2
!
appn link-station LINK2ENB
    port FDDI0
    lan-dest-address 4000.3000.2002
    complete
!
! Link to Primary DLUS NNA via CIP router 1
!
appn link-station LINK1NNA
    port FDDI0
    lan-dest-address 4000.3000.1003
    complete
!
! Link to Primary DLUS NNA via CIP router 2
!
appn link-station LINK2NNA
    port FDDI0
    lan-dest-address 4000.3000.2003
    complete
!
! Link to Backup DLUS NNB via CIP router 1
!
appn link-station LINK1NNB
    port FDDI0
    lan-dest-address 4000.3000.1004
    complete
!
! Link to Backup DLUS NNB via CIP router 2
!
appn link-station LINK2NNB
    port FDDI0
    lan-dest-address 4000.3000.2004
    complete
```

As shown in the preceding configuration, NN1 defines two APPN transmission groups to ENA, ENB, NNA and NNB. There are two channel attachments to each host and each attachment is connected to separate hardware (for example, a CIP card, CIP router, ESCON Director). Reasons to have duplicate hardware include provision for the loss of any physical component; if this happens the host is still accessible using the alternative path.

From an APPN perspective, there are two transmission groups that connect a DLUR router and every host. One transmission group traverses CIP Router 1 and the other traverses CIP Router 2. When one path fails, the APPN transmission group becomes inoperative. The second transmission group provides an alternative route for host connection through the other path.

All the subarea SSCP/PU and SSCP/LU sessions flow on one of the transmission groups between the DLUR router and the primary DLUS host. As for the LU-LU sessions, the two possible routes between the DLUR router and a VTAM host are available. The DLUR router and a VTAM host select one of these two routes at random for the LU-LU sessions. This randomization provides a certain amount of load distribution across the two CIP routers, although it might not necessarily be statistically load balanced.

There are multiple DLUR routers that support downstream SNA devices. The following is a sample configuration for DLUR router NN1:

```
source-bridge ring-group 100
dlsw local-peer peer-id 172.18.3.111 promiscuous
!
interface FDDI0
 ip address 172.18.3.111 255.255.255.0
!
appn control-point NETA.NN1
  complete
!
appn port VDLC1 vdlc
  vdlc 100 4000.1000.2000
  complete
```

The following is a sample configuration for DLUR router NN2:

```
source-bridge ring-group 200
dlsw local-peer peer-id 172.18.3.112 promiscuous
!
interface FDDI0
 ip address 172.18.3.112 255.255.255.0
!
appn control-point NETA.NN2
  complete
!
appn port VDLC2 vdlc
  vdlc 200 4000.1000.2000
  complete
```

A workstation gains access to the host through the DLUR router. A workstation defines 4000.1000.2000 as the destination MAC address in the emulation software. This virtual MAC address is defined to every DLUR router. When initiating a connection, a workstation sends an all-routes broadcast Test command frame to the MAC address to which it wants to connect. The remote DLSw+ router sends an explorer frame to its peers. Both NN1 and NN2 respond with **ICANREACH**. The DLSw+ router is configured to use the load balancing mode. This means that the DLSw+ router caches both NN1 and NN2 as peers that can reach the host. Host sessions are established through NN1 and NN2 in a round robin fashion. This allows the company to spread its SNA traffic over two or more DLUR routers. If NN1 becomes unavailable, sessions that traverse NN1 are disruptive but they can be re-established through NN2 with negligible impact.

This design increases overall availability by using duplicate virtual MAC address on the DLUR router. The dual paths provide the option for a secondary path to be available for use when the primary path is unavailable. Another advantage is that this design allows for easy scaling. For example, when the number of SNA devices increases, buffer memory might become a constraint on the DLUR routers. The company can add a DLUR router to support the increased session load. This topology change does not require any network administration from any remote routers or the data center routers.

Example of APPN with FRAS BNN

This section describes the design considerations when building a large enterprise APPN network. It lists the current technologies that allow the company in this example to build a large APPN network. Each option is discussed in detail. FRAS BNN is chosen as an interim scalability solution to reduce the number of network nodes in the network. This allows the network to scale to meet the company's expanding requirements.

In this example, a government agency has a network that consists of one data center and approximately 100 remote sites. Within the next few years, its network is expected to increase to 500 remote sites.

Figure 6–32 shows a simplified version of the agency's current APPN network.

The data center consists of 20 mainframe processors from IBM and a variety of other vendors. The IBM mainframes are MVS-based and are running VTAM. They are also configured as NN/DLUS and EN data hosts. No subarea protocol exists in this network. Other non-IBM mainframes are configured as either an EN or LEN node.

The user platform is OS/2 running Communications Server at all the remote sites with connectivity needs to the data center mainframe computers. Initially, there are no any-to-any communication requirements in this network. The applications supported are LU type 2 and LU6.2.

APPN in the Data Center

The host mainframes in Figure 6–32 are connected using the external communication adapter (XCA) connection over the 3172 Interconnect Controllers. The non-IBM data hosts (Companies A, B, and C) use the VTAM IBM mainframe as the network-node server. To keep the amount of TDU flows to a minimum, CP-CP sessions exist only between VTAM and the data center routers. There are no CP-CP sessions among the routers located at the data center.

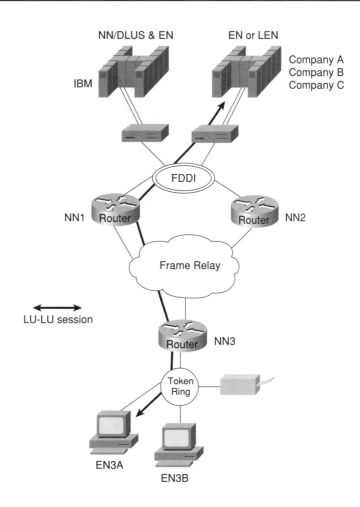

Figure 6–32
Sample APPN network for a government agency.

To achieve the optimal route calculation without explicitly defining meshed connection definitions, every end node and network node at the data center is connected to the same connection network. This allows a session to be directly established between two data center resources without traversing the VTAM network node. As Figure 6–32 shows, when an LU-LU session between resources at EN3A and Company A's mainframe is set up, the optimal route is directly through the FDDI ring to NN1 and NN3.

To reduce the number of broadcast searches to a maximum of one per resource, VTAM is configured as the CDS in this network. The CDS function is very effective in this network because the resources in the network require access only to resources at the host mainframes in the data center. These host mainframes register their resources with VTAM, which is their network-node server. Consequently, VTAM always has location information for every resource at the data center. This means that VTAM never has to perform LOCATE broadcast searches.

APPN in the Remote Site

The network depicted in Figure 6–32 has approximately 30 to 40 CS/2 workstations in every remote site. Every user workstation is configured as an end node. Each end node supports eight independent LU6.2 sessions and four dependent LU sessions. A Cisco router at every location forwards the traffic to the data center. The router's network node function provides the intermediate routing node function for the independent LUs. The DLUR function provides the dependent LU routing function for the dependent LUs.

Future Configuration

This network will eventually consist of 500 remote network node routers, 100 data center routers, and eight mainframe computers. Typically, a 600-node APPN network will have scalability issues. The rest of this section examines the following two options that you can use to address scalability issues in an APPN network:

- Implementing border node on VTAM to partition the network into smaller subnets
- Using FRAS BNN to reduce the number of network nodes in the network

Using Border Node on VTAM to Partition the Network into Smaller Subnets

By implementing the concept of border node on VTAM, a peripheral subnetwork boundary is introduced between NN1 and VTAM, and between NN2 and VTAM, as shown in Figure 6–33.

There would be no topology information exchange between VTAM and the data center NN routers. The eight mainframe computers would be in the same subnet. Every data center router would support multiple access routers and they would form their own subnet. Each subnet is limited to a maximum of 100 network nodes. This configuration would prevent topology information from being sent from one subnet to another, thus allowing the network to scale to over 600 network nodes.

Although this approach addresses the TDU flow issue, there is a considerable loss of functions, however, by configuring VTAM as a border node in this environment. First, two APPN subnetworks cannot be connected through a connection network. LU-LU sessions between resources at Company A's host and remote resources would be set up through an indirect route through the VTAM border node. This is clearly not an optimal route. Second, the central directory server function is lost because the VTAM border node portrays an end node image to NN1. This prevents NN1 from discovering the central directory server in the network.

The next section examines an alternative approach of using FRAS BNN to reduce the number of network nodes in the network.

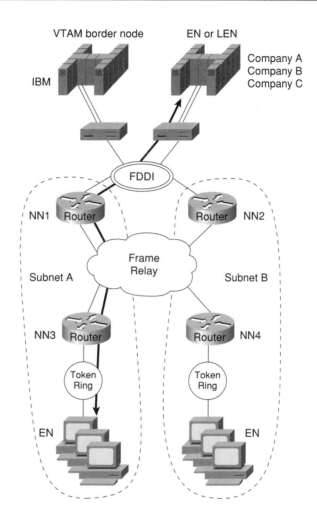

Figure 6–33
APPN network with VTAM
extended border node.

Using FRAS BNN to Reduce the Number of Network Nodes

Figure 6–34 shows how FRAS BNN can be used to reduce the number of network nodes in the company's network. All the server applications are on the mainframe computers and devices only require host access. APPN routing is not essential for this company.

Implementing FRAS BNN rather than a full APPN network node on the access routers directly reduces the number of network nodes. This allows the network to scale without the concern of TDU flows. This is proven to be a viable solution for this company for the time being because LAN-to-LAN connectivity is not an immediate requirement. The remote routers can be migrated to support APPN border node when it becomes available.

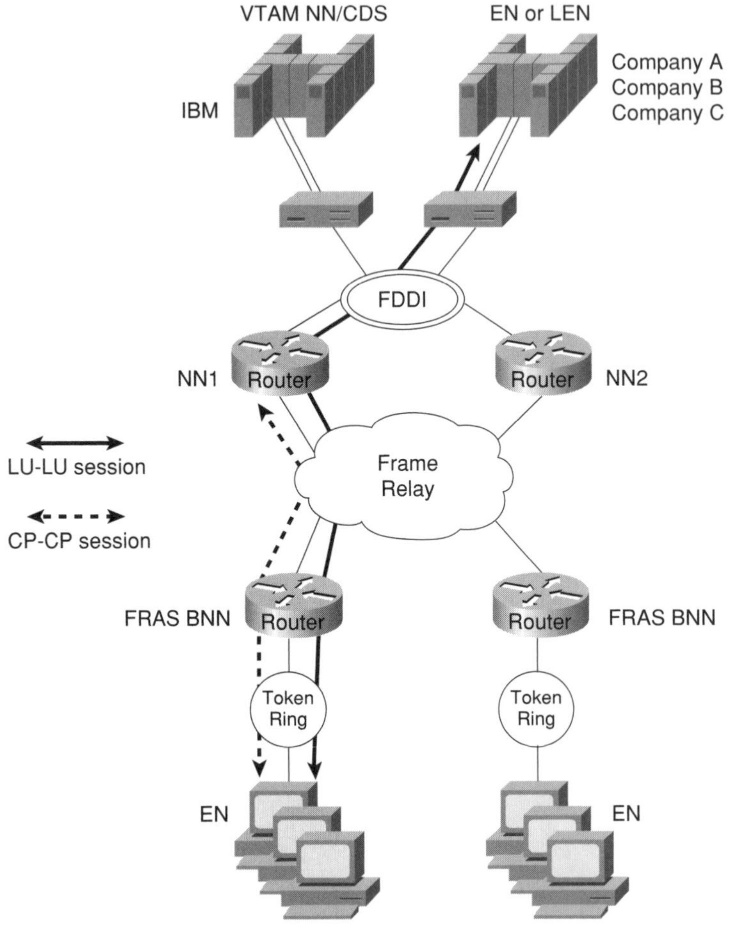

Figure 6–34
APPN network with FRAS
BNN.

Figure 6–34
APPN network with FRAS BNN.

In this environment, CP-CP sessions are supported over the Frame Relay network. The central directory server and the concept of Connection Network are fully supported. LU-LU sessions can be set up using the direct route without traversing VTAM, as shown in Figure 6–34. The only function that is lost with FRAS BNN is COS for traffic traveling from the remote FRAS BNN router to the data center.

SUMMARY

Recall that this chapter discussed developing the network design and planning a successful migration to APPN. It covered the following topics:

- Evolution of SNA
- When to Use APPN as Part of a Network Design
- When to Use APPN Versus Alternative Methods of SNA Transport
- Overview of APPN
- Scalability Issues
- Backup Techniques in an APPN Network
- APPN in a Multiprotocol Environment
- Network Management
- Configuration Examples

Designing DLSw+ Internetworks

This chapter contains the following information:

- Introduction to DLSw+
- Getting Started with DLSw+
- DLSw+ Advanced Features

INTRODUCTION TO DLSw+

This section describes *Data Link Switching Plus* (DLSw+) and provides configuration examples to enable you to quickly design and configure simple DLSw+ networks. It reviews the key components of the data-link switching (DLSw+) features and describes the extensions to the standard that are included in DLSw+. This section also describes advanced features, tells when to use them, and includes examples of how to use these features. It provides tuning, hierarchical design, meshed design, debug, and migration guidance. Finally, it recommends how to proceed with designing your network. This section can be used as a reference only (for configuration examples), as a tuning guide, or as a guide to design a complete DLSw+ network.

DLSw+ Defined

DLSw+ is a means of transporting Systems Network Architecture (SNA) and NetBIOS traffic over a campus or wide-area network (WAN). The end systems can attach to the network over Token Ring, Ethernet, Synchronous Data Link Control (SDLC) protocol, Qualified Logical Link Control (QLLC), or Fiber Distributed Data Interface (FDDI). (FDDI is supported on the Cisco 7000 series only and requires Cisco IOS Release11.2 or later.) DLSw+ switches between diverse media and locally terminates the data links, keeping acknowledgments, keepalives, and polling off the WAN. Local termination of data links also eliminates data-link control timeouts that can occur during transient network congestion or when rerouting around failed links. Finally, DLSw+ provides a mechanism for dynamically searching a network for SNA or NetBIOS resources and includes caching algorithms that minimize broadcast traffic.

In this document, DLSw+ routers are referred to as peer routers, peers, or partners. The connection between two DLSw+ routers is referred to as a peer connection. A DLSw+ circuit compromises the data-link control connection between the originating end system and the originating router, the connection between the two routers (typically a Transport Control Protocol [TCP] connection), and the data-link control connection between the target router and the target end system. A single peer connection can carry multiple circuits.

DLSw+ supports circuits between SNA physical units (PUs) or between NetBIOS clients and servers. The SNA PU connectivity supported is PU 2.0/2.1-to-PU 4 (attached via any supported data-link controls), PU 1-to-PU 4 (SDLC only), PU 4-to-PU 4 (Token Ring only), and PU 2.1-to-PU 2.1 (any supported data-link control). See Appendix B for details about DLSw+ connectivity.

NOTES

N PU 4-to-PU 4 connectivity supports only a single path between front-end processors (FEPs) because of an idiosyncrasy in how FEPs treat duplicate source-route bridged paths. In addition, remote load is not supported.

DLSw Standard

The DLSw standard was defined at the Advanced Peer-to-Peer Networking (APPN) Implementers Workshop (AIW) in the DLSw-related interest group. The current standard is Version 1, which is documented in RFC 1795. RFC 1795 makes obsolete RFC 1434, which described IBM's original 6611 implementation of DLSw.

The DLSw standard describes the Switch-to-Switch Protocol (SSP) used between routers (called data-link switches) to establish DLSw peer connections, locate resources, forward data, handle flow control, and perform error recovery. RFC 1795 requires that data-link connections are terminated at the peer routers, that is, the data-link connections are locally acknowledged and, in the case of Token Ring, the routing information field (RIF) ends at a virtual ring in the peering router.

By locally terminating data-link control connections, the DLSw standard eliminates the requirement for link-layer acknowledgments and keepalive messages to flow across the WAN. In addition, because link-layer frames are acknowledged locally, link-layer timeouts should not occur. It is the responsibility of the DLSw routers to multiplex the traffic of multiple data-link controls to the appropriate TCP pipe and to transport the data reliably across an IP backbone. Before any end-system communication can occur over DLSw, the following must take place:

- Establish peer connections
- Exchange capabilities
- Establish circuit

Establish Peer Connections

Before two routers can switch SNA or NetBIOS traffic, they must establish two TCP connections between them. The standard allows one of these TCP connections to be dropped if it is not required. (Cisco routers will drop the extra TCP connection unless they are communicating with another vendor's router that requires two TCP connections.) The standard also allows additional TCP connections to be made to allow for different levels of priority.

Exchange Capabilities

After the TCP connections are established, the routers exchange their capabilities. Capabilities include the DLSw version number, initial pacing windows (receive window size), NetBIOS support, list of supported link service access points (SAPs), and the number of TCP sessions supported. Media Access Control (MAC) address lists and NetBIOS name lists can also be exchanged at this time, and if desired, a DLSw partner can specify that it does not want to receive certain types of search frames. It is possible to configure the MAC addresses and NetBIOS names of all resources that will use DLSw and thereby avoid any broadcasts. After the capabilities exchange, the DLSw partners are ready to establish circuits between SNA or NetBIOS end systems.

Establish Circuit

Circuit establishment between a pair of end systems includes locating the target resource (based on its destination MAC address or NetBIOS name) and setting up data-link control connections between each end system and its data-link switch (local router). SNA and NetBIOS are handled differently. SNA devices on a LAN find other SNA devices by sending an explorer frame (a TEST or an exchange identification [XID] frame) with the MAC address of the target SNA device. When a DLSw router receives an explorer frame, the router sends a *canureach frame* to each of the DLSw partners. If one of its DLSw partners can reach the specified MAC address, the partner replies with an *icanreach frame*. The specific sequence includes a *canureach ex* (explorer) to find the resource and a *canureach cs* (circuit setup) that triggers the peering routers to establish a circuit.

At this point, the DLSw partners establish a *circuit* that consists of three connections: the two data-link control connections between each router and the locally attached SNA end system, and the TCP connection between the DLSw partners. This circuit is uniquely identified by the source and destination circuit IDs, which are carried in all steady state data frames in lieu of data-link control addresses such as MAC addresses. Each circuit ID is defined by the destination and source MAC addresses, destination and source link service access points (LSAPs), and a data-link control port ID. The circuit concept simplifies management and is important in error processing and cleanup. Once the circuit is established, information frames can flow over the circuit.

NetBIOS circuit establishment is similar, but instead of forwarding a canureach frame that specifies a MAC address, DLSw routers send a name query (NetBIOS NAME-QUERY) frame that specifies a NetBIOS name. Instead of an icanreach frame, there is a *name recognized* (NetBIOS NAME-RECOGNIZED) frame.

Most DLSw implementations cache information learned as part of the explorer processing so that subsequent searches for the same resource do not result in the sending of additional explorer frames.

Flow Control

The DLSw standard describes adaptive pacing between DLSw routers but does not indicate how to map this to the native data-link control flow control on the edges. The DLSw standard specifies flow control on a per-circuit basis and calls for two independent, unidirectional circuit flow-control mechanisms. Flow control is handled by a windowing mechanism that can dynamically adapt to buffer availability, TCP transmit queue depth, and end-station flow-control mechanisms. Windows can be incremented, decremented, halved, or reset to zero.

The granted units (the number of units that the sender has permission to send) are incremented with a flow-control indication from the receiver (similar to classic SNA session-level pacing). Flow-control indicators can be one of the following types:

- *Repeat*—Increment granted units by the current window size
- *Increment*—Increment the window size by one and increment granted units by the new window size
- *Decrement*—Decrement window size by one and increment granted units by the new window size
- *Reset*—Decrease window to zero and set granted units to zero to stop all transmission in one direction until an increment flow-control indicator is sent
- *Half*—Cut the current window size in half and increment granted units by the new window size

Flow-control indicators and flow-control acknowledgments can be piggybacked on information frames or can be sent as independent flow-control messages, but reset indicators are always sent as independent messages.

DLSw+ Features

DLSw+ is Cisco's implementation of DLSw. It goes beyond the standard to include the advanced features of Cisco's current remote source-route bridging (RSRB) and provides additional functionality to increase the overall scalability of DLSw. DLSw+ includes enhancements in the following areas:

- *Scalability*—Constructs IBM internetworks in a way that reduces the amount of broadcast traffic and therefore enhances their scalability
- *Availability*—Dynamically finds alternative paths quickly, and optionally load-balances across multiple active peers, ports, and channel gateways
- *Transport flexibility*—Higher-performance transport options when there is enough bandwidth to handle the traffic load without risk of timeouts, and the option to use

lower-overhead solutions when bandwidth is at a premium and nondisruptive rerouting is not required

- *Modes of operation*—Dynamically detects the capabilities of the peer router, and operates according to those capabilities

DLSw+ Improved Scalability

One of the most significant factors that limits the size of LAN internetworks is the amount of explorer traffic that traverses the WAN. There are several optimizations in DLSw+ to reduce the number of explorers.

Peer Group Concept

Perhaps the most significant optimization in DLSw+ is a feature known as *peer groups*. Peer groups are designed to address the broadcast replication that occurs in a fully meshed network. When any-to-any communication is required (for example, for NetBIOS or APPN environments), RSRB or standard DLSw implementations require peer connections between every pair of routers.

This setup is not only difficult to configure, it results in branch access routers having to replicate search requests for each peer connection. This wastes bandwidth and router cycles. A better concept is to group routers into clusters and designate a focal router to be responsible for broadcast replication. This capability is included in DLSw+.

With DLSw+, a cluster of routers in a region or a division of a company can be combined into a peer group. Within a peer group, one or more of the routers are designated to be the *border peer*s. Instead of all routers peering to one another, each router within a group peers to the border peer; border peers establish peer connections with each other (see Figure 7–1). When a DLSw+ router receives a TEST frame or NetBIOS NAME-QUERY, it sends a single explorer frame to its border peer. The border peer forwards the explorer on behalf of the peer group member. This setup eliminates duplicate explorers on the access links and minimizes the processing required in access routers.

Figure 7–1
The peer group concept can be used to simplify and scale any-to-any networks.

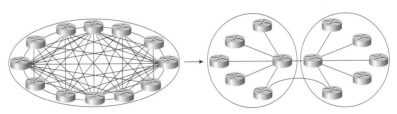

Once the correct destination router is found, an end-to-end peer connection (TCP or IP) is established to carry end-system traffic. This connection remains active as long as there is end-system traffic on it, and it is dynamically torn down when not in use, permitting casual, any-to-any communication without the burden of specifying peer connections in advance. It also allows any-to-any routing in large internetworks in which persistent TCP connections between every pair of routers would not be possible.

Explorer Firewalls

To further reduce the amount of explorer traffic that enters the WAN, there are a number of filter and firewall techniques to terminate the explorer traffic at the DLSw+ router. A key feature is the explorer firewall.

An explorer firewall permits only a single explorer for a particular destination MAC address to be sent across the WAN. While an explorer is outstanding and awaiting a response from the destination, subsequent explorers for that MAC address are not propagated. After the explorer response is received at the originating DLSw+, all subsequent explorers receive an immediate local response. This eliminates the start-of-day explorer storm that many networks experience.

DLSw+ Enhanced Availability

One way DLSw+ offers enhanced availability is by maintaining a reachability cache of multiple paths for local and remote destination MAC addresses or NetBIOS names. For remote resources, the path specifies the peer to use to reach this resource. For local resources, the path specifies a port number. If there are multiple paths to reach a resource, the router will mark one path preferred and all other paths capable. If the preferred path is not available, the next available path is promoted to the new preferred path, and recovery over an alternative path is initiated immediately. The way that multiple capable paths are handled with DLSw+ can be biased to meet the needs of the network:

- *Fault tolerance*—Biases circuit establishment over a preferred path, but also rapidly reconnects on an active alternative path if the preferred path is lost

- *Load balancing*—Distributes circuit establishment over multiple DLSw+ peers in the network or ports on the router

The default for DLSw+ is to use fault-tolerant mode. In this mode, when a DLSw+ peer receives a TEST frame for a remote resource, it checks its cache. If it finds an entry and the entry is fresh (that is, if it is not verified within the last verify interval), the DLSw+ peer responds immediately to the test frame and does not send a canureach frame across the network. If the cache entry is stale, the originating DLSw+ peer sends a canureach directly to each peer in the cache to validate the cache entries (this is known as a directed verify). If any peer does not respond, it is deleted from the list. This may result in reordering the cache. The SNA-VERIFY-INTERVAL is configurable and is the length of time a router waits before marking the cache entry stale. The SNA-CACHE-TIMEOUT is the interval that cache entries are maintained before they are deleted. It defaults to 16 minutes and is configurable.

At the destination DLSw+ router, a slightly different procedure is followed using the local cache entries. If the cache entry is fresh, the response is sent immediately. If the cache entry is stale, a single route broadcast test frame is sent over all the ports in the cache. If a positive response is received, an icanreach frame is sent to the originating router. Test frames are sent every 30 seconds (SNA-RETRY-INTERVAL) for a three-minute period (SNA-EXPLORER-TIMEOUT). These timers are configurable.

Alternatively, when there are duplicate paths to the destination end system, you can configure load balancing, which causes DLSw+ to alternate new circuit requests in a round-robin fashion through the list of capable peers or ports.

This feature is especially attractive in SNA networks. A very common practice used in the hierarchical SNA environment is assigning the same MAC address to different mainframe channel gateways—for example, FEPs or Cisco routers with Channel Interface Processors (CIPs). If one channel gateway is unavailable, alternative channel gateways are dynamically located without any operator intervention. Duplicate MAC addressing also allows load balancing across multiple active channel gateways or Token Ring adapters.

DLSw+ ensures that duplicate MAC addresses are found, and it caches up to four DLSw peers or interface ports that can be used to find the MAC address. This technique can be used for fault tolerance and load balancing. When using this technique for fault tolerance, it facilitates a timely reconnection after circuit outages. When using this technique for load balancing, it improves overall SNA performance by spreading traffic across multiple active routers, Token Ring or FDDI adapters, or channel gateways, as shown in Figure 7–2. Load balancing not only enhances performance, it also speeds up recovery from the loss of any component in a path through the network because a smaller portion of the network is affected by the loss of any single component.

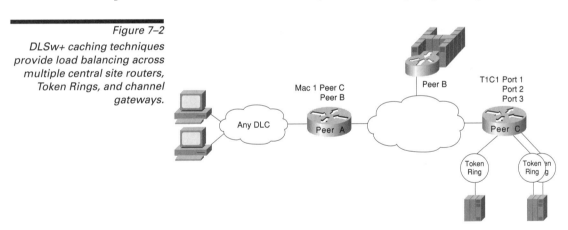

Figure 7–2

DLSw+ caching techniques provide load balancing across multiple central site routers, Token Rings, and channel gateways.

In addition to supporting multiple active peers, DLSw+ supports *backup peers*, which are only connected when the primary peer is unreachable.

DLSw+ Transport Flexibility

The transport connection between DLSw+ routers can vary according to the needs of the network and is not tied to TCP/IP as the DLSw standard is. Cisco supports four transport protocols between DLSw+ routers:

- *TCP/IP*—Transports SNA and NetBIOS traffic across WANs when local acknowledgment is required to minimize unnecessary traffic and prevent data-link control timeouts and when nondisruptive rerouting around link failures is critical; this transport option is required when DLSw+ is operating in DLSw standard mode.

- *FST/IP*—Transports SNA and NetBIOS traffic across WANs with an arbitrary topology; this solution allows rerouting around link failures, but recovery may be disruptive depending on the time required to find an alternative path; this option does not support local acknowledgment of frames.

- *Direct*—Transports SNA and NetBIOS traffic across a point-to-point or Frame Relay connection when the benefits of an arbitrary topology are not important and when nondisruptive rerouting around link failures is not required; this option does not support local acknowledgment of frames.

- *DLSw Lite*—Transports SNA and NetBIOS traffic across a point-to-point connection (currently only Frame Relay is supported) when local acknowledgment and reliable transport are important, but when nondisruptive rerouting around link failures is not required; DLSw Lite uses RFC 1490 encapsulation of Logical Link Control type 2 (LLC2).

DLSw+ Modes of Operation

Cisco has been shipping IBM internetworking products for many years. There is a substantial installed base of Cisco routers running RSRB today. Therefore, it is essential for DLSw+ and RSRB to coexist in the same network and in the same router. In addition, because DLSw+ is based on the new DLSw standard, it must also interoperate with other vendors' implementations that are based on that DLSw standard.

There are three modes of operation for DLSw+:

- *Dual mode*—A Cisco router can communicate with some remote peers using RSRB and with others using DLSw+, providing a smooth migration path from RSRB to DLSw+. In dual mode, RSRB and DLSw+ coexist on the same box; the local peer must be configured for both RSRB and DLSw+; and the remote peers must be configured for either RSRB or DLSw, but not both.

- *Standards compliance mode*—DLSw+ can detect automatically (via the DLSw capabilities exchange) if the participating router is manufactured by another vendor, therefore operating in DLSw standard mode.

- *Enhanced mode*—DLSw+ can detect automatically that the participating router is another DLSw+ router, therefore operating in enhanced mode, making all the features of DLSw+ available to the SNA and NetBIOS end systems.

Some of the enhanced DLSw+ features are also available when a Cisco router is operating in standards-compliance mode with another vendor's router. In particular, enhancements that are locally controlled options on a router can be accessed even though the remote router does not have DLSw+. These enhancements include load balancing, local learning (the capability to determine whether a destination is on a LAN before sending canureach frames across a WAN), explorer firewalls, and media conversion.

How to Proceed

If you have a simple hierarchical network with a small volume of SNA traffic, read the "Getting Started with DLSw+" section, which describes what configuration commands are required in all DLSw+ implementations and provides configuration examples for SDLC, Token Ring, Ethernet, and QLLC. After reading the "Getting Started" section, you can read about advanced features, customization, and bandwidth management.

This chapter describes how to use DLSw+ in conjunction with downstream physical unit (DSPU) concentration, LAN Network Manager, APPN, and native client interface architecture (NCIA).

GETTING STARTED WITH DLSW+

This section describes the basic configuration commands required for a DLSw+ network. It begins with a description of the minimum required configuration and then provides examples for Token Ring, Ethernet, SDLC, and QLLC environments. If you are unfamiliar with router configuration, you should also review the examples in Appendix A, "Subnetting an IP Address Space." These examples illustrate how to configure not only routers, but also the attaching end systems. They show how to configure canonical addresses, static routes, and loopback addresses.

Minimum Required Configuration

Configuring DLSw+ on most networks is not difficult. Every router that supports DLSw+ must have a **dlsw local-peer** command; **dlsw remote-peer** commands are optional, but usually at least one side of a peer connection must configure a remote peer. If a DLSw+ peer configuration omits **dlsw remote-peer** commands, the **dlsw local-peer** command must specify the **promiscuous** keyword. Promiscuous routers will accept peer connection requests from routers that are not preconfigured. This feature allows you to minimize changes to central site routers when branch offices are added or deleted. It also minimizes required coordination of configurations.

If you have used RSRB in the past, you need to know what *not* to configure. With DLSw+, you do not need proxy explorer, NetBIOS name caching, SDLC-to-LLC2 conversion (SDLLC), or source-route translational bridging (SR/TLB). All of these features are built into DLSw+.

In Figure 7–3, the branch router specifies both a **dlsw local-peer** and a **dlsw remote-peer** command. The headquarters router specifies only a **dlsw local-peer** command, but it specifies **promiscuous** on the **dlsw local-peer** command to allow it to dynamically accept connections from branch routers. The peer ID specified on the **dlsw local-peer** command is the router's IP address. It can be a loopback address configured via **interface loopback 0** or the IP address associated with a specific LAN or WAN interface. However, if you use a LAN or WAN IP address, the interface must be up for DLSw to work.

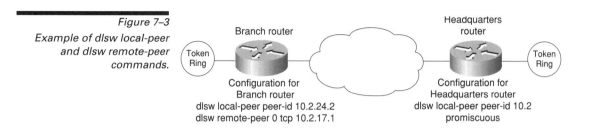

Figure 7–3

Example of dlsw local-peer and dlsw remote-peer commands.

Configuration for
Branch router
dlsw local-peer peer-id 10.2.24.2
dlsw remote-peer 0 tcp 10.2.17.1

Configuration for
Headquarters router
dlsw local-peer peer-id 10.2
promiscuous

The number following **dlsw remote-peer** is the ring list number. Ring lists are an advanced topic, so for now, specify zero in this space, which indicates that ring lists are not in use. There are other options on the **dlsw local-peer** and **dlsw remote-peer** commands, but they are not required. These options are covered in the "DLSw+ Advanced Features" section later in this chapter.

In addition to specifying local and remote peers, you must map the following local data-link controls to DLSw:

- *Token Ring*—Define a virtual ring using the source-bridge ring-group command and include a source-bridge command that tells the router to bridge from the external Token Ring to that virtual ring.

- *Ethernet*—Map a specific Ethernet bridge group to DLSw.

- *SDLC*—Define the SDLC devices and map the SDLC addresses to DLSw+ virtual MAC addresses.

- *QLLC*—Define the X.25 devices and map the X.25 addresses to DLSw+ virtual MAC addresses.

- *FDDI*—Define a virtual ring using the source-bridge ring-group command and include an SRB statement that tells the router to bridge from the external FDDI to that virtual ring; FDDI is supported in Cisco IOS Release 11.2 on the Cisco 7000 series.

The rest of this section provides sample configurations for Token Ring, Ethernet, SDLC, and QLLC.

Token Ring

Figure 7–4 shows a sample DLSw+ configuration for Token Ring. Traffic that originates on Token Ring is source-route bridged from the local ring onto a source-bridge ring group and then picked up by DLSw+. You must include a **source-bridge ring-group** command that specifies a virtual ring number. In addition, you must include a **source-bridge** command that tells the router to bridge from the physical Token Ring to the virtual ring.

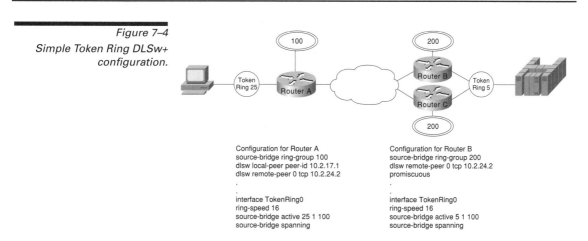

Figure 7–4
Simple Token Ring DLSw+
configuration.

Configuration for Router A
source-bridge ring-group 100
dlsw local-peer peer-id 10.2.17.1
dlsw remote-peer 0 tcp 10.2.24.2
.

.
interface TokenRing0
ring-speed 16
source-bridge active 25 1 100
source-bridge spanning

Configuration for Router B
source-bridge ring-group 200
dlsw remote-peer 0 tcp 10.2.24.2
promiscuous
.

.
interface TokenRing0
ring-speed 16
source-bridge active 5 1 100
source-bridge spanning

DLSw+ supports RIF termination, which means that all remote devices appear to be attached to the virtual ring specified in the **source-bridge** command. In Figure 7–4, from the host end, all the devices attached to Router A appear to reside on Virtual Ring 200. Conversely, from the remote site, the FEP appears to reside on Virtual Ring 100. As illustrated in this figure, the virtual rings specified in peer routers do not have to match. If multiple routers are attached to the same physical ring, as shown in Routers B and C, by specifying the same ring group number in each of them, you can prevent explorers from coming in from the WAN and being forwarded back onto the WAN.

Ethernet

Traffic that originates on Ethernet is picked up from the local Ethernet bridge group and transported across the DLSw network. DLSw always transfers data in noncanonical format. In Figure 7–5, you do not need to configure the left router for translational bridging or worry about what media resides on the other side of the WAN. DLSw will automatically make the correct MAC address conversion depending on the destination media. When DLSw+ receives a MAC address from an Ethernet-attached device, it assumes it is canonical and converts it to noncanonical for transport to the remote peer. At the remote peer, the address is either passed unchanged to Token Ring-attached end systems or converted back to canonical if the destination media is Ethernet. Note that when an SNA resource resides on Ethernet, if you configure a destination SNA address in that device, you must use canonical format. For example, Ethernet-attached 3174s must specify the MAC address of the FEP in canonical format. If the Token Ring or noncanonical format of the MAC address of the FEP is 4000.3745.0001, the canonical format is 0200.ECA2.0080

In Figure 7–5, the data is transferred directly to a Cisco router with a Channel Interface Processor (CIP), but it can be any DLSw-compliant router, and the upstream SNA end system can reside on any supported media.

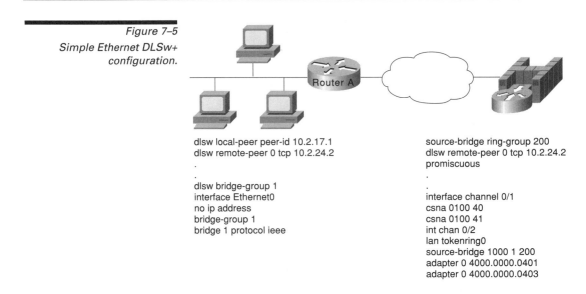

dlsw local-peer peer-id 10.2.17.1
dlsw remote-peer 0 tcp 10.2.24.2
.
.
dlsw bridge-group 1
interface Ethernet0
no ip address
bridge-group 1
bridge 1 protocol ieee

source-bridge ring-group 200
dlsw remote-peer 0 tcp 10.2.24.2
promiscuous
.
.
interface channel 0/1
csna 0100 40
csna 0100 41
int chan 0/2
lan tokenring0
source-bridge 1000 1 200
adapter 0 4000.0000.0401
adapter 0 4000.0000.0403

SDLC

Configuring SDLC devices is a bit more complicated. For SDLC devices, you must know whether the device is a PU 1, PU 2.0, or PU 2.1. For PU 2.0 devices, you must know the IDBLK and IDNUM that was specified in the virtual telecommunications access method (VTAM) for that device because the router plays a greater role in XID processing when SDLC PU 2.0 is involved. You must know if the router is the primary or secondary end of the SDLC line. In addition, if the attachment to the upstream SNA device is over a LAN, you must configure the MAC address of the destination upstream SNA device. In all cases, you must configure a virtual MAC address that will be mapped to an SDLC polling address.

In Figure 7–6, the SDLC-attached devices are each given a common base virtual MAC address of 4000.3174.0000. The router will replace the last two digits of the virtual MAC address with the SDLC address of the device. The device at SDLC address C1 appears to have MAC address 4000.3174.00C1, and the device at SDLC address C2 appears to have MAC address 4000.3174.00C2. In this example, both devices are PU 2.0 devices, so their XID must be configured, and it must match what is specified as the IDBLK and IDNUM in VTAM. In addition, the router always assumes the primary role when attaching upstream from PU 2.0 devices.

The router can be the secondary end of an SDLC line (for example, when connecting to a FEP over SDLC). In this case, specify **secondary** in the **sdlc role** command, and for PU 2.1 devices, specify **xid-passthru** in the **sdlc address** command. In Cisco IOS Release 11.0 and later, DLSw+ supports multidrop PU 2.0/2.1. In Figure 7–7, the multidrop PU 2.0 configuration includes an **sdlc xid** command for each PU 2.0 device.

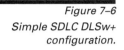

Figure 7–6
Simple SDLC DLSw+
configuration.

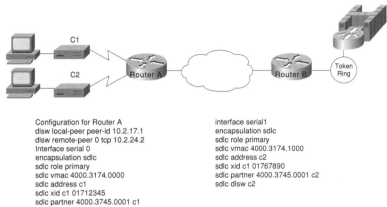

Configuration for Router A
dlsw local-peer peer-id 10.2.17.1
dlsw remote-peer 0 tcp 10.2.24.2
Interface serial 0
encapsulation sdlc
sdlc role primary
sdlc vmac 4000.3174.0000
sdlc address c1
sdlc xid c1 01712345
sdlc partner 4000.3745.0001 c1
sdlc dlsw c1

interface serial1
encapsulation sdlc
sdlc role primary
sdlc vmac 4000.3174.1000
sdlc address c2
sdlc xid c1 01767890
sdlc partner 4000.3745.0001 c2
sdlc dlsw c2

For multidrop lines with a mix of PU 2.1 and 2.0 devices, specify **primary** in the **sdlc role** command. For PU 2.0 devices, you must code the IDBLK and IDNUM in the **sdlc xid** command. For PU 2.1 devices, you can omit the **sdlc xid** command. However, in the **sdlc address** command, you need to specify **xid-poll**. Alternatively, when all devices on a line are PU 2.1, you can specify **sdlc role prim-xid-poll**, in which case you do not need to specify **xid-poll** in each **sdlc address** command.

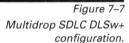

Figure 7–7
Multidrop SDLC DLSw+
configuration.

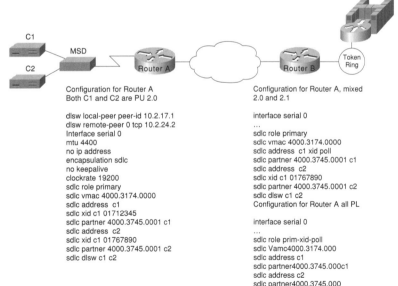

Configuration for Router A
Both C1 and C2 are PU 2.0

dlsw local-peer peer-id 10.2.17.1
dlsw remote-peer 0 tcp 10.2.24.2
Interface serial 0
mtu 4400
no ip address
encapsulation sdlc
no keepalive
clockrate 19200
sdlc role primary
sdlc vmac 4000.3174.0000
sdlc address c1
sdlc xid c1 01712345
sdlc partner 4000.3745.0001 c1
sdlc address c2
sdlc xid c1 01767890
sdlc partner 4000.3745.0001 c2
sdlc dlsw c1 c2

Configuration for Router A, mixed
2.0 and 2.1

interface serial 0
...
sdlc role primary
sdlc vmac 4000.3174.0000
sdlc address c1 xid poll
sdlc partner 4000.3745.0001 c1
sdlc address c2
sdlc xid c1 01767890
sdlc partner 4000.3745.0001 c2
sdlc dlsw c1 c2
Configuration for Router A all PL

interface serial 0
...
sdlc role prim-xid-poll
sdlc Vamc4000.3174.000
sdlc address c1
sdlc partner4000.3745.000c1
sdlc address c2
sdlc partner4000.3745.000

QLLC

QLLC is the data link used by SNA devices when connecting to X.25 networks. QLLC is a legacy protocol developed by IBM to allow the Network Control Program (NCP) to support remote connections over X.25. The software feature on NCP that supports QLLC is called Network Packet Switching Interface. The QLLC protocol derives its name from using the Q-bit in the X.25 header to identify QLLC protocol primitives. QLLC essentially emulates SDLC over X.25. Thus, DLSw+ performs QLLC conversion in a manner similar to SDLC conversion. Cisco's DLSw+ implementation added support for QLLC in Cisco IOS Release 11.0. Because QLLC is more complicated than Token Ring, Ethernet, or SDLC, three examples are included here.

Figure 7–8 shows DLSw+ being used to allow remote devices to connect to a DLSw+ network over an X.25 public packet switched network. In this example, all QLLC traffic is addressed to destination address 4000.1161.1234, which is the MAC address of the FEP. The remote X.25-attached 3174 is given a virtual MAC address of 1000.0000.0001. This virtual MAC address is mapped to the X.121 address of the 3174 (31104150101) in the X.25 attached router.

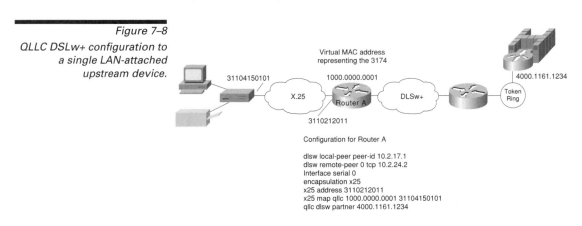

Figure 7–8

QLLC DSLw+ configuration to a single LAN-attached upstream device.

In Figure 7–9, a single 3174 needs to communicate with both an AS/400 and a FEP. The FEP is associated with subaddress 150101, and the AS/400 is associated with subaddress 150102. If an X.25 call comes in for 33204150101, the call is mapped to the FEP and forwarded to MAC address 4000.1161.1234. The 3174 appears to the FEP as a Token Ring-attached resource with MAC address 1000.0000.0001. The 3174 uses a source SAP of 04 when communicating with the FEP.

If an X.25 call comes in for 33204150102, the call is mapped to the AS/400 and forwarded to MAC address 4000.2034.5678. The 3174 appears to the AS/400 as a Token Ring-attached resource with MAC address 1000.0000.0001. The 3174 uses a source SAP of 08 when communicating with the AS/400.

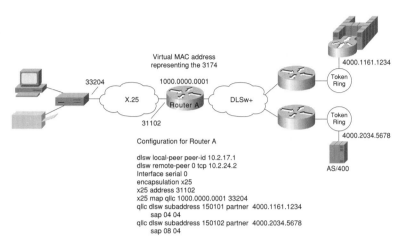

Figure 7–9
QLLC DLSw+ configuration for
support of multiple upstream
LAN-attached devices.

In Figure 7–10, two X.25 resources want to communicate over X.25 to the same FEP. In the router attached to the X.25 network, every X.25 connection request for X.121 address 31102150101 is directed to DLSw+. The **qllc dlsw** command creates a pool of two virtual MAC addresses, starting with 1000.0000.0001. The first switched virtual circuit (SVC) established will be mapped to virtual MAC address 1000.0000.0001. The second SVC will be mapped to virtual MAC address 1000.0000.0002.

Figure 7–10
QLLC DLSw+ configuration for
support of multiple
downstream X.25-attached
devices communicating
through an upstream DLSw+
network.

DLSw+ Advanced Features

This section describes advanced features of DLSw+, the benefits they provide, and a brief description of when and how to use them. Use this section to determine which options you want to use and to learn how to configure those options to address your requirements.

DLSw+ includes features to enhance availability (load balancing, redundancy, and backup peers), improve performance (encapsulation options), minimize broadcasts (ring lists), and build meshed networks (border peers and peer groups). DLSw+ also provides a feature to maximize central site resources and minimize carrier costs (dynamic peers). Advanced features are optional and do not apply in all networks. Each feature includes a description of where it should be used.

How DLSw+ Peers Establish Connections

To understand load balancing, it is useful to understand how DLSw+ peers establish peer connections and find resources. When DLSw+ routers are activated, the first thing they do is establish peer connections with each configured remote peer (unless **passive** is specified, in which case a peer will wait for the remote peer to initiate a peer connection). The routers then exchange their capabilities. Included in the capabilities exchange are any resources configured in **dlsw icanreach** or **dlsw icannotreach** commands. After the capabilities exchange, the DLSw+ peers are idle until an end system sends an explorer frame (explorer frames are SNA TEST or XID frames or NetBIOS NAME-QUERY or ADD NAME-QUERY frames). Explorer frames are forwarded to every active peer and any local ports (other than the port it was received on). It is possible that an end system can be found through multiple remote peers or local ports. The path selected for a given circuit depends on certain advanced configuration options described in this section.

Load Balancing and Redundancy

If you have multiple central site routers supporting DLSw+ for either load balancing or redundancy, this section contains important information. It describes how to balance traffic across multiple central site routers or multiple ports on a single router. Load balancing in this case does not refer to balancing traffic across multiple WAN links or IP paths. That load balancing is done by the underlying IP protocol and is transparent to DLSw+.

If DLSw+ gets multiple positive replies to an explorer, it will cache up to four peers that can be used to reach a remote end system and up to four ports that can be used to reach a local end system. How these cache entries are used depends on whether load balancing is specified on the **dlsw duplicate-path-bias** command. If load balancing is specified, each new circuit request is established over the next path (remote peer or local port) in the cache in a round-robin fashion.

If load balancing is not specified, the peer selects the first path in the cache and sets up all circuits via that path unless the path is unavailable. The first path in the cache list can be one of the following:

- Peer from which the first positive response was received
- Peer with the least cost
- Port over which the first positive response was received

Cost can be specified on either a **dlsw local-peer** or a **dlsw remote-peer** command. When specified on a **dlsw local-peer** command, it is exchanged with remote DLSw+ peers as part of the capabilities exchange. The following example shows how cost can be used to control the path that sessions use.

In Figure 7–11, there are two channel gateways and three Token Ring adapters that can be used to access mainframe applications. All three adapters have been assigned the same MAC address. Assigning duplicate addresses is a common technique for providing load balancing and redundancy in SRB environments. It works because SRB assumes that there are three paths to find the same device and not duplicate LAN addresses. (This technique does not work with transparent bridging.)

Figure 7–11

Possible configuration and the resulting cache entries created when all channel gateways have the same MAC address.

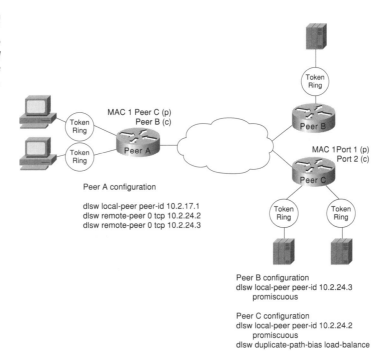

Peer A configuration

dlsw local-peer peer-id 10.2.17.1
dlsw remote-peer 0 tcp 10.2.24.2
dlsw remote-peer 0 tcp 10.2.24.3

Peer B configuration
dlsw local-peer peer-id 10.2.24.3
    promiscuous

Peer C configuration
dlsw local-peer peer-id 10.2.24.2
    promiscuous
dlsw duplicate-path-bias load-balance

In this example, Peer A has **dlsw remote-peer** commands for both Peer B and Peer C. Peer B specifies a cost of four in its **dlsw local-peer** command and Peer C specifies a cost of two. This cost information is exchanged with Peer A during the capabilities exchange.

When the SNA end system (that is, the PU) on the left sends an explorer packet, Peer A forwards the explorer to both Peer B and Peer C. Peer B and Peer C forward the explorer on their local LAN. Peer B will receive a positive reply to the explorer and send a positive response back to Peer A. Peer C will receive two positive replies (one from each port) and will send a positive reply back to Peer A. Peer C records that it has two ports it can use to reach the MAC address of the channel gateway, and Peer A records that it has two peers it can use to reach the MAC address of the channel gateway.

Peer A will forward a positive response to the SNA PU and then establish an end-to-end circuit using Peer C. Peer C is selected because it has a lower cost specified. When the next PU attempts to set up a connection to the same MAC address, it will be set up using Peer C, if available. This is the default method to handle duplicate paths in DLSw+.

At Peer C, the first circuit will be established using Port 1, but the next circuit will use Port 2. This is because Peer C has specified load balancing in the **dlsw duplicate-path-bias** command. Each new SNA PU will use the next path in the list in a round-robin fashion.

Figure 7–11 shows how to cause all remote connections to prefer one peer over another, but the central site load balances traffic across all the LAN adapters on a given channel gateway. Alternatively, load balancing can be specified everywhere to load balance traffic across all central site routers, channel gateways, and LANs. Note that this feature does not require the end systems to be Token Ring-attached. The remote end systems can connect over SDLC, Ethernet, or QLLC, and this feature will still work. The central site channel gateway must be LAN-attached (preferably Token Ring-attached). Duplicate MAC addresses for channel gateways on Ethernet will only work when 1) you have a unique bridged Ethernet segment and a unique DLSw+ router for each duplicate MAC address, and 2) you load balance from the remote sites. (Ethernet has no provision to prevent loops, so care must be taken when building redundant networks with Ethernet LANs. Token Ring networks can rely on SRB for loop prevention.)

An alternative way to specify cost is to use the **dlsw remote-peer** command as shown in Figure 7–12. Specifying **cost** in the **dlsw remote-peer** commands allows different divisions or parts of the country to favor different central site gateways. In addition, you must specify **cost** if you want to split SNA traffic across multiple central site routers, but each remote site has only a single SNA PU (all logical unit sessions flow over the same circuit that the PU session flows over). In Figure 7–12, Peer A always favors Peer B and Peer D always favors Peer C.

Controlling Peer Selection

A higher-cost peer can be used for a connection even when the lower-cost peer is active if the higher-cost peer responds to the explorer before the lower-cost peer. If your network configuration allows this possibility, you can prevent it by adjusting a timer.

Setting the **dlsw explorer-wait-time** command causes DLSw+ to wait the specified amount of time (for example, one second) before selecting a peer to use for connections. This timer can be set in Cisco IOS Release 11.0 and later. Prior to Cisco IOS Release 11.0, this timer did not exist.

Backup Peers

Having multiple active peers is one way to provide dynamic and immediate recovery from the loss of a central site router. However, in some configurations you may prefer the alternative peer to be active only when required. This may be the case when the backup router resides at a disaster recovery site, or when there are more than 300 to 400 remote sites and a single central site router is providing backup for multiple central site routers.

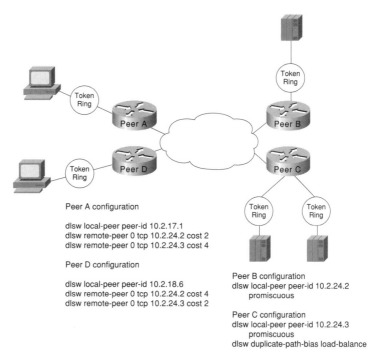

Figure 7–12

Configuration where cost is specified in the disw remote-peer command instead of the disw local-peer command.

Peer A configuration

dlsw local-peer peer-id 10.2.17.1
dlsw remote-peer 0 tcp 10.2.24.2 cost 2
dlsw remote-peer 0 tcp 10.2.24.3 cost 4

Peer D configuration

dlsw local-peer peer-id 10.2.18.6
dlsw remote-peer 0 tcp 10.2.24.2 cost 4
dlsw remote-peer 0 tcp 10.2.24.3 cost 2

Peer B configuration
dlsw local-peer peer-id 10.2.24.2
   promiscuous

Peer C configuration
dlsw local-peer peer-id 10.2.24.3
   promiscuous
dlsw duplicate-path-bias load-balance

In this case, use the backup peer capability (first available in Cisco IOS Release 10.3, but enhanced in Release 11.1). Figure 7–13 illustrates how to configure a backup peer. To use backup peers, the encapsulation method used to access the primary peer must be either TCP or Fast-Sequenced Transport (FST).

In this example, there are 400 remote sites. All the routers on the east coast use Router A as the primary router, and all the routers on the west coast use Router C as the primary router. In either case, the backup router is Router B. The configuration shown is the configuration in Router D, an east coast router. (All the east coast routers will have the same two **dlsw remote-peer** commands.) Both the primary router (Router A) and the backup router (Router B) are configured in **dlsw remote-peer** commands. Router B is configured as a backup only, and the IP address of the router it is backing up is specified.

In the event of a failure in Router A, all SNA sessions are terminated and will reestablish through Router B. When Router A becomes available again, all new sessions are established through Router A, but sessions active on Router B will remain on Router B until the linger timer expires. Omitting the **linger** keyword will cause sessions on Router B to remain active until they terminate on their own. The **linger** keyword can be used to minimize line costs if the backup peer is accessed over dial lines, but will provide enough time for an operator warning to be sent to all the SNA end users.

Figure 7–13

How to use backup peers to enhance availability in a large DLSw+ network.

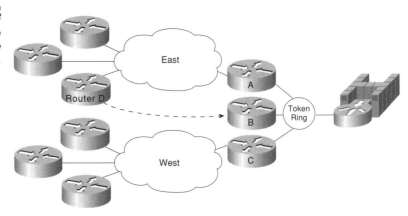

Router D configuration

dlsw local-peer peer-id 10.2.17.1
dlsw remote-peer 0 tcp 10.2.24.2
dlsw remote-peer 0 tcp 10.2.24.3 backup-peer 10.2.24.2 linger 20

NOTES

Prior to Cisco IOS Release 11.1, when the primary peer was activated again, all sessions using the backup peer were terminated immediately and reestablished over the primary router. If that is not the action you want to take and you are running a level of Cisco IOS software earlier than Release 11.1, consider using duplicate active peers instead (described in the previous section).

Backup Peers Compared to Multiple Active Peers

Backup peers and multiple active peers (with one preferred and others capable) are two ways to ensure that a capable peer can back up the failure of a primary peer. One of the key differences in backup peers is that the peer connections are not active until they are needed. Suppose you have 1000 branch offices, and you want to design a network at minimal cost that will recover dynamically from the failure of any single central site router. Assume four routers at the central site can handle your traffic load. You can install four primary routers at the central site and define 250 branches to peer to each central site router.

To address your availability requirement, one option is multiple concurrently active peer connections. In this case, you configure each remote router to have two peer connections: one to a preferred router and one to a capable router. The preferred router is the router configured with lower cost. The capable router can be the same router for all remote sites, but in that case, it has 1,000 peer connections. The largest number of peering routers we have seen is 400, and that was in an environment with extremely low traffic. Although 1,000 idle peer connections are conceivable, as soon as the capable router takes over for another router, those peer connections could put a strain on the router. The other alternative is to have multiple central site routers as capable routers, but this is not the most cost-effective design.

By using a backup peer statement in each remote branch instead of concurrently peering to two routers, a single backup router at a central site can easily back up any other central site router. There is no work on a backup router until a primary router fails.

Encapsulation Options

DLSw+ offers four encapsulation options. These options vary in terms of the processing path they use, their WAN overhead, and the media they support. The encapsulation options are TCP, Fast Sequenced Transport (FST), direct, and LLC2.

TCP Encapsulation

TCP is the standard DLSw encapsulation method and is the only encapsulation method supported by RFC 1795. TCP offers the most functionality of the encapsulation options. It provides reliable delivery of frames and local acknowledgment. It is the only option that offers nondisruptive rerouting around link failures. With TCP encapsulation, you can take advantage of dial-on-demand to dynamically dial additional bandwidth if primary links reach a preconfigured amount of congestion. In most environments, it is the recommended encapsulation because its performance is generally more than adequate, it offers the highest availability, and the overhead generally has no negative impact on response time or throughput.

TCP is process switched, so it uses more cycles than FST or direct encapsulation. A Cisco 4700 router running DLSw+ with TCP encapsulation can switch up to 8 Mbps of data, so TCP encapsulation addresses the processing requirements of most SNA environments. When higher throughput is required, additional routers or alternative encapsulation options can be used.

TCP encapsulation adds the most overhead to each frame (20 bytes for TCP and 20 bytes for IP in addition to the 16-byte DLSw header). TCP header compression or payload compression can be used to reduce the amount of bandwidth required, if necessary. At 56 Kbps or higher line speeds, the 40 bytes of overhead adds less than 5.7 ms to the round trip delay, so its impact is negligible.

DLSw+ with TCP encapsulation provides local acknowledgment and local polling and minimizes keepalive traffic across the WAN. It supports any local media and any WAN media. Load balancing across multiple WAN links or IP paths is possible because TCP resequences traffic before forwarding the traffic.

When using TCP encapsulation, you can assign different types of traffic to different TCP ports so that queuing can be granular. LLC2 traffic can be distinguished by SAP (to distinguish NetBIOS and SNA traffic), and SNA devices can be prioritized by LOCADDR or a MAC/SAP pair. The following is a sample **dlsw remote-peer** command specifying TCP encapsulation:

```
dlsw remote-peer 0 tcp 10.2.24.3
```

FST Encapsulation

FST is a high-performance option used over higher-speed links (256 KB or higher) when high throughput is required. FST uses an IP header with sequencing numbers to ensure that all frames are delivered in sequence (out-of-order frames are discarded and the end system must retransmit them).

FST is fast-switched, not process-switched, so using this encapsulation allows DLSw+ to process more packets per second than TCP encapsulation. FST does not use TCP, so the header is 20 bytes smaller.

FST, however, provides neither reliable delivery of frames nor local acknowledgment. All keepalive frames flow end to end. FST is supported only when the end systems reside on Token Ring. Two FST peers can connect over High-Level Data Link Control (HDLC), Ethernet, Token Ring, FDDI, Asynchronous Transfer Mode (ATM), or Frame Relay. (Some transport media are not available with early maintenance releases. See Appendix B for details.) FST will reroute around link failures, but rerouting may be disruptive. In addition, load balancing across multiple WAN links or IP paths is not recommended with FST because frames may arrive out of order and FST will discard them, causing end systems to retransmit and reducing overall network performance.

Finally, queuing is not as granular with FST because you cannot assign different types of traffic to different TCP ports. This means that when using FST encapsulation, queuing algorithms cannot be distinguished by SAP (so NetBIOS and SNA are treated as LLC2 traffic), and they cannot be distinguished by LOCADDR or MAC address. The following is a sample **dlsw remote-peer fst** command specifying FST encapsulation:

```
dlsw remote-peer 0 fst 10.2.24.3
```

Direct Encapsulation

Direct encapsulation is a minimal-overhead option for transport across point-to-point lines when rerouting is not required. Direct encapsulation is supported over HDLC lines and Frame Relay. It includes a DLSw 16-byte header and the data-link control header. Direct encapsulation is fast-switched, not process-switched, so using this encapsulation allows DLSw+ to process more packets per second than TCP encapsulation.

Direct encapsulation provides neither reliable delivery of frames nor local acknowledgment. All keepalive frames flow end-to-end. Direct encapsulation is supported only when the end systems reside on Token Ring. Direct encapsulation does not provide any rerouting.

Finally, queuing is not as granular with direct encapsulation because you cannot assign different types of traffic to different TCP ports. This means that when using direct encapsulation, queuing algorithms cannot be distinguished by SAP (so NetBIOS and SNA are treated as LLC2 traffic), and they cannot be distinguished by SDLC or MAC address.

Direct encapsulation is sometimes considered for very low-speed lines to minimize overhead, but TCP encapsulation with payload compression may offer lower WAN overhead without the limitations of direct encapsulation. The following is a sample **dlsw remote-peer interface** command specifying direct encapsulation on an HDLC line:

```
dlsw remote-peer 0 interface serial 01
```

The following is a sample **dlsw remote-peer frame relay** command specifying direct encapsulation on a Frame Relay line:

```
dlsw remote-peer 0 frame-relay interface serial 01 33 pass-thru
frame-relay map dlsw 33
```

In this example, data-link connection identifier (DLCI) 33 on serial interface 1 is used to transport DLSw traffic. Specifying **pass-thru** implies that the traffic is not locally acknowledged. Leaving **pass-thru** off causes the traffic to be locally acknowledged, which means it is transported in LLC2 to ensure reliable delivery. The next section describes LLC2 encapsulation.

LLC2 Encapsulation (DLSw Lite)

DLSw+ with LLC2 encapsulation is also known as DLSw Lite. It supports many DLSw+ features, including local acknowledgment, media conversion, minimizing keepalive traffic, and reliable delivery of frames, but it uses less overhead (16 bytes of DLSw header and 4 bytes of LLC2). It is currently supported over Frame Relay and assumes a point-to-point configuration over Frame Relay (that is, the peering router at the central site is also the WAN router). DLSw Lite supports Token Ring-, SDLC-, QLLC-, or Ethernet-attached end systems. DLSw Lite is process-switched and processes approximately the same traffic volume as TCP encapsulation.

With DLSw Lite, link failures are disruptive. Availability can be achieved by having multiple active central site peers, which allows for dynamic, but disruptive, recovery from the loss of either a link or a central site peer. Backup peers are not yet supported for DLSw Lite.

Queuing with DLSw Lite is not as granular as with TCP encapsulation because you cannot assign different types of traffic to different TCP ports. This means that when using DLSw Lite, queuing algorithms cannot distinguish traffic by SAP (so NetBIOS and SNA are treated as LLC2 traffic), and they cannot distinguish traffic by SDLC or MAC address. The following is a sample **dlsw remote-peer frame-relay** command specifying LLC2 encapsulation on a Frame Relay line:

```
dlsw remote-peer 0 frame-relay interface serial 01 33
frame-relay map llc2 33
```

NOTES

The **frame-relay map llc2** command will not work on point-to-point subinterfaces. Instead, you must provide the DLCI number in the **frame-relay interface-dlci** command and specify the same DLCI number in the **dlsw remote-peer frame relay** command.

The following is a sample **dlsw remote-peer** command for point-to-point subinterfaces:

```
dlsw remote-peer 0 frame-relay interface serial 0.1 60
interface s0.1 point-to-point
frame-relay interface-dlci 60
```

Encapsulation Overhead

Different types of encapsulation incur different amounts of overhead on a per-frame basis. But with TCP and LLC2, local acknowledgment and keepalive traffic are removed from the WAN, reducing the number of packets. Also, such techniques as payload or header compression and packing multiple SNA frames in a single TCP packet can further reduce the overhead. The percentage of overhead created by DLSw depends on the encapsulation method used.

Figure 7–14 illustrates the frame format for TCP, FST, DLSw Lite, and direct encapsulation. The percentage shown is the amount of overhead assuming SNA transactions of 40 in, 1920 out (a screen refresh) and 40 in, 1200 out. With smaller transactions, the overhead is larger. The TCP encapsulation numbers are worst-case numbers because they assume that each SNA path information unit (PIU) is encapsulated in a separate TCP packet. In fact, if there is more than one SNA PIU in the output queue, multiple frames will be encapsulated in a single TCP packet, reducing the overhead. The percentages in Figure 7–14 do not take into consideration the fact that DLSw+ eliminates keepalive packets and acknowledgments.

Figure 7–14

Frame format and per-packet overhead of various encapsulation types and transaction sizes.

Encapsulation		40/1920 SDLC	40/1920 LAN	40/1200 SDLC	40/1200 LAN
TCP	DLC | IP | TCP | DLSw | Data	5.7%	4.5%	9%	7%
FST	DLC | IP | DLSw | Data	3.7%	2.4%	5.8%	3.9%
Lite	FR | LLC2 | DLSw | Data	2%	1%	3.2%	1.3%
Direct	FR | DLSw | Data	1.8%	.6%	2.9%	1%

The effective per-packet overhead of DLSw for LAN traffic is lower than SDLC because DLSw+ eliminates the need to carry MAC addresses and RIFs in every frame. DLSw does not carry this data because the DLSw circuit ID (part of the 16-byte DLSw header) is used for circuit correlation. The overhead of MAC addresses and RIFs can range from 12 to 28 bytes of data. The percentages in Figure 7–14 assume the minimum overhead (no RIF).

Port Lists

Port lists allow you to create virtual LANs (VLANs) or broadcast domains in a DLSw+ network. Using port lists, you can control where broadcasts are forwarded. For example, in Figure 7–15, there are three rings at the distribution site (where Peer A resides).

All the rings have SNA end systems, but Ring 15 is the only ring with NetBIOS servers. The branch with Peer B needs access to the NetBIOS servers on Ring 15, but does not need access to other rings. Port lists allow you keep all broadcasts from Peer B off Rings 12 and 22 (and prevent Peer B from communicating with devices on Rings 12 or 22).

You can distinguish among different Token Ring ports and serial ports using port lists, but all Ethernet ports are treated as a single entity (Ethernet bridge group).

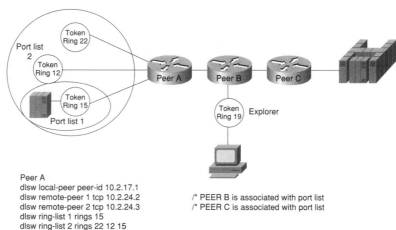

Figure 7–15
Ring lists used to limit
broadcast domains in a DLSw+
network.

Peer A
dlsw local-peer peer-id 10.2.17.1
dlsw remote-peer 1 tcp 10.2.24.2
dlsw remote-peer 2 tcp 10.2.24.3
dlsw ring-list 1 rings 15
dlsw ring-list 2 rings 22 12 15

/* PEER B is associated with port list
/* PEER C is associated with port list

Peer Groups, Border Peers, and On-Demand Peers

Peer groups and border peers can be used to minimize the number of peer connections required for any-to-any communication. Prior to the introduction of border peers, any two DLSw routers that required connectivity needed a peer connection active at all times. This peer connection is used to find resources and to carry circuit traffic. In a fully meshed network of *n* routers, this requires nx(n-1)/2 TCP connections. This is complex to configure and can result in unnecessary explorer traffic. To address this issue, DLSw+ supports the concept of peer groups and border peers. Peer groups are arbitrary groups of routers with one or more designated border peers. Border peers form peer connections with every router in their group and with border peers in other groups. The role of a border peer is to forward explorers on behalf of other routers.

Use peer groups and border peers only when you need branch-to-branch communication between NetBIOS or APPN end systems. In Figure 7–16, the "before" network shows the required TCP connections for fully meshed connectivity without using border peers. Without border peers, any time a router wants to find a resource that is not in its cache, it must create an explorer frame and replicate it for each TCP connection. This creates excessive explorer traffic on the WAN links and processing load on the router.

Figure 7–16

Using border peers and peer groups to minimize the number of required TCP connections while maintaining full any-to-any connectivity.

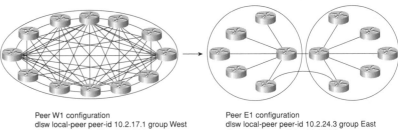

Peer W1 configuration
dlsw local-peer peer-id 10.2.17.1 group West
dlsw remote-peer 0 tcp 10.2.24.1
dlsw peer-on-demand-defaults tcp

Peer WBP configuration
dlsw local-peer peer-id 10.2.24.1 group West
border promiscuous

Peer E1 configuration
dlsw local-peer peer-id 10.2.24.3 group East
dlsw remote-peer 0 tcp 10.2.18.2
dlsw peer-on-demand-defaults tcp

Peer EBP configuration
dlsw local-peer peer-id 10.2.18.2 group East
border promiscuous

After configuring border peers and peer groups, the same fully meshed connectivity is possible without the overhead. In the "after" network, two peer groups are defined (West Group and East Group). Within each group, one or more peers is configured as border peers. Every peer within the West Group establishes a peer connection with the west border peer (WBP). Every peer within the East Group establishes a peer connection with east border peer (EBP). The border peers establish a peer connection with each other. When a peer in the West Group wants to find a resource, it sends a single explorer to its border peer. The border peer forwards this explorer to every peer in its group and to every other border peer. The EBP, after receiving this explorer, forwards it to every peer in its group. When the resource is found (in this case at E1), a positive reply flows back to the origin (W1) via the two border peers. At this point, W1 establishes a direct peer connection to E1. Peer connections that are established via border peers without the benefit of preconfiguration are called *peer-on-demand connections*. The rules for establishing on-demand peers are defined in the **dlsw peer-on-demand-defaults tcp** commands in each router.

Dynamic Peers

Dynamic peers (available in Cisco IOS Release 11.1 and later) are configured remote peers that are connected only when circuits use them. When a **dlsw remote-peer** command specifies **dynamic**, the remote peer is activated only when an end system sends an explorer frame that passes all the filter conditions specified in the **dlsw remote-peer** command. Once the dynamic peer connection is established, the explorer is forwarded to the remote peer. If the resource is found, a circuit is established, and the remote peer will remain active until all circuits using that remote peer terminate and five minutes elapse. You can specify the **no-llc** keyword to modify the elapsed time to something other than five minutes. Optionally, the remote peer can be configured to disconnect when there is no activity on any of the circuits for a prespecified amount of time (inactivity timer).

Filters that minimize how many explorers are sent to a remote peer can be included in **dlsw remote-peer** commands. In the case of dynamic peers, these filters are also used to prevent the dynamic peer from being activated. The remote peer statement allows you to point to lists of SAPs, MAC addresses, NetBIOS names, or byte offset filters. You can also specify a MAC address on the

dlsw remote-peer command for a dynamic peer, in which case that remote peer is activated only when there is an explorer for the specified MAC address. Figure 7–17 shows an example of how to use this feature. In Figure 7–17, the dynamic peer is only established if an explorer frame is received that is destined for the MAC address of the FEP. After the peer connection is established, if there is no activity on this peer connection for 20 minutes, the peer connection and any circuits using the connection are terminated because **inactivity 20** was specified.

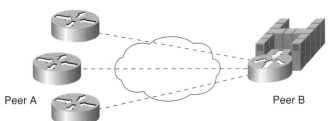

Figure 7–17
DLSw+ routers configure to take advantage of the dynamic peer feature.

Peer A

Peer B

Peer A configuration
dlsw local-peer peer-id 10.2.17.1
dlsw remote-peer 0 tcp 10.2.24.2 dynamic
    inactivity 20 dest-mac 4000.3745.0000

Peer B configuration
dlsw local-peer peer-id 10.2.24.3

When to Use Dynamic Peers

Use dynamic peers if you have a large network, but do not require all remote sites to be connected at the same time. By using dynamic peers, you can minimize the number of central site routers needed to support the network. You can also use dynamic peers for occasional communication between a pair of remote sites. Dynamic peers differ from on-demand peers because they must be preconfigured. Finally, for small networks, dynamic peers can be used to dial out during error recovery.

SNA Dial-on-Demand Routing

SNA Dial-on-Demand Routing (DDR) refers to the capability for DLSw+ to transfer SNA data over a dial-up connection and automatically drop the dial connection when there is no data to send. The SNA session remains active. To use SNA DDR, configure the following on the **dlsw remote-peer** command:

```
dlsw remote-peer list-number tcp ip-address dynamic keepalive 0 timeout seconds
```

The **dynamic** keyword is optional but recommended because it will prevent the remote peer connection from being established unnecessarily. The **dynamic** option is described in the previous section and can be used in conjunction with the **dmac-out** or **dmac-output-list** options on the **dlsw remote-peer** command to ensure that peer connections are only brought up when desired (for example, when a device is trying to locate the FEP).

The **keepalive** keyword is required. DLSw+ locally acknowledges SNA (or more precisely, SDLC or LLC2) traffic, so no data-link control acknowledgments or receiver ready frames will bring up the dial connection. However, DLSw+ peers send peer keepalives to each other periodically, and these keepalives will bring up the dial connection. The **keepalive** option refers to how often DLSw+ peers send peer keepalives to each other. If you set this to zero, no keepalives will be sent and, therefore, the peer keepalive will not keep the dial line up. You must specify **keepalive 0** in *both* peers; that is, either you must specify the remote peers at both the local and remote DLSw+ routers, or you must use the **prom-peer-default** command to set **keepalive** to zero for all promiscuous peer connections. The **prom-peer-default** command has the same options as the **peer-on-demand-defaults** command and is available in the later maintenance release of all DLSw+ releases.

The keepalive parameter refers to how often DLSw+ peers send peer keepalives to each other. If you set this to zero, no keepalives are sent, and the peer keepalive will not keep the dial line up. This parameter must be specified in *both* peers, which means that you must either specify the remote peers at both the local and remote DLSw+ routers, or you must use the **dlsw prom-peer-default** command to set keepalive to 0 for all promiscuous peer connections. The **dlsw prom-peer-default** command is similar to the **dlsw peer-on-demand-defaults** command and is available in the later maintenance releases of all DLSw+ releases.

The **timeout** keyword is recommended. Without peer keepalives, DLSw+ is dependent on TCP timers to determine when the SNA session has come down. TCP will only determine that it has lost a partner if it does not get an acknowledgment after it sends data. By default, TCP may wait up to 15 minutes for an acknowledgment before tearing down the TCP connection. Therefore, when **keepalive 0** is specified, you should also set the **timeout** keyword, which is the number of seconds that TCP will wait for an acknowledgment before tearing down the connection. Timeout should be long enough to allow acknowledgments to get through in periods of moderate to heavy congestion, but short enough to minimize the time it takes to recover from a network outage. SNA data-link control connections typically wait 150 to 250 seconds before timing out.

Other Considerations

In addition to preventing keepalive traffic from bringing up the Integrated Services Digital Network (ISDN) lines, you need to worry about routing updates. In hub and spoke environments, to prevent route table updates from bringing up the dial connections, use static routes. Alternatively, you can use Routing Interface Protocol (RIP) Version 2 or on-demand routing for IP routing from the dial-up branches to the central site. On-demand routing (ODR) is a mechanism that provides minimum-overhead IP routing for sub sites. Define RIP Version 2 or on-demand routing on the ISDN interface of the central router as passive mode. Then redistribute RIP Version 2 or ODR routes into the main routing protocol (Enhanced Interior Gateway Routing Protocol [IGRP] or Open Shortest Path First [OSPF]). This allows you to have multiple routers at the central site for load balancing or redundancy. Whichever router receives the call from the remote site will have the route installed dynamically. At the remote site, the routing protocol (RIP or ODR) must be denied from the dialer list.

For meshed topologies, you can minimize routing table updates by using a distance-vector protocol, such as RIP or IGRP, in combination with Cisco's snapshot routing feature. Snapshot routing prevents regular routing updates from bringing up the ISDN connection. The changes in routing tables are sent either when the link is opened by end-user traffic or at a regular configurable interval. Snapshot routing supports not only IP routing updates, but also Novell's IPX routing and SAP updates.

Many NetBIOS implementations use a session keepalive (in addition to a data-link control keepalive) to maintain sessions, so DDR may not work with NetBIOS. (The session level keepalive will keep the dial line up.)

Local Switching

Local switching (available in Cisco IOS Release 11.1 and later) allows a single router to provide media conversion between SDLC and Token Ring and between QLLC and LAN. This is useful in environments that need simplified SNA network design and improved availability. For example, by converting SDLC to Token Ring, fewer FEP expansion frames are required; moves, adds, and changes are easier; and recovery from a FEP or Token Ring interface coupler (TIC) failure can be automatic (by using duplicate TIC addresses). Local switching can be used to connect SDLC devices directly to a Cisco router with a CIP card. Local switching can also be used over a WAN in which the remote branch has SNA devices on LANs, but the central site FEP still requires serial connectivity (for example, when the FEP is a Cisco 3725 router). To use local switching, omit **dlsw remote-peer** commands. In the **dlsw local-peer** command, the peer ID is unnecessary. A sample network and its configuration are shown in Figure 7–18.

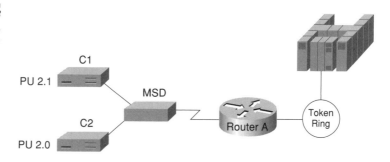

Figure 7–18
Local switching configuration in a mixed PU 2.0 and PU 2.1 environment.

Peer A Router A
dlsw local-peer
interface serial 0
...
sdlc role primary
sdlc vmac 4000.3174.0000
sdlc address c1 xid-poll
sdlc partner 4000.3745.0001 c1
sdlc address c2
sdlc xid c2 01767890
sdlc partner 4000.3745.0001 c2
sdlc dlsw c1 c2

SUMMARY

This chapter provided an introduction to DLSw+, including a description of DLSw+ and configuration examples to enable you to quickly design and configure simple DLSw+ networks. It reviewed the key components of the data-link switching (DLSw+) features and described the extensions to the standard that are included in DLSw+. Finally, advanced features of DLSw+, the benefits they provide, and a brief description of when and how to use them were discussed.

Designing ATM Internetworks

This chapter describes current Asynchronous Transfer Mode (ATM) technologies that network designers can use in their networks today. It also makes recommendations for designing non-ATM networks so that those networks can take advantage of ATM in the future without sacrificing current investments in cable.

This chapter focuses on the following topics:

- ATM overview
- Cisco's ATM WAN solutions

ATM DEFINED

ATM is an evolving technology designed for the high-speed transfer of voice, video, and data through public and private networks in a cost-effective manner. ATM is based on the efforts of Study Group XVIII of the International Telecommunication Union Telecommunication Standardization Sector (ITU-T, formerly the Consultative Committee for International Telegraph and Telephone [CCITT]) and the American National Standards Institute (ANSI) to apply very large-scale integration (VLSI) technology to the transfer of data within public networks. Officially, the ATM layer of the Broadband Integrated Services Digital Network (BISDN) model is defined by CCITT I.361.

Current efforts to bring ATM technology to private networks and to guarantee interoperability between private and public networks is being done by the ATM Forum, which was jointly founded by Cisco Systems, NET/ADAPTIVE, Northern Telecom, and Sprint in 1991.

ROLE OF ATM IN INTERNETWORKS

Today, 90 percent of computing power resides on desktops, and that power is growing exponentially. Distributed applications are increasingly bandwidth-hungry, and the emergence of

305

the Internet is driving most LAN architectures to the limit. Voice communications have increased significantly with increasing reliance on centralized voice mail systems for verbal communications. The internetwork is the critical tool for information flow. Internetworks are being pressured to cost less yet support the emerging applications and higher number of users with increased performance.

To date, local and wide-area communications have remained logically separate. In the LAN, bandwidth is free and connectivity is limited only by hardware and implementation cost. The LAN has carried data only. In the WAN, bandwidth has been the overriding cost, and such delay-sensitive traffic as voice has remained separate from data. New applications and the economics of supporting them, however, are forcing these conventions to change.

The Internet is the first source of multimedia to the desktop and immediately breaks the rules. Such Internet applications as voice and real-time video require better, more predictable LAN and WAN performance. In addition, the Internet also necessitates that the WAN recognize the traffic in the LAN stream, thereby driving LAN/WAN integration.

Multiservice Networks

ATM has emerged as one of the technologies for integrating LANs and WANs. ATM can support any traffic type in separate or mixed streams, delay-sensitive traffic, and nondelay-sensitive traffic, as shown in Figure 8–1.

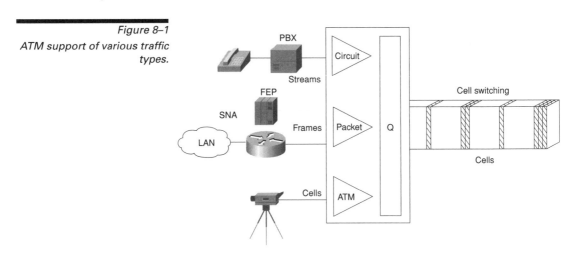

Figure 8–1

ATM support of various traffic types.

ATM can also scale from low to high speeds. It has been adopted by all the industry's equipment vendors, from LAN to private branch exchange (PBX). With ATM, network designers can integrate LANs and WANs, support emerging applications with economy in the enterprise, and support legacy protocols with added efficiency.

TDM Network Migration

In addition to using ATM to combine multiple networks into one multiservice network, network designers are deploying ATM technology to migrate from TDM networks for the following reasons:

- To reduce WAN bandwidth cost
- To improve performance
- To reduce downtime

Reduced WAN Bandwidth Cost

The Cisco line of ATM switches provide additional bandwidth through the use of voice compression, silence compression, repetitive pattern suppression, and dynamic bandwidth allocation. The Cisco implementation of ATM combines the strengths of TDM—whose fixed time slots are used by telephone companies to deliver voice without distortion—with the strengths of packet-switching data networks—whose variable size data units are used by computer networks, such as the Internet, to deliver data efficiently.

While building on the strengths of TDM, ATM avoids the weaknesses of TDM (which wastes bandwidth by transmitting the fixed time slots even when no one is speaking) and PSDNs (which cannot accommodate time-sensitive traffic, such as voice and video, because PSDNs are designed for transmitting bursty data). By using fixed-size cells, ATM combines the isochronicity of TDM with the efficiency of PSDN.

Improved Performance

ATM offers improved performance through performance guarantees and robust WAN traffic management that support the following capabilities:

- Large buffers that guarantee Quality of Service (QoS) for bursty data traffic and demanding multimedia applications
- Per-virtual circuit (VC) queuing and rate scheduling
- Feedback—congestion notification

Reduced Downtime

ATM offers high reliability, thereby reducing downtime. This high reliability is available because of the following ATM capabilities:

- The capability to support redundant processors, port and trunk interfaces, and power supplies
- The capability to rapidly reroute around failed trunks

INTEGRATED SOLUTIONS

The trend in internetworking is to provide network designers greater flexibility in solving multiple internetworking problems without creating multiple networks or writing off existing data communications investments. Routers can provide a reliable, secure network and act as a barrier against inadvertent broadcast storms in the local networks. Switches, which can be divided into two main categories—LAN switches and WAN switches—can be deployed at the workgroup, campus backbone, or WAN level, as shown in Figure 8–2.

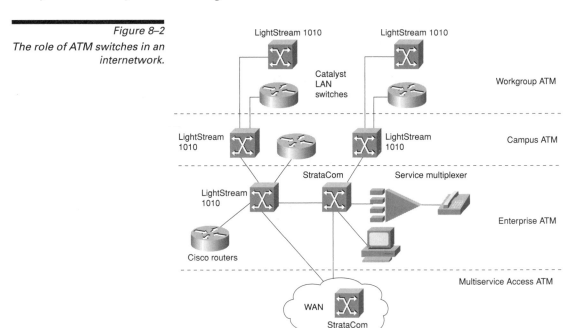

Figure 8–2
The role of ATM switches in an internetwork.

Underlying and integrating all Cisco products is the Cisco IOS software. The Cisco IOS software enables disparate groups, diverse devices, and multiple protocols all to be integrated into a highly reliable and scalable network.

DIFFERENT TYPES OF ATM SWITCHES

Even though all ATM switches perform cell relay, ATM switches differ markedly in the following ways:

- Variety of interfaces and services that are supported
- Redundancy
- Depth of ATM internetworking software
- Sophistication of traffic management mechanism

Just as there are routers and LAN switches available at various price/performance points with different levels of functionality, ATM switches can be segmented into the following four distinct types that reflect the needs of particular applications and markets:

- Workgroup ATM switches

- Campus ATM switches

- Enterprise ATM switches

- Multiservice access switches

As Figure 8–2 shows, Cisco offers a complete range of ATM switches.

Workgroup and Campus ATM Switches

Workgroup ATM switches are characterized by having Ethernet switch ports and an ATM uplink to connect to a campus ATM switch. An example of a workgroup ATM switch is the Cisco Catalyst 5000.

The Catalyst 5500 switch provides high-performance switching between workstations, servers, switches, and routers in wiring closet, workgroup, and campus backbone environments.

The Catalyst 5500 LAN is a 13-slot switch. Slot 1 is reserved for the supervisor engine module, which provides switching, local and remote management, and dual Fast Ethernet uplinks. Slot 2 is available for a second, redundant supervisor engine, or any of the other supported modules. Slots 3–12 support any of the supported modules.

Slot 13 can be populated only with a LightStream 1010 ATM Switch Processor (ASP). If an ASP is present in slot 13, slots 9–12 support any of the standard LightStream 1010 ATM switch port adapter modules (PAMs).

The Catalyst 5500 has a 3.6-Gbps media-independent switch fabric and a 5-Gbps cell-switch fabric. The backplane provides the connection between power supplies, supervisor engine, interface modules, and backbone module. The 3.6-Gbps media-independent fabric supports Ethernet, Fast Ethernet, FDDI/CDDI, ATM LAN Emulation, and RSM modules. The 5-Gbps cell-based fabric supports a LightStream 1010 ASP module and ATM PAMs.

Campus ATM switches are generally used for small-scale ATM backbones (for instance, to link ATM routers or LAN switches). This use of ATM switches can alleviate current backbone congestion while enabling the deployment of such new services as virtual LANs (VLANs). Campus switches need to support a wide variety of both local backbone and WAN types but be price/performance optimized for the local backbone function. In this class of switches, ATM routing capabilities that allow multiple switches to be tied together is very important. Congestion control mechanisms for optimizing backbone performance is also important. The LightStream 1010 family of ATM switches is an example of a campus ATM switch. For more information on deploying workgroup and campus ATM switches in your internetwork, see Chapter 12, "Designing Switched LAN Internetworks."

Enterprise ATM Switches

Enterprise ATM switches are sophisticated multiservice devices that are designed to form the core backbones of large, enterprise networks. They are intended to complement the role played by today's high-end multiprotocol routers. Enterprise ATM switches are used to interconnect campus ATM switches. Enterprise-class switches, however, can act not only as ATM backbones but can serve as the single point of integration for all of the disparate services and technology found in enterprise backbones today. By integrating all of these services onto a common platform and a common ATM transport infrastructure, network designers can gain greater manageability and eliminate the need for multiple overlay networks.

Cisco's BPX/AXIS is a powerful broadband ATM switch designed to meet the demanding, high-traffic needs of a large private enterprise or public service provider. This chapter focuses on this category of ATM switches.

Multiservice Access Switches

Beyond private networks, ATM platforms will also be widely deployed by service providers both as customer premises equipment (CPE) and within public networks. Such equipment will be used to support multiple MAN and WAN services—for instance, Frame Relay switching, LAN interconnect, or public ATM services—on a common ATM infrastructure. Enterprise ATM switches will often be used in these public network applications because of their emphasis on high availability and redundancy, their support of multiple interfaces, and capability to integrate voice and data.

ATM Overview

This section discusses the following ATM concepts:

- Structure of an ATM Network
- ATM Functional Layers
- ATM Addressing
- ATM Media
- ATM Data Exchange Interface

Structure of an ATM Network

ATM is based on the concept of two end-point devices communicating by means of intermediate switches. As Figure 8–3 shows, an ATM network is made up of a series of switches and end-point devices. The end-point devices can be ATM-attached end stations, ATM-attached servers, or ATM-attached routers.

As Figure 8–3 shows, there are two types of interfaces in an ATM network:

- User-to-Network Interface (UNI)
- Network-to-Network Interface (NNI)

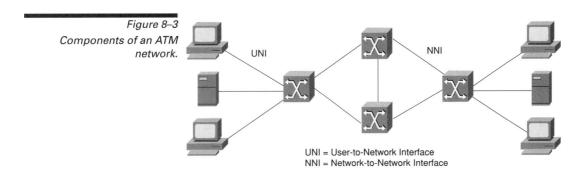

Figure 8–3
Components of an ATM network.

UNI = User-to-Network Interface
NNI = Network-to-Network Interface

The UNI connection is made up of an end-point device and a private or public ATM switch. The NNI is the connection between two ATM switches. The UNI and NNI connections can be carried by different physical connections.

In addition to the UNI and NNI protocols, the ATM Forum has defined a set of LAN Emulation (LANE) standards and a Private Network to Network Interface (PNNI) Phase 0 protocol. LANE is a technology network designers can use to internetwork legacy LANs such as Ethernet and Token Ring with ATM-attached devices. Most LANE networks consist of multiple ATM switches and typically employ the PNNI protocol.

The full PNNI 1.0 specification was released by the ATM Forum in May 1996. It enables extremely scalable, full function, dynamic multi-vendor ATM networks by providing both PNNI routing and PNNI signaling. PNNI is based on UNI 3.0 signaling and static routes. The section "Role of LANE" later in this chapter discusses ATM LANE networks in detail.

General Operation on an ATM Network

Because ATM is connection-oriented, a connection must be established between two end points before any data transfer can occur. This connection is accomplished through a signaling protocol as shown in Figure 8–4.

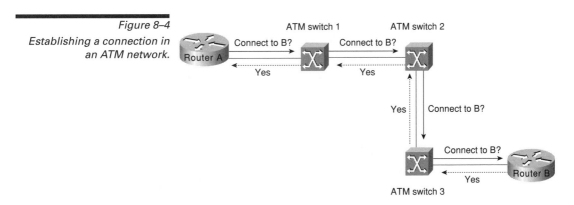

Figure 8–4
Establishing a connection in an ATM network.

As Figure 8–4 shows, for Router A to connect to Router B the following must occur:

1. Router A sends a signaling request packet to its directly connected ATM switch (ATM Switch 1).

   This request contains the ATM address of the Router B as well as any QoS parameters required for the connection.

2. ATM Switch 1 reassembles the signaling packet from Router A, and then examines it.

3. If ATM Switch 1 has an entry for Router B's ATM address in its switch table and it can accommodate the QoS requested for the connection, it sets up the virtual connection and forwards the request to the next switch (ATM Switch 2) along the path.

4. Every switch along the path to Router B reassembles and examines the signaling packet, and then forwards it to the next switch if the QoS parameters can be supported. Each switch also sets up the virtual connection as the signaling packet is forwarded.

   If any switch along the path cannot accommodate the requested QoS parameters, the request is rejected and a rejection message is sent back to Router A.

5. When the signaling packet arrives at Router B, Router B reassembles it and evaluates the packet. If Router B can support the requested QoS, it responds with an accept message. As the accept message is propagated back to Router A, the switches set up a virtual circuit.

NOTES

A *virtual channel* is equivalent to a virtual circuit—that is, both terms describe a logical connection between the two ends of a communications connection. A *virtual path* is a logical grouping of virtual circuits that allows an ATM switch to perform operations on groups of virtual circuits.

---

6. Router A receives the accept message from its directly connected ATM switch (ATM Switch 1), as well as the Virtual path identifier (VPI) and Virtual channel identifier (VCI) values that it should use for cells sent to Router B.

NOTES

ATM cells consist of five bytes of header information and 48 bytes of payload data. The VPI and VCI fields in the ATM header are used to route cells through ATM networks. The VPI and VCI fields of the cell header identify the next network segment that a cell needs to transmit on its way to its final destination.

ATM Functional Layers

Just as the *Open System Interconnection* (OSI) reference model describes how two computers communicate over a network, the ATM protocol model describes how two end systems communicate through ATM switches. The ATM protocol model consists of the following three functional layers:

- ATM physical layer
- ATM layer
- ATM adaptation layer

As Figure 8–5 shows, these three layers correspond roughly to Layer 1 and parts of Layer 2 (such as error control and data framing) of the OSI reference model.

Figure 8–5
Relationship of ATM functional layers to the OSI reference model.

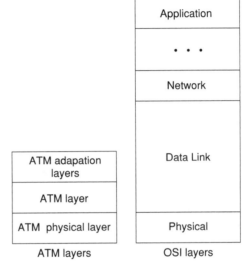

Physical Layer

The ATM physical layer controls transmission and receipt of bits on the physical medium. It also keeps track of ATM cell boundaries and packages cells into the appropriate type of frame for the physical medium being used. The ATM physical layer is divided into two parts:

- Physical medium sublayer
- Transmission convergence sublayer

Physical Medium Sublayer

The physical medium sublayer is responsible for sending and receiving a continuous flow of bits with associated timing information to synchronize transmission and reception. Because it includes only physical-medium-dependent functions, its specification depends on the physical medium used. ATM can use any physical medium capable of carrying ATM cells. Some existing standards that can carry ATM cells are SONET (Synchronous Optical Network)/SDH, DS-3/E3, 100-Mbps local fiber (Fiber Distributed Data Interface [FDDI] physical layer), and 155-Mbps local fiber (Fiber

Channel physical layer). Various proposals for use over twisted-pair wire are also under consideration.

Transmission Convergence Sublayer

The transmission convergence sublayer is responsible for the following:

- *Cell delineation*—Maintains ATM cell boundaries.

- *Header error control sequence generation and verification*—Generates and checks the header error control code to ensure valid data.

- *Cell rate decoupling*—Inserts or suppresses idle (unassigned) ATM cells to adapt the rate of valid ATM cells to the payload capacity of the transmission system.

- *Transmission frame adaptation*—Packages ATM cells into frames acceptable to the particular physical-layer implementation.

- *Transmission frame generation and recovery*—Generates and maintains the appropriate physical-layer frame structure.

ATM Layer

The ATM layer establishes virtual connections and passes ATM cells through the ATM network. To do this, it uses the information contained in the header of each ATM cell. The ATM layer is responsible for performing the following four basic functions:

- Multiplexing and demultiplexing the cells of different virtual connections. These connections are identified by their VCI and VPI values.

- Translating the values of the VCI and VPI at the ATM switches or cross connects.

- Extracting and inserting the header before or after the cell is delivered to or from the higher ATM adaptation layer.

- Handling the implementation of a flow control mechanism at the UNI.

ATM Adaptation Layer (AAL)

The AAL translates between the larger service data units (SDUs) (for example, video streams and data packets) of upper-layer processes and ATM cells. Specifically, the AAL receives packets from upper-level protocols (such as AppleTalk, Internet Protocols [IP], and NetWare) and breaks them into the 48-byte segments that form the payload field of an ATM cell. Several ATM adaptation layers are currently specified. Table 8–1 summarizes the characteristics of each AAL.

Table 8–1 *ATM Adapter Layers*

Characteristics	AAL1	AAL3/4	AAL4	AAL5
Requires timing between source and destination	Yes	No	No	No
Data rate	Constant	Variable	Variable	Variable
Connection mode	Connection-oriented	Connection-oriented	Connectionless	Connection-oriented
Traffic types	Voice and circuit emulation	Data	Data	Data

AAL1

AAL1 prepares a cell for transmission. The payload data consists of a synchronous sample (for example, one byte of data generated at a sampling rate of 125 microseconds). The sequence number field (SN) and sequence number protection (SNP) fields provide the information that the receiving AAL1 needs to verify that it has received the cells in the correct order. The rest of the payload field is filled with enough single bytes to equal 48 bytes.

AAL1 is appropriate for transporting telephone traffic and uncompressed video traffic. It requires timing synchronization between the source and destination and, for that reason, depends on a media that supports clocking, such as SONET. The standards for supporting clock recovery are currently being defined.

AAL3/4

AAL3/4 was designed for network service providers and is closely aligned with Switched Multi-megabit Data Service (SMDS). AAL3/4 is used to transmit SMDS packets over an ATM network. The convergence sublayer (CS) creates a protocol data unit (PDU) by prepending a Beginning/End Tag header to the frame and appending a length field as a trailer as shown in Figure 8–6.

The segmentation and reassembly (SAR) sublayer fragments the PDU and prepends to each PDU fragment a header consisting of the following fields:

- *Type*—Identifies whether the cell is the beginning of a message, continuation of a message, or end of a message.

- *Sequence number*—Identifies the order in which cells should be reassembled.

- *Multiplexing identifier*—Identifies cells from different traffic sources interleaved on the same virtual circuit connection (VCC) so that the correct cells are reassembled at the destination.

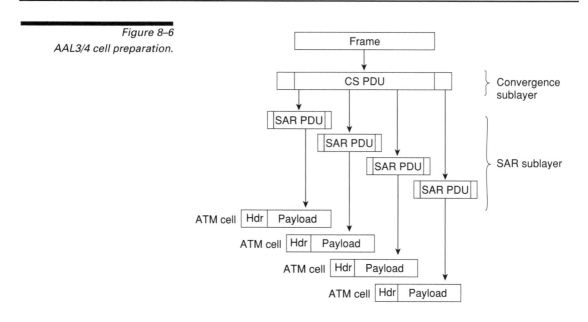

Figure 8–6
AAL3/4 cell preparation.

The SAR sublayer also appends a CRC-10 trailer to each PDU fragment. The completed SAR PDU becomes the payload field of an ATM cell to which the ATM layer prepends the standard ATM header.

AAL5

AAL5 prepares a cell for transmission as shown in Figure 8–7.

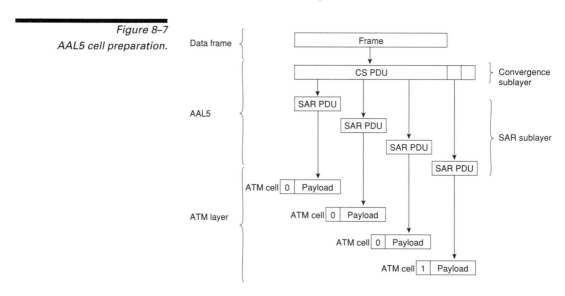

Figure 8–7
AAL5 cell preparation.

First, the convergence sublayer of AAL5 appends a variable-length pad and an 8-byte trailer to a frame. The pad is long enough to ensure that the resulting PDU falls on the 48-byte boundary of the ATM cell. The trailer includes the length of the frame and a 32-bit CRC computed across the entire PDU, which allows AAL5 at the destination to detect bit errors and lost cells or cells that are out of sequence.

Next, the segmentation and reassembly segments the CS PDU into 48-byte blocks. Then the ATM layer places each block into the payload field of an ATM cell. For all cells except the last cell, a bit in the PT field is set to zero to indicate that the cell is not the last cell in a series that represents a single frame. For the last cell, the bit in the PT field is set to one. When the cell arrives at its destination, the ATM layer extracts the payload field from the cell; the SAR sublayer reassembles the CS PDU; and the CS uses the CRC and the length field to verify that the frame has been transmitted and reassembled correctly.

AAL5 is the adaptation layer used to transfer most non-SMDS data, such as classical IP over ATM and local-area network (LAN) emulation.

ATM Addressing

The ATM Forum has adapted the subnetwork model of addressing in which the ATM layer is responsible for mapping network-layer addresses to ATM addresses. Several ATM address formats have been developed. Public ATM networks typically use E.164 numbers, which are also used by Narrowband ISDN (N-ISDN) networks.

Figure 8–8 shows the format of private network ATM addresses. The three formats are Data Country Code (DCC), International Code Designator (ICD), and Network Service Access Point (NSAP) encapsulated E.164 addresses.

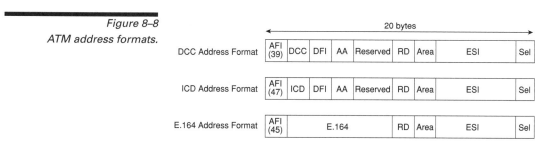

Figure 8–8
ATM address formats.

Fields of an ATM Address

The fields of an ATM address are as follows:

- *AFI*—One byte of authority and format identifier. The AFI field identifies the type of address. The defined values are 45, 47, and 39 for E.164, ICD, and DCC addresses, respectively.

- *DCC*—Two bytes of data country code.

- *DFI*—One byte of domain specific part (DSP) format identifier.
- *AA*—Three bytes of administrative authority.
- *RD*—Two bytes of routing domain.
- *Area*—Two bytes of area identifier.
- *ESI*—Six bytes of end system identifier, which is an IEEE 802 Media Access Control (MAC) address.
- *Sel*—One byte of Network Service Access Point (NSAP) selector.
- *ICD*—Two bytes of international code designator.
- *E.164*—Eight bytes of Integrated Services Digital Network (ISDN) telephone number.

The ATM address formats are modeled on ISO NSAP addresses, but they identify subnetwork point of attachment (SNPA) addresses. Incorporating the MAC address into the ATM address makes it easy to map ATM addresses into existing LANs.

ATM Media

The ATM Forum has defined multiple standards for encoding ATM over various types of media. Table 8–2 lists the framing type and data rates for the various media, including unshielded twisted-pair (UTP) and shielded twisted-pair (STP) cable.

Table 8–2 *ATM Physical Rates*

		Media					
Framing	Data Rate (Mbps)	Multimode Fiber	Single Mode Fiber	Coaxial Cable	UTP-3	UTP-5	STP
DS-1	1.544			√			
E1	2.048			√			
DS-3	45			√			
E3	34			√			
STS-1	51				√		
SONET STS3c SDH STM1	155	√	√	√		√	
SONET STS12c SDH STM4	622	√	√				

Table 8–2 *ATM Physical Rates, Continued*

Framing	Data Rate (Mbps)	Media					
		Multimode Fiber	Single Mode Fiber	Coaxial Cable	UTP-3	UTP-5	STP
TAXI 4B/5B	100	√					
8B/10B (Fiber Channel)	155	√					√

Because the FDDI chipset standard, TAXI 4B/5B, was readily available, the ATM Forum encouraged initial ATM development efforts by endorsing TAXI 4B/5B as one of the first ATM media encoding standards. Today, however, the most common fiber interface is STS3c/STM.

There are two standards for running ATM over copper cable: UTP-3 and UTP-5. The UTP-5 specification supports 155 Mbps with NRZI encoding, while the UTP-3 specification supports 51 Mbps with CAP-16 encoding. CAP-16 is more difficult to implement, so, while it may be cheaper to wire with UTP-3 cable, workstation cards designed for CAP-16-based UTP-3 may be more expensive and will offer less bandwidth.

Because ATM is designed to run over fiber and copper cable, investments in these media today will maintain their value when networks migrate to full ATM implementations as ATM technology matures.

ATM Data Exchange Interface

To make ATM functionality available as soon as possible, the ATM Forum developed a standard known as the *ATM Data Exchange Interface* (DXI). Network designers can use DXI to provide UNI support between Cisco routers and ATM networks, as shown in Figure 8–9.

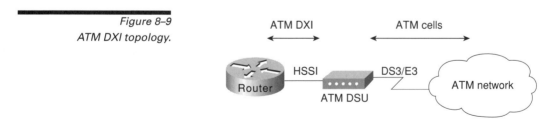

Figure 8–9
ATM DXI topology.

The ATM data service unit (ADSU) receives data from the router in ATM DXI format over a High-Speed Serial Interface (HSSI). The DSU converts the data into ATM cells and transfers them to the ATM network over a DS-3/E3 line.

ATM DXI is available in several modes:

- *Mode 1a*—Supports AAL5 only, a 9232 octet maximum, and a 16-bit FCS, and provides 1023 virtual circuits.

- *Mode 1b*—Supports AAL3/4 and AAL5, a 9224 octet maximum, and a 16-bit FCS. AAL5 support is the same as Mode 1a. AAL3/4 is supported on one virtual circuit.

- *Mode 2*—Supports AAL3/4 and AAL5 with 16,777,215 virtual circuits, a 65535 octet maximum, and 32-bit FCS.

On the router, data from upper-layer protocols is encapsulated into ATM DXI frame format. Figure 8–10 shows the format of a Mode 1a ATM DXI frame.

Figure 8–10
ATM DXI frame format.

Flag	Header	SDU	FCS	Flag
1	2	0-9232	2	1

Field size in octets

In Figure 8–11, a router configured as a data terminal equipment (DTE) device is connected to an ADSU. The ADSU is configured as a data communications equipment (DCE) device. The router sends ATM DXI frames to the ADSU, which converts the frames to ATM cells by processing them through the AAL5 CS and the SAR sublayer. The ATM layer attaches the header, and the cells are sent out the ATM UNI interface.

Figure 8–11
ATM DXI Mode 1a and Mode 1b protocol architecture for AAL5.

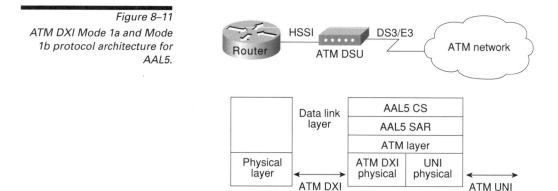

ATM DXI addressing consists of a DFA, which is equivalent to a Frame Relay data link connection identifier (DLCI). The DSU maps the DFA into appropriate VPI and VCI values in the ATM cell. Figure 8–12 shows how the DSU performs address mapping.

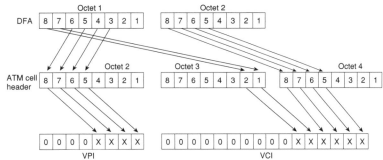

Figure 8–12
ATM DXI address mapping.

Figure 8–12
ATM DXI address mapping.

NOTES

ATM DXI 3.2 is supported in the Cisco IOS Software Release 9.21 or later. Mode 1a is the only mode supported.

ROLE OF LANE

The ATM Forum has defined a standard for LANE. LANE is a technology that network designers can deploy to internetwork their legacy LANs (for example, Ethernet and Token Ring LANs), with ATM-attached devices. LANE uses MAC encapsulation (OSI Layer 2) because this approach supports the largest number of existing OSI Layer 3 protocols. The end result is that all devices attached to an emulated LAN (ELAN) appear to be on one bridged segment. In this way, Apple-Talk, IPX, and other protocols should have similar performance characteristics as in a traditional bridged environment.

In ATM LANE environments, the ATM switch handles traffic that belongs to the same ELAN, and routers handle inter-ELAN traffic. Figure 8–13 shows an example of an ATM LANE network.

As Figure 8–13 shows, network designers can use the LANE technology to interconnect legacy LANs to any of the following types of ATM-attached devices:

- End stations (for example, ATM-attached servers or ATM-attached workstations)
- Edge devices that bridge the legacy LANs onto an ATM backbone (for example, the Catalyst 5000 or Catalyst 3000 switches that have an ATM uplink)
- ATM-attached routers that are used to route between ELANs

Figure 8–13
Components of an ATM LANE
network.

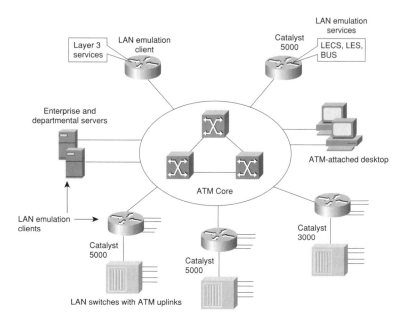

LANE Components

LANE components include the following:

- *LAN emulation client (LEC)*—End systems that support LANE, such as network interface card (NIC)-connected workstations, LAN switches with ATM uplinks (for example, the Catalyst family of switches), and Cisco 7500, 7000, 4500, and 4000 series routers that support ATM attachment, all require the implementation of a LEC. The LEC emulates an interface to a legacy LAN to the higher-level protocols. It performs data forwarding, address resolution, and registration of MAC addresses with the LANE server and communicates with other LECs via ATM virtual channel connections (VCCs).

- *LAN emulation configuration server (LECS)*—The LECS maintains a database of ELANs and the ATM addresses of the LESs that control the ELANs. It accepts queries from LECs and responds with the ATM address of the LES that serves the appropriate ELAN/VLAN. This database is defined and maintained by the network administrator.

  The following is an example of this database.

ELAN Name	LES ATM Address
finance	47.0091.8100.0000.0800.200c.1001. 0800.200c.1001.01
marketing	47.0091.8100.0000.0800.200c.1001. 0800.200c.1001.02

- *LAN emulation server (LES)*—The LES provides a central control point for all LECs. LECs maintain a Control Direct VCC to the LES to forward registration and control information. The LES maintains a point-to-multipoint VCC, known as the *Control Distribute VCC*, to all LECs. The Control Distribute VDD is used only to forward control information. As new LECs join the ATM ELAN, each LEC is added as a leaf to the control distribute tree.

- *Broadcast and unknown server (BUS)*—The BUS acts as a central point for distributing broadcasts and multicasts. ATM is essentially a point-to-point technology without "any-to-any" or "broadcast" support. LANE solves this problem by centralizing the broadcast support in the BUS. Each LEC must set up a Multicast Send VCC to the BUS. The BUS then adds the LEC as a leaf to its point-to-multipoint VCC (known as the *Multicast Forward VCC*).

  The BUS also acts as a multicast server. LANE is defined on ATM adaptation layer 5 (AAL5), which specifies a simple trailer to be appended to a frame before it is broken into ATM cells. The problem is that there is no way to differentiate between ATM cells from different senders when multiplexed on a virtual channel. It is assumed that cells received will be in sequence, and when the End of Message (EOM) cell arrives, you should just have to reassemble all of the cells that have already arrived.

  The BUS takes the sequence of cells on each Multicast Send VCC and reassembles them into frames. When a full frame is received, it is queued for sending to all of the LECs on the Multicast Forward VCC. This way, all the cells from a particular data frame can be guaranteed to be sent in order and not interleaved with cells from any other data frames on the point-to-multipoint VCC.

Note that because LANE is defined at OSI Layer 2, the LECS is the only security checkpoint available. Once it has been told where to find the LES and it has successfully joined the ELAN, the LEC is free to send any traffic (whether malicious or not) into the bridged ELAN. The only place for any OSI Layer 3 security filters is in the router that routes this ELAN to other ELANs. Therefore, the larger the ELAN, the greater the exposure to security violations.

How LANE Works

An ELAN provides Layer 2 communication between all users on an ELAN. One or more ELANs can run on the same ATM network. However, each ELAN is independent of the others and users on separate ELANs cannot communicate directly. Communication between ELANs is possible only through routers or bridges.

Because an ELAN provides Layer 2 communication, it can be equated to a broadcast domain. VLANs can also be thought of as broadcast domains. This makes it possible to map an ELAN to a VLAN on Layer 2 switches with different VLAN multiplexing technologies such as Inter-Switch Link (ISL) or 802.10. In addition, IP subnets and IPX networks that are defined on Layer 3-capable devices such as routers frequently map into broadcast domains (barring secondary addressing). This makes it possible to assign an IP subnetwork or an IP network to an ELAN.

An ELAN is controlled by a single LES/BUS pair and the mapping of an ELAN to its LES ATM address is defined in the LECS database. ELANs consists of multiple LECs and can be Ethernet or Token Ring but not both at the same time.

In order for ELAN to operate properly, the LECs on that ELAN need to be operational. Each LEC goes through a boot up sequence that is described in the following sections.

LANE Operation

In a typical LANE operation, the LEC must first find the LECS to discover which ELAN it should join. Specifically, the LEC is looking for the ATM address of the LECS that serves the desired ELAN.

Finding the LECS

To find the ATM address of the LECS, the LEC does the following:

1. Queries the ATM switch via Interim Local Management Interface (ILMI). The switch has a MIB variable set up with the ATM address of the LECS. The LEC can then use UNI signaling to contact the LECS.

2. Looks for a fixed ATM address that is specified by the ATM Forum as the LECS ATM address.

3. Accesses permanent virtual circuit (PVC) 0/17, a "well-known" PVC.

Contacting the LECS

The LEC creates a signaling packet with the ATM address of the LECS. It signals a Configure Direct VCC and then issues an LE_CONFIGURE_REQUEST on that VCC. The information in this request is compared with the data in the LECS database. The source ATM address is most commonly used to place a LEC into a specific ELAN. If a matching entry is found, a successful LE_CONFIGURE_RESPONSE is returned with the ATM address of the LES that serves the desired ELAN.

Configuring the LECS database

You can configure the LECS database in any of the following three ways:

- *Configure ELAN names at the LEC*—In this configuration, all the LECs are configured with an ELAN name that they can embed in their Configure_Requests. This is the most basic form of the LECS database and it needs only to contain the list of ELANs and their corresponding LES ATM addresses. In such a configuration, all LECs that specifically request to join a given ELAN are returned the ATM address of the corresponding LES. A LEC that does not know which ELAN to join can be assigned to a default ELAN if such an ELAN is configured in the LECS database.

  The following is an example of LEC-to-ELAN mapping at the LEC:
  ```
  lane database test-1
  name finance server-atm-address 47.0091.8100.0000.0800.200c.1001. 0800.200c.1001.01
  ```

```
name marketing server-atm-address 47.0091.8100.0000.0800.200c.1001. 0800.200c.1001.02
default-name finance
```

- *Configure LEC to ELAN assignment in the LECS database*—In this configuration, all the information is centralized in the LECS database. The LECs do not need to be intelligent, and they can simply go to the LECS to determine which ELAN they should join. Although this is a more time-intensive configuration, it provides tighter control over all the ELANs. Consequently, it can be useful when security is important.

  With this method, the LECs are identified by their ATM addresses or MAC addresses. Because wildcarding of ATM address prefixes is also supported, it is useful to make such relationships as "Assign any LEC joining with a prefix of A to ELAN X." The following is an example of LEC-to-ELAN mapping in the LECS database:

```
lane database test-2
name finance server-atm-address 47.0091.8100.0000.0800.200c.1001. 0800.200c.1001.01
name marketing server-atm-address 47.0091.8100.0000.0800.200c.1001. 0800.200c.1001.02
default-name finance

client-atm-address    47.0091.8100.0000.08…   name finance
client-atm-address    47.0091.8100.0000.09…   name marketing

mac-address 00c0.0000.0100 name finance
mac-address 00c0.1111.2222 name marketing
```

- *Hybrid combination*—You can configure a combination of the preceding two methods.

Joining the LES

After the LEC has discovered the ATM address of the desired LES, it drops the connection to the LECS, creates a signaling packet with the ATM address of the LES, and signals a Control Direct VCC. Upon successful VCC setup, the LES sends an LE_JOIN_REQUEST. This request contains the LEC ATM address as well as a MAC address that the LEC wants to register with the ELAN. This information is maintained so that no two LECs can register the same MAC or ATM addresses.

Upon receipt of the LE_JOIN_REQUEST, the LES checks with the LECS via its own open connection with the LECS and verifies the request, thus confirming the client's membership. Upon successful verification, the LES adds the LEC as a leaf of its point-to-multipoint Control Distribute VCC. Finally, the LES issues the LEC a successful LE_JOIN_RESPONSE that contains a LANE client ID (LECID), which is an identifier that is unique to the new client. This ID is used by the LEC to filter its own broadcasts from the BUS. Figure 8–14 shows examples of LES connections.

Finding the BUS

After the LEC has successfully joined the LES, its first task is to find the ATM address of the BUS and join the broadcast group. The LEC creates an LE_ARP_REQUEST packet with the MAC address 0xFFFFFFFF. This special LE_ARP packet is sent on the Control Direct VCC to the LES. The LES recognizes that the LEC is looking for the BUS, responds with the ATM address of the BUS, and forwards that response on the Control Distribute VCC.

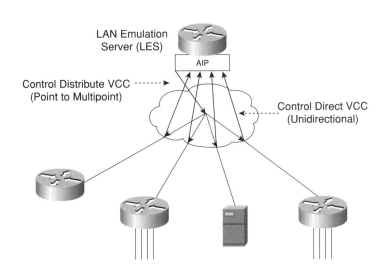

Figure 8–14
LAN emulation server (LES)
connections.

Joining the BUS

When the LEC has the ATM address of the BUS, its next action is to create a signaling packet with that address and signal a Multicast Send VCC. Upon receipt of the signaling request, the BUS adds the LEC as a leaf on its point-to-multipoint Multicast Forward VCC. At this time, the LEC has become a member of the ELAN. Figure 8–15 shows examples of BUS connections.

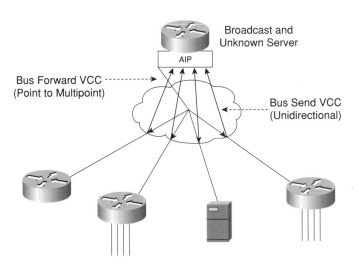

Figure 8–15
BUS connections.

Address Resolution

The real value of LANE is the ATM forwarding path that it provides for unicast traffic between LECs. When a LEC has a data packet to send to an unknown destination, it issues an LE_ARP_REQUEST to the LES on the Control Direct VCC. The LES forwards the request on the Control Distribute VCC, so all LEC stations hear it. In parallel, the unicast data packets are sent to the BUS, to be forwarded to all endpoints. This "flooding" is not the optimal path for unicast traffic, and this transmission path is rate-controlled to 10 packets per second (per the LANE standard). Unicast packets continue using the BUS until the LE_ARP_REQUEST has been resolved.

If bridging or switching devices with LEC software participate in the ELAN, they translate and forward the ARP on their LAN interfaces. One of the LECs should issue an LE_ARP_RESPONSE and send it to the LES, which forwards it to the Control Distribute VCC so that all LECs can learn the new MAC-to-ATM address binding.

When the requesting LEC receives the LE_ARP_RESPONSE, it has the ATM address of the LEC that represents the MAC address being sought. The LEC should now signal the other LEC directly and set up a Data Direct VCC that will be used for unicast data between the LECs.

While waiting for LE_ARP resolution, the LEC forwards unicasts to the BUS. With LE_ARP resolution, a new "optimal" path becomes available. If the LEC switches immediately to the new path, it runs the risk of packets arriving out of order. To guard against this situation, the LANE standard provides a flush packet.

When the Data Direct VCC becomes available, the LEC generates a flush packet and sends it to the BUS. When the LEC receives its own flush packet on the Multicast Forward VCC, it knows that all previously sent unicasts must have already been forwarded. It is now safe to begin using the Data Direct VCC. Figure 8–16 shows an example of a fully connected ELAN.

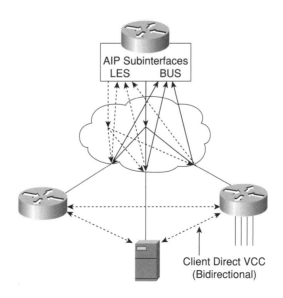

Figure 8–16
Fully connected ELAN.

LANE IMPLEMENTATION

As Table 8–3 indicates, the LANE functionality (the LECS, LEC, LES, and BUS) can be implemented in different Cisco devices.

Table 8–3   *Cisco LANE Implementation*

Cisco Product	Available LANE Components	Required Software Release
Family of Catalyst 5000 switches	LECS, LES, BUS, LEC	ATM Module Software Version 2.0 or later
Family of Catalyst 3000 switches	LECS, LES, BUS, LEC	ATM Module Software Version 2.1 or later
Family of Cisco 7000 routers	LECS, LES, BUS, LEC	Cisco IOS Software Release 11.0 or later
Family of Cisco 7500 routers	LECS, LES, BUS, LEC	Cisco IOS Software Release 11.1 or later
Family of Cisco 4500 and 4000 routers	LECS, LES, BUS, LEC	Cisco IOS Software Release 11.1 or later

These functions will be defined on ATM physical interfaces and subinterfaces. A subinterface can be defined as a logical interface and is a part of a physical interface such as an Optical Carrier 3 (OC-3) fiber. ATM interfaces on the Cisco routers and the ATM module on the Catalyst 5000 switch can be logically divided into up to 255 logical subinterfaces. On the Catalyst 3000 switch, although the same Cisco IOS Software code is used, the subinterface concept does not apply. The LEC can be configured using the menu-driven interface.

This section examines the implementation of ATM LANE networks and covers the following topics:

- LANE Design Considerations
- LANE Redundancy

LANE Design Considerations

The following are some general LANE design considerations:

- The AIP provides an interface to ATM switching fabrics for transmitting and receiving data at rates of up to 155 Mbps bidirectionally. The actual rate is determined by the Physical layer interface module (PLIM).
- One active LECS supports all ELANs.
- In each ELAN, there is one LES/BUS pair and some number of LECs.
- The LES and BUS functionality must be defined on the same subinterface and cannot be separated.

- There can be only one active LES/BUS pair per subinterface.

- There can be only one LES/BUS pair per ELAN.

- The current LANE Phase 1 standard does not provide for any LES/BUS redundancy.

- The LECS and LES/BUS can be different routers, bridges, or workstations.

- VCCs can be either switched virtual circuits (SVCs) or permanent virtual circuits (PVCs), although PVC design configuration and complexity might make anything more than a very small network prohibitively unmanageable and complex.

- When defining VLANs with the Catalyst 5000 switch, each VLAN should be assigned to a different ELAN. The LES/BUS pair for each ELAN can reside on any of the following:
  - Different subinterfaces on the same AIP
  - Different AIPs in the same router
  - Different AIPs in different routers

- There can be only one LEC per subinterface. If a LEC and a LES/BUS pair share a subinterface, they are (by definition) in the same ELAN.

- If a LEC on a router subinterface is assigned an IP, IPX, or AppleTalk address, that protocol is routable over that LEC. If there are multiple LECs on a router and they are assigned protocol addresses, routing will occur between the ELANs. For routing between ELANs to function correctly, an ELAN should be in only one subnet for a particular protocol.

PNNI in LANE Networks

Network designers can deploy PNNI as a Layer 2 routing protocol for bandwidth management, traffic distribution, and path redundancy for LANE networks. PNNI is an ATM routing protocol used for routing call setups and is implemented in the ATM switches. Most LANE networks consist of multiple ATM switches and typically employ the PNNI protocol.

NOTES

Although PNNI is an advanced routing protocol and supports QoS-based routing, this particular aspect of PNNI is not discussed in this chapter because most LANE networks are based on the best-effort traffic category.

The LightStream 1010 ATM switch supports some PNNI-related features that can be useful in scaling LANE networks:

- To load balance call setup requests across multiple paths between two end stations

- To load balance call setups across multiple parallel links

- To support link and path redundancy with fast convergence

- To provide excellent call setup performance across multiple hops using the background routing feature

Figure 8–17 shows how the LightStream 1010 switch supports load balancing.

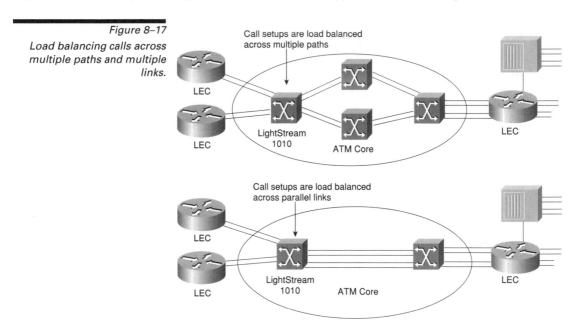

Figure 8–17

Load balancing calls across multiple paths and multiple links.

As Figure 8–17 shows, load balancing of calls is enabled by default on the LightStream 1010 switch. Background routing, however, is not enabled by default. Background routing can be thought of as routing of call setups using a path from a precomputed route database. The background routing process computes a list of all possible paths to all destinations across all the service categories (for example, constant bit rate [CBR], virtual bit rate-real time [VBR-RT], virtual bit rate and nonreal time [VBR-NRT] and available bit rate-unspecified bit rate [ABR-UBR]).

When a call is placed from Point A to Point B, PNNI picks a cached routed from the background route table instead of computing a route on demand. This eases the CPU load and provides a faster rate of processing the call setups.

Background routing can be useful in networks that have a stable topology with respect to QoS. It is, however, not very effective in networks that have rapidly changing topologies (for example, Internet Service Providers [ISP] networks or carrier networks). Campus LANE networks can use this feature effectively because all the SVCs in the network belong to the UBR or ABR category. To enable this feature, use the following command:

```
atm router pnni
    node 1 level 56
    bg-routes
```

The current implementation of PNNI on the LightStream 1010 switch is full, ATM Forum-PNNI Version 1 compliant. The LightStream default PNNI image license supports a single level of hierarchy, where multiple peer groups can be interconnected by IISP or by other switches that support full PNNI hierarchy; extra PNNI image license will support multiple levels of routing hierarchy.

The PNNI protocols have been designed to scale across all sizes of ATM networks, from small campus networks of a handful of switches, to the possible global ATM Internet of millions of switches. This level of scalability is greater than that of any existing routing protocol, and requires very significant complexity in the PNNI protocol. Specifically, such scalability mandates the support of multiple levels of routing hierarchy based upon the use of prefixes of the 20-byte ATM address space. The lowest level of the PNNI routing hierarchy consists of a single peer group within which all switches flood all reachability and QoS metrics to one another. This is analogous, for instance, to a single area in the OSPF protocol.

Subsequently, multiple peer groups at one level of the hierarchy are aggregated into higher-level peer groups, within which each lower-level peer group is represented by a single *peer group leader*, and so on iteratively up the PNNI hierarchy. Each level of the hierarchy is identified by a prefix of the ATM address space, implying that PNNI could theoretically contain over 100 levels of routing hierarchy. However, a handful of levels would be adequate for any conceivable network. The price to be paid for such scalability is the need for highly complex mechanisms for supporting and bringing up the multiple levels of hierarchy and for electing the peer group leaders within each peer group at each level.

Scaling an ELAN—Spanning-Tree Protocol Issues

Spanning-Tree Protocol is implemented in Layer 2 switches/bridges to prevent temporary loops in networks with redundant links. Because a LEC essentially bridges Ethernet/Token Ring traffic over an ATM backbone, the Spanning-Tree Bridge Protocol Data Units (BPDUs) are transmitted over the entire ELAN. The ATM network appears as a shared Ethernet/Token Ring network to the spanning-tree process at the edge of the Layer 2 switches.

The spanning-tree topology of a LANE-based network is substantially simpler than a pure frame-switched network that employs the Spanning-Tree Protocol. It follows that spanning-tree convergence times, which can be a major issue in large frame-switched networks, can be less of an issue in LANE networks. Note that Spanning Tree must reconverge if there are failures at the edge devices or inside the ATM network. If there is a need to tune the convergence time to a lower or higher value, the forward delay parameter can be used.

LANE Redundancy

Although LANE allows network designers to connect their legacy LANs to an ATM network, LANE Version 1.0 does not define mechanisms for building redundancy and fault tolerance into the LANE services. Consequently, this makes the LANE services a single point of failure. Moreover, router redundancy and path/link redundancy are also issues that the network designer needs to consider.

Network designers can use the following techniques to build fault-tolerant and resilient LANE networks:

- Simple Server Replication Protocol (SSRP) for LANE Services redundancy that works with Cisco and any third-party LECs.

- Hot Standby Router Protocol (HSRP) over LANE provides redundancy for the default router configured at IP end stations.

- Dual PHY LANE card on the Catalyst 5000 switch, or multiple ATM uplinks on the Catalyst 3000 switch.

- Spanning-Tree Protocol on the Ethernet-ATM switches.

The following subsections examine these various mechanisms and highlights design rules and issues to consider while implementing redundant LANE networks. It begins with a discussion on SSRP that was developed to provide redundant LANE services.

Although many vendors have implemented redundant LANE services of some fashion, they violate the LANE 1.0 specification and therefore are not interoperable with other third-party implementations. SSRP, however, does not violate the LANE 1.0 specification and is interoperable with third-party LEC implementations, which is important when implementing an interoperable ATM network.

The discussion on SSRP is followed by a description of HSRP over LANE, which provides a mechanism for building router redundancy. Following this is a discussion on the Spanning-Tree Protocol and other product-specific features that can be used to build link and path redundancy into edge devices.

Issues in a LANE 1.0 Network

The main issue with a LANE 1.0 network is that only one set of LANE service components can be accessed by a LEC at any given time. This results in the following limitations:

- Only a single LECS supports all ELANs.
- There can be only one LES/BUS pair per ELAN.

A failure in any of these service components has the following impact on network operation:

- *LECS failure*—A failed LECS impacts all the ELANs under its control because it provides access control for all the ELANs under its control. Although the existing ELANs would continue to work normally (assuming only Cisco LECs), no new LEC can join any ELAN under the control of that LECS. Also, any LEC that needs to rejoin its ELAN or change its membership to another ELAN cannot because the LES cannot verify any LEC trying to join an ELAN.

- *LES/BUS failure*—The LES/BUS pair is needed to maintain an operational ELAN. The LES provides the LE_ARP service for ATM-MAC address mappings and the BUS provides broadcast and unknown services for a given ELAN. Therefore, a failure of either the LES or the BUS immediately affects normal communication on the ELAN. However, a LES/BUS failure impacts only the ELAN served by that pair.

It is clear that these issues can be limiting to networks where resiliency and robustness is a requirement and might even be a deciding factor in your design of whether to implement LANE-based ATM networks. In addition, there are other design considerations such as the placement of the LANE service components within an ATM network that can have implications on the overall robustness of the LANE environment.

Resiliency in LANE 1.0 Networks

Increasing the resiliency of a LANE-based network essentially includes delivering increased robustness in the LANE service components such as the LECS, LES, and BUS. Such robustness is provided by SSRP through a primary-secondary combination of the LANE services. For LECS redundancy, one primary LECS is backed up by multiple secondary LECSs. LES/BUS redundancy is also handled in a similar fashion where one primary LES/BUS pair is backed up by multiple secondaries. Note that the LES/BUS functions are always co-located in a Cisco implementation and the pair is handled as one unit with respect to redundancy.

LECS Redundancy

In the LANE 1.0 specification, the first step for a LEC during initialization is to connect with the LECS to obtain the LES ATM address for the ELAN it wants to join. In order for the LEC to connect to the LECS, multiple mechanisms are defined. The first mechanism that a LEC should use is to query the ATM switch it is attached to for the LECS address. This address discovery process is done using the ILMI protocol on VPI, VCI - 0, 16.

The following is an example of the configuration command to add a LECS address to a LightStream 1010 switch:

```
atm lecs-address <LECS NSAP address> <index>
```

With SSRP, multiple LECS addresses are configured into the ATM switches. An LEC, which requests the LECS address from the ATM switch, gets the entire table of LECS addresses in response. The behavior of the LEC should be to attempt to connect to the highest ranking LECS address. If this fails, it should try the next one in the list and so on until it connects to the LECS.

Whereas the LEC always tries to connect to the highest ranking LECS available, SSRP ensures that there is only a single primary that responds to the Configure Request queries coming from the LEC. The establishment of a primary LECS and placing the others in backup goes to the heart of SSRP. The following describes the mechanism used by SSRP to establish a primary LECS. Upon initialization, a LECS obtains the LECS address table from the switch. The LECS then tries to connect to all the LECSs that are below itself in rank. The rank is derived from the index entry in the LECS address table.

If a LECS has a connection (VCC) from a LECS whose rank is higher than its own, it is in backup mode. The highest ranking LECS does not have any other LECS that connect to it from above and assumes the role of the primary LECS.

Figure 8–18 shows the procedure of a backup taking over in the case of a failed primary LECS. The LANE network shown in Figure 8–18 has four LECS entities (LECS A, B, C, and D). All the ATM switches in the network are configured with the same LECS address table. After startup, LECS A obtains the LECS address table from the ATM switch it is attached to and finds that it has three LECSs below itself and therefore tries to connect to LECS B, C, and D. LECS B connects to LECS C and LECS D, and LECS C connects to LECS D. There is a downward establishment of VCCs. Because LECS A does not have any VCCs from above, it becomes the primary LECS.

Figure 8–18

LECS redundancy.

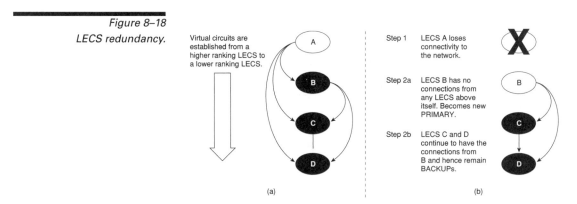

(a)   (b)

During normal network operation, LECS A responds to all the configure requests and the backup LECS (LECS B, C and D) do not respond to any queries. If for some reason the primary LECS (LECS A) fails due to such conditions as a box failure, LECS B loses its VCC from LECS A as do the other LECS.

At this point, LECS B does not have any VCCs from above and therefore is now the highest ranking available LECS in the network. LECS B now becomes the primary LECS. LECS C and LECS D still have connections from higher ranking LECSs and therefore continue to operate in backup mode as shown in Step 2b of Figure 8–18.

LES/BUS Redundancy

The LES/BUS redundancy portion of SSRP supports the configuration of multiple LES/BUS pairs that work in a primary-secondary fashion. However, the mechanisms used here are different from those used for the LECS redundancy described in the preceding section.

Multiple LES/BUS pairs for a given ELAN are first configured into the LECS database. Within this database, each LES/BUS pair is assigned a priority. After initialization, each LES/BUS opens a VCC with the primary LECS using the LECS address discovery mechanism. The LES/BUS pair with the highest priority that has an open VCC to the LECS is assigned as the primary LES/BUS by the primary LECS.

SSRP Usage Guidelines

There are no theoretical limits on the number of LECSs that can be configured using SSRP, however a recommended number is two (one primary plus one backup) or three LECSs (one primary plus two backups). Any more redundancy should be implemented only after very careful consideration because it will add a significant amount of complexity to the network. This added complexity can result in a substantial increase in the amount of time required to manage and troubleshoot such networks.

SSRP Configuration Guidelines

To support the LECS redundancy scheme, you must adhere to the following configuration rules. Failure to do so will result in improper operation of SSRP and a malfunctioning network.

- Each LECS must maintain the same database of ELANs. Therefore, you must maintain the same ELAN database across all the LECSs.

- You must configure the LECS addresses in the LECS address table in the same order on each ATM switch in the network.

- When using SSRP with the Well Known Address, do not place two LECSs on the same ATM switch. If you place two LECs on the same ATM switch, only one LECS can register the Well Known Address with the ATM switch (through ILMI) and this can cause problems during initialization.

SSRP Interoperability Notes

SSRP can be used with independent third-party LECs if they use ILMI for LECS address discovery and can appropriately handle multiple LECS addresses returned by the ATM switch. For example, the LEC should step through connecting to the list of LECS addresses returned by the ATM switch. The first LECS that responds to the configuration request is the master LECS.

Behavior of SSRP with the Well Known LECS Address

SSRP also works with LECS Well Known Address (47.0079....) defined in the LANE 1.0 specification. The Cisco LECS can listen on multiple ATM addresses at the same time. Therefore, it can listen on the Well Known Address and the auto-configured ATM address, which can be displayed using the **show lane default** command.

When the LECS is enabled to listen on the Well Known Address, it registers the Well Known Address with the ATM switch so that the ATM switches can advertise routes to the Well Known Address and route any call setups requests to the correct place.

Under SSRP, there are multiple LECSs in the network. If each LECS registers the Well Known Address to the ATM switches that it is connected to, call setups are routed to different places in the network. Consequently, under SSRP you must configure an autoconfigured address so that the negotiation of the master first takes place and then the master registers the Well Known Address with the ATM switch. If the master fails, the Well Known Address moves with the master LECS.

The PNNI code on the LightStream 1010 switch takes care of advertising the new route to the Well Known Address when there is a change of LECS mastership. Therefore, third-party LECs that use only the Well Known Address can also interoperate with SSRP. SSRP is the only redundancy scheme that can be used with almost any LEC in the industry.

To implement SSRP with the Well Known Address, use the following steps:

Step 1   Configure the LECS to listen on the autoconfigured address (or if you want a separate ATM address that you have predetermined). This autoconfigured (or other) address should be programmed into the ATM switches for the LECS address discovery mechanism.

Step 2   Configure each LECS to listen on the Well Known address using the **lane config fixed-config-atm-address** command. After the master LECS is determined using the LECS redundancy procedure, the master registers the Well Known Address to the ATM switch.

NOTES

SSRP with the Well Known Address does not work properly under certain circumstances (during failover) if two LECS are attached to the same ATM switch. This is due to the possibility of duplicate address registration on the same switch, which ILMI does not allow. Make sure each LECS is on a separate ATM switch.

Behavior of SSRP in Network Partitions

In the event of network partitions where two separate ATM clouds are formed due to an interconnecting link or switch failure, each cloud has its own set of LANE services if SSRP is configured to handle network partitions.

When configuring SSRP, use the following guidelines to accommodate the possibility of network partition:

- Configure each partition with its own LANE services that can become active during a network partition. For example, if you are connecting two sites or campuses across a MAN and you want the same ELANs at both locations, configure each campus/site with its own LANE services.

- Routing behavior should be carefully examined during a network partition in the case where an ELAN maps to a Layer 3 network (for example, an IP subnet or IPX network) because there are now two routes to the same subnet (assuming there are redundant routers in the network). If there are no redundant routers, one of the partitions will be effectively isolated from the rest of the network. Intra-ELAN traffic will continue to behave properly.

HSRP over LANE

HSRP is a protocol that network designers can use to guard against router failures in the network. The HSRP protocol is exchanged between two routers and one of them is elected as the primary router interface (or subinterface) for a given subnet. The other router acts as the *hot standby* router.

In HSRP, a default IP address and a default MAC address are shared between the two routers exchanging the HSRP protocol. This default IP address is used as the default gateway at all IP end stations for them to communicate with end stations outside their immediate subnet. Therefore, when there is a primary router failure, the hot standby router takes over the default gateway address and the MAC address so that the end station can continue communicating with end stations that are not in their immediate subnet.

Because HSRP is a Layer 2 mechanism and needs a MAC address-based Layer 2 network, it is possible to implement HSRP style recovery over LANE. The mechanisms used are the same as for any Ethernet interface and can be configured at a subinterface level.

Redundant ATM Port Card for the Catalyst 5000

Another aspect of addressing the redundancy needs from a physical network perspective is the addition of a redundant PHY portion of an ATM card. The Catalyst 5000 switch employs the dual PHY redundant ATM card. This redundancy is only at a physical level and is useful in cases where the primary link to the ATM switch goes down.

ROLE OF STRATM TECHNOLOGY

Stratm Technology is a new approach to ATM switching technology that incorporates patented standards-based Cisco technology into custom silicon. These application-specific integrated circuits (ASICs) dramatically increase ATM efficiency and scalability and significantly lower the absolute cost of delivering ATM solutions. Stratm Technology can be implemented in switches and routers across LANs, campus networks, and WANs, enabling the delivery of high-performance, end-to-end ATM services to meet a wide range of needs.

Benefits of Stratm Technology

The benefits of Stratm Technology include the following:

- Dramatic improvement in network price/performance scalability
- Increased application *goodput*
- Protection of technology investments
- Increased portability
- Guaranteed infrastructure

Each of these benefits is described in more detail in the following sections.

Improved Network Price/Performance Scalability

Stratm Technology features can dramatically improve network price/performance and scalability as follows:

- Support of up to eight OC-3 (155-Mbps) port interfaces per card slot, and up to 12 digital signal Level 3 T3/E3 (45-Mbps) port interfaces per card slot

- A 30 percent increase in SVC completions to more than 4,000 per second per node

- An increase in connection density per switch by 500 percent

- An increase in the buffering capability of each card to 200,000 cells per card, upgradable to nearly one million cells

- A reduction in the price per port for high-speed connections by up to 50 percent

- The ability to support per-virtual-connection control queuing, rate scheduling, statistics collection, and fair sharing of network resources on an individual connection basis

Increased Application Goodput

Intelligent ATM features are embodied in Stratm Technology. These features are designed to increase application goodput dramatically through advanced features, which are distributed throughout the BXM module in silicon.

- *Distributed ATM functions*—Stratm distributes such ATM services as traffic management, per-VC queuing, class of service (COS) management, SVCs, and multicasting to each card on a silicon chip. Distributed functionality ensures faster, more efficient processing, and it eliminates the possibility of a single point of failure disrupting the entire network.

- *Highest bandwidth efficiency*—Stratm delivers guaranteed bandwidth on demand, QoS, and fair sharing of network resources to each individual connection. With fast, efficient processing and guaranteed bandwidth, application performance is significantly enhanced.

- *Advanced traffic management capabilities*—Stratm incorporates the industry's first commercially available Virtual Source/Virtual Destination (VS/VD) implementation of the full ATM Forum's Traffic Management Specification Version 4.0. This ensures the highest efficiency in bandwidth utilization and provides support for the multicasting capabilities required to successfully deliver multimedia and switched internetworking services.

- *End-to-end intelligence*—With VS/VD implementation, Stratm also represents the industry's first complete LAN-to-WAN ARB implementation. This feature enables ATM services to be delivered to the desktop, ensuring high performance for the most demanding applications.

Industry-Leading Investment Protection

Stratm allows you to protect your current investments by integrating with today's network infrastructures, and providing advanced features and functionality to protect investments far into the future. You can protect your technology investment because of the following Stratm capabilities:

- *Seamlessly integrates with existing switches*—Stratm Technology integrates into Cisco's ATM switching platforms, allowing you to enhance your investment in Cisco technology.

- *Delivers unparalleled performance*—Current ATM switching platforms deliver performance that enables end-to-end delivery of high-quality, high-performance network services.

- *Delivers the future*—Stratm Technology extends the features and functionality of current switches to support next generation requirements. With this technology, you can easily deliver multiple services from a single network infrastructure and ensure the highest QoS possible.

Increases Portability and Guarantees an Infrastructure

With a modular chip set, Stratm increases the portability of standards-based ATM. ATM in silicon stabilizes the transport layer of networks, thereby guaranteeing the necessary infrastructure for efficient, high-performance delivery of emerging multimedia and Internet-based applications.

CISCO ATM WAN PRODUCTS

As Figure 8–19 shows, Cisco provides end-to-end network ATM solutions for internetworks.

Figure 8–19
End-to-end network solutions.

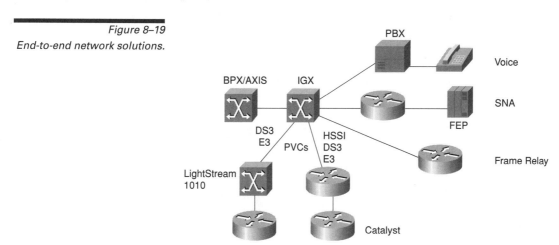

The Cisco ATM products suited for WAN deployment include the following:

- Cisco/StrataCom IGX switch, which is well suited for deployment in an enterprise WAN environment
- Cisco/StrataCom BPX/AXIS switch, which meets the needs of high-end, enterprise WAN and service provider environments
- Cisco AIP for the Cisco 7500 and 7000 series of routers

- Cisco ATM Network Interface Module (NIM) for the Cisco 4700 and 4500 series of routers

- Cisco edge devices such as the Catalyst 5000 and Catalyst 3000 switches, which connect legacy LANs with an ATM network

— **NOTES** —————————————————————————————

The LightStream 1010 is a Cisco campus ATM switch that is specifically designed for workgroup and campus backbone deployment. However, it can also meet the needs of a low-end enterprise environment. For more information on the LightStream 1010 switch as a workgroup switch, see Chapter 12, "Designing Switched LAN Internetworks."

Stratm-Based Cisco WAN Products

Stratm Technology is the basis for a new class of ATM WAN switch products. These products are designed to take users to the next level in building the world's most efficient and scalable ATM networks. High-speed, high-density products based on Stratm Technology provide advanced features, such as the following:

- Standards-based traffic management

- Fair sharing of bandwidth

- Unmatched port density and switch scalability

- High-performance SVCs

- Multicast capability

Cisco/StrataCom BPX

The Cisco/StrataCom BPX Service Node is a standards-based, multiservice ATM switch designed to deliver the highest levels of network scalability, flexibility, and efficiency. The BPX achieves multiservice functionality, efficient use of bandwidth, high performance for all users, and guaranteed QoS for all traffic types through its advanced traffic management features. These advanced traffic management capabilities are based on the first fully compliant implementation of the ATM Forum's Traffic Management Specification V. 4.0, as well as the International Telecommunications Union (ITU) Recommendations I.371 and I.35B.

The BPX incorporates Stratm Technology, which is implemented in custom silicon ASICs. Stratm distributes advanced ATM capabilities throughout the switch modules, resulting in unmatched port density, support for hundreds of thousands of connections, and new functionality. Advanced traffic management features, together with an optimized hardware architecture, enable the switch to simultaneously support ATM, Frame Relay, Internet, voice, wireless communication, video, switched internetworking, and circuit emulation services.

The BPX also offers operational ease. With the BPX's 20-Gbps capacity of high-throughput, low-latency switching, and support for multiple classes of service, service providers can deliver innovative revenue-generating data, voice, and video services. Large enterprises can combine LAN, Systems Network Architecture (SNA), voice, and other types of traffic over a single WAN backbone, as shown in Figure 8–20. The BPX enables organizations to migrate to a new generation of ATM networks and complement existing investments in routers and Frame Relay switches.

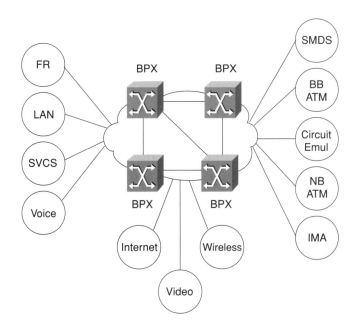

Figure 8–20
BXP multiservice platform.

As Table 8–4 indicates, Stratm allows the BPX to deliver high application performance and guaranteed network responsiveness for all users.

Table 8–4 *BPX Metrics with Stratm*

Category	Amount
Ports/Node	
• DS3/E3	144
• OC-3/STM-1	96
• OC-12/STM-4	24
SVCs/Node	
• Active	384,000
• Calls/Second	4,000
Buffers/Node	22,000,000 cells

Table 8–4 *BPX Metrics with Stratm, Continued*

Buffers/Card	900,000 cells
Nodes/Network	
• Peer group nodes	100
• Number of peer groups	Unlimited

The BPX includes high-density, Broadband Switch Module (BXM) cards that provide standard interfaces for connecting to cell-based customer premises equipment via ATM UNI or to non-Cisco networks via NNI.

Cisco/StrataCom BXM Switch Modules

The Stratm-based BXM cards are a family of highly configurable interface modules that extend today's central crosspoint ATM switch architecture to highly scalable distributed architectures. By integrating Stratm into its ATM platforms, Cisco delivers dramatically increased connections and port density as well as new features and functionality. Equipped with these Stratm-based products, network designers can deploy the most efficient, scalable ATM networks possible.

The major functions of the BXM modules include the following:

- Available Bit Rate Engine (ABRE)
- Serial interface and multicast buffer subsystem (SIMBS)
- Routing, control, monitoring, and policing (RCMP)
- SONET/Synchronous Digital Hierarchy (SDH) UNI (SUNI)

Table 8–5 provides a summary of the BXM switch modules.

Table 8–5 *BXM Family of Switch Modules*

BXM Switch Module	Description
BXM-T3/E3 Broadband Switch Module	A 6- or 12-port, Digital Signal 3 (DS3) (45 or 34 Mbps) ATM interface card, which supports E3/DS3 native ATM access and trunk ports, for the BPX switch. The interface can be configured for trunk, public, or private UNI applications on a per-port basis to provide a high-density, low-cost, broadband ATM networking solution.

Table 8–5 *BXM Family of Switch Modules, Continued*

BXM-155 Broadband Switch Module	An OC-3c/STM-1 version of the BXM interface card, which supports OC-3/STM-1 native ATM access and trunk ports for the BPX switch. It operates at the SONET/SDH rate of 155.520 Mbps. The card provides four or eight OC-3/STM-1 ATM ports per card, each of which can be configured for either trunk or access application.
BXM-622 Broadband Switch Module	An OC-12c/STM-4 version of the BXM interface card, which supports OC-12/STM-4 native ATM access and trunk ports for the BPX switch. It operates at the SONET/SDH rate of 622.08 Mbps. One- or two-port versions of the card are available; both can be configured for either trunk or access application.

The BXM cards support ATM-Frame Relay internetworking and service internetworking. They also allow you to configure PVCs or SVCs for the following defined service classes:

- Constant Bit Rate (CBR)
- Variable Bit Rate-Real Time (VBR-RT)
- Variable Bit Rate-Non-Real Time (VBR-NRT)
- Unspecified Bit (UBR)
- Available Bit Rate (ABR)

The BPX with Stratm architecture supports up to 16 independent classes of service, thereby protecting your hardware investment as the industry defines additional traffic types.

AXIS Interface Shelf

The AXIS interface shelf enables the BPX Service Node to support a wide range of user services. AXIS modules adapt incoming data to 53-byte ATM cells using industry-standard ATM adaptation layers (AALs) for transport over the ATM network.

Because the AXIS interface shelf will support a range of services from a single platform, organizations can reduce equipment costs, fully utilize their investments in existing premises equipment, and rapidly deploy new services as required.

Services below 34 Mbps are provisioned on the AXIS shelf, and the following interfaces are supported:

- Frame Relay
- High-speed Frame Relay
- ATM Frame UNI

- SMDS
- T1/E1 ATM UNI
- n x T1/E1 inverse multiplexing for ATM (IMATM) UNI
- Circuit emulation
- ISDN switched access

Each AXIS shelf aggregates traffic from as many as 80 T1 or E1 ports onto a single port of the multi-port broadband interface card. This high-port density maximizes use of the BPX high-capacity switch fabric. A compact footprint minimizes the space required within central offices. Each 9-inch, rack-mounted shelf supports more than 2,000 64-Kbps users.

Cisco/StrataCom IGX Family of Switches

For wide-area networking, LAN data flowing between different enterprise sites is aggregated by the router and then mixed with voice and other legacy data streams across the corporate wide-area backbone. Traditionally, these corporate backbones use TDM technology. However, as the use of LAN data has exploded and older TDM equipment has been fully depreciated, newer solutions can be cost justified. Enterprises are increasingly turning to a new public service officers (for example, VPN, Frame Relay, and intranets) and a new generation of Frame Relay/ATM-based enterprise switches to maximize the efficiency and minimize the cost of their networks.

The Cisco/StrataCom IGX family of switches provides the needed linkage to integrate the high-speed LAN data and the lower-speed voice and legacy data across the enterprise backbone in the most cost-effective manner. The IGX family of switches is specifically designed for enterprise integration.

The IGX family of ATM enterprise WAN switches includes the IGX8 (8-slot switch), the IGX16 (16-slot switch), and IGX32 (32-slot switch). The IGX family can provide the following enterprise WAN support:

- *Voice*—UVM and CVM
- *Legacy data*—HDM and LDM
- *ATM*—ALM
- *Frame Relay*—UFM and FRM
- *Trunks*—NTM, BTM, and ALM

Benefits of the IGX

With the IGX switch, you can leverage ATM to save costs as follows:

- Apply utilization rates in your network design to source PVCs
- Combine multiple networks into one multiservice network
- Optimize the transmission network with design tools

For example, you can use StrataView+, a network management tool, for network discovery. You can also use the Configuration Extraction Tool (CET) to populate the design data set with existing facilities. With such design tools, incremental network design is possible.

In addition to lower costs of networks, other major benefits of deploying the IGX in an enterprise internetwork include the following:

- Multiband/multiservice
- Better application performance
- Reliability
- Investment protection

Sample IGX Configuration

This section provides an example of how IGX switches can be deployed in an enterprise internetwork. In this example, a postal service has 180,000 employees and 180 mail-sorting offices. The current network design, which is a TDM network, has 750 LANs, 350 routers, 220 X.25 switches, and 110 PBXs. The network handles approximately 70 million voice minutes of traffic per year.

Currently, the enterprise is confronted with the following problems with the existing network design and network requirements:

- Poor performance on the existing TDM network
- Exponential growth of LAN traffic
- Many new applications
- Inability of the existing WAN to scale up

Figure 8–21 shows an example of how the IGX switches can be deployed throughout the network to address these problems.

By deploying the IGX switches throughout the enterprise internetwork, the following benefits are obtained:

- Integration of the voice and data networks
- Improved performance for each type of traffic
- Better response times for new applications
- Reduced downtime
- Higher bandwidth utilization (fivefold increase in traffic using existing trunks)
- Implementation of a scalable network that supports rapid deployment of new services
- Simplification of network design with a reduction in management costs

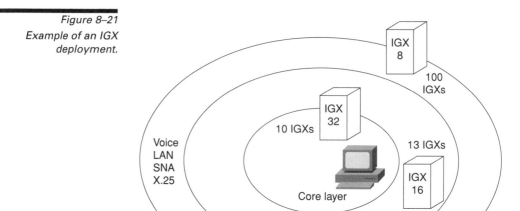

Figure 8–21
Example of an IGX deployment.

Cisco ATM LANE Products

Cisco offers a complete ATM LANE solution by providing the following:

- Inter-ATM ELAN communication through routing
- LEC/BUS/LECS/LES on Cisco 7500, 7000, 4500, and 4000 series routers
- LEC/BUS/LECS/LES on the Catalyst 5000 and Catalyst 3000 switches
- Cisco LightStream 1010 ATM switch

Cisco 7500 Router Series

Data center consolidation, client-server architectures using centralized servers, and growth in remote sites all drive the rapidly growing need for WAN bandwidth. High-performance routing provides critical functionality in the high-speed WAN environment.

The Cisco 7500 router series extends the capabilities of the Cisco 7000 family and incorporates distributed switching functions. The distributed switching capability allows network designers to provide the high-performance routing necessary to support networks using ATM, multilayer LAN switching, and VLAN technologies.

The Cisco 7500 family of routers offers a broad support of high-speed ATM and WAN interfaces. The higher port densities supported the Cisco 7500 series easily handles the large number of interfaces that result from more remote site connectivity. The Cisco IOS software adaptive rerouting increases network availability, and its flexible interfaces provide support for multiple services and a migration path to ATM. Network designers can deploy the Cisco 7500 series in the WAN environment to access multiple types of carrier service offerings as they migrate from TDM backbones to ATM backbones. The Cisco 7500 series also provides network security and minimizes the loss of transparency. The Cisco 7500 series running Cisco IOS Software Release 11.0 or later provides tools for network configuration, fault detection, and minimizing unnecessary traffic across expensive wide-area links.

NOTES

The features discussed for the Cisco 7000 series are also applicable to the Cisco 7500 series.

Cisco 7000 Series

With a CxBus card, the AIP can be installed in a Cisco 7000 and Cisco 7500 series routers and is compatible with all the interface processors as well as the Route Processor (RP), the Switch Processor (SP), the Silicon Switch Processor (SSP), and the new Route Switch Processor (RSP). The AIP supports the following features:

- Single, native ATM port with transmission rates up to 155 Mbps over a variety of ATM physical layer interface media modules (PLIM), eliminating the need for an external ATM data service unit (DSU).

- Multiprotocol support over ATM for all the popular network operating systems and the internet protocol: IP, AppleTalk, Novell IPX, DECnet, Banyan VINES, XNS, and OSI CLNS.

- ATM Adaptation Layers (AALs) 3/4 and 5.

- Dual RISC and dual-SAR design for high-speed cell and packet processing.

- Interim Local Management Interface (ILMI) for ATM address acquisition/registration.

NOTES

Cisco IOS Software Release 10.0 supports AAL5 PVCs only.

Cisco IOS Software Release 10.0 and later support ATM Forum UNI Specification V3.0, which includes the user-to-network ATM signaling specification. The AIP card uses RFC 1483 (Multiprotocol Encapsulation over AAL5) to transport data through an ATM network. RFC 1483 specifies the use of an LLC/SNAP 8-byte header to identify the encapsulated protocol. It also specifies a null encapsulation (VC Mux) which, instead of headers, creates a separate virtual circuit per protocol.

The following physical layer interface modules (PLIMs) are available for the AIP:

- TAXI 4B/5B 100-megabits-per-second (Mbps) multimode fiber-optic cable
- SONET/SDH 155-Mbps multimode fiber-optic (STS-3c or STM1) cable
- SONET/SDH 155-Mbps single mode fiber-optic (STS-3c or STM1) cable
- E3 34-Mbps coaxial cable
- DS-3 45-Mbps cable

The total bandwidth through all the AIPs configured in a router should be limited to 200 Mbps full duplex. For that reason, only the following combinations are supported:

- Two TAXI interfaces
- One SONET and one E3 interface
- Two SONET interfaces, one of which is lightly used
- Five E3 interfaces

The AIP includes hardware support for various traffic-shaping functions. Virtual circuits can be assigned to one of eight rate queues, each of which is programmable for a different peak rate. Each virtual circuit can be assigned an average rate and specific burst size. The signaling request specifies the size of the burst that is sent at the peak rate, and after that burst, the rest of the data is sent at the average rate.

The following are the configurable traffic parameters on the AIP:

- Forward peak cell rate
- Backward peak cell rate
- Forward sustainable cell rate
- Backward sustainable cell rate
- Forward maximum burst
- Backward maximum burst

Figure 8–22 shows how the routing table and address resolution table on Router A are used to forward data to a workstation behind Router C.

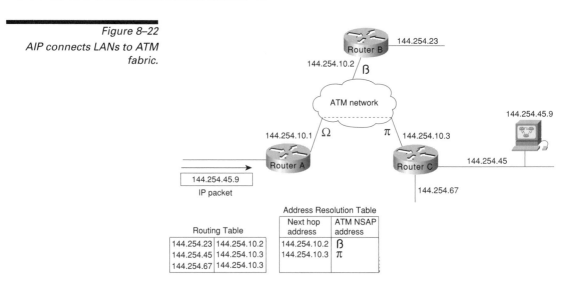

Figure 8–22
AIP connects LANs to ATM fabric.

The routing table on Router A performs its usual function of determining the next hop by mapping the network number of the destination (in this case 144.254.45 from the incoming packet) to the IP address of the router to which the destination network is connected (in this case, 144.254.10.3, which is the IP address of Router C). An address resolution table maps the next-hop IP address to an ATM NSAP address (in this case, represented by π). Router A signals Router C over the ATM network to establish a virtual connection, and Router A uses that connection to forward the packet to Router C. Figure 8–23 shows the layers through which the packet travels.

Figure 8–23

Path of an IP packet over the ATM fabric.

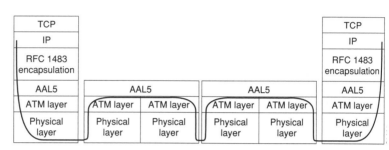

Configuring the AIP for ATM Signaling

The following commands configure an AIP for ATM signaling:

```
interface atm 4/0
ip address 128.24.2.1 255.255.255.0
no keepalive
atm nsap-address AB.CDEF.01.234567.890A.BCDE.F012.3456.7890.1234.12
atm pvc 1 0 5 qsaal
map-group shasta
atm rate-queue 0 155
atm rate-queue 1 45

map-list shasta
ip 144.222.0.0 atm-nsap BB.CDEF.01.234567.890A.BCDE.F012.3456.7890.1234.12
ip 144.3.1.2 atm-nsap BB.CDEF.01.234567.890A.BCDE.F012.3456.7890.1234.12 class QOSclass

map-class QOSclass
atm forward-peak-cell-rate-clp0 15000
atm backward-max-burst-size-clp0 96
```

The following explains relevant portions of the ATM signaling configuration:

- **no keepalive**—Required because Cisco IOS Software Release 10.0 does not support the ILMI, an ATM Forum specification.

- **atm nsap-address**—Required for signaling.

- **atm pvc**—Sets up a PVC to carry signaling requests to the switch. In this case, the command sets up a circuit whose VPI value is 0 and whose VCI value is 5, as recommended by the ATM Forum.

- **map-group**—Associates a map list named **shasta** to this interface.

- **atm rate-queue**—Sets up two rate queues. Rate queue number 0 is for 155-Mbps transfers, and rate queue number 1 is for 45-Mbps transfers.

- **map-list** and **ip 144.222.0.0**—Sets up the static mapping of an IP network number to an ATM NSAP address without any QoS parameters. The **ip 144.3.1.2** command maps an IP host address to an ATM NSAP address with the QoS parameters specified in the map class named **QOSclass**.

- **map-class, atm forward-peak-cell-rate-clp0,** and **atm backward-max-burst-size-clp0**—Sets up QoS parameters associated with this connection. The connection must support a forward peak cell rate of 15 Kbps and a backward burst size of 96 cells.

Interoperability with DXI

When configuring an AIP to communicate with a Cisco router that uses ATM DXI to connect to the ATM network, the AIP requires Network Layer Protocol Identifier (NLPID) encapsulation, which is provided in Cisco IOS Software Release 10.2, or the ATM DXI requires LLC/SNAP encapsulation.

Cisco 4500/4700 ATM NIM

The NIM is the midrange ATM router interface for the Cisco 4500 and Cisco 4700 series of routers. The function of this ATM module is internally much different than that of the AIP module. With the Cisco 4500 and 4700 series router, the packet memory is kept in a 4-Mbps pool that is shared by all of the NIMs. The Cisco IOS software also runs on these routers so the same ATM functionality and commands work on both the Cisco AIP and NIM. The performance of the NIM is actually better in the NIM for process and fast-switched protocols, but the Autonomous/SSE switching available in the Cisco 7000 series, and fast switching available on the Cisco 7500 series remain the fastest in the product family.

In this regard, network designers can deploy the Cisco 4700 series of routers to offer LANE services because the BUS is in the fast switching path. It is important to note that the NIM supports 1024 VCCs and this should be taken into consideration in SVC-intensive LANE networks.

ATM Edge Devices

The Catalyst 5000, 5500, and Catalyst 3000 switches are LAN switches that have ATM uplinks. Consequently, network designers can use these switches as edge devices to interconnect legacy LANs to an ATM network.

Catalyst 5000 as an ATM Edge Device

The Catalyst 5000 ATM LANE Dual PHY modules integrates high-speed, switched LANs across an ATM campus network providing legacy LANs with access to ATM-based services in the backbone. The ATM module supports two (one primary and one secondary) 155-Mbps OC-3c interfaces with a wide range of media options (for example, single-mode fiber, multimode fiber, and unshielded twisted pair [UTP Category 5]).

A maximum of three ATM LANE modules can be supported simultaneously in one Catalyst 5000 switch to provide redundant, fault-tolerant connections. This module delivers redundant LANE services through Cisco's LANE SSRP.

The Catalyst 5000 ATM module is designed to provide Ethernet to ATM functionality by acting as a LANE client. The BUS functionality on the Catalyst 5000 ATM card was designed for very high performance. The data path for the BUS is implemented entirely in firmware/hardware.

Catalyst 3000 as an ATM Edge Device

The Catalyst 3000 switch can also function as an ATM LANE edge device. Like the Catalyst 5000 switch, the Catalyst 3000 switch also supports an ATM LANE module. The Catalyst 3000 ATM module supports a 155-Mpbs OC-3c multimode optical interface that is compliant with the ATM Forum UNI 3.0 and UNI 3.1 specifications. The ATM module in conjunction with other Catalyst 3000 modules can also be used to connect Fast Ethernet hubs, switches, and routers to the ATM backbone.

Support for Cisco's VLAN Trunking Protocol (VTP) allows multiple Catalyst 3000 and Catalyst 5000 switches within a network to share ELAN or VLAN configuration information. For example, VTP will automatically map VLANs based upon Fast Ethernet trunks (ISL) to ELANs based upon ATM trunks.

LightStream 1010 ATM Switches

The LightStream 1010 family of switches are modular switches designed for campuses or workgroups depending upon the types of interfaces used. Its central processor is dedicated to a single, field replaceable ATM Switch/Processor module (ASP).

Single-Switch Designs

Because ATM can use existing multimode fiber networks, FDDI campus backbones can be easily upgraded from 100-Mbps FDDI to 155-Mbps point-to-point ATM. If the network has spare fiber, AIPs can be installed in each router and interconnected with a LightStream 1010 switch, as shown in Figure 8–24. In this topology, each router has a 155-Mbps point-to-point connection to every other router on the ring.

The addition of the ATM switch creates a parallel subnet. During the migration to ATM, a routing protocol, such as the Interior Gateway Routing Protocol (IGRP), can be used to force FDDI routing, as shown by the following commands:

```
interface fddi 1/0
ip address 4.4.4.1 255.255.255.0
interface atm 2/0
ip address 4.4.5.1 255.255.255.0
router igrp 109
network 4.4.0.0
distance 150 4.4.5.0 0.0.0.255
```

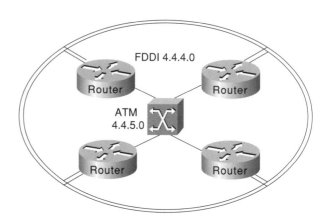

Figure 8–24
Parallel FDDI and ATM
backbone.

The **distance** command causes ATM to appear as a less desirable network and forces routing over FDDI. If the network does not have spare fiber, a concentrator can be installed. Later, an ATM switch can be installed, as shown in Figure 8–25, which can be used to migrate ATM slowly throughout the network, using FDDI as a backup.

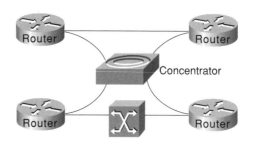

Figure 8–25
FDDI topology with
concentrator and ATM switch.

Broadcasting in Single-Switch ATM Networks

There are two ways to configure broadcasting in a single-switch ATM network. First, the routers can be configured for *pseudo* broadcasting over point-to-point PVCs, as shown in Figure 8–26.

The following commands on each router set up a PVC between each router:

```
atm pvc 1 1 1 aal5snap
atm pvc 2 2 1 aal5snap
atm pvc 3 3 1 aal5snap
```

The following commands on each router cause that router to replicate broadcast packets and send them out on each PVC:

```
ip 4.4.5.1 atm-vc 1 broadcast
ip 4.4.5.2 atm-vc 2 broadcast
ip 4.4.5.3 atm-vc 3 broadcast
```

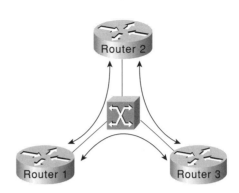

Figure 8–26
Router-based pseudo
broadcasting using
point-to-point PVCs.

The disadvantage of router-based broadcasting is that it places the burden of replicating packets on the routers instead of on the switch, which has the resources to replicate packets at a lower cost to the network.

The second way to configure broadcasting is to configure the routers for *switch-based* broadcasting, as shown in Figure 8–27. With switch-based broadcasting, each router sets up a point-to-multipoint PVC to the other routers in the network. When each router maintains a point-to-multipoint PVC to every other router in the network, the broadcast replication burden is transferred to the switch.

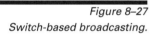

Figure 8–27
Switch-based broadcasting.

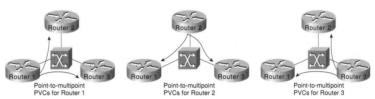

The following commands configure a point-to-multipoint PVC on each router:

```
ip 4.4.4.1 atm-vc 1
ip 4.4.4.2 atm-vc 2
ip 4.4.4.3 atm-vc 3
ip 4.4.4.0 atm-vc broadcast
```

In Figure 8–27, the routers still have full-mesh connectivity to every other router in the network, but the connections are not set up as broadcast PVCs. Instead, each router designates the point-to-multipoint PVC as a broadcast PVC and lets the switch handle replication, which is a function for which the switch is optimized.

The LightStream 1010 switch supports the ATM Forum Private Network-Network Interface (PNNI) Phase 0 protocol, which uses static maps to switch around failed links. Figure 8–28 shows the static maps on the switch to which Router A is connected.

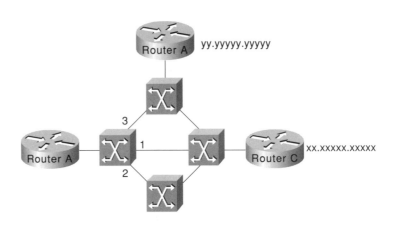

Figure 8–28

*Example of a multiswitch
network that uses the PNNI
phase 0 protocol.*

When a physical link fails, the ATM switch tears down the virtual circuits for that link. When the AIP in Router A detects that a virtual circuit has been torn down, it resignals the network to reestablish the VCC. When the switch receives the new signaling packet and realizes that the primary interface is down, it forwards the request on the alternative interface.

SUMMARY

ATM is an efficient technology to integrate LANs and WANs as well as to combine multiple networks into one multiservice network. This chapter has described the current Asynchronous Transfer Mode (ATM) technologies that network designers can use in their networks. It also made recommendations for designing non-ATM networks.

Designing Packet Service Internetworks

This chapter focuses on the implementation of packet-switching services and addresses internetwork design in terms of the following packet-switching service topics:

- Hierarchical internetwork design
- Topology design
- Broadcast issues
- Performance issues

Information provided in this chapter is organized around these central topics. An introductory discussion outlines the general issues; subsequent discussions focus on considerations for the specific packet-switching technologies.

NOTES

This chapter focuses on general packet-switching considerations and Frame Relay internetworks. Frame Relay was selected as the focus for this chapter because it presents a comprehensive illustration of design considerations for interconnection to packet-switching services.

UNDERSTANDING PACKET-SWITCHED INTERNETWORK DESIGN

The chief trade-off in linking local-area networks (LANs) and private wide-area networks (WANs) into packet-switching data network (PSDN) services is between cost and performance. An ideal design optimizes packet-services. Service optimization does not necessarily translate into picking the service mix that represents the lowest possible tariffs. Successful packet-service implementations result from adhering to two basic rules:

- When implementing a packet-switching solution, be sure to balance cost savings derived by instituting PSDN interconnections with your computing community's performance requirements.

- Build an environment that is manageable and that can scale up as more WAN links are required.

These rules recur as underlying themes in the discussions that follow. The introductory sections outline the overall issues that influence the ways in which packet-switched internetworks are designed.

Hierarchical Design

The objective of a hierarchical internetwork design is to modularize the elements of a large internetwork into layers of internetworking. The general model of this hierarchy is described in Chapter 2, "Internetworking Design Basics." The key functional layers in this model are the access, distribution, and backbone (or core) routing layers. In essence, a hierarchical approach strives to split networks into subnetworks so that traffic and nodes can be more easily managed. Hierarchical designs also facilitate scaling of internetworks because new subnetwork modules and internetworking technologies can be integrated into the overall scheme without disrupting the existing backbone. Figure 9–1 illustrates the basic approach to hierarchical design.

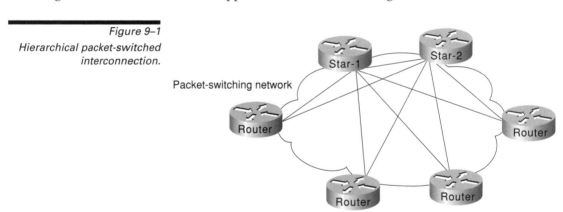

Figure 9–1

Hierarchical packet-switched interconnection.

Packet-switching network

Three basic advantages tilt the design decision in favor of a hierarchical approach:

- Scalability of Hierarchical Internetworks
- Manageability of Hierarchical Internetworks
- Optimization of Broadcast and Multicast Control Traffic

Scalability of Hierarchical Internetworks

Scalability is a primary advantage that supports using a hierarchical approach to packet-service connections. Hierarchical internetworks are more scalable because they allow you to grow your internetwork in incremental modules without running into the limitations that are quickly encountered with a flat, nonhierarchical structure.

However, hierarchical internetworks raise certain issues that require careful planning. These issues include the costs of virtual circuits, the complexity inherent in a hierarchical design (particularly when integrated with a meshed topology), and the need for additional router interfaces to separate layers in your hierarchy.

To take advantage of a hierarchical design, you must match your hierarchy of internetworks with a complementary approach in your regional topologies. Design specifics depend on the packet services you implement, as well as your requirements for fault tolerance, cost, and overall performance.

Manageability of Hierarchical Internetworks

Hierarchical designs offer several management advantages:

- *Internetwork simplicity*—Adopting a hierarchical design reduces the overall complexity of an internetwork by partitioning elements into smaller units. This partitioning of elements makes troubleshooting easier, while providing inherent protection against the propagation of broadcast storms, routing loops, or other potential problems.

- *Design flexibility*—Hierarchical internetwork designs provide greater flexibility in the use of WAN packet services. Most internetworks benefit from using a hybrid approach to the overall internetwork structure. In many cases, leased lines can be implemented in the backbone, with packet-switching services used in the distribution and access internetworks.

- *Router management*—With the use of a layered, hierarchical approach to router implementation, the complexity of individual router configurations is substantially reduced because each router has fewer neighbors or peers with which to communicate.

Optimization of Broadcast and Multicast Control Traffic

The effect of broadcasting in packet-service networks (discussed in "Broadcast Issues" later in this chapter) require you to implement smaller groups of routers. Typical examples of broadcast traffic are the routing updates and Novell Service Advertisement Protocol (SAP) updates that are broadcast between routers on a PSDN. An excessively high population of routers in any area or layer of the overall internetwork might result in traffic bottlenecks brought on by broadcast replication. A hierarchical scheme allows you to limit the level of broadcasting between regions and into your backbone.

Topology Design

After you have established your overall internetwork scheme, you must settle on an approach for handling interconnections among sites within the same administrative region or area. In designing any regional WAN, whether it is based on packet-switching services or point-to-point interconnections, there are three basic design approaches that you can adopt:

- Star Topologies
- Fully Meshed Topologies
- Partially Meshed Topologies

The following discussions introduce these topologies. Technology-specific discussions presented in this chapter address the applicability of these topologies for the specific packet-switching services.

NOTES

Illustrations in this chapter use lines to show the interconnections of specific routers on the PSDN network. These interconnections are virtual connections, facilitated by mapping features within the routers. Actual physical connections generally are made to switches within the PSDN. Unless otherwise specified, the connecting lines represent these virtual connections in the PSDN.

Star Topologies

A star topology features a single internetworking hub providing access from leaf internetworks into the backbone and access to each other only through the core router. Figure 9–2 illustrates a packet-switched star topology for a regional internetwork.

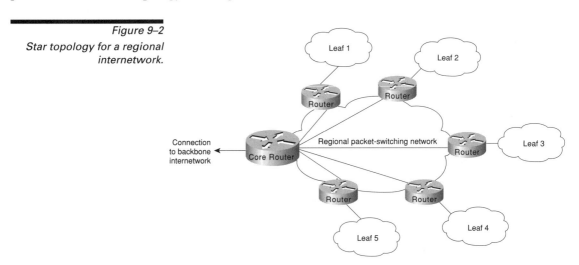

Figure 9–2
Star topology for a regional internetwork.

The advantages of a star approach are simplified management and minimized tariff costs. However, the disadvantages are significant. First, the core router represents a single point of failure. Second, the core router limits overall performance for access to backbone resources because it is a single pipe through which all traffic intended for the backbone (or for the other regional routers) must pass. Third, this topology is not scalable.

Fully Meshed Topologies

A fully meshed topology means that each routing node on the periphery of a given packet-switching network has a direct path to every other node on the cloud. Figure 9–3 illustrates this kind of arrangement.

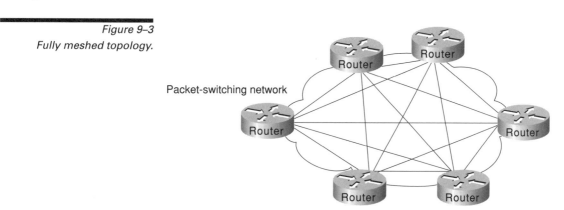

Figure 9–3
Fully meshed topology.

Packet-switching network

The key rationale for creating a fully meshed environment is to provide a high level of redundancy. Although a fully meshed topology facilitates support of all network protocols, it is not tenable in large packet-switched internetworks. Key issues are the large number of virtual circuits required (one for every connection between routers), problems associated with the large number of packet/broadcast replications required, and the configuration complexity for routers in the absence of multicast support in nonbroadcast environments.

By combining fully meshed and star approaches into a partially meshed environment, you can improve fault tolerance without encountering the performance and management problems associated with a fully meshed approach. The next section discusses the partially meshed approach.

Partially Meshed Topologies

A partially meshed topology reduces the number of routers within a region that have direct connections to all other nodes in the region. All nodes are not connected to all other nodes. For a non-meshed node to communicate with another nonmeshed node, it must send traffic through one of the collection point routers. Figure 9–4 illustrates such a situation.

There are many forms of partially meshed topologies. In general, partially meshed approaches are considered to provide the best balance for regional topologies in terms of the number of virtual circuits, redundancy, and performance.

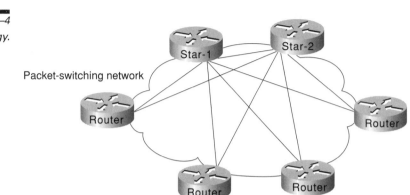

Figure 9–4
Partially meshed topology.

Broadcast Issues

The existence of broadcast traffic can present problems when introduced into packet-service inter-networks. Broadcasts are necessary for a station to reach multiple stations with a single packet when the specific address of each intended recipient is not known by the sending node. Table 9–1 lists common networking protocols and the general level of broadcast traffic associated with each, assuming a large-scale internetwork with many routing nodes.

Table 9–1   *Broadcast Traffic Levels of Protocols in Large-Scale Internetworks*

Network Protocol	Routing Protocol	Relative Broadcast Traffic Level
AppleTalk	Routing Table Maintenance Protocol (RTMP)	High
	Enhanced Interior Gateway Routing Protocol (Enhanced IGRP)	Low
Novell Internetwork Packet Exchange (IPX)	Routing Information Protocol (RIP)	High
	Service Advertisement Protocol (SAP)	High
	Enhanced IGRP	Low
Internet Protocol (IP)	RIP	High
	Interior Gateway Routing Protocol (IGRP)	High
	Open Shortest Path First (OSPF)	Low
	Intermediate System-to-Intermediate System (IS-IS)	Low
	Enhanced IGRP	Low
	Border Gateway Protocol (BGP)	None
	Exterior Gateway Protocol (EGP)	None

Table 9–1 *Broadcast Traffic Levels of Protocols in Large-Scale Internetworks, Continued*

Network Protocol	Routing Protocol	Relative Broadcast Traffic Level
DECnet Phase IV	DECnet Routing	High
DECnet Phase V	IS-IS	Low
International Organization for Standardization (ISO) Connectionless Network Service (CLNS)	IS-IS ISO-IGRP	Low High
Xerox Network Systems (XNS)	RIP	High
Banyan Virtual Integrated Network Service (VINES)	Routing Table Protocol (RTP) Sequenced RTP	High Low

The relative values *high* and *low* in Table 9–1 provide a general range for these protocols. Your situation and implementation will determine the magnitude of broadcast traffic. For example, the level of broadcast traffic generated in an AppleTalk Enhanced IGRP environment depends on the setting of the Enhanced IGRP hello-timer interval. Another issue relates to the size of the internetwork. In a small-scale internetwork, the amount of broadcast traffic generated by Enhanced IGRP nodes might be *higher* than with a comparable RTMP-based internetwork. However, for large-scale internetworks, Enhanced IGRP nodes generate substantially less broadcast traffic than RTMP-based nodes.

Managing packet replication is an important design consideration when integrating broadcast-type LANs (such as Ethernet) with nonbroadcast packet services (such as X.25). With the multiple virtual circuits that are characteristic of connections to packet-switched environments, routers must replicate broadcasts for each virtual circuit on a given physical line.

With highly meshed environments, replicating broadcasts can be expensive in terms of increased required bandwidth and number of CPU cycles. Despite the advantages that meshed topologies offer, they are generally impractical for large packet-switching internetworks. Nonetheless, some level of circuit meshing is essential to ensure fault tolerance. The key is to balance the trade-off in performance with requirements for circuit redundancy.

Performance Issues

When designing a WAN around a specific packet service type, you must consider the individual characteristics of the virtual circuit. For example, performance under certain conditions will depend on a given virtual circuit's capability to accommodate mixed protocol traffic. Depending on how the multiprotocol traffic is queued and streamed from one node to the next, certain protocols may require special handling. One solution might be to assign specific virtual circuits to specific protocol types. Performance concerns for specific packet-switching services include *committed information rates* (CIR) in Frame Relay internetworks and window size limitations in X.25 internetworks. (The CIR corresponds to the maximum average rate per connection [PVC] for a period of time.)

FRAME RELAY INTERNETWORK DESIGN

One of the chief concerns when designing a Frame Relay implementation is *scalability*. As your requirements for remote interconnections grow, your internetwork must be able to grow to accommodate changes. The internetwork must also provide an acceptable level of performance, while minimizing maintenance and management requirements. Meeting all these objectives simultaneously can be quite a balancing act. The discussions that follow focus on several important factors for Frame Relay internetworks:

- Hierarchical design
- Regional topologies
- Broadcast issues
- Performance issues

The guidelines and suggestions that follow are intended to provide a foundation for constructing scalable Frame Relay internetworks that balance performance, fault tolerance, and cost.

Hierarchical Design for Frame Relay Internetworks

In general, the arguments supporting hierarchical design for packet-switching networks discussed in the section "Hierarchical Design" earlier in this chapter apply to hierarchical design for Frame Relay internetworks. To review, the three factors driving the recommendation for implementing a hierarchical design are the following:

- Scalability of hierarchical internetworks
- Manageability of hierarchical internetworks
- Optimization of broadcast and multicast control traffic

The method by which many Frame Relay vendors tariff services is by Data Link Connection Identifier (DLCI), which identifies a Frame Relay permanent virtual connection. A Frame Relay permanent virtual connection is equivalent to an X.25 permanent virtual circuit, which, in X.25 terminology, is identified by a logical channel number (LCN). The DLCI defines the interconnection between Frame Relay elements. For any given internetwork implementation, the number of Frame Relay permanent virtual connections is highly dependent on the protocols in use and actual traffic patterns.

How many DLCIs can be configured per serial port? It varies depending on the traffic level. You can use all of them (about 1,000), but in common use, 200–300 is a typical maximum. If you broadcast on the DLCIs, 30–50 is more realistic due to CPU overhead in generating broadcasts. Specific guidelines are difficult because overhead varies by configuration. However, on low-end boxes (4,500 and below), the architecture is bound by the available I/O memory. The specific number depends on several factors that should be considered together:

- *Protocols being routed*—Any broadcast-intensive protocol constrains the number of assignable DLCIs. For example, AppleTalk is a protocol that is characterized by high levels of broadcast overhead. Another example is Novell IPX, which sends both routing and service updates resulting in higher broadcast bandwidth overhead. In contrast, IGRP is less broadcast intensive because it sends routing updates less often (by default, every 90 seconds). However, IGRP can become broadcast intensive if its IGRP timers are modified so that updates are sent more frequently.

- *Broadcast traffic*—Broadcasts, such as routing updates, are the single most important consideration in determining the number of DLCIs that can be defined. The amount and type of broadcast traffic will guide your ability to assign DLCIs within this general recommended range. Refer to Table 9–1 earlier in this chapter for a list of the relative level of broadcast traffic associated with common protocols.

- *Speed of lines*—If broadcast traffic levels are expected to be high, you should consider faster lines and DLCIs with higher CIR and excess burst (B_e) limits. You should also implement fewer DLCIs.

- *Static routes*—If static routing is implemented, you can use a larger number of DLCIs per line, because a larger number of DLCIs reduces the level of broadcasting.

- *Size of routing protocol and SAP updates*—The larger the internetwork, the larger the size of these updates. The larger the updates, the fewer the number of DLCIs that you can assign.

Two forms of hierarchical design can be implemented:

- Hierarchical Meshed Frame Relay Internetworks
- Hybrid Meshed Frame Relay Internetworks

Both designs have advantages and disadvantages. The brief discussions that follow contrast these two approaches.

Hierarchical Meshed Frame Relay Internetworks

The objectives of implementing a hierarchical mesh for Frame Relay environments are to avoid implementing excessively large numbers of DLCIs and to provide a manageable, segmented environment. The hierarchical meshed environment features full meshing within the core PSDN and full meshing throughout the peripheral internetworks. The hierarchy is created by strategically locating routers between internetwork elements in the hierarchy.

Figure 9–5 illustrates a simple hierarchical mesh. The internetwork illustrated in Figure 9–5 illustrates a fully meshed backbone, with meshed regional internetworks and broadcast networks at the outer periphery.

The key advantages of the hierarchical mesh are that it scales well and localizes traffic. By placing routers between fully meshed portions of the internetwork, you limit the number of DLCIs per physical interface, segment your internetwork, and make the internetwork more manageable. However, consider the following two issues when implementing a hierarchical mesh:

- *Broadcast and packet replication*—In an environment that has a large number of multiple DLCIs per router interface, excessive broadcast and packet replication can impair overall performance. With a high level of meshing throughout a hierarchical mesh, excessive broadcast and packet replication is a significant concern. In the backbone, where traffic throughput requirements are typically high, preventing bandwidth loss due to broadcast traffic and packet replication is particularly important.

- *Increased costs associated with additional router interfaces*—Compared with a fully meshed topology, additional routers are needed to separate the meshed backbone from the meshed peripheral internetworks. However, by using these routers, you can create much larger internetworks that scale almost indefinitely in comparison to a fully meshed internetwork.

Hybrid Meshed Frame Relay Internetworks

The economic and strategic importance of backbone environments often force internetwork designers to implement a hybrid meshed approach to WAN internetworks. Hybrid meshed internetworks feature redundant, meshed leased lines in the WAN backbone and partially (or fully) meshed Frame Relay PSDNs in the periphery. Routers separate the two elements. Figure 9–6 illustrates such a hybrid arrangement.

Hybrid hierarchical meshes have the advantages of providing higher performance on the backbone, localizing traffic, and simplifying scaling of the internetwork. In addition, hybrid meshed internetworks for Frame Relay are attractive because they can provide better traffic control in the backbone and they allow the backbone to be made of dedicated links, resulting in greater stability.

The disadvantages of hybrid hierarchical meshes include high costs associated with the leased lines as well as broadcast and packet replication that can be significant in access internetworks.

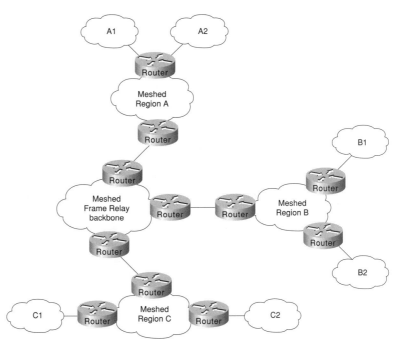

Figure 9–5
Fully meshed hierarchical
Frame Relay environment.

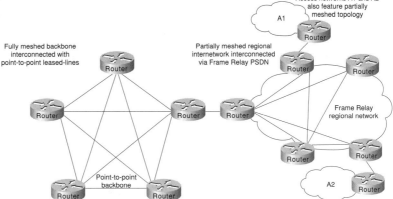

Figure 9–6
Hybrid hierarchical Frame
Relay internetwork.

Regional Topologies for Frame Relay Internetworks

You can adopt one of three basic design approaches for a Frame Relay-based packet service regional internetwork:

- Star Topologies
- Fully Meshed Topologies
- Partially Meshed Topologies

Each of these is discussed in the following sections. In general, emphasis is placed on partially meshed topologies integrated into a hierarchical environment. Star and fully meshed topologies are discussed for structural context.

Star Topologies

The general form of the star topology is addressed in the section "Topology Design" earlier in this chapter. Stars are attractive because they minimize the number of DLCIs required and result in a low-cost solution. However, a star topology presents some inherent bandwidth limitations. Consider an environment where a backbone router is attached to a Frame Relay cloud at 256 Kbps, while the remote sites are attached at 56 Kbps. Such a topology will throttle traffic coming off the backbone intended for the remote sites.

As suggested in the general discussion, a strict star topology does not offer the fault tolerance needed for many internetworking situations. If the link from the hub router to a specific leaf router is lost, all connectivity to the leaf router is lost.

Fully Meshed Topologies

A fully meshed topology mandates that every routing node connected to a Frame Relay internetwork is logically linked via an assigned DLCI to every other node on the cloud. This topology is not tenable for larger Frame Relay internetworks for several reasons:

- Large, fully meshed Frame Relay internetworks require many DLCIs. One is required for each logical link between nodes. As shown in Figure 9–7, a fully connected topology requires the assignment of $[n(n-1)]/2$ DLCIs, where n is the number of routers to be directly connected.

Figure 9–7
Fully meshed Frame Relay.

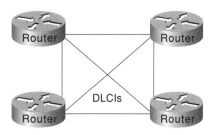

- Broadcast replication will choke internetworks in large, meshed Frame Relay topologies. Routers inherently treat Frame Relay as a broadcast medium. Each time a router sends a multicast frame (such as a routing update, spanning tree update, or SAP update), the router must copy the frame to each DLCI for that Frame Relay interface.

These problems combine to make fully meshed topologies unworkable and unscalable for all but relatively small Frame Relay implementations.

Partially Meshed Topologies

Combining the concepts of the star topology and the fully meshed topology results in the partially meshed topology. Partially meshed topologies are generally recommended for Frame Relay regional environments because they offer superior fault tolerance (through redundant stars) and are less expensive than a fully meshed environment. In general, you should implement the minimum meshing to eliminate single point-of-failure risk.

Figure 9–8 illustrates a twin-star, partially meshed approach. This arrangement is supported in Frame Relay internetworks running IP, ISO CLNS, DECnet, Novell IPX, AppleTalk, and bridging.

Figure 9–8

Twin-star, partially meshed Frame Relay internetwork.

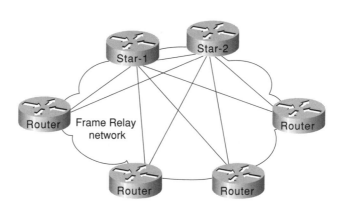

A feature called *virtual interfaces* (introduced with Software Release 9.21) allows you to create internetworks using partially meshed Frame Relay designs, as shown in Figure 9–8.

To create this type of internetwork, individual physical interfaces are split into multiple virtual (logical) interfaces. The implication for Frame Relay is that DLCIs can be grouped or separated to maximize utility. For example, small fully meshed clouds of Frame Relay-connected routers can travel over a group of four DLCIs clustered on a single virtual interface, whereas a fifth DLCI on a separate virtual interface provides connectivity to a completely separate internetwork. All of this connectivity occurs over a single physical interface connected to the Frame Relay service.

Prior to Software Release 9.21, virtual interfaces were not available and partially meshed topologies posed potential problems, depending on the internetwork protocols used. Consider the topology illustrated in Figure 9–9.

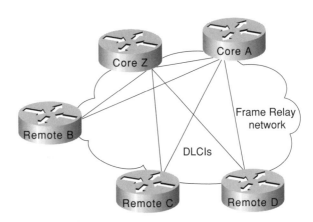

Figure 9–9
Partially meshed Frame Relay internetwork.

Given a standard router configuration and router software predating Software Release 9.21, the connectivity available in the internetwork shown in Figure 9–9 can be characterized as follows:

- Core A and Core Z can reach all the remote routers.

- Remote B, Remote C, and Remote D cannot reach each other.

For Frame Relay implementations running software prior to Software Release 9.21, the only way to permit connectivity among all these routers is by using a distance vector routing protocol that can disable split horizon, such as RIP or IGRP for IP. Any other internetwork protocol, such as AppleTalk or ISO CLNS, does not work. The following configuration listing illustrates an IGRP configuration to support a partially meshed arrangement.

```
router igrp 20
network 45.0.0.0
!
interface serial 3
encapsulation frame-relay
ip address 45.1.2.3 255.255.255.0
no ip split-horizon
```

This topology only works with distance vector routing protocols, assuming you want to establish connectivity from Remote B, C, or D to Core A or Core Z, but not across paths. This topology does not work with link state routing protocols because the router cannot verify complete adjacencies. Note that you will see routes and services of the leaf nodes that cannot be reached.

Broadcast Issues for Frame Relay Internetworks

Routers treat Frame Relay as a broadcast media, which means that each time the router sends a multicast frame (such as a routing update, spanning tree update, or SAP update), the router must replicate the frame to each DLCI for the Frame Relay interface. Frame replication results in substantial overhead for the router and for the physical interface.

Consider a Novell IPX environment with multiple DLCIs configured for a single physical serial interface. Every time a SAP update is detected, which occurs every 60 seconds, the router must replicate it and send it down the virtual interface associated with each DLCI. Each SAP frame contains up to seven service entries, and each update is 64 bytes. Figure 9–10 illustrates this situation.

NOTES

One way to reduce broadcasts is to implement more efficient routing protocols, such as Enhanced IGRP, and to adjust timers on lower speed Frame Relay services.

Figure 9–10
SAP replication in Frame Relay virtual interface environment.

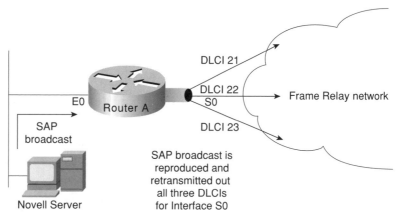

Creating a Broadcast Queue for an Interface

Very large Frame Relay networks might have performance problems when many DLCIs terminate in a single router or access server that must replicate routing updates and service advertising updates on each DLCI. The updates can consume access-link bandwidth and cause significant latency variations in user traffic; the updates can also consume interface buffers and lead to higher packet rate loss for both user data and routing updates.

To avoid such problems, you can create a special broadcast queue for an interface. The broadcast queue is managed independently of the normal interface queue, has its own buffers, and has a configurable size and service rate.

A broadcast queue is given a maximum transmission rate (throughput) limit measured in both bytes per second and packets per second. The queue is serviced to ensure that no more than this maximum is provided. The broadcast queue has priority when transmitting at a rate below the configured maximum, and hence has a guaranteed minimum bandwidth allocation. The two transmission rate limits are intended to avoid flooding the interface with broadcasts. The actual transmission rate limit in any second is the first of the two rate limits that is reached.

Performance Issues for Frame Relay Internetworks

Two important performance concerns must be addressed when you are implementing a Frame Relay internetwork:

- Packet-Switched Service Provider Tariff Metrics
- Multiprotocol Traffic Management Requirements

Each of these must be considered during the internetwork planning process. The following sections briefly discuss the impact that tariff metrics and multiprotocol traffic management can have on overall Frame Relay performance.

Packet-Switched Service Provider Tariff Metrics

When you contract with Frame Relay packet-switched service providers for specific capabilities, CIR, measured in bits per second, is one of the key negotiated tariff metrics. CIR is the maximum permitted traffic level that the carrier will allow on a specific DLCI into the packet-switching environment. CIR can be anything up to the capacity of the physical limitation of the connecting line.

Other key metrics are committed burst (B_c) and excess burst (B_e). B_c is the number of bits that the Frame Relay internetwork is committed to accept and transmit at the CIR. B_e sets the absolute limit for a DLCI in bits. This is the number of bits that the Frame Relay internetwork will attempt to transmit after B_c is accommodated. B_e determines a peak or maximum Frame Relay data rate (Max_R), where $Max_R = (B_c + B_e)/B_c * CIR$, measured in bits per second.

Consider the situation illustrated in Figure 9–11. In this environment, DLCIs 21, 22, and 23 are assigned CIRs of 56 Kbps. Assume the Max_R for each line is 112 Kbps (double the CIR). The serial line to which Router A is connected is a T1 line capable of 1.544 Mbps total throughput. Given that the type of traffic being sent into the Frame Relay internetwork consists of FTP file transfers, the potential is high that the router will attempt to transmit at a rate in excess of Max_R. If this occurs, traffic might be dropped without notification if the B_e buffers (allocated at the Frame Relay switch) overflow.

Unfortunately, there are relatively few ways to automatically prevent traffic on a line from exceeding the Max_R. Although Frame Relay itself uses the Forward Explicit Congestion Notification (FECN) and Backward Explicit Congestion Notification (BECN) protocols to control traffic in the Frame Relay internetwork, there is no formally standardized mapping between the Frame Relay (link) level and most upper-layer protocols. At this time, an FECN bit detected by a router is mapped to the congestion notification byte for DECnet Phase IV or ISO CLNS. No other protocols are supported.

The actual effect of exceeding specified CIR and derived Max_R settings depends on the types of application running on the internetwork. For instance, TCP/IP's backoff algorithm will see dropped packets as a congestion indication and sending hosts might reduce output. However, NFS has no backoff algorithm, and dropped packets will result in lost connections. When determining the CIR, B_c, and B_e for Frame Relay connection, you should consider the actual line speed and applications to be supported.

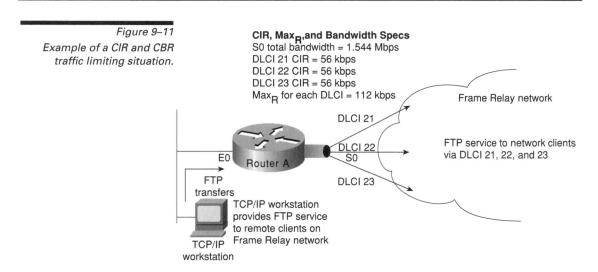

Figure 9-11
Example of a CIR and CBR
traffic limiting situation.

CIR, Max$_R$, and Bandwidth Specs
S0 total bandwidth = 1.544 Mbps
DLCI 21 CIR = 56 kbps
DLCI 22 CIR = 56 kbps
DLCI 23 CIR = 56 kbps
Max$_R$ for each DLCI = 112 kbps

Most Frame Relay carriers provide an appropriate level of buffering to handle instances when traffic exceeds the CIR for a given DLCI. These buffers allow excess packets to be spooled at the CIR and reduce packet loss, given a robust transport protocol such as TCP. Nonetheless, overflows can happen. Remember that although routers can prioritize traffic, Frame Relay switches cannot. You can specify which Frame Relay packets have low priority or low time sensitivity and will be the first to be dropped when a Frame Relay switch is congested. The mechanism that allows a Frame Relay switch to identify such packets is the discard eligibility (DE) bit.

This feature requires that the Frame Relay network be able to interpret the DE bit. Some networks take no action when the DE bit is set. Other networks use the DE bit to determine which packets to discard. The most desirable interpretation is to use the DE bit to determine which packets should be dropped first and also which packets have lower time sensitivity. You can define DE lists that identify the characteristics of packets to be eligible for discarding, and you can also specify DE groups to identify the DLCI that is affected.

You can specify DE lists based on the protocol or the interface, and on characteristics such as fragmentation of the packet, a specific TCP or User Datagram Protocol (UDP) port, an access list number, or a packet size.

NOTES

To avoid packet loss, implement unacknowledged application protocols (such as packetized video) carefully. With these protocols, there is a greater potential for buffer overflow.

Multiprotocol Traffic Management Requirements

With multiple protocols being transmitted into a Frame Relay internetwork through a single physical interface, you might find it useful to separate traffic among different DLCIs based on protocol type. To split traffic in this way, you must assign specific protocols to specific DLCIs. This can be done by specifying static mapping on a per virtual interface basis or by defining only specific types of encapsulations for specific virtual interfaces.

Figure 9–12 illustrates the use of virtual interfaces (assigned using subinterface configuration commands) to allocate traffic to specific DLCIs. In this case, traffic of each configured protocol is sent down a specific DLCI and segregated on a per-circuit basis. In addition, each protocol can be assigned a separate CIR and a separate level of buffering by the Frame Relay service provider.

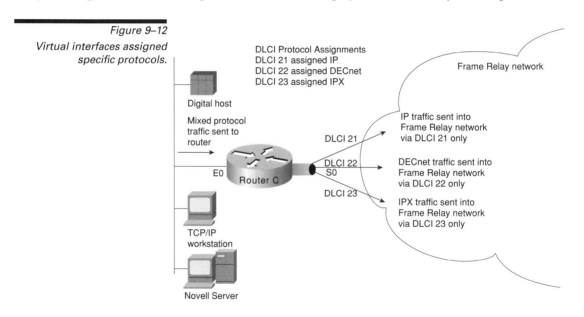

Figure 9–12

Virtual interfaces assigned specific protocols.

Figure 9–13 provides a listing of the subinterface configuration commands needed to support the configuration illustrated in Figure 9–12. The command listing in Figure 9–13 illustrates the enabling of the relevant protocols and the assignment of the protocols to the specific subinterfaces and associated Frame Relay DLCIs. Software Release 9.1 and later uses Frame Relay Inverse Address Resolution Protocol (IARP) to map protocol addresses to Frame Relay DLCIs dynamically. For that reason, Figure 9–13 does not show Frame Relay mappings.

You can use the following commands in Software Release 9.1 to achieve a configuration that is similar to the configuration shown in Figure 9–13:

Figure 9–13
Virtual interface configuration
example.

```
interface Ethernet 0
ip address 192.198.78-9 255.255.255.0
ipx network AC
denet cost 4
no mcp enabled
!
interface Serial0
no ip address
encapsulation frame–realy
!
interface Serial0.1 point–to–point
ip address 131.108.3.12.255.255.255.0
frame–relay interface–dlci 21 broadcast
no frame–relay inverse–arp IP 21
no frame–relay inverse–arp NOVELL 21
no frame–relay inverse–arp APPLETALK 21
no frame–relay inverse–arp INS 21
!
interface Serial0.2 point–to–point
no ip address
decnet cost 10
frame–relay interface–dlci 22 broadcast
no frame–relay inverse–arp IP 22
no frame–relay inverse–arp NOVELL 22
no frame–relay inverse–arp APPLETALK 22
no frame–relay inverse–arp INS 22
!
interface Serial0.3 point–to–point
no ip address
ipx network A3
frame–relay interface–dlci 23 broadcast
no frame–relay inverse–arp IP 23
no frame–relay inverse–arp NOVELL 23
no frame–relay inverse–arp APPLETALK 23
no frame–relay inverse–arp INS 23
!
router igrp 109
network 192.198.78.0
!
ip name–server 255.255.255.255
!
snmp–server community
!
line oon 0
line aux 0
line vty 0 4
end
```

Subinterface command configuration defining Frame Relay DLCIs and assigning protocols to specific DLCIs

You can use the following commands in Software Release 9.1 to achieve a configuration that is similar to the configuration shown in Figure 9–13:

```
Version 9.1
interface serial 0
ip address 131.108.3.12 255.255.255.0
decnet cost 10
novell network A3
frame-relay map IP 131.108.3.62 21 broadcast
frame-relay map DECNET 10.3 22 broadcast
frame-relay map NOVELL C09845 23 broadcast
```

CONFIGURING FRAME RELAY TRAFFIC SHAPING

Beginning with Release 11.2, Cisco IOS supports Frame Relay traffic shaping, which provides the following features:

- *Rate enforcement on a per-virtual circuit basis*—The peak rate for outbound traffic can be set to the CIR or some other user-configurable rate.

- *Dynamic traffic throttling on a per-virtual circuit basis*—When BECN packets indicate congestion on the network, the outbound traffic rate is automatically stepped down; when congestion eases, the outbound traffic rate is stepped up again. This feature is enabled by default.

- *Enhanced queuing support on a per-virtual circuit basis*—Either custom queuing or priority queuing can be configured for individual virtual circuits.

By defining separate virtual circuits for different types of traffic and specifying queuing and an outbound traffic rate for each virtual circuit, you can provide guaranteed bandwidth for each type of traffic. By specifying different traffic rates for different virtual circuits over the same time, you can perform virtual time division multiplexing. By throttling outbound traffic from high-speed lines in central offices to low-speed lines in remote locations, you can ease congestion and data loss in the network; enhanced queuing also prevents congestion-caused data loss. Traffic shaping applies to both PVCs and SVCs.

SUMMARY

This chapter has focused on the implementation of packet-switching services and addresses internetwork design in terms of the packet-switching service topics including hierarchical internetwork design, topology design, broadcast issues, and performance issues.

Designing DDR Internetworks

Dial-on-Demand Routing (DDR) provides network connections across Public Switched Telephone Networks (PSTNs). Dedicated wide-area networks are typically implemented on leased lines or more modern service provider options such as Frame Relay, SMDS, or ATM. Dial-on-Demand Routing provides session control for wide-area connectivity over circuit switched networks, which in turn provides on-demand services and decreased network costs.

DDR can be used over synchronous serial interfaces, Integrated Services Digital Network (ISDN) interfaces, or asynchronous serial interfaces. V.25bis and DTR dialing are used for Switched 56 CSU/DSUs, ISDN terminal adapters (TAs), or synchronous modems. Asynchronous serial lines are available on the auxiliary port on Cisco routers and on Cisco communication servers for connections to asynchronous modems. DDR is supported over ISDN using BRI and PRI interfaces.

INTRODUCTION TO DDR

Cisco IOS Dial-on-Demand Routing (DDR) provides several functions. First DDR spoofs routing tables to provide the image of full-time connectivity using Dialer interfaces. When the routing table forwards a packet to a Dialer interface, DDR then filters out the interesting packets for establishing, maintaining, and releasing switched connections. Internetworking is achieved over the DDR maintained connection using PPP or other WAN encapsulation techniques (such as HDLC, X.25, SLIP). Internetwork engineers can use the model presented in this chapter to construct scalable, DDR internetworks that balance performance, fault tolerance, and cost.

DDR Design Stack

Similar to the model provided by the OSI for understanding and designing internetworking, a stacked approach, shown in Figure 10–1, can be used to design DDR networks.

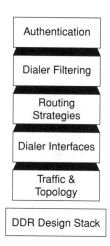

Figure 10–1
DDR design stack.

Dialer Clouds

The network formed by the interconnected DDR devices can generically be labeled the *dialer media* or *dialer cloud*. The scope of the dialer cloud includes only the intended interconnected devices and does not include the entire switched media (the entire ISDN spans the globe and is beyond the scope of the dialer cloud). The exposure to the ISDN must be considered when designing security.

The fundamental characteristics of dialer clouds are as follows:

- Dialer clouds are collective bundles of potential and active point-to-point connections.
- On active connections, dialer clouds form an NBMA (non-broadcast multiaccess) media similar to Frame Relay.
- For outbound dialing on switched circuits (such as ISDN) network protocol address to directory number mapping must be configured.
- Inactive DDR connections are spoofed to appear as active to routing tables.
- Unwanted broadcast or other traffic causing unneeded connections can be prohibitively expensive. Potential costs on Tariffed media (such as ISDN) should be closely analyzed and monitored to prevent such loss.

The characteristics of dialer clouds affect every stage of DDR internetworking design. A solid understanding of network protocol addressing, routing, and filtering strategies can result in very robust and cost-effective internetworks.

TRAFFIC AND TOPOLOGY OF DDR

To determine the optimum topology, the DDR designer should perform a traffic analysis of internetworking applications that must be supported. This includes answering the following questions:

- How often does data traffic need to move between the DDR sites?
- What side of the DDR connection can establish the connection? How many remote sites?
- Is this a point-to-point solution or a multipoint solution?

Topologies

The most important factor in selecting the topology is the number of sites that will be supported. If only two sites will be involved, the point-to-point topology is used. If more than two sites are to be supported, the hub-and-spoke topology is typically used. For small numbers of sites with very low traffic volumes, the fully meshed topology may be the most appropriate solution.

Topologies for DDR covered in this section include:

- Point-to-point
- Fully meshed
- Hub-and-spoke

Point-to-Point Topology

In a simple point-to-point topology (see Figure 10–2), two sites are connected to each other. Each site has a dialer interface and maps the other site's address to a telephone number. If additional bandwidth is required, multiple links can be aggregated using Multilink PPP.

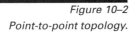

Figure 10–2
Point-to-point topology.

Fully Meshed Topology

The fully meshed configuration (see Figure 10–3) is recommended only for very small DDR networks. Fully meshed topologies can streamline the dialing process for any-to-any connectivity as each site can call any other site directly, rather than having to call through a central site, which then places another call to the target site. However, the configuration for each site is more complex because each site must have mapping information for every other site.

If load sharing is desired, interfaces can be configured for MultiLink PPP capability. In addition to the complexity of the configuration, either sufficient interfaces must be available on each device to deal with the possibility of all of the other devices calling in, or the possibility of contention for interfaces needs to be understood and dealt with.

Hub-and-Spoke DDR Solutions

In a hub-and-spoke topology (see Figure 10–4), a central site is connected to several remote sites. The remote sites communicate with the central site directly; they do not call any of the other remote sites. This topology works very well for scaling large solutions.

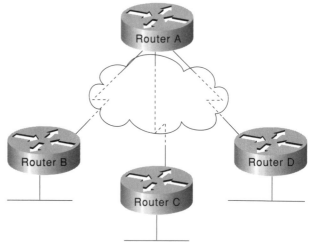

Figure 10–3
Fully meshed topology

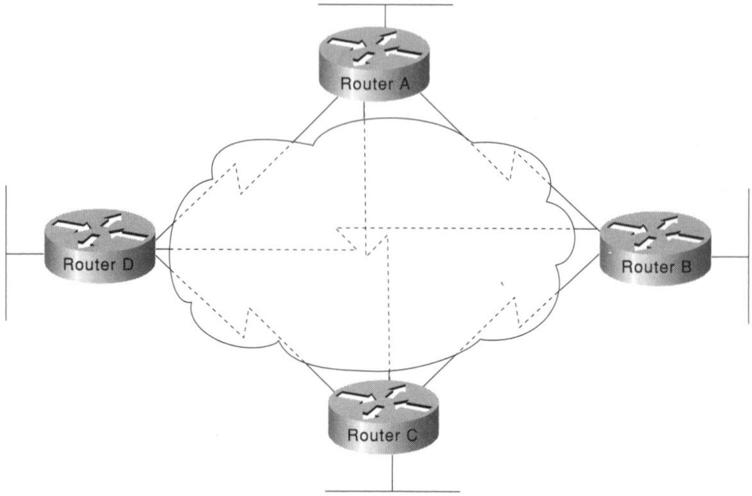

Figure 10–4
Hub-and-spoke topology.

Hub-and-spoke topologies are easier to configure than fully meshed topologies when multipoint topologies are required because remote site dialer interfaces are mapped only to the central site. This allows most of the design complexity (such as addressing, routing, and authentication) to be managed on the DDR Hub. Configuration support of the remote sites can be greatly simplified (similar to one end of a point-to-point topology).

If any-to-any connectivity initiation is required between remote sites, routing behavior may need to be modified depending on dialer interface behavior (that is, it may be necessary to disable split-horizon on distance vector routing protocols).

Multiple hubs can be used to provide further scaling of hub-and-spoke technologies. When using MultiLink PPP, as is very common in ISDN solutions, designers can implement Cisco IOS Multi-Chassis MultiLink PPP to scale the dial-in rotary group between multiple Network Access Servers. MultiChassis MultiLink PPP (MMP) is discussed further in Chapter 11, "Designing ISDN Internetworks," in the section "ISDN Scaling Techniques."

Traffic Analysis

For traffic analysis, develop a chart of which protocols need to be able to support DDR-based dialing from which devices. This will form the basis of the rest of the DDR design.

For example, Company KDT has selected a hub-and-spoke topology (to provide for scaling) and has developed the needs shown in Table 10–1 for its DDR cloud requirements.

Table 10–1 *DDR Protocol Connectivity Requirements for KDT*

Remote Site	Dial-In Protocols	Dial-Out Protocols	Notes
c700A	IP, IPX	None	
c700B	IP	None	
c1600A	IP, AppleTalk	IP	
c2500A	IP, IPX, AppleTalk	IP, IPX, AppleTalk	
c2500B	IP, IPX	IP	
NAS3600A	IP, IPX, AppleTalk	IP, IPX, AppleTalk	

The purpose of Table is to identify which sites and protocols require the capability to initiate the DDR connections. Once connectivity is established, each protocol requires two-way connectivity via routing tables and dialer cloud address mapping. Dial-in versus dial-out is from the perspective of the hub.

Often a primary goal of a DDR network is to offer a cost improvement over WAN charges associated with dedicated connections. Additional traffic analysis must be performed for each protocol at this or the Dialer Filtering design stage. Network applications use the infrastructure provided by the internetwork in many different and often unexpected ways. It is critical to perform a thorough analysis of real-world network traffic that will transit the dialer media in order to determine whether a DDR network can operate in a feasible manner. Packet capture and analysis tools provide the most valuable tool for this analysis.

DIALER INTERFACES

Access to the dialer media is via Cisco ISO Dialer interfaces. ISDN B channels, Synchronous Serial interfaces, and Asynchronous interfaces can all be converted to dialer interfaces using dialer interface configuration commands. To understand dialer interfaces, the following concepts are covered:

- Supported physical interfaces
- Dialer rotary groups
- Dialer profiles
- Dialer addressing
- Dialer mapping

Dialer Interfaces also provide the basis for support of routing table spoofing and dialer filtering. This section focuses on lower-layer characteristics of dialer interfaces.

Supported Physical Interfaces

Several types of physical interfaces can be enabled as dialer interfaces.

Synchronous Serial Interfaces

Dialing on synchronous serial lines can be initiated using V.25bis dialing or DTR dialing. V.25bis is the ITU standard for in-band dialing. With in-band dialing, dialing information is sent over the same connection that carries the data. V.25bis is used with a variety of devices, including synchronous modems, ISDN terminal adapters (TAs), and Switched 56 DSU/CSUs.

With DTR dialing, the DTR signal on the physical interface is activated, which causes some devices to dial a number configured into that device. When using DTR dialing, the interface cannot receive calls. But using DTR dialing allows lower-cost devices to be used in cases where only a single number needs to be dialed. Synchronous Serial Lines support PPP, HDLC, and X.25 datagram encapsulation.

To convert a synchronous serial interface into a dialer interface, use the Cisco IOS command **dialer in-band** or **dialer dtr**.

ISDN Interfaces

All ISDN devices subscribe to services provided by an ISDN service provider, usually a telephone company. ISDN DDR connections are made on B channels at 56 or 64 Kbps depending on the bearer capabilities of the end-to-end ISDN switching fabric. MultiLink PPP is often used to allow BRI devices to aggregate both B channels for great bandwidth and throughput. See Chapter 11, "Designing ISDN Internetworks," for guidance when designing ISDN internetworks.

ISDN BRI and PRI interfaces are automatically configured as dialer in-band interfaces. ISDN can support PPP, HDLC, X.25, and V.120 encapsulation. Typically, PPP will be used for DDR solutions. ISDN interfaces are automatically configured as dialer in-band interfaces.

For example, when examining a BRI interface on a Cisco IOS router, you can see that it is in the spoofing (pretending to be up/up so the routing table can point to this interface):

```
c1600A#sh int bri 0
BRI0 is up, line protocol is up (spoofing)
```

However, the physical interfaces are the individual B (BRI0:1 and BRI0:2) channels being managed by the dialer interface (BRI0).

```
c1600A#sh int bri 0 1
BRI0:1 is down, line protocol is down
  Hardware is BRI
  MTU 1500 bytes, BW 64 Kbit, DLY 20000 usec, rely 255/255, load 1/255
  Encapsulation PPP, loopback not set, keepalive set (10 sec)
  LCP Closed, multilink Closed
  Closed: IPCP, CDPCP
```

Asynchronous Modem Connections

Asynchronous connections are used by communication servers or through the auxiliary port on a router. Asynchronous DDR connections can be used to support multiple network layer protocols. When considering asynchronous DDR solutions, designers should consider if the internetworking applications can tolerate the longer call setup time and lower throughput of analog modems (in comparison with ISDN). For some design applications, DDR over asynchronous modem connections may provide a very cost-effective option.

In order to dial out using asynchronous connections, chat scripts must be configured so that modem dialing and login commands are sent to remote systems. For design flexibility, multiple chat scripts can be configured on *dialer maps*. Modem scripts can be used to configure modems for outbound calls. Login scripts are intended to deal with logging onto remote systems and preparing the link for establishment of PPP. Chat scripts are configured with expect-send pairs and keywords to modify settings, as follows:

```
chat-script dialnum "" "atdt\T" TIMEOUT 60 CONNECT \c
```

If you are using asynchronous DDR and calling a system that requires a character-mode login, use the **system-script** keyword with the **dialer map** command.

Chat scripts often encounter problems with timing due to the fact that they are run with much greater precision than when a human is controlling the connection. For example, sometimes when a modem sends the CONNECT message, it is not actually ready to send data, and may even disconnect if any data is received on the TX circuitry. To avoid such failure modes, pauses are added at the head of some send strings.

Each send string is terminated with a carriage return, even when it's a null string (""). Often the chat script will be set up without the final "send" string. This may produce unexpected results. Ensure that all chat scripts have complete expect-send pairs. If the final element in the chat script logic turns out to be an expect (as in the previous example), use the \c as the final send to suppress unwanted output.

Use the **debug chat** commands to troubleshoot chat script problems. Line-specific debugging can provide additional details when expect-send logic is failing. For an example of a large-scale Async DDR solution, see Chapter 25, "Scaling Dial-on-Demand Routing."

Dialer Rotary Groups

For hub-and-spoke or fully meshed topologies that support multiple connections between sites, physical interfaces can be grouped into rotary groups with the **dialer rotary-group** command. Physical interfaces assigned to the dialer rotary-group inherit their configuration from the corresponding interface dialer.

If one of the physical interfaces in a rotary group is busy, the next available interface can be used to place or receive a call. It is not necessary to configure rotary groups for BRI or PRI interfaces as ISDN B channels are automatically placed into a **rotary-group**, however multiple BRI or PRI interfaces can be grouped using **dialer rotary-group**.

Dialer Profiles

Dialer profiles introduced in Cisco IOS 11.2 offer additional design flexibility such as multisite bridging over ISDN. Dialer profiles provide an alternative methodology for designing DDR networks by removing the logical definition of dialer sites from the physical dialer interfaces.

Encapsulation Methods

When a clear DataLink is established between two DDR peers, internetworking datagrams must be encapsulated and framed for transport across the Dialer media. The encapsulation methods available depend on the physical interface being used. Cisco supports Point-to-Point Protocol (PPP), High-Level Data Link Control (HDLC), Serial Line Interface Protocol (SLIP), and X.25 data-link encapsulations for DDR:

- PPP is the recommended encapsulation method because it supports multiple protocols and is used for synchronous, asynchronous, or ISDN connections. In addition, PPP performs address negotiation and authentication and is interoperable with different vendors.

- HDLC is supported on synchronous serial lines and ISDN connections only. HDLC supports multiple protocols. However, HDLC does not provide authentication, which may be required if using dialer rotary groups.

- SLIP works on asynchronous interfaces only and is supported by IP only. Addresses must be configured manually. SLIP does not provide authentication and is interoperable only with other vendors that use SLIP.

- X.25 is supported on synchronous serial lines and a single ISDN B channel.

Addressing Dialer Clouds

There are two ways of setting up addressing on dialer clouds, as follows:

- Applying a subnet to the dialer cloud

  Each site connected to the dialer cloud is given a unique node address on a shared subnet for use on its dialer interface. This method is similar to numbering a LAN or multipoint WAN and simplifies the addressing scheme and creation of static routes.

- Using unnumbered interfaces

  Similar to using unnumbered addressing on leased line point-to-point interfaces, the address of another interface on the router is borrowed for use on the dialer interface. Unnumbered addressing takes advantage of the fact that there are only two devices on the point-to-point link. The routing table points to an interface (the dialer interface) and a next-hop address (which must match a dialer map: static or dynamic).

  Building static routes for unnumbered interfaces can be a little more complex because the router must be configured with the interface that finds the next-hop out.

Dialer Maps

Similar to the function provided by an ARP table, **dialer map** statements translate next-hop protocol addresses to telephone numbers. Without statically configured dialer maps, DDR call initiation cannot occur. When the routing table points at a dialer interface, and the next-hop address is not found in a dialer map, the packet is dropped.

In the following example, packets received for a host on network 172.20.0.0 are routed to a next-hop address of 172.20.1.2, which is statically mapped to telephone number 555-1212:

```
interface dialer 1
ip address 172.20.1.1 255.255.255.0
dialer map ip 172.20.1.2 name c700A 5551212
!
ip route 172.20.0.0 255.255.255.0 172.20.1.2
```

Checks against **dialer map** statements for broadcasts will fail because a broadcast packet is transmitted with a next-hop address of the broadcast address. If you want broadcast packets transmitted to remote sites defined by **dialer map** statements, use the **broadcast** keyword with the **dialer map** command.

To configure whether calls are placed at 56 or 64 Kbps for ISDN calls, you can use the speed option with the **dialer map** command when configuring interfaces. See Chapter 11, "Designing ISDN Internetworks," for details on ISDN media.

When setting up DDR between more than two sites, it is necessary to use PPP authentication and to use the **name** keyword with the **dialer map** command, as dialer maps for inbound calls are maps between protocol addresses and authenticated user names.

To facilitate building of dialer maps, the internetwork designer should build an Address Mapping Table as an aid for configuration. In Table , the dialer cloud has been assigned IP subnet 172.20.1.0/24, IPX network 100, and AppleTalk cable-range 20-20. Table forms the basis for building proper dialer maps for each site.

Table 10–2   *DDR Address Mapping Table for KDT*

Remote Site	Dial-In Protocols	Directory#	Notes
c700A	IP: 172.20.1.2 IPX: 100.0000.0c00.0002	4085551212	
c700B	IP:172.20.1.3	4155558888	56K
c1600A	IP: 172.20.1.4 AT: 20.4	5305551000	
c2500A	IP: 172.20.1.5 IPX: 100.0000.0c00.0005 AT: 20.5	5125558085	
c2500B	IP: 172.20.1.6 IPX: 100.0000.0c00.0006	2105552020	
NAS3600A	IP: 172.20.1.1 IPX: 100.0000.0c00.0001	8355558661	Hub

As NAS3600A forms the hub in the hub-and-spoke topology, each remote site is configured with the dialer maps to get to the central site. For example, the dialer map configuration for c1600A would be as follows:

```
interface dialer1
encapsulation ppp
ip address 172.20.1.4 255.255.255.0
appletalk cable-range 20-20 20.4
appletalk zone ZZ DDR
dialer in-band
dialer map ip 172.20.1.1 name nas3600A speed 56 18355558661
dialer map appletalk 20.1 name nas3600A speed 56 18355558661
dialer-group 5
ppp authentication chap callin
```

The dialer map configuration for NAS3600A would be as follows:

```
interface dialer1
encapsulation ppp
ip address 172.20.1.1 255.255.255.0
appletalk cable-range 20-20 20.1
appletalk zone ZZ DDR
ipx network 100
dialer in-band
dialer map ip 172.20.1.2 name c700A
dialer map ipx 100.0000.0c00.0002 c700A
dialer map ip 172.20.1.3 name c700B
dialer map ip 172.20.1.4 name speed 56 c1600A 15305551000
```

```
dialer map appletalk 20.4 name c1600A
dialer map ip 172.20.1.5 name c2500A 15125558085
dialer map ipx 100.0000.0c00.0005 name c2500A 15125558085
dialer map appletalk 20.5 name c2500A 15125558085
dialer map ip 172.20.1.6 name c2500B 12105552020
dialer map ipx 100.0000.0c00.0006 name c2500B
dialer-group 5
ppp authentication chap callin
```

Note that dialer maps provide mapping between remote site protocol addresses, remote site names, and remote site directory numbers. For dial-in only sites, directory numbers are not required and can be left off to avoid inadvertent dialing. Table was used to determine which sites do not require dial-out support. For dial-in sites, the ppp authentication name is mapped to the protocol address to ensure outbound packets are placed on the correct PPP connection.

Recent Cisco IOS releases can build dynamic dialer maps using for IP (using IPCP address negotiation) and IPX (using IPXCP address negotiation), eliminating the need for dialer maps for dial-in only sites.

The DDR designer should familiarize themselves with the use of the Cisco IOS exec commands **show dialer** and **show dialer map** to examine the state of the DDR sites, the physical interfaces, and the dialer map table. Use **debug dialer** to troubleshoot DDR connection problems.

```
c1600A#sh dialer
BRI0 - dialer type = ISDN
Dial String      Successes   Failures   Last called   Last status
1835558661 0          0      never                -
0 incoming call(s) have been screened.
BRI0:1 - dialer type = ISDN
Idle timer (60 secs), Fast idle timer (20 secs)
Wait for carrier (30 secs), Re-enable (5 secs)
Dialer state is idle
BRI0:2 - dialer type = ISDN
Idle timer (60 secs), Fast idle timer (20 secs)
Wait for carrier (30 secs), Re-enable (5 secs)
Dialer state is idle

c1600A#sh dialer map
Static dialer map ip 172.20.1.4 name nas (8355558661) on BRI0
```

ROUTING STRATEGIES

The nature of DDR networks is that routing and some directory services tables must be maintained over idle connections. DDR designers may use a combination of static, dynamic, and snapshot routing techniques to meet design needs. Default routing and remote node spoofing techniques (such as Cisco 700 Series PAT and Cisco IOS EZIP) can be used to greatly simplify routing design.

Often the backbone at the NAS site will use a fast-converging routing protocol such as OSPF or EIGRP; however, these protocols do not operate easily on the dialer media due to their broadcast and link-state nature. Typically, static routing and/or distance vector routing protocols are selected for the DDR connections. Routing redistribution may be required to support propagation of routing information between the different routing protocols.

A complete discussion of routing redistribution techniques is beyond the scope of this chapter; however, DDR designers do need to develop and verify their routing strategy for each network protocol.

Static Routing

With static routes, network protocol routes are entered manually, eliminating the need for a routing protocol to broadcast routing updates across the DDR connection. Static routes can be effective in small networks that do not change often. Routing protocols can generate traffic that causes connections to be made unnecessarily.

When designing with IP unnumbered environments, older versions of Cisco IOS required multiple static routes for each site: one route to define the next-hop IP address and a second to define the interface on which to find the next-hop (and dialer map). The following code:

```
interface Dialer1
      ip unnumbered Ethernet0/0
      dialer in-band
      dialer map ip 172.17.1.100 name kdt-NAS speed 56 5558660
      dialer-group 5
      !
      ip classless
      ip route 0.0.0.0 0.0.0.0 172.17.1.100 200
      ip route 172.17.1.100 255.255.255.255 Dialer1 200
      dialer-list 5 protocol ip permit
```

creates the following routing table:

```
kdt-3640#sh ip route
      ...<snip>...
      Gateway of last resort is 172.17.1.100 to network 0.0.0.0

172.17.0.0/32 is subnetted, 1 subnets
      S       172.17.1.100 is directly connected, Dialer1
         172.20.0.0/24 is subnetted, 1 subnets
      S*   0.0.0.0/0 [200/0] via 172.17.1.100
```

Recent Cisco IOS versions allow configuration of this as one route. For example, the example configuration here:

```
ip route 0.0.0.0 0.0.0.0 Dialer1 172.17.1.100 200 permanent
```

results in a simplified routing table, as follows:

```
kdt-3640#sh ip route
      ...<snip>...
      Gateway of last resort is 172.17.1.100 to network 0.0.0.0

172.20.0.0/24 is subnetted, 1 subnets
      C       172.20.1.0 is directly connected, Ethernet0/0
      S*   0.0.0.0/0 [200/0] via 172.17.1.100, Dialer1
```

It is typically necessary to configure redistribution of static routes into the backbone dynamic routing protocol to ensure end-to-end connectivity. For example, to redistribute the static route to other networks in IGRP autonomous system 20, use the following configuration commands:

```
router igrp 20
 network 172.20.0.0
 redistribute static
```

Dynamic Routing

Dynamic routing can be used in DDR network design in a number of ways. Dynamic routing can be used with snapshot routing (as described in the "Snapshot Routing" section later in this chapter) to cache routes learned by dynamic routing protocols, thus allowing the automation of static routing maintenance. Dynamic routing can be used as a trigger for routing convergence in large and complex DDR designs.

When the DDR link is connected, routing updates will flow to the peer, allowing redundant designs to converge on the physical connection by redistribution of trigger routing updates.

Selecting a Dynamic Routing Protocol

The routing protocol selected for DDR link is typical of a Distance Vector protocol such as RIP, RIP II, EIGRP, IGRP, or RTMP. Selecting the simplest protocol that meets the needs of the internetwork design and that is supported by the DDR routers is recommended.

Passive Interfaces

Interfaces that are tagged as passive will not send routing updates. To prevent routing updates from establishing DDR connections on dialer interfaces that do not rely on dynamic routing information, configure DDR interfaces with the **passive-interface** command or use access lists as described in the sections "IP Access Lists" and "IPX Access Lists" later in this chapter. Using either the **passive-interface** command or an access list prevents routing updates from triggering a call. However, if you want routing updates to be passed when the link is active, use an access list rather than the **passive-interface** command.

Split Horizons

Routers connected to broadcast-type IP networks and routers that use distance-vector routing protocols use split horizons to reduce the possibility of routing loops. When split horizons are enabled, information about routes that comes in on an interface is not advertised out on that same interface.

NOTES

If remote sites need to communicate with one another, split horizons should be disabled for hub-and-spoke topologies. In hub-and-spoke topologies, spokes learn about one another through the hub site to which they are connected by a single interface. In order for spokes to send and receive information to one another, split horizons may need to be disabled so that full routing tables are built at each site.

Dynamic Connected Routes

Dynamic connected routes include the two following:

- *Per-user AAA Installed Routes*—AAA servers can install routes associated with users by using AAA authorization to download and install routes as remote sites connect.

- *PPP Peer Routes*—IPCP address negotiation installs host-routes (/32 subnet mask) for the remote peer. This host-route can be propagated to backbone routers to provide robust routing convergence. In most applications, the peer host-route will be beneficial (or innocuous) to the internetwork design. If PPP peer host-routes interact poorly with existing routing strategies, they can be turned off with the interface configuration command **no peer neighbor-route**.

Snapshot Routing

With snapshot routing, the router is configured for dynamic routing. Snapshot routing controls the update interval of the routing protocols. Snapshot routing works with the following distance vector protocols:

- Routing Information Protocol (RIP) for IP
- Interior Gateway Routing Protocol (IGRP) for IP
- Routing Information Protocol (RIP) and Service Advertisement Protocol (SAP) for Novell Internet Packet Exchange (IPX)
- Routing Table Maintenance Protocol (RTMP) for AppleTalk
- Routing Table Protocol (RTP) for Banyan VINES

Under normal circumstances, these routing protocols broadcast updates every 10 to 60 seconds, so an ISDN link would be made every 10 to 60 seconds simply to exchange routing information. From a cost perspective, this frequency is prohibitive. Snapshot routing solves this problem.

NOTES

Snapshot routing is available in Cisco IOS Software Release 10.2 or later.

Snapshot Model

Snapshot routing uses the client-server design model. When snapshot routing is configured, one router is designated as the snapshot server and one or more routers are designated as snapshot clients. The server and clients exchange routing information during an active period. At the beginning of the active period, the client router dials the server router to exchange routing information. At the end of the active period, each router takes a snapshot of the entries in its routing table. These entries remain frozen during a quiet period. At the end of the quiet period, another active period begins, and the client router dials the server router to obtain the latest routing information. The client router determines the frequency at which it calls the server router. The quiet period can be as long as 100,000 minutes (approximately 69 days).

When the client router transitions from the quiet period to the active period, the line might be down or busy. If this happens, the router would have to wait through another entire quiet period before it could update its routing table, which might severely affect connectivity if the quiet period is very long. To avoid having to wait through the quiet period, snapshot routing supports a retry period. If the line is not available when the quiet period ends, the router waits for the amount of time specified by the retry period and then transitions to an active period once again.

The retry period is also useful in dial-up environments in which there are more remote sites than interface lines. For example, the central site might have one PRI (with 23 B channels available) but might dial more than 23 remote sites. In this situation, there are more dialer map commands than available lines. The router tries the **dialer map** commands in order and uses the retry time for the lines that it cannot immediately access (see Figure 10–5).

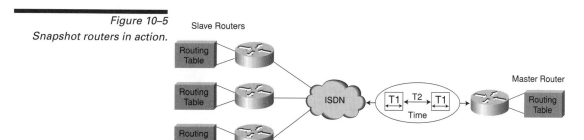

Figure 10–5
Snapshot routers in action.

Enabling Snapshot Routing

Snapshot routing is enabled through interface configuration commands (see Figure 10–6). The central router is configured for snapshot routing by applying the **snapshot server** interface configuration command to its ISDN interfaces. The **snapshot server** command specifies the length of the active period and whether the router is allowed to dial remote sites to exchange routing updates in the absence of regular traffic.

The remote routers are configured for snapshot routing by applying the **snapshot client** command to each ISDN interface. The **snapshot client** interface configuration command specifies the following variables:

- The length of the active period (which must match the length specified on the central router)
- The length of the quiet period

- Whether the router can dial the central router to exchange routing updates in the absence of regular traffic

- Whether connections that are established to exchange user data can be used to exchange routing updates

When the backbone routing protocol is not supported by snapshot routing (for example, OSPF or EIGRP), standard routing redistribution techniques can be used to ensure that routing updates are propagated between routing protocols, as required. Care should be taken to ensure redistribution of subnets if needed and to avoid routing loops.

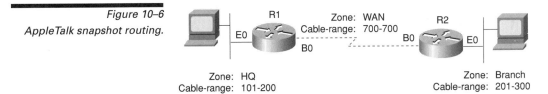

Figure 10–6
AppleTalk snapshot routing.

- R1 configuration is as follows:
  ```
  username R2 password SECRET
  appletalk routing
  isdn switch-type basic-5ess
  !
  interface BRI0
   encapsulation ppp
   appletalk cable-range 700-700 700.1
   appletalk zone WAN
   dialer map appletalk 700.2 name R2 speed 56 broadcast 5552222
   dialer map snapshot 2 name R2 speed 56 broadcast 5552222
   dialer-group 1
   snapshot client 5 60 dialer
   isdn spid1 5550066
   ppp authentication chap
  !
  dialer-list 1 protocol appletalk permit
  ```

- R2 configuration is as follows:
  ```
  username R1 password SECRET
  appletalk routing
  isdn switch-type basic-5ess
  interface BRI0
   encapsulation ppp
   appletalk cable-range 700-700 700.2
   appletalk zone WAN
   dialer wait-for-carrier-time 60
   dialer map appletalk 700.1 name R1 speed 56 broadcast 5550066
   dialer-group 1
  ```

```
snapshot server 5 dialer
isdn spid1 5552222
ppp authentication chap
!
dialer-list 1 protocol appletalk permit
```

For a further examination of snapshot routing, see Chapter 21, "Using ISDN Effectively in Multi-protocol Networks."

Dial Backup for Leased Lines

Dial backup protects against wide-area network (WAN) downtime by allowing a dedicated serial connection to be backed up by a circuit-switched connection. Dial backup can be performed in several ways: either with floating static routes or with backup interfaces.

Dial backup challenges the designer with different traffic patterns than DDR-supported SOHO and ROBO sites. When designing Dial backup port densities, consider how many links might fail concurrently in a mass-failure scenario, as well as how many ports will be required on the central site in a worst-case scenario. Typical design involves selecting only dial-in or dial-out to avoid contention when both sides are trying to re-establish connectivity.

Backup Interfaces

A primary/dedicated serial line is configured to have a backup interface in the event of link failure or exceeded load thresholds. If the interface line or line protocol state goes down, the backup interface is used to establish a connection to the remote site.

Once configured, the dial backup interface remains inactive until one of the following conditions is met:

1. Line Protocol on the primary link goes down. The backup line is then activated, re-establishing the connection between the two sites.

2. The traffic load on the primary line exceeds a defined limit—The traffic load is monitored and a five-minute moving average is computed. If the average exceeds the user-defined value for the line, the backup line is activated. Depending on how the backup line is configured, some or all of the traffic flows onto it.

A Cisco IOS interface is placed into backup mode by applying the **backup interface** command:

- The **backup interface** interface configuration command specifies the interface that is to act as the backup.

- The **backup load** command specifies the traffic threshold at which the backup interface is to be activated and deactivated.

- The **backup delay** command specifies the amount of time that is to elapse before the backup interface is activated or deactivated after a transition on the primary interface.

Backup interfaces traditionally lock the backup interface into BACKUP state so it is unavailable for other use. Dialer Profiles eliminates this lock and allows the physical interface to be used for multiple purposes. Floating Static Route DDR design also eliminates this lock on the dialer interface.

In Figure 10–7, a leased line connects Router A to Router B, and BRI 0 on Router B is used as a backup line.

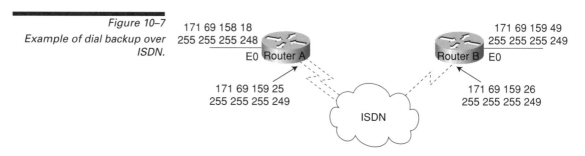

Figure 10–7
Example of dial backup over ISDN.

171 69 158 18
255 255 255 248

171 69 159 49
255 255 255 249

E0 Router A

Router B E0

171 69 159 25
255 255 255 249

171 69 159 26
255 255 255 249

ISDN

Using the configuration that follows, BRI 0 is activated only when serial interface 1/0 (the primary line) goes down. The **backup delay** command configures the backup connection to activate 30 seconds after serial interface 0 goes down and to remain activated for 60 seconds after the serial interface 1/0 comes up:

```
interface serial 1/0
    ip address 172.20.1.4 255.255.255.0
    backup interface bri 2/0
    backup delay 30 60
```

Using the configuration that follows, BRI 2/0 is activated only when the load on serial 0 (the primary line) exceeds 75 percent of its bandwidth. The backup line is deactivated when the aggregate load between the primary and backup lines is within five percent of the primary line's bandwidth:

```
interface serial 1/0
    ip address 172.20.1.4 255.255.255.0
    backup interface bri 2/0
    backup load 75 5
```

Using the following configuration, BRI 2/0 is activated only when serial interface 1/00 goes down or when traffic exceeds 25 percent. If serial interface 1/0 goes down, 10 seconds will elapse before BRI 0 becomes active. When serial interface 1/0 comes up, BRI 2/0 will remain active for 60 seconds. If BRI 2/0 is activated by the load-threshold on serial interface 1/0, BRI 2/0 is deactivated when the aggregate load of serial interface 1/0 and BRI 2/0 returns to within five percent of the bandwidth of serial interface 1/0:

```
interface serial 1/0
ip address 172.20.1.4 255.255.255.0
backup interface bri 2/0
backup load 25 5
backup delay 10 60
```

Floating Static Routes

Backup interface operation is determined by the state of the line and line protocol on the primary link. It is possible that end-to-end connectivity is lost, but line protocol stays up. For example, line protocol on a FrameRelay link is determined by the status of ILMI messages between the FrameRelay DCE (switch). Connectivity to the Frame Relay DCE does not guarantee end-to-end connectivity.

Designing Dial Backup with floating static routes utilizes Cisco IOS routing table maintenance and dynamic routing protocols. See Chapter 15, "Dial-on-Demand Routing," for examples of using Floating Static Routes to provide backup to leased lines.

IPX Static Routes and SAP Updates

With DDR, you need to configure static routes because routing updates are not received across inactive DDR connections. To create static routes to specified destinations, use the **ipx route** command. You can also configure static Service Advertisement Protocol (SAP) updates with the **ipx sap** command so that clients can always find a particular server. In this way, you can determine the areas on your internetwork where SAP updates will establish DDR connections.

In the following example, traffic to network 50 will always be sent to address 45.0000.0c07.00d3. Traffic to network 75 will always be sent to address 45.0000.0c07.00de. The router will respond to GNS queries with the server WALT if there are no dynamic SAPs available:

```
ipx route 50 45.0000.0c07.00d3
ipx route 75 45.0000.0c07.00de
ipx sap 4 WALT 451 75.0000.0000.0001 15
```

Configuring AppleTalk Static Zones

Static AppleTalk routes and zones are created using the **appletalk static** command as in the following example:

```
appletalk static cable-range 110-110 to 45.2 zone Marketing
```

In many cases, manual configuration of static appletalk cable-ranges and zones will prove to be onerous. Snapshot routing should be investigated to provide automated route caching.

DIALER FILTERING

Dialer filtering (see Figure 10–8) is used to classify all packets traversing the DDR connection as either *interesting* or *uninteresting* using Access Control Lists (ACLs). Only interesting packets can bring up and keep up DDR connections. It is the task of the DDR designer to determine which kinds of packets are to be deemed uninteresting and develop ACLs to prevent these uninteresting packets from causing unnecessary DDR connections.

If a packet is uninteresting and there is no connection established, the packet is dropped. If the packet is uninteresting, but a connection is already established to the specified destination, the packet is sent across the connection, but the idle timer is not reset. If the packet is interesting, and there is no connection on the available interface, the router attempts to establish a connection.

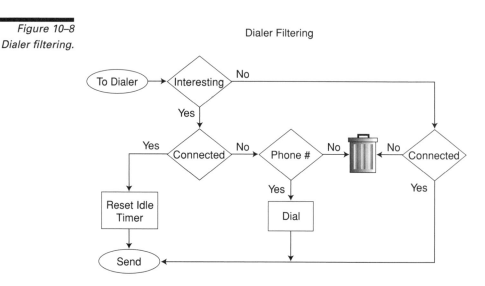

Figure 10–8
Dialer filtering.

Each packet arriving at a dialer interface is filtered and determined to be interesting or uninteresting based on **dialer-group** and **dialer-list** configuration. The following Cisco IOS configuration interface dialer 1 uses dialer-group 5 to determine interesting packets, as defined by the dialer-list 5 commands. Dialer-group 5 is defined by dialer-list 5 commands which in this case deems all IP, IPX, and AppleTalk packets to be interesting.

```
interface Dialer1
dialer-group 5
!
dialer-list 5 protocol ip permit
dialer-list 5 protocol ipx permit
dialer-list 5 protocol appletalk permit
!
```

Cisco IOS now supports many dialer-filtering protocols, as seen by the dialer-list online help:

```
kdt-3640(config)#dialer-list 5 protocol ?
    appletalk          AppleTalk
    bridge             Bridging
    clns               OSI Connectionless Network Service
    clns_es            CLNS End System
    clns_is            CLNS Intermediate System
    decnet             DECnet
    decnet_node        DECnet node
    decnet_router-L1   DECnet router L1
    decnet_router-L2   DECnet router L2
    ip                 IP
    ipx                Novell IPX
    llc2               LLC2
    vines              Banyan Vines
    xns                XNS
```

Defining Interesting Packets Using ACLs

Further dialer-filtering granularity is provided for each protocol by definition of Cisco IOS Access Control Lists (ACLs). For example, the following configuration defines SNMP traffic as not interesting using dialer-list 3 and extended IP ACLs:

```
dialer-list protocol ip 3 list 101

!
access-list 101 deny udp any any eq snmp
access-list 101 permit ip any any
```

Routing updates and directory services effects on Dialer interfaces can be managed by several techniques: static and default routing, passive-interfaces, or non-broadcast dialer maps. For solutions that require dynamic routing and cannot use SnapShot, routing can still be supported on the ISDN link, and then deemed uninteresting by the dialer filtering.

For example, if the internetwork design requires IGRP routing update packets, the IGRP packets can be filtered with access lists to prevent unwanted DDR connections as follows:

```
access-list 101 deny igrp 0.0.0.0 255.255.255.255 0.0.0.0 255.255.255.255
access-list 101 permit ip 0.0.0.0 255.255.255.255 0.0.0.0 255.255.255.255
```

You can use one of the following two access lists to classify Enhanced IGRP traffic as uninteresting:

```
access-list 101 deny eigrp any any
access-list 101 deny ip any 224.0.0.10 0.0.0.0
```

The first access list denies all Enhanced IGRP traffic and the second access list denies the multicast address (224.0.0.10) that Enhanced IGRP uses for its updates. When you use access lists to control Enhanced IGRP traffic, you need to configure static routes to create routes across the ISDN link. When the DDR link is connected, routing updates will be able to flow across the line. In the design of DDR filtering, it is important to understand where updates and service requests are useful and where these packet types can be safely filtered.

It is important to consider closely the directory service protocols and the internetworking applications that need to be supported at each site. Numerous protocols and applications can cause DDR connections to be established and maintained, and may result in extraordinary WAN charges if not properly monitored and filtered. Don't wait until you get a phone bill surprise to perform careful traffic and costing analysis for your network. If you are concerned about WAN costs, implement network monitoring tools to provide quick feedback on connection frequency and duration. Cost-containment issues are discussed in Chapter 11, "Designing ISDN Internetworks."

SNMP

Although SNMP can provide useful information about ISDN connections and how they are used, using SNMP can result in excessive uptime for ISDN links. For example, HP OpenView gathers information by regularly polling the network for SNMP events. These polls can cause the ISDN connections to be made frequently in order to check that the remote routers are there, which results in higher ISDN usage charges. To control ISDN charges, the central site should filter SNMP packets destined for remote sites over ISDN. Incoming SNMP packets from remote sites can still be permitted, which allows SNMP traps to flow to the SNMP management platform. That way, if an SNMP device fails at the remote site, the alarm will reach the SNMP management platform at the central site.

To control SNMP traffic, create an access list that denies SNMP packets. The following is an example of SNMP filtering:

```
access-list 101 deny tcp any any eq 161
access-list 101 deny udp any any eq snmp
access-list 101 permit ip any any
!
dialer-list 1 list 101
```

IPX Packets

On Novell IPX internetworks, it is important to consider filtering routing updates on DDR interfaces for the protocols listed in Table 10–3.

Table 10–3 *Novell IPX Update Packet Cycles*

Packet Type	Periodic Update Cycle
RIP	60 seconds
SAP	60 seconds
Serialization	66 seconds

You can use access lists to declare as uninteresting packets intended for the Novell serialization socket (protocol number 0, socket number 457), RIP packets (protocol number 1, socket number 453), SAP packets (protocol number 4, socket number 452), and diagnostic packets generated by the autodiscovery feature (protocol number 4, socket number 456). Uninteresting packets are dropped and do not cause connections to be initiated. For a sample IPX access list, see Chapter 21, "Using ISDN Effectively in Multiprotocol Networks."

IPX sends out several types of packets that, if not controlled, cause unnecessary connections: IPX watchdog packets and SPX keepalive packets. In addition, NetWare includes a time synchronization protocol that, if not controlled, causes unnecessary connections.

Novell IPX internetworks use several types of update packets that may need to be filtered with access lists. Novell hosts broadcast serialization packets as a copy-protection precaution. Routing Information Protocol (RIP) routing table updates and SAP advertisements are broadcast every 60 seconds. Serialization packets are sent approximately every 66 seconds.

In the following example, access list 901 classifies SAP (452), RIP (453), and serialization (457) packets as uninteresting and classifies IPX packet types unknown/any (0), any or RIP (1), any or SAP (4), SPX (5), NCP (17), and NetBIOS (20) as interesting:

```
access-list 901 deny 0 FFFFFFFF 452
access-list 901 deny 4 FFFFFFFF 452
access-list 901 deny 0 FFFFFFFF 453
```

```
access-list 901 deny 1 FFFFFFFF 453
access-list 901 deny 0 FFFFFFFF 457
access-list 901 deny 0 FFFFFFFF 0 FFFFFFFF 452
access-list 901 deny 0 FFFFFFFF 0 FFFFFFFF 453
access-list 901 deny 0 FFFFFFFF 0 FFFFFFFF 457
access-list 901 permit 0
access-list 901 permit 1
access-list 901 permit 2
access-list 901 permit 4
access-list 901 permit 5
access-list 901 permit 17
```

You can permit any other type of IPX packet as needed. With Cisco IOS 10.2, the configuration of Novell IPX access lists is improved with the support of wildcard (–1), so the previous example would be as follows:

```
access-list 901 deny -1 FFFFFFFF 452
access-list 901 deny -1 FFFFFFFF 453
access-list 901 deny -1 FFFFFFFF 457
access-list 901 deny -1 FFFFFFFF 0 FFFFFFFF 452
access-list 901 deny -1 FFFFFFFF 0 FFFFFFFF 453
access-list 901 deny -1 FFFFFFFF 0 FFFFFFFF 457
access-list 901 permit -1
```

Controlling IPX Watchdog Packets

NetWare servers send *watchdog* packets to clients and disconnect any clients that do not respond. When IPX watchdog spoofing is enabled, the router local to the NetWare server responds to watchdog packets on behalf of the server's clients. IPX watchdog spoofing allows clients to remain attached to servers without having to constantly send packets across the ISDN link to do so. This feature is particularly important when trying to control ISDN link uptime. The interface configuration command for enabling IPX watchdog spoofing is **ipx watchdog-spoof**.

Controlling SPX Keepalive Packets

Some Sequenced Packet Exchange (SPX)-based services in the Novell environment use SPX keepalive packets. These packets are used to verify the integrity of end-to-end communications when guaranteed and sequenced packet transmission is required. The keepalive packets are generated at a rate that can be adjusted by the user from a default of one every five seconds to a minimum of one every 15 minutes. SPX spoofing as implemented in the Cisco IOS software receives, recognizes, and successfully acknowledges keepalive packets both at the server end and the client end.

Time Server and NDS Replica Packets

NetWare 4.x includes a time synchronization protocol that causes NetWare 4.x time servers to send an update every 10 minutes. To prevent the time server from generating update packets that would cause unwanted connections, you need to load a NetWare-loadable module (NLM) named TIMESYNC.NLM that allows you to increase the update interval for these packets to several days.

A similar problem is caused by efforts to synchronize NDS replicas. NetWare 4.1 includes two NLMs: DSFILTER.NLM and PINGFILT.NLM. They work together to control NDS synchronization updates. Use these two modules to ensure that NDS synchronization traffic is sent to specified servers only at the specified times.

AppleTalk Filtering

AppleTalk's user-friendly directory services are based on Zone names and the Name Binding Protocol (NBP). Applications (such as the MacOS Chooser) use NBP Lookups to look for services (such as AppleShare and Printing) by zone names. Some applications may abuse NBP services assuming that DDR networks do not exist and send broadcasts to all zones. This in turn can cause excessive dial-on-demand triggers. Applications such as QuarkXpress and 4D use all zone NBP broadcasts to periodically probe the network either for licensing purposes or to provide links to other networked resources. The **test appletalk:nbp lookup** command combined with the **debug dialer** command monitors NBP traffic and can help you determine the kinds of packets that cause connections to be made.

Beginning with Cisco IOS 11.0, you can filter NBP packets based on the name, type, and zone of the entity that originated the packet. AppleTalk NBP filtering allows Cisco routers to build firewalls, dial-on-demand triggers, and queuing options based on any NBP type or object. For a configuration example, see Chapter 21, "Using ISDN Effectively in Multiprotocol Networks." Ultimately, if the applications that use NBP have been isolated, consult the individual vendors and ask for their advice on how to control or eliminate NBP traffic.

Some Macintosh applications periodically send out NBP Lookup to all zones for numerous reasons; checking same serial number for copy protection, automatic search of other servers, and so on. As a result, the ISDN link will get brought up frequently and waste usages. In 11.0(2.1) or later, Cisco routers allow the user to configure NBP Filtering for dialer-list to prevent this problem. To do this, you should replace this line on both routers:

```
dialer-list 1 protocol appletalk permit
```

with these lines:

```
dialer-list 1 list 600

access-list 600 permit nbp 1 type AFPServer
access-list 600 permit nbp 2 type LaserWriter
access-list 600 deny other-nbps
access-list 600 permit other-access broadcast-deny
```

The previous example indicates you want to permit only two kinds of service for NBP Lookup to bring up the ISDN line. If you want to permit additional types, add to the example before the **denyother-nbps** statement. Make sure you have a different sequence number or it will overwrite the previous one. For example, if you want to also permit NBP Lookup for DeskWriter to bring up the line, the list will look like this:

```
dialer-list 1 list 600

access-list 600 permit nbp 1 type AFPServer
access-list 600 permit nbp 2 type LaserWriter
```

```
access-list 600 permit nbp 3 type DeskWriter
access-list 600 deny other-nbps
access-list 600 permit other-access broadcast-deny
```

NOTES

AppleShare servers use the Apple Filing Protocol (AFP) to send out tickles approximately every 30 seconds to connected AppleShare clients. These tickles will cause DDR connections to stay up. To avoid unwanted DDR connections, you must manually unmount AppleTalk servers or install software on the servers that automatically disconnects idle users after a timeout period.

Banyan VINES, DECnet IV, and OSI Packets

Cisco IOS 10.3 introduced access lists for Banyan VINES, DECnet IV, and the Open Systems Integration (OSI) protocol. When a dialer map is configured for these protocols, access lists can be used to define interesting packets (that is, packets that will trigger the DDR link).

AUTHENTICATION

Authentication in DDR network design provides two functions: security and dialer state. As most DDR networks connect to the Public Switched Telephone Network, it is imperative that a strong security model be implemented to prevent unauthorized access to sensitive resources. Authentication also allows the DDR code to keep track of what sites are currently connected and provides for building of MultiLink PPP bundles. The following issues are addressed:

- PPP Authentication
- CHAP
- PAP
- ISDN Security
- DDR Callback
- IPX Access Lists

PPP Authentication

PPP Authentication via CHAP or PAP (as described in RFC 1334) should be used to provide security on DDR connections. PPP authentication occurs after LCP is negotiated on the DDR connection, but before any network protocols are allowed to flow. PPP Authentication is negotiated as an LCP option, and is bidirectional, meaning each side can authenticate the other. In some environments, it may be necessary to enable PPP authentication on the call-in side only (meaning the calling side does not authenticate the called side).

CHAP

With CHAP, a remote device attempting to connect to the local router is presented with a CHAP challenge containing the host name and a challenge seed. When the remote router receives the challenge, it looks up the hostname received in the challenge and replies with the hostname and a CHAP response derived from the challenge seed and the password for that hostname. The passwords must be identical on the remote device and the local router. The names and passwords are configured using the **username** command. In the following example, Router nas3600A will allow Router c1600A to call in using the password "bubble":

```
hostname nas3600A
username c1600A password bubble
!
interface dialer 1
ppp authentication chap callin
```

In the following example, Router Macduff will allow Router Macbeth to call in using the password "bubble":

```
hostname c1600A
username nas3600A password bubble
!
interface dialer 1
encapsulation ppp
dialer in-band
dialer-group 5
dialer map ip 172.20.1.1 name nas3600A 18355558661
ppp authentication chap callin
```

The following steps illustrate the CHAP process:

Step 1   c1600A calls nas3600A and LCP is negotiated.

Step 2   nas3600A challenges c1600A with: <nas3600A/challenge_string>.

Step 3   c1600A looks up the password for username nas3600A and generates response_string.

Step 4   c1600A sends response to c3600A: <nas1600A/response_string>.

Step 5   c3600A looks up the password for username c1600A and generates the expected response_string. If the response_string received matches the response string expected, PPP authorization passes, and the PPP can negotiate the network control protocols (such as IPCP). If it fails, the remote site is disconnected.

PAP

Like CHAP, PAP is an authentication protocol used with PPP. However, PAP is less secure than CHAP. CHAP passes an encrypted version of the password on the physical link, but PAP passes the password in clear text, which makes it susceptible to sniffer attack.

When being authenticated with PAP, the router looks up the username that matches the dialer map used to initiate the call. When being authenticated with PAP on a receiving call, PAP looks up the username associated with its hostname (because no dialer map was used to initiate the connection).

In the following configuration, the NAS router will authenticate the peer with PAP when answering the DDR call, and compare the result to the local database:

```
hostname nas3600A
aaa new-model
aaa authentication ppp default local
username c2500A password freedom
username nas3600A password texas
!
interface Dialer1
encapsualtion ppp
ppp authentication pap
```

ISDN Security

ISDN DDR can use caller-ID for enhanced security by configuring ISDN caller on the incoming ISDN interfaces. Incoming calls are screened to verify that the calling line ID is from an expected origin. However, caller-ID screening requires an end-to-end ISDN connection that can deliver the caller-ID to the router. See Chapter 11, "Designing ISDN Internetworks," for more information.

DDR Callback

DDR environments can be configured for callback operations. When a remote site dials into a central site (or the opposite), the central site can be configured to disconnect and initiate an outbound DDR connection to the remote site.

DDR callback provides enhanced security by ensuring that the remote site can connect only from a single location as defined by the callback number. DDR callback can also enhance administration by centralizing billing for remote DDR connections.

IPX Access Lists

Access lists determine whether packets are interesting or uninteresting. Interesting packets activate DDR connections automatically. Uninteresting packets do not trigger DDR connections, although if a DDR connection is already active, uninteresting packets will travel across the existing connection.

SUMMARY

When designing DDR internetworks, consider the topology type: point-to-point, hub-and-spoke, and fully meshed. With the topology type, consider the type of addressing scheme used and security issues. Keep in mind that media choice affects how packets are sent. Define where packets are sent by configuring static routes, zones, and services. Determine how packets reach their destination by configuring dialer interfaces and mapping addresses to telephone numbers. Finally, determine when the router should connect by configuring interesting versus uninteresting packets, eliminating unwanted AppleTalk broadcasts, and spoofing IPX watchdog packets. Following these guidelines will help you construct scalable DDR internetworks that balance performance, fault tolerance, and cost.

For further guidance on building DDR networks, including protocol-specific examples, see Chapter 11, "Designing ISDN Internetworks," Chapter 25, "Scaling Dial-on-Demand Routing," and Chapter 21, "Using ISDN Effectively in Multiprotocol Networks."

Designing ISDN Internetworks

The Public Switched Telephone Network (PSTN) has been transformed into an Integrated Systems Digital Network (ISDN). Implementation of Signalling System 7 (SS7) in the PSTN backbone has made possible such widespread services as Caller-ID and Dialed-Number delivery, 800 Directory Number lookup, Calling Card services, and Digital Data Services. Using BRI and PRI services, ISDN call switching can be extended to customer premises equipment (CPE) and provide end-to-end digital paths.

Previous to ISDN availability, data connectivity over the Public Switched Telephone Network (PSTN) was via Plain Old Telephone Service (POTS) using analog modems. Connectivity over ISDN offers the internetworking designer increased bandwidth, reduced call setup time, reduced latency, and lower signal/noise ratios.

ISDN is now being deployed rapidly in numerous applications including Dial-on-Demand Routing, Dial Backup, SOHO and ROBO connectivity, and modem pool aggregation. This chapter covers the design of these applications. The purpose of this chapter is to discuss the design issues associated with building ISDN internetworks. For specific examples, please see the relevant case study chapters.

Figure 11–1 shows ISDN being used to concurrently serve ISDN and POTS (analog modem) connected remote sites in a hybrid dial solution.

APPLICATIONS OF ISDN IN INTERNETWORKING

ISDN has many applications in internetworking. The Cisco IOS has long been building Dial-On-Demand Routing and Dial Backup solutions for Remote Office/Branch Office connectivity. Recently, ISDN has seen incredible growth in the support of mass Small Office/Home Office (SOHO) dial-up connectivity. For the purposes of this book, the ISDN calling side will be referred to as SOHO and the answering side will be referred to as the NAS (Network Access Server) unless otherwise stated. In this section, the following issues are addressed:

Figure 11–1
ISDN can support hybrid (analog and digital) dial solutions.

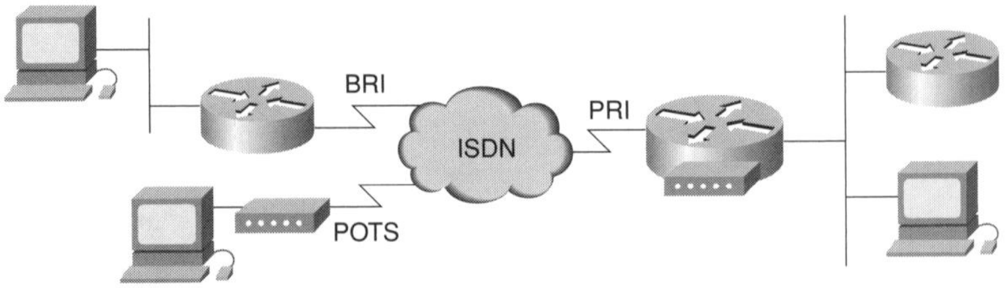

- Dial-On-Demand Routing
- Dial Backup
- SOHO Connectivity
- Modem Aggregation

Dial-On-Demand Routing

Full-time connectivity across the ISDN is spoofed by Cisco IOS routers using DDR. When qualified packets arrive at a Dialer interface, connectivity is established over the ISDN. After a configured period of inactivity, the ISDN connection is disconnected. Additional ISDN B channels can be added and removed from the MultiLink PPP bundles using configurable thresholds. Figure 11–2 illustrates the use of DDR for internetworking between ISDN connected sites.

Figure 11–2
DDR creates connectivity between ISDN sites.

Dial Backup

ISDN can be used as a backup service for a leased-line connection between the remote and central offices. If the primary connectivity goes down, an ISDN circuit-switched connection is established and traffic is rerouted over ISDN. When the primary link is restored, traffic is redirected to the leased line, and the ISDN call is released.

Dial Backup can be accomplished with floating static routes and DDR or by using the interface backup commands. ISDN dial backup can also be configured based on traffic thresholds as a dedicated primary link. If traffic load exceeds a user-defined value on the primary link, the ISDN link is activated to increase bandwidth between the two sites, as shown in Figure 11–3.

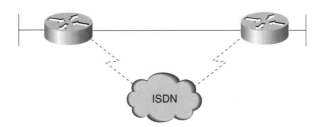

Figure 11–3
ISDN can back up primary connectivity between sites.

SOHO Connectivity

Small Office and Home Office sites can be now be economically supported with ISDN BRI services. This offers to the casual or full-time SOHO sites the capability to connect to their corporate site or the Internet at much higher speeds than available over POTS and modems.

SOHO designs typically involve dial-up only (SOHO initiated connections) and can take advantage of emerging address translation technology (such as Cisco 700 series PAT and Cisco IOS EZIP) to simplify design and support. Using these features, the SOHO site can support multiple devices, but appears to the Cisco IOS NAS as a single IP address, as shown in Figure 11–4.

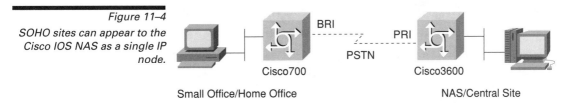

Figure 11–4
SOHO sites can appear to the Cisco IOS NAS as a single IP node.

Modem Aggregation

Modem racking and cabling has been eliminated by integration of digital modem cards on Cisco IOS Network Access Servers (NAS). Digital integration of modems makes possible 56 Kbps modem technologies. Hybrid dial solutions can be built using a single phone number to provide analog modem and ISDN conductivity, as shown in Figure 11–1.

BUILDING BLOCKS OF ISDN SOLUTIONS

ISDN itself does not solve internetworking problems. By using either DDR or user-initiated sessions, ISDN can provide the internetwork designer a clear data path over which to negotiate PPP links. A Public Switched Telephone Network to provide internetwork connectivity requires careful consideration of network security and cost containment.

This section includes overviews of the following ISDN design issues, which are then covered more fully in the following main sections of this chapter:

- ISDN Connectivity
- Datagram Encapsulation
- DDR: Dial-On-Demand Routing
- Security Issues
- Cost Containment Issues

ISDN Connectivity

Connectivity to ISDN is provided by physical PRI and BRI interfaces. A single PRI or BRI interface provides a multiplexed bundle of B and D channels. The B channel provides bearer services such as high bandwidth data (up to 64 Kbps per B channel) or voice services. The D channel provides the signalling and control channel and can also be used for low-bandwidth data applications.

BRI service is provided over a groomed local loop that is traditionally used for switch to analog phone service. BRI delivers to the subscriber 2 64 Kbps B channels and 1 16 Kbps D channel (2B+D).

PRI service is provided on traditional T1 & E1 leased lines between the customer premise equipment (CPE) and the ISDN switch:

- T1-based PRI provides 23 B channels and 1 D channel (23B+D).
- E1-based PRI provides 30 64 Kbps B channels and 1 64 Kbps D channel (30B+D).

Provisioning of both PRI and BRI services have very stringent requirements on the physical equipment and cabling in the path from ISDN switch to ISDN CPE. Typical installations can require additional lead times as well as require working with dedicated support groups within your ISDN service provider organizations. See Figure 11–5.

Figure 11–5
Connectivity to ISDN using BRI and PRI.

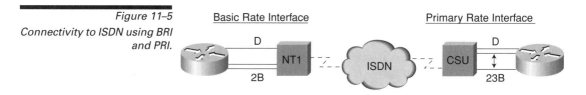

Datagram Encapsulation

When DDR (or a user) creates an end-to-end path over the ISDN, some method of datagram encapsulation is needed to provide data connectivity. Available encapsulations for ISDN designs are PPP, HDLC, X.25, and V.120. X.25 can also be used for datagram delivery over the D channel.

Most internetworking designs use PPP as the encapsulation. The point-to-point protocol (PPP) is a powerful and modular peer-to-peer mechanism to establish data links, provide security, and encapsulate data traffic. PPP is negotiated between the internetworking peers each time a connection is established. PPP links can then be used by network protocols such as IP and IPX to establish internetwork connectivity. PPP solutions can support bandwidth aggregation using MultiLink PPP to provide greater throughput for internetworking applications.

DDR: Dial-On-Demand Routing

When building internetworking applications, designers must determine how ISDN connections will be initiated, maintained, and released. DDR is a sophisticated set of Cisco IOS features that intelligently establishes and releases circuit switched connections as needed by internetworking traffic. DDR can spoof internetwork routing and directory services in numerous ways to provide the illusion of full-time connectivity over circuit switched connections. Refer to Chapter 10, "Designing DDR Internetworks" for a discussion of DDR design.

Security Issues

Because your internetwork devices can now be connected to over the PSTN, it is imperative to design and confirm a robust security model for protecting your network. Cisco IOS uses the AAA model for implementing security. ISDN offers the use of Caller-ID and DNIS information to provide additional security design flexibility.

Cost Containment Issues

A primary goal of selecting ISDN for your internetwork is to avoid the cost of full-time data services (such as leased lines or frame relay). As such, it is very important to evaluate your data traffic profiles and monitor your ISDN usage patterns to ensure your WAN costs are controlled. Dialer Callback can also be implemented to centralize billing.

Each of these building blocks of ISDN (connectivity, data encapsulation, DDR, security, and cost containment) is discussed in further detail in the remaining sections of this chapter.

ISDN CONNECTIVITY ISSUES

Based on application need and traffic engineering, BRI or PRI services are selected for ISDN connectivity from each site. Traffic engineering may require multiple BRI services or multiple PRIs at some sites. Once connected to the ISDN fabric by BRI or PRI interfaces, design of ISDN end-to-end services must be implemented. This section covers the following issues related to ISDN connectivity:

- Establishing BRI Connectivity
- Establishing ISDN Primary Rate Interface (PRI)
- ISDN End-to-End Considerations
- Datagram Encapsulation Issues

Establishing BRI Connectivity

The BRI local loop is terminated at the customer premise at an NT1. The interface of the local loop at the NT1 is called the *U reference point*. On the customer premise side of the NT1 is the S/T reference point. The S/T reference point can support a multipoint bus of ISDN devices (Terminal Adapters). Figure 11–6 shows a typical BRI installation.

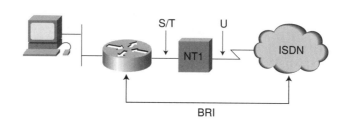

Figure 11–6
The BRI local loop connected to ISDN.

BRI Hardware

Two common types of ISDN CPE are available for BRI Services: ISDN routers and PC Terminal Adapters. Some BRI devices offer integrated NT1s and integrated Terminal Adapters for analog telephones.

- *LAN Routers*—ISDN Routers provide routing between ISDN BRI and the LAN by using Dial-on-Demand Routing (DDR).

  - DDR automatically establishes and releases circuit switched calls providing transparent connectivity to remote sites based on internetworking traffic. DDR also controls establishing and releasing secondary B channels based on load thresholds. MultiLink PPP is used to provide bandwidth aggregation when using multiple B channels. For more information on DDR, see Chapter 10, "Designing DDR Internetworks."

  - Some ISDN applications may require the SOHO user to take direct control over ISDN calls. Emerging Cisco IOS features can bring this control to the user desktop. New Cisco 700 models provide a *call* button on the front of the router for direct control.

  - Cisco 700 series and Cisco IOS based 1000, 1600, 2500 routers provide single BRI interfaces. Multiple-BRI interfaces are available for the Cisco3600 and Cisco4x00 Series.

- *PC Terminal Adapters (PC-TA)*—These devices connect to PC workstations either by the PC Bus or externally through the communications ports (such as RS-232) and can be used similar to analog (such as V.34) internal and external modems.

  - PC Terminal Adapters can provide a single PC user with direct control over ISDN session initiation and release similar to using an analog modem. Automated mechanisms must be provided to support the addition and removal of the secondary B channel. Cisco200 Series PC Cards can provide ISDN services to a PC.

BRI Configuration

BRI configuration involves configuration of ISDN switch-type, and ISDN SPIDs, as follows:

- *ISDN switch types*—ISDN central office switches (also known as *local exchange equipment*) provide two functions at the local exchange: local termination and exchange termination. The local termination function deals with the transmission facility and termination of the local loop. The exchange termination function deals with the switching portion of the local exchange. First, the exchange termination function de-multiplexes the bits on the B and D channels. Next, B channel information is routed to the first stage of the circuit switch, and D channel packets are routed to D channel packet separation circuitry.

  ○ For proper ISDN operation, it is imperative that the correct switch type is configured on the ISDN device. For Cisco IOS releases up to 11.2, the configured ISDN switch-type is a global command (note this also means you cannot use BRI and PRI cards in the same Cisco IOS chassis). In Cisco IOS 11.3T or later, multiple switch-types in a single Cisco IOS chassis are now supported.

  ○ *Cisco IOS switch types*
  The following Cisco IOS command helps illustrate the supported BRI switch types. In North America, the most common types are 5ESS, DMS100, and NI-1.
  ```
  kdt-3640(config)#isdn switch-type ?
    basic-1tr6     1TR6 switch type for Germany
    basic-5ess     AT&T 5ESS switch type for the U.S.
    basic-dms100   Northern DMS-100 switch type
    basic-net3     NET3 switch type for UK and Europe
    basic-ni1      National ISDN-1 switch type
    basic-nwnet3   NET3 switch type for Norway
    basic-nznet3   NET3 switch type for New Zealand
    basic-ts013    TS013 switch type for Australia
    ntt            NTT switch type for Japan
    vn2            VN2 switch type for France
    vn3            VN3 and VN4 switch types for France
  ```

  ○ *Cisco 700 switch types.*
  On Cisco 700 Series routers, use the **set switch** command, which has the following options when running the US software image:
  ```
  SEt SWitch 5ESS ¦ DMS ¦ NI-1 ¦ PERM64 ¦ PERM128
  ```

- *Service profile identifiers (SPIDs)*—A service profile identifier (SPID) is a number provided by the ISDN carrier to identify the line configuration of the BRI service. SPIDs allow multiple ISDN devices, such as voice and data, to share the local loop. SPIDs are required by DMS-100 and National ISDN-1 switches. Depending on the software version it runs, an AT&T 5ESS switch might require SPIDs as well.

Each SPID points to line setup and configuration information. When a device attempts to connect to the ISDN network, it performs a D channel Layer 2 initialization process that causes a TEI to be assigned to the device. The device then attempts D channel Layer 3 initialization. If SPIDs are necessary but not configured or configured incorrectly on the device, the Layer 3 initialization fails, and the ISDN services cannot be used.

○ The AT&T 5ESS switch supports up to eight SPIDs per BRI. Because multiple SPIDs can be applied to a single B channel, multiple services can be supported simultaneously. For example, the first B channel can be configured for data, and the second B channel can be configured for both voice (using an ISDN telephone) and data.

○ DMS-100 and National ISDN-1 switches support only two SPIDs per BRI: one SPID for each B channel. If both B channels will be used for data only, configure the router for both SPIDs (one for each B channel). You cannot run data and voice over the same B channel simultaneously. The absence or presence of a channel's SPID in the router's configuration dictates whether the second B channel can be used for data or voice.

NOTES

There is no standard format for SPID numbers. As a result, SPID numbers vary depending on the switch vendor and the carrier.

- A typical Cisco IOS SPID configuration is as follows:
  ```
  interface BRI0
  isdn spid1 0835866201 8358662
  isdn spid2 0835866401 8358664
  ```

  ○ These commands also specify the local directory number (LDN), which is the seven-digit number assigned by the service provider and used for call routing. The LDN is not necessary for establishing ISDN-based connections, but it must be specified if you want to receive incoming calls on B channel 2. The LDN is required only when two SPIDs are configured (for example, when connecting to a DMS or NI1 switch). Each SPID is associated with an LDN. Configuring the LDN causes incoming calls to B channel 2 to be answered properly. If the LDN is not configured, incoming calls to B channel 2 may fail.

- A typical Cisco 700 Series SPID configuration is as follows:
  ```
  SET 1 SPID 51255500660101
  SET 1 DIRECTORYNUMBER 5550066
  SET PHONE1 = 5550066
  SET 2 SPID 51255500670101
  ```

Confirming BRI Operations

To confirm BRI operations in Cisco IOS, use the **show isdn status** command to inspect the status of your BRI interfaces. In the following example, the TEIs have been successfully negotiated and ISDN Layer3 (end-to-end) is ready to make or receive calls:

```
kdt-1600#sh isdn status
The current ISDN Switchtype = basic-ni1
ISDN BRI0 interface
    Layer 1 Status:
        ACTIVE
    Layer 2 Status:
        TEI = 109, State = MULTIPLE_FRAME_ESTABLISHED
        TEI = 110, State = MULTIPLE_FRAME_ESTABLISHED
    Spid Status:
        TEI 109, ces = 1, state = 8(established)
            spid1 configured, spid1 sent, spid1 valid
            Endpoint ID Info: epsf = 0, usid = 1, tid = 1
        TEI 110, ces = 2, state = 8(established)
            spid2 configured, spid2 sent, spid2 valid
            Endpoint ID Info: epsf = 0, usid = 3, tid = 1
    Layer 3 Status:
        0 Active Layer 3 Call(s)
    Activated dsl 0 CCBs = 0
    Total Allocated ISDN CCBs = 0
```

Troubleshooting SPID problems is done with the **debug isdn q921** command. In the example that follows, you can see that **isdn spid1** was rejected by the ISDN switch:

```
kdt-1600#debug isdn q921
ISDN Q921 packets debugging is on
kdt-1600#clear int bri 0
kdt-1600#
*Mar  1 00:09:03.728: ISDN BR0: TX ->  SABMEp sapi = 0  tei = 113
*Mar  1 00:09:04.014: ISDN BR0: RX <-  IDREM ri = 0  ai = 127
*Mar  1 00:09:04.018: %ISDN-6-LAYER2DOWN:
        Layer 2 for Interface BRI0, TEI 113 changed to down
*Mar  1 00:09:04.022: %ISDN-6-LAYER2DOWN:
        Layer 2 for Interface BR0, TEI 113 changed to down
*Mar  1 00:09:04.046: ISDN BR0: TX ->  IDREQ  ri = 44602  ai = 127
*Mar  1 00:09:04.049: ISDN BR0: RX <-  IDCKRQ  ri = 0  ai = 113
*Mar  1 00:09:05.038: ISDN BR0: RX <-  IDCKRQ  ri = 0  ai = 113
*Mar  1 00:09:06.030: ISDN BR0: TX ->  IDREQ  ri = 37339  ai = 127
*Mar  1 00:09:06.149: ISDN BR0: RX <-  IDREM  ri = 0  ai = 113
*Mar  1 00:09:06.156: ISDN BR0: RX <-  IDASSN  ri = 37339  ai = 114
*Mar  1 00:09:06.164: ISDN BR0: TX ->  SABMEp sapi = 0  tei = 114
*Mar  1 00:09:06.188: ISDN BR0: RX <-  UAf sapi = 0  tei = 114
*Mar  1 00:09:06.188: %ISDN-6-LAYER2UP:
        Layer 2 for Interface BR0, TEI 114 changed to up
*Mar  1 00:09:06.200: ISDN BR0: TX ->
        INFOc sapi = 0  tei = 114  ns = 0  nr = 0  i = 0x08007B3A06383932393833
*Mar  1 00:09:06.276: ISDN BR0: RX <-
        INFOc sapi = 0  tei = 114  ns = 0  nr = 1  i = 0x08007B080382E43A
*Mar  1 00:09:06.283: ISDN BR0: TX ->  RRr sapi = 0  tei = 114  nr = 1
*Mar  1 00:09:06.287: %ISDN-4-INVALID_SPID: Interface BR0, Spid1 was rejected
```

Check the status of the Cisco 700 ISDN line with the **show status** command, as follows:

```
kdt-776> sh status
Status    01/04/1995 18:15:15
Line Status
  Line Activated
```

```
Terminal Identifier Assigned   SPID Accepted
Terminal Identifier Assigned   SPID Accepted
Port Status                         Interface Connection Link
  Ch: 1      Waiting for Call
  Ch: 2      Waiting for Call
```

BRI Notes

Note the following issues regarding BRI configuration that must be addressed:

- *TEI negotiation*—Some switches deactivate Layer 2 of the D channel when no calls are active, so the router must be configured to perform TEI negotiation at the first call instead of at router power-up (the default). To enable TEI negotiation at the first call, use the following **global** configuration command:

  ```
  isdn tei-negotiation first-call
  ```

- *ISDN Sub-Addressing*—The S/T bus is a point to multipoint bus. Multiple ISDN CPE devices can share the same S/T bus. Call routing to individual devices on an S/T bus is achieved by using ISDN Sub-Addressing.

- *Voice routing*—Cisco 700 Series routers can provide POTS jacks for connecting traditional analog telephone sets. SOHO sites can benefit from the capability to concurrently route data and voice calls over the same ISDN BRI interface. Voice port phone numbers and voice priority must be configured for the needs of the SOHO site. The example that follows shows the voice routing setup for a typical Cisco 700:

  ```
  SET SWITCH NI-1
  SET 1 SPID 51255500660101
  SET 1 DIRECTORYNUMBER 5550066
  SET PHONE1 = 5550066
  SET 2 SPID 51255500670101
  SET 2 DIRECTORYNUMBER 5550067
  SET PHONE2 = 5550067
  SET VOICEPRIORITY INCOMING INTERFACE PHONE1 NEVER
  SET VOICEPRIORITY OUTGOING INTERFACE PHONE1 NEVER
  SET CALLWAITING INTERFACE PHONE1 OFF
  SET VOICEPRIORITY INCOMING INTERFACE PHONE2 ALWAYS
  SET VOICEPRIORITY OUTGOING INTERFACE PHONE2 ALWAYS
  SET CALLWAITING INTERFACE PHONE2 ON
  kdt-776> sh voicerouting
  Interface    VoicePriority  VoicePriority  Call      Directory  Ring
               In             Out            Waiting   Number     Cadence
     PHONE1    NEVER          NEVER          OFF       6720066
     PHONE2    ALWAYS         ALWAYS         ON        6720067
     DOV       N/A            N/A            N/A
     UNSPECIFIED N/A          N/A            N/A
  ```

Establishing ISDN Primary Rate Interface (PRI)

Cisco IOS routers support PRI interfaces using MultiChannel Interface Processor (MIP) cards. MIP cards can support Channelized T1/E1 or PRI timeslots. MIP cards are available for Cisco 4x000, Cisco 36x0, Cisco 5x00, and Cisco 7x00 Series routers.

To specify that the MIP card is to be used as an ISDN PRI, use the **pri-group timeslots** controller configuration command.

Cisco IOS routers supporting PRI interfaces become Network Access Servers. Cisco 5x00 and 36x0 Series routers support hybrid dial solutions (POTS and ISDN) by providing access to analog modems over the NAS backplane.

PRI Configuration

Configure the ISDN switch-type for the PRI interface using the **isdn switch-type** command:

```
AS5200-2(config)#isdn switch-type ?
  primary-4ess    AT&T 4ESS switch type for the U.S.
  primary-5ess    AT&T 5ESS switch type for the U.S.
  primary-dms100  Northern Telecom switch type for the U.S.
  primary-net5    European switch type for NET5
  primary-ntt     Japan switch type
  primary-ts014   Australia switch type
```

Normally, this is a global configuration command. Cisco IOS 11.3T or later will provide support for multiple switch-types in a single Cisco IOS chassis. Enable PRI services on the Cisco IOS NAS by configuring the T1 (or E1) controllers. The configuration that follows shows a typical T1 controller configuration on a Cisco5200.

```
controller T1 0
 framing esf
 clock source line primary
 linecode b8zs
 pri-group timeslots 1-24
!
controller T1 1
 framing esf
 clock source line secondary
 linecode b8zs
 pri-group timeslots 1-24
!
```

Note that PRI channels 0–23 map to pri-group timeslots 1–24. The same +1 mapping is used on E1-based PRI.

To configure a T1-based PRI, apply the configuration commands to the PRI D channel, that is, interface Serial0:23. All B channels in an ISDN PRI (or BRI) interface are automatically bundled into a dialer interface. When calls are made or received on the B channels, the configuration is cloned from the dialer interface (Serial0:23). If a NAS contains multiple PRIs, these PRIs can be grouped into a single dialer interface by the **dialer rotary-group** interface command, as shown in this example:

```
interface Serial0:23
 dialer rotary-group 1
!
interface Serial1:23
 dialer rotary-group 1
!
interface Dialer1
 ip unnumbered Ethernet0
```

```
encapsulation ppp
peer default ip address pool default
dialer in-band
dialer idle-timeout 120
dialer-group 1
no fair-queue
no cdp enable
ppp authentication pap chap
ppp multilink
```

With this configuration, every B channel configuration or multilink PPP bundle is cloned from **interface Dialer1.**

Confirming PRI Operations

The state of the T1 controller is inspected with the Cisco IOS exec command: **show controller t1,** as follows:

```
AS5200-1#sh contr t1
T1 0 is up.
  No alarms detected.
  Version info of slot 0:  HW: 2, Firmware: 14, NEAT PLD: 14, NR Bus PLD: 22
  Framing is ESF, Line Code is B8ZS, Clock Source is Line Primary.
  Data in current interval (685 seconds elapsed):
     0 Line Code Violations, 0 Path Code Violations
     0 Slip Secs, 0 Fr Loss Secs, 0 Line Err Secs, 0 Degraded Mins
     0 Errored Secs, 0 Bursty Err Secs, 0 Severely Err Secs, 0 Unavail Secs
  Total Data (last 24 hours)
     0 Line Code Violations, 0 Path Code Violations,
     0 Slip Secs, 0 Fr Loss Secs, 0 Line Err Secs, 8 Degraded Mins,
     0 Errored Secs, 0 Bursty Err Secs, 0 Severely Err Secs, 0 Unavail Secs
T1 1 is up.
  No alarms detected.
  Version info of slot 0:  HW: 2, Firmware: 14, NEAT PLD: 14, NR Bus PLD: 22
  Framing is ESF, Line Code is B8ZS, Clock Source is Line Secondary.
  Data in current interval (197 seconds elapsed):
     0 Line Code Violations, 0 Path Code Violations
     0 Slip Secs, 0 Fr Loss Secs, 0 Line Err Secs, 0 Degraded Mins
     0 Errored Secs, 0 Bursty Err Secs, 0 Severely Err Secs, 0 Unavail Secs
  Total Data (last 24 hours)
     0 Line Code Violations, 0 Path Code Violations,
     0 Slip Secs, 0 Fr Loss Secs, 0 Line Err Secs, 4 Degraded Mins,
     0 Errored Secs, 0 Bursty Err Secs, 0 Severely Err Secs, 0 Unavail Secs
```

Excessive line code violations and other errors will cause significant performance loss. Work with your ISDN PRI service provider to ensure that these counters show relatively clean operation. Use the Cisco IOS exec command **show isdn status** to verify ISDN is operational, as follows:

```
AS5200-1#sh isdn status
The current ISDN Switchtype = primary-dms100
ISDN Serial0:23 interface
    Layer 1 Status:
        ACTIVE
    Layer 2 Status:
        TEI = 0, State = MULTIPLE_FRAME_ESTABLISHED
```

```
        Layer 3 Status:
            0 Active Layer 3 Call(s)
        Activated dsl 0 CCBs = 0
    ISDN Serial1:23 interface
        Layer 1 Status:
            ACTIVE
        Layer 2 Status:
            TEI = 0, State = MULTIPLE_FRAME_ESTABLISHED
        Layer 3 Status:
            0 Active Layer 3 Call(s)
        Activated dsl 1 CCBs = 0
        Total Allocated ISDN CCBs = 0
```

Inspect B channel status with the **show isdn service** exec command, as follows:

```
AS5200-1#sh isdn service
PRI Channel Statistics:
ISDN Se0:23, Channel (1-31)
  Activated dsl 0
  State (0=Idle 1=Propose 2=Busy 3=Reserved 4=Restart 5=Maint)
  0 0 0 0 0 0 0 0 0 0 0 0 0 0 0 0 0 0 0 0 0 0 0 3 3 3 3 3 3 3 3
  Channel (1-31) Service (0=Inservice 1=Maint 2=Outofservice)
  0 0 0 0 0 0 0 0 0 0 0 0 0 0 0 0 0 0 0 0 0 0 0 0 0 0 0 0 0 0 0
ISDN Se1:23, Channel (1-31)
  Activated dsl 1
  State (0=Idle 1=Propose 2=Busy 3=Reserved 4=Restart 5=Maint)
  0 0 0 0 0 0 0 0 0 0 0 0 0 0 0 0 0 0 0 0 0 0 0 3 3 3 3 3 3 3 3
  Channel (1-31) Service (0=Inservice 1=Maint 2=Outofservice)
  0 0 0 0 0 0 0 0 0 0 0 0 0 0 0 0 0 0 0 0 0 0 0 0 0 0 0 0 0 0 0
```

ISDN End-to-End Considerations

The following ISDN end-to-end considerations are covered in this section:

- Signaling System 7 (SS7)
- Data Path Speed

Signaling System 7

Signaling System 7 (SS7) provides telephone switches with out-of-band signalling capabilities for telephony trunks (switch to switch DS0 connections). End-to-End call management (such as setup and tear-down) uses ITU specification Q.931 and is extended to PRI/BRI internetworking devices over the ISDN D channel.

Out-of-Band signalling via SS7 provides numerous benefits to internetworking design, including reduced call setup time, bearer capability and other progress indicators, 64 Kbps data paths, caller-ID, and dialed number information (DNIS). The output that follows of Cisco IOS **debug isdn q931** shows typical ISDN Q.931 setup messages received by an NAS.

The Q.931 setup message includes a bearer capability Information Element (IE), which indicates to the ISDN fabric and receiving side the type of application carried on the B channel. It is the responsibility of the ISDN to provide an end-to-end channel capable of carrying the bearer service, and to provide to the receiving side progress indication to help it better utilize the ISDN connection.

The Cisco IOS **debug isdn q931** output has different bearer capabilities for each incoming call type, as follows:

- Incoming 64 Kbps data call

```
ISDN Se0:23: RX <- SETUP pd = 8  callref = 0x0470
        Bearer Capability i = 0x8890
        Channel ID i = 0xA98382
        Calling Party Number i = '!', 0x83, '5125558084'
        Called Party Number i = 0xC9, '52000'
```

- Incoming 56 Kbps data call

```
ISDN Se0:23: RX <- SETUP pd = 8  callref = 0x05DC
        Bearer Capability i = 0x8890218F
        Channel ID i = 0xA98382
        Calling Party Number i = '!', 0x83, '5125558084'
        Called Party Number i = 0xC9, '52000'
```

- Incoming voice call

```
ISDN Se0:23: RX <- SETUP pd = 8  callref = 0x015C
        Bearer Capability i = 0x8090A2
        Channel ID i = 0xA98383
        Progress Ind i = 0x8283 - Origination address is non-ISDN
        Called Party Number i = 0xC1, '5552000'
```

To support routing of voice calls to integrated modem cards, use the Cisco IOS interface configuration command **isdn incoming-voice modem**. In some network designs, data calls may be made with the Q.931 setup message indicating that it is a voice call. In some regions, ISDN tariff structures may make this type of call more cost effective. (This design is commonly referred to as *ISDN data-over-voice*.) However, indicating to the ISDN switching fabric that the bearer capability is voice allows the call to be placed through non-digital trunks. Designers, therefore, must carefully consider the potential risk in such a design. To support incoming ISDN data-over-voice calls on the Cisco IOS, use the configuration command **isdn incoming-voice data**, as follows:

```
NAS-522(config)#int serial 0:23
NAS-522(config-if)#isdn incoming ?
  data   Incoming voice calls will be handled as data.
  modem  Incoming voice calls will be handled as modems.
```

Data Path Speed

Prior to SS7 implementation, end-to-end call management signalling was provided in-band by robbing bits from the DS0 trunks. Utilizing the occasional eighth and least significant bit of each voice byte was not detrimental to voice quality, but provided switch-to-switch signalling. End-to-end out-of-band signalling via SS7 and PRI/BRI D channels allows data calls to be placed through ISDN networks utilizing the full DS0 trunk (64 Kbps). Some trunks of the PSTN still do not support out-of-band signalling, and can provide only robbed-bit trunking (Channelized T1/E1), limiting the available data channel to 56 Kbps.

It is the responsibility of the ISDN switching fabric to provide an end-to-end path matching the requirement of the bearer capability. If a call is made at 64 Kbps and there is not a 64 Kbps clear end-to-end path for the call, a busy signal should be received. Internetwork designers must consider the possibility of occasional ISDN call blocking at 64 Kbps. Robust design may require that some sites be supported with 56 Kbps data calls. See Table 11–1 for outgoing speeds.

Table 11–1 *Outgoing Speeds and the Cisco IOS Dialer Maps and Profiles*

Outgoing Speed	Cisco IOS Dialer Maps	Cisco IOS Dialer Profile	Cisco 700
64 Kbps	dialer map ... speed 64 (default)	??	set speed 64
56 Kbps	dialer map ... speed 56	??	set speed 56
Auto	Multiple Dialer Maps	??	set speed auto (default)

When originating calls are made at 64 Kbps improperly delivered to the destination by the ISDN network over at 56 Kbps path, the transmitted data will be corrupted. The troubleshooting indication will be that **debug isdn q931** shows the call being delivered, but no output is ever seen as received from **debug ppp negotiation** on one side. The packets have been corrupted and are being discarded. If calls are being delivered and PPP is not negotiating LCP, it is always a prudent idea to test outgoing calls at 56 Kbps.

- Outgoing call speed
  - Cisco IOS speed configuration—Use the **speed** parameter on the **dialer map** configuration command to make outgoing calls at 56 Kbps as in the following example.
    ```
    int dialer 1
    dialer map ip 172.20.1.1 name nas speed 56 5558084
    ```
  - Cisco IOS dialer profiles speed configuration—The following example illustrates how to configure a Cisco IOS dialer profile to make outgoing calls at 56 Kbps:
    ```
    interface dialer 1
    dialer remote-name nas
    dialer string 5558084 class unameit
    !
    map-class dialer unameit
    dialer isdn speed 56
    ```
  - Cisco 700 speed configuration—Use the Cisco 700 series **set speed** configuration command to control the speed for outgoing calls.
- Incoming call speed
  - The ISDN Q.931 bearer capability and other IEs are used to determine the speed of the incoming call and in most circumstances will operate properly. However, in some country-to-country applications, the incoming call setup message will be delivered with a bearer capability that does not match the originating call. If an **isdn not end-to-end** Information Element is also received, it can be used to override the received bearer capability using the Cisco IOS configuration command **isdn not end-to-end**.

Datagram Encapsulation Issues

ISDN can use PPP, HDLC, or X.25 for encapsulation. PPP is used most frequently as it provides an excellent mechanism for authentication and negotiation of compatible link and protocol configuration.

Point-to-Point Protocol (PPP)

PPP provides a standard method for transporting multiprotocol packets over point-to-point links. PPP is defined in RFC 1661. PPP consists of several components, each of which are of concern to the internetwork designer:

- PPP framing

  RFC 1662 discusses the implementation of PPP in HDLC-like framing. There are differences in the way PPP is implemented on asynchronous and synchronous links.

  When one end of the link uses synchronous PPP (such as an ISDN router) and the other uses asynchronous PPP (such as an ISDN TA connected to a PC serial port), two techniques are available to provide framing compatibility. The preferable method is to enable synchronous to asynchronous PPP frame conversion in the ISDN TA. If this is not available, V.120 can be used to encapsulate the asynchronous PPP frames for transport across the ISDN.

- Link Control Protocol (LCP)

  The PPP LCP provides a method of establishing, configuring, maintaining, and terminating the point-to-point connection. Before any network-layer datagrams (for example, IP) can be exchanged, LCP must first open the connection and negotiate configuration parameters. This phase is complete when a configuration acknowledgment frame has been both sent and received.

- PPP authentication

  The PPP authentication protocols (PAP and CHAP) are defined in RFC 1334. After LCP has established the PPP connection, an optional authentication protocol can be implemented before proceeding to the negotiation and establishment of the Network Control Protocols. If authentication is desired, it must be negotiated as an option at the LCP establishment phase. Authentication can be bidirectional (both sides authenticate the other) or unidirectional (one side, typically the called side, authenticates the other).

  Most ISDN designs require the called device to authenticate the calling device. Besides the obvious security benefits, authentication also provides a sense of state for DDR and MultiLink PPP bundling.

- Network Control Protocols (NCP)

  This is a family of NCPs for establishing and configuring different network-layer protocols. PPP is designed to allow the simultaneous use of multiple network-layer protocols.

  After LCP has been established and authentication has passed, the PPP nodes sends NCP frames to negotiate and establish connectivity for one or more network-layer protocols.

For example, to support IP over a PPP connection, the IPCP is negotiated and established as per RFC 1332. Once IPCP is successfully established, IP datagrams can be transmitted over the PPP connection.

- MultiLink PPP (MP)

Multilink PPP (MP) is a standard for aggregating multiple PPP links that allows for multi-vendor interoperability, and is defined in RFC 1717. MP defines a way of sequencing and transmitting packets over multiple physical interfaces. To reduce potential latency issues, MP also defines a method of fragmenting and reassembling large packets. Figure 11–7 provides a conceptual view of MP in action.

Figure 11–7
MultiLink PPP in action.

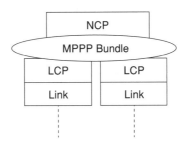

When an NCP packet arrives at an MLP master-interface for transmitting and is over 30 bytes, it is fragmented and sent on each physical link in the MLP bundle. When MLP packet fragments arrive on PPP destination, MLP reassembles the original packets and sequences them correctly in the data stream.

Using MP, BRI devices can double their connection bandwidth across the link: from 56/64 Kbps to 112/128 Kbps. MPPP is supported as long as all devices are part of the same dialer rotary-group or pool.

Cisco IOS and Cisco 700 DDR intelligence is used to determine when to add and remove links from the MP master-interface. Cisco IOS DDR provides a load-threshold configuration to determine when to add and remove the additional link. The load-factor can be calculated on incoming, outgoing, or two-way traffic.

The following partial configuration for NAS places two BRI interfaces into a dialer rotary-group, enables MP support, and defines a load-threshold for determining when to bring up additional B channels.

```
interface BRI2/0
 encapsulation ppp
 dialer rotary-group 1
 isdn spid1 0835866201
 isdn spid2 0835866401
!
interface BRI2/1
 encapsulation ppp
```

```
dialer rotary-group 1
isdn spid1 0835867201
isdn spid2 0835967401
!
interface Dialer1
 ip unnumbered Ethernet0/0
 encapsulation ppp
 dialer in-band
 dialer map ip 172.20.2.1 name kdt-nas 8358661
 dialer load-threshold 100 either
 dialer-group 1
 ppp authentication chap callin
 ppp multilink
```

MP state and sessions can be investigated using the **show user** and the **show ppp multilink** commands:

```
KDT-5200#sh user
    Line     User     Host(s)              Idle Location
* 51 vty 1   admin    idle                 00:00:00
   Vi1       jack-isdn Virtual PPP (Bundle) 00:00:46
   Vi9       cisco776  Virtual PPP (Bundle) 00:00:46
   Se0:18    jack-isd  Sync PPP             00:09:06
   Se0:21    cisco776  Sync PPP             00:18:59
   Se0:22    jack-isdn Sync PPP             00:08:49


KDT-AS5200#sh ppp multi

Bundle cisco776, 1 member, Master link is Virtual-Access9
Dialer Interface is Dialer1
   0 lost fragments, 3 reordered, 0 unassigned, sequence 0x2068/0x1A7C rcvd/sent
   0 discarded, 0 lost received, 1/255 load

Member Link: 1
Serial0:21


Bundle jack-isdn, 2 members, Master link is Virtual-Access1
Dialer Interface is Dialer1
   0 lost fragments, 8 reordered, 0 unassigned, sequence 0x5DEB/0x1D7E4 rcvd/sent
   0 discarded, 0 lost received, 1/255 load

Member Links: 2
Serial0:18
Serial0:22
```

As seen previously, MP uses the PPP authentication name to build and maintain MP bundles. To enable MP on a Cisco 700, apply the following configuration command:

```
set ppp multilink on
```

• Compression Control Protocol (CCP)

The Point-to-Point (PPP) Compression Control Protocol (CCP) is an Internet Engineering Task Force (IETF) draft RFC that defines a method for negotiating data compression over

PPP links. These links can be either leased lines or circuit-switched WAN links, including ISDN. Compression increases throughput and shortens file transfer times.

Use the **compress** interface configuration command at both ends of the link to enable compression. Use the **stac** keyword to enable the Stacker (LZS) compression algorithm or the **predictor** keyword to enable the RAND algorithm (a predictor algorithm). The Stacker algorithm is appropriate for LAPB and PPP encapsulation, and the RAND algorithm is appropriate for HDLC and PPP encapsulation. The Stacker algorithm is preferred for PPP encapsulation.

On the Cisco IOS, to determine what components have been negotiated (such as LCP, IPCP, CCP, and so on), use the **show interface** command on the master interface. To troubleshoot PPP negotiation problems, use **debug ppp negotiation** and **debug ppp authentication**.

ISDN SECURITY

Using SS7, the ISDN can deliver end-to-end Information Elements such as Caller-ID and Dialed Number Information Service (DNIS). This information can be used to provide additional security when designing ISDN solutions. It is recommended that PPP authentication always be implemented.

- PPP authentication

  PPP authentication is used to provide primary security on ISDN and other PPP encapsulated links. The authenticated username is also used by MultiLink PPP to maintain bundles and by DDR to determine which dialer sites are currently connected.

  PPP authentication is enabled with the **ppp authentication** interface command. PAP and/or CHAP can be used to authenticate the remote connection. CHAP is considered a superior authentication protocol since it uses a three-way handshake to avoid sending the password in clear-text on the PPP link.

  Often, it may be necessary to authenticate the remote side only when receiving calls (not when originating).

- Caller ID screening

  The **isdn caller** interface configuration command configures caller ID screening. For example, the following command configures an ISDN to accept a call with a delivered caller ID having 41555512 and any numbers in the last two positions.

  ```
  isdn caller 41555512xx
  ```

  Multiple **isdn caller** commands can be entered as needed. If a call is received that does not contain a caller ID or does not match a configured **isdn caller** statement, the call will be rejected.

- Dialer Callback

  Callback allows a router (typically a remote router) to initiate a circuit-switched WAN link to another device and request that device to call back. The device, such as a central site router, responds to the callback request by calling the device that made the initial call. Callback uses the Point-to-Point Protocol (PPP) and the facilities specified in RFC 1570. Figure 11–8 shows a typical negotiation.

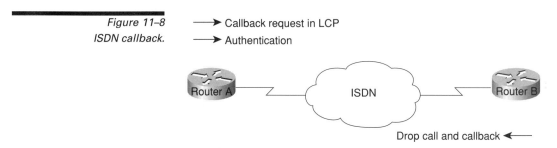

Figure 11–8
ISDN callback.

In Figure 11–8, callback is completed in the following sequence of steps, as follows:

Step 1   Router A brings up a circuit-switched connection to Router B.

Step 2   Routers A and B negotiate PPP Link Control Protocol (LCP). Router A can request a callback, or Router B can initiate a callback.

Step 3   Router A authenticates itself to Router B using PPP PAP or CHAP. Router B can optionally authenticate itself to Router A.

Step 4   Both routers drop the circuit-switched connection.

Step 5   Router B brings up a circuit-switched connection to Router A.

Callback provides centralized billing for synchronous dial-up services. It also allows you to take advantage of tariff disparities on both a national and international basis. However, because callback requires a circuit-switched connection to be established before the callback request can be passed, a small charge (dependent on local tariffing) is always incurred by the router initiating the call that requests a callback.

See Chapter 10 for a further discussion of DDR callback. See Chapter 21, "Using ISDN Effectively in Multiprotocol Networks" for a callback configuration example.

- Called party number verification

    When multiple devices and a router share the same ISDN local loop, you can ensure that the correct device answers an incoming call. This is done by configuring the device to verify the called party number and the subaddress delivered by the switch as part of the setup message against the device's configured number and subaddress.

    To configure called party number verification on the router, apply the **isdn answer1** or **isdn answer2** interface configuration commands to the BRI. These commands allow you to specify the called party number, the subaddress number, or both. If you do not use either the **isdn answer1** command or the **isdn answer2** command, the router processes and accepts all incoming calls.

ISDN SCALING TECHNIQUES

ISDN scaling techniques covered in this section include the following:

- Virtual Remote Nodes
- Virtual Profiles
- Multichassis MultiLink PPP (MMP)

Virtual Remote Nodes

By using Network Address Translations (NAT) features such as Cisco 700 PAT and Cisco IOS EZIP, remote sites can appear to the ISDN NAS as a single remote node IP address. This alleviates IP address consumption problems and the routing design complexity often associated with large-scale ISDN DDR deployment while still supporting a LAN and DDR-based connectivity from the remote site.

These NAT features use the IP address received from the NAS during IPCP negotiation. All packets routed between the LAN and the PPP link have IP address and UDP/TCP port addresses translated to appear as a single IP address. The port number translation is used to determine which packets need to be returned to which IP addresses on the LAN. The following Cisco 700 configuration commands set NAT up for PAT.

Cisco 700 PAT and DHCP

The following configuration sets up a Cisco 700 for PAT and DHCP service:

```
cd internal
set ip address 172.24.4.254
set ip netmask 255.255.255.0
set ip routing on
set ip rip update off
cd
set user access-gw1
set ip routing on
set ip framing none
set number 18005552626
set ip rip update off
set encap ppp
set ip route destination 0.0.0.0 gateway 0.0.0.0
set ip pat on
cd lan
set bridging on
set encaps ppp
set ip routing on
cd
set ip pat porthandler default 172.24.4.1
set ip pat porthandler http 172.24.4.1
set bridging on
set dhcp server
set dhcp domain cisco.com
set dhcp address 172.24.1.1 10
```

```
set dhcp netmask 255.255.255.0
set dhcp gateway primary 172.24.4.254
set dhcp dns primary 172.30.1.100
set dhcp dns secondary 172.30.2.100
set dhcp wins primary 172.30.1.101
set dhcp wins secondary 172.30.2.101
set ppp authentication incoming chap
set ppp authentication outgoing chap
set ppp secret client
 <insert_secret>
 <insert_secret>
set ppp secret host
 <insert_secret>
 <insert_secret>
```

If support is required for outbound initiated network connections to the remote site, port handler configuration can be added so that the SOHO router knows which IP address to forward packets on to for individual connection types.

```
kdt-776> sh ip pat
Dropped - icmp 0, udp 0, tcp 0, map 0, frag 0
Timeout - udp 5 minutes, tcp 30 minutes
Port handlers [default 172.24.4.1]:
Port      Handler           Service
------------------------------------------
0         172.24.4.1        DEFAULT
23        Router            TELNET
67        Router            DHCP Server
68        Router            DHCP Client
69        Router            TFTP
80        172.24.4.1        HTTP
161       Router            SNMP
162       Router            SNMP-TRAP
520       Router            RIP


Translation Table - 11 Entries.
Inside          Outside         Orig. Port/ID    Trans. Port/ID  Timeout
------------------------------------------------------------------------
172.24.4.1      172.17.190.5    0x414            0xff7d              1
172.24.4.1      172.17.190.5    0x415            0xff7c             30
172.24.4.1      172.17.190.26   0x40d            0xff88             27
172.24.4.1      172.17.114.11   0x416            0xff7b              4
172.24.4.1      172.17.114.11   0x417            0xff7a              4
172.24.4.1      172.17.114.11   0x40f            0xff82              4
172.24.4.1      172.17.190.19   0x418            0xff79              1
172.24.4.1      172.17.190.5    0x410            0xff81              1
172.24.4.1      172.17.114.11   0x411            0xff80              4
172.24.4.1      172.17.114.11   0x412            0xff7f              4
172.24.4.1      172.17.190.5    0x413            0xff7e              1
```

Virtual Profiles

Virtual Profiles (introduced in Cisco IOS 11.3) are PPP applications that create virtual-access interfaces for each connected user. Virtual Profiles allow additional design flexibility when building ISDN networks for SOHO support. Using Virtual Profiles for dial-in can provide simplified node addressing and address mapping that was previously provided by using DDR on ISDN interfaces. (As of Cisco IOS 11.3, Virtual Profile based dial-out is not supported.)

The virtual-access interface configuration can be cloned from a Dialer or Virtual-Template. To learn more about virtual-access interfaces, see: http://cio.cisco.com/warp/customer/131/4.html. Virtual Profiles use Virtual Templates and can use AAA based on per-user configuration to create virtual-access interfaces. Per-user configuration can be added to meet the specific protocol needs of individual users or groups.

Cisco IOS virtual-access interfaces can simplify remote node support for IPX and AppleTalk by using the same configuration used on traditional group-async interfaces. The following configuration provides peer addressing for IP, IPX, and AppleTalk using a Virtual-Template interface:

```
interface Virtual-Template1
 ip unnumbered Ethernet0/0
 appletalk client-mode
 ipx ppp-client Loopback0
 peer default ip address pool default
```

Multichassis MultiLink PPP (MMP)

When designing MultiLink PPP without Multichassis support, telco hunt-groups cannot span more than a single Cisco IOS NAS or there exists a risk that the multiple B channels will not be reassembled. For example, an AS5300 can support up to four PRI interfaces providing a maximum of 120 B channels (E1-based) in a single dial-in hunt group. Additional NAS capacity would need to be provided by configuring a new hunt-group (with a new pilot directory number) for each Network Access Server, as shown in Figure 11–9. This has the negative effect of fragmenting the dial-up pool.

Cisco recognized that no matter what size NAS they can develop, there will always be customers needing larger pools of access ports. As such, Cisco IOS 11.2 released Multichassis MultiLink Point-to-Point Protocol (MMP), which extends MultiLink PPP (MLP) by providing a mechanism to aggregate B channels transparently across multiple NASs.

MMP consists of two primary components to complement MLP, as follows:

- *The dial StackGroup*—NASs that operate as a group when receiving MLP calls. Every MLP session receiving any NAS is sent out to bid using the Stack Group Bidding Protocol (SGBP). Primarily, this allows secondary MLP links to be bundled to the MLP master interface. Different bidding strategies (such as off-load and load-sharing) can be used to determine who should win master-interface bidding.

Figure 11–9

MMP allows a telco hunt-group to span more than a single NAS.

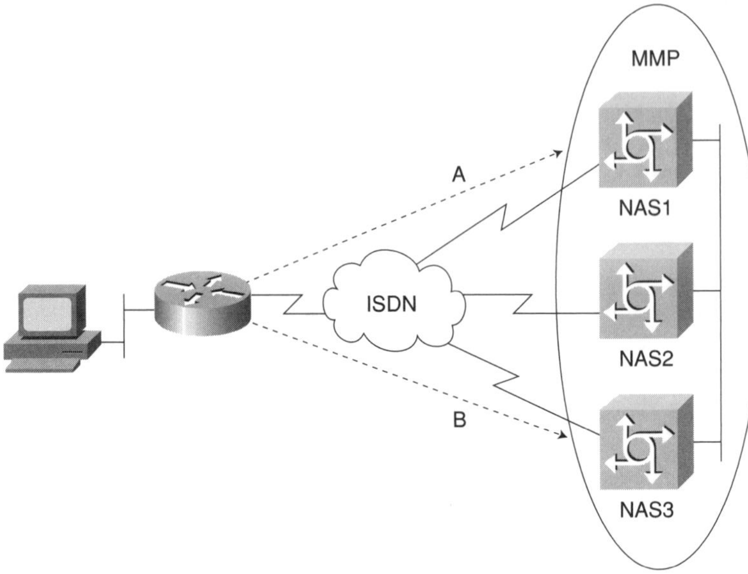

- *Level 2 Forwarding (L2F) protocol*—A draft IETF standard, L2F provides for tunneling of the MLP fragments between the MLP physical interface and the MLP master-interface.

By using MMP, MLP capacity can be easily added and removed from large dial pools as needed. CPU processing capacity can be added to dialup pools through the use of off-load servers. Tasks such as MLP fragmentation and reassembly, PPP compression, and encryption can be intensive and may benefit from execution in off-load servers (see Figure 11–10).

To configure MMP on a Cisco IOS NAS, use the **SGBP** commands, as follows:

```
kdt-3640(config)#sgbp ?
  group         SGBP group name
  member        SGBP group member configuration
  ppp-forward   SGBP participation for non-Multilink PPP also
  seed-bid      mastership query seed bid
  source-ip     SGBP source ip address
```

To monitor and troubleshoot MMP, use both SGBP and VPDN (for L2F).

```
sh sgbp
sh vpdn
debug sgbp
debug vpdn
```

MMP provides an interoperable multivendor solution because it does not require any special software capabilities at the remote sites. The only remote requirement is support for the industry standard MLP (RFC 1717).

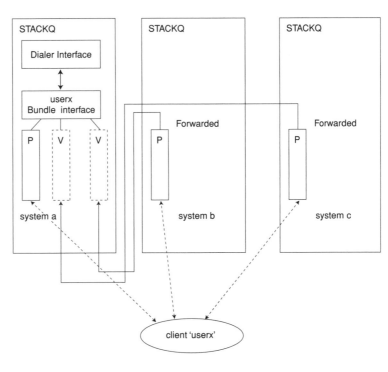

Figure 11–10
Active MMP sessions.

Legend

←——————→	Client PPP MP links across stack members STACKQ
←- - - - - - -→	L2F projected links to the stack member containing bundle interface 'userx'
Bundle Interface	Bundle Interface for client 'userx' (Virtual Access interface)
P	Physical interface
V	Projected PPP link (Virtual Access Interface)

ISDN COST CONTAINMENT ISSUES

As a circuit-switched connection, ISDN is billed, or tariffed, based on usage. Given this model, the configuration goal is to minimize uptime by controlling the kinds of packets that bring the link up. Minimizing uptime becomes a challenge when routing protocols are used because of their need to send regular broadcasts that contain routing information.

ISDN charges in some installations have easily exceeded $4,000/month for a single site as a result of being poorly designed and managed. When the outrageous phone bill is received, it is too late; the cost has been occurred. Cisco highly recommends the use of proper network management to back up careful design to ensure excessive charges are not experienced. Depending on the protocols your network runs, you might want to use a combination of the techniques described in this section, which are as follows:

- Traffic Analysis
- Tariff Structure
- User Education
- Using SNMP
- Cisco Enterprise Accounting (CEA) for ISDN
- AAA Accounting

Traffic Analysis

Most ISDN solutions can remain cost effective only as long as the ISDN B channels are kept idle most of the day. The general rule of thumb is that Frame Relay will make a more cost effective solution at some application-dependent number of hours per day. (The point at which it is more cost effective to use a leased-line solution depends on the cost structures for each point-to-point application.)

Each internetworking application and protocol has its own set of challenges. E-mail clients may be set to periodically poll POP servers. Network Time Protocol might be desired to support clock synchronization. To provide total control over when the DDR connections are made, the network designer must carefully consider the following issues:

- Which sites can initiate connections based on traffic?
- Is dial-out required to SOHO sites? For network or workstation management?
- Which sites can terminate connections based on idle links?
- How are directory services and routing tables supported across an idle connection?
- What applications need to be supported over DDR connections? For how many users?
- What unexpected protocols might cause DDR connections? Can they be filtered?
- Are dialer filters performing as expected?

Guidelines should be provided to users as to how to avoid and/or eliminate excessive ISDN charges. These guidelines will be the result of first determining what applications are required over these connections. Packet-tracing tools can be used very effectivity to determine how to minimize or eliminate unnecessary DDR connections. For example,

- Sending and receiving e-mail should be manual if possible.
- Windows Networking may require periodic directory services traffic.
- AppleShare servers will need to be disconnected to avoid tickle packets.
- DB-accessing applications, such as scheduling software, may require logging out when not in use.

Tariff Structure

Some ISDN service providers charge a per-connection and per-minute charge even for local calls. It is important to consider local and long-distance tariff charges when selecting DDR design and parameters. ISDN Callback can be used to centralize long-distance charges, which can significantly reduce administrative overhead and provide opportunities for reduced rate structures. ISDN Callback can also enhance the security environment.

User Education

End users should be trained to keep their ISDN routers visible and monitor the status of their B channel LEDs on their BRI devices. If B channels are up when they are not using networking applications, they should alert network managers. User education can be very effective in helping to avoid excessive ISDN charges.

Using SNMP

The Simple Network Management Protocol (SNMP) uses management information bases (MIBs) to store information about network events. Currently, no industry-standard ISDN MIB is available, but as of Cisco IOS Software Release 10.3(3), two Cisco ISDN MIBs are available. With these MIBs, SNMP-compliant management platforms (for example, HP OpenView or SunNet Manager) can query Cisco routers for ISDN-related statistics.

The Cisco ISDN MIB focuses primarily on ISDN interface and neighbor information. It defines two MIB groups: demandNbrTable and demandNbrEntry. Table 11–2 lists some of the MIB variables that are available in the ISDN MIB. Cisco Enterprise Accounting for ISDN can provide management access to Call History Data using this MIB.

Table 11–2 *Cisco ISDN MIB Variables*

MIB Object	Description
demandNbrPhysIf	Index value of the physical interface that the neighbor will be called on; on an ISDN interface, this is the ifIndex value of the D channel.
demandNbrMaxduration	Maximum call duration in seconds.
demandNbrLastduration	Duration of last call in seconds.
demandNbrAcceptCalls	Number of calls accepted from the neighbor.
demandNbrRefuseCalls	Number of calls from neighbor that the router has refused.

The Cisco Call History MIB stores call information for accounting purposes. The goal is to provide a historical view of an ISDN interface, including the number of calls that have been placed and call length. Most call history MIB variables are in the ciscoCallHistory MIB group. Table 11–3 lists some of the MIB variables.

Table 11–3 *Cisco Call History Variables*

MIB Object	Description
ciscoCallHistoryStartTime	The value of sysUpTime when this call history entry was created; this variable can be used to retrieve all calls after a specific time.
ciscoCallHistoryCalledNumber	The number that was used to place this call.
ciscoCallHistoryCallConnection Time	The value of sysUpTime when the call was connected.
ciscoCallHistoryCallDisconnect Time	The value of sysUpTime when the call was disconnected.

The Cisco ISDN MIBs assume SNMP support on the network. If an SNMP-compliant management platform is present, the Cisco ISDN MIBs deliver valuable information about ISDN links. In particular, the Call History MIB provides critical information about ISDN uptime, which is useful for tracking ISDN charges.

Cisco offers a wide range of ISDN-based products in response to a variety of internetworking needs. The Cisco IOS software provides a number of features that maximize ISDN performance and minimize ISDN usage charges, such as snapshot routing, access lists, NBP filtering (for AppleTalk), and watchdog and keepalive packet control (for IPX).

Cisco Enterprise Accounting (CEA) for ISDN

CEA for ISDN is a software application that runs on Windows NT. CEA for ISDN can be utilized to monitor the ISDN Call-History-MIB and provide network managers with Call Detail Records, including cost estimates.

AAA Accounting

AAA Accounting can be implemented to provide feedback of PPP Session connect times. AAA Accounting is transported to TACACS+ or RADIUS servers where the data can often be accessed with standard SQL tools for scheduled and immediate reporting. The following command enables AAA Accounting records for PPP sessions:

```
aaa accounting network stop-only
```

SUMMARY

Increasing availability and decreasing costs are making ISDN an excellent choice for many internetworking applications. Cisco IOS features allow the building of large and flexible ISDN solutions. DDR is used for call initiation and termination. Virtual Profiles can be used to easily scale mass ISDN dial-in solutions. However, extra care must be taken to ensure ISDN costs are controlled.

Designing Switched LAN Internetworks

This chapter describes the following three technologies that network designers can use to design switched LAN internetworks:

- LAN switching
- Virtual LANs (VLANs)
- ATM switching

EVOLUTION FROM SHARED TO SWITCHED NETWORKS

In the past, network designers had only a limited number of hardware options when purchasing a technology for their campus networks. Hubs were for wiring closets and routers were for the data center or main telecommunications operations. The increasing power of desktop processors and the requirements of client-server and multimedia applications, however, have driven the need for greater bandwidth in traditional shared-media environments. These requirements are prompting network designers to replace hubs in their wiring closets with switches, as shown in Figure 12–1.

This strategy allows network managers to protect their existing wiring investments and boost network performance with dedicated bandwidth to the desktop for each user. Coinciding with the wiring closet evolution is a similar trend in the network backbone. Here, the role of Asynchronous Transfer Mode (ATM) is increasing as a result of standardizing protocols, such as LAN emulation (LANE), that enable ATM devices to coexist with existing LAN technologies. Network designers are collapsing their router backbones with ATM switches, which offer the greater backbone bandwidth required by high-throughput data services.

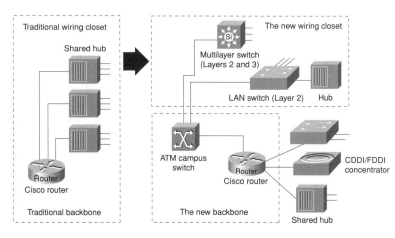

Figure 12–1
Evolution from shared to switched internetworks.

TECHNOLOGIES FOR BUILDING SWITCHED LAN INTERNETWORKS

With the advent of such technologies as Layer 3 switching, LAN switching, and VLANs, building campus LANs is becoming more complex than in the past. Today, the following three technologies are required to build successful campus networks:

- LAN switching technologies
  - Ethernet switching—Provides Layer 2 switching and offers broadcast domain segmentation using VLANs. This is the base fabric of the network.
  - Token Ring switching—Offers the same functionality as Ethernet switching but uses Token Ring technology. You can use a Token Ring switch as either a transparent bridge or source-route bridge.
  - Copper Data Distributed Interface (CDDI)—Provides a single-attachment station (SAS) or dual-attachment station (DAS) to two Category 5 unshielded twisted-pair (UTP), 100 Mbps RJ-45 connectors.
  - Fiber Distributed Data Interface (FDDI)—Provides an SAS or DAS connection to the FDDI backbone network using two multimode, media interface connector (MIC) fiber-optic connections.
- ATM switching technologies

ATM switching offers high-speed switching technology for voice, video, and data. Its operation is similar to LAN switching technologies for data operations. ATM, however, offers superior voice, video, and data integration today.

- Routing technologies

Routing is a key technology for connecting LANs in a campus network. It can be either Layer 3 switching or more traditional routing with Layer 3 switching features and enhanced Layer 3 software features.

NOTES

Switched LAN internetworks are also referred to as *campus LANs*.

Role of LAN Switching Technology in Campus Networks

Most network designers are beginning to integrate switching devices into their existing shared-media networks to achieve the following goals:

- Increase the bandwidth that is available to each user, thereby alleviating congestion in their shared-media networks.

- Employ the manageability of VLANs by organizing network users into logical workgroups that are independent of the physical topology of wiring closet hubs. This, in turn, can reduce the cost of moves, adds, and changes while increasing the flexibility of the network.

- Deploy emerging multimedia applications across different switching platforms and technologies, making them available to a variety of users.

- Provide a smooth evolution path to high-performance switching solutions, such as Fast Ethernet and ATM.

Segmenting shared-media LANs divides the users into two or more separate LAN segments, reducing the number of users contending for bandwidth. LAN switching technology, which builds upon this trend, employs *microsegmentation,* which further segments the LAN to fewer users and ultimately to a single user with a dedicated LAN segment. Each switch port provides a dedicated, 10MB Ethernet segment, or dedicated 4/16MB Token Ring segment.

Segments are interconnected by internetworking devices that enable communication between LANs while blocking other types of traffic. Switches have the intelligence to monitor traffic and compile address tables, which then allows them to forward packets directly to specific ports in the LAN. Switches also usually provide nonblocking service, which allows multiple conversations (traffic between two ports) to occur simultaneously.

Switching technology is quickly becoming the preferred solution for improving LAN traffic for the following reasons:

- Unlike hubs and repeaters, switches allow multiple data streams to pass simultaneously.

- Switches have the capability through microsegmentation to support the increased speed and bandwidth requirements of emerging technologies.

- Switches deliver dedicated bandwidth to users through high-density group switched and switched 10BaseT or 100BaseT Ethernet, flexible 10/100 BaseT Ethernet, fiber-based Fast

Ethernet, Fast EtherChannel, Token Ring, CDDI/FDDI, and ATM LAN Emulation (LANE).

Switched Internetwork Solutions

Network designers are discovering, however, that many products offered as switched internetwork solutions are inadequate. Some offer a limited number of hardware platforms with little or no system integration with the current infrastructure. Others require complete abandonment of all investments in the current network infrastructure. To be successful, a switched internetwork solution must accomplish the following:

- Leverage strategic investments in the existing communications infrastructure while increasing available bandwidth.

- Reduce the costs of managing network operations.

- Offer options to support multimedia applications and other high-demand traffic across a variety of platforms.

- Provide scalability, traffic control, and security that is at least as good or better than that of today's router-based internetworks.

- Provide support for embedded remote monitoring (RMON) agent.

The key to achieving these benefits is to understand the role of the internetworking software infrastructure within the switched internetworks. Within today's networks, routers allow for the interconnection of disparate LAN and WAN technologies, while also implementing security filters and logical firewalls. It is these capabilities that have allowed current internetworks to scale globally while remaining stable and robust.

As networks evolve toward switched internetworks, similar logical internetworking capabilities are required for stability and scalability. Although LAN and ATM switches provide great performance improvements, they also raise new internetworking challenges. Switched internetworks must integrate with existing LAN and WAN networks. Such services as VLANs, which will be deployed with switched internetworks, also have particular internetworking requirements.

A true switched internetwork, therefore, is more than a collection of boxes. Rather, it consists of a system of devices integrated and supported by an intelligent internetworking software infrastructure. Presently, this network intelligence is centralized within routers. However, with the advent of switched internetworks, the intelligence will often be dispersed throughout the network, reflecting the decentralized nature of switching systems. The need for an internetworking infrastructure, however, will remain.

COMPONENTS OF THE SWITCHED INTERNETWORKING MODEL

A switched internetwork is composed of the following three basic components:

- Physical switching platforms
- A common software infrastructure
- Network management tools and applications

Cisco provides network designers with a complete, end-to-end solution for implementing and managing scalable, robust, switched internetworks.

Scalable Switching Platforms

The first component of the switched internetworking model is the physical switching platform. This can be an ATM switch, a LAN switch, or a router.

ATM Switches

Although switched internetworks can be built with a variety of technologies, many network designers will deploy ATM in order to utilize its unique characteristics. ATM provides scalable bandwidth that spans both LANs and WANs. It also promises Quality of Service (QoS) guarantees—bandwidth on demand—that can map into and support higher-level protocol infrastructures for emerging multimedia applications and provide a common, multiservice network infrastructure.

ATM switches are one of the key components of ATM technology. All ATM switches, however, are not alike. Even though all ATM switches perform cell relay, ATM switches differ markedly in the following capabilities:

- Variety of interfaces and services that are supported
- Redundancy
- Depth of ATM internetworking software
- Sophistication of traffic management mechanism
- Blocking and non-blocking switching fabrics
- SVC and PVC support

Just as there are routers and LAN switches available at various price/performance points with different levels of functionality, ATM switches can be segmented into the following four distinct types that reflect the needs of particular applications and markets:

- Workgroup ATM switches
- Campus ATM switches
- Enterprise ATM switches
- Multiservice access switches

As Figure 12–2 shows, Cisco offers a complete range of ATM switches.

Workgroup and Campus ATM Switches

Workgroup ATM switches are optimized for deploying ATM to the desktop over low-cost ATM desktop interfaces, with ATM signaling interoperability for ATM adapters and QoS support for multimedia applications.

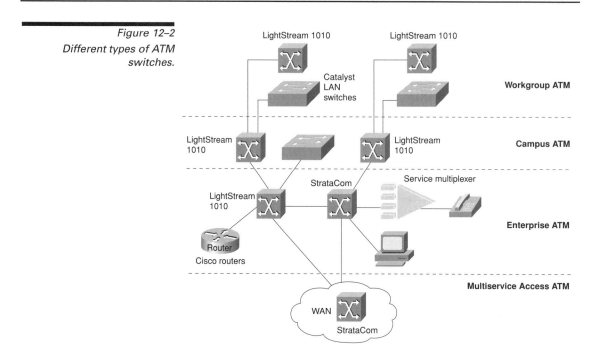

Figure 12–2

Different types of ATM switches.

Campus ATM switches are generally used for small-scale ATM backbones (for example, to link ATM routers or LAN switches). This use of ATM switches can alleviate current backbone congestion while enabling the deployment of such new services as VLANs. Campus switches need to support a wide variety of both local backbone and WAN types but be price/performance optimized for the local backbone function. In this class of switches, ATM routing capabilities that allow multiple switches to be tied together is very important. Congestion control mechanisms for optimizing backbone performance is also important.

Enterprise ATM Switches

Enterprise ATM switches are sophisticated multiservice devices that are designed to form the core backbones of large, enterprise networks. They are intended to complement the role played by today's high-end multiprotocol routers. Enterprise ATM switches, much as campus ATM switches, are used to interconnect workgroup ATM switches and other ATM-connected devices, such as LAN switches. Enterprise-class switches, however, can act not only as ATM backbones but can serve as the single point of integration for all of the disparate services and technology found in enterprise backbones today. By integrating all of these services onto a common platform and a common ATM transport infrastructure, network designers can gain greater manageability while eliminating the need for multiple overlay networks.

LAN Switches

A LAN switch is a device that typically consists of many ports that connect LAN segments (Ethernet and Token Ring) and a high-speed port (such as 100-Mbps Ethernet, Fiber Distributed Data Interface [FDDI], or 155-Mbps ATM). The high-speed port, in turn, connects the LAN switch to other devices in the network.

A LAN switch has dedicated bandwidth per port, and each port represents a different segment. For best performance, network designers often assign just one host to a port, giving that host dedicated bandwidth of 10 Mbps, as shown in Figure 12–3, or 16 Mbps for Token Ring networks.

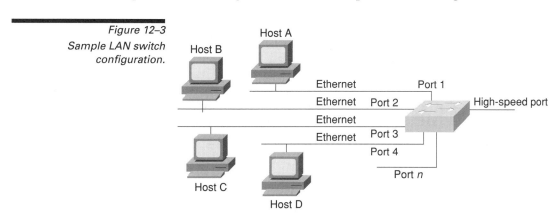

Figure 12–3
Sample LAN switch configuration.

When a LAN switch first starts up and as the devices that are connected to it request services from other devices, the switch builds a table that associates the MAC address of each local device with the port number through which that device is reachable. That way, when Host A on Port 1 needs to transmit to Host B on Port 2, the LAN switch forwards frames from Port 1 to Port 2, thus sparing other hosts on Port 3 from responding to frames destined for Host B. If Host C needs to send data to Host D at the same time that Host A sends data to Host B, it can do so because the LAN switch can forward frames from Port 3 to Port 4 at the same time it forwards frames from Port 1 to Port 2.

Whenever a device connected to the LAN switch sends a packet to an address that is not in the LAN switch's table (for example, to a device that is beyond the LAN switch), or whenever the device sends a broadcast or multicast packet, the LAN switch sends the packet out all ports (except for the port from which the packet originated)—a technique known as *flooding*.

Because they work like traditional "transparent" bridges, LAN switches dissolve previously well-defined workgroup or department boundaries. A network built and designed only with LAN switches appears as a *flat* network topology consisting of a single broadcast domain. Consequently, these networks are liable to suffer the problems inherent in flat (or *bridged*) networks—that is, they do not scale well. Note, however, that LAN switches that support VLANs are more scalable than traditional bridges.

Multiservice Access Switches

Beyond private networks, ATM platforms will also be widely deployed by service providers both as customer premises equipment (CPE) and within public networks. Such equipment will be used to support multiple MAN and WAN services—for example, Frame Relay switching, LAN interconnect, or public ATM services—on a common ATM infrastructure. Enterprise ATM switches will often be used in these public network applications because of their emphasis on high availability and redundancy, and their support of multiple interfaces.

Routing Platforms

In addition to LAN switches and ATM switches, typically network designers use routers as one of the components in a switched internetwork infrastructure. While LAN switches are being added to wiring closets to increase bandwidth and to reduce congestion in existing shared-media hubs, high-speed backbone technologies, such as ATM switching and ATM routers are being deployed in the backbone. Within a switched internetwork, routing platforms also allow for the interconnection of disparate LAN and WAN technologies while also implementing broadcast filters and logical firewalls. In general, if you need advanced internetworking services, such as broadcast firewalling and communication between dissimilar LANs, routers are necessary.

Common Software Infrastructure

The second level of a switched internetworking model is a common software infrastructure. The function of this software infrastructure is to unify the variety of physical switching platforms: LAN switches, ATM switches, and multiprotocol routers. Specifically, the software infrastructure should perform the following tasks:

- Monitor the logical topology of the network
- Logically route traffic
- Manage and control sensitive traffic
- Provide firewalls, gateways, filtering, and protocol translation

Cisco offers network designers Cisco Internetwork Operating System (Cisco IOS) switching software. This subset of the Cisco IOS software is optimized for switching and provides the unifying element to Cisco's line of switching platforms in a switched internetwork. The Cisco IOS software is found on standalone routers, router modules for shared-media hubs, PC and workstations file servers, multiservice WAN access switches, LAN switches, ATM switches, and ATM-capable PBXs. It provides optional levels of routing and switching across a switched internetwork in addition to new capabilities, such as VLANs, ATM internetworking software services, multilayer switching, extensions to support new networked multimedia applications, and traffic management and analysis tools.

VLANs

A VLAN consists of several end systems, either hosts or network equipment (such as switches and routers), all of which are members of a single logical broadcast domain. A VLAN no longer has physical proximity constraints for the broadcast domain. This VLAN is supported on various pieces of network equipment (for example, LAN switches) that support VLAN trunking protocols between them. Each VLAN supports a separate Spanning Tree (IEEE 802.1d).

First-generation VLANs are based on various OSI Layer 2 bridging and multiplexing mechanisms, such as IEEE 802.10, LAN Emulation (LANE), and Inter-Switch Link (ISL), that allow the formation of multiple, disjointed, overlaid broadcast groups on a single network infrastructure. Figure 12–4 shows an example of a switched LAN network that uses VLANs. Layer 2 of the OSI reference model provides reliable transit of data across a physical link. The data link layer is concerned with physical addressing, network topology, line discipline, error notification, ordered delivery frames, and flow control. The IEEE has divided this layer into two sublayers: the MAC sublayer and the LLC sublayer, sometimes simply called link layer.

In Figure 12–4, 10-Mbps Ethernet connects the hosts on each floor to switches A, B, C, and D. 100-Mbps Fast Ethernet connects these to Switch E. VLAN 10 consists of those hosts on Ports 6 and 8 of Switch A and Port 2 on Switch B. VLAN 20 consists of those hosts that are on Port 1 of Switch A and Ports 1 and 3 of Switch B.

VLANs can be used to group a set of related users, regardless of their physical connectivity. They can be located across a campus environment or even across geographically dispersed locations. The users might be assigned to a VLAN because they belong to the same department or functional team, or because data flow patterns among them is such that it makes sense to group them together. Note, however, that without a router, hosts in one VLAN cannot communicate with hosts in another VLAN.

Network Management Tools and Applications

The third and last component of a switched internetworking model consists of network management tools and applications. As switching is integrated throughout the network, network management becomes crucial at both the workgroup and backbone levels. Managing a switch-based network requires a radically different approach than managing traditional hub and router-based LANs.

As part of designing a switched internetwork, network designers must ensure that their design takes into account network management applications needed to monitor, configure, plan, and analyze switched internetwork devices and services. Cisco offers such tools for emerging switched internetworks.

Figure 12–4
Typical VLAN topology.

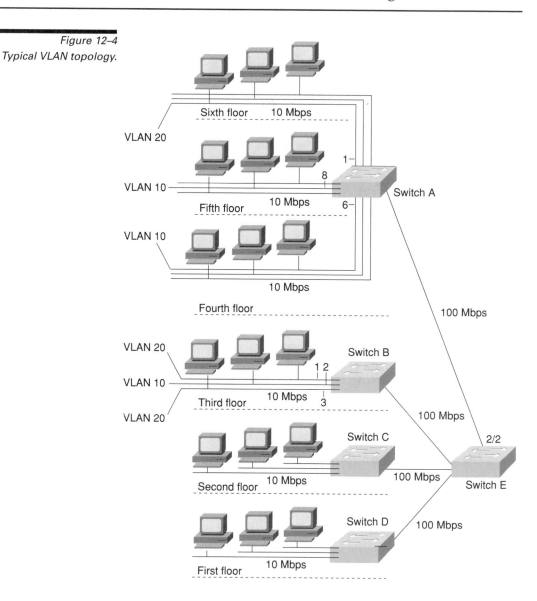

CISCO SWITCHED INTERNETWORKING PRODUCTS

Cisco offers the following products that meet the needs of a switched internetwork, all discussed in the following sections:

- Cisco ATM Switches
- Cisco LAN Switches
- Cisco Routing Platforms

Cisco ATM Switches

Cisco's LightStream 1010 family of ATM switches is specifically designed for workgroup and campus backbone deployment. It incorporates support for the latest ATM Forum specifications and builds upon the Cisco IOS software. The LightStream 1010 is a five-slot, modular switch that features the option of dual, load-sharing, hot-swappable power supplies, 5-Gbps of shared memory, nonblocking switch fabric, and 65,536 cells of shared ATM cell buffers. It supports a wide range of modular, hot-swappable, desktop, backbone, and wide-area ATM interfaces. These characteristics allow network managers to deploy it in a variety of scenarios ranging from high-density, 155-Mbps copper UTP-5 workgroups to high-performance OC-12 backbones.

In order to support the bursty, best-effort traffic generated by LAN switches and routes, the LightStream 1010 provides advanced traffic management mechanisms. The LightStream 1010's intelligent early packet discard mechanism allows it to discard entire packets rather than individual cells when necessary, which greatly increases performance for current protocols, such as TCP/IP and IPX. It also supports the latest ATM Forum Available Bit Rate (ABR) congestion control specifications, which allows the LightStream 1010 to slow traffic sources before congestion becomes excessive. Because of its support for the ATM Forum private network-network interface (PNNI) protocols, networks of LightStream 1010s can scale to hundreds of nodes.

In addition, the LightStream 1010 offers a high degree of manageability. Advanced port snooping and connection-steering capabilities allow the connections on any port to be directed to a monitor port for analysis by an external ATM analyzer. This capability is critical for the monitoring and troubleshooting of ATM switching systems, which unlike shared-media LANs, cannot be monitored easily with external devices. Simple Network Management Protocol (SNMP) monitoring and configuration invoked through the CiscoView graphical user interface (GUI) device configuration applications and the AtmDirector CiscoWorks ATM system management application, allow for comprehensive network management.

By building on the Cisco IOS software, the LightStream 1010 switch also shares the advanced serviceability capabilities found today on Cisco's multiprotocol routers. As with all Cisco routers, the LightStream 1010 switch supports such protocols as BOOTP, DHCP, Telnet, and Trivial File Transfer Protocol (TFTP) for remote access and autoconfiguration. It also offers the access protections of the Cisco IOS software, from multiple password levels to TACACS for remote access validation, to preclude unauthorized changes to the switch configuration. These capabilities are clearly essential to safeguard the operation of the mission-critical campus backbones in which the LightStream 1010 will typically be deployed.

The Cisco/StrataCom BPX/AXIS is a powerful broadband 9.6-Gbps ATM switch designed to meet the demanding, high-traffic needs of a large private enterprise or public service provider. The Cisco/StrataCom IGX is a 1.2-Gbps ATM-based enterprise WAN switch that can be used to provide enterprise WAN features in your internetwork. For more information on these enterprise ATM switches, see Chapter 8, "Designing ATM Internetworks."

Cisco LAN Switches

Cisco's Catalyst family is a comprehensive line of high-performance switches designed to help network managers easily migrate from traditional shared LANs to fully switched internetworks. The Catalyst family delivers the varying levels of flexibility and cost-effectiveness required for today's desktop, workgroup, and backbone applications while enabling enterprise-wide switched internetworks. Using these LAN switches instead of traditional shared hubs increase performance and provides new capabilities, such as VLANs.

Figure 12–5 shows an example of switches that can be used in a campus backbone. In this example, the Cisco switches are used to interconnect the four buildings that comprise the campus network.

Figure 12–5
LAN switches in a campus backbone.

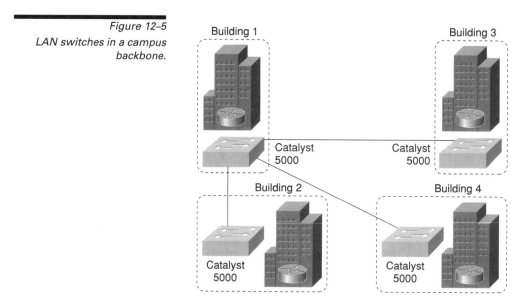

Table 12–1 summarizes the LAN switches that Cisco offers.

Table 12–1 *List of Cisco LAN Switches*

Cisco LAN Switch	Description
Catalyst 5500 switching system	The Catalyst 5500 switch chassis has 13 slots. Slot 1 is for the Supervisor Engine II model which provides switching, local and remote management, and dual Fast Ethernet interfaces. Slot 2 contains an additional redundant Supervisor Engine II in case the first module fails. A failure of the active Supervisor Engine II is detected by the standby module, which takes control of the Supervisor Engine II switching functions. If a redundant Supervisor Engine II is not required, slot 2 is available for any interface module.
	The Catalyst 5500 has a 3.6-Gbps media-independent switch fabric and a 5-Gbps cell-switch fabric. The backplane provides the connection between power supplies, Supervisor Engine II, interface modules, and backbone module. The 3.6-Gbps media-independent fabric supports Ethernet, Fast Ethernet, FDDI/CDDI, ATM LAN Emulation, and RSM modules. The 5-Gbps cell-based fabric supports an ATM switch processor (ASP) module and ATM port adapter modules (PAMS).
Route switch module	The Cisco Catalyst 5000 series route switch module builds upon the Route Switch Processor (RSP) featured in Cisco's 7500 routing platform. The route switch module provides high-performance multilayer switching and routing services between switched Virtual LANs (VLANs), emulated LANs (ELANs) within an Asynchronous Transfer Mode (ATM) fabric, or across mixed media via an optional Versatile Interface Processor (VIP) and port adapters.
Catalyst 5000 switching system	A modular switching platform that meets high performance needs, bandwidth-intensive networking switching applications. It offers five slots that can be populated with any combination of 10BaseT, 10BaseFL modules, switched 10-Mbps Fast Ethernet, FDDI, or ATM modules.
	It delivers high performance both for client and server connections as well as for backbone connections. Its switching backplane operates at 1.2 Gbps and provides nonblocking performance for all switched 10-Mbps Ethernet interfaces.
	It supports enterprise-wide VLAN communications across Ethernet, Fast Ethernet, CDDI/FDDI, and ATM connections via the following protocols: ISL for Fast Ethernet interfaces, 802.10 for FDDI interfaces, and LANE v1.0 for ATM.

Table 12–1   *List of Cisco LAN Switches, Continued*

Catalyst 3000 stackable switching system	A 16-port 10BaseT switch that has two open expansion bays that can be populated with 100BaseTX/FX, 10BaseFL, 10BaseT, 100VG-AnyLAN, or ATM. With the Matrix module, up to eight Catalyst 3000 switches can be stacked together as one logical switching system. The Catalyst 3000 system can also be populated with the Catalyst 3011 WAN router module. A fully loaded Catalyst 3000 system can support up to 192 10BaseT ports, or 128 10BaseT ports with 16 high-speed ports. Supports up to 64 VLANs within the stack. Also supports ISL for Fast Ethernet, and ATM LANE.
Catalyst 2900 Fast Ethernet switch	A 14-port, fixed-configuration, Fast Ethernet switch that provides media-rate Fast Ethernet switching in backbone, server cluster, and high-performance workgroup applications. Its software architecture combines superior traffic throughput, complete VLAN solutions, traffic management, and fault tolerance.
Catalyst 1800 Token Ring switch	A Token Ring switch that has 16 dedicated or shared ports in the base unit plus two feature-card slots that is designed for the workgroup switching environment. Using the four-port Token Ring unshielded twisted-pair/shielded twisted-pair (UTP/STP) feature cards, it supports eight additional Token Ring ports.
Catalyst 1900 and Catalyst 2820 Ethernet switches	Ideally suited to replace shared 10BaseT hubs in the wiring closet with feature-rich switched Ethernet capability to the desktop. The Catalyst 1900 Ethernet switch features 25 switched Ethernet ports providing attachment to individual workstations and 10BaseT hubs. It also has two 100BaseT ports for high speed connectivity to servers and backbones. The Catalyst 2820 Ethernet switch has 25 switched Ethernet ports and two high-speed expansion slots. Field-installable modules provide configuration, wiring, and backbone flexibility with a choice of 100BaseT, FDDI, and future ATM modules available, which support Category 5 UTP or fiber-optic cabling.
Catalyst 1200 workgroup switch	A multilayer switch for workgroup applications that can benefit from OSI Layer 3 as well as Layer 2 capabilities. It offers eight 10BaseT or 10BaseFL ports and one expansion slot. The expansion slot can be populated with either one A/B CDDI interface or one A/B FDDI interface. IP routing only supports 802.10 over FDDI VLANs. In addition to meeting a wide range of performance needs for Ethernet and FDDI, it offers such unique features as embedded Remote Monitoring (RMON) functionality, which helps network managers monitor and control the growth and changes of client-server workgroups.

Cisco Routing Platforms

Both the Cisco 7000 and Cisco 4000 family of multiprotocol routers are particularly well suited for switched internetworking. In particular, the first native-mode ATM router interface, the ATM Interface Processor (AIP) for the Cisco 7000 family of routers, is a key enabler for integrating existing LAN and WAN networks with evolving, ATM-based switched internetworks.

The sophisticated ATM signaling and traffic management capabilities of the AIP also allows it to play a crucial role in the deployment of new services such as VLANs. The AIP, a key enabler for the production deployment of switched internetworks, allows VLANs to internetwork either with each other or with external networks. The Cisco 4000 family of multiprotocol routers also support such capabilities, thereby providing network designers with a wide choice of price/performance points for ATM-capable routers.

Because the Cisco 7000 and Cisco 4000 families support FDDI, Fast Ethernet, and ATM, they provide network designers with a full set of options for high-speed connectivity. Both router families also support routing between VLANs on all media for ease of migration.

SWITCHED LAN NETWORK DESIGNS

A successful switched internetworking solution must combine the benefits of both routers and switches in every part of the network, as well as offer a flexible evolution path from shared-media networking to switched internetworks.

In general, incorporating switches in campus network designs results in the following benefits:

- High bandwidth
- Quality of Service (QoS)
- Low cost
- Easy configuration

If you need advanced internetworking services, however, routers are necessary. Routers offer the following services:

- Broadcast firewalling
- Hierarchical addressing
- Communication between dissimilar LANs
- Fast convergence
- Policy routing
- QoS routing
- Security
- Redundancy and load balancing
- Traffic flow management
- Multimedia group membership

Some of these router services will be offered by switches in the future. For example, support for multimedia often requires a protocol, such as Internet Group Management Protocol (IGMP), that allows workstations to join a group that receives multimedia multicast packets. In the future, Cisco will allow switches to participate in this process by using the Cisco Group Management Protocol (CGMP). One router will still be necessary, but you will not need a router in each department because CGMP switches can communicate with the router to determine whether any of their attached users are part of a multicast group.

Switching and bridging sometimes can result in nonoptimal routing of packets. This is because every packet must go through the root bridge of the spanning tree. When routers are used, the routing of packets can be controlled and designed for optimal paths. Cisco now provides support for improved routing and redundancy in switched environments by supporting one instance of the spanning tree per VLAN.

When designing switched LAN networks, you should consider the following:

- Comparison of LAN Switches and Routers
- Benefits of LAN Switches (Layer 2 Services)
- Benefits of Routers (Layer 3 Services)
- Benefits of VLANs
- VLAN Implementation
- General Network Design Principles
- Switched LAN Network Design Principles

Comparison of LAN Switches and Routers

The fundamental difference between a LAN switch and a router is that the LAN switch operates at Layer 2 of the OSI model and the router operates at Layer 3. This difference affects the way that LAN switches and routers respond to network traffic. This section compares LAN switches and routers with regard to the following network design issues:

- Loops
- Convergence
- Broadcasts
- Subnetworking
- Security
- Media Dependence

— **NOTES**

Because routers implement Layer 2 functionality and switches are beginning to implement Layer 3 functionality, the functions of a LAN switch and a router are merging.

Loops

Switched LAN topologies are susceptible to loops, as shown in Figure 12–6.

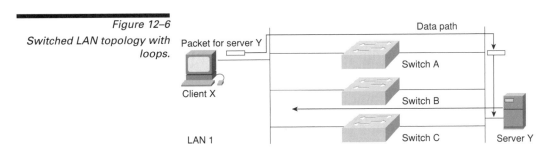

Figure 12–6
Switched LAN topology with loops.

In Figure 12–6, it is possible for packets from Client X to be switched by Switch A and then for Switch B to put the same packet back on to LAN 1. In this situation, packets loop and undergo multiple replications. To prevent looping and replication, topologies that may contain loops need to run the Spanning-Tree Protocol. The Spanning-Tree Protocol uses the spanning-tree algorithm to construct topologies that do not contain any loops. Because the spanning-tree algorithm places certain connections in blocking mode, only a subset of the network topology is used for forwarding data. In contrast, routers provide freedom from loops and make use of optimal paths.

Convergence

In transparent switching, neighboring switches make topology decisions locally based on the exchange of Bridge Protocol Data Units (BPDUs). This method of making topology decisions means that convergence on an alternative path can take an order of magnitude longer than in a routed environment.

In a routed environment, sophisticated routing protocols, such as Open Shortest Path First (OSPF) and Enhanced Interior Gateway Routing Protocol (Enhanced IGRP), maintain concurrent topological databases of the network and allow the network to converge quickly.

Broadcasts

LAN switches do not filter broadcasts, multicasts, or unknown address frames. The lack of filtering can be a serious problem in modern distributed networks in which broadcast messages are used to resolve addresses and dynamically discover network resources such as file servers. Broadcasts originating from each segment are received by every computer in the switched internetwork. Most devices discard broadcasts because they are irrelevant, which means that large amounts of bandwidth are wasted by the transmission of broadcasts.

In some cases, the circulation of broadcasts can saturate the network so that there is no bandwidth left for application data. In this case, new network connections cannot be established, and existing connections may be dropped (a situation known as a *broadcast storm*). The probability of broadcast storms increases as the switched internetwork grows. Routers do not forward broadcasts, and, therefore, are not subject to broadcast storms. For more information about the impact of broadcasts, see Appendix E, "Broadcasts in Switched LAN Internetworks."

Subnetworking

Transparently switched internetworks are composed of physically separate segments, but are logically considered to be one large network (for example, one IP subnet). This behavior is inherent to the way that LAN switches work—they operate at OSI Layer 2 and have to provide connectivity to hosts as if each host were on the same cable. Layer 2 addressing assumes a flat address space with universally unique addresses.

Routers operate at OSI Layer 3, so can formulate and adhere to a hierarchical addressing structure. Routed networks can associate a logical addressing structure to a physical infrastructure so that each network segment has, for example, a TCP/IP subnet or IPX network. Traffic flow on routed networks is inherently different from traffic flow on switched networks. Routed networks have more flexible traffic flow because they can use the hierarchy to determine optimal paths depending on dynamic factors such as network congestion.

Security

Information is available to routers and switches that can be used to create more secure networks. LAN switches may use custom filters to provide access control based on destination address, source address, protocol type, packet length, and offset bits within the frame. Routers can filter on logical network addresses and provide control based on options available in Layer 3 protocols. For example, routers can permit or deny traffic based on specific TCP/IP socket information for a range of network addresses.

Media Dependence

Two factors need to be considered with regard to mixed-media internetworks. First, the maximum transfer unit (MTU) differs for various network media. Table 12–2 lists the maximum frame size for various network media.

Table 12–2 *MTUs for Various Network Media*

Media	Minimum Valid Frame	Maximum Valid Size
Ethernet	64 bytes	1518 bytes
Token Ring	32 bytes	16 KB theoretical, 4 KB normal
Fast Ethernet	64 bytes	1518 bytes

Table 12–2 *MTUs for Various Network Media, Continued*

Media	Minimum Valid Frame	Maximum Valid Size
FDDI	32 bytes	4400 bytes
ATM LANE	64 bytes	1518 bytes
ATM Classical IP	64 bytes	9180 bytes
Serial HDLC	14 bytes	No limit, 4.5 KB normal

When LANs of dissimilar media are switched, hosts must use the MTU that is the lowest common denominator of all the switched LANs that make up the internetwork. This requirement limits throughput and can seriously compromise performance over a relatively fast link, such as FDDI or ATM. Most Layer 3 protocols can fragment and reassemble packets that are too large for a particular subnetwork, so routed networks can accommodate different MTUs, which maximizes throughput.

Second, because they operate at Layer 2, switches must use a translation function to switch between dissimilar media. The translation function can result in serious problems such as non-canonical versus canonical Token Ring-to-Ethernet MAC format conversion. One issue with moving data from a Token Ring to a Ethernet network is Layer 2 addressing. Token Ring devices read the Layer 2 MAC address as most significant bit starting from left to right. Ethernet devices read the Layer 2 MAC address as most significant bit starting from right to left.

By working at Layer 3, routers are essentially independent of the properties of any physical media and can use a simple address resolution algorithm (such as *Novell-node-address = MAC-address*) or a protocol, such as the Address Resolution Protocol (ARP), to resolve differences between Layer 2 and Layer 3 addresses.

Benefits of LAN Switches (Layer 2 Services)

An individual Layer 2 switch might offer some or all of the following benefits:

- *Bandwidth*—LAN switches provide excellent performance for individual users by allocating dedicated bandwidth to each switch port (for example, each network segment). This technique is known as *microsegmenting*.

- *VLANs*—LAN switches can group individual ports into logical switched workgroups called VLANs, thereby restricting the broadcast domain to designated VLAN member ports. VLANs are also known as switched domains and autonomous switching domains. Communication between VLANs requires a router.

- *Automated packet recognition and translation*—Cisco's unique Automatic Packet Recognition and Translation (APaRT) technology recognizes and converts a variety of Ethernet protocol formats into industry-standard CDDI/FDDI formats. With no changes needed in either client or server end stations the Catalyst solution can provide an easy migration to

100-Mbps server access while preserving the user's investment in existing shared 10Base-T LANs.

Benefits of Routers (Layer 3 Services)

Because routers use Layer 3 addresses, which typically have structure, routers can use techniques (such as address summarization) to build networks that maintain performance and responsiveness as they grow in size. By imposing structure (usually hierarchical) on a network, routers can effectively use redundant paths and determine optimal routes even in a dynamically changing network. This section describes the router functions that are vital in switched LAN designs:

- Broadcast and Multicast Control
- Broadcast Segmentation
- Media Transition

Broadcast and Multicast Control

Routers control broadcasts and multicasts in the following ways:

- *By caching the addresses of remote hosts.* When a host sends a broadcast packet to obtain the address of a remote host that the router already knows about, the router responds on behalf of the remote host and drops the broadcast packet (sparing hosts from having to respond to it).

- *By caching advertised network services.* When a router learns of a new network service, it caches the necessary information and does not forward broadcasts related to it. When a client of that network service sends a broadcast to locate that service, the router responds on behalf of that service and drops the broadcast packet (sparing hosts from having to respond to it). For example, Novell clients use broadcasts to find local services. In a network without a router, every server responds to every client broadcast by multicasting its list of services. Routers manage Novell broadcasts by collecting services not local to the switch and sending out periodic updates that describe the services offered on the entire network. Each router sends out one frame for every seven services on the network.

- *By providing special protocols, such as the IGMP and Protocol Independent Multicast (PIM).* These new protocols allow a multicasting application to "negotiate" with routers, switches, and clients to determine the devices that belong to a multicast group. This negotiation helps limit the scope and impact of the multicast stream on the network as a whole. For information about IP multicasting, see Chapter 13, "Designing Internetworks for Multimedia."

Successful network designs contain a mix of appropriately scaled switching and routing. Given the effects of broadcast radiation on CPU performance, well-managed switched LAN designs must include routers for broadcast and multicast management.

Broadcast Segmentation

In addition to preventing broadcasts from radiating throughout the network, routers are also responsible for generating services to each LAN segment. The following are examples of services that the router provides to the network for a variety of protocols:

- *IP*—Proxy ARP and Internet Control Message Protocol (ICMP)
- *IPX*—SAP table updates
- *AppleTalk*—ZIP table updates
- *Network management*—SNMP queries

In a flat virtual network, a single router would be bombarded by myriad requests needing replies, severely taxing its processor. Therefore, the network designer needs to consider the number of routers that can provide reliable services to a given subset of VLANs. Some type of hierarchical design needs to be considered.

Media Transition

In the past, routers have been used to connect networks of different media types, taking care of the OSI Layer 3 address translations and fragmentation requirements. Routers continue to perform this function in switched LAN designs. Most switching is done within like media (such as Ethernet, Token Ring, and FDDI switches) with some capability of connecting to another media type. However, if a requirement for a switched campus network design is to provide high-speed connectivity between unlike media, routers play a significant part in the design.

Benefits of VLANs

In a flat, bridged network all broadcast packets generated by any node in the network are sent to and received by all other network nodes. The ambient level of broadcasts generated by the higher layer protocols in the network—known as *broadcast radiation*—will typically restrict the total number of nodes that the network can support. In extreme cases, the effects of broadcast radiation can be so severe that an end station spends all of its CPU power on processing broadcasts.

VLANs have been designed to address the following problems inherent in a flat, bridged network:

- Scalability issues of a flat network topology
- Simplification of network management by facilitating network reconfigurations

VLANs solve some of the scalability problems of large flat networks by breaking a single bridged domain into several smaller bridged domains, each of which is a virtual LAN. Note that each virtual LAN is itself constrained by the scalability issues described in Appendix E, "Broadcasts in Switched LAN Internetworks." It is insufficient to solve the broadcast problems inherent to a flat switched network by superimposing VLANs and reducing broadcast domains. VLANs without routers do not scale to large campus environments. Routing is instrumental in the building of scalable VLANs and is the only way to impose hierarchy on the switched VLAN internetwork.

VLANs offer the following features:

- *Broadcast control*—Just as switches isolate collision domains for attached hosts and only forward appropriate traffic out a particular port, VLANs refine this concept further and provide complete isolation between VLANs. A VLAN is a bridging domain, and all broadcast and multicast traffic is contained within it.

- *Security*—VLANs provide security in two ways:

  - High-security users can be grouped into a VLAN, possibly on the same physical segment, and no users outside of that VLAN can communicate with them.

  - Because VLANs are logical groups that behave like physically separate entities, inter-VLAN communication is achieved through a router. When inter-VLAN communication occurs through a router, all the security and filtering functionality that routers traditionally provide can be used because routers are able to look at OSI Layer 3 information. In the case of nonroutable protocols, there can be no inter-VLAN communication. All communication must occur within the same VLAN.

- *Performance*—The logical grouping of users allows, for example, an engineer making intensive use of a networked CAD/CAM station or testing a multicast application to be assigned to a VLAN that contains just that engineer and the servers he or she needs. The engineer's work does not affect the rest of the engineering group, which results in improved performance for the engineer (by being on a dedicated LAN) and improved performance for the rest of the engineering group (whose communications are not slowed down by the engineer's use of the network).

- *Network management*—The logical grouping of users, divorced from their physical or geographic locations, allows easier network management. It is no longer necessary to pull cables to move a user from one network to another. Adds, moves, and changes are achieved by configuring a port into the appropriate VLAN. Expensive, time-consuming recabling to extend connectivity in a switched LAN environment is no longer necessary because network management can be used to logically assign a user from one VLAN to another.

VLAN Implementation

This section describes the different methods of creating the logical groupings (or broadcast domains) that make up various types of VLANs. There are three ways of defining a VLAN:

- *By port*—Each port on the switch can support only one VLAN. With port-based VLANs, no Layer 3 address recognition takes place, so Internet Protocol (IP), Novell, and AppleTalk networks must share the same VLAN definition. All traffic within the VLAN is switched, and traffic between VLANs is routed (by an external router or by a router within the switch). This type of VLAN is also known as a *segment-based VLAN*.

- *By protocol*—VLANs based on network addresses (that is, OSI Layer 3 addresses) can differentiate between different protocols, allowing the definition of VLANs to be made on a per-protocol basis. With network address-based VLANs, it will be possible to have a different virtual topology for each protocol, with each topology having its own set of rules, firewalls, and so forth. Routing between VLANs comes automatically, without the need for an external router or card. Network address-based VLANs will mean that a single port on a switch can support more than one VLAN. This type of VLAN is also known as a *virtual subnet VLAN*.

- *By a user-defined value*—This type of VLAN is typically the most flexible, allowing VLANs to be defined based on the value of any field in a packet. For example, VLANs could be defined on a protocol basis or could be dependent on a particular IPX or NetBIOS service. The simplest form of this type of VLAN is to group users according to their MAC addresses.

Cisco's initial method of implementing VLANs on routers and Catalyst switches is by port. To efficiently operate and manage protocols, such as IP, IPX, and AppleTalk, all nodes in a VLAN should be in the same subnet or network.

Cisco uses three technologies to implement VLANs:

- IEEE 802.10
- Inter-Switch Link (ISL)
- LAN Emulation

The three technologies are similar in that they are based on OSI Layer 2 bridge multiplexing mechanisms.

— **NOTES** —————————————————————————————————

With respect to this chapter and the discussions in it, VLANs are differentiated by assigning each VLAN a "color" (or VLAN ID). For example, Engineering might be the "blue" VLAN, and Manufacturing might be the "green" VLAN.

IEEE 802.10

IEEE 802.10 defines a method for secure bridging of data across a shared metropolitan area network (MAN) backbone. Cisco has initially implemented the relevant portions of the standard to allow the "coloring" of bridged traffic across high-speed backbones (FDDI, Ethernet, Fast Ethernet, Token Ring, and serial links). There are two strategies using IEEE 802.10 to implement VLANs, depending on how traffic is handled through the backbone:

- Switched Backbone
- Routed Backbone

Switched Backbone

In the switched backbone topology shown in Figure 12–7, you want to ensure that intra-VLAN traffic goes only between Segment A and Segment D (both in VLAN 10) and Segment B and Segment C (both in VLAN 20).

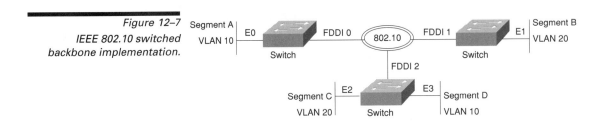

Figure 12–7
IEEE 802.10 switched
backbone implementation.

In Figure 12–7, all Ethernet ports on Switches X, Y, and Z are in a VLAN and are to be VLAN interfaces. All FDDI interfaces in Switches X, Y, and Z are called *VLAN trunk interfaces*. To ensure that traffic from Segment A destined for Segment D on Switch Z is forwarded onto Ethernet 3 and not onto Ethernet 2, it is colored when it leaves Switch X. Switch Z recognizes the color and knows that it must forward these frames onto Ethernet 3 and not onto Ethernet 2.

The coloring of traffic across the FDDI backbone is achieved by inserting a 16-byte header between the source MAC address and the Link Service Access Point (LSAP) of frames leaving a switch. This header contains a 4-byte VLAN ID or "color." The receiving switch removes the header and forwards the frame to interfaces that match that VLAN color.

Routed Backbone

In the routed backbone topology shown in Figure 12–8, the goal is the same as for the switched topology—that is, to ensure that intra-VLAN traffic goes only between Segment A and Segment D (both in VLAN 10) and Segment B and Segment C (both in VLAN 20).

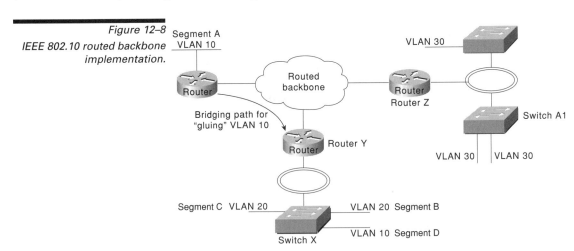

Figure 12–8
IEEE 802.10 routed backbone
implementation.

It is important that a single VLAN use only one subnet. In Figure 12–8, VLAN 10 (subnet 10) is "split" and therefore must be "glued" together by maintaining a bridged path for it through the network. For Switch X and nodes in VLAN 20 (subnet 20), traffic is switched locally if appropriate. If traffic is destined for a node in VLAN 30 (subnet 30) from a node in VLAN 20, Router Y routes it through the backbone to Router Z. If traffic from Segment D on VLAN 10 is destined for a node in VLAN 20, Router Y routes it back out the FDDI interface.

Fast EtherChannel

Fast Ether Channel is a trunking technology based on grouping together multiple full duplex 802.3 Fast Ethernets to provide fault-tolerant high-speed links between switches, routers, and servers. Fast EtherChannels can be composed of two to four industry-standard Fast Ethernet links to provide load sharing of traffic with up to 800 Mbps of usable bandwidth. Fast EtherChannels can interconnect LAN switches, routers, servers, and clients. Since its load balancing is integrated with the Catalyst 5000 families LAN switch architectures, there is no performance degradation for adding links to a channel—high throughput and low latencies can be maintained while gaining more total available bandwidth. Fast EtherChannel provides link resiliency within a channel—if links should fail the traffic is immediately directed to the remaining links. Finally, Fast EtherChannel is not dependent on any type of media—it can be used with Fast Ethernet running on existing Unshielded Twisted Pair (UTP) wiring, or single mode and multimode fiber. Figure 12–9 shows a collapsed backbone topology design using the Fast EtherChannel modules to provide links of 400 Mb between switches in the wiring closets and the data center.

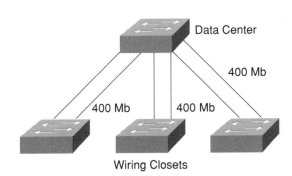

Figure 12–9
Collapsed backbone topology design using the Fast EtherChannel modules.

Data Center

400 Mb

400 Mb 400 Mb

Wiring Closets

IEEE 802.10 Design Issues

- Routers fast switch IEEE 802.10, which means that the fast-switching throughput of the platform must be considered.
- VLANs must be consistent with the routed model. (That is, subnets cannot be split.)

○ If subnets must be split, they must be "glued" together by a bridged path.

○ Normal routed behavior needs to be maintained for end nodes to correctly achieve routing between VLANs.

○ Networks need to be designed carefully when integrating VLANs; the simplest choice is to avoid splitting VLANs across a routed backbone.

The difference between these two strategies is subtle. Table 12–3 compares the advantages and disadvantages of the two strategies.

Table 12–3   *Advantages and Disadvantages of Switched and Routed Backbones*

Switched Backbone		Routed Backbone	
Advantages	**Disadvantages**	**Advantages**	**Disadvantages**
Propagates color information across entire network.	Backbone is running bridging.	No bridging in backbone.	Color information is not propagated across backbone and must be configured manually.
Allows greater scalability by extending bridge domains.	Broadcast traffic increases drastically on the backbone.	Easy to integrate into existing internetwork.	If subnets are split, a bridged path has to be set up between switches.
		Can run native protocols in the backbone.	

A VLAN interface can have only one VLAN ID, and VLAN trunk interfaces support multiple VLANs across them.

Inter-Switch Link

ISL is a Cisco-proprietary protocol for interconnecting multiple switches and maintaining VLAN information as traffic goes between switches. This technology is similar to IEEE 802.10 in that it is a method of multiplexing bridge groups over a high-speed backbone. It is defined only on Fast Ethernet. The discussion of routing and switching in the backbone in the section "IEEE 802.10," earlier in this chapter, also applies to ISL.

With ISL, an Ethernet frame is encapsulated with a header that maintains VLAN IDs between switches. A 30-byte header is prepended to the Ethernet frame, and it contains a two-byte VLAN ID. In Figure 12–10, Switch Y switches VLAN 20 traffic between segments A and B if appropriate. Otherwise, it encapsulates traffic with an ISL header that identifies it as traffic for VLAN 20 and sends it through the interim switch to Router X.

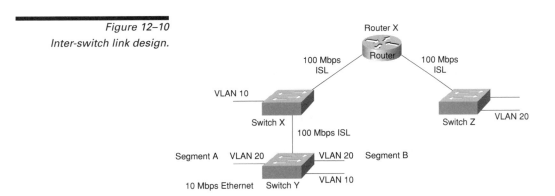

Figure 12–10
Inter-switch link design.

Router X routes the packet to the appropriate interface, which could be through a routed network beyond Router X (as in this case) out the Fast Ethernet interface to Switch Z. Switch Z receives the packet, examines the ISL header noting that this packet is destined for VLAN 20, and switches it to all ports in VLAN 20 (if the packet is a broadcast or multicast) or the appropriate port (if the packet is a unicast).

NOTES

Routers fast switch ISL, which means that the fast-switching throughput of the platform must be considered.

LAN Emulation

LAN Emulation (LANE) is a service that provides interoperability between ATM-based workstations and devices connected to existing legacy LAN technology. The ATM Forum has defined a standard for LANE that provides to workstations attached via ATM the same capabilities that they are used to obtaining from legacy LANs.

LANE uses MAC encapsulation (OSI Layer 2) because this approach supports the largest number of existing OSI Layer 3 protocols. The end result is that all devices attached to an emulated LAN appear to be on one bridged segment. In this way, AppleTalk, IPX, and other protocols should have similar performance characteristics as in a traditional bridged environment. In ATM LANE environments, the ATM switch handles traffic that belongs to the same emulated LAN (ELAN), and routers handle inter-ELAN traffic. For more information about LANE, see Chapter 8, "Designing ATM Internetworks."

Virtual Multihomed Servers

In traditional networks, there are usually several well-known servers, such as e-mail and corporate servers, that almost everyone in an enterprise needs to access. If these servers are located in only one VLAN, the benefits of VLANs will be lost because all of the different workgroups will be forced to route to access this common information source.

This problem can be solved with LANE and virtual multihomed servers, as shown in Figure 12–11. Network interface cards (NICs) allow workstations and servers to join up to eight different VLANs. This means that the server will appear in eight different ELANs and that to other members of each ELAN, the server appears to be like any other member. This capability greatly increases the performance of the network as a whole because common information is available directly through the optimal Data Direct VCC and does not need to be routed. This also means that the server must process all broadcast traffic in each VLAN that it belongs to, which can decrease performance.

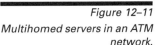

Figure 12–11
Multihomed servers in an ATM network.

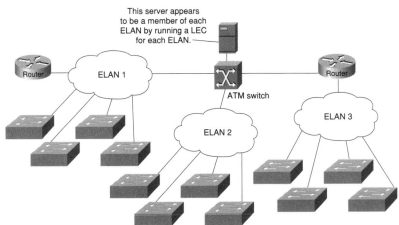

To multihome servers in non-ATM environments, there are two possible choices:

- Use servers with multiple NICs (different connections into each VLAN).
- Use servers with NICs that support the VLAN trunking technology (IEEE 802.10 or ISL) used in the backbone.

Virtual Trunk Protocol

The Catalyst 5000 switch implements Cisco's Virtual Trunk Protocol (VTP). VTP is the industry's first protocol implementation specifically designed for large VLAN deployments. VTP enhances VLAN deployment by providing the following:

- Integration of ISL, 802.10, and ATM LAN-based VLANs
- Auto-intelligence within the switches for configuring VLANs
- Configuration consistency across the network

- An automapping scheme for going across mixed-media backbones
- Accurate tracking and monitoring of VLANs
- Dynamic reporting of added VLANs across the network
- Plug-and-play setup and configuration when adding new VLANs

General Network Design Principles

Good network design is based on many concepts that are summarized by the following key principles:

- *Examine single points of failure carefully*—There should be redundancy in the network so that a single failure does not isolate any portion of the network. There are two aspects of redundancy that need to be considered: backup and load balancing. In the event of a failure in the network, there should be an alternative or backup path. Load balancing occurs when two or more paths to a destination exist and can be utilized depending on the network load. The level of redundancy required in a particular network varies from network to network.

- *Characterize application and protocol traffic*—For example, the flow of application data will profile client-server interaction and is crucial for efficient resource allocation, such as the number of clients using a particular server or the number of client workstations on a segment.

- *Analyze bandwidth availability*—For example, there should not be an order of magnitude difference between the different layers of the hierarchical model. It is important to remember that the hierarchical model refers to conceptual layers that provide functionality. The actual demarcation between layers does not have to be a physical link—it can be the backplane of a particular device.

- *Build networks using a hierarchical or modular model*—The hierarchy allows autonomous segments to be internetworked together.

Figure 12–12 shows a high-level view of the various aspects of a hierarchical network design. A hierarchical network design presents three layers—core, distribution, and access—with each layer providing different functionality.

The core layer is a high-speed switching backbone and should be designed to switch packets as fast as possible. This layer of the network should not perform any packet manipulation access lists and filtering that would slow down the switching of packets.

The distribution layer of the network is the demarcation point between the access and core layers and helps to define and differentiate the core. The purpose of this layer is to provide boundary definition and is the place at which packet manipulation can take place. In the campus environment, the distribution layer can include several functions, such as the following:

- Address or area aggregation
- Departmental or workgroup access
- Broadcast/multicast domain definition
- VLAN routing
- Any media transitions that need to occur
- Security

Figure 12–12
Hierarchical network design
model.

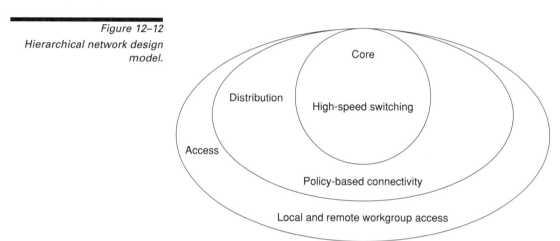

In the non-campus environment, the distribution layer can be a redistribution point between routing domains or the demarcation between static and dynamic routing protocols. It can also be the point at which remote sites access the corporate network. The distribution layer can be summarized as the layer that provides policy-based connectivity.

The access layer is the point at which local end users are allowed into the network. This layer may also use access lists or filters to further optimize the needs of a particular set of users. In the campus environment, access-layer functions can include the following:

- Shared bandwidth
- Switched bandwidth
- MAC layer filtering
- Microsegmentation

In the non-campus environment, the access layer can give remote sites access to the corporate network via some wide-area technology, such as Frame Relay, ISDN, or leased lines.

It is sometimes mistakenly thought that the three layers (core, distribution, and access) must exist in clear and distinct physical entities, but this does not have to be the case. The layers are defined to aid successful network design and to represent functionality that must exist in a network. The instantiation of each layer can be in distinct routers or switches, can be represented by a physical media, can be combined in a single device, or can be omitted altogether. The way the layers are implemented depends on the needs of the network being designed. Note, however, that for a network to function optimally, hierarchy must be maintained.

With respect to the hierarchical model, traditional campus LANs have followed one of two designs—single router and distributed backbone—as shown in Figure 12–13.

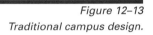

Figure 12–13
Traditional campus design.

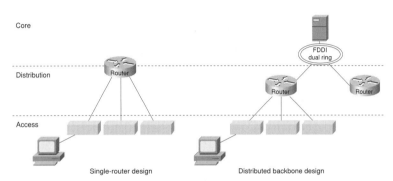

In the single-router design, the core and distribution layers are present in a single entity—the router. Core functionality is represented by the backplane of the router and distribution is represented by the router. Access for end users is through individual- or chassis-based hubs. This design suffers from scalability constraints because the router can be only be in one physical location, so all segments end at the same location—the router. The single router is responsible for all distribution functionality, which can cause CPU overload.

The distributed backbone design uses a high-speed backbone media, typically FDDI, to spread routing functionality among several routers. This also allows the backbone to traverse floors, a building, or a campus.

Switched LAN Network Design Principles

When designing switched LAN campus networks, the following factors must be considered:

- *Broadcast radiation*—Broadcast radiation can become fatal—that is, 100 percent of host CPU cycles can be consumed by processing broadcast and multicast packets. Because of delays inherent in carrier sense multiple access collision detect (CMSA/CD) technologies, such as Ethernet, any more than a small amount of broadcast traffic will adversely affect the operation of devices attached to a switch. Although VLANs reduce the effect of broadcast radiation on all LANs, there is still a scaling issue as to how many hosts should reside on a given VLAN. A router allows for larger network designs because a VLAN can be subsegmented depending on traffic patterns. However, in a nonoptimal network design, a single router can be burdened with large amounts of traffic.

- *Well-behaved VLANs*—A well-behaved VLAN is a VLAN in which 80 percent or more of the traffic is local to that VLAN. In an example in which the Marketing, MIS, and Engineering departments each have an individual VLAN segment, the 80 percent rule is violated when a user in the Marketing VLAN reads mail from the MIS VLAN, mounts servers from the Engineering VLAN, and sends e-mail to members of the Engineering VLAN.

- *Available bandwidth to access routing functionality*—Inter-VLAN traffic must be routed, so the network design must allocate enough bandwidth to move inter-VLAN traffic from the source, through the device that provides routing functionality, and to the destination.

- *Appropriate placement of administrative boundaries*—Switching has the effect of flattening networks, and the deployment of switching outside of your administrative boundary can adversely affect the network within your administrative boundary.

Campus network designs are evolving rapidly with the deployment of switching at all levels of the network—from the desktop to the backbone. Three topologies have emerged as generic network designs:

- Scaled Switching
- Large Switching/Minimal Routing
- Distributed Routing/Switching

Scaled Switching

The scaled switching design shown in Figure 12–14 deploys switching at all levels of the network without the use of routers. In this design, each layer consists of switches, with switches in the access layer providing 10-Mbps Ethernet or 16-Mbps Token Ring to end users.

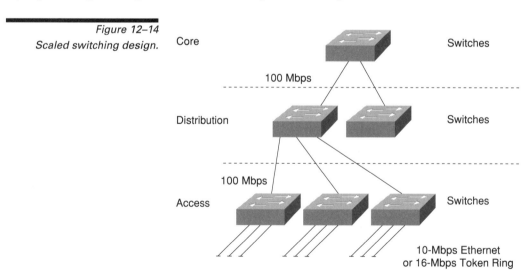

Figure 12–14
Scaled switching design.

Scaled switching is a low-cost and easy-to-install solution for a small campus network. It does not require knowledge of address structure, is easy to manage, and allows all users to communicate with one another. However, this network comprises a single broadcast domain. If a scaled switched network needs to grow beyond the broadcast domain, it can use VLANs to create multiple broadcast domains. Note that when VLANs are used, end users in one VLAN cannot communicate with end users in another VLAN unless routers are deployed.

Large Switched/Minimal Routing

The large switched/minimal routing design deploys switching at the access layer of the network, either ATM switching or LAN switching at the distribution layer of the network, and ATM/LAN switching at the core. Figure 12–15 shows an example of this network design.

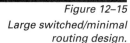

Figure 12–15
Large switched/minimal routing design.

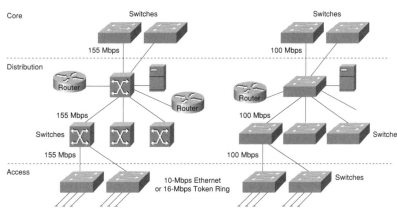

In the case of ATM in the distribution layer, the following key issues are relevant:

- LANE support on routers and switches.
- Support for UNI 3.X signaling (including point-to-multipoint).
- If redundancy is provided by a virtual PVC or SVC mesh, the mesh is a single point of failure.

In the case of LAN switching in the distribution layer, the following key issues are relevant:

- Support for VLAN trunking technology in each device.
- The switches in the distribution layer must run the Spanning-Tree Protocol to prevent loops, which means that some connections will be blocked and load balancing cannot occur.

To scale the large switched/minimal routing design, a logical hierarchy must be imposed. The logical hierarchy consists of VLANs and routers that enable inter-VLAN communication. In this topology, routing is used only in the distribution layer, and the access layer depends on bandwidth through the distribution layer to gain access to high-speed switching functionality in the core layer.

The large switched/minimal routing design scales well when VLANs are designed so that the majority of resources are available in the VLAN. Therefore, if this topology can be designed so that 80 percent of traffic is intra-VLAN and only 20 percent of traffic is inter-VLAN, the bandwidth needed for inter-VLAN routing is not a concern. However, if inter-VLAN traffic is greater than 20 percent, access to routing in the core becomes a scalability issue. For optimal network operation, scalable routing content is needed at the distribution layer of the network.

Distributed Routing/Switching

The distributed routing/switching design deploys switching in the access layer, routing in the distribution layer, and some form of high-speed switching in the core layer, as shown in Figure 12–16.

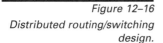

Figure 12–16
Distributed routing/switching design.

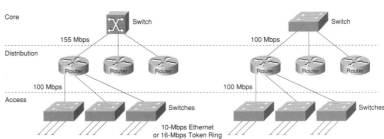

The distributed routing/switching design follows the classic hierarchical network model both physically and logically. Because it provides high bandwidth for access to routing functionality, this design scales very well. This design is optimized for networks that do not have the 80/20 pattern rule. If servers are centralized, most traffic is inter-VLAN; therefore, high routing content is needed.

SUMMARY

Campus LAN designs use switches to replace traditional hubs and use an appropriate mix of routers to minimize broadcast radiation. With the appropriate pieces of software and hardware in place, and adhering to good network design, it is possible to build topologies, such as the examples described in the section "Switched LAN Network Designs" earlier in this chapter.

Designing Internetworks for Multimedia

Networked multimedia applications are rapidly being deployed in campus LAN and WAN environments. From the corporate perspective, network multimedia applications, such as network TV or videoconferencing, hold tremendous promise as the next generation of productivity tools. The use of digital audio and video across corporate network infrastructures has tremendous potential for internal and external applications. The World Wide Web is a good example of network multimedia and its manifold capabilities.

More than 85 percent of personal computers sold are multimedia capable. This hardware revolution has initiated a software revolution that has brought a wide range of audio- and video-based applications to the desktop. It is not uncommon for computers to run video editing or image processing applications (such as Adobe Premier and Photoshop) in addition to basic "productivity" applications (word processing, spreadsheet, and database applications).

The proliferation of multimedia-enabled desktop machines has spawned a new class of multimedia applications that operate in network environments. These network multimedia applications leverage the existing network infrastructure to deliver video and audio applications to end users, such as videoconferencing and video server applications. With these application types, video and audio streams are transferred over the network between peers or between clients and servers.

To successfully deliver multimedia over a network, it is important to understand both multimedia and networking. Three components must be considered when deploying network multimedia applications in campus LAN and WAN environments:

- *Bandwidth*—How much bandwidth do the network multimedia applications demand and how much bandwidth can the network infrastructure provide?

- *Quality of service*—What level of service does the network multimedia application require and how can this be satisfied through the network?

- *Multicasting*—Does the network multimedia application utilize bandwidth-saving multicasting techniques and how can multicasting be supported across the network?

This chapter addresses the underpinnings of effectively deploying network multimedia applications. Specifically, this chapter addresses the following topics:

- Multimedia Basics, including analog video, digital video, video compression, and digital audio standards

- Using Networked Multimedia Applications, including bandwidth and quality of service requirements

- Understanding Multicasting, including Internet Group Management Protocol, Distance Vector Multicast Routing Protocol, Multicast Open Shortest Path First, Protocol Independent Multicast, and Simple Multicast Routing Protocol

- Network Designs for Multimedia Applications, including traditional LAN designs, WAN designs, and high-speed LAN designs

MULTIMEDIA BASICS

Much of today's video starts out as an analog signal, so a working knowledge of analog standards and formats is essential for understanding digital video and the digitization process. The following topics are fundamental for understanding analog video:

- Broadcast Standards
- Video Signal Standards
- Video Storage Formats
- Digitizing Video
- Digitizing Audio

Broadcast Standards

The principal standards for analog broadcast transmission are as follows:

- *National Television Standards Committee (NTSC)*—The broadcast standard in Canada, Japan, the United States, and Central America. NTSC defines 525 vertical scan lines per frame and yields 30 frames per second. The scan lines refer to the number of lines from top to bottom on the television screen. The frames per second refer to the number of complete images that are displayed per second.

- *Phase Alternation Line (PAL)*—The broadcast standard in Europe and in the Middle East, Africa, and South America. PAL defines 625 vertical scan lines and refreshes the screen 25 times per second.

- *Système Electronique pour Couleur Avec Mémoire (SECAM)*—The broadcast standard in France, Russia, and regions of Africa. SECAM is a variant of PAL but it delivers the same number of vertical scan lines as PAL and uses the same refresh rate.

To produce an image on a television screen, an electron gun scans across the television screen from left to right moving from top to bottom, as shown in Figure 13–1.

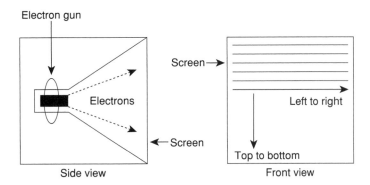

Figure 13–1
Television scan gun operation.

Early television sets used a phosphor-coated tube, which meant that by the time the gun finished scanning all the lines that the broadcast standard required, the lines at the top were starting to fade. To combat fading, the NTSC adopted an interlace technique so that on the first pass from top to bottom, only every other line is scanned. With NTSC, this means that the first pass scans 262 lines. The second pass scans another 262 lines that are used to fill in the rest of the TV image.

A frame represents the combination of the two passes, known as *fields*, as Figure 13–2 indicates. For NTSC to deliver 30 frames per second, it must generate 60 fields per second. The rate at which fields are delivered depends on the clocking source. NTSC clocks its refresh intervals from AC power. In the United States, the AC power runs at 60 hertz or 60 oscillations per second. The 60 hertz yields 60 fields per second with every two fields yielding a frame. In Europe, AC power clocks at 50 hertz. This yields 50 fields per second or 25 frames per second.

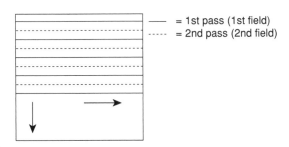

Figure 13–2
Interlace scan process.

—— = 1st pass (1st field)
----- = 2nd pass (2nd field)

Video Signal Standards

Black-and-white televisions receive one signal called *luminance* (also know as the *Y signal*). Each screen pixel is defined as some range of intensity between white (total intensity) and black (no intensity). In 1953, the NTSC was faced with the task of revising their standard to handle color. To maintain compatibility with older black-and-white sets, the NTSC set a color standard that kept the luminance signal separate and that provided the color information required for newer color television sets.

In the digital world, colors are typically expressed using red, green, and blue (RGB). The analog world has also embraced the RGB standard, at least on the acquisition side, where most cameras break the analog signal into RGB components.

Unfortunately, the NTSC could not use RGB as the color television standard because the old black-and-white sets could not decode RGB signals. Instead, they had to send a luminance signal for black-and-white sets and fill in the color information with other signals, called hue and saturation, (also known as the *U* and *V signals*). For this reason, digital color technology uses RGB and analog color technology, especially broadcast television, uses YUV (Y, U, and V signals).

Figure 13–3 traces an analog video signal from capture to NTSC output. On the far left is the RGB capture in which storage channels are maintained for each of the three primary colors. RGB, however, is an inefficient analog video storage format for two reasons:

- First, to use RGB, all three color signals must have equal bandwidth in the system, which is often inefficient from a system design perspective.

- Second, because each pixel is the sum of red, green and blue values, modifying the pixel forces an adjustment of all three values. In contrast, when images are stored as luminance and color formats (that is, YUV format), a pixel can be altered by modifying only one value.

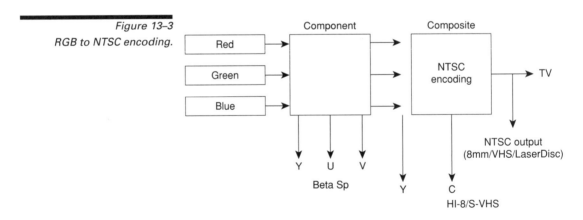

Figure 13–3
RGB to NTSC encoding.

Component video maintains separate channels for each color value, both in the recording device and the storage medium. Component video delivers the highest fidelity because it eliminates noise that would otherwise occur if two signals were combined in one channel.

After NTSC encoding, the hue and saturation channels (U and V signals) are combined into one chrominance channel, the C channel. A video signal, called *S-Video*, carries separate channels for the luminance and chrominance signals. S-Video is also known as *Y/C video*.

All color and other information must be combined into one YUV channel, called the *composite signal*, to play on old black-and-white televisions. Technically, a composite signal is any signal that contains all the information necessary to play video. In contrast, any one individual channel of component or Y/C video is not sufficient to play video.

A video signal can be transmitted as composite, S-Video, or component video. The type of video signal affects the connector that is used. The composite signal, which carries all the information in one electrical channel, uses a one-hole jack called the *RCA Phono connector*. The S-Video signal, composed of two electrical channels, uses a four-pin connector called the *mini-DIN connector*. Finally, the component signal uses three connectors.

Video Storage Formats

There are six video storage formats: 8 mm, Beta SP, HI-8, Laserdisc, Super VHS (SVHS), and VHS. The six formats use different signals to store color. The composite signal provides the lowest quality because all signals are combined, which in turn has the highest potential for noise. The S-Video signal produces less noise because the two signals are isolated in separate channels. The component signal provides the highest quality signal because all components are maintained in separate channels. The image quality that a video capture board produces can only be as good as the signal it accepts. Table 13–1 lists the analog capture and storage standards for video.

Table 13–1 *Analog Video Storage Formats*

	Beta SP	SVHS/HI-8	VHS/8mm	Laserdisc
Color signal	Component	Y/C	Composite	Composite
Lines of resolution	750	400	200	400
Signal-to-noise ratio	50 db	47 db	47 db	47 db

As Table indicates, the storage formats deliver different lines of resolution. Resolution is a measure of an image's quality. From the viewer's perspective, an image with higher resolution yields sharper picture quality than a lower resolution image.

Most consumer televisions display roughly 330 lines of horizontal resolution. Broadcast environments typically used high-end cameras to capture video. These cameras and their associated storage formats can deliver horizontal resolutions of approximately 700 lines. Each time a copy is made, the copied image loses some of its resolution. When an image is recorded in high-resolution, multiple generations of the video can be copied without a noticeable difference. When an image is recorded in a lower resolution, there is less room to manipulate the image before the viewer notices the effects.

Digitizing Video

Digitizing video involves taking an analog video signal and converting it to a digital video stream using a video capture board, as shown in Figure 13–4. Today, a variety of computer platforms, including PC, Macintosh, and UNIX workstations, offer video capture capabilities. In some cases, though, the capture equipment is a third-party add-on. The analog video source can be stored in any video storage format or it can be a live video feed from a camera. The source can be connected to the video capture card using any three connectors types (component, S-Video, or composite) depending on the connector type that the card supports.

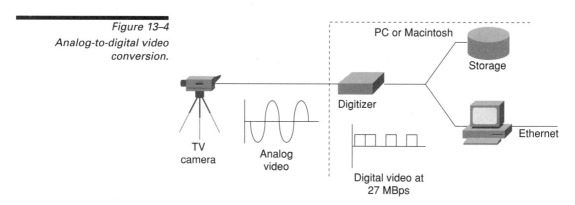

Figure 13–4
Analog-to-digital video conversion.

PC or Macintosh

Storage

Digitizer

TV camera

Analog video

Digital video at 27 MBps

Ethernet

When capturing and digitizing video, the following components are critical:

- *Resolution*—The horizontal and vertical dimensions of the video session. A full-screen video session is typically 640 horizontal pixels by 480 vertical pixels. Full-screen video uses these dimensions because it yields the 4:3 aspect ratio of standard television. Of the 525 vertical scan lines in the NTSC standard, 483 lines are used to display video. The other lines are used for signaling and are referred to as the *vertical blanking interval*. Because the NTSC standard uses 483 vertical lines, capturing at 640 by 480 means that three lines are dropped during the digitization process.

- *Color depth*—The number of bits that are used to express color. At the high end is 24-bit color, which is capable of displaying 16.7 million colors and is the aggregate of 8 bits of red, 8 bits of green, and 8 bits of blue. The 8 bits are used to express color intensity from 0 to 255. Other common color depths are 16-bit and 8-bit, which yield roughly 65,000 and 256 colors, respectively.

- *Frame rate*—The number of frames that are displayed per second. To deliver NTSC-quality video, 30 frames per second are displayed. PAL and SECAM display 25 frames per second.

Based on these criteria, it is a simple mathematical operation to determine how much bandwidth a particular video stream requires. For example, to deliver uncompressed NTSC-quality digitized video to the network, a bandwidth of approximately 27 megabytes per second (Mbps) is needed. This number is derived from the following calculation:

$$640 \times 480 \times 3 \times 30 = 27.648 \text{ MBps (or 221.184 megabits per second [Mbps])}$$

where 640 and 480 represent the resolution in pixels, 3 represents 24-bit color (3 bytes), and 30 represents the number of frames per second.

As this calculation indicates, full-motion, full-color digital video requires considerably more bandwidth than today's typical packet-based network can support. Fortunately, two techniques reduce bandwidth consumption:

- Video Capture Manipulation
- Video Compression

Video Capture Manipulation

Manipulating video capture parameters involves changing resolution, color depth, and frame rate. To reduce bandwidth consumption, all three variables are often changed. For example, some multimedia applications capture video at 320×240 with 8-bit color and at a frame rate of 15 frames per second. With these parameters, bandwidth requirements drop to 9.216 Mbps. Although this level of bandwidth is difficult for a 10-Mbps Ethernet network to achieve, it can be provided by 16-Mbps Token Ring, 100-Mbps Fast Ethernet, and other higher-speed technologies.

Video Compression

Video compression is a process whereby a collection of algorithms and techniques replace the original pixel-related information with more compact mathematical descriptions. Decompression is the reverse process of decoding the mathematical descriptions back to pixels for display. At its best, video compression is transparent to the end user. The true measure of a video compression scheme is how little the end user notices its presence, or how effectively it can reduce video data rates without adversely affecting video quality. An example of post-digitization video compression is shown in Figure 13–5.

Video compression is performed using a CODEC (Coder/Decoder or Compressor/Decompressor). The CODEC, which can be implemented either in software or hardware, is responsible for taking a digital video stream and compressing it and for receiving a precompressed video stream and decompressing it. Although most PC, Macintosh, and UNIX video capture cards include the CODEC, capture and compression remain separate processes.

There are two types of compression techniques:

Figure 13–5
Post-digitization video
compression.

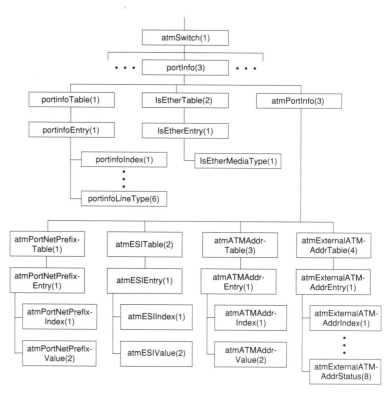

- *Lossless*—A compression technique that creates compressed files that decompress into exactly the same file as the original. Lossless compression is typically used for executables (applications) and data files for which any change in digital makeup renders the file useless. In general, lossless techniques identify and utilize patterns within files to describe the content more efficiently. This works well for files with significant redundancy, such as database or spreadsheet files. However, lossless compression typically yields only about 2:1 compression, which barely dents high-resolution uncompressed video files. Lossless compression is used by products such as STAC and Double Space to transparently expand hard drive capacity, and by products like PKZIP to pack more data onto floppy drives. STAC and another algorithm called Predictor are supported in the Cisco IOS software for data compression over analog and digital circuits.

- *Lossy*—Lossy compression, used primarily on still image and video image files, creates compressed files that decompress into images that look similar to the original but are different in digital makeup. This "loss" allows lossy compression to deliver from 2:1 to 300:1 compression. Lossy compression cannot be used on files, such as executables, that when decompressed must match the original file. When lossy compression is used on a

24-bit image, it may decompress with a few changed pixels or altered color shades that cannot be detected by the human eye. When used on video, the effect of lossy compression is further minimized because each image is displayed for only a fraction of a second (1/15 or 1/30 of a second, depending on the frame rate).

A wide range of lossy compression techniques is available for digital video. This simple rule applies to all of them: the higher the compression ratio, the higher the loss. As the loss increases, so does the number of artifacts. (An *artifact* is a portion of a video image for which there is little or no information.)

In addition to lossy compression techniques, video compression involves the use of two other compression techniques:

- *Interframe compression*—Compression between frames (also known as *temporal compression* because the compression is applied along the time dimension).

- *Intraframe compression*—Compression within individual frames (also known as *spatial compression*).

Some video compression algorithms use both interframe and intraframe compression. For example, Motion Picture Experts Group (MPEG) uses Joint Photographic Experts Group (JPEG), which is an intrafame technique, and a separate interframe algorithm. Motion-JPEG (M-JPEG) uses only intraframe compression.

Interframe Compression

Interframe compression uses a system of key and delta frames to eliminate redundant information between frames. Key frames store an entire frame, and delta frames record only changes. Some implementations compress the key frames, and others don't. Either way, the key frames serve as a reference source for delta frames. Delta frames contain only pixels that are different from the key frame or from the immediately preceding delta frame. During decompression, delta frames look back to their respective reference frames to fill in missing information.

Different compression techniques use different sequences of key and delta frames. For example, most video for Windows CODECs calculate interframe differences between sequential delta frames during compression. In this case, only the first delta frame relates to the key frame. Each subsequent delta frame relates to the immediately preceding delta frame. In other compression schemes, such as MPEG, all delta frames relate to the preceding key frame.

All interframe compression techniques derive their effectiveness from interframe redundancy. Low-motion video sequences, such as the head and shoulders of a person, have a high degree of redundancy, which limits the amount of compression required to reduce the video to the target bandwidth.

Until recently, interframe compression has addressed only pixel blocks that remained static between the delta and the key frame. Some new CODECs increase compression by tracking moving blocks of pixels from frame to frame. This technique is called *motion compensation* (also known as *dynamic carry forwards*) because the data that is carried forward from key frames is dynamic. Consider a video clip in which a person is waving an arm. If only static pixels are tracked between frames, no interframe compression occurs with respect to the moving parts of the person because those parts are not located in the same pixel blocks in both frames. If the CODEC can track the motion of the arm, the delta frame description tells the decompressor to look for particular moving parts in other pixel blocks, essentially tracking the moving part as it moves from one pixel block to another.

Although dynamic carry forwards are helpful, they cannot always be implemented. In many cases, the capture board cannot scale resolution and frame rate, digitize, and hunt for dynamic carry forwards at the same time.

Dynamic carry forwards typically mark the dividing line between hardware and software CODECs. Hardware CODECs, as the name implies, are usually add-on boards that provide additional hardware compression and decompression operations. The benefit of hardware CODECs is that they do not place any additional burden on the host CPU in order to execute video compression and decompression.

Software CODECs rely on the host CPU and require no additional hardware. The benefit of software CODECs is that they are typically cheaper and easier to install. Because they rely on the host's CPU to perform compression and decompression, software CODECs are often limited in their capability to use techniques such as advanced tracking schemes.

Intraframe Compression

Intraframe compression is performed solely with reference to information within a particular frame. It is performed on pixels in delta frames that remain after interframe compression and on key frames. Although intraframe techniques are often given the most attention, overall CODEC performance relates more to interframe efficiency than intraframe efficiency. The following are the principal intraframe compression techniques:

- *Run Length Encoding (RLE)*—A simple lossless technique originally designed for data compression and later modified for facsimile. RLE compresses an image based on "runs" of pixels. Although it works well on black-and-white facsimiles, RLE is not very efficient for color video, which have few long runs of identically colored pixels.

- *JPEG*—A standard that has been adopted by two international standards organizations: the ITU (formerly CCITT) and the ISO. JPEG is most often used to compress still images using discrete cosine transform (DCT) analysis. First, DCT divides the image into 8×8 blocks and then converts the colors and pixels into frequency space by describing each block in terms of the number of color shifts (frequency) and the extent of the change (amplitude). Because most natural images are relatively smooth, the changes that occur most often have low amplitude values, so the change is minor. In other words, images have many subtle shifts among similar colors but few dramatic shifts between very different colors.

  Next, quantization and amplitude values are categorized by frequency and averaged. This is the lossy stage because the original values are permanently discarded. However, because most of the picture is categorized in the high-frequency/low-amplitude range, most of the loss occurs among subtle shifts that are largely indistinguishable to the human eye.

After quantization, the values are further compressed through RLE using a special zigzag pattern designed to optimize compression of like regions within the image. At extremely high compression ratios, more high-frequency/low-amplitude changes are averaged, which can cause an entire pixel block to adopt the same color. This causes a blockiness artifact that is characteristic of JPEG-compressed images. JPEG is used as the intraframe technique for MPEG.

- *Vector quantization (VQ)*—A standard that is similar to JPEG in that it divides the image into 8×8 blocks. The difference between VQ and JPEG has to do with the quantization process. VQ is a recursive, or multistep algorithm with inherently self-correcting features. With VQ, similar blocks are categorized and a reference block is constructed for each category. The original blocks are then discarded. During decompression, the single reference block replaces all of the original blocks in the category.

After the first set of reference blocks is selected, the image is decompressed. Comparing the decompressed image to the original reveals many differences. To address the differences, an additional set of reference blocks is created that fills in the gaps created during the first estimation. This is the self-correcting part of the algorithm. The process is repeated to find a third set of reference blocks to fill in the remaining gaps. These reference blocks are posted in a lookup table to be used during decompression. The final step is to use lossless techniques, such as RLE, to further compress the remaining information.

VQ compression is by its nature computationally intensive. However, decompression, which simply involves pulling values from the lookup table, is simple and fast. VQ is a public-domain algorithm used as the intraframe technique for both Cinepak and Indeo.

End-User Video Compression Algorithms

The following are the most popular end-user video compression algorithms. Note that some algorithms require dedicated hardware.

- *MPEG1*—A bit stream standard for compressed video and audio optimized to fit into a bandwidth of 1.5 Mbps. This rate is special because it is the data rate of uncompressed audio CDs and DATs. Typically, MPEG1 is compressed in non-real time and decompressed in real time. MPEG1 compression is typically performed in hardware; MPEG1 decompression can be performed in software or in hardware.

- *MPEG2*—A standard intended for higher quality video-on-demand applications for products such as the "set top box." MPEG2 runs at data rates between 4 and 9 Mbps. MPEG2 and variants are being considered for use by regional Bell carriers and cable companies to deliver video-on-demand to the home as well as for delivering HDTV broadcasts. MPEG2 chip sets that perform real-time encoding are available. Real-time MPEG2 decompression boards are also available. A specification for MPEG2 adaptation over ATM AAL5 has been developed.

- *MPEG4*—A low-bit-rate compression algorithm intended for 64-Kbps connections. MPEG4 can be used for a wide range of applications including mobile audio, visual applications, and electronic newspaper sources.

- *M-JPEG (Motion-JPEG)*—The aggregation of a series of JPEG-compressed images. M-JPEG can be implemented in software or in hardware.

- *Cell B*—Part of a family of compression techniques developed by Sun Microsystems. Cell B is designed for real-time applications, such as videoconferencing, that require real-time video transmission. Cell A is a counterpart of Cell B that is intended for non-real time applications where encoding does not need to take place in real time. Both Cell A and Cell B use VQ and RLE techniques.

- *Indeo*—Developed by Intel. Indeo uses VQ as its intraframe engine. Intel has released three versions of Indeo:

  - *Indeo 2.1*—Focused on Intel's popular capture board, the Smart Video Recorder, using intraframe compression.

  - *Indeo 3.1*—Introduced in late 1993 and incorporated interframe compression.

  - *Indeo 3.2*—Requires a hardware add-on for video compression but decompression can take place in software on a high-end 486 or Pentium processor.

- *Cinepak*—Developed by SuperMatch, a division of SuperMac Technologies. Cinepak was first introduced as a Macintosh CODEC and then migrated to the Windows platform in 1993. Like Indeo, Cinepak uses VQ as its intraframe engine. Of all the CODECs, Cinepak offers the widest cross-platform support, with versions for 3D0, Nintendo, and Atari platforms.

- *Apple Video*—A compression technique used by applications such as Apple Computer's QuickTime Conferencing.

- *H.261*—The compression standard specified under the H.320 videoconferencing standard. H.261 describes the video coding and decoding methods for the moving picture component of audio-visual services at the rate of $p \times 64$ Kbps, where p is in the range 1 to 30. It describes the video source coder, the video multiplex coder, and the transmission coder. H.261 defines two picture formats:

  - *Common Intermediate Format (CIF)*—Specifies 288 lines of luminance information (with 360 pixels per line) and 144 lines of chrominance information (with 180 pixels per line).

  - *Quarter Common Intermediate Format (QCIF)*—Specifies 144 lines of luminance (with 180 pixels per line) and 72 lines of chrominance information (with 90 pixels per line). The choice between CIF and QCIF depends on available channel capacity—that is, QCIF is normally used when p is less than 3.

The actual encoding algorithm of H.261 is similar to (but incompatible with) MPEG. Also, H.261 needs substantially less CPU power for real-time encoding than MPEG. The H.261 algorithm includes a mechanism for optimizing bandwidth usage by trading picture quality against motion so that a quickly changing picture has a lower quality than a relatively static picture. When used in this way, H.261 is a constant-bit-rate encoding rather than a constant-quality, variable-bit-rate encoding.

Hardware Versus Software CODECs

In many cases, the network multimedia application dictates the video compression algorithm used. For example, Intel's ProShare videoconferencing application uses the Indeo standard or H.261, and Insoft Communique! uses Cell B compression. In some cases, such as Apple Computer's QuickTime Conferencing, the end user can specify the compression algorithm.

In general, the more CPU cycles given to video compression and decompression, the better the performance. This can be achieved either by running less expensive software CODECs on fast CPUs (Pentium, PowerPC, or RISC processors) or by investing more money in dedicated hardware add-ons such as an MPEG playback board. In some cases, the application dictates hardware or software compression and decompression. Insoft's INTV! video multicast package, for instance, uses a hardware-based compressor in the UNIX workstation, but uses a software-based decompressor for the PC workstations. The implication is that to use INTV, the PCs might need to be upgraded to deliver the requisite processing capabilities.

Compression Ratios

Any of the compression standards discussed in this chapter are helpful in reducing the amount of bandwidth needed to transmit digital video. In fact, digital video can be compressed up to 20:1 and still deliver a VHS-quality picture. Table 13–2 shows digital video compression ratios and the approximate quality that they yield in terms of video formats.

Table 13–2 *Image Quality as a Function of Compression Ratio*

Video Compression Ratio	Analog Picture Quality Equivalent
20:1	VHS
10:1	SVHS/HI-8
04:1	Broadcast quality

As Table 13–2 indicates, fairly high video compression ratios can be used while still preserving high-quality video images. For example, a typical MPEG1 video stream (640×480, 30 frames per second) runs at 1.5 Mbps.

Digitizing Audio

Many of today's multimedia applications include audio support. Some applications include hardware for digitizing audio, and other applications rely on third-party add-ons for audio support. Check with the application vendor to learn how audio is handled.

Like digital video, digital audio often begins from an analog source, so an analog-to-digital conversion must be made. Converting an analog signal to a digital signal involves taking a series of samples of the analog source. The aggregation of the samples yields the digital equivalent of the analog sound wave. A higher sampling rate delivers higher quality because it has more reference points to replicate the analog signal.

The sampling rate is one of three criteria that determine the quality of the digital version. The other two determining factors are the number of bits per sample and the number of channels.

Sampling rates are often quoted Hertz (Hz) or Kilohertz (KHz). Sampling rates are always measured per channel, so for stereo data recorded at 8,000 samples per second (8 KHz), there would actually be 16,000 samples per second (16 KHz). Table lists common sampling rates.

Table 13–3   *Common Audio Sampling Rates*

Samples per Second	Description
08,000	A telephony standard that works with μ-LAW encoding.
˙1 K	Either 11025 (a quarter of the CD sampling rate) or half the Macintosh sampling rate (perhaps the most popular rate on Macintosh computers).
16,000	Used by the G.722 compression standard
18.9 K	CD-ROM/XA standard
22 K	Either 22050 (half the CD sampling rate) or the Macintosh rate, which is precisely 22254.545454545454.
32,000	Used in digital radio; Nearly Instantaneous Compandable Audio Matrix (NICAM) (IBA/BREMA/BB), and other TV work in the U.K.; long play Digital Audio Tape (DAT); and Japanese HDTV.
37.8 K	CD-ROM/XA standard for higher quality.
44,056	Used by professional audio equipment to fit an integral number of samples in a video frame.
44,100	CD sampling rate. DAT players recording digitally from CD also use this rate.
48,000	DAT sampling rate for domestic rate.

An emerging tendency is to standardize on only a few sampling rates and encoding styles, even if the file formats differ. The emerging rates and styles are listed in Table 13–4.

Table 13–4 *Sample Rates and Encoding Styles*

Samples Per Second	Encoding Style
08,000	8-bit μ-LAW mono
2,050	8-bit linear unsigned mono and stereo
44,100	16-bit linear unsigned mono and stereo

Audio Compression

Audio data is difficult to compress effectively. For 8-bit data, a Huffman encoding of the deltas between successive samples is relatively successful. Companies such as Sony and Philips have developed proprietary schemes for 16-bit data. Apple Computer has an audio compression/expansion scheme called ACE on the Apple IIGS and called MACE on the Macintosh. ACE/MACE is a lossy scheme that attempts to predict where the wave will go on the next sample. There is very little quality change on 8:4 compression, with somewhat more quality degradation at 8:3 compression. ACE/MACE guarantees exactly 50 percent or 62.5 percent compression.

Public standards for voice compression using Adaptive Delta Pulse Code Modulation (ADPCM) are as follows:

- CCIU G.721 sampling at 32 Kbps
- CCIU G.723 sampling at 24 Kbps and 40 Kbps
- GSM 06.10 is a European speech encoding standard that compresses 160 13-bit samples into 260 bits (33 bytes), or 1,650 bytes per second (at 8,000 samples per second).

There are also two U.S. federal standards:

- 1016 using code excited linear prediction (CELP) at 4,800 bits per second)
- 1015 (LPC-10E) at 2,400 bits per second)

USING NETWORKED MULTIMEDIA APPLICATIONS

There is a wide range of network multimedia applications to choose from, so it is important to understand why a particular application is being deployed. Additionally, it is important to understand the bandwidth implications of the chosen application. Table 13–5 lists some of the popular network multimedia applications.

Table 13–5 *Popular Network Multimedia Applications*

Application	Type	Platform
Apple QuickTime Conferencing	Videoconferencing	Macintosh
AT&T Vistium	Videoconferencing	PC
CU-seeMe	Videoconferencing	Macintosh/PC/UNIX
InPerson	Videoconferencing	UNIX
Insoft Communique!	Videoconferencing	PC/UNIX
Intel CNN at Work	LAN broadcast	PC
Intel ProShare	Videoconferencing	PC
InVision	Videoconferencing	PC
Novell Video for NetWare	Video server	NetWare
PictureTel	Videoconferencing	PC
Starlight Starworks	Video server	UNIX/NetWare

Types of Applications

Network multimedia applications fall into the following categories:

- Point-to-Point Bidirectional Applications
- Point-to-Multipoint Bidirectional Applications
- Point-to-Point Unidirectional Applications
- Point-to-Multipoint Unidirectional Applications

Point-to-Point Bidirectional Applications

Point-to-point bidirectional applications, as shown in Figure 13–6, deliver real-time, point-to-point communication. The process is bidirectional, meaning that video can be transmitted in both directions in real time.

Examples of point-to-point bidirectional applications include the following:

- Audio and videoconferencing
- Shared whiteboard
- Shared application

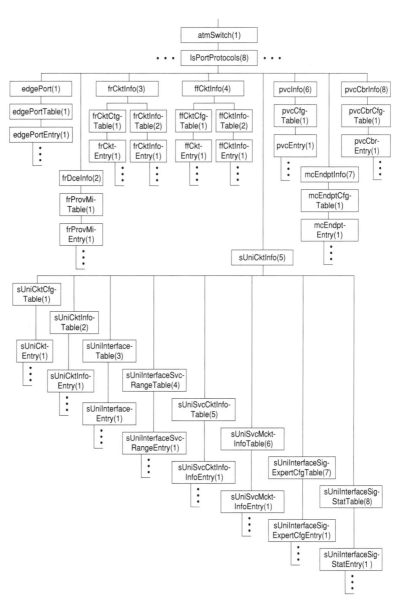

Figure 13–6
Point-to-point bidirectional applications.

Audio and videoconferencing applications provide a real-time interactive environment for two users. Often, these applications also include a shared whiteboard application or an application-sharing functionality. Shared whiteboard applications provide a common area that both users can see and draw on. Shared whiteboards (also known as *collaborative workspaces*) are particularly useful in conversations where "a picture is worth a thousand words." Application sharing is also a useful and productive tool. With application sharing, one user can launch an application, such as Microsoft Access, and the user at the other end can view and work with it as though the application were installed on that user's computer. Coworkers at opposite ends of a network can collaborate in an application regardless of where the application resides.

Point-to-Multipoint Bidirectional Applications

Point-to-multipoint bidirectional applications as shown in Figure 13–7, use multiple video senders and receivers. In this model, multiple clients can send and receive a video stream in real time.

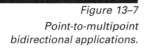

Figure 13–7

Point-to-multipoint bidirectional applications.

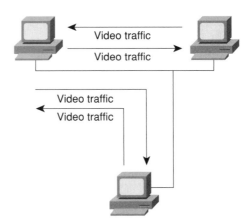

Interactive video, such as video kiosks, deliver video to multiple recipients. The recipients, however, can interact with the video session by controlling start and stop functions. The video content can also be manipulated by end-user interaction. Some kiosks, for example, have a touch pad that delivers different videos based on the user's selection. Examples of point-to-multipoint bidirectional applications include the following:

- Interactive video
- Videoconferencing

Like a telephone call in which multiple listeners participate, the same can be done with certain videoconferencing applications. For example, a three-way video conference call can occur in which each person can receive video and audio from the other two participants.

Point-to-Point Unidirectional Applications

Point-to-point unidirectional applications, as shown in Figure 13–8, use point-to-point communications in which video is transmitted in only one direction. The video itself can be a stored video stream or a real-time stream from a video recording source.

Figure 13–8
Point-to-point unidirectional applications.

Server

Client

Video traffic

Examples of point-to-point unidirectional applications include the following:

- Video server applications
- Multimedia-enabled email applications

In point-to-point unidirectional applications, compressed video clips are stored centrally. The end user initiates the viewing process by downloading the stream across the network to the video decompressor, which decompresses the video clip for viewing.

Point-to-Multipoint Unidirectional Applications

Point-to-multipoint unidirectional applications, as shown in Figure 13–9, are similar to point-to-point unidirectional applications except that the video is transmitted to a group of clients. The video is still unidirectional. The video can come from a storage device or a recording source.

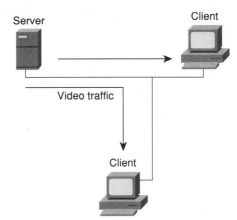

Figure 13–9
Point-to-multipoint unidirectional applications.

Server

Client

Video traffic

Client

Examples of point-to-multipoint unidirectional applications include the following:

- Video server applications
- LAN TV

Both of these applications provide unidirectional video services. Video server applications deliver to multiple clients video streams that have already been compressed. LAN TV applications deliver stored video streams or real-time video from a camera source. Distance learning, in which classes are videotaped and then broadcast over the LAN and WAN to remote employees, is a popular example of a point-to-multipoint unidirectional video application.

Quality of Service Requirements

Data and multimedia applications have different quality of service requirements. Unlike traditional "best effort" data services, such as File Transfer Protocol (FTP), Simple Mail Transfer Protocol (SMTP), and X Window, in which variations in latency often go unnoticed, audio and video data are useful only if they are delivered within a specified time period. Delayed delivery only impedes the usefulness of other information in the stream. In general, *latency* and *jitter* are the two primary forces working against the timely delivery of audio and video data.

Latency

Real-time, interactive applications, such as desktop conferencing, are sensitive to accumulated delay, which is known as *latency*. Telephone networks are engineered to provide less than 400 milliseconds (ms) round-trip latency. Multimedia networks that support desktop audio and videoconferencing also must be engineered with a latency budget of less than 400 ms per round-trip. The network contributes to latency in several ways:

- *Propagation delay*—The length of time that information takes to travel the distance of the line. Propagation delay is mostly determined by the speed of light; therefore, the propagation delay factor is not affected by the networking technology in use.

- *Transmission delay*—The length of time a packet takes to cross the given media. Transmission delay is determined by the speed of the media and the size of the packet.

- *Store-and-forward delay*—The length of time an internetworking device (such as a switch, bridge, or router) takes to send a packet that it has received.

- *Processing delay*—The time required by a networking device for looking up the route, changing the header, and other switching tasks. In some cases, the packet also must be manipulated. For example, the encapsulation type or the hop count must be changed. Each of these steps can contribute to the processing delay.

Jitter

If a network delivers data with variable latency, it introduces jitter. Jitter is particularly disruptive to audio communications because it can cause pops and clicks that are noticeable to the user. Many multimedia applications are designed to minimize jitter. The most common technique is to store incoming data in an insulating buffer from which the display software or hardware pulls data. The buffer reduces the effect of jitter in much the same way that a shock absorber reduces the effect of road irregularities on a car: Variations on the input side are smaller than the total buffer size and therefore are not normally perceivable on the output side. Figure 13–10 shows a typical buffering strategy that helps to minimize latency and jitter inherent in a given network.

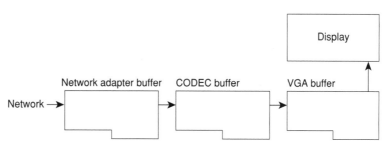

Figure 13–10
Hardware buffering minimizes latency and jitter.

Buffering can also be performed within the network itself. Consider a client that connects to a video server. During the video playback session, data moving from the video server to the client can be buffered by the network interface cards and the video decompressor. In this case, buffering acts as a regulator to offset inherent irregularities (latency/jitter) that occur during transmission. The overall effect is that even though the traffic may be bursty coming over the network, the video image is not impaired because the buffers store incoming data and then regulate the flow to the display card.

Buffers can play a large role in displaying video, especially over existing networks, but because they are not large enough to accommodate the entire audio or video file, the use of buffers cannot guarantee jitter-free delivery. For that reason, multimedia networks should also make use of techniques that minimize jitter.

One way of providing predictable performance is to increase line speeds to assure that adequate bandwidth is available during peak traffic conditions. This approach may be reasonable for backbone links, but it may not be cost effective for other links. A more cost-effective approach may be to use lower-speed lines and give mission-critical data priority over less critical transmissions during peak traffic conditions through the use of queuing techniques. The Cisco IOS software offers the following queuing strategies:

- Priority Queuing
- Custom Queuing
- Weighted Fair Queuing

Priority Queuing

Priority queuing allows the network administrator to define four priorities of traffic—high, normal, medium, and low—on a given interface. As traffic comes into the router, it is assigned to one of the four output queues. Packets on the highest priority queue are transmitted first. When that queue empties, packets on the next highest priority queue are transmitted, and so on.

Priority queuing ensures that during congestion, the highest-priority data is not delayed by lower-priority traffic. Note that, if the traffic sent to a given interface exceeds the bandwidth of that interface, lower-priority traffic can experience significant delays.

Custom Queuing

Custom queuing allows the network administrator to reserve a percentage of bandwidth for specified protocols. Cisco IOS Software Release 11.0 allows the definition of up to 16 output queues for normal data (including routing packets) with a separate queue for system messages, such as LAN keepalive messages. The router services each queue sequentially, transmitting a configurable percentage of traffic on each queue before moving on to the next queue. Custom queuing guarantees that mission-critical data is always assigned a certain percentage of the bandwidth but also assures predictable throughput for other traffic. For that reason, custom queuing is recommended for networks that need to provide a guaranteed level of service for all traffic.

Custom queuing works by determining the number of bytes that should be transmitted from each queue, based on the interface speed and the configured percentage. When the calculated byte count from a given queue has been transmitted, the router completes transmission of the current packet and moves on to the next queue, servicing each queue in a round-robin fashion.

With custom queuing, unused bandwidth is dynamically allocated to any protocol that requires it. For example, if SNA is allocated 50 percent of the bandwidth but uses only 30 percent, the next protocol in the queue can take up the extra 20 percent until SNA requires it. Additionally, custom queuing maintains the predictable throughput of dedicated lines by efficiently using packet-switching technologies such as Frame Relay.

Weighted Fair Queuing

Weighted fair queuing was introduced with Cisco IOS Software Release 11.0. Weighted fair queuing is a traffic priority management algorithm that identifies conversations (traffic streams) and then breaks up the streams of packets that belong to each conversation to ensure that capacity is shared fairly between individual conversations. By examining fields in the packet header, the algorithm automatically separates conversations.

Conversations are sorted into two categories—those that are attempting to use a lot of bandwidth with respect to the interface capacity (for example, FTP) and those that need less (for example, interactive traffic). For streams that use less bandwidth, the queuing algorithm always attempts to provide access with little or no queuing and shares the remaining bandwidth between the other conversations. In other words, low-bandwidth traffic has effective priority over high-bandwidth traffic, and high-bandwidth traffic shares the transmission service proportionally.

Weighted fair queuing provides an automatic way of stabilizing network behavior during congestion and results in increased performance and reduced retransmission. In most cases, weighted fair queuing provides smooth end-to-end performance over a given link and, in some cases, may resolve link congestion without an expensive increase in bandwidth.

NOTES

Weighted fair queuing is enabled by default on most serial interfaces; priority queuing or custom queuing can be configured instead. By default, weighted fair queuing is disabled on serial interfaces that are configured for X.25, LAPB, and SDLC, and on all LAN interfaces.

Bandwidth Requirements

Bandwidth requirements for network multimedia applications can range anywhere from 100 Kbps to 70 or 100 Mbps. Figure 13–11 shows the amount of bandwidth that the various types of network multimedia applications require.

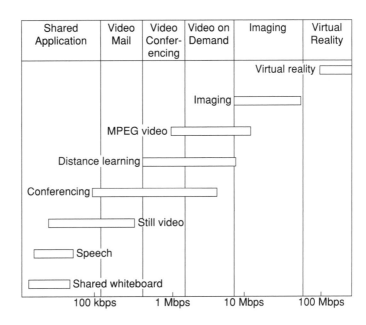

Figure 13–11
Network bandwidth usage.

As Figure 13–11 indicates, the type of application has a direct impact on the amount of LAN or WAN bandwidth needed. Assuming that bandwidth is limited, the choice is either to select a lower quality video application that works within the available bandwidth, or consider modifying the network infrastructure to deliver more overall bandwidth.

UNDERSTANDING MULTICASTING

Traditional network applications, including most of today's network multimedia applications, involve communication only between two computers. A two-user videoconferencing session using Intel ProShare, for example, is a strictly unicast transaction. However, a new breed of network multimedia applications, such as LAN TV, desktop conferencing, corporate broadcasts, and collaborative computing, requires simultaneous communication between groups of computers. This process is known generically as *multipoint communications*.

When implementing multipoint network multimedia applications, it is important to understand the traffic characteristics of the application in use. In particular, the network designer needs to know whether an application uses unicast, broadcast, or multicast transmission facilities, defined as follows:

- *Unicast*—In a unicast design, applications can send one copy of each packet to each member of the multipoint group. This technique is simple to implement, but it has significant scaling restrictions if the group is large. In addition, unicast applications require extra bandwidth, because the same information has to be carried multiple times—even on shared links.

- *Broadcast*—In a broadcast design, applications can send one copy of each packet and address it to a broadcast address. This technique is even simpler than unicast for the application to implement. However, if this technique is used, the network must either stop broadcasts at the LAN boundary (a technique that is frequently used to prevent broadcast storms) or send the broadcast everywhere. Sending the broadcast everywhere is a significant burden on network resources if only a small number of users actually want to receive the packets.

- *Multicast*—In a multicast design, applications can send one copy of each packet and address it to a group of computers that want to receive it. This technique addresses packets to a group of receivers (at the multicast address) rather than to a single receiver (at a unicast address), and it depends on the network to forward the packets to only those networks that need to receive them. Multicasting helps control network traffic and reduces the amount of processing that hosts have to do.

Many network multimedia applications, such as Insoft INTV! 3.0 and Apple QuickTime Conferencing 1.0, implement multicast transmission facilities because of the added efficiency that multicasting offers to the network and to the client. From the network perspective, multicast dramatically reduces overall bandwidth consumption and allows for more scalable network multimedia applications.

Consider an MPEG-based video server. Playback of an MPEG stream requires approximately 1.5 Mbps per client viewer. In a unicast environment, the video server send $1.5 \times n$ (where n=number of client viewers) Mbps of traffic to the network. With a 10-Mbps connection to the server, roughly six to seven streams could be supported before the network runs out of bandwidth. In a multicast environment, the video server need send only one video stream to a multicast address. Any number of clients can listen to the multicast address and receive the video stream. In this scenario, the server requires only 1.5 Mbps and leaves the rest of the bandwidth free for other uses.

Multicast can be implemented at both OSI Layer 2 and OSI Layer 3. Ethernet and Fiber Distributed Data Interface (FDDI), for example, support unicast, multicast, and broadcast addresses. A host can respond to a unicast address, several multicast addresses, and the broadcast address. Token Ring also supports the concept of multicast addressing but uses a different technique. Token Rings have functional addresses that can be used to address groups of receivers.

If the scope of an application is limited to a single LAN, using an OSI Layer 2 multicast technique is sufficient. However, many multipoint applications are valuable precisely because they are not limited to a single LAN.

When a multipoint application is extended to an Internet consisting of different media types, such as Ethernet, Token Ring, FDDI, Asynchronous Transfer Mode (ATM), Frame Relay, SMDS, and other networking technologies, multicast is best implemented at OSI Layer 3. OSI Layer 3 must define several parameters in order to support multicast communications:

- *Addressing*—There must be an OSI Layer 3 address that is used to communicate with a group of receivers rather than a single receiver. In addition, there must be a mechanism for mapping this address onto OSI Layer 2 multicast addresses where they exist.

- *Dynamic registration*—There must be a mechanism for the computer to communicate to the network that it is a member of a particular group. Without this capability, the network cannot know which networks need to receive traffic for each group.

- *Multicast routing*—The network must be able to build packet distribution trees that allow sources to send packets to all receivers. A primary goal of packet distribution trees is to ensure that only one copy of a packet exists on any given network—that is, if there are multiple receivers on a given branch, there should be only one copy of each packet on that branch.

IP Multicast

The Internet Engineering Task Force (IETF) has developed standards that address the parameters that are required to support multicast communications:

- *Addressing*—The IP address space is divided into four sections: Class A, Class B, Class C, and Class D. Class A, B, and C addresses are used for unicast traffic. Class D addresses are reserved for multicast traffic and are allocated dynamically.

- *Dynamic registration*—RFC 1112 defines the Internet Group Management Protocol (IGMP). IGMP specifies how the host should inform the network that it is a member of a particular multicast group.

- *Multicast routing*—There are several standards for routing IP multicast traffic:

  ○ Distance Vector Multicast Routing Protocol (DVMRP) as described in RFC 1075.

  ○ Multicast Open Shortest Path First (MOSPF), which is an extension to Open Shortest Path First (OSPF) that allows it to support IP multicast, as defined in RFC 1584.

  ○ Protocol Independent Multicast (PIM), which is a multicast protocol that can be used with all unicast IP routing protocols, as defined in the two Internet standards-track drafts entitled *Protocol Independent Multicast (PIM): Motivation and Architecture* and *Protocol Independent Multicast (PIM): Protocol Specification*.

IP Multicast Group Addressing

Figure 13–12 shows the format of a Class D IP multicast address.

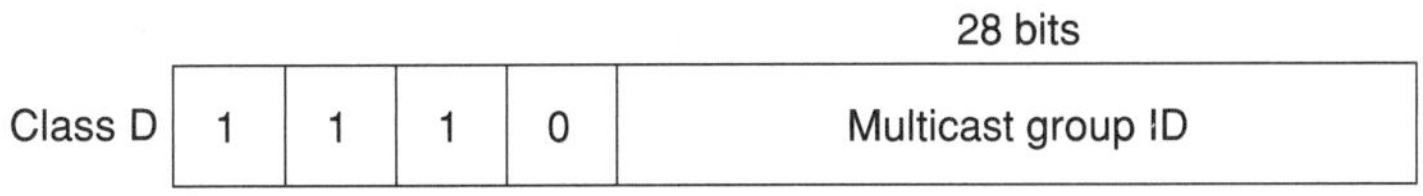

Figure 13–12
Class D address format.

| Class D | 1 | 1 | 1 | 0 | 28 bits
Multicast group ID |

Unlike Class A, B, and C IP addresses, the last 28 bits of a Class D address have no structure. The multicast group address is the combination of the high-order 4 bits of 1110 and the multicast group ID. These are typically written as dotted-decimal numbers and are in the range 224.0.0.0 through 239.255.255.255. Note that the high-order bits are 1110. If the bits in the first octet are 0, this yields the 224 portion of the address.

The set of hosts that responds to a particular IP multicast address is called a *host group*. A host group can span multiple networks. Membership in a host group is dynamic—hosts can join and leave host groups. For a discussion of IP multicast registration, see the section called "Internet Group Management Protocol" later in this chapter.

Some multicast group addresses are assigned as well-known addresses by the Internet Assigned Numbers Authority (IANA). These multicast group addresses are called *permanent host groups* and are similar in concept to the well-known TCP and UDP port numbers. Address 224.0.0.1 means "all systems on this subnet," and 224.0.0.2 means "all routers on this subnet."

Table 13–6 lists the multicast address of some permanent host groups.

Table 13–6   *Example of Multicast Addresses for Permanent Host Groups*

Permanent Host Group	Multicast Address
Network Time Protocol	224.0.1.1
RIP-2	224.0.0.9
Silicon Graphics Dogfight application	224.0.1.2

The IANA owns a block of Ethernet addresses that in hexadecimal is 00:00:5e. This is the high-order 24 bits of the Ethernet address, meaning that this block includes addresses in the range 00:00:5e:00:00:00 to 00:00:5e:ff:ff:ff. The IANA allocates half of this block for multicast addresses. Given that the first byte of any Ethernet address must be 01 to specify a multicast address, the Ethernet addresses corresponding to IP multicasting are in the range 01:00:5e:00:00:00 through 01:00:5e:7f:ff:ff.

This allocation allows for 23 bits in the Ethernet address to correspond to the IP multicast group ID. The mapping places the low-order 23 bits of the multicast group ID into these 23 bits of the Ethernet address, as shown in Figure 13–13. Because the upper five bits of the multicast address are ignored in this mapping, the resulting address is not unique. Thirty-two different multicast group IDs map to each Ethernet address.

Because the mapping is not unique and because the interface card might receive multicast frames in which the host is really not interested, the device driver or IP modules must perform filtering.

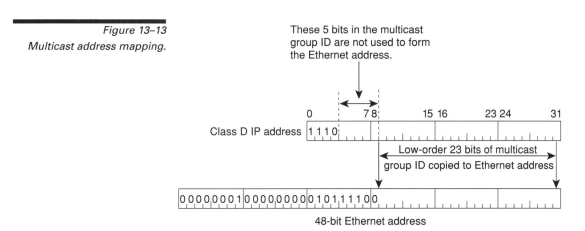

Figure 13–13
Multicast address mapping.

These 5 bits in the multicast group ID are not used to form the Ethernet address.

Class D IP address

Low-order 23 bits of multicast group ID copied to Ethernet address

48-bit Ethernet address

Multicasting on a single physical network is simple. The sending process specifies a destination IP address that is a multicast address, and the device driver converts this to the corresponding Ethernet address and sends it. The receiving processes must notify their IP layers that they want to receive datagrams destined for a given multicast address and the device driver must somehow enable reception of these multicast frames. This process is handled by joining a multicast group.

When a multicast datagram is received by a host, it must deliver a copy to all the processes that belong to that group. This is different from UDP where a single process receives an incoming unicast UDP datagram. With multicast, multiple processes on a given host can belong to the same multicast group.

Complications arise when multicasting is extended beyond a single physical network and multicast packets pass through routers. A protocol is needed for routers to know if any hosts on a given physical network belong to a given multicast group. This function is handled by the Internet Group Management Protocol.

Internet Group Management Protocol

The Internet Group Management Protocol (IGMP) is part of the IP layer and uses IP datagrams (consisting of a 20-byte IP header and an 8-byte IGRP message) to transmit information about multicast groups. IGMP messages are specified in the IP datagram with a protocol value of 2. Figure 13–14 shows the format of the 8-byte IGMP message.

Figure 13–14
IGMP message format.

4-bit IGMP Version (1)	4-bit IGMP Type (1-2)	(Unused)	16-bit checksum	32-bit group address (Class D IP address)

The value of the *version* field is 1. The value of the *type* field is 1 for a query sent by a multicast router and 2 for a report sent by a host. The value of the *checksum* field is calculated in the same way as the ICMP checksum. The group address is a class D IP address. In a query, the group address is set to 0, and in a report, it contains the group address being reported.

The concept of a process joining a multicast group on a given host interface is fundamental to multicasting. Membership in a multicast group on a given interface is dynamic (that is, it changes over time as processes join and leave the group). This means that end users can dynamically join multicast groups based on the applications that they execute.

Multicast routers use IGMP messages to keep track of group membership on each of the networks that are physically attached to the router. The following rules apply:

- A host sends an IGMP report when the first process joins a group. The report is sent out the same interface on which the process joined the group. Note that if other processes on the same host join the same group, the host does *not* send another report.

- A host does not send a report when processes leave a group, even when the last process leaves a group. The host knows that there are no members in a given group, so when it receives the next query, it doesn't report the group.

- A multicast router sends an IGMP query at regular intervals to see whether any hosts still have processes belonging to any groups. The router sends a query out each interface. The group address in the query is 0 because the router expects one response from a host for every group that contains one or more members on a host.

- A host responds to an IGMP query by sending one IGMP report for each group that still contains at least one process.

Using queries and reports, a multicast router keeps a table of its interfaces that have one or more hosts in a multicast group. When the router receives a multicast datagram to forward, it forwards the datagram (using the corresponding multicast OSI Layer 2 address) on only those interfaces that still have hosts with processes belonging to that group.

The Time to Live (TTL) field in the IP header of reports and queries is set to 1. A multicast datagram with a TTL of 0 is restricted to the same host. By default, a multicast datagram with a TTL of 1 is restricted to the same subnet. Higher TTL field values can be forwarded by the router. By increasing the TTL, an application can perform an expanding ring search for a particular server. The first multicast datagram is sent with a TTL of 1. If no response is received, a TTL of 2 is tried, and then 3, and so on. In this way, the application locates the server that is closest in terms of hops.

The special range of addresses 224.0.0.0 through 224.0.0.255 is intended for applications that never need to multicast further than one hop. A multicast router should never forward a datagram with one of these addresses as the destination, regardless of the TTL.

Multicast Routing Protocols

A critical issue for delivering multicast traffic in a routed network is the choice of multicast routing protocol. Three multicast routing protocols have been defined for this purpose:

- Distance Vector Multicast Routing Protocol
- Multicast OSPF
- Protocol Independent Multicast

The goal in each protocol is to establish paths in the network so that multicast traffic can effectively reach all group members.

Distance Vector Multicast Routing Protocol

Distance Vector Multicast Routing Protocol (DVMRP) uses a technique known as *reverse path forwarding*. When a router receives a packet, it floods the packet out all paths except the path that leads back to the packet's source. Reverse path forwarding allows a data stream to reach all LANs (possibly multiple times). If a router is attached to a set of LANs that does not want to receive a particular multicast group, the router sends a "prune" message up the distribution tree to prevent subsequent packets from traveling where there are no members.

New receivers are handled by using grafts. Consequently, only one round-trip time (RTT) from the new receiver to the nearest active branch of the tree is required for the new receiver to start getting traffic.

To determine which interface leads back to the source of the data stream, DVMRP implements its own unicast routing protocol. This unicast routing protocol is similar to RIP and is based on hop counts. As a result, the path that the multicast traffic follows might not be the same as the path that the unicast traffic follows. The need to flood frequently means that DVMRP has trouble scaling. This limitation is exacerbated by the fact that early implementations of DVMRP did not implement pruning.

DVMRP has been used to build the MBONE—a multicast backbone across the public Internet—by building tunnels between DVMRP-capable machines. The MBONE is used widely in the research community to transmit the proceedings of various conferences and to permit desktop conferencing.

Multicast OSPF

Multicast OSPF (MOSPF) is an extension of the OSPF unicast routing protocol and works only in internetworks that use OSPF. OSPF works by having each router in a network understand all of the available links in the network. Each OSPF router calculates routes from itself to all possible destinations. MOSPF works by including multicast information in OSPF link-state advertisements so that an MOSPF router learns which multicast groups are active on which LANs.

MOSPF builds a distribution tree for each source-group pair and computes a tree for active sources sending to the group. The tree state is cached and must be recomputed when a link state change occurs or when the cache times out.

MOSPF works well in environments that have relatively few source-group pairs active at any given time. It works less well in environments that have many active sources or in environments that have unstable links.

Protocol Independent Multicast

Unlike MOSPF, which is OSPF dependent, Protocol Independent Multicast (PIM) works with all existing unicast routing protocols. Unlike DVMRP, which has inherent scaling problems, PIM solves potential scalability problems by supporting two different types of multipoint traffic distribution patterns: dense mode and sparse mode. Dense mode is most useful when the following conditions occur:

- Senders and receivers are in close proximity to one another.
- There are few senders and many receivers.
- The volume of multicast traffic is high.
- The stream of multicast traffic is constant.

Dense-mode PIM uses reverse path forwarding and is similar to DVMRP. The most significant difference between DVMRP and dense-mode PIM is that PIM works with whatever unicast protocol is being used—it does not require any particular unicast protocol.

In dense mode, PIM floods the network and prunes back based on multicast group member information. Dense mode is effective, for example, in a LAN TV multicast environment because it is likely that there will be a group member on each subnet. Flooding the network is effective because little pruning is necessary. An example of PIM dense-mode operation is shown in Figure 13–15.

Figure 13–15
PIM dense-mode operation.

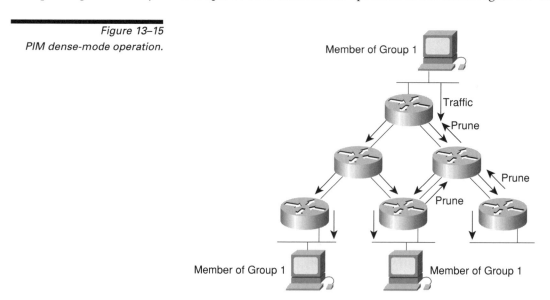

Sparse-mode PIM is most useful when the following conditions occur:

- There are few receivers in a group.

- Senders and receivers are separated by WAN links.
- The stream of multicast traffic is intermittent.

Sparse-mode PIM is optimized for environments where there are many multipoint data streams. Each data stream goes to a relatively small number of the LANs in the internetwork. For these types of groups, reverse path forwarding would make inefficient use of the network bandwidth.

In sparse-mode, PIM assumes that no hosts want the multicast traffic unless they specifically ask for it. It works by defining a rendezvous point (RP). The RP is used by senders to a multicast group to announce their existence and by receivers of multicast packets to learn about new senders. When a sender wants to send data, it first sends the data to the RP. When a receiver wants to receive data, it registers with the RP. Once the data stream begins to flow from sender to RP to receiver, the routers in the path automatically optimize the path to remove any unnecessary hops. An example of PIM sparse-mode operation is shown in Figure 13–16.

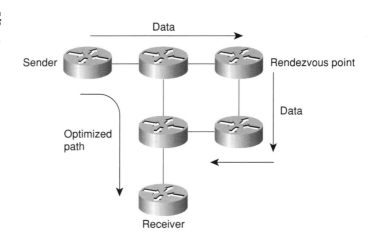

Figure 13–16
PIM sparse-mode operation.

NOTES

The administrators of the MBONE plan to adopt PIM because it is more efficient than DVMRP.

Simple Multicast Routing Protocol

Simple Multicast Routing Protocol (SMRP) is a transport layer multicast protocol standard for multicast AppleTalk and IPX traffic.

NOTES

Initial support for SMRP is provided by Cisco IOS Software Release 11.0 or later for AppleTalk only.

With SMRP, a router on each local network segment is elected as the primary node. The primary node handles requests from local devices to create multicast groups on that segment. When it wants to send multicast data, a device sends a Create Group Request packet to ask the primary node to assign a group address. The primary node responds by sending to the requesting device a Create Group Response packet that contains the assigned group address.

Devices that want to receive multicast data from this group send a Join Request packet to ask their local router to join the group. The local router forwards the Join Request to the primary node that created the group. The primary node responds by sending a Join Response.

Multicast data sent by the source is forwarded by router downstream interfaces toward receivers. Receivers can join and leave a group at any time, and a sender can delete the group at any time. The routers ensure that multicast data is transmitted as efficiently as possible, without duplication, from senders to receivers.

Routers maintain and update SMRP multicast groups by periodically sending Creator Query and Member Query packets to poll the network for the presence of senders and receivers. A router that detects the disappearance of a sender deletes the group. A router that senses the disappearance of a receiver informs its upstream neighbor to stop forwarding multicast data if no other receivers exist on the segment. Each router periodically informs its neighbors of its presence by sending Hello packets.

NETWORK DESIGNS FOR MULTIMEDIA APPLICATIONS

This section examines network designs that work well with network multimedia applications. The following topics are covered:

- Traditional LAN Designs
- WAN Designs
- High-Speed LAN Designs

Traditional LAN Designs

Some campus LAN environments already have adequate bandwidth for running certain network multimedia applications, but most do not. In many cases, lack of bandwidth is *not* caused by a slow LAN medium—instead, lack of bandwidth is caused by inefficient LAN design and segmentation. A considerable amount of bandwidth can be gained by using switches to resegment the campus LAN environment.

Consider three different campus designs. In Figure 13–17, Campus A has 500 users on five separate 100-node shared Ethernet segments. Each of the five segments are connected via a Cisco 7x00 series router.

With 100 users per segment, the net bandwidth per user is 100 Kbps. Using the graph shown in Figure 13–17, an audio conferencing package is the most that Campus A can handle. In Figure 13–18, Campus B uses a combination of shared Ethernet hubs (repeaters) and Ethernet switches to deliver substantially more bandwidth per user.

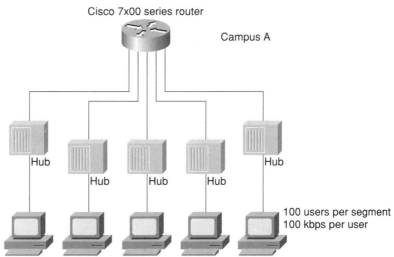

Figure 13–17
Shared Ethernet campus LAN design.

Cisco 7x00 series router

Campus A

Hub

Hub Hub Hub

Hub

100 users per segment
100 kbps per user

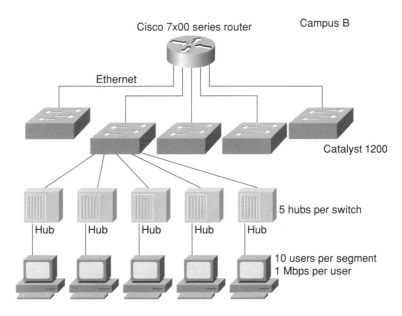

Figure 13–18
Shared Ethernet and switched Ethernet campus LAN design.

Cisco 7x00 series router

Campus B

Ethernet

Catalyst 1200

Hub Hub Hub Hub Hub

5 hubs per switch

10 users per segment
1 Mbps per user

In Figure 13–18, ten users are connected to a shared Ethernet hub. The hub is then connected to dedicated 10-Mbps Ethernet switch ports. Each of the Ethernet switches is connected together over a routed Ethernet backbone. In this scenario, each hub gets 10 Mbps, which yields roughly 1 Mbps for each of the ten users on the hub. Based on this network design, Campus B can run medium-quality video applications.

Campus C, shown in Figure 13–19, eliminates the shared Ethernet hubs. Each user has a dedicated l0-Mbps connection to the LAN via a direct connection to an Ethernet switch port. Like Campus B, the switches are interconnected over a routed Ethernet backbone. With 10 Mbps of bandwidth per user, Campus C can easily support high-quality network multimedia applications.

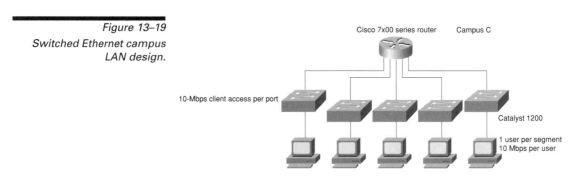

Figure 13–19
Switched Ethernet campus LAN design.

The comparison of Campus A, Campus B, and Campus C illustrates that the first step in delivering more bandwidth is *not* ripping out the existing Ethernet or Token Ring infrastructure and moving to a 100-Mbps technology. Instead, the proper first step is to deploy switches thereby improving bandwidth per user by assigning a small number of users to each switch port or by assigning one user to each switch port, thereby providing dedicated 10-Mbps bandwidth to that user. This technique is known as *microsegmenting*.

The majority of today's network multimedia applications require less than 10 Mbps for operation, so Ethernet is still an acceptable LAN medium. The problem with Ethernet is that more of its 10 Mbps needs to be delivered to each user than is delivered by the typical shared network.

Figure 13–20 shows how microsegmentation can affect per-user bandwidth, thus allowing network multimedia applications that have high bandwidth requirements to run.

When using LAN switches to design networks to support multimedia applications, it is important to remember the following design constraints:

- Multicast packets are basically equivalent to broadcast packets.
- Switches flatten the network and cause broadcast packets (and multicast packets) to be flooded throughout the network.
- Virtual LANs (VLANs) can be used to control the size and scope of the broadcast domain and, therefore, the networks on which multicast packets are sent.

- Routers are required to allow VLANs to communicate with each other and to control the spread of multicast packets.

- VLANs and routers are required for scalability in switched LAN networks.

- Because it supports IGMP, the Catalyst 1200 switch is well-suited for networks that support network multimedia applications.

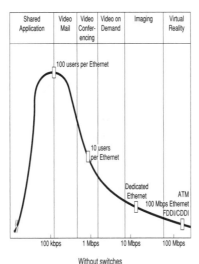
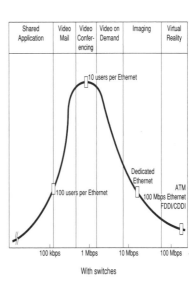

Figure 13–20
Effect of switches on usage patterns.

For more information about using LAN switches in your network design, see Chapter 12, "Designing Switched LAN Internetworks."

WAN Designs

Although there are many different ways to increase LAN bandwidth, increasing WAN bandwidth is not so easy. Because it is expensive, WAN bandwidth is a scarce resource in many environments. Running multimedia applications across a WAN is a challenge.

If additional bandwidth is needed in the WAN, first look at available circuit-switched technologies: switched-56, switched-T1, and ISDN. With these services, charges are based on connect time, which in the case of multimedia means that charges will be based on the length of the multimedia session. In cases where the circuit switched service is used with another connecting WAN service (switched or leased), the circuit-switched service can be configured as a backup service.

One way to improve utilization of WAN connections is to schedule WAN usage appropriately. On-demand applications (such as videoconferencing) typically consume WAN bandwidth during the working day, but other applications (such as video server applications) can be scheduled so that they consume bandwidth during off hours. A typical video server environment might have multiple video servers deployed in various sites. During the day, users access their local video server for training material or other video feeds. At night, when the WAN is idle, the video servers can replicate information and receive updates of new video content. By arranging to make use of unutilized WAN bandwidth at night, video servers can be maintained without adding to network traffic during the day.

Several Cisco IOS features can be used to control connect time and the type of data that flows over a WAN link, including snapshot routing, IPX and SPX spoofing, Name Binding Protocol (NBP) filtering, bandwidth on demand, and access lists. WAN connections should also take advantage of policy-based routing, which was introduced with Cisco IOS Software Release 11.0.

Policy-based routing is designed for networks in which both circuit-switched WAN and leased line connections are used. With policy-based routing, traffic can be routed over redundant WAN links based on traffic type (such as protocol or UDP port number). For example, policy-based routing can be used to route email and FTP traffic over a serial link and to route Intel ProShare traffic across an ISDN link. In Figure 13–21, policy-based routing is used to configure a T1 interface for regular traffic and an ISDN interface for video-conferencing traffic.

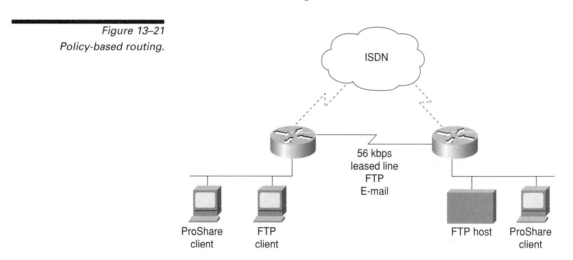

Figure 13–21
Policy-based routing.

In Figure 13–21, the multimedia gets the required bandwidth from the circuit-switched service. Because the circuit-switched service is up only when the application is in use, WAN costs are controlled. Traditional LAN traffic runs separately on the leased line and experiences uninterrupted service.

Until WAN bandwidth becomes affordable at any speed, delivering bandwidth to applications over the WAN will remain a difficult task. Wherever possible, take advantage of circuit-switched technologies and Cisco IOS features such as policy-based routing and bandwidth on demand.

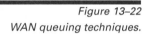

NOTES

The Cisco IOS software includes two lossless data compression algorithms, STAC and Predictor, that compress data that is transmitted over WAN links. Neither algorithm should be used to compress video because they cannot achieve the compression ratios that are achieved by video and audio compression algorithms. In addition, do not use STAC and Predictor to compress video that has already been compressed. In most cases, instead of decreasing the size of a video or audio transmission, these algorithms increase it.

Additionally, take advantage of the priority queuing, custom queuing, and weighted fair queuing to optimize WAN traffic patterns. For example, set up a queue for a particular multicast session or use weighted fair queuing to dynamically queue the multicast stream, as shown in Figure 13–22.

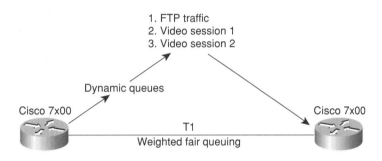

Figure 13–22
WAN queuing techniques.

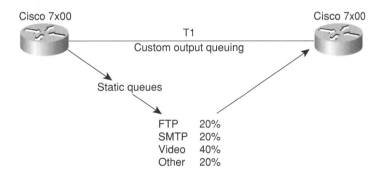

High-Speed LAN Designs

Many of today's network multimedia applications are packet-based audio or video applications. These applications are transmitted using the traditional OSI Layer 3 protocols: IP, IPX, and Apple-Talk. Stream-based applications are best exemplified in ATM environments in which audio or video is captured and converted directly into ATM cells and transmitted *natively* using ATM through the

ATM switch fabric. Typically, these multimedia applications are constant bit rate (CBR) and use AAL1 and circuit emulation for transmission.

It is important to ask the following questions of each network multimedia application in use:

- Is the application packet-based or stream-based?
- What are the bandwidth requirements?
- Does the application support multicast transmission?
- Does the application support quality of service parameters?

Designing a network to support packet-based video is quite different from designing a network for stream-based applications. Packet-based video is best deployed in networks built around switches and routers. To further tailor the network, virtual LAN (VLAN) technology can also be leveraged across the campus LAN and WAN.

In this model, ATM can be deployed as a backbone technology to interconnect different switches and VLANs. From an implementation standpoint, if IP is the only protocol on the network, the ATM part of the network can run classical IP over ATM, as defined in RFC 1577. However, if the ATM network needs to support additional protocols or IP multicast, the ATM network must run LAN Emulation (LANE) instead.

If resegmenting and microsegmenting an existing network, as described in the section "Multimedia and Traditional Network Designs" earlier in this chapter, does not yield enough bandwidth to run network multimedia applications, or if a new network is being designed, consider the following high-speed LAN technologies:

- Fast Ethernet
- Fiber Distributed Data Interface and Copper Distributed Data Interface (FDDI and CDDI)
- Asynchronous Transfer Mode (ATM)

The combination of switches and routers interconnected using a high-speed backbone technology (Fast Ethernet, FDDI, or ATM) provides sufficient bandwidth for most network multimedia applications in the campus environment.

Fast Ethernet

Fast Ethernet (IEEE 802.3u), delivers 100-Mbps bandwidth over category 5 unshielded twisted-pair (UTP) wire or fiber-optic cable. Like 10-Mbps Ethernet, Fast Ethernet uses carrier sense multiple access collision detection (CSMA/CD) network access method. Perhaps the two best advantages of Fast Ethernet are that it is relatively inexpensive (assuming category 5 UTP is present) and that migration from traditional 10-Mbps Ethernet is simple. Fast Ethernet delivers bandwidth that allows for a variety of different network design scenarios:

- High-speed client-server connectivity
- High-speed interswitch communication
- High-speed backbone

High-speed client-server connectivity is a popular use for Fast Ethernet. In this scenario, servers (Novell NetWare, Windows NT, and SPARC servers) are on Fast Ethernet and transmit to clients connected via Fast Ethernet or switched 10-Mbps Ethernet. Fast Ethernet server connectivity works particularly well in video server environments where the server needs to deliver multiple video streams to its clients. The capability to take advantage of a high-speed connection is a product of the server's architecture and the operating system that it runs. Novell NetWare, for example, can deliver substantial I/O caching, which in turn generates high-speed transfers. Figure 13–23 shows a design that gives users on 10-Mbps Ethernet access to file, print, and video servers located on 100-Mbps segments.

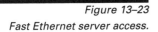

Figure 13–23
Fast Ethernet server access.

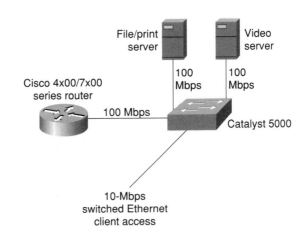

Using Fast Ethernet for high-speed client connectivity is also effective. Today, reasonably priced Fast Ethernet adapters are available for PCs (EISA and PCI) and SPARCstations (S-bus). Because installation is simple, Fast Ethernet provides a straightforward migration path to 100-Mbps bandwidth.

Fast Ethernet can also be used to interconnect Ethernet switch workgroups. In this scenario, a group of switches is interconnected using Fast Ethernet. This is particularly useful in a microsegmented environment in which each client has a dedicated 10-Mbps segment. With a Fast Ethernet connection between switches, a client can communicate with a client attached to a different switch without sacrificing bandwidth, as shown in Figure 13–24.

Fast Ethernet connections over category 5 UTP are limited to 100 meters in length. With fiber, Fast Ethernet can deliver connections up to two kilometers in length, allowing Fast Ethernet over fiber to be used as a backbone technology to interconnect various switched segments in a campus environment, as shown in Figure 13–25.

Figure 13–24
Fast Ethernet interswitch connections.

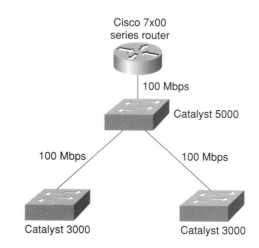

In practice, Fast Ethernet is rarely used as a core backbone technology because FDDI and ATM offer advanced features that make them more viable for backbone implementations.

Figure 13–25
Fast Ethernet backbone.

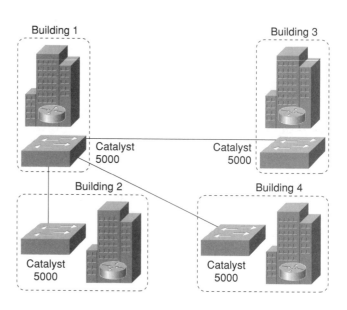

The design shown in Figure 13–26 works well for low-port density switched Ethernet environments, using switches for client and server access and routers for core connectivity. This design controls multicast traffic by deploying IGMP at the switch port, which allows multicast traffic to be sent only to ports that have registered an IGMP Join.

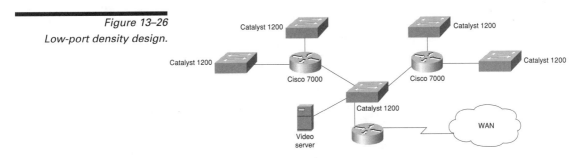

Figure 13–26
Low-port density design.

For high-port density Ethernet or Token Ring environments, a combination of routers and Catalyst 3000, Catalyst 1600, or Catalyst 5000 switches is effective. The design relies on VLAN technology to control multicast traffic. VLAN technology permits the creation of multiple bridge groups within a switch or across high-speed backbones with remote switches. With VLANs, multicast transmission can be limited to only the desired ports by creating a specific VLAN that includes only the multicast sender and the multicast recipients.

Designing VLANs to support multicast applications hinges largely on the application in use. Figure 13–27 is an example of a campus design that uses a single network TV multicast application.

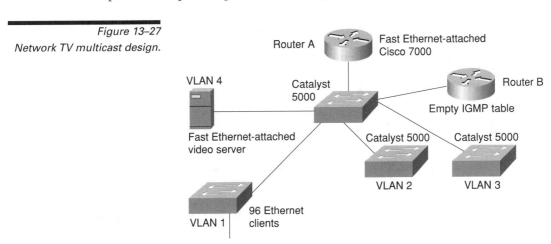

Figure 13–27
Network TV multicast design.

In Figure 13–27, there is only one VLAN per switch, resulting in a large number of clients per VLAN. The video source resides on the high-speed backbone and is in its own VLAN. During the multicast transmission, the video source sends a video stream out the high-speed connection.

Router A receives the video stream and sends it out its high-speed link to the VLANs on the Catalyst 5000 switches.

When a VLAN receives a multicast stream from the router, it forwards it to all members of that VLAN. Therefore, this design works well for environments in which every client tunes in to the network TV transmission. If only a few clients per VLAN tune in to the broadcast and the remaining clients task the network for other services, the multicast traffic can hinder overall network performance.

The routers support IGMP, which limits multicast traffic to only those interfaces that have registered IGMP Joins from clients. In Figure 13–27, Router B has no IGMP receivers in its table and therefore multicast traffic is not forwarded out any of its interfaces.

To impose greater control over multicast transmission, a microVLAN strategy can be used. In this scenario, a switch has multiple VLANs (thereby limiting the multicast traffic to fewer ports). MicroVLANs are best used in multipoint videoconferencing environments and environments where there are multiple multicast video sources. In these environments, many different multicast transmissions may occur simultaneously, which can impose some scalability issues unless the multicast traffic can be contained.

Figure 13–28 shows a microVLAN design in which the VLANs are aligned based on multicast demands. VLAN 1, for example, contains clients that primarily receive video from Video server 1. VLAN 1 also receives video from Video server 2, which is the corporate broadcast service.

The microVLAN approach minimizes the effects of multicast traffic by creating many small broadcast domains using VLANs.

One issue to keep in mind with the microVLAN design is that it might violate the 80/20 rule for designing VLANs. VLAN design is optimized when at least 80 percent of the traffic is intraVLAN and at most 20 percent of the traffic is interVLAN. Essentially, performance is optimized when traffic remains within the local VLAN. If VLANs are aligned based on multicast clients and servers, there is a good chance that access to other servers, such as the email server, will be interVLAN. Because interVLAN communication must be handled by a router, as interVLAN communication increases, route processing increases. Ultimately, the number of VLANs per router port should be determined by the multicast applications in use and their respective bandwidth requirements. Compared with low-bandwidth multicast applications, high-bandwidth multicast applications place a greater constraint on the number of VLANs on a router interface. For additional information about VLANs, see Chapter 12, "Designing Switched LAN Internetworks."

Fiber Distributed Data Interface and Copper Distributed Data Interface

Fiber Distributed Data Interface (FDDI) and Copper Distributed Data Interface (CDDI) deliver bandwidth that allows for a variety of different network design scenarios. FDDI is particularly attractive as a backbone technology for the following reasons:

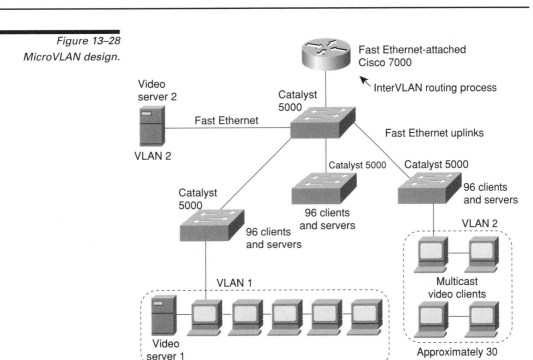

Figure 13–28 MicroVLAN design.

- *Distance capabilities*—With multimode fiber, an FDDI connection can span 2 kilometers. With single mode fiber, an FDDI connection can span 10 kilometers. This capability allows tremendous flexibility for interconnecting LAN segments in a campus environment.

- *Fault tolerance and redundancy*—FDDI's inherent fault tolerance and its ability to support designs such as dual-homing also make the technology attractive in backbone environments.

- *Security*—Optical transmission makes it more difficult for hackers to tap into compared to traditional copper transmission.

Like Fast Ethernet, FDDI and CDDI can deliver high-speed client connectivity, but most often, FDDI and CDDI are used for server and backbone connections, especially in video server environments where multiple video streams are sent to video clients, as shown in Figure 13–29.

In addition to delivering high bandwidth, FDDI and CDDI deliver better redundancy than Fast Ethernet. With FDDI and CDDI, a server can be *dual-homed* to FDDI or CDDI concentrators, as shown in Figure 13–30. Dual-homing gives a server access to two FDDI or CDDI rings. Under normal circumstances, the server uses only one ring. If the primary ring fails, the server can fall back to the secondary ring, maintaining connectivity with no down time. Dual-homing requires that the server FDDI or CDDI adapter be a Dual Attached Station (DAS) adapter (as opposed to a Single Attached Station [SAS] connector, which provides a single physical connection).

Figure 13–29
FDDI or CDDI server access.

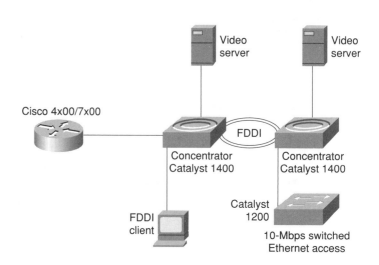

Figure 13–29
FDDI or CDDI server access.

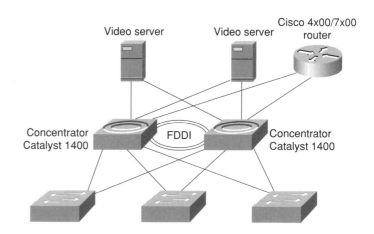

Figure 13–30
FDDI dual-homed design.

Clients attached to different Ethernet switch workgroups can gain high-speed intercommunication, which allows a client connected to one Ethernet switch to access a video server or initiate a video-conferencing session with a resource connected to another Ethernet switch. In this design, dual-homing can be implemented. An FDDI-equipped switch can be dual-homed to two different concentrators, providing greater redundancy and fault tolerance.

The design shown in Figure 13–31 works for point-to-point applications that only impose bandwidth demands on the network, but it is vulnerable to multicast applications. The switch transmits OSI Layer 2 multicast frames to all ports in the same manner as it transmits OSI Layer 2 broadcast frames. For example, if a client accesses a multicast video stream on a server, the multicast transmission is forwarded to all switch ports, which undermines the performance benefits of switching.

Figure 13–31
Switch/router campus design.

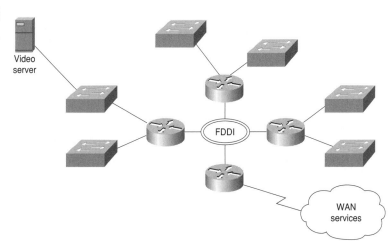

Asynchronous Transfer Mode

Asynchronous Transfer Mode (ATM) has gained much attention as the next-generation LAN and WAN technology. Much of the excitement about ATM centers around the fact that ATM delivers an entirely switch-based fabric and offers high-speed connectivity (100-Mbps TAXI, 155-Mbps OC-3 and in the future 622-Mbps OC-12). Besides the raw bandwidth that ATM provides, the technology also offers extensive support for transporting video, voice, and data. As Figure 13–32 illustrates, a variety of different design scenarios are possible using ATM equipment.

From a bandwidth perspective, ATM offers considerable flexibility for running network multimedia applications. Although ATM provides features, such as quality of service support, that make it an attractive environment in which to run network multimedia applications, ATM is not a prerequisite for running network multimedia applications. Rather, today's existing LAN technologies can also support many network multimedia applications.

LAN Emulation

LAN Emulation (LANE) defines a service interface for Open Systems Interconnection (OSI) Layer 3 protocols that is identical to that of existing LANs and encapsulates data sent across the ATM network in the appropriate LAN MAC packet format. It makes no attempt to emulate the actual media access control protocol of the specific LAN concerned (that is, CSMA/CD for Ethernet or token passing for IEEE 802.5).

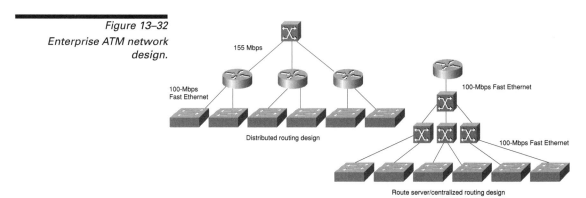

Figure 13–32
Enterprise ATM network design.

155 Mbps

100-Mbps Fast Ethernet

100-Mbps Fast Ethernet

Distributed routing design

100-Mbps Fast Ethernet

Route server/centralized routing design

Currently, LANE does not define a separate encapsulation for FDDI. FDDI packets are mapped into Ethernet or Token Ring-emulated LANs (ELANs) using existing translational bridging techniques. Because they use the same packet formats, the two most prominent new LAN standards, Fast Ethernet (100BaseT) and IEEE 802.12 (100VG-AnyLAN), can be mapped unchanged into either the Ethernet or Token Ring LANE formats and procedures.

LANE supports a range of maximum packet (MPDU) sizes, corresponding to maximum size Ethernet, 4-Mbps and 16-Mbps Token Ring packets, and to the value of the default MPDU for IP over ATM. Typically, the size of the MPDU depends on the type of LAN that is being emulated and on the support provided by LAN switches bridged to the ELAN. An ELAN with only native ATM hosts, however, may optionally use any of the available MPDU sizes, even if a size does not correspond to the actual MPDU in a real LAN of the type being emulated. All LAN Emulation clients (LECs) within a given ELAN must use the same MPDU size. Put simply, LANE makes an ATM network look and behave like an Ethernet or Token Ring LAN—albeit one operating much faster than such a network.

The advantage of LANE is that it allows higher-layer protocols to work without modification over ATM networks. Because LANE presents the same service interface of existing MAC protocols to network-layer drivers (for example, an NDIS- or ODI-like driver interface), no changes are required in those drivers. See Figure 13–33 for a representation of the LANE protocol architecture.

The goal of LANE is to accelerate the deployment of ATM at the same time that work continues on the full definition and implementation of native mode network-layer protocols.

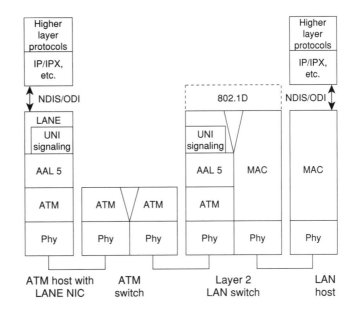

Figure 13–33
LANE protocol architecture.

LANE Designs

When designing with LANE, the primary issues typically center on the scalability of LAN Emulation servers (LESs) and broadcast and unknown servers (BUSs). Currently, all multicast transmission relies on the BUS for delivery to all LAN Emulation clients (LECs) within a given ELAN.

In a Cisco ATM network, the router operates as the BUS for a given ELAN. If the router supports multiple ELANs, it runs multiple BUS processes. Router performance is a function of the number of ELANs the router is a member of and the number of BUS processes that it executes. In environments in which there are a large number of ELANs, additional routers should be deployed to handle BUS functionality for each ELAN. Essentially, BUS functionality is distributed across a set of routers in the ATM network, as shown in Figure 13–34.

Currently, LANE is the only ATM technology that addresses multicast packet-based video. Classical IP over ATM (RFC 1577) has no provision for resolving OSI Layer 2 multicast addresses into ATM addresses. For more information about LANE, see Chapter 8, "Designing ATM Internetworks."

Native Mode ATM

Native mode ATM protocols bypass the MAC address encapsulation of LANE. In native mode, address resolution mechanisms map network-layer addresses directly into ATM addresses, and the network-layer packets are then carried across the ATM network. Currently, IP is the only protocol for which extensive native-mode work has been done.

From the perspective of running network multimedia applications, one of the most compelling reasons for running native mode protocols is quality of service support. LANE deliberately hides ATM so any network-layer protocol that operates over ATM cannot gain access to the quality of service properties of ATM and must therefore use unspecified bit rate (UBR) or available bit rate (ABR) connections only. Currently, this is not a major restriction because all network protocols were developed for use over existing LAN and WAN technologies, none of which can deliver a guaranteed quality of service. Consequently, no existing network-layer protocol can request a specific quality of service from the network or deliver it to a higher-layer protocol or application. In turn, most network applications today do not expect to receive any guaranteed quality of service from the underlying network protocol, so they do not request it.

Figure 13–34
Distributed LES/BUS design.

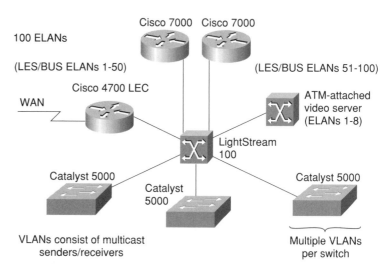

For a long time, IP has had optional support for type of service (TOS) indications within the IP header that could theoretically be used to provide a rudimentary form of quality of service support. In practice, however, almost no end-system or intermediate-system IP implementations have any support for TOS because TOS indications cannot be mapped into any common underlying networking technology. Few, if any, IP routing protocols use the TOS bits, and no applications set them.

At best, all current network-layer protocols expect and deliver only a "best effort" service—precisely the type of service that the ABR service was designed to offer. Just as LANE adapts the connection-oriented nature of ATM to offer the same type of connectionless service that is expected by network-layer protocols, so ABR hides the guaranteed quality of services features of ATM to offer the best effort service expected by these protocols. As such, ABR and LANE perfectly complement each other.

As ATM networks proliferate, it is likely that demand will grow to use the quality of service features of ATM, which will spur application development expressly designed to take advantage of ATM and ATM quality of service.

Native ATM Designs

As mentioned earlier in this chapter, LANE is best suited for "best effort" traffic (that is, ABR traffic) but is not well-suited for applications that require more predictable network service, such as CBR and VBR multimedia applications. For these applications, it is best to run native ATM. In a native ATM environment, digital video and audio is sent to a service multiplexer that segments the audio and video streams into cells and forwards them out to ATM-attached clients that receive the streams.

MPEG2, which is a VBR application, is a good example of a native ATM application. With MPEG2, video can be digitized and compressed in real time and then put into ATM cells for delivery to ATM-attached clients. Figure 13–35 shows an example of MPEG2 running over ATM.

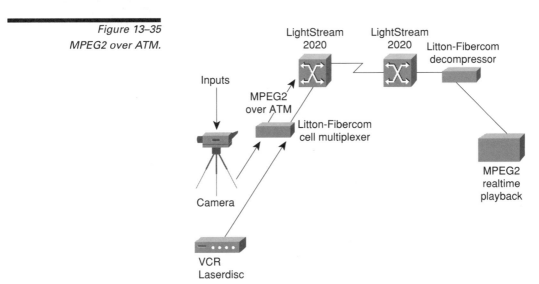

Figure 13–35
MPEG2 over ATM.

Multimedia Applications in ATM Networks

Within an ATM network, connections are categorized into various quality-of-service types: constant bit rate (CBR), variable bit rate (VBR), available bit rate (ABR), and unspecified bit rate (UBR). For the most part, network multimedia applications are CBR or VBR. CBR video applications are designed to run over traditional 64-Kbps or multiple 64-Kbps lines. With ATM, CBR video is transported using circuit emulation, which means that the ATM switch must support circuit emulation.

ATM switches that do not have CBR line cards must have a service multiplexer. The multiplexer has inputs for CBR traffic at T1/E1 and T3/E3 speeds and can adapt those streams to ATM. For example, the Litton-FiberCom ATM multiplexer features real-time video encoding and provides ATM adaptation with an OC-3 (155 Mbps) ATM port.

VBR video applications, which are commonly seen in traditional LAN environments, are more bursty than CBR applications. VBR applications are often referred to as *packetized video*. The video compression algorithm, such as MPEG, generates VBR output that is packetized onto the LAN. In ATM, VBR applications can run using LANE or can run natively using IP over ATM.

MPEG2 is a special case of VBR that can run directly on ATM, bypassing LANE and IP altogether. In this case, there is an MPEG2-to-ATM convergence layer in which MPEG2 information is translated into ATM cells. Figure 13–36 shows how CBR and VBR map into ATM.

Figure 13–36

Video stream protocol mappings.

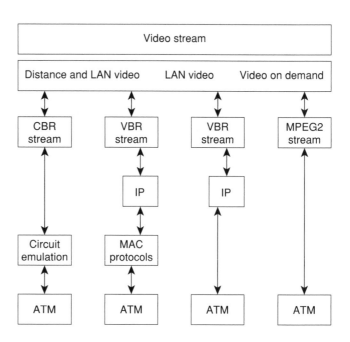

Depending on the type of ATM service requested, the network is expected to deliver guarantees on the particular mix of quality of service elements (such as cell loss ratio, cell delay, and cell delay variation) that are specified at the connection setup.

In UNI 3.0/3.1, the traffic parameters and requested quality of service for a connection cannot be negotiated at setup, nor can they be changed over the life of the connection. UNI 4.0 will support connection quality of service negotiation.

ATM Multicasting

There are two fundamental types of ATM connections:

- Point-to-point connections, which connect two ATM end systems. Such connections can be unidirectional or bidirectional.

- Point-to-multipoint connections, which connect a single source end system (known as the *root node*) to multiple destination end systems (known as *leaves*). Cell replication is done within the network by the ATM switches at which the connection splits into two or more branches. Such connections are unidirectional, permitting the root to transmit to the leaves but not permitting the leaves to transmit to the root, or to each other, on the same connection.

An analog to the multicasting or broadcasting capability common in many shared-media LAN technologies, such as Ethernet and Token Ring, is notably missing from these types of ATM connections. In such technologies, multicasting allows multiple end systems to receive data from other multiple systems and to transmit data to these multiple systems. Such capabilities are easy to implement in shared-media technologies such as LANs, where all nodes on a single LAN segment must necessarily process all packets sent on that segment. The obvious analog in ATM to a multicast LAN group would be a bidirectional, multipoint-to-multipoint connection. Unfortunately, this obvious solution cannot be implemented when using ATM Adaptation Layer 5 (AAL5), the most common ATM adaptation layer used to transmit data across ATM networks.

Unlike AAL3/4, with its Message Identifier (MID) field, AAL5 does not have any provision within its cell format for the interleaving of cells from different AAL5 packets on a single connection. Therefore, all AAL5 packets sent to a particular destination across a particular connection must be received in sequence, with no interleaving between the cells of different packets on the same connection, or the destination reassembly process would not be able to reconstruct the packets.

Despite the problems that AAL5 has with multicast support, it is not feasible to use AAL3/4 as an alternative for data transport. AAL3/4 is a much more complex protocol than AAL5 and would lead to much more complex and expensive implementations. Indeed, AAL5 was developed specifically to replace AAL3/4. Although the MID field of AAL3/4 could preclude cell interleaving problems, allowing for bidirectional, multipoint-to-multipoint connections, this would also require some mechanism for ensuring that all nodes in the connection use a unique MID value. There is no such mechanism currently in existence or development; the number of possible nodes within a given multicast group would also be severely limited due to the small size of the MID field.

ATM AAL5 point-to-multipoint connections can be only unidirectional because if a leaf node were to transmit an AAL5 packet onto the connection, it would be received by both the root node and all other leaf nodes. However, at these nodes, the packet sent by the leaf could be interleaved with packets sent by the root, and possibly other leaf nodes; this would preclude the reassembly of any of the interleaved packets. Clearly, this is not acceptable.

Notwithstanding this problem, ATM requires some form of multicast capability because most existing protocols (having been developed initially for LAN technologies) rely on the existence of a low-level multicast/broadcast facility. Three methods have been proposed for solving this problem:

- *VP-multicasting*—With this mechanism, a multipoint-to-multipoint VP links all nodes in the multicast group, and each node is given a unique VCI value within the VP. Interleaved packets can be identified by the unique VCI value of the source. Unfortunately, this mechanism requires a protocol that uniquely allocates VCI values to nodes, and such a protocol does not currently exist. It is also not clear whether current segmentation and reassembly (SAR) devices could easily support such a mode of operation. Moreover, UNI 3.0/3.1 does not support switched virtual paths. UNI 4.0, however, should add this capability.

• *Multicast server*—With this mechanism as illustrated in Figure 13–37, all nodes wanting to transmit onto a multicast group set up a point-to-point connection with an external device known as a multicast server (perhaps better described as a resequencer or serializer). The multicast server, in turn, is connected to all nodes that want to receive the multicast packets through a point-to-multipoint connection. The multicast server receives packets across the point-to-point connections, and then retransmits them across the point-to-multipoint connection—but only after ensuring that the packets are serialized (that is, one packet is fully transmitted prior to the next being sent). In this way, cell interleaving is precluded.

Figure 13–37
Multicast server operation.

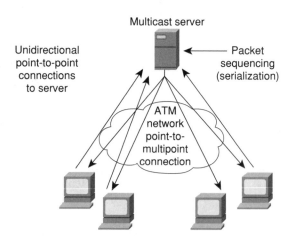

• *Overlaid point-to-multipoint connections*—With this mechanism, all nodes in the multicast group establish a point-to-multipoint connection with each of the other nodes in the group, and, in turn, become a leaf in the equivalent connections of all other nodes. Therefore, as shown in Figure 13–38, all nodes can both transmit to and receive from all other nodes.

Overlaid point-to-multipoint connections require each node to maintain *n* connections for each group, where *n* is the total number of transmitting nodes within the group. The multicast server mechanism requires only two connections. Overlaid point-to-multipoint connections also require a registration process for telling a node that joins a group what the other nodes in the group are, so that the joining node can form its own point-to-multipoint connection. The other nodes also need to know about the new node so they can add the new node to their own point-to-multipoint connections. The multicast server mechanism is more scalable in terms of connection resources but has the problem of requiring a centralized resequencer, which is both a potential bottleneck and a single point of failure.

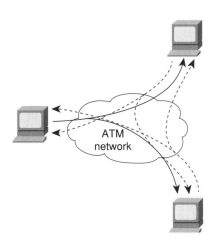

In short, there is no ideal solution within ATM for multicast. Higher layer protocols within ATM networks use both the multicast server solution and the overlaid point-to-multipoint connection solution. This is one example of why using existing protocols with ATM is so complex. Most current protocols, particularly those developed for LANs, implicitly assume a network infrastructure similar to existing LAN technologies—that is, a shared-medium, connectionless technology with implicit broadcast mechanisms. ATM violates all of these assumptions.

WORK IN PROGRESS

In the case of IP, the IETF has developed the notion of an Integrated Services Internet, which envisages a set of enhancements to IP to allow it to support integrated or multimedia services. These enhancements include traffic management mechanisms that closely match the traffic management mechanisms of ATM. For instance, protocols such as Resource Reservation Protocol (RSVP) are being defined to allow for resource reservation across an IP network, much as ATM signaling does within ATM networks.

RSVP is an advanced method for dynamically allocating bandwidth to network-based applications running in traditional packet-based networks. RSVP will be particularly useful for CBR multimedia applications because it will allow a network application to request a specific quality of service from the network. It will be the responsibility of internetworking devices (such as routers) to respond to the RSVP request and to establish a connection through the network that can support the requested quality of service.

The IP Version 6 (IPv6) protocol (formally known as the IP Next Generation [IPng] protocol), which the IETF is now developing as a replacement for the current IPv4 protocol, incorporates support for a flow ID within the packet header. The network uses the flow ID to identify flows, much as VPI/VCI (virtual path identifier/virtual channel identifier) are used to identify streams of ATM cells. Protocols such as RSVP will be used to associate with each flow a flow specification that characterizes the traffic parameters of the flow, much as the ATM traffic contract is associated with an ATM connection.

The IETF is also in the process of developing a new transport protocol, the Real-Time Transport Protocol (RTP). RTP is designed to provide end-to-end network transport functions for applications transmitting real-time data (such as audio, video, or simulation data) over multicast or unicast network services. RTP builds on protocols like RSVP for resource reservation and on transport technologies such as ATM for quality of service guarantees. The services provided by RTP to real-time applications include payload type identification, sequence numbering, time stamping, and delivery monitoring.

The concept of a Multicast Address Resolution Server (MARS), which can be considered the analog of the ARP server in RFC 1577, is also in development. A MARS serves a group of nodes known as a *cluster*. All end systems within the cluster are configured with the ATM address of the MARS. The MARS supports multicast through *multicast meshes* of overlaid point-to-multipoint connections, or through multicast servers.

SUMMARY

This chapter addressed how to effectively deploy network multimedia applications. Specifically, this chapter addressed the following topics:

- Multimedia basics, including analog video, digital video, video compression, and digital audio standards

- Using networked multimedia applications, including bandwidth and quality of service requirements

- Understanding multicasting, including Internet Group Management Protocol, Distance Vector Multicast Routing Protocol, Multicast Open Shortest Path First, Protocol Independent Multicast, and Simple Multicast Routing Protocol

- Network designs for multimedia applications, including traditional LAN designs, WAN designs, and high-speed LAN designs

PART II

Internetworking Case Studies

RIP and OSPF
Redistribution

This case study addresses the issue of integrating Routing Information Protocol (RIP) networks with Open Shortest Path First (OSPF) networks. Most OSPF networks also use RIP to communicate with hosts or to communicate with portions of the internetwork that do not use OSPF. Cisco supports both the RIP and OSPF protocols and provides a way to exchange routing information between RIP and OSPF networks. This case study provides examples of how to complete the following phases in redistributing information between RIP and OSPF networks, including the following topics:

- Configuring a RIP Network
- Adding OSPF to the Center of a RIP Network
- Adding OSPF Areas
- Setting Up Mutual Redistribution

CONFIGURING A RIP NETWORK

Figure 14–1 illustrates a RIP network. Three sites are connected with serial lines. The RIP network uses a Class B address and an 8-bit subnet mask. Each site has a contiguous set of network numbers.

Table 14–1 lists the network address assignments for the RIP network, including the network number, subnet range, and subnet masks. All interfaces indicate network 130.10.0.0; however, the specific address includes the subnet and subnet mask. For example, serial interface 0 on Router C has an IP address of 130.10.63.3 with a subnet mask of 255.255.255.0.

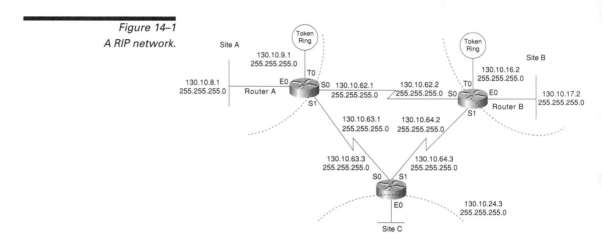

Figure 14–1
A RIP network.

Table 14–1 *RIP Network Address Assignments*

Network Number	Subnets	Subnet Masks
130.10.0.0	**Site A:** 8 through 15	255.255.255.0
130.10.0.0	**Site B:** 16 through 23	255.255.255.0
130.10.0.0	**Site C:** 24 through 31	255.255.255.0
130.10.0.0	**Serial Backbone:** 62 through 64	255.255.255.0

Configuration File Examples

The following commands in the configuration file for Router A determine the IP address for each interface and enable RIP on those interfaces:

```
interface serial 0
ip address 130.10.62.1 255.255.255.0
interface serial 1
ip address 130.10.63.1 255.255.255.0
interface ethernet 0
ip address 130.10.8.1 255.255.255.0
interface tokenring 0
ip address 130.10.9.1 255.255.255.0
router rip
network 130.10.0.0
```

The following commands in the configuration file for Router B determine the IP address for each interface and enable RIP on those interfaces:

```
interface serial 0
ip address 130.10.62.2 255.255.255.0
interface serial 1
ip address 130.10.64.2 255.255.255.0
interface ethernet 0
```

```
ip address 130.10.17.2 255.255.255.0
interface tokenring 0
ip address 130.10.16.2 255.255.255.0
router rip
network 130.10.0.0
```

The following commands in the configuration file for Router C determine the IP address for each interface and enable RIP on those interfaces:

```
interface serial 0
ip address 130.10.63.3 255.255.255.0
interface serial 1
ip address 130.10.64.3 255.255.255.0
interface ethernet 0
ip address 130.10.24.3 255.255.255.0
router rip
network 130.10.0.0
```

ADDING OSPF TO THE CENTER OF A RIP NETWORK

A common first step in converting a RIP network to OSPF is to add backbone routers that run both RIP and OSPF, while the remaining network devices run RIP. These backbone routers are OSPF autonomous system boundary routers. Each autonomous system boundary router controls the flow of routing information between OSPF and RIP. In Figure 14–2, Router A is configured as the autonomous system boundary router.

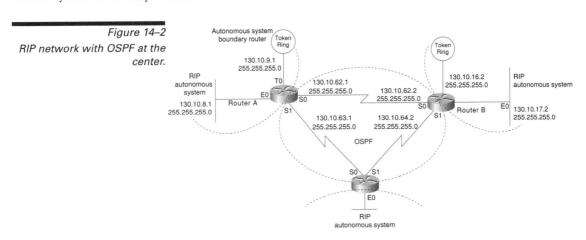

Figure 14–2
RIP network with OSPF at the center.

RIP does not need to run between the backbone routers; therefore, RIP is suppressed on Router A with the following commands:

```
router rip
passive-interface serial 0
passive-interface serial 1
```

The RIP routes are redistributed into OSPF by all three routers with the following commands:

```
router ospf 109
redistribute rip subnets
```

The **subnets** keyword tells OSPF to redistribute all subnet routes. Without the **subnets** keyword, only networks that are not subnetted will be redistributed by OSPF. Redistributed routes appear as external type 2 routes in OSPF. Each RIP domain receives information about networks in other RIP domains and in the OSPF backbone area from the following commands that redistribute OSPF routes into RIP:

```
router rip
redistribute ospf 109 match internal external 1 external 2
default-metric 10
```

The **redistribute** command uses the **ospf** keyword to specify that OSPF routes are to be redistributed into RIP. The keyword **internal** indicates the OSPF intra-area and interarea routes: External 1 is the external route type 1, and external 2 is the external route type 2. Because the command in the example uses the default behavior, these keywords may not appear when you use the **write terminal** or **show configuration** commands.

Because metrics for different protocols cannot be directly compared, you must specify the default metric in order to designate the cost of the redistributed route used in RIP updates. All routes that are redistributed will use the default metric.

In Figure 14–2, there are no paths directly connecting the RIP clouds. However, in typical networks, these paths, or "back doors," frequently exist, allowing the potential for feedback loops. You can use access lists to determine the routes that are advertised and accepted by each router. For example, access list 11 in the configuration file for Router A allows OSPF to redistribute information learned from RIP only for networks 130.10.8.0 through 130.10.15.0:

```
router ospf 109
redistribute rip subnet
distribute-list 11 out rip
access-list 11 permit 130.10.8.0 0.0.7.255
access-list 11 deny 0.0.0.0 255.255.255.255
```

These commands prevent Router A from advertising networks in other RIP domains onto the OSPF backbone, thereby preventing other boundary routers from using false information and forming a loop.

Configuration File Examples

The full configuration for Router A follows:

```
interface serial 0
ip address 130.10.62.1 255.255.255.0
interface serial 1
ip address 130.10.63.1 255.255.255.0
interface ethernet 0
ip address 130.10.8.1 255.255.255.0
interface tokenring 0
ip address 130.10.9.1 255.255.255.0
!
router rip
default-metric 10
network 130.10.0.0
passive-interface serial 0
passive-interface serial 1
```

```
redistribute ospf 109 match internal external 1 external 2
!
router ospf 109
network 130.10.62.0 0.0.0.255 area 0
network 130.10.63.0 0.0.0.255 area 0
redistribute rip subnets
distribute-list 11 out rip
!
access-list 11 permit 130.10.8.0 0.0.7.255
access-list 11 deny 0.0.0.0 255.255.255.255
```

The full configuration for Router B follows:

```
interface serial 0
ip address 130.10.62.2 255.255.255.0
interface serial 1
ip address 130.10.64.2 255.255.255.0
interface ethernet 0
ip address 130.10.17.2 255.255.255.0
interface tokenring 0
ip address 130.10.16.2 255.255.255.0
!
router rip
default-metric 10
network 130.10.0.0
passive-interface serial 0
passive-interface serial 1
redistribute ospf 109 match internal external 1 external 2
!
router ospf 109
network 130.10.62.0 0.0.0.255 area 0
network 130.10.64.0 0.0.0.255 area 0
redistribute rip subnets
distribute-list 11 out rip
access-list 11 permit 130.10.16.0 0.0.7.255
access-list 11 deny 0.0.0.0 255.255.255.255
```

The full configuration for Router C follows:

```
interface serial 0
ip address 130.10.63.3 255.255.255.0
interface serial 1
ip address 130.10.64.3 255.255.255.0
interface ethernet 0
ip address 130.10.24.3 255.255.255.0
!
router rip
default-metric 10
!
network 130.10.0.0
passive-interface serial 0
passive-interface serial 1
redistribute ospf 109 match internal external 1 external 2
!
router ospf 109
network 130.10.63.0 0.0.0.255 area 0
network 130.10.64.0 0.0.0.255 area 0
```

```
redistribute rip subnets
distribute-list 11 out rip
access-list 11 permit 130.10.24.0 0.0.7.255
access-list 11 deny 0.0.0.0 255.255.255.255
```

ADDING OSPF AREAS

Figure 14–3 illustrates how each of the RIP clouds can be converted into an OSPF area. All three routers are area border routers. Area border routers control network information distribution between OSPF areas and the OSPF backbone. Each router keeps a detailed record of the topology of its area and receives summarized information from the other area border routers on their respective areas.

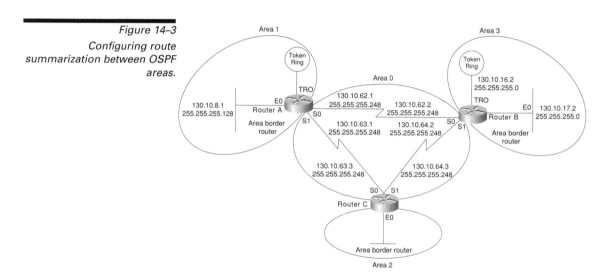

Figure 14–3

Configuring route summarization between OSPF areas.

Figure 14–3 also illustrates *variable-length subnet masks* (VLSMs). VLSMs use different size network masks in different parts of the network for the same network number. VLSM conserves address space by using a longer mask in portions of the network that have fewer hosts. Table 14–2 lists the network address assignments for the network, including the network number, subnet range, and subnet masks. All interfaces indicate network 130.10.0.0.

Table 14–2 *OSPF Address Assignments*

Network Number	Subnets	Subnet Masks
130.10.0.0	**Area 0:** 62 through 64	255.255.255.248
130.10.0.0	**Area 1:** 8 through 15	255.255.255.0
130.10.0.0	**Area 2:** 16 through 23	255.255.255.0
130.10.0.0	**Area 3:** 24 through 31	255.255.255.0

To conserve address space, a mask of 255.255.255.248 is used for all the serial lines in area 0. If an area contains a contiguous range of network numbers, an area border router uses the **range** keyword with the **area** command to summarize the routes that are injected into the backbone:

```
router ospf 109
network 130.10.8.0 0.0.7.255 area 1
area 1 range 130.10.8.0 255.255.248.0
```

These commands allow Router A to advertise one route, 130.10.8.0 255.255.248.0, which covers all subnets in Area 1 into Area 0. Without the **range** keyword in the **area** command, Router A would advertise each subnet individually; for example, one route for 130.10.8.0 255.255.255.0, one route for 130.10.9.0 255.255.255.0, and so forth.

Because Router A no longer needs to redistribute RIP routes, the **router rip** command can now be removed from the configuration file; however, it is common in some environments for hosts to use RIP to discover routers. When RIP is removed from the routers, the hosts must use an alternative technique to find the routers. Cisco routers support the following alternatives to RIP:

- *ICMP Router Discovery Protocol (IRDP)*—This technique is illustrated in the example at the end of this section. IRDP is the recommended method for discovering routers. The **ip irdp** command enables IRDP on the router. Hosts must also run IRDP.

- *Proxy Address Resolution Protocol (ARP)*—If the router receives an ARP request for a host that is not on the same network as the ARP request sender, and if the router has the best route to that host, the router sends an ARP reply packet giving the router's own local data link address. The host that sent the ARP request then sends its packets to the router, which forwards them to the intended host. Proxy ARP is enabled on routers by default. Proxy ARP is transparent to hosts.

Configuration File Examples

The full configuration for Router A follows:

```
interface serial 0
ip address 130.10.62.1 255.255.255.248
interface serial 1
ip address 130.10.63.1 255.255.255.248
interface ethernet 0
ip address 130.10.8.1 255.255.255.0
ip irdp
interface tokenring 0
ip address 130.10.9.1 255.255.255.0
ip irdp
router ospf 109
network 130.10.62.0 0.0.0.255 area 0
network 130.10.63.0 0.0.0.255 area 0
network 130.10.8.0 0.0.7.255 area 1
area 1 range 130.10.8.0 255.255.248.0
```

The full configuration for Router B follows:

```
interface serial 0
ip address 130.10.62.2 255.255.255.248
interface serial 1
```

```
ip address 130.10.64.2 255.255.255.248
interface ethernet 0
ip address 130.10.17.2 255.255.255.0
ip irdp
interface tokenring 0
ip address 130.10.16.2 255.255.255.0
ip irdp
router ospf 109
network 130.10.62.0 0.0.0.255 area 0
network 130.10.64.0 0.0.0.255 area 0
network 130.10.16.0 0.0.7.255 area 2
area 2 range 130.10.16.0 255.255.248.0
```

The full configuration for Router C follows:

```
interface serial 0
ip address 130.10.63.2 255.255.255.248
interface serial 1
ip address 130.10.64.2 255.255.255.248
interface ethernet 0
ip address 130.10.24.3 255.255.255.0
ip irdp
router ospf 109
network 130.10.63.0 0.0.0.255 area 0
network 130.10.64.0 0.0.0.255 area 0
network 130.10.24.0 0.0.0.255 area 3
area 3 range 130.10.24.0 255.255.248.0
```

SETTING UP MUTUAL REDISTRIBUTION

It is sometimes necessary to accommodate more complex network topologies such as independent RIP and OSPF clouds that must perform mutual redistribution. In this scenario, it is critically important to prevent potential routing loops by filtering routes. The router in Figure 14–4 is running both OSPF and RIP.

Figure 14–4

Mutual redistribution between RIP and OSPF networks.

With the following commands, OSPF routes will be redistributed into RIP. You must specify the default metric to designate the cost of the redistributed route in RIP updates. All routes redistributed into RIP will have this default metric.

```
! passive interface subcommand from previous example is left out for clarity!
router rip
default-metric 10
network 130.10.0.0
redistribute ospf 109
```

It is a good practice to strictly control which routes are advertised when redistribution is configured. In the following example, a **distribute-list out** command causes RIP to ignore routes coming from the OSPF that originated from the RIP domain.

```
router rip
distribute-list 10 out ospf 109
!
access-list 10 deny 130.10.8.0 0.0.7.255
access-list 10 permit 0.0.0.0 255.255.255.255
```

Router A

The full configuration for the router follows:

```
interface serial 0
ip add 130.10.62.1 255.255.255.0
!
interface serial 1
ip add 130.10.63.1 255.255.255.0
!
interface ethernet 0
ip add 130.10.8.1 255.255.255.0
!
interface tokenring 0
ip add 130.10.9.1 255.255.255.0
!
router rip
default-metric 10
network 130.10.0.0
passive-interface serial 0
passive-interface serial 1
redistribute ospf 109
distribute-list 10 out ospf 109
!
router ospf 109
network 130.10.62.0 0.0.0.255 area 0
network 130.10.63.0 0.0.0.255 area 0
redistribute rip subnets
distribute-list 11 out rip
!
access-list 10 deny 130.10.8.0 0.0.7.255
access-list 10 permit 0.0.0.0 255.255.255.255
access-list 11 permit 130.10.8.0 0.0.7.255
access-list 11 deny 0.0.0.0 255.255.255.255
```

SUMMARY

Because it is common for OSPF and RIP to be used together, it is important to use the practices described here in order to provide functionality for both protocols on an internetwork. You can configure autonomous system boundary routers that run both RIP and OSPF and redistribute RIP routes into the OSPF and vice versa. You can also create OSPF areas using area border routers that provide route summarizations. Use VLSM to conserve address space.

Dial-on-Demand Routing

Cisco's dial-on-demand routing (DDR) feature allows you to use existing telephone lines to form a wide-area network (WAN). While using existing telephone lines, you can analyze traffic patterns to determine whether the installation of leased lines is appropriate. DDR provides significant cost savings over leased lines for links that are utilized for only a few hours each day or that experience low traffic flow.

DDR over serial lines requires the use of dialing devices that support V.25bis. V.25bis is an International Telecommunication Union Telecommunication (ITU-T) Standardization Sector standard for in-band signaling to bit synchronous data communications equipment (DCE) devices. A variety of devices support V.25bis, including analog V.32 modems, ISDN terminal adapters, and inverse multiplexers. Cisco's implementation of V.25bis supports devices that use the 1984 version of V.25bis (which requires the use of odd parity), as well as devices that use the 1988 version of V.25bis (which does not use parity).

NOTES

The ITU-T carries out the functions of the former Consultative Committee for International Telegraph and Telephone (CCITT).

This case study describes the use of DDR to connect a worldwide network that consists of a central site located in San Francisco and remote sites located in Tokyo, Singapore, and Hong Kong. The following scenarios and configuration file examples are described:

- Having the Central Site Dial Out

  Describes the central and remote site configurations for three setups: a central site with one interface per remote site, a single interface for multiple remote sites, and multiple interfaces for multiple remote sites. Includes examples of the usage of rotary groups and access lists.

- Having the Central and Remote Sites Dial In and Dial Out

  Describes the central and remote site configurations for three setups: central site with one interface per remote site, a single interface for multiple remote sites, and multiple interfaces for multiple remote sites. Also describes the usage of Point-to-Point Protocol (PPP) encapsulation and the Challenge Handshake Authentication Protocol (CHAP).

- Having Remote Sites Dial Out

  A common configuration is one in which the remote sites place calls to the central site but the central site does not dial out. In a "star" topology, it is possible for all of the remote routers to have their serial interfaces on the same subnet as the central site serial interface.

- Using DDR as a Backup to Leased Lines

  Describes the use of DDR as a backup method to leased lines and provides examples of how to use floating static routes on single and shared interfaces.

- Using Leased Lines and Dial Backup

  Describes the use of Data Terminal Ready (DTR) dialing and V.25bis dialing with leased lines.

Figure 15–1 shows the topology of the DDR network that is the subject of this case study.

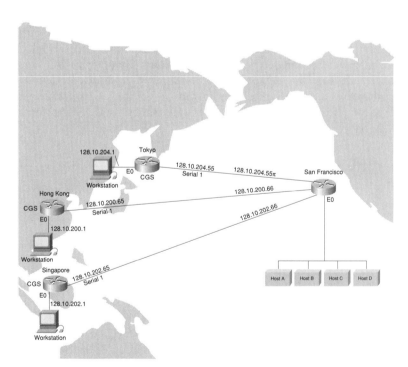

Figure 15–1

DDR internetwork topology.

NOTES

All examples and descriptions in this case study refer to features available in Software Release 9.1(9) or later. Some features are available in earlier releases. Features that are available only in Software Release 9.21 are indicated as such.

HAVING THE CENTRAL SITE DIAL OUT

In this example, the central site calls the remote sites. The cost of initiating a call from the United States to international sites is often lower than if the remote sites initiate the call, and it is expected that remote offices need to connect to the central site network only periodically. This section provides the following configuration examples in which the central site is configured to dial out:

- Configuring One Interface Per Remote Site
- Configuring a Single Interface for Multiple Remote Sites
- Configuring Multiple Interfaces for Multiple Remote Sites

Configuring One Interface Per Remote Site

For the initial configuration, the San Francisco central site is configured to have one interface per remote site.

Central Site: Dial Out Only

In the following configuration, the central site places the calls with a separate interface configured for each remote site. There is no support for answering calls in this configuration.

```
interface serial 5
description DDR connection to Hong Kong
ip address 128.10.200.66 255.255.255.192
dialer in-band
dialer wait-for-carrier-time 60
dialer string 0118527351625
pulse-time 1
dialer-group 1
!
interface serial 6
description DDR connection to Singapore
ip address 128.10.202.66 255.255.255.192
dialer in-band
dialer wait-for-carrier-time 60
dialer string 011653367085
pulse-time 1
dialer-group 1
!
interface serial 7
description DDR connection to Tokyo
ip address 128.10.204.66 255.255.255.192
dialer in-band
dialer wait-for-carrier-time 60
```

```
dialer string 0118127351625
pulse-time 1
dialer-group 1
!
router igrp 1
network 128.10.0.0
redistribute static
! route to Hong Kong
ip route 128.10.200.0 255.255.255.192 128.10.200.65
! route to Singapore
ip route 128.10.202.0 255.255.255.192 128.10.202.65
! route to Tokyo
ip route 128.10.204.0 255.255.255.192 128.10.204.65
access-list 101 deny igrp 0.0.0.0 255.255.255.255 255.255.255.255 0.0.0.0
access-list 101 permit ip 0.0.0.0 255.255.255.255 0.0.0.0 255.255.255.255
dialer-list 1 list 101
```

Interface Configuration

The configuration of the individual interfaces and Internet Protocol (IP) addresses is straightforward. The IP address for each interface is provided. The example uses a 6-bit host portion in IP addresses. The **dialer in-band** command enables DDR and V.25bis dialing on the interface. V.25bis is a ITU-T standard for in-band signaling to bit synchronous DCE devices. A variety of devices support V.25bis, ranging from analog V.32 modems to ISDN terminal adapters to inverse multiplexers.

The **dialer wait-for-carrier-time** command is set to 60 seconds. When using V.25bis, the router does not parse any responses it receives from the DCE. Instead, the router depends on the modem's Carrier Detect (CD) signal to indicate that a call has been connected. If the modem's CD signal is not activated before the time allotted with the **dialer wait-for-carrier-time** command, the router assumes that the call has failed and disconnects the line. Because the calls are international, and thus take longer to connect than local calls, the wait for carrier time is set to 60 seconds. Even for local calls, analog modems can take 20 to 30 seconds to synchronize to each other, including the time to dial and answer.

The **dialer string** command identifies the telephone number of the targeted destination. Because the central site is calling only a single destination, this dialer string is the simplest possible configuration. The **pulse-time** command specifies how long Data Terminal Ready (DTR) is held inactive. When using DDR and V.25bis modems, the router disconnects calls by deactivating DTR. This command is automatically inserted into the configuration when the **dialer in-band** command is entered.

The **dialer-group** command is used to identify each interface with a dialer list set. The **dialer-list** command associates each interface with access lists that determine which packets are "interesting" versus "uninteresting" for an interface. For details on access lists and dialer lists, see the "Access List Configuration" section that follows.

Routing Configuration

The Interior Gateway Routing Protocol (IGRP) is used to route traffic on the network. The first two commands in the routing section of the configuration file are **router igrp** and **network**. These define the IGRP number and the network over which IGRP runs.

The **redistribute** command causes the static route information (defined with the **ip route** commands shown in the configuration example) to be sent to other routers in the same IGRP area. Without this command, other routers connected to the central site will not have routes to the remote routers. The three static routes define the subnets on the Ethernet backbone of the remote routers. DDR tends to use static routes extensively because routing updates are not received when the dial-up connection is not active.

Access List Configuration

The last section of the configuration file provides the access lists that DDR uses to classify "interesting" and "uninteresting" packets. Interesting packets are packets that pass the restrictions of the access lists. These packets either initiate a call (if one is not already in progress) or reset the idle timer if a call is in progress. Uninteresting packets are transmitted if the link is active, but dropped if the link is not active. Uninteresting packets do not initiate calls or reset the idle timer. Access list 101 provides the following filters:

- IGRP packets that are sent to the broadcast address (255.255.255.255) do not cause dialing.
- All other IP packets are interesting and thus may cause dialing and reset the idle timer.

Remote Sites: Dial In Only

Except for the IP address and the default route, each of the remote sites is configured identically as an answer-only site. The following example lists Hong Kong's configuration:

```
interface serial 1
description interface to answer calls from San Francisco
ip address 128.10.200.65 255.255.255.192
dialer in-band
!
ip route 0.0.0.0 0.0.0.0 128.10.200.66
```

The answering site will not disconnect the call. It is up to the calling site to disconnect the call when the line is idle. In this case, the answering site is using static routing. The default route points to the serial interface at the central site.

Configuring a Single Interface for Multiple Remote Sites

It is possible to use a single interface to call multiple destinations, such as a site in Hong Kong and a site in Paris, France. Because of the time differences, these sites would never need to be connected at the same time. Therefore, a single interface could be used for both sites without the possibility of contention for the interface and without the cost of dedicating a serial port and modem to each destination.

Central Site: Dial Out Only

In the following configuration, the central site places the calls. A single interface is configured to call multiple remote sites. There is no support for answering calls in this configuration.

```
interface serial 5
description DDR connection to Hong Kong and Singapore
ip address 128.10.200.66 255.255.255.192
ip address 128.10.202.66 255.255.255.192 secondary
dialer in-band
dialer wait-for-carrier-time 60
! map Hong Kong to a phone number
dialer map ip 128.10.200.65 0118527351625
! map Singapore to a phone number
dialer map ip 128.10.202.65 011653367085
pulse-time 1
dialer-group 1
!
router igrp 1
network 128.10.0.0
passive-interface serial 5
redistribute static
! route to Hong Kong
ip route 128.10.200.0 255.255.255.192 128.10.200.65
! route to Singapore
ip route 128.10.202.0 255.255.255.192 128.10.202.65
!
access-list 101 deny igrp 0.0.0.0 255.255.255.255 255.255.255.255 0.0.0.0
access-list 101 permit ip 0.0.0.0 255.255.255.255 0.0.0.0 255.255.255.255
dialer-list 1 list 101
```

Interface Configuration

The configuration of the interface in this example is slightly more complicated than the configuration described in the "Configuring One Interface Per Remote Site" section. In addition to the original IP address, there is a secondary IP address configured for serial interface 5 because the Singapore and Hong Kong offices are on different subnets.

The **dialer in-band, dialer wait-for-carrier-time, pulse-time,** and **dialer-group** commands are used in the same manner as described previously in the "Configuring One Interface Per Remote Site" section. However, the previous **dialer string** command has been removed and replaced with two **dialer map** commands.

The first **dialer map** command maps the telephone number for Hong Kong to its next hop address, which is the IP address of the serial port of the router in Hong Kong. The second **dialer map** command maps the telephone number for the Singapore router to the next hop address for Singapore.

Routing Configuration

The IP static routes define the next hops used in the **dialer map** commands. When a packet is received for a host on network 128.10.200.0, it is routed to a next hop address of 128.10.200.65. This route goes out serial interface 5. DDR uses the next hop address to obtain the telephone number of the destination router.

NOTES

The use of the **passive-interface** command states that routing updates are not to be sent out serial interface 5. Because the remote sites are using a default route, there is no need to send routing updates over the wire.

Access List Configuration

The use of **dialer map** commands provides an additional level of filtering. When a packet is received for a host on network 128.10.200.0, it is routed to a next hop address of 128.10.200.65. This route goes out serial interface 5. The packet is compared to the access lists. If the packet is deemed "interesting," the packet's next hop address is compared to the **dialer map** commands defined for that interface. If a match is found, the interface is checked to determine whether it is connected to the telephone number for that next hop address. If the interface is not connected, a call is placed to the telephone number. If the interface is currently connected to that number, the idle timer is reset. If the interface is connected to another number (from another **dialer map** command), the fast-idle timer is started due to contention for the interface. If there is no match of the next hop address to any of the dialer maps and there is no dialer string defined (which matches all next hop addresses), the packet is dropped.

This additional layer of filtering for the next hop address causes problems for broadcast packets such as routing updates. Because a broadcast packet is transmitted with a next hop address of the broadcast address, the check against the **dialer map** commands will fail. If you want broadcast packets transmitted to telephone numbers defined by **dialer map** commands, additional **dialer map** commands must specify the broadcast address as the next hop address with the same telephone number. For example, you might add the following **dialer map** commands:

```
dialer map ip 255.255.255.255 0118527351625
dialer map ip 255.255.255.255 011653367085
```

If the interface is currently connected to one of these telephone numbers, and if it receives an IGRP broadcast packet, that packet will now be transmitted because it matches a **dialer map** command to an already connected telephone number. (If the connection is already established, both "interesting" and "uninteresting" packets are sent.) If a connection is not already established, adding the **dialer map** commands will not cause an IGRP packet sent to the broadcast address to cause dialing because the access lists determine that the IGRP packet is uninteresting.

NOTES

In the configuration example described in the "Configuring a Single Interface for Multiple Remote Sites" section, the **dialer string** command permits broadcast packets to be sent when the link is connected because the dialer string matches all next hop addresses that did not have a dialer map.

Remote Sites: Dial In Only

Except for the IP address and the default route, each of the remote sites is configured identically as an answer-only site. The following example illustrates the Hong Kong configuration:

```
interface serial 1
description interface to answer calls from San Francisco
ip address 128.10.200.65 255.255.255.192
dialer in-band
!
ip route 0.0.0.0 0.0.0.0 128.10.200.66
```

The answering site will not disconnect the call. It is up to the calling site to disconnect the call when the line is idle. A default route is defined back to the central site.

Configuring Multiple Interfaces for Multiple Remote Sites

When using a single interface with dialer maps, contention for the interface can occur. This contention starts a fast-idle timer that causes lines to remain connected for a shorter idle time than usual, allowing other destinations to use the interface. Dialer rotary groups prevent contention by creating a set of interfaces that can be used to dial out. Rather than statically assigning an interface to a destination, dialer rotary groups allow dynamic allocation of interfaces to telephone numbers. Before a call is placed, the rotary group is searched for an interface that is not in use to place the call. It is not until all of the interfaces in the rotary group are in use that the fast-idle timer is started.

NOTES

The following configurations appear as they would be entered at the command line. Due to the way dialer rotary groups function, the output from a **write terminal** command on the router may differ slightly from what is shown here.

Central Site: Dial Out Only

The following configuration defines dialer rotary groups on the central site router:

```
interface dialer 1
description rotary group for Hong Kong, Tokyo, and Singapore
ip address 128.10.200.66 255.255.255.192
ip address 128.10.202.66 255.255.255.192 secondary
ip address 128.10.204.66 255.255.255.192 secondary
dialer in-band
dialer wait-for-carrier-time 60
! map Hong Kong to a phone number
dialer map ip 128.10.200.65 0118527351625
! map Singapore to a phone number
dialer map ip 128.10.202.65 011653367085
! map Tokyo to a phone number
dialer map ip 128.10.204.65 0118127351625
pulse-time 1
dialer-group 1
!
interface serial 5
```

```
dialer rotary-group 1
!
interface serial 6
dialer rotary-group 1
!
router igrp 1
network 128.10.0.0
passive-interface dialer 1
redistribute static
!
! route to Hong Kong
ip route 128.10.200.0 255.255.255.192 128.10.200.65
! route to Singapore
ip route 128.10.202.0 255.255.255.192 128.10.202.65
! route to Tokyo
ip route 128.10.204.0 255.255.255.192 128.10.204.65
!
access-list 101 deny igrp 0.0.0.0 255.255.255.255 255.255.255.255 0.0.0.0
access-list 101 permit ip 0.0.0.0 255.255.255.255 0.0.0.0 255.255.255.255
dialer-list 1 list 101
```

Interface Configuration

Specifying a dialer interface is the first step in defining a dialer rotary group. While a dialer interface is not a physical interface, all of the configuration commands that can be specified for a physical interface can be used for a dialer interface. For example, the commands listed under the **interface dialer** command are identical to those used for physical serial interface 5 as described in the "Configuring a Single Interface for Multiple Remote Sites" section. Also, an additional **dialer map** command has been added to map the next hop address for Tokyo to the telephone number.

The **dialer rotary-group** command places physical serial interface 5 and serial interface 6 in the rotary group. Either of these interfaces can be used to dial any of the destinations defined by the **interface dialer** command.

As mentioned earlier, when you look at the configuration on the router using the **write terminal** command, the configuration may look slightly different from your input. For example, the **pulse-time** command associated with the dialer interface will appear with all of the serial interfaces that were added with the **dialer rotary-group** command. Certain configuration information associated with the dialer interface is propagated to all of the interfaces that are in the rotary group.

Routing Configuration

The routing section of this configuration has not changed from the example in the "Configuring a Single Interface for Multiple Remote Sites" section. But if you were to examine the routing table for one of the remote networks using the **show ip route** command (for example, **show ip route 128.10.200.0**), you would see that the output interface for packets sent to this subnet is interface dialer 1. The actual physical interface over which the packet will be transmitted is not determined until the DDR steps described in the following paragraph are performed.

Before a packet is sent out the dialer interface, DDR checks to determine whether the packet is "interesting" or "uninteresting." DDR then checks the dialer map. Next, all of the physical interfaces in the rotary group are checked to determine whether they are connected to the telephone number. If an appropriate interface is found, the packet is sent out that physical interface. If an interface is not found and the packet is deemed interesting, the rotary group is scanned for an available physical interface. The first available interface found is used to place a call to the telephone number.

— ◁ **NOTES** ▷ ————————————————————————————————

To use dynamic routing, in which two of the remote sites communicate with each other via the central site, the **no ip split-horizon** command is required and the **passive-interface** command must be removed.

Access List Configuration

This configuration uses the same access lists as the example in the "Configuring a Single Interface for Multiple Remote Sites" section. A default route is defined back to the central site.

Remote Sites: Dial In Only

Except for the IP address and the default route, each of the remote sites is configured identically as an answer-only site. The following example illustrates the Hong Kong configuration:

```
interface serial 1
description interface to answer calls from San Francisco
ip address 128.10.200.65 255.255.255.192
dialer in-band
!
ip route 0.0.0.0 0.0.0.0 128.10.200.66
```

The answering site will not disconnect the call. It is up to the calling site to disconnect the call when the line is idle.

HAVING THE CENTRAL AND REMOTE SITES DIAL IN AND DIAL OUT

It is often more convenient to have the remote sites call the central site as its users require, instead of depending on the central site to poll the remote sites. This section provides the following configuration examples in which both the central site and the remote sites are placing calls:

- Configuring One Interface Per Remote Site
- Configuring a Single Interface for Multiple Remote Sites
- Configuring Multiple Interfaces for Multiple Remote Sites

Configuring One Interface Per Remote Site

In order to support dial-in and dial-out for both the central and remote sites using one interface per remote site, each remote site must call in on the specific central site interface that has the dialer string corresponding to the respective remote site telephone number.

Central Site: Dial In and Dial Out

In the following example, the central San Francisco site is configured to place and answer calls. One interface is configured per remote site.

```
interface serial 5
description DDR connection to Hong Kong
ip address 128.10.200.66 255.255.255.192
dialer in-band
dialer wait-for-carrier-time 60
dialer string 0118527351625
pulse-time 1
dialer-group 1
!
interface serial 6
description DDR connection to Singapore
ip address 128.10.202.66 255.255.255.192
dialer in-band
dialer wait-for-carrier-time 60
dialer string 011653367085
pulse-time 1
dialer-group 1
!
interface serial 7
description DDR connection to Tokyo
ip address 128.10.204.66 255.255.255.192
dialer in-band
dialer wait-for-carrier-time 60
dialer string 0118127351625
pulse-time 1
dialer-group 1
!
router igrp 1
network 128.10.0.0
redistribute static
!
! route to Hong Kong
ip route 128.10.200.0 255.255.255.192 128.10.200.65
! route to Singapore
ip route 128.10.202.0 255.255.255.192 128.10.202.65
! route to Tokyo
ip route 128.10.204.0 255.255.255.192 128.10.204.65
!
access-list 101 deny igrp 0.0.0.0 255.255.255.255 255.255.255.255 0.0.0.0
access-list 101 permit ip 0.0.0.0 255.255.255.255 0.0.0.0 255.255.255.255
dialer-list 1 list 101
```

Remote Sites: Dial In and Dial Out

All of the remote configurations are similar. Each defines a default route back to the central site and a dialer string that contains the telephone number of the central site.

Hong Kong

In the following example, the remote Hong Kong site is configured to place and answer calls. Hong Kong's configuration file contains a dialer string of 14155551212, which should call serial interface 5 in San Francisco.

```
interface serial 1
description DDR connection to San Francisco
ip address 128.10.200.65 255.255.255.192
dialer in-band
dialer wait-for-carrier-time 60
dialer string 14155551212
pulse-time 1
dialer-group 1
!
router igrp 1
network 128.10.0.0
!
ip route 128.10.0.0 255.255.0.0 128.10.200.66
!
access-list 101 deny igrp 0.0.0.0 255.255.255.255 255.255.255.255 0.0.0.0
access-list 101 permit ip 0.0.0.0 255.255.255.255 0.0.0.0 255.255.255.255
dialer-list 1 list 101
```

Singapore

In the following example, the remote Singapore site is configured to place and answer calls. The Singapore configuration file contains a dialer string of 14155551213, which should call serial interface 6 in San Francisco.

```
interface serial 1
description DDR connection to San Francisco
ip address 128.10.202.65 255.255.255.192
dialer in-band
dialer wait-for-carrier-time 60
dialer string 14155551213
pulse-time 1
dialer-group 1
!
router igrp 1
network 128.10.0.0
!
ip route 128.10.0.0 255.255.0.0 128.10.202.66
!
access-list 101 deny igrp 0.0.0.0 255.255.255.255 255.255.255.255 0.0.0.0
access-list 101 permit ip 0.0.0.0 255.255.255.255 0.0.0.0 255.255.255.255
dialer-list 1 list 101
```

Tokyo

In the following example, the remote Tokyo site is configured to place and answer calls. The Tokyo configuration file contains a dialer string of 14155551214, which should call serial interface 7 in San Francisco.

```
interface serial 1
description DDR connection to San Francisco
ip address 128.10.204.65 255.255.255.192
dialer in-band
dialer wait-for-carrier-time 60
dialer string 14155551214
pulse-time 1
dialer-group 1
router igrp 1
network 128.10.0.0
!
ip route 128.10.0.0 255.255.0.0 128.10.204.66
!
access-list 101 deny igrp 0.0.0.0 255.255.255.255 255.255.255.255 0.0.0.0
access-list 101 permit ip 0.0.0.0 255.255.255.255 0.0.0.0 255.255.255.255
dialer-list 1 list 101
```

Because all incoming calls are assumed to be from the telephone number configured with the **dialer string** command, it is important to configure the central and remote sites correctly. For example, if the Singapore dialer string uses the telephone number that Hong Kong uses to call the central site, packets from the central site intended for Hong Kong would be sent to Singapore whenever Singapore called in because Singapore called in using the Hong Kong interface.

Configuring a Single Interface for Multiple Remote Sites

When multiple sites are calling into a central site, an authentication mechanism must be used unless that central site has one interface dedicated to each incoming call. Without the authentication mechanism, the central site router has no way of identifying the sites to which it is currently connected and cannot ensure that additional calls are not made. Point-to-Point Protocol (PPP) encapsulation with CHAP or Password Authentication Protocol (PAP) provides the mechanism to identify the calling party.

NOTES

A router with a built-in ISDN port may be able to use calling party identification. Because calling party identification is not available everywhere, PPP with CHAP provides the identification mechanism. In Software Release 9.21, PPP and Password Authentication Protocol (PAP) can be used in place of CHAP, although PAP is less secure than CHAP. The configuration of PAP would differ slightly from the configuration for CHAP illustrated in this section.

Central Site: Dial In and Dial Out

In the following example, the central San Francisco site is configured to place and answer calls. A single interface is configured for multiple remote sites.

```
hostname SanFrancisco
interface serial 5
description DDR connection to Hong Kong and Singapore
ip address 128.10.200.66 255.255.255.192
ip address 128.10.202.66 255.255.255.192 secondary
```

```
encapsulation ppp
ppp authentication chap
dialer in-band
dialer wait-for-carrier-time 60
dialer map ip 128.10.200.65 name HongKong 0118527351625
dialer map ip 128.10.202.65 name Singapore 011653367085
pulse-time 1
dialer-group 1
!
router igrp 1
network 128.10.0.0
passive-interface serial 5
redistribute static
!
! route to Hong Kong
ip route 128.10.200.0 255.255.255.192 128.10.200.65
! route to Singapore
ip route 128.10.202.0 255.255.255.192 128.10.202.65
access-list 101 deny igrp 0.0.0.0 255.255.255.255 255.255.255.255 0.0.0.0
access-list 101 permit ip 0.0.0.0 255.255.255.255 0.0.0.0 255.255.255.255
dialer-list 1 list 101
!
username HongKong password password1
username Singapore password password2
```

The command **encapsulation ppp** enables PPP encapsulation. The command **ppp authentication chap** enables CHAP authentication. In addition, **username** commands are entered for each of the remote sites that place calls. The **username** command defines the name of the remote router and a password to be associated with that router. When **ppp authentication chap** is configured, authentication must be verified or else network traffic will not be transmitted.

The **dialer map** command contains the host name of the remote router. This associates the remote router with a next hop address and a telephone number. When a packet is received for a host on network 128.10.200.0, it is routed to a next hop address of 128.10.200.65 via serial interface 5. The packet is compared to the access lists and then the packet's next hop address is compared to the **dialer map** commands for serial interface 5.

If the packet is "interesting" and a connection to the number in the **dialer map** command is already active on the interface, the idle timer is reset. If a match is found, DDR checks the interface to determine whether it is connected to the telephone number for the next hop address. The comparison to the telephone number is useful only if the router placed the call or if the telephone number was received via calling party ID on an ISDN router. With CHAP and the **name** keyword included in the **dialer map** command, both the telephone number and the name for a given next hop address are compared to the names of the routers already connected. In this way, calls to destinations to which connections are already established can be avoided.

Remote Sites: Dial In and Dial Out

In the following configuration examples, the remote sites are configured to place and receive calls to or from a single interface at the central site.

Hong Kong

The following configuration allows Hong Kong to place and receive calls to and from the central site in San Francisco:

```
hostname HongKong
interface serial 1
description DDR connection to SanFrancisco
ip address 128.10.200.65 255.255.255.192
encapsulation ppp
dialer in-band
dialer wait-for-carrier-time 60
dialer string 14155551212
pulse-time 1
dialer-group 1
!
router igrp 1
network 128.10.0.0
!
ip route 128.10.0.0 255.255.0.0 128.10.200.66
!
access-list 101 deny igrp 0.0.0.0 255.255.255.255 255.255.255.255 0.0.0.0
access-list 101 permit ip 0.0.0.0 255.255.255.255 0.0.0.0 255.255.255.255
dialer-list 1 list 101
!
username SanFrancisco password password1
```

Singapore

The following configuration allows Singapore to place and receive calls to and from the central site in San Francisco:

```
hostname Singapore
interface serial 1
description DDR connection to San Francisco
ip address 128.10.202.65 255.255.255.192
encapsulation ppp
dialer in-band
dialer wait-for-carrier-time 60
dialer string 14155551212
pulse-time 1
dialer-group 1
!
router igrp 1
network 128.10.0.0
ip route 128.10.0.0 255.255.0.0 128.10.202.66
!
access-list 101 deny igrp 0.0.0.0 255.255.255.255 255.255.255.255 0.0.0.0
access-list 101 permit ip 0.0.0.0 255.255.255.255 0.0.0.0 255.255.255.255
dialer-list 1 list 101
!
username SanFrancisco password password2
```

Unlike the central site, the remote sites do not contain the **ppp authentication chap** command. This is because only one site, the central site, is calling in to the remote sites. If only one site is calling in,

DDR assumes the call is from the number defined with the **dialer string** command; therefore, the command **ppp authentication chap** is not required.

NOTES

If the remote sites use **dialer map** commands instead of **dialer string**, the **ppp authentication chap** command is required, and the **dialer map** commands require the **name** keyword. This is because the assumption is made that if the **dialer map** command is used, multiple sites either can be called or can call in.

Also, the remote sites have a **username** entry for the San Francisco router, and the San Francisco router contains the username passwords for Singapore and Hong Kong.

Configuring Multiple Interfaces for Multiple Remote Sites

The configurations in this section are similar to the examples provided in the earlier "Configuring a Single Interface for Multiple Remote Sites" section. The encapsulation is set to PPP and CHAP authentication is required.

Central Site: Dial In and Dial Out

The following example configures the central site router to dial in and dial out on multiple interfaces to multiple remote sites:

```
hostname SanFrancisco
interface dialer 1
description rotary group for Hong Kong, Tokyo, and Singapore
ip address 128.10.200.66 255.255.255.192
ip address 128.10.202.66 255.255.255.192 secondary
ip address 128.10.204.66 255.255.255.192 secondary
encapsulation ppp
ppp authentication chap
dialer in-band
dialer wait-for-carrier-time 60
dialer map ip 128.10.200.65 name HongKong 0118527351625
dialer map ip 128.10.202.65 name Singapore 011653367085
dialer map ip 128.10.204.65 name Tokyo 0118127351625
pulse-time 1
dialer-group 1
!
interface serial 5
dialer rotary-group 1
!
interface serial 6
dialer rotary-group 1
!
router igrp 1
network 128.10.0.0
passive-interface dialer 1
redistribute static
```

```
! route to Hong Kong
ip route 128.10.200.0 255.255.255.192 128.10.200.65
! route to Singapore
ip route 128.10.202.0 255.255.255.192 128.10.202.65
! route to Tokyo
ip route 128.10.204.0 255.255.255.192 128.10.204.65
!
access-list 101 deny igrp 0.0.0.0 255.255.255.255 255.255.255.255 0.0.0.0
access-list 101 permit ip 0.0.0.0 255.255.255.255 0.0.0.0 255.255.255.255
dialer-list 1 list 101
!
username HongKong password password1
username Singapore password password2
username Tokyo password password3
```

Remote Sites: Dial In and Dial Out

In the following configuration examples, the remote sites are configured to place and receive calls to or from multiple interfaces at the central site. All of the remote sites dial the same telephone number. At the San Francisco site, that single telephone number will connect to either serial interface 5 or serial interface 6. This capability is provided by the telephone service provider.

Hong Kong

The following configuration allows Hong Kong to place and receive calls to and from the central site in San Francisco:

```
hostname HongKong
interface serial 1
description DDR connection to SanFrancisco
ip address 128.10.200.65 255.255.255.192
encapsulation ppp
dialer in-band
dialer wait-for-carrier-time 60
dialer string 14155551212
pulse-time 1
dialer-group 1
router igrp 1
network 128.10.0.0
ip route 128.10.0.0 255.255.0.0 128.10.200.66
!
access-list 101 deny igrp 0.0.0.0 255.255.255.255 255.255.255.255 0.0.0.0
access-list 101 permit ip 0.0.0.0 255.255.255.255 0.0.0.0 255.255.255.255
dialer-list 1 list 101
!
username SanFrancisco password password1
```

Singapore

The following configuration allows Singapore to place and receive calls to and from the central site in San Francisco:

```
hostname Singapore
interface serial 1
```

```
description DDR connection to San Francisco
ip address 128.10.202.65 255.255.255.192
encapsulation ppp
dialer in-band
dialer wait-for-carrier-time 60
dialer string 14155551212
pulse-time 1
dialer-group 1
router igrp 1
network 128.10.0.0
ip route 128.10.0.0 255.255.0.0 128.10.202.66
!
access-list 101 deny igrp 0.0.0.0 255.255.255.255 255.255.255.255 0.0.0.0
access-list 101 permit ip 0.0.0.0 255.255.255.255 0.0.0.0 255.255.255.255
dialer-list 1 list 101
!
username SanFrancisco password password2
```

Tokyo

The following configuration allows Tokyo to place and receive calls to and from the central site in San Francisco:

```
hostname Tokyo
interface serial 1
description DDR connection to San Francisco
ip address 128.10.204.65 255.255.255.192
encapsulation ppp
dialer in-band
dialer wait-for-carrier-time 60
dialer string 14155551212
pulse-time 1
dialer-group 1
router igrp 1
network 128.10.0.0
ip route 128.10.0.0 255.255.0.0 128.10.204.66
!
access-list 101 deny igrp 0.0.0.0 255.255.255.255 255.255.255.255 0.0.0.0
access-list 101 permit ip 0.0.0.0 255.255.255.255 0.0.0.0 255.255.255.255
dialer-list 1 list 101
!
username SanFrancisco password password3
```

The remote sites do not use the **ppp authentication chap**. This is because only one site, the central site, is calling in to the remote sites. If only one site is calling in, DDR assumes the call is from the number defined with the **dialer string** command; therefore, the command **ppp authentication chap** is not required. However, if the remote sites use **dialer map** commands instead of **dialer string**, the **ppp authentication chap** command is required, and the **dialer map** commands require the **name** keyword.

Also, each remote site has a **username SanFrancisco** entry containing the same password that the central San Francisco site uses to identify the remote site.

HAVING REMOTE SITES DIAL OUT

A common configuration is to have the remote sites place calls to the central site, which does not dial out.

Configuring Multiple Interfaces for Multiple Remote Sites

In a "star" topology, all the remote routers can have their serial interfaces on the same subnet as the central site serial interface. (See Figure 15–2.)

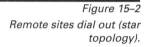

Figure 15–2
Remote sites dial out (star topology).

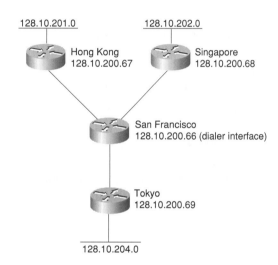

Central Site: Dial In Only

The following example configures the central site router to accept dial-ins on multiple interfaces:

```
hostname SanFrancisco
interface dialer 1
description rotary group for inbound calls
ip address 128.10.200.66 255.255.255.192
encapsulation ppp
ppp authentication chap
dialer in-band
dialer wait-for-carrier-time 60
dialer map ip 128.10.200.67 name HongKong
dialer map ip 128.10.200.68 name Singapore
dialer map ip 128.10.200.69 name Tokyo
pulse-time 1
dialer-group 1
!
interface serial 5
dialer rotary-group 1
!
interface serial 6
```

```
dialer rotary-group 1
!
router igrp 1
network 128.10.0.0
passive-interface dialer 1
redistribute static
! route to Hong Kong
ip route 128.10.201.0 255.255.255.192 128.10.200.67
! route to Singapore
ip route 128.10.202.0 255.255.255.192 128.10.200.68
! route to Tokyo
ip route 128.10.204.0 255.255.255.192 128.10.200.69
!
access-list 101 deny igrp 0.0.0.0 255.255.255.255 255.255.255.255 0.0.0.0
access-list 101 permit ip 0.0.0.0 255.255.255.255 0.0.0.0 255.255.255.255
dialer-list 1 list 101
!
username HongKong password password1
username Singapore password password2
username Tokyo password password3
```

Remote Sites: Dial Out Only

In the following configurations, the remote sites are configured to place calls to multiple interfaces at the central site. The assumption here is that a single telephone number on the central site will get any one of two possible inbound serial interfaces (serial interface 5 or serial interface 6).

Hong Kong

The following configuration allows Hong Kong to place calls to the central site in San Francisco:

```
hostname HongKong
interface ethernet 0
ip address 128.10.201.1 255.255.255.192
interface serial 1
description DDR connection to SanFrancisco
ip address 128.10.200.67 255.255.255.192
encapsulation ppp
dialer in-band
dialer wait-for-carrier-time 60
dialer string 14155551212
pulse-time 1
dialer-group 1
router igrp 1
network 128.10.0.0
ip route 128.10.0.0 255.255.0.0 128.10.200.66
!
access-list 101 deny igrp 0.0.0.0 255.255.255.255 255.255.255.255 0.0.0.0
access-list 101 permit ip 0.0.0.0 255.255.255.255 0.0.0.0 255.255.255.255
dialer-list 1 list 101
!
username SanFrancisco password password1
```

Singapore

The following configuration allows Singapore to place calls to the central site in San Francisco:

```
hostname Singapore
interface ethernet 0
ip address 128.10.202.1 255.255.255.192
interface serial 1
description DDR connection to San Francisco
ip address 128.10.200.68 255.255.255.192
encapsulation ppp
dialer in-band
dialer wait-for-carrier-time 60
dialer string 14155551212
pulse-time 1
dialer-group 1
router igrp 1
network 128.10.0.0
ip route 128.10.0.0 255.255.0.0 128.10.200.66
!
access-list 101 deny igrp 0.0.0.0 255.255.255.255 255.255.255.255 0.0.0.0
access-list 101 permit ip 0.0.0.0 255.255.255.255 0.0.0.0 255.255.255.255
dialer-list 1 list 101
!
username SanFrancisco password password2
```

Tokyo

The following configuration allows Tokyo to place calls to the central site in San Francisco:

```
hostname Tokyo
interface ethernet 0
ip address 128.10.204.1 255.255.255.192
interface serial 1
description DDR connection to San Francisco
ip address 128.10.200.69 255.255.255.192
encapsulation ppp
dialer in-band
dialer wait-for-carrier-time 60
dialer string 14155551212
pulse-time 1
dialer-group 1
router igrp 1
network 128.10.0.0
ip route 128.10.0.0 255.255.0.0 128.10.200.66
!
access-list 101 deny igrp 0.0.0.0 255.255.255.255 255.255.255.255 0.0.0.0
access-list 101 permit ip 0.0.0.0 255.255.255.255 0.0.0.0 255.255.255.255
dialer-list 1 list 101
!
username SanFrancisco password password3
```

USING DDR AS A BACKUP TO LEASED LINES

DDR allows you to quickly enable a WAN connection through the use of existing analog telephone lines. Also, DDR provides cost savings because the line is used on an as-needed basis, whereas a leased line is paid for when the line is not in use. However, there are times when a leased line may provide benefits.

Figure 15–3 shows that there can be a point (when a connection needs to be maintained for more than a certain number of hours per day) at which a DDR link no longer has cost savings, and a leased line may be more cost effective. Additionally, DDR links have a variable cost. It is difficult to predict what a DDR link may cost per month, given that users can initiate traffic at any time.

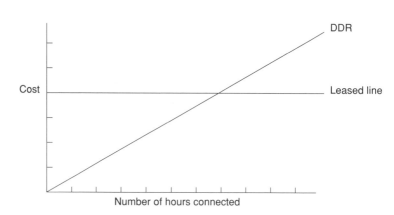

Figure 15–3
DDR-to-Leased Line Cutover.

With leased lines, you can still continue to use dial-up lines as a backup by using either of the following methods:

- Floating static routes (single and shared interfaces) and DDR
- DTR dialing or V.25bis dialing

Floating Static Routes

Floating static routes are static routes that have an administrative distance greater than the administrative distance of dynamic routes. Administrative distances can be configured on a static route so that the static route is less desirable than a dynamic route. In this manner, the static route is not used when the dynamic route is available. However, if the dynamic route is lost, the static route can take over, and traffic can be sent through this alternative route. If this alternative route is provided by a DDR interface, DDR can be used as a backup mechanism.

Central Site

The following example outlines a configuration of a central site using leased lines for primary connectivity and DDR for backup:

```
interface serial 1
description Leased connection to Hong Kong
ip address 128.10.200.66 255.255.255.192
!
interface serial 2
description leased connection to Singapore
ip address 128.10.202.66 255.255.255.192
!
interface serial 5
description backup DDR connection to Hong Kong
ip address 128.10.200.130 255.255.255.192
dialer in-band
dialer wait-for-carrier-time 60
dialer string 0118527351625
pulse-time 1
dialer-group 1
!
interface serial 6
description backup DDR connection to Singapore
ip address 128.10.202.130 255.255.255.192
dialer in-band
dialer wait-for-carrier-time 60
dialer string 011653367085
pulse-time 1
dialer-group 1
!
interface serial 7
description DDR connection to Tokyo
ip address 128.10.204.66 255.255.255.192
dialer in-band
dialer wait-for-carrier-time 60
dialer string 0118127351625
pulse-time 1
dialer-group 1
!
router igrp 1
network 128.10.0.0
redistribute static
!
! route to Hong Kong with administrative distance
ip route 128.10.200.0 255.255.255.192 128.10.200.129 150
! route to Singapore with administrative distance
ip route 128.10.202.0 255.255.255.192 128.10.202.129 150
! route to Tokyo
ip route 128.10.204.0 255.255.255.192 128.10.204.65
!
access-list 101 deny igrp 0.0.0.0 255.255.255.255 255.255.255.255 0.0.0.0
access-list 101 permit ip 0.0.0.0 255.255.255.255 0.0.0.0 255.255.255.255
dialer-list 1 list 101
```

Serial interfaces 1 and 2 are used as leased lines to Hong Kong and Singapore. Serial interface 5 backs up serial interface 1; serial interface 6 backs up serial interface 2; and serial interface 7 is used for DDR to Tokyo.

Remote Sites

Each remote sites has a leased line as a primary link and a DDR line as a backup. For example:

```
interface serial 0
description leased line from San Francisco
ip address 128.10.200.65 255.255.255.192
!
interface serial 1
description interface to answer backup calls from San Francisco
ip address 128.10.200.129 255.255.255.192
dialer in-band
!
router igrp 1
network 128.10.0.0
! route back to San Francisco with administrative distance
ip route 128.10.0.0 255.255.0.0 128.10.200.130 150
```

The first serial interface is the leased line, whereas the second answers calls from the central site in case the central site needs to use DDR as a backup method.

Floating Static Routes on Shared Interfaces

The central site configuration requires a large number of serial ports because each primary port has its own backup. For true redundancy, backup is a requirement. But in many cases, an interface or a set of interfaces can be shared as backup for a set of primary lines. The following configuration shows how to set up a single interface to back up all of the primary lines:

```
interface serial 1
description Leased connection to Hong Kong
ip address 128.10.200.66 255.255.255.192
!
interface serial 2
description leased connection to Singapore
ip address 128.10.202.66 255.255.255.192
!
interface serial 5
description backup DDR connection for all destinations except Tokyo
ip address 128.10.200.130 255.255.255.192
ip address 128.10.202.130 255.255.255.192 secondary
dialer in-band
dialer wait-for-carrier-time 60
! map Hong Kong to a phone number
dialer map ip 128.10.200.129 0118527351625
! map Singapore to a phone number
dialer map ip 128.10.202.129 011653367085
pulse-time 1
dialer-group 1
!
interface serial 7
description DDR connection to Tokyo
ip address 128.10.204.66 255.255.255.192
dialer in-band
dialer wait-for-carrier-time 60
dialer string 0118127351625
```

```
pulse-time 1
dialer-group 1
!
router igrp 1
network 128.10.0.0
passive-interface serial 5
redistribute static
!
! route to Hong Kong with administrative distance
ip route 128.10.200.0 255.255.255.192 128.10.200.129 150
! route to Singapore with administrative distance
ip route 128.10.202.0 255.255.255.192 128.10.202.129 150
! route to Tokyo
ip route 128.10.204.0 255.255.255.192 128.10.204.65
!
access-list 101 deny igrp 0.0.0.0 255.255.255.255 255.255.255.255 0.0.0.0
access-list 101 permit ip 0.0.0.0 255.255.255.255 0.0.0.0 255.255.255.255
dialer-list 1 list 101
```

Serial interface 5 is the DDR backup interface for all destinations and is configured with multiple IP addresses for routing. The **dialer map** commands map the next hop addresses to the telephone numbers for each of the destinations. If a dynamic route is lost, the floating static route takes over. The next hop address sends the packets to serial interface 5, where the **dialer map** commands place the telephone call.

If two primary lines fail at the same time, there will be contention to use serial interface 5. The fast-idle timer may disconnect the calls. If serial interface 5 were in constant use, one of the primary lines would be disconnected and packets would be dropped. The fact that the backup route is unavailable is not communicated because there is no way to announce that one of the two IP addresses on the interface are unavailable. If you use a dialer rotary group, the contention problem can be avoided.

USING LEASED LINES AND DIAL BACKUP

This section describes how to use the following two methods for dial backup with leased lines:

- DTR Dialing
- V.25bis Dialing

DTR Dialing

Since Software Release 8.3, a dial backup capability has been provided. Although it is somewhat more restrictive than floating static routes, dial backup can be used if V.25bis modems are not available or if protocols that do not have support for floating static routes are used.

Central Site

Dial backup requires that the modems place a call when the Data Terminal Ready (DTR) signal is raised. The telephone number is configured into the modem or other DCE device. That number is called when DTR is raised. The call is disconnected when DTR is lowered. The following configuration illustrates how to take advantage of dial backup and DTR dialing:

```
interface serial 1
description Leased connection to Hong Kong
ip address 128.10.200.66 255.255.255.192
backup interface serial 4
backup delay 0 20
!
interface serial 2
description leased connection to Singapore
ip address 128.10.202.66 255.255.255.192
backup interface serial 5
backup delay 0 20
!
interface serial 4
description backup connection for Hong Kong
ip address 128.10.200.67 255.255.255.192
pulse-time 10
!
interface serial 5
description backup connection for Singapore
ip address 128.10.202.67 255.255.255.192
pulse-time 10
!
interface serial 7
description DDR connection to Tokyo
ip address 128.10.204.66 255.255.255.192
dialer in-band
dialer wait-for-carrier-time 60
dialer string 0118127351625
pulse-time 1
dialer-group 1
!
router igrp 1
network 128.10.0.0
```

This solution requires one serial port per primary line. Because the backup ports are placed on the same subnet as the primary serial port, no static routes are required. The **backup delay** command is used to specify how long to wait after the primary has failed before activating the backup line, and how long to delay before deactivating the backup line after the primary line comes back up. In this case, the primary link will be active for 20 seconds before disabling the backup line. This delay allows for flapping in the primary link when it returns to functioning.

Remote Sites

For the remote sites, the floating static route is not needed. The IP address of the backup interface must be on the same subnet as the primary interface. The following example illustrates the Hong Kong router configuration. Serial interface 0 is the leased line, whereas serial interface 1 answers calls as a backup method:

```
interface serial 0
description leased line from San Francisco
```

```
ip address 128.10.200.65 255.255.255.192
!
interface serial 1
description interface to answer backup calls from San Francisco
ip address 128.10.200.68 255.255.255.192
!
router igrp 1
network 128.10.0.0
```

V.25bis Dialing

V.25bis dialing capability can be preferable to DTR dialing when multiple telephone numbers are required. Using DTR dialing, most devices will call only a single number. With V.25bis, the router can attempt to call several numbers if the first number does not answer. The following configuration illustrates V.25bis dialing:

```
interface serial 1
description Leased connection to Hong Kong
ip address 128.10.200.66 255.255.255.192
backup interface serial 4
backup delay 0 20
!
interface serial 2
description leased connection to Singapore
ip address 128.10.202.66 255.255.255.192
backup interface serial 5
backup delay 0 20
!
interface serial 4
description backup connection for Hong Kong
ip address 128.10.200.67 255.255.255.192
dialer in-band
dialer wait-for-carrier-time 60
dialer map IP 128.10.200.68 0118527351625
dialer map IP 128.10.200.68 0118527351872
dialer-group 1
pulse-time 1
!
interface serial 5
description backup connection for Singapore
ip address 128.10.202.67 255.255.255.192
dialer in-band
dialer wait-for-carrier-time 60
dialer string 011653367085
dialer-group 1
pulse-time 1
!
interface serial 7
description DDR connection to Tokyo
ip address 128.10.204.66 255.255.255.192
dialer in-band
dialer wait-for-carrier-time 60
dialer string 0118127351625
pulse-time 1
```

```
dialer-group 1
!
router igrp 1
network 128.10.0.0
redistribute static
!
! route to Hong Kong
ip route 128.10.200.0 255.255.255.192 128.10.200.68
! route to Singapore
ip route 128.10.202.0 255.255.255.192 128.10.202.68
! route to Tokyo
ip route 128.10.204.0 255.255.255.192 128.10.204.65
!
dialer-list 1 protocol IP PERMIT
```

Multiple telephone numbers are configured for serial interface 4. The two **dialer map** commands have the same next hop address. The software first attempts to call the telephone number specified in the first **dialer map** command. If this number fails—that is, if no connection is made before the wait-for-carrier timer expires—the second number is dialed. Each of the other backup interfaces uses a dialer string for the backup telephone number. When using V.25bis with dial backup, the **dialer-list protocol** command shown in the preceding example should be used. The dialer list states that all IP traffic is interesting and will, therefore, cause dialing. Routing updates are included. When a serial line is used as a backup, it is normally the state of the primary link, not the fast-idle timer, that determines when to disconnect the call.

SUMMARY

As this case study indicates, there are many ways that dial-on-demand routing (DDR) can be used both for primary access and backup access. Sites can place calls, receive calls, and both place and receive calls. Additionally, using dialer rotary groups provides increased flexibility.

Increasing Security on IP Networks

Network security is a broad topic that can be addressed at the *data* link, or media, level (where packet snooping and encryption problems can occur), at the *network,* or protocol, layer (the point at which Internet Protocol (IP) packets and routing updates are controlled), and at the *application* layer (where, for example, host-level bugs become issues).

As more users access the Internet and as companies expand their networks, the challenge to provide security for internal networks becomes increasingly difficult. Companies must determine which areas of their internal networks they must protect, learn how to restrict user access to these areas, and determine which types of network services they should filter to prevent potential security breaches.

Cisco Systems provides several network, or protocol, layer features to increase security on IP networks. These features include controls to restrict access to routers and communication servers by way of console port, Telnet, Simple Network Management Protocol (SNMP), Terminal Access Controller Access Control System (TACACS), vendor token cards, and access lists. Firewall architecture setup is also discussed.

CAUTION

Although this case study addresses network-layer security issues, which are the most relevant in the context of an Internet connection, ignoring host-level security, even with network-layer filtering in place, can be dangerous. For host-level security measures, refer to your application's documentation and the recommended reading list at the end of this case study.

UNDERSTANDING CISCO'S APPROACH TO NETWORK SECURITY

When most people talk about security, they mean ensuring that users can only perform tasks they are authorized to do, can only obtain information they are authorized to have, and cannot cause damage to the data, applications, or operating environment of a system.

The word *security* connotes protection against malicious attack by outsiders. Security also involves controlling the effects of errors and equipment failures. Anything that can protect against a deliberate, intelligent, calculated attack will probably prevent random misfortune as well.

Security measures keep people honest in the same way that locks do. This case study provides specific actions you can take to improve the security of your network. Before going into specifics, however, it will help if you understand the following basic concepts that are essential to any security system:

- *Know your enemy*

  This case study refers to *attackers* or *intruders*. Consider who might want to circumvent your security measures and identify their motivations. Determine what they might want to do and the damage that they could cause to your network.

  Security measures can never make it impossible for a user to perform unauthorized tasks with a computer system. They can only make it harder. The goal is to make sure the network security controls are beyond the attacker's ability or motivation.

- *Count the cost*

  Security measures almost always reduce convenience, especially for sophisticated users. Security can delay work and create expensive administrative and educational overhead. It can use significant computing resources and require dedicated hardware.

  When you design your security measures, understand their costs and weigh those costs against the potential benefits. To do that, you must understand the costs of the measures themselves and the costs and likelihoods of security breaches. If you incur security costs out of proportion to the actual dangers, you have done yourself a disservice.

- *Identify your assumptions*

  Every security system has underlying assumptions. For example, you might assume that your network is not tapped, or that attackers know less than you do, that they are using standard software, or that a locked room is safe. Be sure to examine and justify your assumptions. Any hidden assumption is a potential security hole.

- *Control your secrets*

  Most security is based on secrets. Passwords and encryption keys, for example, are secrets. Too often, though, the secrets are not really all that secret. The most important part of keeping secrets is knowing the areas you need to protect. What knowledge would enable someone to circumvent your system? You should jealously guard that knowledge and assume that everything else is known to your adversaries. The more secrets you have, the harder it will be to keep all of them. Security systems should be designed so that only a limited number of secrets need to be kept.

- *Remember human factors*

  Many security procedures fail because their designers do not consider how users will react to them. For example, because they can be difficult to remember, automatically generated "nonsense" passwords are often found written on the undersides of keyboards. For convenience, a "secure" door that leads to the system's only tape drive is sometimes propped open. For expediency, unauthorized modems are often connected to a network to avoid onerous dial-in security measures.

If your security measures interfere with essential use of the system, those measures will be resisted and perhaps circumvented. To win compliance, you must make sure that users can get their work done, and you must sell your security measures to users. Users must understand and accept the need for security.

Any user can compromise system security, at least to some degree. Passwords, for instance, can often be found simply by calling legitimate users on the telephone, claiming to be a system administrator, and asking for them. If your users understand security issues, and if they understand the reasons for your security measures, they are far less likely to make an intruder's life easier.

At a minimum, users should be taught never to release passwords or other secrets over unsecured telephone lines (especially cellular telephones) or electronic mail (email). Users should be wary of questions asked by people who call them on the telephone. Some companies have implemented formalized network security training for their employees; that is, employees are not allowed access to the Internet until they have completed a formal training program.

- *Know your weaknesses*

  Every security system has vulnerabilities. You should understand your system's weak points and know how they could be exploited. You should also know the areas that present the largest danger and prevent access to them immediately. Understanding the weak points is the first step toward turning them into secure areas.

- *Limit the scope of access*

  You should create appropriate barriers inside your system so that if intruders access one part of the system, they do not automatically have access to the rest of the system. The security of a system is only as good as the weakest security level of any single host in the system.

- *Understand your environment*

  Understanding how your system normally functions, knowing what is expected and what is unexpected, and being familiar with how devices are usually used, help you to detect security problems. Noticing unusual events can help you to catch intruders before they can damage the system. Auditing tools can help you to detect those unusual events.

- *Limit your trust*

  You should know exactly which software you rely on, and your security system should not have to rely upon the assumption that all software is bug-free.

- *Remember physical security*

  Physical access to a computer (or a router) usually gives a sufficiently sophisticated user total control over that computer. Physical access to a network link usually allows a person to tap that link, jam it, or inject traffic into it. It makes no sense to install complicated software security measures when access to the hardware is not controlled.

- *Security is pervasive*

  Almost any change you make in your system may have security effects. This is especially true when new services are created. Administrators, programmers, and users should consider the security implications of every change they make. Understanding the security implications of a change is something that takes practice. It requires lateral thinking and a willingness to explore every way in which a service could potentially be manipulated.

CONTROLLING ACCESS TO CISCO ROUTERS

It is important to control access to your Cisco routers. You can control access to the router using the following methods:

- Console Access
- Telnet Access
- Simple Network Management Protocol (SNMP) Access
- Controlling Access to Network Servers That Contain Configuration Files

You can secure the first three of these methods by employing features within the router software. For each method, you can permit nonprivileged access and privileged access for a user (or group of users). Nonprivileged access allows users to monitor the router, but not to configure the router. Privileged access allows the user to fully configure the router.

For console port and Telnet access, you can set up two types of passwords. The first type of password, the login password, allows the user nonprivileged access to the router. After accessing the router, the user can enter privileged mode by entering the **enable** command and the proper password. Privileged mode provides the user with full configuration capabilities.

SNMP access allows you to set up different SNMP community strings for both nonprivileged and privileged access. Nonprivileged access allows users on a host to send the router SNMP get-request and SNMP get-next-request messages. These messages are used for gathering statistics from the router. Privileged access allows users on a host to send the router SNMP set-request messages in order to make changes to the router's configurations and operational state.

Console Access

A console is a terminal attached directly to the router via the console port. Security is applied to the console by asking users to authenticate themselves via passwords. By default, there are no passwords associated with console access.

Nonprivileged Mode Password

You configure a password for nonprivileged mode by entering the following commands in the router's configuration file. Passwords are case-sensitive. In this example, the password is "1forAll."

```
line console 0
login
password 1forAll
```

When you log in to the router, the router login prompt is as follows:

```
User Access Verification
Password:
```

You must enter the password "1forAll" to gain nonprivileged access to the router. The router response is as follows:

```
router>
```

Nonprivileged mode is signified on the router by the > prompt. At this point, you can enter a variety of commands to view statistics on the router, but you cannot change the configuration of the router. Never use "cisco," or other obvious derivatives, such as "pancho," for a Cisco router password. These will be the first passwords intruders will try if they recognize the Cisco login prompt.

Privileged Mode Password

Configure a password for privileged mode by entering the following commands in the router's configuration file. In this example, the password is "san-fran."

```
enable-password san-fran
```

To access privileged mode, enter the following command:

```
router> enable
Password:
```

Enter the password "san-fran" to gain privileged access to the router. The router responds as follows:

```
router#
```

Privileged mode is signified by the # prompt. In privileged mode, you can enter all commands to view statistics and configure the router.

Session Timeouts

Setting the login and enable passwords may not provide enough security in some cases. The timeout for an unattended console (by default 10 minutes) provides an additional security measure. If the console is left unattended in privileged mode, any user can modify the router's configuration. You can change the login timeout via the command **exec-timeout** *mm ss* where *mm* is minutes and *ss* is seconds. The following commands change the timeout to 1 minute and 30 seconds:

```
line console 0
exec-timeout 1 30
```

Password Encryption

All passwords on the router are visible via the **write terminal** and **show configuration** privileged mode commands. If you have access to privileged mode on the router, you can view all passwords in cleartext by default.

There is a way to hide cleartext passwords. The command **service password-encryption** stores passwords in an encrypted manner so that anyone performing a **write terminal** and **show configuration** will not be able to determine the cleartext password. However, if you forget the password, regaining access to the router requires you to have physical access to the router.

NOTES ───

Although encryption is helpful, it can be compromised and thus should not be your only network-security strategy.

Telnet Access

You can access both nonprivileged and privileged mode on the router via Telnet. As with the console port, Telnet security is provided when users are prompted by the router to authenticate themselves via passwords. In fact, many of the same concepts described in the "Console Access" section earlier in this chapter apply to Telnet access. You must enter a password to go from nonprivileged mode to privileged mode, and you can encrypt passwords and specify timeouts for each Telnet session.

Nonprivileged Mode Password

Each Telnet port on the router is known as a *virtual terminal*. There are a maximum of five virtual terminal (VTY) ports on the router, allowing five concurrent Telnet sessions. (The communication server provides more VTY ports.) On the router, the virtual terminal ports are numbered from 0 through 4. You can set up nonprivileged passwords for Telnet access via the virtual terminal ports with the following configuration commands. In this example, virtual terminal ports 0 through 4 use the password "marin":

```
line vty 0 4
login
password marin
```

When a user telnets to a router IP address, the router provides a prompt similar to the following:

```
% telnet router
Trying ...
Connected to router.
Escape character is '^]'.
User Access Verification
Password:
```

If the user enters the correct nonprivileged password, the following prompt appears:

```
router>
```

Privileged Mode Password

The user now has nonprivileged access to the router and can enter privileged mode by entering the **enable** command as described in the "Privileged Mode Password" section earlier in this chapter.

Restricting Telnet Access to Particular IP Addresses

If you want to allow only certain IP addresses to use Telnet to access the router, you must use the **access-class** command. The command **access-class** *nn* **in** defines an access list (from 1 through 99) that allows access to the virtual terminal lines on the router. The following configuration commands allow incoming Telnet access to the router only from hosts on network 192.85.55.0:

```
access-list 12 permit 192.85.55.0 0.0.0.255
line vty 0 4
access-class 12 in
```

Restricting Telnet Access to Cisco Products via TCP Ports

It is possible to access Cisco products via Telnet to specified TCP ports. The type of Telnet access varies, depending upon the following Cisco software releases:

- Software Release 9.1 (11.4) and earlier and 9.21 (3.1) and earlier
- Software Release 9.1 (11.5), 9.21 (3.2), and 10.0 and later

Earlier Software Releases

For Software Release 9.1 (11.4) and earlier and Software Release 9.21 (3.1) and earlier, it is possible, by default, to establish TCP connections to Cisco products via the TCP ports listed in Table 16–1.

Table 16–1 *TCP Port Telnet Access to Cisco Products (Earlier Releases)*

TCP Port Number	Access Method
7	Echo
9	Discard
23	Telnet (to virtual terminal VTY ports in rotary fashion)
79	Finger
1993	SNMP over TCP
2001 through 2999	Telnet to auxiliary (AUX) port, terminal (TTY) ports, and virtual terminal (VTY) ports
3001 through 3999	Telnet to rotary ports (access via these ports is only possible if the rotaries have been explicitly configured first with the **rotary** command)
4001 through 4999	Telnet (stream mode) mirror of 2000 range

Table 16–1   *TCP Port Telnet Access to Cisco Products (Earlier Releases), Continued*

TCP Port Number	Access Method
5001 through 5999	Telnet (stream mode) mirror of 3000 range (access via these ports is possible only if the rotaries have been explicitly configured first)
6001 through 6999	Telnet (binary mode) mirror of 2000 range
7001 through 7999	Telnet (binary mode) mirror of 3000 range (access via these ports is possible only if the rotaries have been explicitly configured first)
8001 through 8999	Xremote (communication servers only)
9001 through 9999	Reverse Xremote (communication servers only)
10001 through 19999	Reverse Xremote rotary (communication servers only; access via these ports is possible only if the ports have been explicitly configured first)

CAUTION

Because Cisco routers have no TTY lines, configuring access (on communication servers) to terminal ports 2002, 2003, 2004, and greater could potentially provide access (on routers) to virtual terminal lines 2002, 2003, 2004, and greater. To provide access only to TTY ports, you can create access lists to prevent access to VTYs.

When configuring rotary groups, keep in mind that access through any available port in the rotary group is possible (unless access lists are defined). Cisco recommends that if you are using firewalls that allow in-bound TCP connection to high-number ports, remember to apply appropriate in-bound access lists to Cisco products.

The following is an example illustrating an access list denying all in-bound Telnet access to the auxiliary port and allowing Telnet access to the router only from IP address 192.32.6.7:

```
access-class 51 deny 0.0.0.0 255.255.255.255
access-class 52 permit 192.32.6.7

line aux 0
access-class 51 in
line vty 0 4
access-class 52 in
```

To disable connections to the echo and discard ports, you must disable these services completely with the **no service tcp-small-servers** command.

CAUTION

If the **ip alias** command is enabled on Cisco products, TCP connections to any destination port are considered valid connections. You may want to disable the **ip alias** command.

You might want to create access lists to prevent access to Cisco products via these TCP ports. For information on how to create access lists for routers, see the "Configuring the Firewall Router" section later in this chapter. For information on how to create access lists for communication servers, see the "Configuring the Firewall Communication Server" section later in this chapter.

Software Releases 9.1 (11.5), 9.21 (3.2), and 10.0 and Later

With Software Release 9.1 (11.5), 9.21 (3.2), and any version of Software Release 10, the following enhancements have been implemented:

- Direct access to virtual terminal lines (VTYs) through the 2000, 4000, and 6000 port ranges has been disabled. If you want to keep access open, you can set up one-to-one mapping of VTY-to-rotary ports.

- Connections to echo and discard ports (7 and 9) can be disabled with the **no service tcp-small-servers** command.

- All Cisco products allow connections to IP alias devices only on destination port 23.

For later releases, a Cisco router accepts TCP connections on the ports listed in Table 16–2 by default.

Table 16–2 *TCP Port Telnet Access to Cisco Products (Later Releases)*

TCP Port Number	Access Method
7	Echo
9	Discard
23	Telnet
79	Finger
1993	SNMP over TCP
2001	Auxiliary (AUX) port
4001	Auxiliary (AUX) port (stream)
6001	Auxiliary (AUX) port (binary)

Access via port 23 can be restricted by creating an access list and assigning it to virtual terminal lines. Access via port 79 can be disabled with the **no service finger** command. Access via port 1993 can be controlled with SNMP access lists. Access via ports 2001, 4001, and 6001 can be controlled with an access list placed on the auxiliary port.

Terminal Access Controller Access Control System (TACACS)

Nonprivileged and privileged mode passwords are global and apply to every user accessing the router from either the console port or from a Telnet session. As an alternative, the Terminal Access

Controller Access Control System (TACACS) provides a way to validate every user on an individual basis before they can gain access to the router or communication server. TACACS was derived from the United States Department of Defense and is described in Request For Comments (RFC) 1492. TACACS is used by Cisco to allow finer control over who can access the router in nonprivileged and privileged mode.

With TACACS enabled, the router prompts the user for a username and a password. Then, the router queries a TACACS server to determine whether the user provided the correct password. A TACACS server typically runs on a UNIX workstation. Public domain TACACS servers can be obtained via anonymous ftp to *ftp.cisco.com* in the */pub* directory. Use the */pub/README* file to find the filename. A fully supported TACACS server is bundled with CiscoWorks Version 3.

The configuration command **tacacs-server host** specifies the UNIX host running a TACACS server that will validate requests sent by the router. You can enter the **tacacs-server host** command several times to specify multiple TACACS server hosts for a router.

Nonprivileged Access

If all servers are unavailable, you may be locked out of the router. In that event, the configuration command **tacacs-server last-resort [password | succeed]** allows you to determine whether to allow a user to log in to the router with no password (**succeed** keyword) or to force the user to supply the standard login password (**password** keyword).

The following commands specify a TACACS server and allow a login to succeed if the server is down or unreachable:

```
tacacs-server host 129.140.1.1
tacacs-server last-resort succeed
```

To force users who access the router via Telnet to authenticate themselves using TACACS, enter the following configuration commands:

```
line vty 0 4
login tacacs
```

Privileged Access

This method of password checking can also be applied to the privileged mode password with the **enable use-tacacs** command. If all servers are unavailable, you may be locked out of the router. In that event, the configuration command **enable last-resort [succeed | password]** allows you to determine whether to allow a user to log in to the router with no password (**succeed** keyword) or to force the user to supply the enable password (**password** keyword). There are significant risks to using the **succeed** keyword. If you use the **enable use-tacacs** command, you must also specify the **tacacs-server authenticate enable** command.

The **tacacs-server extended** command enables a Cisco device to run in extended TACACS mode. The UNIX system must be running the extended TACACS daemon, which can be obtained via anonymous ftp to *ftp.cisco.com*. The filename is *xtacacsd.shar*. This daemon allows communication servers and other equipment to talk to the UNIX system and update an audit trail with information on port usage, accounting data, or any other information the device can send.

The command **username <user> password [0 | 7] <password>** allows you to store and maintain a list of users and their passwords on a Cisco device instead of on a TACACS server. The number 0 stores the password in cleartext in the configuration file. The number 7 stores the password in an encrypted format. If you do not have a TACACS server and still want to authenticate users on an individual basis, you can set up users with the following configuration commands:

```
username steve password 7 steve-pass
username allan password 7 allan-pass
```

The two users, Steve and Allan, will be authenticated via passwords that are stored in encrypted format.

Token Card Access

Using TACACS service on routers and communications servers, support for physical card key devices, or token cards, can also be added. The TACACS server code can be modified to provide support for this without requiring changes in the setup and configuration of the routers and communication servers. This modified code is not directly available from Cisco.

The token card system relies on a physical card that must be in your possession in order to provide authentication. By using the appropriate hooks in the TACACS server code, third-party companies can offer these enhanced TACACS servers to customers. One such product is the Enigma Logic SafeWord security software system. Other card-key systems, such as Security Dynamics SmartCard, can be added to TACACS as well.

Simple Network Management Protocol (SNMP) Access

SNMP is another method you can use to access your routers. With SNMP, you can gather statistics or configure the router. Gather statistics with get-request and get-next-request messages, and configure routers with set-request messages. Each of these SNMP messages has a community string that is a cleartext password sent in every packet between a management station and the router (which contains an SNMP agent). The SNMP community string is used to authenticate messages sent between the manager and agent. Only when the manager sends a message with the correct community string will the agent respond.

The SNMP agent on the router allows you to configure different community strings for nonprivileged and privileged access. You configure community strings on the router via the configuration command **snmp-server community <*string*> [RO | RW]** [*access-list*]. The following sections explore the various ways to use this command.

Unfortunately, SNMP community strings are sent on the network in cleartext ASCII. Thus, anyone who has the ability to capture a packet on the network can discover the community string. This may allow unauthorized users to query or modify routers via SNMP. For this reason, using the **no snmp-server trap-authentication** command may prevent intruders from using trap messages (sent between SNMP managers and agents) to discover community strings.

The Internet community, recognizing this problem, greatly enhanced the security of SNMP version 2 (SNMPv2) as described in RFC 1446. SNMPv2 uses an algorithm called *MD5* to authenticate communications between an SNMP server and agent. MD5 verifies the integrity of the communications, authenticates the origin, and checks for timeliness. Further, SNMPv2 can use the data encryption standard (DES) for encrypting information.

Nonprivileged Mode

Use the **RO** keyword of the **snmp-server community** command to provide nonprivileged access to your routers via SNMP. The following configuration command sets the agent in the router to allow only SNMP get-request and get-next-request messages that are sent with the community string "public":

```
snmp-server community public RO 1
```

You can also specify a list of IP addresses that are allowed to send messages to the router using the *access-list* option with the **snmp-server community** command. In the following configuration example, only hosts 1.1.1.1 and 2.2.2.2 are allowed nonprivileged mode SNMP access to the router:

```
access-list 1 permit 1.1.1.1
access-list 1 permit 2.2.2.2
snmp-server community public RO 1
```

Privileged Mode

Use the **RW** keyword of the **snmp-server community** command to provide privileged access to your routers via SNMP. The following configuration command sets the agent in the router to allow only SNMP set-request messages sent with the community string "private":

```
snmp-server community private RW 1
```

You can also specify a list of IP addresses that are allowed to send messages to the router by using the *access-list* option of the **snmp-server community** command. In the following configuration example, only hosts 5.5.5.5 and 6.6.6.6 are allowed privileged mode SNMP access to the router:

```
access-list 1 permit 5.5.5.5
access-list 1 permit 6.6.6.6
snmp-server community private RW 1
```

Controlling Access to Network Servers That Contain Configuration Files

If a router regularly downloads configuration files from a Trivial File Transfer Protocol (TFTP) or Maintenance Operations Protocol (MOP) server, anyone who can access the server can modify the router configuration files stored on the server.

Communication servers can be configured to accept incoming local area transport (LAT) connections. Protocol translators and their translating router brethren can accept X.29 connections. These different types of access should be considered when creating a firewall architecture.

SETTING UP YOUR FIREWALL ARCHITECTURE

A firewall architecture is a structure that exists between you and the outside world to protect you from intruders. In most circumstances, intruders are represented by the global Internet and the thousands of remote networks it interconnects. Typically, a network firewall consists of several different machines as shown in Figure 16–1.

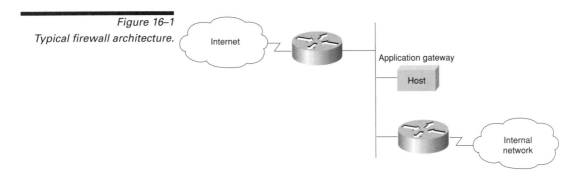

Figure 16–1
Typical firewall architecture.

In this architecture, the router that is connected to the Internet (exterior router) forces all incoming traffic to go to the application gateway. The router that is connected to the internal network (interior router) accepts packets only from the application gateway.

The application gateway institutes per-application and per-user policies. In effect, the gateway controls the delivery of network-based services both into and from the internal network. For example, only certain users might be allowed to communicate with the Internet, or only certain applications are permitted to establish connections between an interior and exterior host.

The route and packet filters should be set up to reflect the same policies. If the only application that is permitted is mail, only mail packets should be allowed through the router. This protects the application gateway and avoids overwhelming it with packets that it would otherwise discard.

CONTROLLING TRAFFIC FLOW

This section uses the scenario illustrated in Figure 16–2 to describe the use of access lists to restrict traffic to and from a firewall router and a firewall communication server.

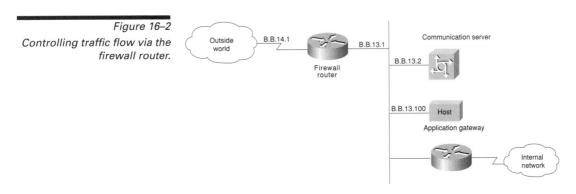

Figure 16–2
Controlling traffic flow via the firewall router.

In this case study, the firewall router allows incoming new connections to one or more communication servers or hosts. Having a designated router act as a firewall is desirable because it clearly identifies the router's purpose as the external gateway and avoids encumbering other routers with this task. In the event that the internal network needs to isolate itself, the firewall router provides the point of isolation so that the rest of the internal network structure is not affected.

Connections to the hosts are restricted to incoming file transfer protocol (FTP) requests and email services as described in the "Configuring the Firewall Router" section later in this chapter. The incoming Telnet, or modem, connections to the communication server are screened by the communication server running TACACS username authentication, as described in the "Configuring the Firewall Communication Server" section later in this chapter.

NOTES

Connections from one communication server modem line to another outgoing modem line (or to the outside world) should be disallowed to prevent unauthorized users from using your resources to launch an attack on the outside world. Because intruders have already passed the communication server TACACS authentication at this point, they are likely to have someone's password. It is an excellent idea to keep TACACS passwords and host passwords distinct from one another.

Configuring the Firewall Router

In the firewall router configuration that follows, subnet 13 of the Class B network is the firewall subnet, whereas subnet 14 provides the connection to the worldwide Internet via a service provider:

```
interface ethernet 0
ip address B.B.13.1 255.255.255.0
interface serial 0
ip address B.B.14.1 255.255.255.0
router igrp
network B.B.0.0
```

This simple configuration provides *no security* and allows all traffic from the outside world onto all parts of the network. To provide security on the firewall router, use access lists and access groups as described in the next section.

Defining Access Lists

Access lists define the actual traffic that will be permitted or denied, whereas an access group applies an access list definition to an interface. Access lists can be used to deny connections that are known to be a security risk and then permit all other connections, or to permit those connections that are considered acceptable and deny all the rest. For firewall implementation, the latter is the more secure method.

In this case study, incoming email and news are permitted for a few hosts, but FTP, Telnet, and rlogin services are permitted only to hosts on the firewall subnet. IP *extended* access lists (range 100 to 199) and transmission control protocol (TCP) or user datagram protocol (UDP) port numbers are used to filter traffic. When a connection is to be established for email, Telnet, FTP, and so forth, the connection will attempt to open a service on a specified port number. You can, therefore, filter out selected types of connections by denying packets that are attempting to use that service. For a list of well-known services and ports, see the "Filtering TCP and UDP Services" section later in this chapter.

An access list is invoked after a routing decision has been made but before the packet is sent out on an interface. The best place to define an access list is on a preferred host using your favorite text editor. You can create a file that contains the **access-list** commands, place the file (marked *readable*) in the default TFTP directory, and then network load the file onto the router.

The network server storing the file must be running a TFTP daemon and have TCP network access to the firewall router. Before network loading the access control definition, any previous definition of this access list is removed by using the following command:

```
no access-list 101
```

The **access-list** command can now be used to permit any packets returning to machines from already established connections. With the **established** keyword, a match occurs if the TCP datagram has the acknowledgment (ACK) or reset (RST) bits set.

```
access-list 101 permit tcp 0.0.0.0 255.255.255.255 0.0.0.0 255.255.255.255 established
```

If any firewall routers share a common network with an outside provider, you may want to allow access from those hosts to your network. In this case study, the outside provider has a serial port that uses the firewall router Class B address (B.B.14.2) as a source address as follows:

```
access-list 101 permit ip B.B.14.2 0.0.0.0 0.0.0.0 255.255.255.255
```

The following example illustrates how to deny traffic from a user attempting to spoof any of your internal addresses from the outside world (*without* using 9.21 input access lists):

```
access-list 101 deny ip B.B.0.0 0.0.255.255 0.0.0.0 255.255.255.255
```

The following commands allow domain name system (DNS) and network time protocol (NTP) requests and replies:

```
access-list 101 permit udp 0.0.0.0 255.255.255.255 0.0.0.0 255.255.255.255 eq 53
access-list 101 permit udp 0.0.0.0 255.255.255.255 0.0.0.0 255.255.255.255 eq 123
```

The following command denies the network file server (NFS) user datagram protocol (UDP) port:

```
access-list 101 deny udp 0.0.0.0 255.255.255.255 0.0.0.0 255.255.255.255 eq 2049
```

The following commands deny OpenWindows on ports 2001 and 2002 and deny X11 on ports 6001 and 6002. This protects the first two screens on any host. If you have any machine that uses more than the first two screens, be sure to block the appropriate ports.

```
access-list 101 deny tcp 0.0.0.0 255.255.255.255 0.0.0.0 255.255.255.255 eq 6001
access-list 101 deny tcp 0.0.0.0 255.255.255.255 0.0.0.0 255.255.255.255 eq 6002

access-list 101 deny tcp 0.0.0.0 255.255.255.255 0.0.0.0 255.255.255.255 eq 2001
access-list 101 deny tcp 0.0.0.0 255.255.255.255 0.0.0.0 255.255.255.255 eq 2002
```

The following command permits Telnet access to the communication server (B.B.13.2):

```
access-list 101 permit tcp 0.0.0.0 255.255.255.255 B.B.13.2 0.0.0.0 eq 23
```

The following commands permit FTP access to the host on subnet 13:

```
access-list 101 permit tcp 0.0.0.0 255.255.255.255 B.B.13.100 0.0.0.0 eq 21
access-list 101 permit tcp 0.0.0.0 255.255.255.255 B.B.13.100 0.0.0.0 eq 20
```

For the following examples, network B.B.1.0 is on the internal network. The following commands permit TCP and UDP connections for port numbers greater than 1023 to a very limited set of hosts. Make sure no communication servers or protocol translators are in this list.

```
access-list 101 permit tcp 0.0.0.0 255.255.255.255 B.B.13.100 0.0.0.0 gt 1023
access-list 101 permit tcp 0.0.0.0 255.255.255.255 B.B.1.100 0.0.0.0 gt 1023
access-list 101 permit tcp 0.0.0.0 255.255.255.255 B.B.1.101 0.0.0.0 gt 1023
access-list 101 permit udp 0.0.0.0 255.255.255.255 B.B.13.100 0.0.0.0 gt 1023
access-list 101 permit udp 0.0.0.0 255.255.255.255 B.B.1.100 0.0.0.0 gt 1023
access-list 101 permit udp 0.0.0.0 255.255.255.255 B.B.1.101 0.0.0.0 gt 1023
```

NOTES

Standard FTP uses ports above 1023 for its data connections; therefore, for standard FTP operation, ports above 1023 must all be open. For more details, see the "File Transfer Protocol (FTP) Port" section that follows.

The following commands permit DNS access to the DNS server(s) listed by the Network Information Center (NIC):

```
access-list 101 permit tcp 0.0.0.0 255.255.255.255 B.B.13.100 0.0.0.0 eq 53
access-list 101 permit tcp 0.0.0.0 255.255.255.255 B.B.1.100 0.0.0.0 eq 53
```

The following commands permit incoming simple mail transfer protocol (SMTP) email to only a few machines:

```
access-list 101 permit tcp 0.0.0.0 255.255.255.255 B.B.13.100 0.0.0.0 eq 25
access-list 101 permit tcp 0.0.0.0 255.255.255.255 B.B.1.100 0.0.0.0 eq 25
```

The following commands allow internal network news transfer protocol (NNTP) servers to receive NNTP connections from a list of authorized peers:

```
access-list 101 permit tcp 16.1.0.18 0.0.0.1 B.B.1.100 0.0.0.0 eq 119
access-list 101 permit tcp 128.102.18.32 0.0.0.0 B.B.1.100 0.0.0.0 eq 119
```

The following command permits Internet control message protocol (ICMP) for error message feedback:

```
access-list 101 permit icmp 0.0.0.0 255.255.255.255 0.0.0.0 255.255.255.255
```

Every access list has an implicit "deny everything else" statement at the end of the list to ensure that attributes that are not expressly permitted are in fact denied.

File Transfer Protocol (FTP) Port

Many sites today choose to block incoming TCP sessions originated from the outside world while allowing outgoing connections. The trouble with this is that blocking incoming connections kills traditional FTP client programs because these programs use the "PORT" command to tell the server where to connect to send the file. The client opens a "control" connection to the server, but the server then opens a "data" connection to an effectively arbitrarily chosen (> 1023) port number on the client.

Fortunately, there is an alternative to this behavior that allows the client to open the "data" socket and allows you to have the firewall and FTP too. The client sends a PASV command to the server, receives back a port number for the data socket, opens the data socket to the indicated port, and finally sends the transfer.

In order to implement this method, the standard FTP client program must be replaced with a modified one that supports the PASV command. Most recent implementations of the FTP server already support the PASV command. The only trouble with this idea is that it breaks down when the server site has also blocked arbitrary incoming connections.

CAUTION

Care should be taken in providing anonymous FTP service on the host system. Anonymous FTP service allows anyone to access the hosts, without requiring an account on the host system. Many implementations of the FTP server have severe bugs in this area. Also, take care in the implementation and setup of the anonymous FTP service to prevent any obvious access violations. For most sites, anonymous FTP service is disabled.

Applying Access Lists to Interfaces

After this access list has been loaded onto the router and stored into nonvolatile random-access memory (NVRAM), assign it to the appropriate interface. In this case study, traffic coming from the outside world via serial 0 is filtered before it is placed on subnet 13 (ethernet 0). Therefore, the **access-group** command, which assigns an access list to filter incoming connections, must be assigned to Ethernet 0 as follows:

```
interface ethernet 0
ip access-group 101
```

To control outgoing access to the Internet from the network, define an access list and apply it to the outgoing packets on serial 0 of the firewall router. To do this, returning packets from hosts using Telnet or FTP must be allowed to access the firewall subnetwork B.B.13.0.

Filtering TCP and UDP Services

Some well-known TCP and UDP port numbers include the services listed in Table 16–3.

Table 16–3 *Well-Known TCP and UDP Services and Ports*

Service	Port Type	Port Number
File Transfer Protocol (FTP)—Data	TCP	20
FTP—Commands	TCP	21
Telnet	TCP	23
Simple Mail Transfer Protocol (SMTP)—Email	TCP	25
Terminal Access Controller Access Control System (TACACS)	UDP	49

Table 16–3   *Well-Known TCP and UDP Services and Ports, Continued*

Service	Port Type	Port Number
Domain Name Server (DNS)	TCP and UDP	53
Trivial File Transfer Protocol (TFTP)	UDP	69
finger	TCP	79
SUN Remote Procedure Call (RPC)	UDP	111
Network News Transfer Protocol (NNTP)	TCP	119
Network Time Protocol (NTP)	TCP and UDP	123
NeWS	TCP	144
Simple Management Network Protocol (SNMP)	UDP	161
SNMP (traps)	UDP	162
Border Gateway Protocol (BGP)	TCP	179
rlogin	TCP	513
rexec	TCP	514
talk	TCP and UDP	517
ntalk	TCP and UDP	518
Open Windows	TCP and UDP	2000
Network File System (NFS)	UDP	2049
X11	TCP and UDP	6000

CERT Advisory

The Computer Emergency Response Team (CERT) recommends filtering the services listed in Table 16–4.

Table 16–4   *CERT Advisory on TCP and UDP Services and Ports*

Service	Port Type	Port Number
DNS zone transfers	TCP	53
TFTP daemon (tftpd)	UDP	69
link—commonly used by intruders	TCP	87
SUN RPC	TCP and UDP	111[*]
NFS	UDP	2049

Table 16–4 *CERT Advisory on TCP and UDP Services and Ports, Continued*

Service	Port Type	Port Number
BSD UNIX **r** commands (**rsh, rlogin,** and so forth)	TCP	512 through 514
line printer daemon (lpd)	TCP	515
UNIX-to-UNIX copy program daemon (uucpd)	TCP	540
Open Windows	TCP and UDP	2000
X Windows	TCP and UDP	6000+

* Port 111 is only a directory service. If you can guess the ports on which the actual data services are provided, you can access them. Most RPC services do not have fixed port numbers. You should find the ports on which these services can be found and block them. Unfortunately, because ports can be bound anywhere, Cisco recommends blocking all UDP ports except DNS where practical.

NOTES

Cisco recommends that you filter the finger TCP service at port 79 to prevent outsiders from learning about internal user directories and the names of hosts from which users log in.

Input Access Lists

In Software Release 9.21, Cisco introduces the ability to assign input access lists to an interface. This allows a network administrator to filter packets before they enter the router, instead of as they leave the router. In most cases, input access lists and output access lists accomplish the same functionality; however, input access lists are more intuitive to some people and can be used to prevent some types of IP address "spoofing" where output access lists will not provide sufficient security.

Figure 16–3 illustrates a host that is "spoofing," or illegally claiming to be an address that it is not. Someone in the outside world is claiming to originate traffic from network 131.108.17.0. Although the address is spoofed, the router interface to the outside world assumes that the packet is coming from 131.108.17.0. If the input access list on the router allows traffic coming from 131.108.17.0, it will accept the illegal packet. To avoid this spoofing situation, an input access list should be applied to the router interface to the outside world. This access list would not allow any packets with addresses that are from the internal networks of which the router is aware (17.0 and 18.0).

Figure 16–3
A host that is spoofing.

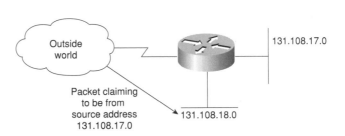

Outside world

Packet claiming to be from source address 131.108.17.0

131.108.17.0

131.108.18.0

If you have several internal networks connected to the firewall router and the router is using output filters, traffic between internal networks will see a reduction in performance created by the access list filters. If input filters are used only on the interface going from the router to the outside world, internal networks will not see any reduction in performance.

— **NOTES** ▸————————————————————————————————

If an address uses source routing, it can send and receive traffic through the firewall router. For this reason, you should always disable source routing on the firewall router with the **no ip source-route** command.

———————————————————————————————————————

Configuring the Firewall Communication Server

In this case study, the firewall communication server has a single inbound modem on line 2:

```
interface Ethernet0
ip address B.B.13.2 255.255.255.0
!
access-list 10 deny B.B.14.0 0.0.0.255
access-list 10 permit B.B.0.0 0.0.255.255
!
access-list 11 deny B.B.13.2 0.0.0.0
access-list 11 permit B.B.0.0 0.0.255.255
!
line 2
login tacacs
location FireWallCS#2
!
access-class 10 in
access-class 11 out
!
modem answer-timeout 60
modem InOut
telnet transparent
terminal-type dialup
flowcontrol hardware
stopbits 1
rxspeed 38400
txspeed 38400
!
tacacs-server host B.B.1.100
tacacs-server host B.B.1.101
tacacs-server extended
!
line vty 0 15
login tacacs
```

Defining Access Lists

In this example, the network number is used to permit or deny access; therefore, standard IP access list numbers (range 1 through 99) are used. For incoming connections to modem lines, only packets from hosts on the internal Class B network and packets from those hosts on the firewall subnetwork are permitted:

```
access-list 10 deny B.B.14.0 0.0.0.255
access-list 10 permit B.B.0.0 0.0.255.255
```

Outgoing connections are allowed only to internal network hosts and to the communication server. This prevents a modem line in the outside world from calling out on a second modem line:

```
access-list 11 deny B.B.13.2 0.0.0.0
access-list 11 permit B.B.0.0 0.0.255.255
```

Applying Access Lists to Lines

Apply an access list to an asynchronous line with the **access-class** command. In this case study, the restrictions from access list 10 are applied to incoming connections on line 2. The restrictions from access list 11 are applied to outgoing connections on line 2.

```
access-class 10 in
access-class 11 out
```

Using Banners to Set Up Unauthorized Use Notifications

It is also wise to use the **banner exec** global configuration command to provide messages and unauthorized use notifications, which will be displayed on all new connections. For example, on the communication server, you can enter the following message:

```
banner exec ^C
If you have problems with the dial-in lines, please send mail to helpdesk@Corporation
X.com. If you get the message "% Your account is expiring", please send mail with name and
voicemail box to helpdesk@CorporationX.com, and someone will contact you to renew your
account. Unauthorized use of these resources is prohibited.
```

SECURING NONSTANDARD SERVICES

There are a number of nonstandard services available from the Internet that provide value-added services when connecting to the outside world. In the case of a connection to the Internet, these services can be very elaborate and complex. Examples of these services are World Wide Web (WWW), Wide Area Information Service (WAIS), gopher, and Mosaic. Most of these systems are concerned with providing a wealth of information to the user in some organized fashion and allowing structured browsing and searching.

Most of these systems have their own defined protocol. Some, such as Mosaic, use several different protocols to obtain the information in question. Use caution when designing access lists applicable to each of these services. In many cases, the access lists will become interrelated as these services become interrelated.

SUMMARY

Although this case study illustrates how to use Cisco network layer features to increase network security on IP networks, in order to have comprehensive security, you must address all systems and layers.

RECOMMENDED READING

This section contains a list of publications that provide internetwork security information.

Books and Periodicals

Cheswick, B. and Bellovin, S. *Firewalls and Internet Security*. Addison-Wesley.

Comer, D.E and Stevens, D.L., *Internetworking with TCP/IP*. Volumes I-III. Englewood Cliffs, New Jersey: Prentice Hall; 1991-1993.

Curry, D. *UNIX System Security—A Guide for Users and System Administrators*.

Garfinkel and Spafford. *Practical UNIX Security*. O'Reilly & Associates.

Quarterman, J. and Carl-Mitchell, S. *The Internet Connection*, Reading, Massachusetts: Addison-Wesley Publishing Company; 1994.

Ranum, M. J. *Thinking about Firewalls*, Trusted Information Systems, Inc.

Stoll, C. *The Cuckoo's Egg*. Doubleday.

Treese, G. W. and Wolman, A. *X through the Firewall and Other Application Relays*.

Requests For Comments (RFCs)

RFC 1118. "The Hitchhiker's Guide to the Internet." September 1989.

RFC 1175. "A Bibliography of Internetworking Information." August 1990.

RFC1244. "Site Security Handbook." July 1991.

RFC 1340. "Assigned Numbers." July 1992.

RFC 1446. "Security Protocols for SNMPv2." April 1993.

RFC 1463. "FYI on Introducing the Internet—A Short Bibliography of Introductory Internetworking Readings for the Network Novice." May 1993.

RFC 1492. "An Access Control Protocol, Sometimes Called TACACS." July 1993.

Internet Directories

Documents at *gopher.nist.gov.*

The "Computer Underground Digest" in the */pub/cud* directory at *ftp.eff.org.*

Documents in the */dist/internet_security* directory at *research.att.com.*

Integrating Enhanced IGRP into Existing Networks

The Enhanced Interior Gateway Routing Protocol (IGRP) combines the ease of use of traditional routing protocols with the fast rerouting capabilities of link-state protocols, providing advanced capabilities for fast convergence and partial updates. When a network topology change occurs, the Diffusing Algorithm (DUAL) used with Enhanced IGRP provides convergence in less than five seconds in most cases. This is equivalent to the convergence achieved by link-state protocols such as Open Shortest Path First (OSPF), Novell Link Services Protocol (NLSP), and Intermediate System-to-Intermediate System (IS-IS). In addition, Enhanced IGRP sends routing update information only when changes occur, and only the changed information is sent to affected routers.

Enhanced IGRP supports three network level protocols: IP, AppleTalk, and Novell Internetwork Packet Exchange (IPX). Each of these has protocol-specific, value-added functionality. IP Enhanced IGRP supports variable-length subnet masks (VLSMs). IPX Novell Enhanced IGRP supports incremental Service Advertisement Protocol (SAP) updates, removes the Routing Information Protocol (RIP) limitation of 15 hop counts, and provides optimal path use. A router running AppleTalk Enhanced IGRP supports partial, bounded routing updates and provides load sharing and optimal path use.

The case study provided here discusses the benefits and considerations involved in integrating Enhanced IGRP into the following types of internetworks:

- *IP*—The existing IP network is running IGRP

- *Novell IPX*—The existing IPX network is running RIP and SAP

- *AppleTalk*—The existing AppleTalk network is running the Routing Table Maintenance Protocol (RTMP)

When integrating Enhanced IGRP into existing networks, plan a phased implementation. Add Enhanced IGRP at the periphery of the network by configuring Enhanced IGRP on a boundary router on the backbone off the core network. Then integrate Enhanced IGRP into the core network.

NOTES

For a discussion of Enhanced IGRP network design considerations and details on DUAL convergence, see the *Internetwork Design Guide*.

CAUTION

If you are using *candidate default route* in IP Enhanced IGRP and have installed multiple releases of Cisco router software within your internetwork that include any versions prior to September 1994, contact your Cisco technical support representative for version compatibility and software upgrade information. Refer to your software release notes for details. If you plan to implement Enhanced IGRP over a Frame Relay network, you should ensure that your network is hierarchical in design and adheres to sound design principles.

IP NETWORK

This case study illustrates the integration of Enhanced IGRP into an IGRP internetwork in two phases: configuring an IGRP network and adding Enhanced IGRP to the network. The key considerations for integrating Enhanced IGRP into an IP network running IGRP are as follows:

- Route selection
- Metric handling
- Redistribution from IGRP to Enhanced IGRP and vice versa
- Route summarization

Configuring an IGRP Network

IGRP is a dynamic distance vector routing protocol designed by Cisco Systems in the mid-1980s for routing in an autonomous system (AS) containing large, arbitrarily complex networks with diverse media.

An autonomous system is a collection of interconnected routers under common management control, or with similar routing policies and requirements. Typically, an autonomous system consists of routers connecting multiple IP network numbers. Routes originating from one autonomous system that need to be advertised into other autonomous systems must be redistributed.

In Figure 17–1, Routers A, B, C, and D are configured to run IGRP in autonomous system 68.

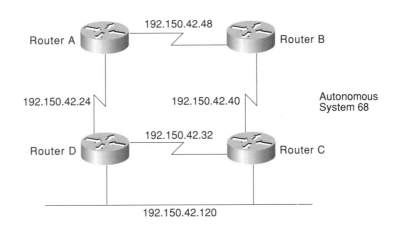

Figure 17–1
Configuring an IGRP network.

The configuration commands to enable IGRP routing for Routers A, B, C, and D are as follows:
```
router igrp 68
network 192.150.42.0
```

Adding Enhanced IGRP to IGRP Networks

This section provides two examples of adding Enhanced IGRP to IGRP networks:

* Adding Enhanced IGRP to a Single IGRP Network
* Adding Enhanced IGRP to Multiple IGRP Networks

Adding Enhanced IGRP to a Single IGRP Network

In Figure 17–2, Router E acts as the boundary router, running both IGRP and Enhanced IGRP, and redistributing information between IGRP autonomous system 68 into the Enhanced IGRP autonomous system 68.

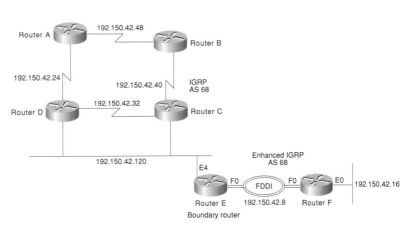

Figure 17–2
Adding Enhanced IGRP to a single IGRP network.

Router E, the boundary router, is configured to run both IGRP and Enhanced IGRP as follows:

```
router igrp 68
network 192.150.42.0
router eigrp 68
network 192.150.42.0
```

— **NOTES** ————————————————————————————————————

Redistribution is automatic because the autonomous system number for IGRP and Enhanced IGRP are the same.

——

Router F runs Enhanced IGRP only:

```
router eigrp 68
network 192.150.42.0
```

A **show ip route** command on Router E shows networks that are directly connected (C), routes learned from IGRP (I), and routes learned from Enhanced IGRP (D):

```
     192.150.42.0 is subnetted (mask is 255.255.255.248), 7 subnets
C       192.150.42.120 is directly connected, Ethernet4
I       192.150.42.48 [100/2860] via 192.150.42.123, 0:00:08, Ethernet4
I       192.150.42.40 [100/2850] via 192.150.42.121, 0:00:08, Ethernet4
I       192.150.42.32 [100/2850] via 192.150.42.121, 0:00:08, Ethernet4
I       192.150.42.24 [100/2760] via 192.150.42.123, 0:00:08, Ethernet4
D       192.150.42.16 [90/30720] via 192.150.42.10, 0:00:38, Fddi0
C       192.150.42.8 is directly connected, Fddi0
```

A **show ip route** command on Router F shows that all routes are learned via enhanced IGRP (D) or are directly connected (C):

```
     192.150.42.0 is subnetted (mask is 255.255.255.248), 7 subnets
D       192.150.42.120 [90/729600] via 192.150.42.9, 0:01:16, Fddi0
D EX    192.150.42.48 [170/757760] via 192.150.42.9, 0:01:16, Fddi0
D EX    192.150.42.40 [170/755200] via 192.150.42.9, 0:01:16, Fddi0
D EX    192.150.42.32 [170/755200] via 192.150.42.9, 0:01:16, Fddi0
D EX    192.150.42.24 [170/732160] via 192.150.42.9, 0:01:16, Fddi0
C       192.150.42.16 is directly connected, Ethernet0
C       192.150.42.8 is directly connected, Fddi0
```

Subnetwork 120 is seen as an internal route. All other routes are external (EX) because they were learned via IGRP in Router E and redistributed into Enhanced IGRP.

A **show ip eigrp topology** command on Router F shows that the state of each of the networks is passive (P) and that each network has one successor and lists the feasible distance (FD) of each successor via a neighbor to the destination. The computed/advertised metric is listed. Then the interface through which the neighbor network is available is provided.

```
     IP-EIGRP Topology Table for process 68
     Codes: P - Passive, A - Active, U - Update, Q - Query, R - Reply,
            r - Reply status
     P 192.150.42.120 255.255.255.248, 1 successors, FD is 2172416
             via 192.150.42.9 (2172416/2169856), Fddi0
     P 192.150.42.8 255.255.255.248, 1 successors, FD is 28160
             via Connected, Fddi0
```

```
P 192.150.42.48 255.255.255.248, 1 successors, FD is 2560515840
          via 192.150.42.9 (2560515840/2560513280), Fddi0
P 192.150.42.16 255.255.255.248, 1 successors, FD is 281600
          via Connected, Ethernet0
P 192.150.42.40 255.255.255.248, 1 successors, FD is 2560026880
          via 192.150.42.9 (2560026880/2560001280), Fddi0
P 192.150.42.32 255.255.255.248, 1 successors, FD is 2560026880
          via 192.150.42.9 (2560026880/2560001280), Fddi0
```

Adding Enhanced IGRP to Multiple IGRP Networks

In Figure 17–3, Routers A, B, and C are connected to each other through several different networks. Routers A, B, and C are configured to run IGRP only within IGRP autonomous system (AS) 68. Router A redistributes static routes for subnetworks of network 9.0.0.0 (not shown). Assume that the IGRP AS continues at network 10.0.0.0.

Figure 17–3
Adding Enhanced IGRP to multiple IGRP networks.

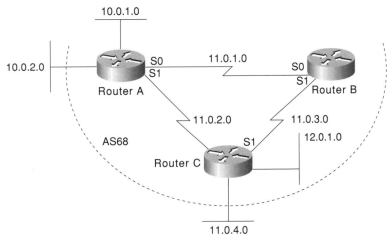

The configuration for Router A is as follows:
```
router igrp 68
network 10.0.0.0
network 11.0.0.0
default-metric 1000 100 1 1 1500
redistribute static
ip route 9.1.0.0 255.255.0.0 e0
ip route 9.2.0.0 255.255.0.0 e1
```

The configuration for Router B is as follows:
```
router igrp 68
network 11.0.0.0
```

The configuration for Router C is as follows:
```
router igrp 68
network 11.0.0.0
network 12.0.0.0
```

This example takes you through the steps to add Enhanced IGRP to the internetwork one router at a time:

Step 1   Configure Enhanced IGRP for Router C as follows:
```
router eigrp 68
network 11.0.0.0
network 12.0.0.0
```

Because they are directly connected networks, Router C automatically summarizes networks 11.0.0.0 and 12.0.0.0 in its routing updates. Router C learns about networks 9.0.0.0 and 10.0.0.0 through IGRP. Networks 9.0.0.0 and 10.0.0.0 are already IGRP- summarized by Router A before they reach Router C.

Step 2   Configure Router A to run Enhanced IGRP as follows:
```
router eigrp 68
network 10.0.0.0
network 11.0.0.0
default-metric 1000 100 1 1 1500
redistribute static
```

Router A now automatically summarizes networks 10.0.0.0 and 11.0.0.0 in its Enhanced IGRP routing updates. It also continues to summarize these networks in its IGRP routing updates. However, automatic summarization of network 9.0.0.0 through Enhanced IGRP is not performed.

Router C now learns Enhanced IGRP routes for specific subnetworks of network 9.0.0.0 from Router A. At the same time, Router C continues to receive a summary route for network 9.0.0.0 though IGRP from Router A. The summary route for network 10.0.0.0, which Router C had previously learned through IGRP from Router A, is replaced with an Enhanced IGRP route in Router C's routing table.

Step 3   Configure Router A to ensure that Router C does not unnecessarily learn about specific subnetworks of network 9.0.0.0. The following commands enable summarization of network 9.0.0.0 at Router A:
```
interface serial 1
ip summary-address eigrp 68 9.0.0.0 255.0.0.0
```

With this configuration on Router A, Router C's IGRP summary route for network 9.0.0.0 is replaced with an Enhanced IGRP summary route, and the more specific subnetworks of network 9.0.0.0 are no longer known by Router C.

Step 4   Enable Enhanced IGRP on Router B as follows:
```
router eigrp 68
network 11.0.0.0
```

Step 5   Ensure that Router B does not unnecessarily learn about specific subnetworks of network 9.0.0.0. Therefore, configure summarization of network 9.0.0.0 at Router A as follows:
```
interface serial 0
ip summary-address eigrp 68 9.0.0.0 255.0.0.0
```

With this configuration on Router A, Router B learns a summary route for network 12.0.0.0 through Enhanced IGRP from Router C. Router B learns summary routes for networks 9.0.0.0 and 10.0.0.0 through Enhanced IGRP from Router A.

Step 6   Now that both of the next hop routers (Routers B and C) are running Enhanced IGRP, it is no longer necessary for these routers to run IGRP. Disable IGRP on Routers B and C with the following command:

```
no router igrp 68
```

Router A continues to run both IGRP and Enhanced IGRP and redistribute static routes.

If there were more routers on the network, you could continue deployment of Enhanced IGRP throughout network 10.0.0.0 one router at a time.

Route Selection

Enhanced IGRP uses three kinds of routes: internal, external, and summary. Internal routes are routes that are learned from Enhanced IGRP. External routes are routes that are learned from another protocol and then redistributed into Enhanced IGRP. Summary routes are routes that Enhanced IGRP may dynamically create due to auto summarization, or due to an explicit summary route configuration. Route selection is based on administrative distance. The default administrative distance for Enhanced IGRP is 90 (internal), 170 (external), or 5 (summary). For IGRP, the default administrative distance is 100 because internal Enhanced IGRP routes take precedence over IGRP routes, and IGRP routes are preferred to external Enhanced IGRP routes.

Metric Handling

The metric calculation and default metric value for IGRP and Enhanced IGRP are the same. By default, the composite metric is the sum of the segment delays and the lowest segment bandwidth (scaled and inverted) for a given route. Although you can adjust the default value with the **metric weights** command, the defaults were carefully selected to provide excellent operation in most networks.

Redistribution

Enhanced IGRP can be added to an IGRP network in two ways: using the same IGRP AS number or using a new AS number. If Enhanced IGRP uses the same AS number as IGRP, redistribution of IGRP into Enhanced IGRP and redistribution of Enhanced IGRP into IGRP occurs. If Enhanced IGRP uses a different AS number, the network administrator needs to configure redistribution manually with the **redistribute** command. For redistributing information from Enhanced IGRP into other dynamic routing protocols besides IGRP and vice versa, the designer must use the **redistribute** and **default-metric** commands. IGRP routes redistributed into Enhanced IGRP are marked as external.

Route Summarization

With IGRP, routing information advertised out an interface is often automatically summarized at major network number boundaries. Specifically, this automatic summarization occurs for those routes whose major network number differs from the major network number of the interface to which the advertisement is being sent. The remaining routes, which are part of the major network number of the interface, are advertised without summarization. For the following example, refer to Figure 17–4.

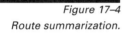

Figure 17–4
Route summarization.

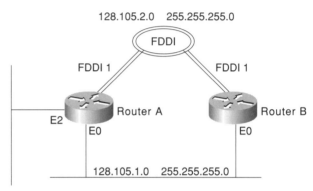

In this example, Router A is directly connected to two different major networks and configured as follows:

```
interface ethernet 0
ip address 128.105.1.1 255.255.255.0
interface fddi 1
ip address 128.105.2.1 255.255.255.0
interface ethernet 2
ip address 128.106.1.1 255.255.255.0
router igrp 5
network 128.105.0.0
network 128.106.0.0
```

When advertising routing information out Ethernet interface 0, IGRP will summarize network 128.106.0.0 and will not summarize network 128.105.0.0. Therefore, IGRP will advertise routes for 128.106.0.0 with a network mask of 255.255.0.0 and routes for 128.105.2.1 with a network mask of 255.255.255.0.

Because it provides automatic route summarization, Enhanced IGRP will advertise the same routing information in the previous IGRP example. However, in the Enhanced IGRP example that follows, the previous configuration is modified so that it allows redistribution of routing information that is not summarized:

```
ip route 128.107.1.0 255.255.255.0 128.106.1.2
router eigrp 5
redistribute static
```

```
network 128.105.0.0
network 128.106.0.0
router igrp 5
redistribute static
```

At this point, there is a third subnetted major network in the IP routing table. When advertising out Ethernet interface 0, IGRP will summarize the route for 128.107.1.0 as 128.107.0.0 with a network mask of 255.255.0.0. However, Enhanced IGRP will not summarize network 128.107.0.0. It will advertise 128.107.1.0 with network mask 255.255.255.0. Enhanced IGRP's automatic summarization only applies to networks that are directly connected, not redistributed. For Enhanced IGRP, you can explicitly cause network 128.107.0.0 to be summarized out all three interfaces as shown in the following example:

```
interface ethernet 0
ip summary-address eigrp 5 128.107.0.0 255.255.0.0
interface fddi 1
ip summary-address eigrp 5 128.107.0.0 255.255.0.0
interface ethernet 2
ip summary-address eigrp 5 128.107.0.0 255.255.0.0
```

Redistribution between Enhanced IGRP and RIP

Figure 17–5 shows a router that connects two networks; one network uses RIP and the other network uses Enhanced IGRP. The goal for the router is to advertise RIP routes in the Enhanced IGRP network and to advertise Enhanced IGRP routes in the RIP network, while preventing the occurrence of route feedback. (That is, the router must be configured so that Enhanced IGRP does not send routes learned from RIP back into the RIP network and so that RIP does not send routes learned from Enhanced IGRP back into the Enhanced IGRP network.)

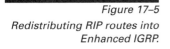

Figure 17–5

Redistributing RIP routes into
Enhanced IGRP.

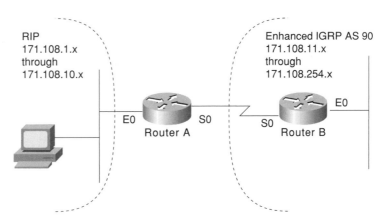

The RIP portion of the configuration for Router A is as follows:

```
router rip
network 171.108.0.0
redistribute eigrp 90
```

```
default-metric 2
passive-interface serial 0
```

The **router rip** global configuration command starts a RIP process.

The **network** router configuration command specifies that the RIP process is to send RIP updates out on the interfaces that are directly connected to network number 171.108.0.0. In this case, the RIP process will send updates out on Ethernet interface 0 and not on serial interface 0 because of the **passive-interface** command applied to serial interface 0.

The **redistribute eigrp** router configuration command specifies that routing information derived from Enhanced IGRP be advertised in RIP routing updates.

The **default-metric** router configuration command causes RIP to use the same metric value (in this case, a hop count of 2) for all routes obtained from Enhanced IGRP. A default metric helps solve the problem of redistributing routes that have incompatible metrics. Whenever metrics do not convert, using a default metric provides a reasonable substitute and enables the redistribution to proceed.

The **passive-interface** router configuration command disables the sending of routing updates on serial interface 0. In this case, the **passive-interface** command is used with RIP, which means the router does not send out any updates on a passive interface, but the router still processes updates that it receives on that interface. The result is that the router still learns of networks that are behind a passive interface. (The same is true when the **passive-interface** command is used with IGRP.)

The Enhanced IGRP portion of the configuration for Router A is as follows:

```
router eigrp 90
network 171.108.0.0
redistribute rip
default-metric 1544 100 255 1 1500
distribute-list 1 in
passive interface ethernet 0
access-list 1 permit ip 171.108.1.0 255.255.255.0
access-list 1 permit ip 171.108.2.0 255.255.255.0
access-list 1 permit ip 171.108.3.0 255.255.255.0
access-list 1 permit ip 171.108.4.0 255.255.255.0
access-list 1 permit ip 171.108.5.0 255.255.255.0
access-list 1 permit ip 171.108.6.0 255.255.255.0
access-list 1 permit ip 171.108.7.0 255.255.255.0
access-list 1 permit ip 171.108.8.0 255.255.255.0
access-list 1 permit ip 171.108.9.0 255.255.255.0
access-list 1 permit ip 171.108.10.0 255.255.255.0
access-list 1 deny ip
```

The **router eigrp** global configuration command starts an Enhanced IGRP process and assigns to it autonomous system number 90.

The **network** router configuration command specifies that the Enhanced IGRP process is to send Enhanced IGRP updates to the interfaces that are directly connected to network number 171.108.0.0. In this case, the Enhanced IGRP process will send updates out on serial interface 0 and not on Ethernet interface 0 because of the **passive-interface** command applied to Ethernet interface 0.

The **redistribute eigrp** router configuration command specifies that routing information derived from RIP be advertised in Enhanced IGRP routing updates.

The **default-metric** router configuration command assigns an Enhanced IGRP metric to all RIP-derived routes. The first value (1544) specifies a minimum bandwidth of 1544 kilobits per second. The second value (100) specifies a route delay in tens of microseconds. The third value (255) specifies the connection is guaranteed to be 100 percent reliable. The fourth value (1) specifies the effective bandwidth of the route. The fifth value (1500) specifies in bytes the maximum transmission unit (MTU) of the route.

The **distribute-list in** router configuration command causes the router to use access list 1 to filter networks learned from RIP and allows only those networks that match the list to be redistributed into Enhanced IGRP. This prevents route feedback loops from occurring.

When used with Enhanced IGRP, the **passive-interface** router configuration command has a different effect than it has when used with RIP or IGRP. When the **passive-interface** command is used with Enhanced IGRP, the router does not send out any updates—including hello messages—on the interface. Because hello messages are not sent, the router cannot discover any neighbors on that interface, which means that the router does not learn about networks that are behind a passive interface.

Access list 1 permits subnetworks 1 through 10 and denies all other networks. Although ten statements have been used, this particular access list could be written with four **access-list** commands if the address space had been divided efficiently. This example illustrates the need to think carefully about how to divide an address space. For example, if the RIP AS had been subnets 0 through 7, a single access list statement would have covered all of the subnetworks. The implication is that, when using a protocol that can summarize, summarization can be achieved much more efficiently when the IP address space is divided optimally. For information about dividing an IP address space optimally, see Appendix A, "Subnetting an IP Address Space."

NOVELL IPX NETWORK

This case study illustrates the integration of Enhanced IGRP into a Novell IPX internetwork in two phases: configuring an IPX network and adding Enhanced IGRP to the IPX network. The key considerations for integrating Enhanced IGRP into an IPX network running RIP and SAP are as follows:

- Route selection
- Redistribution metric handling
- Redistribution from IPX RIP to Enhanced IGRP and vice versa
- Reducing SAP traffic

Configuring a Novell IPX Network

Cisco's implementation of Novell's IPX protocol provides all the functions of a Novell router. In this case study, routers are configured to run Novell IPX. (See Figure 17–6.)

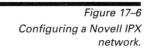

Figure 17–6
Configuring a Novell IPX
network.

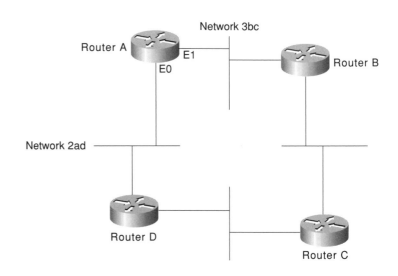

The configuration commands to enable IPX routing for Router A are as follows:

```
ipx routing
interface ethernet 0
ipx network 2ad
interface ethernet 1
ipx network 3bc
```

NOTES

In Software Release 9.21 and later, the command to enable Novell IPX routing is **ipx** rather than **novell**.

Adding Enhanced IGRP to a Novell IPX Network

Enhanced IGRP for a Novell IPX network has the same fast rerouting and partial update capabilities as Enhanced IGRP for IP. In addition, Enhanced IGRP has several capabilities that are designed to facilitate the building of large, robust Novell IPX networks.

The first capability is support for incremental SAP updates. Novell IPX RIP routers send out large RIP and SAP updates every 60 seconds. This can consume substantial amounts of bandwidth. Enhanced IGRP for IPX sends out SAP updates only when changes occur and sends only changed information.

The second capability that Enhanced IGRP adds to IPX networks is the ability to build large networks. IPX RIP networks have a diameter limit of 15 hops. Enhanced IGRP networks can have a diameter of 224 hops.

The third capability that Enhanced IGRP for Novell IPX provides is optimal path selection. The RIP metric for route determination is based on ticks with hop count used as a tie-breaker. If more than one route has the same value for the tick metric, the route with the least number of hops is preferred. Instead of ticks and hop count, IPX Enhanced IGRP uses a combination of these metrics:

delay, bandwidth, reliability, and load. For an illustration of how IPX Enhanced IGRP provides optimal path selection, see Figure 17–7.

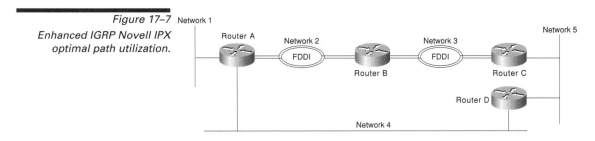

Figure 17–7
Enhanced IGRP Novell IPX
optimal path utilization.

Both Ethernet and FDDI interfaces have a tick value of 1. If configured for Novell RIP, Router A will choose the Ethernet connection via network 4 to reach network 5 because Router D is only one hop away from Router A. However, the fastest path to network 5 is two hops away, via the FDDI rings. With IPX Enhanced IGRP configured, Router A will automatically take the optimal path through Routers B and C to reach network 5.

To add Enhanced IGRP to a Novell RIP and SAP network, configure Enhanced IGRP on the Cisco router interfaces that connect to other Cisco routers also running Enhanced IGRP. Configure RIP and SAP on the interfaces that connect to Novell hosts and or Novell routers that do not support Enhanced IGRP.

In Figure 17–8, Routers E, F, and G are running IPX Enhanced IGRP. Router E redistributes Enhanced IGRP route information via Network AA to Router D.

Figure 17–8
Adding Enhanced IGRP to a
Novell IPX network.

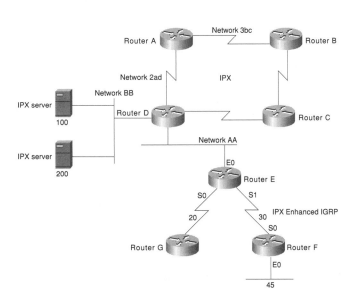

The configuration for Router E is as follows:

```
ipx routing
interface ethernet 0
ipx network AA
interface serial 0
ipx network 20
interface serial 1
ipx network 30
ipx router eigrp 10
network 20
network 30
ipx router rip
no network 20
```

With Enhanced IGRP configured, periodic SAP updates are replaced with Enhanced IGRP incremental updates when an Enhanced IGRP peer is found. Unless RIP is explicitly disabled for an IPX network number, as shown for network 20, both RIP and Enhanced IGRP will be active on the interface associated with that network number. Based on the above configuration, and assuming an Enhanced IGRP peer on each Enhanced IGRP configured interface, RIP updates are sent on networks AA and 30, while Enhanced IGRP routing updates are sent on networks 20 and 30. Incremental SAP updates are sent on network 20 and network 30, and periodic SAP updates are sent on network AA.

The configuration for Router F is as follows:

```
ipx routing
interface ethernet 0
ipx network 45
interface serial 0
ipx network 30
ipx router eigrp 10
network 30
network 45
```

Partial output for a **show ipx route** command on Router E indicates that network 45 was discovered using Enhanced IGRP (E), whereas network BB was discovered via a RIP (R) update:

```
R   Net 3bc
R   Net 2ad
C   Net 20 (HDLC), is directly connected, 66 uses, Serial0
C   Net 30 (HDLC), is directly connected, 73 uses, Serial1
E   Net 45 [2195456/0] via 30.0000.0c00.c47e, age 0:01:23, 1 uses, Serial1
C   Net AA (NOVELL-ETHER), is directly connected, 3 uses, Ethernet0
R   Net BB [1/1] via AA.0000.0c03.8b25,  48 sec, 87 uses, Ethernet0
```

Partial output for a **show ipx route** command on Router F indicates that networks 20, AA, and BB were discovered using Enhanced IGRP (E):

```
E   Net 20 [2681856/0] via 30.0000.0c01.f0ed, age 0:02:57, 1 uses, Serial0
C   Net 30 (HDLC), is directly connected, 47 uses, Serial0
C   Net 45 (NOVELL-ETHER), is directly connected, 45 uses, Ethernet0
E   Net AA [267008000/0] via 30.0000.0c01.f0ed, age 0:02:57, 1 uses, Serial0
E   Net BB [268416000/2] via 30.0000.0c01.f0ed, age 0:02:57, 11 uses, Serial0
```

A **show ipx servers** command on Router E shows that server information was learned via periodic (P) SAP updates:

```
Codes: S - Static, I - Incremental, P - Periodic, H - Holddown
5 Total IPX Servers
Table ordering is based on routing and server info
Type Name             Net Address       Port    RouteHopsItf
P    4 Networkers      100.0000.0000.0001:0666    2/022Et1
P    5 Chicago         100.0000.0000.0001:0234    2/022Et1
P    7 Michigan        100.0000.0000.0001:0123    2/022Et1
P    8 NetTest1        200.0000.0000.0001:0345    2/022Et1
P    8 NetTest         200.0000.0000.0001:0456    2/022Et1
```

A **show ipx servers** command on Router F shows that server information was learned via incremental SAP (I) updates allowed with Enhanced IGRP:

```
Codes: S - Static, I - Incremental, P - Periodic, H - Holddown
5 Total IPX Servers
Table ordering is based on routing and server info
Type Name             Net Address       Port    RouteHopsItf
I    4 Networkers      100.0000.0000.0001:0666 268416000/033Se0
I    5 Chicago         100.0000.0000.0001:0234 268416000/033Se0
I    7 Michigan        100.0000.0000.0001:0123 268416000/033Se0
I    8 NetTest1        200.0000.0000.0001:0345 268416000/033Se0
I    8 NetTest         200.0000.0000.0001:0456 268416000/033Se0
```

A **show ipx eigrp topology** command on Router E shows that the state of the networks is passive (P) and that each network provides one successor, and it lists the feasible distance (FD) of each successor via a neighbor to the destination. For example, for network 45, the neighbor is located at address 0000.0c00.c47e and the computed/advertised cost metric for that neighbor to the destination is 2195456/281600:

```
IPX EIGRP Topology Table for process 10
Codes: P - Passive, A - Active, U - Update, Q - Query, R - Reply,
       r - Reply status
P 20, 1 successors, FD is 1
         via Connected, Serial0
P 30, 1 successors, FD is 1
         via Connected, Serial1
P 45, 1 successors, FD is 2195456
         via 30.0000.0c00.c47e (2195456/281600), Serial1
P AA, 1 successors, FD is 266496000
         via Redistributed (266496000/0),
P BB, 1 successors, FD is 267904000
         via Redistributed (267904000/0),
```

The output for a **show ipx eigrp topology** command on Router F lists the following information:

```
IPX EIGRP Topology Table for process 10
Codes: P - Passive, A - Active, U - Update, Q - Query, R - Reply,
       r - Reply status
P 20, 1 successors, FD is 2681856
         via 30.0000.0c01.f0ed (2681856/2169856), Serial0
P 30, 1 successors, FD is 1
         via Connected, Serial0
P 45, 1 successors, FD is 1
         via Connected, Ethernet0
P AA, 1 successors, FD is 267008000
         via 30.0000.0c01.f0ed (267008000/266496000), Serial0
P BB, 1 successors, FD is 268416000
         via 30.0000.0c01.f0ed (268416000/267904000), Serial0
```

Route Selection

IPX Enhanced IGRP routes are automatically preferred over RIP routes regardless of metrics unless a RIP route has a hop count less than the external hop count carried in the Enhanced IGRP update, for example, a server advertising its own internal network.

Redistribution and Metric Handling

Redistribution is automatic between RIP and Enhanced IGRP, and vice versa. Automatic redistribution can be turned off using the **no redistribute** command. Redistribution is not automatic between different Enhanced IGRP autonomous systems.

The metric handling for integrating RIP into Enhanced IGRP is bandwidth plus delay, left shifted by 8 bits. The metric handling for Enhanced IGRP to RIP is the external metric plus 1. An IPX Enhanced IGRP router that is redistributing RIP into Enhanced IGRP takes the RIP metric associated with each RIP route, increments it, and stores that metric in the Enhanced IGRP routing table as the external metric.

In Figure 17–9, a Novell IPX server with an internal network number of 100 advertises this network number using RIP on network 222. Router A hears this advertisement and installs it in its routing table as being 1 hop and 1 tick away. Router A then announces this network to Router B on network 501 using Enhanced IGRP.

Figure 17–9
IPX metric handling example.

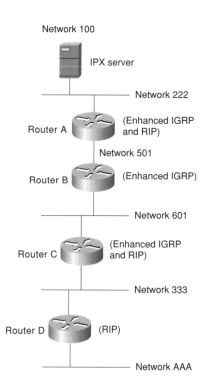

The configuration for Router A is as follows:

```
ipx routing
!
interface ethernet 0
ipx network 222
!
interface serial 0
ipx network 501
!
ipx router eigrp 9000
network 222
network 501
!
!The following commands turn off IPX RIP on the serial interface:
!
ipx router rip
no network 501
```

The configuration for Router B is as follows:

```
ipx routing
!
interface ethernet 0
ipx network 601
!
interface serial 0
ipx network 501


ipx router eigrp 9000
network 501
network 601
!
!The following command turns off IPX RIP on this router:
!
no ipx router rip
```

The configuration for Router C is as follows:

```
ipx routing
!
interface ethernet 0
ipx network 333
!
interface ethernet 1
ipx network 601
!
ipx router eigrp 9000
network 333
network 601
!
!The following commands turn off IPX RIP on ethernet 1:
!
ipx router rip
no network 601
```

The configuration for Router D is as follows:

```
ipx routing
!
interface ethernet 0
ipx network 333
!
interface ethernet 1
ipx network AAA
```

The output from a **show ipx route** command on Router A is as follows:

```
R  Net 100 [1/1] via 222.0260.8c4c.4f22,  59 sec, 1 uses, Ethernet0
C  Net 222 (ARPA), is directly connected, 1252 uses, Ethernet0
E  Net 333 [46277376/0] via 501.0000.0c05.84bc, age 0:04:07, 1 uses, Serial0
C  Net 501 (HDLC), is directly connected, 3908 uses, Serial0
E  Net 601 [46251776/0] via 501.0000.0c05.84bc, age 5:21:38, 1 uses, Serial0
E  Net AAA [268441600/2] via 501.0000.0c05.84bc, age 0:16:23, 1 uses, Serial0
```

The output from a **show ipx route** command on Router B is as follows:

```
E  Net 100 [268416000/2] via 501.0000.0c05.84b4, age 0:07:30, 2 uses, Serial0
E  Net 222 [267008000/0] via 501.0000.0c05.84b4, age 0:07:30, 1 uses, Serial0
E  Net 333 [307200/0] via 601.0000.0c05.84d3, age 0:07:30, 1 uses, Ethernet0
C  Net 501 (HDLC), is directly connected, 4934 uses, Serial0
C  Net 601 (NOVELL-ETHER), is directly connected, 16304 uses, Ethernet0
E  Net AAA [267929600/2] via 601.0000.0c05.84d3, age 0:14:40, 1 uses, Ethernet0
```

The output from a **show ipx route** command on Router C is as follows:

```
E  Net 100 [268441600/2] via 601.0000.0c05.84bf, age 0:07:33, 1 uses, Ethernet1
E  Net 222 [267033600/0] via 601.0000.0c05.84bf, age 0:07:34, 1 uses, Ethernet1
C  Net 333 (NOVELL-ETHER), is directly connected, 15121 uses, Ethernet0
E  Net 501 [46251776/0] via 601.0000.0c05.84bf, age 0:07:32, 9 uses, Ethernet1
C  Net 601 (NOVELL-ETHER), is directly connected, 1346 uses, Ethernet1
R  Net AAA [1/1] via 333.0000.0c05.8b25,  35 sec, 1 uses, Ethernet0
```

The output from a **show ipx route** command on Router D is as follows:

```
R  Net 100 [8/2] via 333.0000.0c05.84d1,  18 sec, 1 uses, Ethernet0
R  Net 222 [6/1] via 333.0000.0c05.84d1,  18 sec, 1 uses, Ethernet0
R  Net 333 [1/1] via 333.0000.0c05.84d1,  18 sec, 1 uses, Ethernet0
R  Net 501 [3/1] via 333.0000.0c05.84d1,  17 sec, 3 uses, Ethernet0
R  Net 601 [1/1] via 333.0000.0c05.84d1,  18 sec, 1 uses, Ethernet0
C  Net AAA (SNAP), is directly connected, 20 uses, Ethernet1
```

The Enhanced IGRP metric is created using the RIP ticks for the delay vector. The hop count is incremented and stored as the external metric. The external delay is also stored. Router B computes the metric to network 100 given the information received from Router A and installs this in its routing table. In this case, the tick value for network 100 is 8.

The "2" after the slash in the routing entry for network 100 is the external metric. This number does not increase again while the route is in the Enhanced IGRP autonomous system. Router C computes the metric to network 100 through Router B and stores it in its routing table. Finally, Router C redistributes this information back into RIP with a hop count of 2 (the external metric) and a tick value derived from the original tick value of the RIP route (1) plus the Enhanced IGRP delay through the autonomous system converted to ticks.

Reducing SAP Traffic

Novell IPX RIP routers send out large RIP and SAP updates every 60 seconds regardless of whether a change has occurred. These updates can consume a substantial amount of bandwidth. You can reduce SAP update traffic by configuring Enhanced IGRP to do incremental SAP updates. When Enhanced IGRP is configured for incremental SAP updates, the updates consist only of information that has changed and the updates are sent out only when a change occurs, thus saving bandwidth.

When you configure Enhanced IGRP for incremental SAP updates, you can do the following:

- Retain RIP, in which case only the reliable transport of Enhanced IGRP is used for sending incremental SAP updates. (This is the preferred configuration over bandwidth-sensitive connections.)
- Turn off RIP, in which case Enhanced IGRP replaces RIP as the routing protocol.

Figure 17–10 shows a bandwidth-sensitive topology in which configuring incremental SAP updates is especially useful. The topology consists of a corporate network that uses a 56-Kbps Frame Relay connection to communicate with a remote branch office. The corporate network has several Novell servers, each of which advertises many services. Depending on the number of servers and the number of advertised services, a large portion of the available bandwidth could easily be consumed by SAP updates.

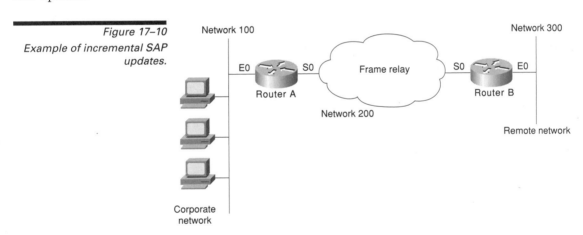

Figure 17–10
Example of incremental SAP updates.

Router A is configured as follows:

```
ipx routing
!
interface ethernet 0
ipx network 100
!
interface serial 0
encapsulation frame-relay
!
interface serial 0.1 point-to-point
```

```
ipx network 200
ipx sap-incremental eigrp 90 rsup-only
frame-relay interface-dlci 101
!
ipx router eigrp 90
network 200
```

The **ipx routing** global configuration command enables IPX routing on the router.

The **ipx network** interface configuration command enables IPX routing on Ethernet interface 0 for network 100.

For serial interface 0, the **encapsulation frame-relay** interface configuration command establishes Frame Relay encapsulation using Cisco's own encapsulation, which is a 4-byte header, with 2 bytes to identify the DLCI and 2 bytes to identify the packet type.

The **interface serial** global configuration command establishes a point-to-point subinterface (**0.1**). Subinterfaces are logical interfaces associated with a physical interface. Using subinterfaces allows Router A to receive multiple simultaneous connections over a single Frame Relay interface.

The **ipx network** interface configuration command enables IPX routing on subinterface serial interface 0.1 for network 200.

The **ipx sap-incremental** interface configuration command enables the incremental SAP feature. The required **eigrp** keyword enables Enhanced IGRP and its transport mechanism and, in this case, specifies an autonomous system number of 90. Because this command uses the **rsup-only** keyword, the router sends incremental SAP updates on this link.

The **frame-relay interface-dlci** interface configuration command associates data link connection identifier (DLCI) 101 with subinterface serial interface 0.1.

The **ipx router eigrp** global configuration command starts an Enhanced IGRP process and assigns to it autonomous system number 90.

The **network** IPX-router configuration command enables Enhanced IGRP for network 200.

Router B is configured as follows:

```
ipx routing
!
interface ethernet 0
ipx network 300
!
interface serial 0
encapsulation frame-relay
ipx network 200
ipx sap-incremental eigrp 90 rsup-only
!
ipx router eigrp 90
network 200
```

The **ipx routing** global configuration command enables IPX routing on the router.

The **ipx network** interface configuration command enables IPX routing on Ethernet interface 0 for network 300.

On serial interface 0, the **encapsulation frame-relay** interface configuration command establishes Frame Relay encapsulation using Cisco's own encapsulation, which is a 4-byte header, with 2 bytes to identify the DLCI and 2 bytes to identify the packet type.

The **ipx network** interface configuration command enables IPX routing on subinterface serial 0 for network 200.

The **ipx sap-incremental** interface configuration command enables the incremental SAP feature. The required **eigrp** keyword enables Enhanced IGRP and its transport mechanism and, in this case, specifies an autonomous system number of 90. Because this command uses the **rsup-only** keyword, the router sends incremental SAP updates on this link.

The **ipx router eigrp** global configuration command starts an Enhanced IGRP process and assigns to it autonomous system number 90.

The **network** IPX-router configuration command enables Enhanced IGRP for network 200.

NOTES

The absence of the **ipx router rip** command means the IPX RIP is still being used for IPX routing, and the use of the **rsup-only** keyword means that the router is sending incremental SAP updates over the Frame Relay link.

APPLETALK NETWORK

This case study illustrates the integration of Enhanced IGRP into an existing AppleTalk internetwork in two phases: configuring an AppleTalk network and adding Enhanced IGRP to an AppleTalk network. The key considerations for integrating Enhanced IGRP into an AppleTalk network are as follows:

- Route selection
- Metric handling
- Redistribution from AppleTalk to Enhanced IGRP and vice versa

Configuring an AppleTalk Network

Cisco routers support AppleTalk Phase 1 and AppleTalk Phase 2. For AppleTalk Phase 2, Cisco routers support both extended and nonextended networks. In this case study, Routers A, B, and C are running AppleTalk, as illustrated in Figure 17–11.

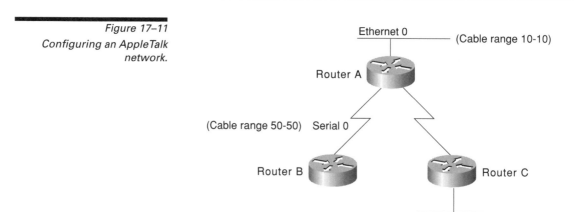

Figure 17–11
Configuring an AppleTalk
network.

The configuration for Router A is as follows:
```
appletalk routing
interface ethernet 0
appletalk cable-range 10-10
appletalk zone casestudy
interface serial 0
appletalk cable-range 50-50
appletalk zone casestudy
```

Adding Enhanced IGRP to an AppleTalk Network

To add Enhanced IGRP to an AppleTalk network, configure Enhanced IGRP on the interface that connects to the routers. Do not disable RTMP on the interfaces that connect to AppleTalk hosts or that connect to AppleTalk routers that do not support Enhanced IGRP. RTMP is the enabled by default when AppleTalk routing is enabled and when an interface is assigned an AppleTalk cable range.

In this case study, Routers D and E are running AppleTalk Enhanced IGRP. Routers F and G run both AppleTalk and AppleTalk Enhanced IGRP. Router G redistributes the routes from the Apple-Talk network to the AppleTalk Enhanced IGRP network, and vice versa. (See Figure 17–12.)

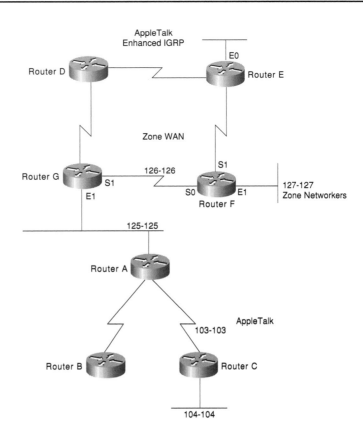

Figure 17–12
Example of adding Enhanced IGRP to an AppleTalk network.

The configuration for Router G is as follows:

```
appletalk routing eigrp 1
interface ethernet 1
appletalk cable-range 125-125
appletalk zone Marketing Lab
appletalk protocol eigrp
interface serial 1
appletalk cable-range 126-126
appletalk zone WAN
appletalk protocol eigrp
no appletalk protocol rtmp
```

The configuration for Router F is as follows:

```
appletalk routing eigrp 2
interface serial 0
appletalk cable-range 126-126
appletalk zone WAN
appletalk protocol eigrp
no appletalk protocol rtmp
```

A **show appletalk route** command on Router G shows that the first set of routes is learned from an RTMP update, that the second set of routes is directly connected, and that the last route is learned by AppleTalk Enhanced IGRP via serial interface 1:

```
R Net 103-103 [1/G] via 125.220, 0 sec, Ethernet1, zone Marketing Lab
R Net 104-104 [1/G] via 125.220, 1 sec, Ethernet1, zone Marketing Lab
R Net 105-105 [1/G] via 125.220, 1 sec, Ethernet1, zone Marketing Lab
R Net 108-108 [1/G] via 125.220, 1 sec, Ethernet1, zone Marketing Lab
C Net 125-125 directly connected, Ethernet1, zone Marketing Lab
C Net 126-126 directly connected, Serial1, zone Wan
E Net 127-127 [1/G] via 126.201, 114 sec, Serial1, zone Networkers
```

A **show appletalk route** command on Router F shows that routes are learned from AppleTalk Enhanced IGRP:

```
E Net 103-103 [2/G] via 126.220, 519 sec, Serial0, zone Marketing Lab
E Net 104-104 [2/G] via 126.220, 520 sec, Serial0, zone Marketing Lab
E Net 105-105 [2/G] via 126.220, 520 sec, Serial0, zone Marketing Lab
E Net 108-108 [2/G] via 126.220, 520 sec, Serial0, zone Marketing Lab
E Net 125-125 [1/G] via 126.220, 520 sec, Serial0, zone Marketing Lab
C Net 126-126 directly connected, Serial0, zone Wan
C Net 127-127 directly connected, Ethernet1, zone Networkers
```

Route Selection

AppleTalk Enhanced IGRP routes are automatically preferred over Routing Table Maintenance Protocol (RTMP) routes. Whereas the AppleTalk metric for route determination is based on hop count only, AppleTalk Enhanced IGRP uses a combination of these configurable metrics: delay, bandwidth, reliability, and load.

Metric Handling

The formula for converting RTMP metrics to AppleTalk Enhanced IGRP metrics is hop count multiplied by 252524800. This is a constant based on the bandwidth for a 9.6-Kbps serial line and includes an RTMP factor. An RTMP hop distributed into Enhanced IGRP appears as a slightly worse path than an Enhanced IGRP-native, 9.6-Kbps serial link. The formula for converting Enhanced IGRP to RTMP is the value of the Enhanced IGRP external metric plus 1.

Redistribution

Redistribution between AppleTalk and Enhanced IGRP and vice versa is automatic by default. Redistribution involves converting the Enhanced IGRP metric back into an RTMP hop count metric. In reality, there is no conversion of an Enhanced IGRP composite metric into a RTMP metric. Because a hop count is carried in an Enhanced IGRP metric tuple as the Enhanced IGRP route spreads through the network, 1 is added to the hop-count carried in the Enhanced IGRP metric blocks through the network and put into any RTMP routing tuple generated.

There is no conversion of an Enhanced IGRP metric back into an RTMP metric because, in reality, what RTMP uses as a metric (the hop count) is carried along the Enhanced IGRP metric all the way through the network. This is true of Enhanced IGRP-derived routes and routes propagated through the network that were originally derived from an RTMP route.

SUMMARY

This case study illustrates the integration of Enhanced IGRP in graduated steps, starting at the periphery of the network before adding Enhanced IGRP into the core network. With Enhanced IGRP for IP networks, route summarization and redistribution of routing updates are key considerations. To add Enhanced IGRP to IPX networks, it is critical to configure RIP and SAP on interfaces connecting to Novell hosts or routers that do not support Enhanced IGRP. When adding Enhanced IGRP to AppleTalk networks, turn off RTMP on the interfaces that are configured to support Enhanced IGRP.

Reducing SAP Traffic in Novell IPX Networks

One of the limiting factors in the operation of large Novell Internetwork Packet Exchange (IPX) internetworks is the amount of bandwidth consumed by the large, periodic Service Advertisement Protocol (SAP) updates. Novell servers periodically send clients information about the services they provide by broadcasting this information onto their connected local-area network (LAN) or wide-area network (WAN) interfaces. Routers are required to propagate SAP updates through an IPX network so that all clients can see the service messages. It is possible to reduce SAP traffic on Novell IPX networks by the following means:

- *Filtering SAP updates through access lists*. SAP updates can be filtered by prohibiting routers from advertising services from specified Novell servers.

- *Configuring Cisco routers on Novell IPX networks to run Enhanced IGRP*. Although filters provide a means of *eliminating* the advertisements of specified services, Enhanced IGRP provides *incremental* SAP updates for a finer granularity of control. Complete SAP updates are sent periodically on each interface only until an IPX Enhanced IGRP neighbor is found. Thereafter, SAP updates are sent only when there are *changes* to the SAP table. In this way, bandwidth is conserved, and the advertisement of services is reduced without being eliminated.

  Incremental SAP updates are automatic on serial interfaces and can be configured on LAN media. Enhanced IGRP also provides partial routing updates and fast convergence for IPX networks. Administrators may choose to run only the partial SAP updates or to run both the reliable SAP protocol and the partial routing update portion of Enhanced IGRP.

- *Configuring Cisco routers on Novell IPX networks to send incremental SAP updates*. With Software Release 10.0, the incremental SAP updates just described can be configured for Cisco routers on Novell IPX networks, *without* the requirement of running the routing update feature of Enhanced IGRP (only the partial SAP updates are enabled). This feature is supported on all interface types. Again, SAP updates are sent only when changes occur on a network. Only the changes to SAP tables are sent as updates.

To illustrate how to reduce SAP traffic, this case study is organized into two parts:

- Configuring Access Lists to Filter SAP Updates
- Configuring Incremental SAP Updates

NOTES

For a detailed case study on configuring Novell IPX Enhanced IGRP, see the "Novell IPX Network" section in Chapter 17, "Integrating Enhanced IGRP into Existing Networks."

The internetwork for this case study is illustrated in Figure 18–1. The following portions of a large-scale Novell IPX network spanning across a Frame Relay WAN are examined:

- Router A connects from the Frame Relay internetwork to the central site with three Novell servers.

- Router B connects from the Frame Relay internetwork to a remote site with one Novell client and one Novell server.

- Router C connects from the Frame Relay internetwork to a remote site with two Novell clients.

Figure 18–1

Large-scale Novell IPX internetwork.

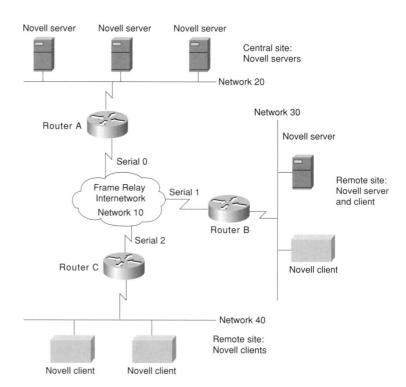

CONFIGURING ACCESS LISTS TO FILTER SAP UPDATES

Access lists can control which routers send or receive SAP updates and which routers do not send or receive SAP updates. SAP access lists can be defined to filter SAP updates based on the source network address of a SAP entry, the type of SAP entry (file server, print server, and so forth), and the name of the SAP server. A SAP access list is made up of entries in the following format:

```
access-list n [deny¦permit] network[.node] [service-type[server-name]]
```

where *n* is between 1000-1099. A network number of -1 indicates any network, and a service type of 0 indicates any service. For example, the following access list accepts print server SAP entries from server PRINTER_1, all file servers, and any other SAP entries from network 123 except those from a server called UNTRUSTED; all other SAP entries are to be ignored:

```
access-list 1000 permit -1 47 PRINTER_1
access-list 1000 permit -1 4
access-list 1000 deny 123 0 UNTRUSTED
access-list 1000 permit 123
```

When checking the entries in a SAP update, each statement in the access list is processed in order, and if there is no match for a SAP entry, it is not accepted. Thus, to block server UNTRUSTED, the **deny** statement must be placed before the **permit** for all other devices on network 123.

Two techniques can be used with filtering. Either the SAP entries that are required can be permitted and the rest denied, or the unwanted SAP entries can be denied and the rest permitted. In general, the first method is preferred because it avoids new and unexpected services being propagated throughout the network.

The most common form of SAP filtering is to limit which services are available across a WAN. For example, it does not, in general, make sense for clients in one location to be able to access print servers in another location because printing is a local operation. In this case study, only file servers are permitted to be visible across the WAN.

Central Site

Router A connects to the central site. The following access lists configured on Router A permit everything except print servers from being announced out the serial interface:

```
access-list 1000 deny -1 47
access-list 1000 permit -1
!
interface serial 0
ipx network 10
ipx output-sap-filter 1000
```

To permit only IPX file servers and to deny all other IPX servers, use the following configuration:

```
access-list 1000 permit -1 4
!
interface serial 0
ipx network 10
ipx out-sap-filter 1000
```

Remote Sites

This section provides information on the configuration of the routers at the remote sites:

- Router B connected to an IPX server and client
- Router C connected to two IPX clients

IPX Server and Client

For Router B, the following access lists permit everything except print servers from being announced out the serial interface.

```
access-list 1000 deny -1 47
access-list 1000 permit -1
!
interface serial 1
ipx network 10
ipx output-sap-filter 1000
```

To permit only IPX file servers and to deny all other IPX servers, use the following configuration:

```
access-list 1000 permit -1 4
!
interface serial 1
ipx network 10
ipx out-sap-filter 1000
```

IPX Clients

Router C does not require an access list configuration because the remote site does not have any servers. Only Novell servers generate SAP updates.

CONFIGURING INCREMENTAL SAP UPDATES

Incremental SAP updates allow any-to-any connectivity with reduced network SAP overhead. Instead of eliminating the receipt of SAP updates entirely, all necessary IPX services can be broadcast to remote sites only as changes to the SAP tables occur.

Central Site

To configure Enhanced IGRP encapsulated SAP updates to be sent only on a incremental basis, use the following configuration. Although the defined Enhanced IGRP autonomous system number is 999, Enhanced IGRP routing (and routing updates) are not performed because of the **rsup-only** keyword used with the **ipx sap-incremental** command. The **rsup-only** keyword indicates a reliable SAP update.

```
interface ethernet 0
ipx network 20
!
interface serial 0
ipx network 10
ipx sap-incremental eigrp 999 rsup-only
!
ipx router eigrp 999
network 10
```

To configure both incremental SAP and Enhanced IGRP routing, simply configure Enhanced IGRP with the following commands:

```
interface ethernet 0
ipx network 20
!
interface serial 0
ipx network 10
!
ipx router eigrp 999
network 10
```

Remote Sites

This section provides information on the configuration of the routers at the remote sites:

- Router B connected to an IPX server and client
- Router C connected to two IPX clients

IPX Server and Client

To configure Enhanced IGRP encapsulated SAP updates to be sent only on a incremental basis, use the following configuration for Router B. Although the defined Enhanced IGRP autonomous system number is 999, Enhanced IGRP routing is not performed because of the **rsup-only** keyword used with the **ipx sap-incremental** command.

```
interface ethernet 1
ipx network 30
!
interface serial 1
ipx network 10
ipx sap-incremental eigrp 999 rsup-only
!
ipx router eigrp 999
network 10
```

To configure both incremental SAP and Enhanced IGRP routing, simply configure Enhanced IGRP with the following commands:

```
interface ethernet 1
ipx network 30
!
interface serial 1
ipx network 10
!
ipx router eigrp 999
network 10
```

IPX Clients

To configure Enhanced IGRP encapsulated SAP updates to be sent only on a incremental basis, use the following configuration for Router C:

```
interface ethernet 2
ipx network 40
```

```
!
interface serial 2
ipx network 10
ipx sap-incremental eigrp 999 rsup-only
!
ipx router eigrp 999
network 10
```

Even though there are no servers, these configuration commands are required to support the incremental SAP updates being advertised from the central site and other remote sites to Router C.

SUMMARY

This case study illustrates two methods of reducing SAP traffic on Novell IPX networks: the use of access lists to eliminate the advertisements of specified services, and the use of the incremental SAP feature to exchange SAP changes as they occur. This technique eliminates periodic SAP updates.

UDP Broadcast Flooding

A *broadcast* is a data packet that is destined for multiple hosts. Broadcasts can occur at the data link layer and the network layer. Data-link broadcasts are sent to all hosts attached to a particular physical network. Network layer broadcasts are sent to all hosts attached to a particular logical network. The Transmission Control Protocol/Internet Protocol (TCP/IP) supports the following types of broadcast packets:

- *All ones*—By setting the broadcast address to all ones (255.255.255.255), all hosts on the network receive the broadcast.

- *Network*—By setting the broadcast address to a specific network number in the network portion of the IP address and setting all ones in the host portion of the broadcast address, all hosts on the specified network receive the broadcast. For example, when a broadcast packet is sent with the broadcast address of 131.108.255.255, all hosts on network number 131.108 receive the broadcast.

- *Subnet*—By setting the broadcast address to a specific network number and a specific subnet number, all hosts on the specified subnet receive the broadcast. For example, when a broadcast packet is set with the broadcast address of 131.108.4.255, all hosts on subnet 4 of network 131.108 receive the broadcast.

Because broadcasts are recognized by all hosts, a significant goal of router configuration is to control unnecessary proliferation of broadcast packets. Cisco routers support two kinds of broadcasts: *directed* and *flooded*. A directed broadcast is a packet sent to a specific network or series of networks, whereas a flooded broadcast is a packet sent to every network. In IP internetworks, most broadcasts take the form of User Datagram Protocol (UDP) broadcasts.

Although current IP implementations use a broadcast address of all ones, the first IP implementations used a broadcast address of all zeros. Many of the early implementations do not recognize broadcast addresses of all ones and fail to respond to the broadcast correctly. Other early implementations forward broadcasts of all ones, which causes a serious network overload known as a *broadcast storm.* Implementations that exhibit these problems include systems based on versions of BSD UNIX prior to Version 4.3.

In the brokerage community, applications use UDP broadcasts to transport market data to the desktops of traders on the trading floor. This case study gives examples of how brokerages have implemented both directed and flooding broadcast schemes in an environment that consists of Cisco routers and Sun workstations. Figure 19–1 illustrates a typical topology. Note that the addresses in this network use a 10-bit netmask of 255.255.255.192.

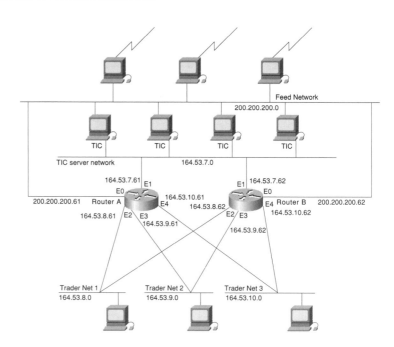

Figure 19–1

Topology that requires UDP broadcast forwarding.

In Figure 19–1, UDP broadcasts must be forwarded from a source segment (Feed network) to many destination segments that are connected redundantly. Financial market data, provided, for example, by Reuters, enters the network through the Sun workstations connected to the Feed network and is disseminated to the TIC servers. The TIC servers are Sun workstations running Teknekron Information Cluster software. The Sun workstations on the trader networks subscribe to the TIC servers for the delivery of certain market data, which the TIC servers deliver by means of UDP broadcasts. The two routers in this network provide redundancy so that if one router becomes unavailable, the other router can assume the load of the failed router without intervention from an operator. The connection between each router and the Feed network is for network administration purposes only and does not carry user traffic.

Two different approaches can be used to configure Cisco routers for forwarding UDP broadcast traffic: IP helper addressing and UDP flooding. This case study analyzes the advantages and disadvantages of each approach.

Regardless of whether you implement IP helper addressing or UDP flooding, you must use the **ip forward-protocol udp** global configuration command to enable the UDP forwarding. By default, the **ip forward-protocol udp** command enables forwarding for ports associated with the following protocols: Trivial File Transfer Protocol, Domain Name System, Time service, NetBIOS Name Server, NetBIOS Datagram Server, Boot Protocol, and Terminal Access Controller Access Control System. To enable forwarding for other ports, you must specify them as arguments to the **ip forward-protocol udp** command.

IMPLEMENTING IP HELPER ADDRESSING

IP helper addressing is a form of static addressing that uses directed broadcasts to forward local and all-nets broadcasts to desired destinations within the internetwork.

To configure helper addressing, you must specify the **ip helper-address** command on every interface on every router that receives a broadcast that needs to be forwarded. On Router A and Router B, IP helper addresses can be configured to move data from the TIC server network to the trader networks. IP helper addressing in not the optimal solution for this type of topology because each router receives unnecessary broadcasts from the other router, as shown in Figure 19–2.

Figure 19–2

Flow of UDP packets from routers to trader networks using IP helper addressing.

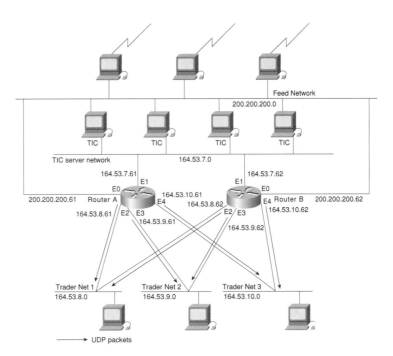

In this case, Router A receives each broadcast sent by Router B *three times*, one for each segment, and Router B receives each broadcast sent by Router A three times, one for each segment. When each broadcast is received, the router must analyze it and determine that the broadcast does not need to be forwarded. As more segments are added to the network, the routers become overloaded with unnecessary traffic, which must be analyzed and discarded.

When IP helper addressing is used in this type of topology, no more than one router can be configured to forward UDP broadcasts (unless the receiving applications can handle duplicate broadcasts). This is because duplicate packets arrive on the trader network. This restriction limits redundancy in the design and can be undesirable in some implementations.

To send UDP broadcasts bidirectionally in this type of topology, a second **ip helper address** command must be applied to every router interface that receives UDP broadcasts. As more segments and devices are added to the network, more **ip helper address** commands are required to reach them, so the administration of these routers becomes more complex over time. Note, too, that bidirectional traffic in this topology significantly impacts router performance.

Although IP helper addressing is well-suited to nonredundant, nonparallel topologies that do not require a mechanism for controlling broadcast loops, in view of these drawbacks, IP helper addressing does not work well in this topology. To improve performance, network designers considered several other alternatives:

- *Setting the broadcast address on the TIC servers to all ones (255.255.255.255)*—This alternative was dismissed because the TIC servers have more than one interface, causing TIC broadcasts to be sent back onto the Feed network. In addition, some workstation implementations do not allow all ones broadcasts when multiple interfaces are present.

- *Setting the broadcast address of the TIC servers to the major net broadcast (164.53.0.0)*—This alternative was dismissed because the Sun TCP/IP implementation does not allow the use of major net broadcast addresses when the network is subnetted.

- *Eliminating the subnets and letting the workstations use Address Resolution Protocol (ARP) to learn addresses*—This alternative was dismissed because the TIC servers cannot quickly learn an alternative route in the event of a primary router failure.

With alternatives eliminated, the network designers turned to a simpler implementation that supports redundancy without duplicating packets and that ensures fast convergence and minimal loss of data when a router fails: UDP flooding.

IMPLEMENTING UDP FLOODING

UDP flooding uses the spanning tree algorithm to forward packets in a controlled manner. Bridging is enabled on each router interface for the sole purpose of building the spanning tree. The spanning tree prevents loops by stopping a broadcast from being forwarded out an interface on which the broadcast was received. The spanning tree also prevents packet duplication by placing certain interfaces in the blocked state (so that no packets are forwarded) and other interfaces in the forwarding state (so that packets that need to be forwarded are forwarded).

To enable UDP flooding, the router must be running software that supports transparent bridging and bridging must be configured on each interface that is to participate in the flooding. If bridging is not configured for an interface, the interface will receive broadcasts, but the router will not forward those broadcasts and will not use that interface as a destination for sending broadcasts received on a different interface.

NOTES

Releases prior to Cisco Internetwork Operating System (Cisco IOS) Software Release 10.2 do not support flooding subnet broadcasts.

When configured for UPD flooding, the router uses the destination address specified by the **ip broadcast-address** command on the output interface to assign a destination address to a flooded UDP datagram. Thus, the destination address might change as the datagram propagates through the network. The source address, however, does not change.

With UDP flooding, both routers shown in Figure 19-1 use a spanning tree to control the network topology for the purpose of forwarding broadcasts. The key commands for enabling UDP flooding are as follows:

```
bridge group protocol protocol
ip forward-protocol spanning tree
bridge-group group input-type-list access-list-number
```

The **bridge protocol** command can specify either the **dec** keyword (for the DEC spanning-tree protocol) or the **ieee** keyword (for the IEEE Ethernet protocol). All routers in the network must enable the same spanning tree protocol. The **ip forward-protocol spanning tree** command uses the database created by the **bridge protocol** command. Only one broadcast packet arrives at each segment, and UDP broadcasts can traverse the network in both directions.

NOTES

Because bridging is enabled only to build the spanning tree database, use access lists to prevent the spanning tree from forwarding non-UDP traffic. The configuration examples later in this chapter configure an access list that blocks all bridged packets.

To determine which interface forwards or blocks packets, the router configuration specifies a path cost for each interface. The default path cost for Ethernet is 100. Setting the path cost for each interface on Router B to 50 causes the spanning tree algorithm to place the interfaces in Router B in forwarding state. Given the higher path cost (100) for the interfaces in Router A, the interfaces in Router A are in the blocked state and do not forward the broadcasts. With these interface states, broadcast traffic flows through Router B. If Router B fails, the spanning tree algorithm will place the interfaces in Router A in the forwarding state, and Router A will forward broadcast traffic.

With one router forwarding broadcast traffic from the TIC server network to the trader networks, it is desirable to have the other forward unicast traffic. For that reason, each router enables the

ICMP Router Discovery Protocol (IRDP), and each workstation on the trader networks runs the **irdp** daemon. On Router A, the **preference** keyword sets a higher IRDP preference than does the configuration for Router B, which causes each **irdp** daemon to use Router A as its preferred default gateway for unicast traffic forwarding. Users of those workstations can use **netstat -rn** to see how the routers are being used.

On the routers, the **holdtime, maxadvertinterval,** and **minadvertinterval** keywords reduce the advertising interval from the default so that the **irdp** daemons running on the hosts expect to see advertisements more frequently. With the advertising interval reduced, the workstations will adopt Router B more quickly if Router A becomes unavailable. With this configuration, when a router becomes unavailable, IRDP offers a convergence time of less than one minute.

IRDP is preferred over the Routing Information Protocol (RIP) and default gateways for the following reasons:

- RIP takes longer to converge, typically from one to two minutes.
- Configuration of Router A as the default gateway on each Sun workstation on the trader networks would allow those Sun workstations to send unicast traffic to Router A, but would not provide an alternative route if Router A becomes unavailable.

NOTES

Some workstation vendors include an **irdp** daemon with their operating systems. Source code for an **irdp** daemon is available by anonymous FTP at *ftp.cisco.com*.

Figure 19–3 shows how data flows when the network is configured for UDP flooding.

Figure 19–3

Data flow with UDP flooding and IRDP.

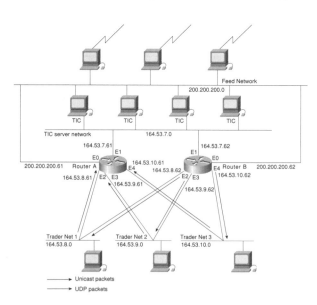

> **NOTES**
>
> This topology is broadcast intensive—broadcasts sometimes consume 20 percent of the Ethernet bandwidth. However, this is a favorable percentage when compared to the configuration of IP helper addressing, which, in the same network, causes broadcasts to consume up to 50 percent of the Ethernet bandwidth.

If the hosts on the trader networks do not support IRDP, the Hot Standby Routing Protocol (HSRP) can be used to select which router will handle unicast traffic. HSRP allows the standby router to take over quickly if the primary router becomes unavailable. For information about configuring HSRP, see Chapter 22, "Using HSRP for Fault-Tolerant IP Routing."

By default, the router performs UDP flooding by process switching the UDP packets. To increase performance on AGS+ and Cisco 7000 series routers, enable fast switching of UDP packets by using the following command:

```
ip forward-protocol turbo-flood
```

> **NOTES**
>
> Turbo flooding increases the amount of processing that is done at interrupt level, which increases the CPU load on the router. Turbo flooding may not be appropriate on routers that are already under high CPU load or that must also perform other CPU-intensive activities.

The following commands configure UDP flooding on Router A. Because this configuration does not specify a lower path cost than the default and because the configuration of Router B specifies a lower cost than the default with regard to UDP flooding, Router A acts as a backup to Router B. Because this configuration specifies an IRDP preference of 100 and because Router B specifies a IRDP preference of 90 (**ip irdp preference 90**), Router A forwards unicast traffic from the trader networks, and Router B is the backup for unicast traffic forwarding.

```
!Router A:
ip forward-protocol spanning-tree
ip forward-protocol udp 111
ip forward-protocol udp 3001
ip forward-protocol udp 3002
ip forward-protocol udp 3003
ip forward-protocol udp 3004
ip forward-protocol udp 3005
ip forward-protocol udp 3006
ip forward-protocol udp 5020
ip forward-protocol udp 5021
ip forward-protocol udp 5030
ip forward-protocol udp 5002
ip forward-protocol udp 1027
ip forward-protocol udp 657
!
interface ethernet 0
ip address 200.200.200.61 255.255.255.0
```

```
ip broadcast-address 200.200.200.255
no mop enabled
!
interface ethernet 1
ip address 164.53.7.61 255.255.255.192
ip broadcast-address 164.53.7.63
ip irdp
ip irdp maxadvertinterval 60
ip irdp minadvertinterval 45
ip irdp holdtime 60
ip irdp preference 100
bridge-group 1
bridge-group 1 input-type-list 201
no mop enabled
!
interface ethernet 2
ip address 164.53.8.61 255.255.255.192
ip broadcast-address 164.53.8.63
ip irdp
ip irdp maxadvertinterval 60
ip irdp minadvertinterval 45
ip irdp holdtime 60
ip irdp preference 100
bridge-group 1
bridge-group 1 input-type-list 201
no mop enabled
!
interface ethernet 3
ip address 164.53.9.61 255.255.255.192
ip broadcast-address 164.53.9.63
ip irdp
ip irdp maxadvertinterval 60
ip irdp minadvertinterval 45
ip irdp holdtime 60
ip irdp preference 100
bridge-group 1
bridge-group 1 input-type-list 201
no mop enabled
!
interface ethernet 4
ip address 164.53.10.61 255.255.255.192
ip broadcast-address 164.53.10.63
ip irdp
ip irdp maxadvertinterval 60
ip irdp minadvertinterval 45
ip irdp holdtime 60
ip irdp preference 100
bridge-group 1
bridge-group 1 input-type-list 201
no mop enabled
!
router igrp 1
network 164.53.0.0
!
```

```
ip name-server 255.255.255.255
snmp-server community public RW
snmp-server host 164.53.7.15 public
bridge 1 protocol dec
bridge 1 priority 255
access-list 201 deny    0xFFFF 0x0000
```

The following commands configure UDP flooding on Router B. Because this configuration specifies a lower path cost than the default (**bridge-group 1 path-cost 50**) and because the configuration of Router A accepts the default, Router B forwards UDP packets. Because this configuration specifies an IRDP preference of 90 (**ip irdp preference 90**) and because Router A specifies a IRDP preference of 100, Router B acts as the backup for Router A for forwarding unicast traffic from the trader networks.

```
!Router B
ip forward-protocol spanning-tree
ip forward-protocol udp 111
ip forward-protocol udp 3001
ip forward-protocol udp 3002
ip forward-protocol udp 3003
ip forward-protocol udp 3004
ip forward-protocol udp 3005
ip forward-protocol udp 3006
ip forward-protocol udp 5020
ip forward-protocol udp 5021
ip forward-protocol udp 5030
ip forward-protocol udp 5002
ip forward-protocol udp 1027
ip forward-protocol udp 657
!
interface ethernet 0
ip address 200.200.200.62 255.255.255.0
ip broadcast-address 200.200.200.255
no mop enabled
!
interface ethernet 1
ip address 164.53.7.62 255.255.255.192
ip broadcast-address 164.53.7.63
ip irdp
ip irdp maxadvertinterval 60
ip irdp minadvertinterval 45
ip irdp holdtime 60
ip irdp preference 90
bridge-group 1
bridge-group 1 path-cost 50
bridge-group 1 input-type-list 201
no mop enabled
!
interface ethernet 2
ip address 164.53.8.62 255.255.255.192
ip broadcast-address 164.53.8.63
ip irdp
ip irdp maxadvertinterval 60
ip irdp minadvertinterval 45
```

```
ip irdp holdtime 60
ip irdp preference 90
bridge-group 1
bridge-group 1 path-cost 50
bridge-group 1 input-type-list 201
no mop enabled
!
interface ethernet 3
ip address 164.53.9.62 255.255.255.192
ip broadcast-address 164.53.9.63
ip irdp
ip irdp maxadvertinterval 60
ip irdp minadvertinterval 45
ip irdp holdtime 60
ip irdp preference 90
bridge-group 1
bridge-group 1 path-cost 50
bridge-group 1 input-type-list 201
no mop enabled
!
interface ethernet 4
ip address 164.53.10.62 255.255.255.192
ip broadcast-address 164.53.10.63
ip irdp
ip irdp maxadvertinterval 60
ip irdp minadvertinterval 45
ip irdp holdtime 60
ip irdp preference 90
bridge-group 1
bridge-group 1 path-cost 50
bridge-group 1 input-type-list 201
no mop enabled
!
router igrp 1
network 164.53.0.0
!
ip name-server 255.255.255.255
snmp-server community public RW
snmp-server host 164.53.7.15 public
bridge 1 protocol dec
bridge 1 priority 255
access-list 201 deny 0xFFFF 0x0000
```

NOTES

In releases prior to Cisco IOS Software Release 10.2, the spanning tree algorithm prevented the forwarding of local broadcast addresses, but allowed the forwarding of local secondary addresses. For that reason, when running a release prior to Cisco IOS Software Release 10.2, a secondary address must be specified for each Ethernet interface that will forward local broadcast address packets. The secondary address is used to forward packets, whereas the primary address is never used. In such configurations, the secondary addresses are assigned to an Interior Gateway Routing Protocol (IGRP) group instead of the primary address.

SUMMARY

Although IP helper addressing is useful in networks that do not require redundancy, when configured in networks that feature redundancy, IP helper addressing results in packet duplication that severely reduces router and network performance.

By configuring UDP flooding, one router forwards UDP traffic without burdening the second router with duplicate packets. By dedicating one router to the task of forwarding UDP traffic, the second router becomes available for forwarding unicast traffic. At the same time, because each router is configured as the backup for the other router, redundancy is maintained; if either router fails, the other router can assume the work of the failed router without intervention from an operator. When compared with IP helper addressing, UDP flooding makes the most efficient use of router resources.

STUN for Front-End Processors

Serial tunneling (STUN) enables the integration of traditional *systems network architecture* (SNA) networks with multiprotocol networks. STUN also lowers operating costs by reducing the need for redundant remote wide-area links. This case study explores three implementations of STUN between Cisco routers and front-end processors (FEPs):

- *Basic STUN*—Presents a STUN implementation that is simple and quick to configure because it does not require the specification of addresses. This implementation is recommended for networks that do not require synchronous data link control (SDLC) address checking or local acknowledgment.

- *SDLC STUN*—Presents a STUN implementation that includes the configuration of addresses. This implementation is recommended for networks that require SDLC address checking.

- *SDLC-Transmission Group STUN*—Presents a STUN implementation that supports enhanced FEP-to-FEP communications features, such as transmission groups, as well as advanced router features. This implementation is recommended for networks that require local acknowledgment.

NOTES

This case study introduces basic SNA concepts, but does not discuss them in detail. For additional information, see Chapters 2–4.

UNDERSTANDING FEP CONFIGURATION

In a traditional SNA environment, serial lines connect FEPs in a master-slave topology, as shown in Figure 20–1. The primary FEP is connected to the IBM host, which is typically an IBM 3090 mainframe. Synchronous modems connect the FEPs.

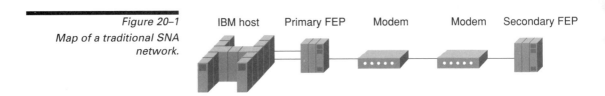

Figure 20–1
Map of a traditional SNA network.

The software running on the FEP is called the *Network Control Program* (NCP). This section describes NCP configuration parameters and optional NCP features that network administrators must consider when they introduce routers into an FEP environment.

Serial Connections

Typically, a serial port on a line interface card in the FEP connects the FEP to a synchronous modem. Depending on the type of line interface card, the serial port may be EIA/TIA-232 or V.35. The modem acts as data communications equipment (DCE) and provides clocking and synchronization. The FEP acts as data terminal equipment (DTE). The NCP statement that configures the FEP for DTE is CLOCKNG=EXT.

Primary and Secondary Roles

The FEPs dynamically determine their primary and secondary roles. Typically, the FEP with the higher subarea address becomes the primary FEP. In some versions of NCP, the role parameter is configurable. Typically, the local FEP (the closest to the mainframe) is the primary FEP, whereas the remote FEP is the secondary FEP.

NRZ and NRZI Encoding

The NRZI parameter specifies whether the FEP should operate in nonreturn-to-zero inverted (NRZI) mode or in nonreturn-to-zero (NRZ) mode. Both techniques encode binary data on a synchronous serial line. The specification depends on the way the modem operates. Old modems and satellite links that are not sensitive to a pattern of repeated binary ones and zeros (that is, 101010...) operate in NRZI mode. Modems that are sensitive to repeated patterns operate in NRZ mode.

The NCP statement that configures the FEP for NRZI is NRZI=YES, which is the default and is correct for most IBM modems. The NCP statement that configures the FEP for NRZ is NRZI=NO, which is correct for most non-IBM modems.

NOTES

All devices on the same SDLC link must use the same encoding scheme.

MODULO and MAXOUT Parameters

The MODULO parameter specifies the number of information frames (I-frames) that NCP can send to the remote device before receiving an acknowledgment. The statement MODULO=8 allows

NCP to send seven unacknowledged I-frames, whereas the statement MODULO=128 and the statement MAXOUT=127 allows NCP to send 127 unacknowledged I-frames. (Note that when the MODULO parameter is set to 128, the NCP MAXOUT parameter specifies the number of I-frames that can be sent before receiving an acknowledgment. MAXOUT can range from 8 [the default] to 127.)

Typically, network administrators configure NCP to allow a high number of outstanding I-frames (that is, MODULO=128 and MAXOUT=127) for slow links or for satellite links. Allowing a high number of outstanding I-frames uses the link more efficiently by reducing the number of acknowledgments and by preventing session timeouts. When the MODULO parameter is 128, make sure the TCP output queue on the router is greater than 128.

The SDLC STUN implementation supports setting the MODULO parameter to 8 as well as 128. Note, however, that setting the MODULO parameter to any legal value other than 8 causes the router to use additional buffers to store unacknowledged I-frames.

When local acknowledgment is configured to reduce supervisory frame traffic and to prevent session timeouts, 8 is the only supported value of the MODULO parameter. When the MODULO value is 8, the router does not use additional buffers unnecessarily.

ADDRESS Parameter

The ADDRESS parameter has the following format: ADDRESS=(*line-number, mode*).

If *mode* is FULL, the FEP can send and receive data at the same time. When mode is HALF, the FEP is limited to sending data and then receiving data. The default value of *mode* is FULL. The value of mode affects the operation of the DUPLEX parameter. For more information, see the "DUPLEX Parameter" section later. The value of *line-number* specifies the channel adapter position or the relative line number of all the telecommunication links defined for this NCP.

When implementing SDLC STUN or SDLC-Transmission Group STUN, the network administrator must specify SDLC addresses in the configuration of the router. The addresses specified in the router configuration are based on the order in which the ADDRESS parameter appears in the NCP configuration. Consider the following NCP configuration:

```
***********************************************************************
*          LOCAL NCP LINKS -- PRIMARY FEP                             *
***********************************************************************

LINK04    GROUP LNCTL=SDLC,                 GROUP LEVEL             X
                NPACOLL=YES,                <== 3745 Dallas         X
                DUPLEX=FULL,                                        X
                NEWSYNC=NO,                                         X
                NRZI=NO,                                            X
                SDLCST=(CPRI4,CSEC4),                               X
                RETRIES=(10,5,10),          PU LEVEL                X
                IRETRY=YES,                                         X
                MAXOUT=7,                                           X
                PASSLIM=254,                                        X
                SERVLIM=254,                                        X
```

```
                    ISTATUS=ACTIVE,          VTAM-ONLY LEVEL           X
                    OWNER=CMC
*
*----------------------------------------------------------------
*
X1010442 LINE   ADDRESS=(005,FULL)        <== 3745 Chicago (01)
S1010442 PU     PUTYPE=4
*
X1030442 LINE   ADDRESS=(132,FULL)        <== 3745 Raleigh (02)
S1030442 PU     PUTYPE=4
*
X1010446 LINE   ADDRESS=(068,FULL),MODULO=128,ISTATUS=ACTIVE, <== 3745 Houston (03) X
                SPEED=56000,SDLCST=(S04PRI,S04SEC)
S1010446 PU     PUTYPE=4,MAXOUT=63
*
X1020412 LINE   ADDRESS=(100,FULL),MODULO=128,ISTATUS=ACTIVE, <== 3745 Lafayette (04) X
                SPEED=56000,SDLCST=(S04PRI,S04SEC)
S1020412 PU     PUTYPE=4,MAXOUT=63
*
X1010412 LINE   ADDRESS=(112,FULL),SPEED=56000,ISTATUS=ACTIVE <== 3745 Atlanta (05) X
S1010412 PU     PUTYPE=4
*
X1010462 LINE   ADDRESS=(080,FULL),       <== 3745 San Francisco (06) X
                NRZI=NO,                                          X
                NEWSYNC=NO,                                       X
                DUPLEX=FULL,                                      X
                ISTATUS=ACTIVE,                                   X
                SERVLIM=254,                                      X
                SDLCST=(S04PRI,S04SEC),                           X
                MODULO=128,                                       X
                SPEED=56000
S1010462 PU     PUTYPE=4,                                         X
                MAXOUT=63
*
********************************************************************
```

Given this configuration, the router configuration uses address 01 for Chicago, address 02 for Raleigh, address 03 for Houston, address 04 for Lafayette, address 05 for Atlanta, and address 06 for San Francisco.

DUPLEX Parameter

The DUPLEX parameter specifies whether the communication line and the modem operate in full- or half-duplex mode, and controls the Request To Send (RTS) signal. If the ADDRESS parameter specifies that the mode is FULL, the value of the DUPLEX parameter has no effect, and RTS is always high (that is, permanent RTS). If the ADDRESS parameter specifies that the mode is HALF, the following applies:

- The statement DUPLEX=FULL causes RTS to be permanently high regardless of whether the FEP is sending or receiving data.

- The statement DUPLEX=HALF causes RTS to be high only when the FEP is sending data.

Enhanced NCP Features

This section describes the following enhanced NCP features that are supported by Cisco routers: transmission groups, echo addressing, and remote NCP loading. Note, however, that the basic STUN and SDLC STUN implementations do not support transmission groups.

Transmission Groups

A *transmission group* is one or more parallel SDLC links that connect FEPs. Transmission groups increase the reliability of the logical link connection between FEPs and provide additional bandwidth. When one link fails or congests, NCP uses one of the other links in the group to send data (see Figure 20–2).

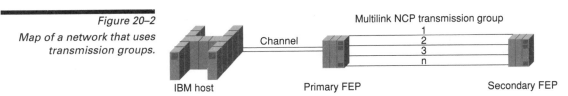

Figure 20–2
Map of a network that uses transmission groups.

NCP uses virtual routes to provide more than one route between two FEPs. This multiple active routing mechanism increases the probability that an SDLC route is available when a session needs to be established.

> **NOTES**
>
> SDLC-TG STUN is the only implementation that supports transmission groups.

Echo Addressing

Later versions of NCP use echo addressing. With echo addressing, the secondary FEP sets the high-order bit of the SDLC address when sending a response to the primary FEP. For example, the primary FEP sends frames with address 0x01, and the secondary FEP sends frames with address 0x81. This addressing scheme limits the range of SDLC addresses from 0x01 to 0x7F. Although echo addressing is a violation of the SDLC standard, it is supported because it occurs only between FEPs.

> **NOTES**
>
> Echo addressing is implicitly supported by the basic STUN implementation because that implementation does not perform any address checking. The **echo** keyword of the **sdlc address** interface configuration command configures support for echo addressing in the SDLC STUN and SDLC-TG STUN implementations.

Remote NCP Loading

When a local FEP is loading a remote FEP with a new NCP configuration, the local FEP uses a non-standard form of SDLC to complete the remote NCP load. This violation of the SDLC standard is supported because it occurs only between FEPs.

NOTES

The basic STUN implementation implicitly supports remote NCP loading. When used with the **stun protocol-group** command, the **sdlc-tg** keyword automatically includes support for remote NCP loading in the SDLC-TG STUN implementation.

UNDERSTANDING FEP-TO-FEP COMMUNICATIONS WITH ROUTERS

Figure 20–3 illustrates the topology of an FEP-based network that includes routers. In this multi-protocol topology, the routers already handle traffic between Token Rings and the IBM host. When used to handle traffic between the FEPs, the routers replace the modems and lines that formerly connected the FEPs.

*Figure 20–3
Map showing the addition of routers.*

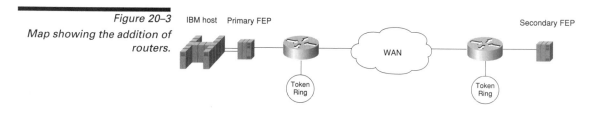

An EIA/TIA-232 (formerly RS-232) cable or a V.35 cable connects each router to its FEP, and a serial T1 line connects each router to the wide-area network (WAN). The FEPs continue to act as DTE devices, and, by providing clocking and synchronization, the serial interfaces on the routers act as DCE devices.

Advanced Router Features

When configured for STUN, Cisco routers can take advantage of the following advanced router features: priority queuing, custom queuing, and local acknowledgment.

NOTES

When priority queuing or custom queuing is enabled, the router takes longer to switch packets because the processor card has to classify each packet.

Priority Queuing

Priority queuing allows the network administrator to set priorities on the traffic that passes through the network. Packets are classified according to various criteria, including protocol and subprotocol type, and then queued on one of four output queues: high, medium, normal, or low.

A FEP-to-FEP STUN implementation can use priority queuing to prioritize SNA traffic over other protocols that share the same link. The following commands distribute transmission control protocol (TCP) traffic among the four queues and assign STUN traffic encapsulated in TCP to the high queue:

```
priority-list 1 ip high tcp 1994
priority-list 1 ip medium tcp 1990
priority-list 1 ip normal tcp 1991
priority-list 1 ip low tcp 1992
priority-list 1 stun high
!
interface serial 0
encapsulation stun
stun group 1
sdlc address 01
stun route address 01 tcp 1.1.1.2 local-ack
priority-group 1
```

NOTES

Configure the **priority-group** interface configuration command on the STUN input interface.

Custom Queuing

Custom queuing, available in Software Release 9.21 and subsequent software releases, is a queuing strategy that imparts a measure of fairness not provided by priority queuing. The network administrator can control on each interface the minimum percentage of bandwidth allocated to a particular kind of traffic.

When custom queuing is enabled on an interface, the router maintains for that interface eleven output queues (numbered 0 to 10). The router reserves queue number 0 for its own use. The router cycles sequentially through queue numbers 1 to 10, delivering packets in the current queue before moving to the next queue.

Each output queue has an associated configurable byte count that specifies how many bytes of data the router should deliver from the current queue before it moves to the next queue. When the router processes a particular queue, it sends packets until the number of bytes sent exceeds the queue byte count or until the queue is empty.

Custom queuing can be used instead of, but not in addition to, the **priority-group** interface configuration command in a single interface. The following configuration commands place STUN traffic on queue 1 with a byte-count limit of 4000 bytes and a maximum of 40 queues:

```
stun peer-name 1.1.1.1
stun protocol-group 1 sdlc-tg
```

```
!
interface serial 0
encapsulation stun
stun route address 01 tcp 1.1.1.2 local-ack
!
interface serial 1
encapsulation hdlc
custom-queue-list 1
!
queue-list 1 protocol stun 1
queue-list 1 protocol novell 2
queue-list 1 default 3
queue-list 1 queue 1 byte-count 4000
queue-list 1 queue 1 limit 40
```

NOTES

Configure the **custom-queue-list** interface configuration command on the output interface that connects to the WAN.

Local Acknowledgment

Local acknowledgment is a router feature that prohibits supervisory frames from traversing the WAN, as shown in Figure 20–4.

Figure 20–4

Local acknowledgment limits the range of supervisory frames.

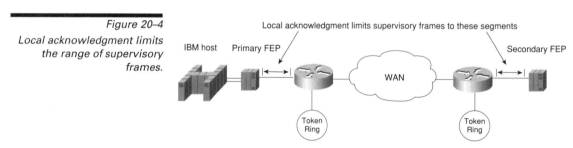

Cisco recommends the use of local acknowledgment when one or both of the following conditions exist:

- *WAN link use is high*—When local acknowledgment is configured, supervisory frames, such as Receiver Ready (RR), Receiver Not Ready (RNR), and Reject (REJ), do not traverse the WAN link. Instead, supervisory frames are locally acknowledged by the router, which reduces the amount of traffic on the WAN link.

- *Network delay causes NCP timers to expire*—Link congestion, busy local-area networks, or high end-station use can cause excessive network delays, which can result in delayed acknowledgment of I-frames. When configured for local acknowledgment, the router acknowledges I-frames locally, which helps to prevent NCP timers from timing out and closing existing sessions.

Basic STUN

Basic STUN is easy to configure because it does not require the router configuration to match line addresses that may be configured on the FEPs. The mainframe sends data to the primary FEP, which passes the data to its router. The router for the primary FEP passes the data over an arbitrary medium (serial, fiber distributed data interface [FDDI], Token Ring, or Ethernet) to the router for the secondary FEP, and the router for the secondary FEP sends the data to the secondary FEP. Data from the secondary FEP flows to the mainframe by the reverse path. Network administrators use basic STUN for three purposes:

- *To accommodate existing addressing schemes*—Some NCP configurations use nonstandard addresses. For example, some configurations use address 0x00 or 0xFF for broadcasts and address 0xC1 for communication. By configuring the router for basic STUN, the network administrator does not have to configure the router to match existing addressing schemes.

- *To test connectivity*—When network administrators plan to implement SDLC STUN or SDLC-TG STUN, they often implement basic STUN first to verify physical connections.

- *To improve performance*—Because basic STUN requires minimal processing, it passes frames faster than SDLC STUN and SDLC-TG STUN.

The basic STUN implementation has the following limitations:

- Lack of support for transmission groups, as well as lack of support for advanced router features. For information about advanced router features, see the "SDLC-Transmission Group STUN" section later in this chapter.

- Limited output from the router debugging commands.

- Lack of support for multidrop environments. (However, multidrop support is usually a requirement for cluster controller environments rather than FEP environments.)

Basic STUN Configuration: Example 1

In Figure 20–5, the routers pass data over an IP WAN. The FEPs are configured for DTE, full-duplex mode, and NRZ encoding. The serial interfaces on the routers are configured for DCE.

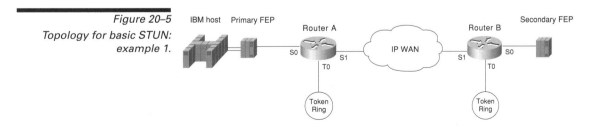

Figure 20–5
Topology for basic STUN: example 1.

The following commands configure basic STUN (example 1) for Router A:

```
stun peer-name 1.1.1.1
stun protocol-group 1 basic
!
interface serial 0
no ip address
encapsulation stun
stun group 1
stun route all tcp 1.1.2.1
clockrate 19200
!
interface tokenring 0
ip address 1.1.4.1 255.255.255.0
!
interface serial 1
ip address 1.1.3.1 255.255.255.0
!
interface loopback 0
ip address 1.1.1.1 255.255.255.0
!
router igrp 1
network 1.0.0.0
```

The following commands configure basic STUN (example 1) for Router B:

```
stun peer-name 1.1.2.1
stun protocol-group 1 basic
!
interface serial 0
no ip address
encapsulation stun
stun group 1
stun route all tcp 1.1.1.1
clockrate 19200

interface tokenring 0
ip address 1.1.5.1 255.255.255.0
!
interface serial 1
ip address 1.1.3.2 255.255.255.0
!
interface loopback 0
ip address 1.1.2.1 255.255.255.0
!
router igrp 1
network 1.0.0.0
```

Basic STUN Configuration: Example 2

In Figure 20–6, the routers transmit data over a Frame Relay WAN. The FEPs are configured for DTE, full-duplex mode, and NRZI encoding. The serial interfaces on the routers are configured for DCE.

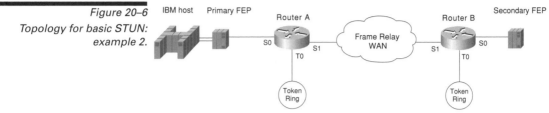

Figure 20–6
Topology for basic STUN:
example 2.

The following commands configure basic STUN (example 2) for Router A:

```
stun peer-name 1.1.1.1
stun protocol-group 1 basic
!
interface serial 0
no ip address
encapsulation stun
stun group 1
stun route all tcp 1.1.2.1
nrzi-encoding
clockrate 56000
!
interface tokenring 0
ip address 1.1.4.1 255.255.255.0
!
interface serial 1
ip address 1.1.3.1 255.255.255.0
encapsulation frame-relay
frame-relay map ip 1.1.3.2 40 broadcast
!
interface loopback 0
ip address 1.1.1.1 255.255.255.0
!
router igrp 1
network 1.0.0.0
```

The following commands configure basic STUN (example 2) for Router B:

```
stun peer-name 1.1.2.1
stun protocol-group 1 basic
!
interface serial 0
no ip address
encapsulation stun
stun group 1
stun route all tcp 1.1.1.1
nrzi-encoding
clockrate 56000
!
interface tokenring 0
ip address 1.1.5.1 255.255.255.0


interface serial 1
```

```
ip address 1.1.3.2 255.255.255.0
encapsulation frame-relay
frame-relay map ip 1.1.3.1 40 broadcast
!
interface loopback 0
ip address 1.1.2.1 255.255.255.0
!
router igrp 1
network 1.0.0.0
```

NOTES

NRZ encoding is the default for all Cisco routers. NRZI encoding is software configurable for Cisco 250x, Cisco 3x04, Cisco 4000 4T, and Cisco 7000 routers. NRZI encoding is hardware configurable for Cisco 4000 2T and AGS+ routers. Full-duplex mode is the default for all router serial cards. Half-duplex mode is software configurable for the Cisco 4000 4T and Cisco 250x routers and is hardware configurable on the EIA/TIA-232/H applique for the AGS+.

SDLC STUN

SDLC STUN is the most commonly used tunneling configuration in Cisco multiprotocol networks. It is frequently implemented for gateways and cluster controllers. SDLC STUN uses the standard SDLC protocol. In most cases, IBM FEPs and compatible FEPs comply with that standard. If an FEP uses a nonstandard form of SDLC, the router must be configured for basic STUN.

The SDLC STUN implementation requires coordination of SDLC addresses between the router and the NCP configuration. To configure the router for SDLC STUN, the network administrator must know the relative position of the ADDRESS parameters in the NCP configuration. For details, see the earlier "ADDRESS Parameter" section. Network administrators use SDLC STUN for two purposes:

- *To support specific addressing schemes*—SDLC STUN allows the network administrator to configure specific line addresses. SDLC STUN is required in certain environments, such as multidrop, that depend on specific addresses.

- *To support network tuning and monitoring*—Occasionally, the network administrator needs to tune and monitor the SNA SDLC and multiprotocol network.

SDLC STUN is limited by its lack of support for transmission groups.

Configuring SDLC STUN

In Figure 20–7, the routers transmit data over a serial line. The FEPs are configured for DTE, full-duplex mode, and NRZ encoding. The router serial interfaces are configured as DCE devices.

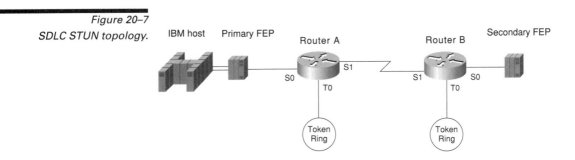

Figure 20–7
SDLC STUN topology.

The following commands configure SDLC STUN for Router A:

```
stun peer-name 1.1.1.1
stun protocol-group 1 sdlc
!
interface serial 0
no ip address
encapsulation stun
sdlc address 04
stun route address 04 interface s1
stun route address ff interface s1
clockrate 19200
!
interface tokenring 0
ip address 1.1.4.1 255.255.255.0
!
interface serial 1
ip address 1.1.3.1 255.255.255.0
!
interface loopback 0
ip address 1.1.1.1 255.255.255.0
!
router igrp 1
network 1.0.0.0
```

The following commands configure SDLC STUN for Router B:

```
stun peer-name 1.1.2.1
stun protocol-group 1 sdlc
!
interface serial 0
no ip address
encapsulation stun
sdlc address 04
stun route address 04 interface s1
stun route address ff interface s1
clockrate 19200
!
interface tokenring 0
ip address 1.1.5.1 255.255.255.0
!
interface serial 1
ip address 1.1.3.2 255.255.255.0
```

```
!
interface loopback 0
ip address 1.1.2.1 255.255.255.0
!
router igrp 1
network 1.0.0.0
```

SDLC-Transmission Group STUN

SDLC-Transmission Group (TG) STUN is a complex implementation that supports enhanced NCP features. When configuring STUN-TG, many network administrators also configure the routers to take advantage of the advanced features described in the "Advanced Router Features" section earlier in this chapter. Because these features increase memory and processor use, they should be used only when necessary to support the existing network or to relieve congestion. SDLC-TG STUN forces local acknowledgment. If you do not want to configure local acknowledgment, use the basic STUN or the SDLC STUN implementation.

The SDLC-TG implementation requires coordination of SDLC addresses between the router and the NCP configuration. To configure the router for SDLC-TG, the network administrator must know the relative position of the ADDRESS parameters in the NCP configuration. For details, see the "ADDRESS Parameter" section earlier in this chapter.

Configuring SDLC-TG STUN

Figure 20–8 illustrates a network that implements SDLC-TG STUN. The routers transmit data over an IP WAN. The FEPs are configured for DTE, full-duplex mode, and NRZ encoding. The serial interfaces on the routers are configured as DCE devices.

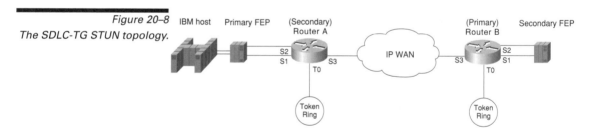

Figure 20–8
The SDLC-TG STUN topology.

To the primary FEP, Router A looks like a secondary FEP. To the secondary FEP, Router B looks like a primary FEP. The following commands configure SDLC-TG STUN for Router A:

```
stun peer-name 1.1.1.1
stun remote-peer-keepalive
stun protocol-group 1 sdlc-tg
!
interface tokenring 0
ip address 1.1.4.1 255.255.255.0
!
interface serial 1
```

```
mtu 4400
hold-queue 150 in
no ip address
encapsulation stun
stun group 1
stun sdlc-role secondary
sdlc n1 35200
sdlc address 01 echo
stun route address 1 tcp 1.1.2.1 local-ack tcp-queue-max 120
clockrate 56000


interface serial 2
mtu 4400
hold-queue 150 in
no ip address
encapsulation stun
stun group 1
stun sdlc-role secondary
sdlc n1 35200
sdlc address 02 echo
stun route address 2 tcp 1.1.2.1 local-ack tcp-queue-max 120
clockrate 56000
!
interface serial 3
ip address 1.1.3.1
interface loopback 0
ip address 1.1.1.1 255.255.255.0
!
router igrp 1
network 1.0.0.0
```

The following commands configure SDLC-TG STUN for Router B:

```
stun peer-name 1.1.2.1
stun remote-peer-keepalive
stun protocol-group 1 sdlc-tg
!
interface tokenring 0
ip address 1.1.5.1 255.255.255.0
!
interface serial 1
mtu 4400
hold-queue 150 in
no ip address
encapsulation stun
stun group 1
stun sdlc-role primary
sdlc line-speed 56000
sdlc n1 35200
sdlc address 01 echo
stun route address 1 tcp 1.1.1.1 local-ack tcp-queue-max 120
clockrate 56000
!
```

```
interface serial 2
mtu 4400
hold-queue 150 in
no ip address
encapsulation stun
stun group 1
stun sdlc-role primary
sdlc line-speed 56000
sdlc n1 35200
sdlc address 02 echo
stun route address 2 tcp 1.1.1.1 local-ack tcp-queue-max 120
clockrate 56000
!
interface serial 3
ip address 1.1.3.2
!
interface loopback 0
ip address 1.1.2.1 255.255.255.0
!
router igrp 1
network 1.0.0.0
```

The **stun peer-name** global configuration command identifies this router as a peer to its peer group.

The **stun remote-peer-keepalive** global configuration command causes Router A and Router B to exchange keepalive messages on each idle line. (An idle line is a line over which no I-frames are flowing.) Keepalive messages allow a router to detect when its peer router is not longer available. A peer router might become unavailable if it goes down or if the line goes down. The routers do not send keepalive traffic to the FEPs.

Routers send keepalive messages over an idle line at a default interval of 30 seconds and waits three times that interval for a response. If the router does not receive a response, it closes the STUN session.

The **stun protocol-group** global configuration command establishes a protocol group that is part of an SNA transmission group. The **sdlc-tg** keyword can be used only when the **stun route address tcp** interface configuration command is used to configure local acknowledgment and TCP encapsulation. The SDLC broadcast address 0xFF is routed automatically for interfaces on which the **sdlc-tg** keyword is configured. The **stun protocol-group** global configuration command also alerts the router that it should support transmission group features, such as the following:

- Echo addressing
- Transmission group rerouting if a single link in a multilink transmission group goes down
- Remote NCP load
- Broadcast addressing

The **mtu** interface configuration command specifies a maximum transmission unit (MTU) of 4400 bytes, which is the highest recommended value, for the interface. The value of the NCP

MAXDATA parameter should be no more than the MTU on the router interface. The recommended value of MAXDATA is 4096 bytes.

NOTES

Depending on the version of NCP, the MAXDATA parameter may or may not take into account the number of bytes in the frame header (which, for example, includes the source and destination address of the frame), so the MTU on the router interface should be at least 100 bytes larger than the value of MAXDATA in the NCP configuration.

The **hold-queue** interface configuration command increases the size of the input hold queue from 75 packets (the default) to 150 packets. The specified value should be greater than the depth of the TCP output queue (as specified by the **tcp-queue-max** keyword of the **stun route address tcp** interface configuration command). Increasing the size of the input hold queue allows flow control to activate when the TCP output queue reaches a threshold of 90 percent, which occurs before the input interface throttling mechanism can activate.

The **stun sdlc-role primary** interface configuration command is used when the router is connected to a secondary FEP. The **stun sdlc-role secondary** interface configuration command is used when the router is connected to a primary FEP.

On the primary router, the **sdlc line-speed** interface configuration command adjusts the SDLC poll timer based on the line speed. The line speed argument should be equal to the speed of the line connected to the interface, regardless of whether the interface is configured as a DCE or a DTE.

The **sdlc n1** interface configuration command specifies the maximum size (in bits) of an incoming frame on the SDLC link and is required when the MTU is not 1500 bytes (the default). The **sdlc n1** command must be eight times larger than the value specified by the **stun** command.

The **sdlc address** interface configuration command specifies an SDLC address. The specified address must be the same as the relative line number at which the ADDRESS parameter is specified in the NCP configuration of the FEP to which the router is connected. (For more information, see the "ADDRESS Parameter" section earlier in this chapter.) The **echo** keyword causes the router to treat nonecho (for example, 0x01) and echo (for example, 0x81) SDLC addresses as the same address. The **sdlc address** interface configuration command is valid only for interfaces on which the **stun protocol-group** command with the **sdlc-tg** keyword is configured. Only one **sdlc address** interface configuration command with **echo** keyword is required per interface.

The **stun route address tcp** interface configuration command specifies TCP encapsulation. The value of *address* specifies the SDLC address, which must be specified with the echo bit turned off. The **local-ack** keyword causes the router to perform local acknowledgment and is required when the **sdlc-tg** keyword appears with the **stun protocol-group** command. The **tcp-queue-max** keyword sets the maximum size of the TCP output queue for a serial line. The default is 100 packets. The recommended minimum is 70, and the recommended maximum is 500. The **clockrate** interface configuration command specifies the clocking speed when the serial interface is in DCE mode.

SUMMARY

This case study presents three types of STUN implementations in SNA environments: basic STUN, SDLC STUN, and SDLC-TG STUN. Although basic STUN is the easiest to configure because it does not require the configuration of line addresses on the router, it does not support local acknowledgment. Compared to basic STUN, the SDLC STUN implementation is the most flexible because it supports, but does not require, local acknowledgment. However, the use of SDLC STUN is limited because it does not support transmission groups. SDLC-TG STUN is not as flexible as SDLC STUN because it enforces local acknowledgment. At the same time, SDLC-TG STUN is the only STUN implementation that supports transmission groups.

Using ISDN Effectively in Multiprotocol Networks

As telephone companies make Integrated Services Digital Network (ISDN) services available, ISDN is becoming an increasingly popular way of connecting remote sites. This case study covers the following ISDN scenarios:

- *Configuring DDR over ISDN*—This telecommuting scenario describes the configuration of home sites that use ISDN to connect to a central company network and shows you how to use calling line identification numbers to prevent unauthorized access to the central network.

- *Configuring Snapshot Routing over ISDN*—Snapshot routing provides cost-effective access to a central company network from branch or home offices. Snapshot routing is used to upgrade the telecommuting network and control routing updates in Novell IPX networks.

- *Configuring AppleTalk over ISDN*—This scenario shows you how to control AppleTalk packets that might otherwise trigger unnecessary ISDN connections.

CONFIGURING DDR OVER ISDN

In the United States, many companies today regard telecommuting as a way to solve space problems, conform to the Clean Air Act, and make employees more productive. In Europe, companies are looking for solutions that allow central offices to connect to remote sites. In the past, analog modems provided the necessary connectivity over serial lines, but they are not fast enough for LAN-to-LAN connections or for remote use of graphical programs, such as computer-aided design (CAD) tools. ISDN provides the needed additional bandwidth without requiring a leased line.

An ISDN Basic Rate Interface (BRI) provides two 64-kilobits-per-second (Kbps) B channels for voice or data and one 16-Kbps D channel for signaling. Voice and data information is carried over the B channels digitally. In the United States, an ISDN Primary Rate Interface (PRI) provides 23 64-Kbps B channels for voice and data over a T1 connection, and one 64-Kbps D channel for signaling. In

Europe, a PRI provides 30 B channels for voice and data and one D channel for signaling over an E1 connection.

Figure 21–1 shows the network that will be discussed in this case study. The ISDN network uses multiple central office ISDN switches.

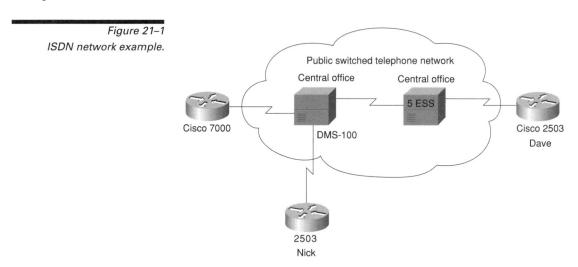

Figure 21–1
ISDN network example.

In this case study, the remote sites (homes) use Cisco 2503 routers, which provide one BRI, an Ethernet interface, and two high-speed serial interfaces. At the central company site, a Cisco 7000 series router equipped with a channelized T1 card answers the calls. The channelized T1 card provides a PRI.

Currently in many parts of the United States, telephone companies have not deployed Signaling System 7, which means that calls between certain central offices must be placed at 56 Kbps. This restriction does not apply to all parts of the United States or to other countries, but it does apply to some of the sample ISDN networks described in this chapter.

Native ISDN Interfaces

If you are using an external ISDN terminal adapter, also known as an *ISDN modem*, you can use the configuration examples provided in Chapter 15, "Dial-on-Demand Routing." Although an ISDN modem provides ISDN connectivity and allows you to use existing serial interfaces, it is not always the optimal solution because of the investment in an external unit and in additional cabling. Also, using V.25bis does not give the router full access to certain information that is available in an ISDN network, such as the speed of the call or the number of the calling party.

The native ISDN interface on the Cisco 2503 router allows the router to be directly connected to an ISDN NT1 device. In many countries, the NT1 is provided by the telephone company. In the United States, however, the NT1 is customer-owned equipment. By directly connecting to the ISDN network, the router has more direct control over ISDN parameters and has access to ISDN information.

Configuring an ISDN Interface

Configuring a native ISDN interface is similar to configuring a serial interface using DDR routing as described in Chapter 15, "Dial-on-Demand Routing." There are two major differences:

- The **dialer in-band** interface configuration command is not required with ISDN. PRI and BRI interfaces are assumed by the router to be a DDR interface.

- The individual B channels cannot be configured separately. The B channels of a BRI appear to be a dialer rotary group with two members. In the United States, the B channels of a PRI appear to be a dialer rotary group with 23 members, and in Europe, the B channels of a PRI appear to be a dialer rotary group with 30 members. Because the PRI or BRI is a dialer rotary group, all configuration commands associated with a PRI or BRI apply to all B channels.

The following sections describe the configurations of the central site and the home site routers. In this case study, both the central site and the home sites can place calls. The central site uses a Cisco 7000 router that connects to a NorTel DMS-100 central office ISDN switch. One remote site router (nick-isdn) connects to the same central office switch that the central site router uses. Connections from the other remote site router (dave-isdn) pass through two central office switches to reach the central site router.

Central Site

Two remote site users, Dave and Nick, dial from their homes into the central site router that is configured as follows. Part of the configuration of the central site router is specific to the DMS-100 switch, whereas other commands apply to any type of ISDN central office switch.

```
hostname central-isdn
!
username dave-isdn password 7 130318111D
username nick-isdn password 7 08274D02A02
isdn switch-type primary-dms100
!
interface ethernet 0
ip address 11.108.40.53 255.255.255.0
no mop enabled
!
controller t1 1/0
framing esf
linecode b8zs
pri-group timeslots 2-6
!
interface serial 1/0:23
ip address 11.108.90.53 255.255.255.0
encapsulation ppp
dialer idle-timeout 300
dialer map ip 11.108.90.1 name dave-isdn speed 56 914085553680
dialer map ip 11.108.90.7 name nick-isdn 8376
dialer-group 1
ppp authentication chap
!
```

```
router igrp 10
network 11.108.0.0
redistribute static
!
! route to nick-isdn
ip route 11.108.137.0 255.255.255.0 11.108.90.7
! route to dave-isdn
ip route 11.108.147.0 255.255.255.0 11.108.90.1
!
access-list 101 deny igrp 0.0.0.0 255.255.255.255 0.0.0.0 255.255.255.255
!NTP
access-list 101 deny udp 0.0.0.0 255.255.255.255 0.0.0.0 255.255.255.255 eq 123
!SNMP
access-list 101 deny udp 0.0.0.0 255.255.255.255 0.0.0.0 255.255.255.255 eq 161
access-list 101 permit ip 0.0.0.0 255.255.255.255 0.0.0.0 255.255.255.255
!
dialer-list 1 list 101
```

The configuration begins by establishing the host name of the router. The **username** global configuration commands establish the names of the routers that are allowed to dial up this router. The names correspond to the host names of Dave's router and Nick's router. The **isdn switch-type** command global configuration command specifies that the central site router connects to a NorTel DMS-100 switch. The host name, usernames, and ISDN switch type vary from router to router.

Controller Configuration

The **controller** global configuration command uses **T1** to specify a T1 controller interface. The "1" indicates that the controller card is located in backplane slot number 1. The "0" indicates port 0.

The **framing** controller configuration command selects the frame type for the T1 data line. In this case, the **framing** command uses the **esf** keyword to indicate the extended super frame (ESF) frame type. The service provider determines which framing type, either sf, esf, or crc4, is required for your T1/E1 circuit.

The **linecode** controller configuration command defines the line-code type for the T1 data line. In this case, the **linecode** command uses the **b8zs** keyword to indicate that the line-code type is bipolar 8 zero substitution (B8ZS). The service provider determines which line-code type, either alternate mark inversion (AMI) or B8ZS, is required for your T1/E1 circuit.

The **pri-group** controller configuration command specifies an ISDN PRI on a channelized T1 card in a Cisco 7000 series router. The **timeslots** keyword establishes the B channels. In this example, only five B channels (channels 2 through 6) are in use on this controller.

Interface Configuration

The **ip address** interface configuration command establishes the IP address of the interface, and the **encapsulation ppp** command establishes the Point-to-Point protocol (PPP) as the encapsulation method. PPP supports Challenge Handshake Authentication Protocol (CHAP) and Password Authentication Protocol (PAP) as authentication mechanisms for identifying the caller and providing a level of security. The **dialer idle-timeout** interface configuration command sets the idle timeout to five minutes.

The **dialer map** interface configuration commands establish the remote sites that the router can call. Because Dave's router connects to a central office switch that does not use Signaling System 7, the **dialer map** command for calling Dave's router uses the **speed** keyword, which is valid for native ISDN interfaces only. The native ISDN interface on the Cisco 2503 operates at either 64 or 56 Kbps. If the calling party and the called party use the same ISDN switch, they can communicate at 64 Kbps. Otherwise, they must communicate at 56 Kbps.

Because Nick's ISDN line connects to the same central office as the line that the central site router uses, the telephone number in the **dialer map** command for connecting to Nick's router does not have to include the three-digit prefix. Note that because the central site router uses lines that are part of a Centrex, the outgoing telephone numbers start with 9 if they are not four-digit numbers.

The **dialer-group** interface configuration command associates the BRI with dialer access group 1. The **ppp authentication chap** interface configuration command enables CHAP authentication.

Routing Configuration

In the routing section of the configuration, the **router igrp** global configuration command enables the Interior Gateway Routing Protocol (IGRP) and sets the autonomous system number to 10. The **network** router configuration command assigns the network number. The **redistribute** router configuration command sends the static route information (defined with the **ip route** global configuration commands) to other routers in the same IGRP area. Without this command, other routers connected to the central site would not have routes to the remote routers.

DDR tends to use static routes extensively because routing updates are not received when the dial-up connection is not active. The first two **ip route** commands create the static routes that define the subnets that Dave and Nick use.

NOTES

The IGRP commands are the same on all central site routers, except that the static routes correspond to the home sites calling into each central site router.

Access List Configuration

DDR uses access lists to determine whether a packet is *interesting* or *uninteresting*. Interesting packets cause a call to be placed if a call is not active or cause a call that has already been placed to be maintained as active. The first extended **access-list** global configuration command states that IGRP updates are uninteresting. The second extended **access-list** command states that Network Time Protocol (NTP) packets are uninteresting. The third extended **access-list** command specifies that Simple Network Management Protocol (SNMP) packets are uninteresting, and the final extended **access-list** command states that all other IP packets are interesting. The **dialer-list list** global configuration command assigns the set of access lists to dialer access group 1.

Home Site

The configurations of the home site routers are similar, but Nick's configuration is simpler because his router connects to the same central office switch as the central site router.

Nick

The configuration for the router at Nick's home is as follows:

```
hostname nick-isdn
!
username central-isdn password 7 050D130C2A5
isdn switch-type basic-dms100
!
interface ethernet 0
ip address 11.108.137.1 255.255.255.0
no mop enabled
!
interface bri 0
ip address 11.108.90.7 255.255.255.0
encapsulation ppp
no ip route-cache
isdn spid1 415555837601 5558376
isdn spid2 415555837802 5558378
dialer idle-timeout 300
dialer map ip 11.108.90.53 name central-isdn 8362
dialer map ip 11.108.90.53 name central-isdn 8370
dialer-group 1
ppp authentication chap
!
ip route 11.108.0.0 255.255.0.0 11.108.90.53
!
access-list 101 deny udp 0.0.0.0 255.255.255.255 0.0.0.0 255.255.255.255 eq 177
access-list 101 permit ip 0.0.0.0 255.255.255.255 0.0.0.0 255.255.255.255
!
dialer-list 1 list 101
```

As with the central site router, the **isdn switch-type** global configuration command specifies that the switch is an NT DMS-100 switch. Because Nick's router connects to the DMS-100, SPIDs are required for the BRI. PPP and CHAP are configured, along with a **username** command for the central site router. The configuration for Nick's router differs from that of the central site with regard to the **dialer map** commands and the routing section. Two **dialer map** commands point to the same next-hop address. If the attempt to call the first number fails, the second number will be used to connect to the next-hop address.

The **isdn spid1** and **isdn spid2** interface configuration commands represent service profile identifiers (SPIDs). SPIDs are used when a BRI connects to a NorTel DMS-100 switch or a National ISDN-1 switch. SPIDs are assigned by the service provider to associate a SPID number with a telephone number. Other switch types do not require SPIDs. Your service provider can tell you if SPIDs are required for your switch. In this example, SPID 1 identifies 415 as the area code, 555 as the exchange, 8376 as the station ID, and 01 as the terminal identifier. The SPID format required by your service provider may differ from the examples shown in this case study.

Dave

The configuration for Dave's router is similar to the configuration for Nick's router, except that Dave's router is not in the same Centrex as the central company site. The configuration for Dave's router is as follows:

```
hostname dave-isdn
!
username central-isdn password 7 08274341
isdn switch-type basic-5ess
!
interface ethernet 0
ip address 11.108.147.1 255.255.255.0
no mop enabled
!
interface bri 0
ip address 11.108.90.1 255.255.255.0
encapsulation ppp
no ip route-cache
bandwidth 56
dialer map ip 11.108.90.53 name central-isdn speed 56 14155558370
dialer-group 1
ppp authentication chap
!
ip route 11.108.0.0 255.255.0.0 11.108.90.53
!
dialer-list 1 list 101
```

Dave's configuration is different from Nick's configuration because Dave's router connects to an AT&T 5ESS central office ISDN switch that does not run Signaling System 7. The **isdn switch-type** global configuration command specifies a basic rate AT&T switch, which does not require Dave's router configuration to use the **isdn spid1** and **isdn spid2** interface configuration commands that the DMS-100 switch requires. The **bandwidth** interface configuration command tells routing protocols that the line operates at 56 Kbps. The **dialer map** interface configuration command uses the **speed** keyword so that when Dave's router dials up the central site router, it sets the line speed to 56 Kbps. This setting is necessary when the connection traverses a switch that does not run Signaling System 7.

Configuring Calling Line Identification Numbers

Because Nick is in the same Centrex as the central company routers, the central router can use the Calling Line Identification (CLID) number received from the ISDN switch to identify Nick. With CLID, the configuration for Nick does not require CHAP or PAP; however, Nick needs to modify his configuration to include CLID. Nick's new configuration and a sample of the central site changed configuration are shown in the following sections.

NOTES

CLID is not available in all parts of the United States and other countries. Some countries do not require Centrex for CLID.

Central Site

Here is the central site PRI interface configuration modified for CLID:

```
controller t1 1/0
framing esf
linecode b8zs
pri-group timeslots 2-6
!
interface serial 1/0:23
ip address 11.108.90.53 255.255.255.0
dialer idle-timeout 300
dialer map ip 11.108.90.7 name 5558376 8376
dialer-group 1
```

The **name** keyword in the **dialer map** interface configuration command specifies the actual string that calling line identification returns. This string differs from the number called: the number called is a four-digit Centrex number, and the number returned is the full seven digits.

Home Site

As with the central site, the major difference in Nick's configuration is the use of the **name** keyword with the **dialer map** command that specifies the actual number being returned as the calling line number.

```
interface bri 0
ip address 11.108.90.7 255.255.255.0
no ip route-cache
isdn spid1 415555837601 5558376
isdn spid2 415555837802 5558378
dialer idle-timeout 300
dialer map ip 11.108.90.53 name 5558362 8362
dialer map ip 11.108.90.53 name 5558370 8370
dialer-group 1
```

— **NOTES** ————————————————————————————

If the **debug isdn-q931** EXEC command is enabled, the decode for an incoming call setup can be seen and the CLID number will be shown.

Configuring Callback

Because Dave is located several miles from the central office, calls to the central office router are metered and billed to Dave's telephone number. The callback feature (introduced in Cisco IOS 11.0) allows Dave's router to place a call to the central site router requesting that the central site router call Dave's router. Then the central site router disconnects the call and places a return call to Dave's router. With callback configured, Dave's telephone bill is reduced because actual data transfers occur when the central office router calls back. The following commands configure callback on Dave's router:

```
interface bri 0
ppp callback request
dialer hold-queue 100 timeout 20
```

The **ppp callback** interface configuration command with the **request** keyword specifies that when the interface places a call, it is to request callback. The **dialer hold-queue** interface configuration command specifies that up to 100 packets can be held in a queue until the central site router returns the call. If the central site router does not return the call within 20 seconds plus the length of the enable timeout configured on the central site router, the packets are dropped. The following commands configure callback on the central office router:

```
map-class dialer class1
dialer callback-server username
interface serial 1/0:23
dialer map ip 11.108.90.1 name dave-isdn speed 56 class class1 914085553680
ppp callback accept
dialer callback-secure
dialer enable-timeout 1
dialer hold-queue
```

The **map-class** global configuration command establishes a quality of service (QoS) parameter that is to be associated with a static map. The **dialer** keyword specifies that the map is a dialer map. The **class1** parameter is a user-defined value that creates a map class to which subsequent encapsulation specific commands apply.

The **dialer map** interface configuration command has been modified to include the **class** keyword and the name of the class, as specified in the **map-class** command. The **name** keyword is required so that, when Dave's router dials in, the interface can locate this dialer map statement and obtain the dial string for calling back Dave's router.

The **ppp callback** interface configuration command with the **accept** keyword allows the interface to accept and honor callback requests that come into the interface. (Callback depends on PPP authentication, using PAP or CHAP.)

The **dialer callback-server** map class configuration command allows the interface to return calls when callback is successfully negotiated. The **username** keyword specifies that the interface is to locate the dial string for making the return call by looking up the authenticated host name in a **dialer map** command.

The **dialer callback-secure** interface configuration command specifies that the router is to disconnect the initial call, and call back only if it has a **dialer map** command with a defined class for the remote router. If the **dialer callback-secure** command is not present, the central router will not drop the connection if it does not have a **dialer map** command with a defined class. The **dialer enable-timeout** interface configuration command specifies that the interface is to wait one second after disconnecting the initial call before making the return call.

Configuring Snapshot Routing over ISDN

Snapshot routing is an easy way to reduce connection time in ISDN networks by suppressing the transfer of routing updates for a configurable period of time. Snapshot routing is best suited for networks whose data-transfer connections typically last longer than five minutes and that are running the following distance-vector protocols:

- Routing Information Protocol (RIP) and Integrated Gateway Routing Protocol (IGRP) for IP
- Routing Table Maintenance Protocol (RTMP) for AppleTalk
- Routing Information Protocol (RIP) and Service Advertisement Protocol (SAP) for Novell Internet Packet Exchange (IPX)
- Routing Table Protocol (RTP) for Banyan VINES

The goal of snapshot routing is to allow routing protocols to exchange updates as they normally would. Because Enhanced IGRP and link-state routing protocols, such as Novell Link Services Protocol (NLSP), Open Shortest Path First (OSPF), and Intermediate System-to-Intermediate System (IS-IS) depend on the frequent sending of hello messages to neighboring routers in order to discover and maintain routes, they are incompatible with snapshot routing.

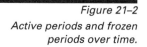

This case study applies snapshot routing to an ISDN network, but other similar media, such as dedicated leased lines, can benefit from the reduction of periodic updates that snapshot routing provides.

Before snapshot routing became available in Cisco Internetwork Operating System (IOS) Software Release 10.2, ISDN interfaces were configured using static routes. Static routes, such as the routes defined by the **ip route** commands in the "Central Site" section earlier in this chapter, prevent bandwidth from being consumed by routing updates, but they are difficult to maintain as the network grows.

Snapshot routing supports dynamic routes by allowing routing updates to occur during an active period and reduces connection cost by suppressing routing updates during a quiet period, which can be up to 65 days long. During the quiet period, the routing tables on the routers at both ends of a link are frozen. Figure 21–2 shows the relationship of active and quiet periods over time.

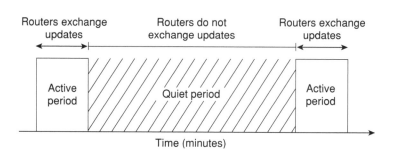

Figure 21–2
Active periods and frozen periods over time.

During the active period, the routers at each end of the connection exchange the routing updates that are normal for their configured routing protocols. They continue to exchange routing updates until the active period ends. When the active period ends, each router freezes its routing tables, stops sending routing updates, and enters the quiet period. Each router remains in the quiet period until a configurable timer expires, at which time one of the routers initiates a connection to send and receive routing updates.

To ensure that routing tables are updated, the active period must be long enough for several routing updates to come through the link. An active period that is too short might allow only one routing update to cross the link. If that update is lost due to noise on the line, the router on the other end would age out a valid route or would not learn about a new valid route. To make sure that updates occur, the active period must be at least five minutes long (that is, three times longer than the routing protocols' update interval). Because the routing protocols update their routing tables during the active period as they normally would, there is no need to adjust any routing protocol timers.

If the line is not available when the router transitions from the quiet period to the active period, it enters a retry period. During the retry period, the router continually attempts to connect until it enters an active period, as shown in Figure 21–3.

Figure 21–3
The router continually
attempts to connect during
the retry period.

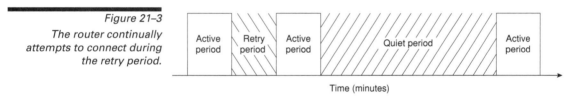

Table 21–1 shows the minimum and maximum lengths of each period.

Table 21–1 *Snapshot Routing Periods*

Period	Configurable	Minimum Length	Maximum Length
Active	Yes	5 minutes	100 minutes
Quiet	Yes	5 minutes	65 days
Retry	No	8 minutes	8 minutes

By default, snapshot routing allows routing updates to be exchanged over connections that are established to transfer user data. This means that, if necessary, snapshot routing forces the connection to last as long as the active period. If you do not want the routers to exchange updates during connections that are established to transfer user data, use the **suppress-statechange-updates** keyword.

Upgrading the Telecommuting Network

Snapshot routing is well-suited to the hub-and-spoke topology of the telecommuting network described in the "Configuring DDR over ISDN" section at the beginning of this chapter. Snapshot routing is designed for a client-server relationship. The client routers, such as the home sites, determine the frequency at which the routers exchange updates by setting the length of the quiet period, and the server router accepts incoming snapshot connections from several client routers.

NOTES

Snapshot routing is not recommended for meshed topologies. In meshed topologies, configuring static routes is more efficient than configuring snapshot routing.

Central Site Modified for Snapshot Routing

The following is the configuration of the central site router after modification for snapshot routing:

```
hostname central-isdn
!
username dave-isdn password 7 130318111D
username nick-isdn password 7 08274D02A02
isdn switch-type primary-dms100
!
interface ethernet 0
ip address 11.108.40.53 255.255.255.0
no mop enabled
!
controller t1 1/0
framing esf
linecode b8zs
pri-group timeslots 2-6
ip address 11.108.90.53 255.255.255.0
encapsulation ppp
dialer idle-timeout 300
dialer map ip 11.108.90.1 name dave-isdn speed 56 914085553680
dialer map ip 11.108.90.7 name nick-isdn 8376
dialer-group 1
isdn spid1 415555836201 5558362
isdn spid2 415555837002 5558370
snapshot server 5
ppp authentication chap
!
router igrp 10
network 11.108.0.0
redistribute static
!
! route to nick-isdn
ip route 11.108.137.0 255.255.255.0 11.108.90.7
! route to dave-isdn
ip route 11.108.147.0 255.255.255.0 11.108.90.1
!
access-list 101 deny igrp 0.0.0.0 255.255.255.255 0.0.0.0 255.255.255.255
!NTP
access-list 101 deny udp 0.0.0.0 255.255.255.255 0.0.0.0 255.255.255.255 eq 123
!SNMP
access-list 101 deny udp 0.0.0.0 255.255.255.255 0.0.0.0 255.255.255.255 eq 161
access-list 101 permit ip 0.0.0.0 255.255.255.255 0.0.0.0 255.255.255.255
!
dialer-list 1 list 101
```

The **ip route** global configuration commands that configured static routes for the home sites have been removed from the configuration. The **snapshot server** interface configuration command enables snapshot routing. The "5" sets the length of the active period to five minutes.

NOTES

Snapshot routing must be configured on rotary interfaces, which are established by the **dialer rotary-group** interface configuration command. ISDN interfaces are rotary interfaces by definition, so you do not need to use the **dialer rotary-group** command in ISDN configurations.

Home Site Modified for Snapshot Routing

The following is the configuration of Dave's home site router after modification for snapshot routing:

```
hostname dave-isdn
!
username central-isdn password 7 08274341
isdn switch-type basic-5ess
!
interface ethernet 0
ip address 11.108.147.1 255.255.255.0
no mop enabled
!
interface bri 0
ip address 11.108.90.1 255.255.255.0
encapsulation ppp
no ip route-cache
bandwidth 56
dialer map snapshot 1 name central-isdn 14155558370
dialer map ip 11.108.90.53 name central-isdn speed 56 14155558370
dialer-group 1
snapshot client 5 43200 suppress-statechange-updates dialer
ppp authentication chap
!
dialer-list 1 list 101
```

The **ip route** commands that configured static routes for the home sites have been removed from the configuration. The **dialer map snapshot** interface configuration command establishes a map (whose sequence number is 1) that the router uses to connect to the central site router for the exchange of routing updates. The **name** keyword specifies the name of the remote router that is associated with the dial string. Because the **ppp authentication** interface configuration command enables CHAP authentication, when this router dials the central router, it receives the host name of the central router and compares it with the name specified by the **name** keyword.

The **snapshot client** interface configuration command sets the length of the active period to five minutes (a value that must match the value set in the snapshot server's configuration) and sets the length of the quiet period to 43,200 seconds (12 hours). The **suppress-statechange-updates** keyword prevents the routers from exchanging updates during connections that are established to transfer user data. The **dialer** keyword allows the client router to dial up the server router in the absence of regular traffic and is required when you use the **suppress-statechange-update** keyword.

Snapshot and Novell IPX Networks

This section describes a Novell IPX network for which snapshot routing has been configured. Client routers at branch offices use DDR to connect to a central router over ISDN. At the central office, NetWare servers use the Novell IPX protocol to provide services to NetWare clients on each branch office network. Some client-to-server connections are required during a limited period of the day. Figure 21–4 illustrates the network.

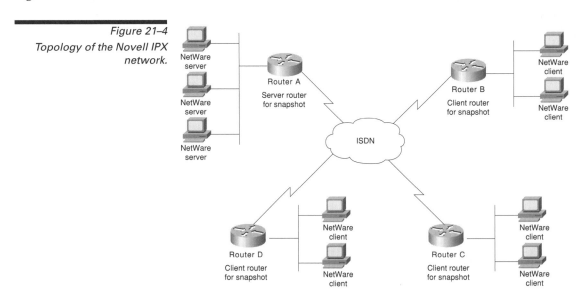

Figure 21–4
Topology of the Novell IPX network.

In this topology, the client routers are responsible for updating their routing tables by connecting to the server router when the quiet period expires. The client routers also retrieve update information if a reload occurs.

NOTES

Snapshot routing works with Novell 3.x and 4.x networks. However, Novell 4.x includes a time synchronization protocol that causes Novell 4.x time servers to send an update every 10 minutes. To prevent the time server from generating update packets that would cause unwanted connections, you should load a NetWare Loadable Module (NLM) named TIMESYNC.NLM that allows you to increase the update interval for these packets to several days. A similar problem is caused by Novell's efforts to synchronize NDS replicas. NetWare 4.1 includes two NLMs, DSFILTER.NLM and PINGFILT.NLM, that work together to control NDS synchronization updates. You should use these two modules to make sure that NDS synchronization traffic is sent to specified servers only at the specified times.

Server Router Configuration

The following is the complete configuration for the server router:

```
hostname RouterA
!
username RouterB password 7 120D0A031D
username RouterC password 7 111D161118
username RouterD password 7 43E7528384
isdn switch-type vn3
!
ipx routing

interface Ethernet 0
ip address 192.104.155.99 255.255.255.0
ipx network 300
!
interface bri 0
ip address 1.0.0.1 255.0.0.0
encapsulation ppp
ipx network 10
no ipx route-cache
ipx update-time 20
ipx watchdog-spoof
dialer idle-timeout 60
dialer wait-for-carrier-time 12
dialer map ipx 10.0000.0000.0002 name RouterB broadcast 041389082
dialer map ipx 10.0000.0000.0003 name RouterC broadcast 041389081
dialer map ipx 10.0000.0000.0004 name RouterD broadcast 041389083
!
dialer-group 1
snapshot server 10
ppp authentication chap
!
access-list 901 deny 0 FFFFFFF 0 FFFFFFFF 457
access-list 901 deny 1 10.0000.0000.0001 0 10.ffff.ffff.ffff 453
access-list 901 deny 4 10.0000.0000.0001 0 10.ffff.ffff.ffff 452
access-list 901 deny 4 FFFFFFF 0 FFFFFFFF 456
access-list 901 permit -1
!
dialer-list 1 list 901
```

The configuration begins with the host name used for CHAP authentication. The usernames correspond to the host names of Router B, Router C, and Router D. The **isdn switch-type** global configuration command specifies that the router connects to a French VN3 ISDN BRI switch.

Interface Configuration

The **dialer idle-timeout** interface configuration command specifies 60 seconds as the amount of idle time that must elapse before the router disconnects the line. The **dialer wait-for-carrier-time** interface configuration command sets the wait-for-carrier time to 60 seconds.

The first **dialer map** interface configuration command sets the next-hop address of Router B to 10.0000.0000.0002. When Router B dials up the server router (Router A), the server router uses the next hop address to transmit packets to Router B. The **broadcast** keyword sets 041389082 as the address to which IPX broadcasts are to be forwarded. The second and third **dialer map** commands set similar values for Router C and Router D.

The **snapshot server** interface configuration command sets the length of the active period to 10 minutes. The **ppp authentication** interface configuration command sets CHAP as the authentication protocol.

Access List Configuration

Access lists are used to determine whether an outgoing packet is interesting or uninteresting. Packets that are not interesting are dropped, and packets that are interesting cause a call to be placed if a call is not active or cause a call that has already been placed to be maintained as active. The access lists defined by this configuration are extended Novell IPX access lists. The first **access-list** global configuration command defines any packets intended for the Novell serialization socket as uninteresting. The second **access-list** command defines RIP packets as uninteresting. The third **access-list** command defines SAP packets as uninteresting. The fourth **access-list** command defines Novell diagnostic packets generated by the Autodiscovery feature as uninteresting, and the final **access-list** command states that all other packets are interesting. The **dialer-list** global configuration command assigns access list 901 to dialer access group 1, which is associated with BRI 0 by the **dialer-group** interface configuration command.

Client Router Configuration

The configurations for the client routers are the same except for the commands that configure the router's host name, the username that it uses when it dials up Router A, and the router's network numbers. The following is the configuration for Router B:

```
hostname RouterB
!
username RouterA password 7 105A060D0A
ipx routing
isdn switch-type vn3
isdn tei first-call
!
interface ethernet 0
ip address 192.104.155.100 255.255.255.0
ipx network 301
!
interface bri 0
no ip address
encapsulation ppp
ipx network 10
no ipx route-cache
ipx update-time 20
ipx watchdog-spoof
dialer idle-timeout 60
dialer wait-for-carrier-time 12
dialer map snapshot 1 name RouterA 46148412
dialer map ipx 10.0000.0000.0001 name RouterA broadcast 46148412
```

```
dialer-group 1
snapshot client 10 86400 dialer
ppp authentication chap
!
access-list 901 deny 0 FFFFFFFF 0 FFFFFFFF 457
access-list 901 deny 1 10.0000.0000.0002 0 10.ffff.ffff.ffff 453
access-list 901 deny 4 10.0000.0000.0002 0 10.ffff.ffff.ffff 452
access-list 901 deny 4 FFFFFFFF 0 FFFFFFFF 456
access-list 901 permit 0
!
dialer-list 1 list 901
```

The configuration begins with the host name used for CHAP authentication. The usernames correspond to the host names of Router B, Router C, and Router D. The **isdn switch-type** global configuration command specifies that the router connects to a French VN3 ISDN BRI switch.

The **isdn tei** global configuration command uses the **first-call** keyword to specify that ISDN terminal *endpoint identifier* (TEI) negotiation is to occur when Router A places or receives its first ISDN call. (The default is for TEI negotiation to occur when the router is powered on.)

Interface Configuration

The **dialer wait-for-carrier** interface configuration command specifies 12 seconds as the number of seconds that the interface will wait for the carrier to come up when it places a call.

The **snapshot client** interface configuration command sets the length of the active period to 10 minutes (a value that must match the value set in the snapshot server's configuration) and sets the length of the quiet period to 86,400 seconds (24 hours). Because the **suppress-statechange-updates** keyword is not used, the routers can exchange updates during connections that are established to transfer user data. The **dialer** keyword allows the client router to dial up the server router in the absence of regular traffic.

CONFIGURING APPLETALK OVER ISDN

To run AppleTalk over an ISDN network effectively, you need to prevent Name Binding Protocol (NBP) packets and RTMP updates from triggering unnecessary connections over ISDN connections.

Figure 21–5 shows a sample AppleTalk network that uses ISDN to connect two networks located in different cities. Users on the district office network occasionally need access to servers located on the main office network and vice versa. In this scenario, both routers dial up each other when user data from one part of the network needs to reach the other part of the network.

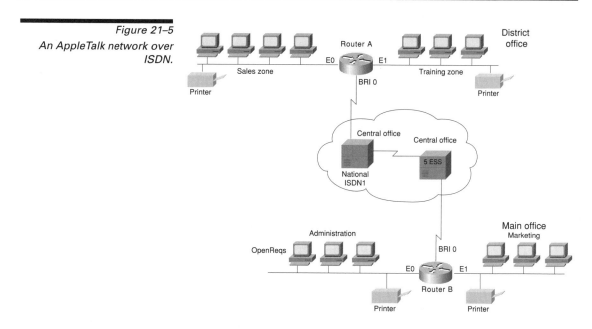

Figure 21–5

An AppleTalk network over ISDN.

Users of hosts connected to the main office network do not need to access the Training zone, so when configuring Router A, one goal is to prevent NBP packets generated by the Training zone from triggering an ISDN connection with the main office network. Another configuration goal for both routers is to prevent NBP packets generated by the printers on each network from triggering an ISDN connection.

To control the forwarding of NBP packets, use AppleTalk-style access lists. AppleTalk-style access lists allow you to control the flow of NBP packets based on the type of the entity that originated the packet, the name of the entity that originated the packet, and the zone of the entity that originated the packet.

NOTES

The capability to control the forwarding of NBP packets was introduced in Cisco IOS Software Release 11.0.

Both routers also need to control RTMP packets. To control RTMP packets, configure static Apple-Talk cable ranges and node numbers and use the **no appletalk send rtmps** command on the ISDN BRI or PRI interface that connects two AppleTalk networks.

Router A Configuration

As shown in Figure 21–5, Router A is located in the district office. The district office network consists of two zones: Sales and Training. On Router A, an AppleTalk-style access list is assigned to BRI 0 to prevent the forwarding of NBP packets that come from printers and NBP packets that come from the Training zone. If the router were to allow the forwarding of these packets, they would trigger an unnecessary ISDN connection to the main office network.

```
hostname RouterA
!
username RouterB password 7 125D063D2E
appletalk routing
appletalk static cable-range 20-20 to 15.43 zone Administration
appletalk static cable-range 25-25 to 15.43 zone Marketing
isdn switch-type basic-ni1
!
interface ethernet 0
appletalk cable-range 5-5 5.128
appletalk zone Sales
!
interface ethernet 1
appletalk cable-range 10-10 10.26
appletalk zone Service
!
interface bri 0
appletalk static cable-range 15-15 15.42
appletalk zone PhoneZone
no appletalk send-rtmps
encapsulation ppp
ppp authentication chap
dialer idle-timeout 240
bandwidth 56
dialer map appletalk 15.43 name RouterA speed 56 912065553240
dialer-group 1
isdn spid1 602555463101 5554631
!
access-list 601 deny nbp 1 type LaserWriter
access-list 601 deny nbp 2 zone Training
access-list 601 permit nbp 3 zone Sales
access-list 601 deny other-nbps
access-list 601 permit other-access
!
dialer-list 1 list 601
```

The **hostname** global configuration command establishes the host name of Router A. The **username** global configuration command establishes the name of the router that is allowed to dial up Router A. The name corresponds to the host name of Router B. The **password** keyword indicates that the **username** command specifies a password. The "7" indicates that the password is encrypted using a Cisco-defined encryption algorithm. The **appletalk routing** global configuration command enables AppleTalk routing.

The **appletalk static cable-range** global configuration commands create static AppleTalk routes to the zones in the main office network. Static AppleTalk routes are required because the **no appletalk send-rtmps** interface configuration command prevents the exchange of RTMP updates between the two networks. Without static routes, zones for the main office would not appear when users open the Chooser on hosts connected to the district office network. The **isdn switch-type** global configuration command specifies that Router A connects to a National ISDN-1 switch.

Interface Configuration

The **appletalk cable-range** interface configuration commands for each Ethernet interface establish the network number for the cable segment to which the interface connects and the node number of the interface. For each interface, the **appletalk zone** interface configuration command establishes the zone name for the network that is connected to the interface. None of the interface configurations specifies an AppleTalk routing protocol, so the interfaces use the default routing protocol, RTMP.

The **no appletalk send-rtmps** interface configuration command prevents Router A from sending RTMP updates out on interface BRI 0. To compensate for the lack of RTMP exchange, you must configure static AppleTalk routes (using the **appletalk static cable-range** global configuration command).

The **encapsulation ppp** interface configuration command specifies PPP encapsulation, and the **ppp authentication chap** command enables CHAP authentication. The **dialer idle-timeout** interface configuration command sets the idle timeout to 240 seconds (four minutes). The **bandwidth** interface configuration command tells routing protocols that the line operates at 56 Kbps.

The **dialer map** interface configuration command establishes the remote site that Router A is to call. In this case, the **dialer map** command establishes 15.43 as the next hop address. The **name** keyword specifies the name of the remote router that is associated with the dial string. The **speed** keyword specifies that Router A is to set the line's rate to 56 Kbps, which is required when the connection traverses a switch that does not support Signaling System 7. The **dialer-group** interface configuration command associates the interface BRI 0 with dialer access group 1.

The **isdn spid1** interface configuration commands represent service profile identifiers (SPIDs) and are required by National ISDN-1 switches. Service providers assign SPIDs to associate a SPID number with a telephone number. Your service provider can tell you if SPIDs are required for your switch. In this example, SPID 1 identifies 602 as the area code, 555 as the exchange, 4631 as the station ID, and 01 as the terminal identifier.

Access List Configuration

The first **access-list nbp** global configuration command defines access list 601 and prevents the forwarding of NBP packets generated by any LaserWriter printer on the district office network. The second **access-list nbp** command prevents the forwarding of NBP packets generated by the Training zone. The third **access-list nbp** command allows the forwarding of NBP packets generated by the Sales zone.

The **access-list other-nbps** global configuration command prevents the forwarding of all other NBP packets that have not been explicitly permitted or denied by previous **access-list nbp** global configuration commands.

The **access-list other-access** global configuration command permits all other access checks that would otherwise be denied because they are not explicitly permitted by an **access-list** command. The **dialer-list** global configuration command assigns the access list 601 to dialer access group 1, which is associated with BRI 0.

Router B Configuration

As shown in Figure 21–5, Router B is located in the main office. The main office network consists of two zones: Marketing and Administration. With the exception of the OpenReqs server in the Administration zone, users of hosts connected to the district office network do not need to access servers located in the Administration zone. Like the district office network, each zone in the main office network has its own printer, so there is no need for Router B to forward NBP packets that the printers originate. The access list for Router B prevents NBP packets that come from printers and NBP packets that come from all servers in the Administration zone (except OpenReqs) from triggering an ISDN connection to the district office network.

```
hostname RouterB
!
username RouterA password 7 343E821D4A
appletalk routing
```

```
appletalk static cable-range 5-5 to 15.42 zone Sales
appletalk static cable-range 10-10 to 15.42 zone Training
isdn switch-type basic-5ess
!
interface ethernet 0
appletalk cable-range 20-20 20.5
appletalk zone Administration
!
interface ethernet 1
appletalk cable-range 25-25 25.36
appletalk zone Marketing
!
interface bri 0
appletalk static cable-range 15-15 15.43
appletalk zone PhoneZone
no appletalk send-rtmps
encapsulation ppp
ppp authentication chap
dialer idle-timeout 240
bandwidth 56
dialer map appletalk 15.42 name RouterB speed 56 917075553287
dialer-group 1
!
access-list 601 deny nbp 1 type LaserWriter
access-list 601 permit nbp 2 object OpenReqs
access-list 601 permit nbp 3 zone Marketing
access-list 601 deny other-nbps
access-list 601 permit other-access
dialer-list 1 list 601
```

The configuration for Router B is similar to the configuration for Router A, with the follwing differences:

- The **isdn switch-type** global configuration command specifies that Router B connects to an AT&T 5ESS central office ISDN switch. This type of switch does not use SPID numbers, so the **isdn spid1** command is not used.

- The first **access-list nbp** global configuration command defines access list 601 and prevents the forwarding of NBP packets generated by the LaserWriter printers connected to the main office network. The second **access-list nbp** command allows the forwarding of packets generated by the server OpenReqs. The third **access-list nbp** command allows the forwarding of packets generated by the Marketing zone.

SUMMARY

When you configure ISDN, controlling packets that trigger unnecessary connections is a major concern. In the past, one way of controlling routing update packets was to configure static routes. Snapshot routing and NBP-packet filtering provide new ways to control routing updates. Snapshot routing allows you to configure the network so that routed protocols update their routing tables dynamically without triggering frequent and costly ISDN connections. Snapshot routing is ideally suited for relatively stable networks in which a single router is a central point through which routing updates flow.

Using HSRP for Fault-Tolerant IP Routing

This case study examines Cisco's Hot Standby Routing Protocol (HSRP), which provides automatic router backup when you configure it on Cisco routers that run the Internet Protocol (IP) over Ethernet, Fiber Distributed Date Interface (FDDI), and Token Ring local-area networks (LANs). HSRP is compatible with Novell's Internetwork Packet Exchange (IPX), AppleTalk, and Banyan VINES, and it is compatible with DECnet and Xerox Network Systems (XNS) in certain configurations.

NOTES

Banyan VINES serverless clients do not respond well to topology changes (regardless of whether HSRP is configured). This case study describes the effect of topology changes in networks that include Banyan VINES serverless clients.

For IP, HSRP allows one router to automatically assume the function of the second router if the second router fails. HSRP is particularly useful when the users on one subnet require continuous access to resources in the network.

Consider the network shown in Figure 22–1. Router A is responsible for handling packets between the Tokyo segment and the Paris segment, and Router B is responsible for handling packets between the Tokyo segment and the New York segment. If the connection between Routers A and C goes down or if either router becomes unavailable, fast converging routing protocols, such as the Enhanced Interior Gateway Routing Protocol (Enhanced IGRP) and Open Shortest Path First (OSPF) can respond within seconds so that Router B is prepared to transfer packets that would otherwise have gone through Router A.

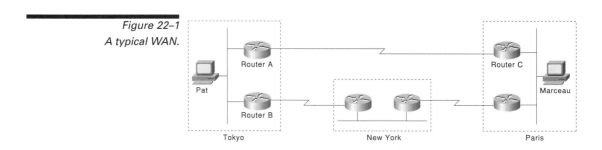

Figure 22–1
A typical WAN.

However, in spite of fast convergence, if the connection between Router A and Router C goes down, or if either router becomes unavailable, the user Pat on the Tokyo segment might not be able to communicate with the user Marceau even after the routing protocol has converged. That's because IP hosts, such as Pat's workstation, usually do not participate in routing protocols. Instead, they are configured statically with the address of a single router, such as Router A. Until someone manually modifies the configuration of Pat's host to use the address of Router B instead of Router A, Pat cannot communicate with Marceau.

Some IP hosts use proxy Address Resolution Protocol (ARP) to select a router. If Pat's workstation were running proxy ARP, it would send an ARP request for the IP address of Marceau's workstation. Router A would reply on behalf of Marceau's workstation and would give to Pat's workstation its own media access control (MAC) address (instead of the IP address of Marceau's workstation). With proxy ARP, Pat's workstation behaves as if Marceau's workstation were connected to the same segment of the network as Pat's workstation. If Router A fails, Pat's workstation will continue to send packets destined for Marceau's workstation to the MAC address of Router A even though those packets have nowhere to go and are lost. Pat either waits for ARP to acquire the MAC address of Router B by sending another ARP request or reboots the workstation to force it to send an ARP request. In either case, for a significant period of time, Pat cannot communicate with Marceau—even though the routing protocol has converged, and Router B is prepared to transfer packets that would otherwise go through Router A.

Some IP hosts use the Routing Information Protocol (RIP) to discover routers. The drawback of using RIP is that it is slow to adapt to changes in the topology. If Pat's workstation is configured to use RIP, 3 to 10 minutes might elapse before RIP makes another router available.

Some newer IP hosts use the ICMP Router Discovery Protocol (IRDP) to find a new router when a route becomes unavailable. A host that runs IRDP listens for *hello* multicast messages from its configured router and uses an alternate router when it no longer receives those hello messages. If Pat's workstation were running IRDP, it would detect that Router A is no longer sending hello messages and would start sending its packets to Router B.

For IP hosts that do not support IRDP, Cisco's HSRP provides a way to keep communicating when a router becomes unavailable. HSRP allows two or more HSRP-configured routers to use the MAC address and IP network address of a virtual router. The virtual router does not physically exist; instead, it represents the common target for routers that are configured to provide backup to each other. Figure 22–2 shows the Tokyo segment of the WAN as it might be configured for HSRP. Each actual router is configured with the MAC address and the IP network address of the virtual router.

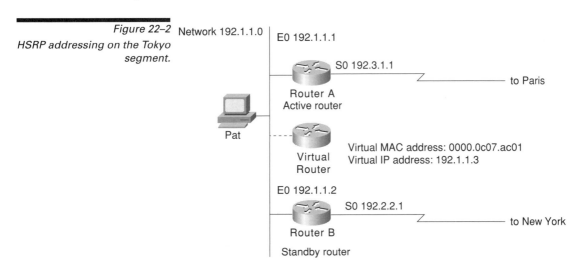

Figure 22–2

HSRP addressing on the Tokyo segment.

In Figure 22–2, the MAC address of the virtual router is 0000.0c07.ac01. When you configure HSRP, the router automatically selects one of the virtual MAC addresses from a range of addresses in the Cisco IOS software that is within the range of Cisco's MAC address block. Ethernet and FDDI LANs use one of the preassigned MAC addresses as a virtual MAC address. Token Ring LANs use a functional address as a virtual MAC address.

In Figure 22–2, instead of configuring the hosts on network 192.1.1.0 with the IP address of Router A, they are configured with the IP address of the virtual router as their default router. When Pat's workstation sends packets to Marceau's workstation on the Paris segment, it sends them to the MAC address of the virtual router.

In Figure 22–2, Router A is configured as the active router. It is configured with the IP address and MAC address of the virtual router and sends any packets addressed to the virtual router out interface 1 to the Paris segment. As the standby router, Router B is also configured with the IP address and MAC address of the virtual router. If for any reason Router A stops transferring packets, the routing protocol converges, and Router B assumes the duties of Router A and becomes the active router. That is, Router B now responds to the virtual IP address and the virtual MAC address. Pat's workstation continues to use the IP address of the virtual router to address packets destined for Marceau's workstation, which Router B receives and sends to the Paris segment via the New York segment. Until Router A resumes operation, HSRP allows Router B to provide uninterrupted service to the users on the Tokyo segment that need to communicate with users on the Paris segment. While it is the active router, Router B continues to perform its normal function: handling packets between the Tokyo segment and the New York segment.

HSRP also works when the hosts are configured for proxy ARP. When the active HSRP router receives an ARP request for a host that is not on the local LAN, the router replies with the MAC address of the virtual router. If the active router becomes unavailable or its connection to the remote LAN goes down, the router that becomes the active router receives packets addressed to the virtual router and transfers them accordingly.

NOTES

You can configure HSRP on any Cisco router that is running Cisco Internetwork Operating System (Cisco IOS) Software Release 10.0 or later. If you configure HSRP for one Cisco router on a Token Ring LAN, all Cisco routers on that LAN must run Cisco IOS Software Release 10.0 or later. Cisco IOS Software Releases 10.2(9), 10.3(6), and 11.0(2) allow standby IP addresses to respond to ping requests. Cisco Software Release 11.0(3)(1) provides improved support for the use of secondary IP addresses with HSRP.

UNDERSTANDING HOW HSRP WORKS

HSRP uses a priority scheme to determine which HSRP-configured router is to be the default active router. To configure a router as the active router, you assign it a priority that is higher than the priority of all the other HSRP-configured routers. The default priority is 100, so if you configure just one router to have a higher priority, that router will be the default active router.

HSRP works by the exchange of multicast messages that advertise priority among HSRP-configured routers. When the active router fails to send a hello message within a configurable period of time, the standby router with the highest priority becomes the active router. The transition of packet-forwarding functions between routers is completely transparent to all hosts on the network.

HSRP-configured routers exchange three types of multicast messages:

- *Hello*—The hello message conveys to other HSRP routers the router's HSRP priority and state information. By default, an HSRP router sends hello messages every three seconds.

- *Coup*—When a standby router assumes the function of the active router, it sends a coup message.

- *Resign*—A router that is the active router sends this message when it is about to shut down or when a router that has a higher priority sends a hello message.

At any time, HSRP-configured routers are in one of the following states:

- *Active*—The router is performing packet-transfer functions.

- *Standby*—The router is prepared to assume packet-transfer functions if the active router fails.

- *Speaking and listening*—The router is sending and receiving hello messages.

- *Listening*—The router is receiving hello messages.

When configured on AGS, AGS+, and Cisco 7000 series routers, HSRP takes advantage of special hardware features that are not available on other Cisco routers. This means that HSRP operates in a slightly different way on these routers. For an example, see the "Using HSRP with Routed Protocols" section later in this chapter.

CONFIGURING HSRP

Figure 22–3 shows the topology of an IP network in which two routers are configured for HSRP.

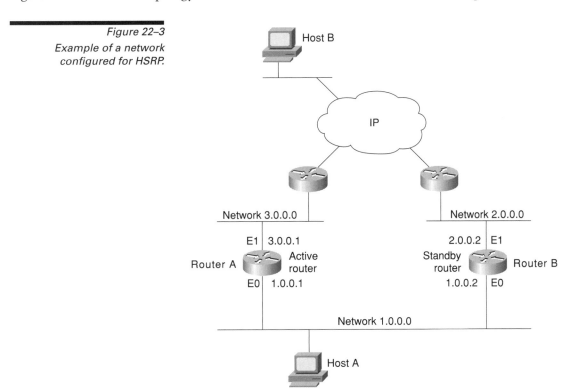

Figure 22–3

Example of a network configured for HSRP.

All hosts on the network are configured to use the IP address of the virtual router (in this case, 1.0.0.3) as the default gateway. The command for configuring the default gateway depends on the host's operating system, TCP/IP implementation, and configuration.

NOTES

The configurations shown in this case study use the Enhanced IGRP routing protocol. HSRP can be used with any routing protocol supported by the Cisco IOS software. Some configurations that use HSRP still require a routing protocol to converge when a topology change occurs. The standby router becomes active, but connectivity does not occur until the protocol converges.

The following is the configuration for Router A:

```
hostname RouterA
!
interface ethernet 0
ip address 1.0.0.1 255.0.0.0
standby 1 ip 1.0.0.3
standby 1 preempt
standby 1 priority 110
standby 1 authentication denmark
standby 1 timers 5 15
!
interface ethernet 1
ip address 3.0.0.1 255.0.0.0
!
router eigrp 1
network 1.0.0.0
network 3.0.0.0
```

The following is the configuration for Router B:

```
hostname RouterB
!
interface ethernet 0
ip address 1.0.0.2 255.0.0.0
standby 1 ip 1.0.0.3
standby 1 preempt
standby 1 authentication denmark
standby 1 timers 5 15
!
interface ethernet 1
ip address 2.0.0.2 255.0.0.0
!
router eigrp 1
network 1.0.0.0
network 2.0.0.0
```

The **standby ip** interface configuration command enables HSRP and establishes 1.0.0.3 as the IP address of the virtual router. The configurations of both routers include this command so that both routers share the same virtual IP address. The 1 establishes Hot Standby group 1. (If you do not specify a group number, the default is group 0.) The configuration for at least one of the routers in the Hot Standby group must specify the IP address of the virtual router; specifying the IP address of the virtual router is optional for other routers in the same Hot Standby group.

The **standby preempt** interface configuration command allows the router to become the active router when its priority is higher than all other HSRP-configured routers in this Hot Standby group.

The configurations of both routers include this command so that each router can be the standby router for the other router. The 1 indicates that this command applies to Hot Standby group 1. If you do not use the **standby preempt** command in the configuration for a router, that router cannot become the active router.

The **standby priority** interface configuration command sets the router's HSRP priority to 110, which is higher than the default priority of 100. Only the configuration of Router A includes this command, which makes Router A the default active router. The 1 indicates that this command applies to Hot Standby group 1.

The **standby authentication** interface configuration command establishes an authentication string whose value is an unencrypted eight-character string that is incorporated in each HSRP multicast message. This command is optional. If you choose to use it, each HSRP-configured router in the group should use the same string so that each router can authenticate the source of the HSRP messages that it receives. The "1" indicates that this command applies to Hot Standby group 1.

The **standby timers** interface configuration command sets the interval in seconds between hello messages (called the *hello time*) to five seconds and sets the duration in seconds that a router waits before it declares the active router to be down (called the *hold time*) to eight seconds. (The defaults are three and 10 seconds, respectively.) If you decide to modify the default values, you must configure each router to use the same hello time and hold time. The "1" indicates that this command applies to Hot Standby group 1.

NOTES

There can be up to 255 Hot Standby groups on any Ethernet or FDDI LAN. There can be no more than three Hot Standby groups on any Token Ring LAN.

CONFIGURING MULTIPLE HOT STANDBY GROUPS

Multigroup HSRP (MHSRP) is an extension of HSRP that allows a single router interface to belong to more than one Hot Standby group. MHSRP requires the use of Cisco IOS Software Release 10.3 or later and is supported only on routers that have special hardware that allows them to associate an Ethernet interface with multiple unicast Media Access Control (MAC) addresses. These routers are the AGS and AGS+ routers and any router in the Cisco 7000 series. The special hardware allows you to configure a single interface in an AGS, AGS+, or Cisco 7000 series router so that the router is the backup router for more than one Hot Standby group, as shown in Figure 22–4.

In Figure 22–4, the Ethernet interface 0 of Router A belongs to group 1. Ethernet interface 0 of Router B belongs to groups 1, 2, and 3. The Ethernet interface 0 of Router C belongs to group 2, and the Ethernet interface 0 of Router D belongs to group 3. When you establish groups, you might want to align them along departmental organizations. In this case, group 1 might support the Engineering Department, group 2 might support the Manufacturing Department, and group 3 might support the Finance Department.

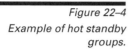

Figure 22–4

Example of hot standby groups.

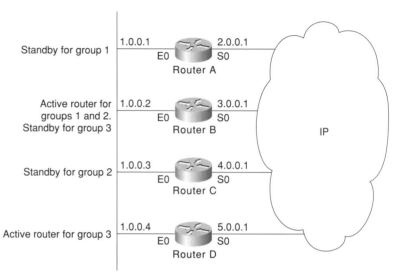

Router B is configured as the active router for groups 1 and 2 and as the standby router for group 3. Router D is configured as the active router for group 3. If Router D fails for any reason, Router B will assume the packet-transfer functions of Router D and will maintain the ability of users in the Finance Department to access data on other subnets. The following is the configuration for Router A:

```
hostname RouterA
!
interface ethernet 0
ip address 1.0.0.1 255.0.0.0
standby 1 ip 1.0.0.5
standby authentication sclara
!
interface serial 0
ip address 2.0.0.1 255.0.0.0
!
router eigrp 1
network 1.0.0.0
network 2.0.0.0
```

The following is the configuration for Router B, which must be an AGS, AGS+, or Cisco 7000 series router:

```
hostname RouterB
!
interface ethernet 0
ip address 1.0.0.2 255.0 0.0
standby 1 ip 1.0.0.5
standby 1 priority 110
standby 1 preempt
standby 1 authentication sclara
standby 2 ip 1.0.0.6
standby 2 priority 110
standby 2 preempt
```

```
standby 2 authentication mtview
standby 3 ip 1.0.0.7
standby 3 preempt
standby 3 authentication svale
!
interface serial 0
ip address 3.0.0.1 255.0.0.0
!
router eigrp 1
network 1.0.0.0
network 3.0.0.0
```

The following is the configuration for Router C:

```
hostname RouterC
!
interface ethernet 0
ip address 1.0.0.3 255.0 0.0
standby 2 ip 1.0.0.6
standby 2 authentication mtview
!
interface serial 0
ip address 4.0.0.1 255.0.0.0
!
router eigrp 1
network 1.0.0.0
network 4.0.0.0
```

The following is the configuration for Router D:

```
hostname RouterD
!
interface ethernet 0
ip address 1.0.0.4 255.0 0.0
standby 3 ip 1.0.0.7
standby 1 priority 110
standby 1 preempt
standby 3 authentication svale
!
interface serial 0
ip address 4.0.0.1 255.0.0.0
!
router eigrp 1
network 1.0.0.0
network 5.0.0.0
```

Interface Tracking

For both HSRP and MHSRP, you can use the tracking feature to adjust the Hot Standby priority of a router based on whether certain of the router's interfaces are available. When a tracked interface becomes unavailable, the HSRP priority of the router is decreased. You can use tracking to automatically reduce the likelihood that a router that already has an unavailable key interface will become the active router. To configure tracking, use the **standby track** interface configuration command. Figure 22–5 shows a network for which tracking is configured.

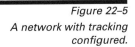

Figure 22–5
A network with tracking
configured.

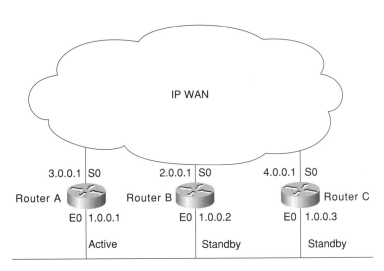

Figure 22–5
A network with tracking
configured.

In Figure 22–5, Router A is configured as the active router. Routers B and C are configured as standby routers for Router A. The following is the configuration for Router A:

```
hostname RouterA
!
interface ethernet 0
ip address 1.0.0.1 255.0.0.0
standby 1 ip 1.0.0.4
standby 1 preempt
standby 1 priority 110
standby authentication microdot
!
interface serial 0
ip address 2.0.0.1 255.0.0.0
!
router eigrp 1
network 1.0.0.0
network 3.0.0.0
```

The **standby ip** interface configuration command enables HSRP and establishes 1.0.0.4 as the IP address of the virtual router. The "1" establishes Hot Standby group 1. The **standby preempt** interface configuration command allows Router A to become the active router when its priority is higher than all other HSRP-configured routers in the Hot Standby group.

The **standby priority** interface configuration command sets the router's HSRP priority to 110, which is highest priority assigned to the three routers in this example. Because Router A has the highest priority, it is the active router under normal operation. The following is the configuration for Router B:

```
hostname RouterB
!
interface ethernet 0
ip address 1.0.0.2 255.0 0.0
standby 1 ip 1.0.0.4
```

```
standby 1 preempt
standby 1 priority 105
standby track serial 0
standby 1 authentication microdot

interface serial 0
ip address 3.0.0.1 255.0.0.0
!
router eigrp 1
network 1.0.0.0
network 2.0.0.0
```

The **standby preempt** interface configuration command allows Router B to become the active router immediately if its priority is highest, even before the current active router fails. The **standby priority** interface configuration command specifies a priority of 105 (lower than the priority of Router A and higher than the priority of Router C), so Router B is a standby router.

The **standby track** interface configuration command causes Ethernet interface 0 to track serial interface 0. If serial interface 0 becomes unavailable, the priority of Router B is reduced by 10 (the default). The following is the configuration for Router C:

```
hostname RouterC
!
interface ethernet 0
ip address 1.0.0.3 255.0 0.0
standby 1 ip 1.0.0.4
standby 1 preempt
standby 1 priority
standby track serial 0
standby 1 authentication microdot
!
interface serial 0
ip address 4.0.0.1 255.0.0.0
!
router eigrp 1
network 1.0.0.0
network 4.0.0.0
```

The **standby preempt** interface configuration command allows Router C to become the active router if its priority is highest when the active router fails. The **standby priority** interface configuration command does not specify a priority, so its priority is 100 (the default).

If Router A becomes unavailable and if serial interface 0 on Router B is available, Router B (with its priority of 105) will become the active router. However, if serial interface 0 on Router B becomes unavailable before Router A becomes unavailable, the HSRP priority of Router B will be reduced from 105 to 95. If Router A then becomes unavailable, Router C (whose priority is 100) will become the active router.

Load Sharing

You can use HSRP or MHSRP when you configure load sharing. In Figure 22–6, half of the workstations on the LAN are configured for Router A, and half of the workstations are configured for Router B.

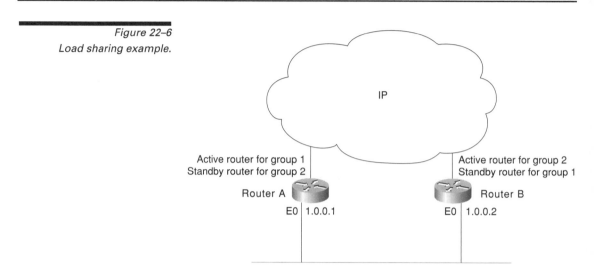

Figure 22–6
Load sharing example.

The following is a partial configuration for Router A:

```
hostname RouterA
!
interface ethernet 0
ip address 1.0.0.1 255.0.0.0
standby 1 ip 1.0.0.3
standby 1 priority 110
standby 1 preempt
standby 2 ip 1.0.0.4
standby 2 preempt
```

The following is a partial configuration for Router B:

```
hostname RouterB
!
interface ethernet 0
ip address 1.0.0.2 255.0.0.0
standby 1 ip 1.0.0.3
standby 1 preempt
standby 2 ip 1.0.0.4
standby 2 priority 110
standby 2 preempt
```

Together, the configuration files for Routers A and B establish two Hot Standby groups. For group 1, Router A is the default active router, and Router B is the standby router. For group 2, Router B is the default active router, and Router A is the standby router. During normal operation, the two routers share the IP traffic load. When either router becomes unavailable, the other router becomes active and assumes the packet-transfer functions of the router that is unavailable. The **standby preempt** interface configuration commands are necessary so that if a router goes down and then comes back up, preemption occurs and restores load sharing.

USING HSRP WITH ROUTED PROTOCOLS

This section describes the interaction between HSRP and the following routed protocols:

- AppleTalk, Banyan VINES, and Novell IPX
- DECnet and XNS

AppleTalk, Banyan VINES, and Novell IPX

You can configure HSRP in networks that, in addition to IP, run AppleTalk, Banyan VINES, and Novell IPX. AppleTalk and Novell IPX continue to function when the standby router becomes the active router, but they take time to adapt to topology changes. In general, AppleTalk hosts discover a new active router in less than 30 seconds. Novell 4.*x* hosts discover a new active router in 10 seconds, on average. Novell 2.*x* or Novell 3.*x* hosts might require more time to adapt.

NOTES

Regardless of whether HSRP is configured, Banyan VINES does not respond well to topology changes. When HSRP is configured, the effect of a topology change varies, depending on the type of router that becomes the active router.

When the active router becomes unavailable, or its connection to the network goes down, all Banyan VINES sessions that rely on that router stop and must be reinitiated. If an AGS, AGS+, or Cisco 7000 series router becomes the active router, Banyan VINES traffic flowing through that router is not affected as it changes from standby to active. That is because these routers have special hardware that allows them to have more than one MAC address at the same time. If the router that becomes the active router is *not* an AGS, AGS+, or Cisco 7000 series router, Banyan VINES traffic flowing through that router pauses and resumes after no more than 90 seconds while the router changes from standby to active.

Regardless of which type of router becomes the active router, any Banyan VINES serverless clients that obtained their network-layer address from the unavailable router might need to reboot to obtain another network-layer address.

DECnet and XNS

DECnet and XNS are compatible with HSRP and MHSRP over Ethernet, FDDI, and Token Ring on the Cisco 7000 and Cisco 7500 routers. Some constraints apply when HSRP and MHSRP are configured on other routers, such as the Cisco 2500, Cisco 3000, Cisco 4000, and Cisco 4500 series routers, which do not have the hardware required to support multiple MAC addresses. Table 22–1 identifies the supported and unsupported combinations.

Table 22–1   *HSRP and MHSRP Compatibility with DECnet and XNS*

Protocol Combination per Interface	Cisco 2500	Cisco 3000	Cisco 4000	Cisco 4500	Cisco 7000	Cisco 7500
MHSRP with or without DECnet or XNS	No	No	No	No	Yes	Yes
HSRP without DECnet or XNS	Yes	Yes	Yes	Yes	Yes	Yes
HSRP with DECnet or XNS	No	No	No	No	Yes	Yes

SUMMARY

HSRP and MHSRP provide fault-tolerant routing of IP packets for networks that require nonstop access by hosts on all segments to resources on all segments. To provide fault tolerance, HSRP and MHSRP require a routing protocol that converges rapidly, such as Enhanced Interior Gateway Routing Protocol (Enhanced IGRP). A fast-converging protocol ensures that router state changes propagate fast enough to make the transition from standby to active mode transparent to network users.

LAN Switching

Today's local-area networks (LANs) are becoming increasingly congested and overburdened. In addition to an ever-growing population of network users, several factors have combined to stress the capabilities of traditional LANs:

- *Faster CPUs*—In the mid-1980s, the most common desktop workstation was a PC. At the time, most PCs could execute 1 million instructions per second (MIPS). Today, workstations with 50 to 75 MIPS of processing power are common, and I/O speeds have increased accordingly. Two modern engineering workstations on the same LAN can easily saturate it.

- *Faster operating systems*—Until recently, operating system design had constrained network access. Of the three most common desktop operating systems (DOS/Windows, the UNIX operating system, and the Mac OS), only the UNIX operating system could multitask. Multitasking allows users to initiate simultaneous network transactions. With the release of Windows 95, which reflected a redesign of DOS/Windows that included multitasking, PC users could increase their demands for network resources.

- *Network-intensive applications*—Use of client-server applications, such as Network File System (NFS), LAN Manager, NetWare, and World Wide Web is increasing. Client-server applications allow administrators to centralize information, thus making it easy to maintain and protect. Client-server applications free users from the burden of maintaining information and the cost of providing enough hard disk space to store it. Given the cost benefit of client-server applications, such applications are likely to become even more widely used in the future.

Switching is a technology that alleviates congestion in Ethernet, Token Ring, and Fiber Distributed Data Interface (FDDI) LANs by reducing traffic and increasing bandwidth. Such switches, known as *LAN switches*, are designed to work with existing cable infrastructures so that they can be installed with minimal disruption of existing networks. Often, they replace shared hubs. This case study describes how LAN switching works, how virtual LANs work, and how to configure virtual LANs (VLANs) in a topology that consists of Catalyst 5000 LAN switches.

UNDERSTANDING SWITCHING BASICS

The term *switching* was originally used to describe packet-switch technologies, such as Link Access Procedure, Balanced (LAPB), Frame Relay, Switched Multimegabit Data Service (SMDS), and X.25. Today, switching refers to a technology that is similar to a bridge in many ways.

The term *bridging* refers to a technology in which a device (known as a *bridge*) connects two or more LAN segments. A bridge transmits datagrams from one segment to their destinations on other segments. When a bridge is powered and begins to operate, it examines the Media Access Control (MAC) address of the datagrams that flow through it to build a table of known destinations. If the bridge knows that the destination of a datagram is on the same segment as the source of the datagram, it drops the datagram because there is no need to transmit it. If the bridge knows that the destination is on another segment, it transmits the datagram on that segment only. If the bridge does not know the destination segment, the bridge transmits the datagram on all segments except the source segment (a technique known as *flooding*). The primary benefit of bridging is that it limits traffic to certain network segments.

Like bridges, switches connect LAN segments, use a table of MAC addresses to determine the segment on which a datagram needs to be transmitted, and reduce traffic. Switches operate at much higher speeds than bridges, and can support new functionality, such as virtual LANs.

SWITCHING IN THE ETHERNET ENVIRONMENT

The most common LAN media is traditional Ethernet, which has a maximum bandwidth of 10 Mbps. Traditional Ethernet is a half-duplex technology. Each Ethernet host checks the network to determine whether data is being transmitted before it transmits and defers transmission if the network is in use. In spite of transmission deferral, two or more Ethernet hosts can transmit at the same time, which results in a collision. When a collision occurs, the hosts enter a back-off phase and retransmit later. As more hosts are added to the network, hosts must wait more often before they can begin transmitting, and collisions are more likely to occur because more hosts are trying to transmit. Today, throughput on traditional Ethernet LANs suffers even more because users are running network-intensive software, such as client-server applications, which cause hosts to transmit more often and for longer periods of time.

An Ethernet LAN switch improves bandwidth by separating collision domains and selectively forwarding traffic to the appropriate segments. Figure 23–1 shows the topology of a typical Ethernet network in which a LAN switch has been installed.

In Figure 23–1, each Ethernet segment is connected to a port on the LAN switch. If Server A on port 1 needs to transmit to Client B on port 2, the LAN switch forwards Ethernet frames from port 1 to port 2, thus sparing port 3 and port 4 from frames destined for Client B. If Server C needs to send data to Client D at the same time that Server A sends data to Client B, it can do so because the LAN switch can forward frames from port 3 to port 4 at the same time it is forwarding frames from port 1 to port 2. If Server A needs to send data to Client E, which also resides on port 1, the LAN switch does not need to forward any frames.

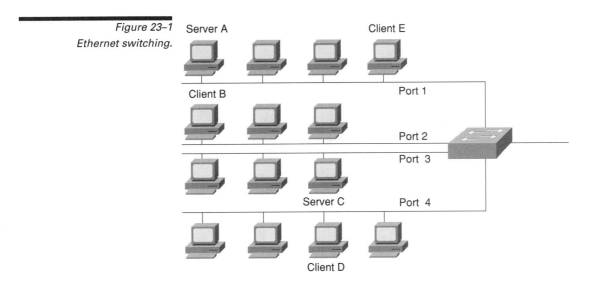

Figure 23–1
Ethernet switching.

Performance improves in LANs in which LAN switches are installed because the LAN switch creates isolated collision domains. By spreading users over several collision domains, collisions are avoided and performance improves. Many LAN switch installations assign just one user per port, which gives that user an effective bandwidth of 10 Mbps.

UNDERSTANDING VIRTUAL LANs

A virtual LAN (VLAN) is a group of hosts or network devices, such as routers (running transparent bridging) and bridges, that forms a single bridging domain. Layer 2 bridging protocols, such as IEEE 802.10 and Inter-Switch Link (ISL), allow a VLAN to exist across a variety of equipment, including LAN switches.

VLANs are formed to group related users regardless of the physical connections of their hosts to the network. The users can be spread across a campus network or even across geographically dispersed locations. A variety of strategies can be used to group users. For example, the users might be grouped according to their department or functional team. In general, the goal is to group users into VLANs so that most of their traffic stays within the VLAN. When you configure VLANs, the network can take advantage of the following benefits:

- *Broadcast control*—Just as switches physically isolate collision domains for attached hosts and only forward traffic out a particular port, VLANs provide logical collision domains that confine broadcast and multicast traffic to the bridging domain.

- *Security*—If you do not include a router in a VLAN, no users outside of that VLAN can communicate with the users in the VLAN and vice versa. This extreme level of security can be highly desirable for certain projects and applications.

- *Performance*—You can assign users that require high-performance networking to their own VLANs. You might, for example, assign an engineer who is testing a multicast application and the servers the engineer uses to a single VLAN. The engineer experiences improved network performance by being on a "dedicated LAN," and the rest of the engineering group experiences improved network performance because the traffic generated by the network-intensive application is isolated to another VLAN.

- *Network management*—Software on the switch allows you to assign users to VLANs and, later, reassign them to another VLAN. Recabling to change connectivity is no longer necessary in the switched LAN environment because network management tools allow you to reconfigure the LAN logically in seconds.

Figure 23–2 shows an example of a switched LAN topology in which VLANs are configured.

Figure 23–2
Typical VLAN topology.

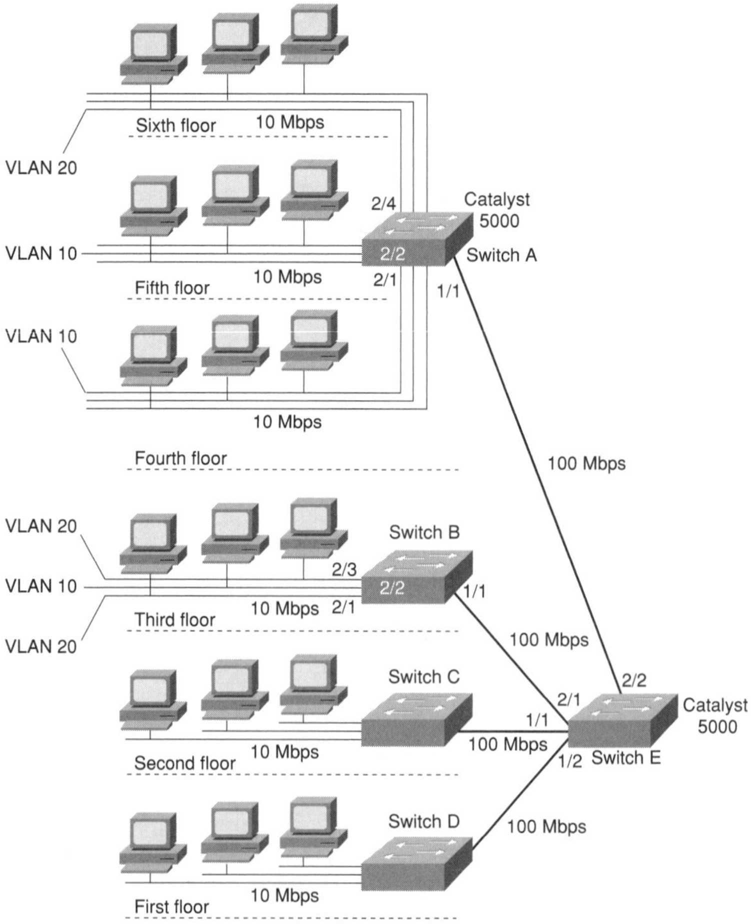

In Figure 23–2, a 10-Mbps Ethernet connects the hosts on each floor to Catalyst 5000 LAN switches. 100-Mbps Fast Ethernet connects switches A, B, C, and D to Switch E.

NOTES

The Catalyst 5000 has five slots in which modules can be installed. The *supervisor engine* module is always installed in slot 1. The supervisor engine module is the main system processor switch; it provides a console port and two 100-Mbps Fast Ethernet ports. A variety of other modules providing 10-Mbps Ethernet and Fast Ethernet interfaces can be installed in slots 2 through 5. Ports are identified by their slot number and their position, from left to right, on the module. For example, port 2/2 is the second port from the left on the module in slot 2.

The switches in Figure 23–2 communicate with each other using ISL, which is a protocol that maintains VLAN information as traffic flows between the switches. With ISL, an Ethernet frame is encapsulated with a 30-byte header that contains a two-byte VLAN ID.

Figure 23–2 shows that VLAN 20 consists of port 4 in slot 2 on Switch A and ports 1 and 3 in slot 4 on Switch B. Frames exchanged between ports 1/4 and 3/4 are switched by Switch B as normal. On Switch B, any frame generated by ports 1/4 and 3/4 that is not destined for ports 1/4 and 3/4 is encapsulated in an ISL header that includes a VLAN 20 identifier and is sent to Switch E. Switch E examines the ISL header and determines that the frame is intended for VLAN 20 and sends the frame out on port 2/2 to Switch A. Switch A examines the ISL header to determine the VLAN for which the frame is destined, removes the header, and switches it to all ports in VLAN 20 (if the frame is broadcast or multicast) or to port 2/4 if the frame is a unicast.

CONFIGURING THE SWITCHES

When a Catalyst 5000 switch first starts up, the following defaults are set:

- The console port is set to 9600 baud, 8 data bits, no parity, and 1 stop bit. If you want to change the baud rate, use the **set system baud** command.
- The Cisco Discovery Protocol (CDP) is enabled on every port to send a CDP message every 60 seconds. If you want to disable CDP on ports that do not have a Cisco device, use the **set cdp disable** command.
- The following Simple Network Management Protocol (SNMP) community strings are defined:
  - "public" for the read-only access type
  - "private" for the read-write access type
  - "secret" for the read-write-all access type

  If you want to set other SNMP community strings, use the **set snmp community** command.
- All modules and all ports are enabled. To disable a module, use the **set module disable** command, and to disable a port, use the **set port disable** command.
- All 10-Mbps Ethernet ports are set to half duplex. Use the **set port duplex** command to set a port to full duplex.

When you first start up a switch, you should set some values that apply to the switch as a whole. For example, you might enter the following commands at the console port of Switch A:

```
set system contact Terry Moran
set system location Norwich
set system name SwitchA
set time fri 9/15/95 14:08:34
set prompt SwitchA>
set password
set enablepass
set interface sc0 131.108.40.1
```

The **set system contact** command establishes "Terry Moran" as the person to contact for system administration. The **set system name** establishes "SwitchA" as the name of this switch. The **set time** command sets the current time, using a 24-hour clock format. The **set prompt** command sets the prompt to "SwitchA>". The default prompt is "Console>".

The **set password** command sets password protection for the administrative interface in normal mode. When you enter the **set password** command, the switch prompts you to enter a password and then prompts you to reenter the password.

The **set enablepass** command sets password protection for the administrative interface in privileged mode. When you enter the **set enablepass** command, the switch prompts you to enter a password and then prompts you to reenter the password.

The **set interface** command assigns an IP address and netmask to interface sc0. After you make this assignment, you can Telnet to the switch to perform administrative tasks. The switch supports up to eight simultaneous Telnet connections. Alternatively, you can use the **set interface** command to enable a Serial Line Interface Protocol (SLIP) connection on the console interface (sl0).

Configuring VLANs on Switch A

The following commands configure VLANs 10 and 20 on Switch A:

```
set vlan 10 2/1,2/2
set vlan 20 2/4
set trunk 1/1 10,20
```

The first **set vlan** command creates VLAN 10 and assigns ports 1 and 2 in slot 2 to it. The second **set vlan** command creates VLAN 20 and assigns port 4 in slot 2 to it.

The **set trunk** command configures port 1 in slot 1 as a trunk and adds VLANs 10 and 20 to it. Trunks are used for Fast Ethernet connections between switches. When a port is configured as a trunk, it runs in ISL mode. To detect and break loops, trunks use the spanning-tree protocol on all VLANs that are carried across the trunk.

Configuring VLANs on Switch B

The following commands configure VLANs 10 and 20 on Switch B:

```
set vlan 10 2/2
set vlan 20 2/1,2/3
set trunk 1/1 10,20
```

The first **set vlan** command creates VLAN 10 and assigns port 2 in slot 2 to it. The second **set vlan** command creates VLAN 20 and assigns ports 1 and 3 in slot 2 to it. The **set trunk** command configures port 1 in slot 1 as a trunk and adds VLANs 10 and 20 to it.

Configuring VLANs on Switch E

The following commands configure VLANs 10 and 20 on Switch E:

```
set trunk 2/1 10,20
set trunk 2/2 10,20
```

The first **set trunk** command configures port 1 in slot 2 as a trunk and adds VLANs 10 and 20 to it. This trunk is used to communicate with Switch B. The second **set trunk** command configures port 2 in slot 2 as a trunk and adds VLANs 10 and 20 to it. This trunk is used to communicate with Switch A.

SUMMARY

LAN switching technology improves the performance of traditional Ethernet, FDDI, and Token Ring technologies without requiring costly wiring upgrades or time-consuming host reconfiguration. The low price per port allows the deployment of LAN switches so that they decrease segment size and increase available bandwidth. VLANs make it possible to extend the benefit of switching over a network of LAN switches and other switching devices.

Multicasting in IP and AppleTalk Networks

Over the past few years, the concept of end-users being able to send and receive audio and video (known collectively as *multimedia*) at the desktop has gained considerable attention and acceptance. With high-performance 486, Pentium, and PowerPC CPUs, more than 80 percent of the personal computers sold during 1995 were multimedia capable. Today, it is not uncommon for end-users to run video editing and image processing applications from the desktop.

The proliferation of more and more multimedia-enabled desktop computers has spawned a new class of multimedia applications that operate in networked environments. These network multimedia applications leverage existing network infrastructure to deliver video and audio applications to end users. Most notable are videoconferencing and video server applications. With these applications, video and audio streams are transferred over the network between peers or between clients and servers. There are three types of multimedia applications:

- *Unicast*—Unicast applications send one copy of each packet to each host that wants to receive the packet. This type of application is easy to implement, but it requires extra bandwidth because the network has to carry the same packet multiple times—even on shared links. Because unicast applications make a copy of each packet, the number of receivers is limited to the number of copies of each packet that can be made by the CPU that runs the unicast application.

- *Broadcast*—Broadcast applications send each packet to a broadcast address. This type of application is easier to implement than unicast applications, but it can have serious effects on the network. Allowing the broadcast to propagate throughout the network is a significant burden on both the network (in terms of traffic volume) and the hosts connected to the network (in terms of the CPU time that each host that does not want to receive the transmission must spend processing and discarding unwanted broadcast packets). You can configure routers to stop broadcasts at the LAN boundary (a technique that is frequently used to prevent broadcast storms), but this technique limits the receivers according to their physical location.

- *Multicast*—Multicast applications send each packet to a multicast group address. Hosts that want to receive the packets indicate that they want to be members of the multicast group. This type of application expects that networks with hosts that have joined a multicast group will receive multicast packets. Multicast applications and underlying multicast protocols control multimedia traffic and shield hosts from having to process unnecessary broadcast traffic.

This case study examines multicast protocols that have been developed for the Internet Protocol (IP) and for AppleTalk, as well as Cisco Internetwork Operating System (Cisco IOS) features that can help your network deliver video and audio smoothly.

IMPLEMENTING MULTICAST APPLICATIONS IN IP NETWORKS

Currently, support for IP multicasting comes from three protocols:

- Internet Group Management Protocol (IGMP)
- Protocol-Independent Multicast (PIM)
- Distance Vector Multicast Routing Protocol (DVMRP)

Network multimedia applications for IP use IGMP to join multicast groups. PIM and DVMRP use IGMP to determine the location of hosts that have joined a multicast group.

This section covers the following topics:

- Addressing
- Internet Group Management Protocol
- Protocol-Independent Multicast

Addressing

IP multicasting applications use Class D addresses to address packets. The high-order four bits of a Class D address are set to 1110, and the remaining 28 bits are set to a specific multicast group ID. Class D addresses are typically written as dotted-decimal numbers and are in the range of 224.0.0.0 through 239.255.255.255.

Some multicast group addresses are assigned as well-known addresses by the Internet Assigned Numbers Authority (IANA). These multicast group addresses are called *permanent host groups* and are similar in concept to the well-known TCP and UDP port numbers. Table 24–1 lists the multicast address of three permanent host groups.

Table 24–1 *Multicast Addresses for Permanent Host Groups*

Permanent Host Group	Multicast Address
Network Time Protocol (NTP)	224.0.1.1
RIP-2	224.0.0.9
Silicon Graphics' Dogfight application	224.0.1.2

Internet Group Management Protocol

The Internet Group Management Protocol (IGMP) uses IP datagrams to allow IP multicast applications to join a multicast group. Membership in a multicast group is dynamic—that is, it changes over time as hosts join and leave the group.

Multicast routers that run IGMP use IGMP host-query messages to keep track of the hosts that belong to multicast groups. These messages are sent to the all-systems group address 224.0.0.1. The hosts then send IGMP report messages listing the multicast groups they would like to join. When the router receives a packet addressed to a multicast group, it forwards the packet to those interfaces that have hosts that belong to that group. If you want to prevent hosts on a particular interface from participating in a multicast group, you can configure a filter on that interface by using the **ip igmp access-group** interface configuration command.

Routers on which GMP is enabled periodically send IGMP host-query messages to refresh their knowledge of memberships present on their interfaces. If, after some number of queries, the router determines that no local hosts are members of a particular multicast group on a particular interface, the router stops forwarding packets for that group and sends a *prune* message upstream toward the source of the packet.

You can configure the router to be a member of a multicast group. This is useful for determining multicast reachability in a network. If a router is configured as a group member it can, for example, respond to an ICMP echo request packet addressed to a group for which it is a member. To configure the router as a member of a multicast group, use the **ip igmp join-group** interface configuration command.

Protocol-Independent Multicast

Protocol-Independent Multicast (PIM) is an IP multicast protocol that works with all existing unicast routing protocols. PIM has two modes that allow it to work effectively with two different types of multicast traffic distribution patterns: dense mode and sparse mode.

Dense mode PIM is designed for the following conditions:

- Senders and receivers are in close proximity to one another.
- There are few senders and many receivers.
- The volume of multicast traffic is high.

Sparse-mode PIM is designed for the following conditions:

- There are few receivers in a group.
- Senders and receivers are separated by WAN links.

Dense Mode

Dense-mode PIM uses a technique known as *reverse path forwarding*. When a router receives a packet, it sends the packet out all interfaces except the interface on which the packet was received. Reverse path forwarding allows a data stream to reach all LANs, possibly multiple times. If the router has interfaces for which no hosts are members of the multicast group for which the packet is intended or for which no downstream multicast router on that LAN has joined the group, the router sends a prune message up the distribution tree to inform the sender that it need not send subsequent packets for this multicast group. Figure 24–1 shows how PIM works in dense mode.

Figure 24–1

PIM dense-mode operation.

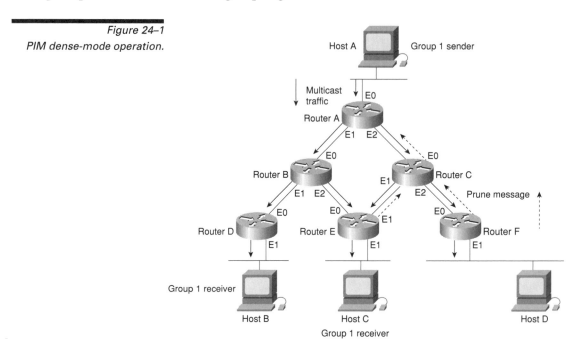

In Figure 24–1, Router A receives multicast traffic from Host A on Ethernet interface 0, duplicates each packet, and sends the packets out on Ethernet interface 1 and Ethernet interface 2 to Routers B and C. Routers B and C duplicate the packets and send them out to Routers D, E, and F. Router D has a host that is a member of Group 1, so Router D does not send a prune message. Router E also has a host that is a member of Group 1, but because it receives the packets on two interfaces, Router E sends a prune message to Router C. (The decision about which router should be pruned is reached through a negotiation process conducted by Router B and Router C. If the connection between Router E and Router B had been a point-to-point link, the prune message would have been sent to Router B automatically, thereby eliminating the need for Routers B and C to negotiate an agreement.)

Router F does not have any hosts that are members of Group 1, so it sends a prune message to Router C. Router C sends a prune message to Router A. After the prune messages are received, Router A sends multicast traffic for Group 1 to Router B only.

When you configure PIM in dense mode, you should enable IP multicast routing on every router over which multicast traffic will flow. The following commands configure dense mode PIM on Router B:

```
ip multicast-routing
interface ethernet 1
ip pim dense-mode
!
interface ethernet 2
ip pim dense-mode
```

The **ip multicast-routing** global configuration command enables IP multicast routing. You should include this command on every router that you want to participate in PIM. If some routers cannot be configured for IP multicast routing (for example, if they do not run a version of the Cisco IOS software release that supports PIM), you need to configure a tunnel so that multicast packets bypass these routers.

The **ip pim** interface configuration command enables PIM on the specified interface, and the **dense-mode** keyword enables dense mode. When you configure PIM in dense mode, you should apply the **ip pim** command with the **dense-mode** keyword to every interface that you want to forward multicast traffic.

NOTES

Enabling PIM automatically enables IGMP.

In dense mode, the PIM-configured interface with the highest IP address on a LAN (subnet) is responsible for sending IGMP host-query messages to all hosts on the LAN. By default, the router that is responsible for sending PIM router-query messages sends them every 30 seconds. If you want to modify this interval, use the **ip pim query-interval** interface configuration command.

By default, a PIM-configured interface forwards all multicast packets. If you want to control the forwarding of packets, use the **ip multicast-threshold ttl** interface configuration command. The **ip multicast-threshold ttl** command changes the value of time-to-live (TTL) threshold, which the router compares with the TTL field in the IP header. Only those multicast packets that have a TTL greater than the TTL threshold are forwarded. You might, for example, want to set the TTL threshold to a very high value (such as 200) to prevent multicast packets from exiting an area.

Sparse Mode

Sparse-mode PIM is designed for environments in which many multipoint data streams go to a relatively small number of the LAN segments. For this type of environment, dense mode PIM would use bandwidth inefficiently.

Sparse-mode PIM assumes that no hosts want to receive multicast traffic unless they specifically request it. In sparse-mode PIM, a router is designated as a rendezvous point. The rendezvous point collects information about multicast senders and makes that information available to potential receivers. When a sender wants to send data, it first sends the data to the rendezvous point. When a receiver wants to receive data, it registers with the rendezvous point. When the data stream begins to flow from sender to rendezvous point to receiver, the routers in the path automatically optimize the path to remove any unnecessary hops. Figure 24–2 shows how PIM works in sparse mode.

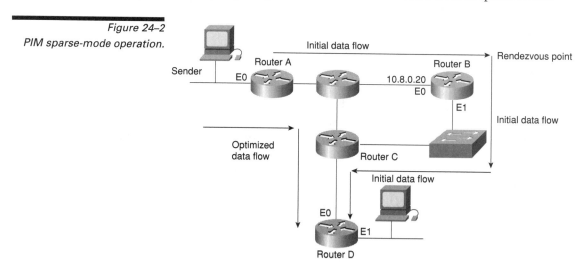

Figure 24–2

PIM sparse-mode operation.

In Figure 24–2, Routers A and D are leaf routers. *Leaf routers* are routers that are directly connected either to a receiver or sender of multicast messages. The sparse-mode configuration of a leaf router designates one or more routers as rendezvous points. In this example, Router B is designated as the rendezvous point.

The leaf router that is directly connected to a sender (in this case, Router A) sends PIM register messages on behalf of the sender to the rendezvous point. The leaf router that is directly connected to a receiver (in this case, Router B) sends PIM join and prune messages to the rendezvous point to inform it about group membership. The following commands configure Router A for sparse mode:

```
ip multicast-routing
ip pim rp-address 10.8.0.20 1
!
interface ethernet 0
ip pim sparse-mode
!
interface ethernet 1
ip pim sparse-mode
!
access-list 1 permit 224.0.1.2
```

The following commands configure Router D for sparse mode:

```
ip multicast-routing
ip pim rp-address 10.8.0.20 1
!
interface ethernet 0
ip pim sparse-mode
```

```
!
interface ethernet 1
ip pim sparse-mode
!
access-list 1 permit 224.0.1.2
```

The **ip multicast-routing** global configuration command enables IP multicast routing. When you configure PIM, IP multicast routing must be enabled on every router over which multicast traffic will flow. If some routers cannot be configured for IP multicast routing (for example, if they do not run a version of the Cisco IOS Software that supports PIM), you need to configure a tunnel so that multicast packets bypass these routers.

The **ip pim rp-address** global configuration command specifies the IP address of an interface on the router that is to be the rendezvous point and specifies that access list 1 is to be used to define the multicast groups for which the rendezvous point is to be used. The **ip pim rp-address** command must be configured on every sparse-mode router.

The **ip pim** interface configuration command enables PIM on the interface, and the **sparse-mode** keyword enables sparse mode. When you configure PIM in sparse mode, you should apply the **ip pim** command with the **sparse-mode** keyword to every interface that you want to forward multicast traffic. The **access-list** global configuration command defines a standard IP access list that permits traffic using the multicast address 224.0.1.2 (the Silicon Graphics Dogfight application).

In sparse mode, the PIM-configured interface with the highest IP address on a LAN (subnet) is responsible for sending IGMP host-query messages to all hosts on the LAN and for sending PIM register and join messages toward the rendezvous point.

NOTES

To configure a router as a rendezvous point, add the **ip multicast-routing** command and the **ip pim** command with the **sparse-mode** keyword to its configuration. The router recognizes its own IP address as the address of the rendezvous point and automatically assumes the functions of a rendezvous-point function.

Interoperability with Distance Vector Multicast Routing Protocol

The Distance Vector Multicast Routing Protocol (DVMRP) is another multicast protocol that has been developed for IP. DVMRP is similar to dense-mode PIM in that it uses reverse path forwarding. When a router receives a packet, it sends the packet out all interfaces except the interface that leads back to the source of the packet. If the router has interfaces for which no hosts are members of the multicast group for which the packet is intended, the router sends a prune message up the distribution tree to inform the sender that it need not send subsequent packets for this multicast group.

Although the Cisco IOS software does not support DVMRP, it does support interoperability with DVMRP-configured routers. PIM-configured routers dynamically discover DVMRP-configured routers on attached networks. When a DVMRP neighbor is discovered, PIM-configured routers periodically transmit DVMRP report messages advertising the unicast sources that are reachable in the PIM domain. By default, directly connected subnets and networks are advertised. The PIM-configured router forwards multicast packets that it receives from DVMRP routers into the PIM domain and, in turn, forwards multicast packets from the PIM domain to DVMRP routers.

NOTES

When PIM-configured routers are directly connected to DVMRP routers or interoperate with DVMRP routers over a tunnel, the DVMRP routers should run *mrouted* Version 3.8. (The mrouted protocol is a public domain implementation of DVMRP.)

Interoperability Between Directly Connected Routers

Figure 24–3 illustrates a topology in which a PIM-configured router is directly connected to a DVMRP-configured router.

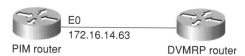

Figure 24–3
PIM and DVMRP
interoperability.

PIM router   DVMRP router

E0
172.16.14.63

The following commands configure the PIM router for interoperability with the DVMRP router:

```
ip multicast-routing
!
interface ethernet 0
ip address 172.16.14.63 255.255.0.0
ip pim dense-mode
ip dvmrp metric 1 list 1
ip dvmrp metric 0 list 2
!
access-list 1 permit 192.168.35.0 0.0.0.255
access-list 1 permit 192.168.36.0 0.0.0.255
access-list 1 permit 192.168.37.0 0.0.0.255
access-list 1 deny 0.0.0.0 255.255.255.255
access-list 2 permit 0.0.0.0 255.255.255.255
```

The **ip dvmrp metric** interface configuration commands configure the metric that is to be associated with a set of destinations for DVMRP reports. The first **ip dvmrp metric** command causes the routes specified by access list 1 to be advertised to the DVMRP router (in this case, networks 192.168.35.0, 192.168.36.0, and 192.168.37.0). The second **ip dvmrp metric** command indicates that the routes specified by access list 2 are not to be advertised (in this case, all other routes). If you do not specify the routes that are to be advertised, only those subnets and networks that are directly connected to the PIM router will be advertised.

Interoperability over a Tunnel

DVMRP tunnels are used when one or more routers on a path do not support multicast routing. The router then sends and receives multicast packets over the tunnel. This allows a PIM domain to connect to a DVMRP router.

When a PIM-configured router interoperates with DVMRP over a tunnel, it advertises source routes in DVMRP report messages. In addition, the router caches any DVMRP report messages that it receives. The router uses the cached report messages as part of its reverse path forwarding calculation. This allows the router to forward multicast packets that it receives over the tunnel. Figure 24-4 illustrates interoperability with DVMRP over a tunnel interface.

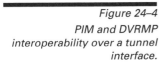
Figure 24-4
PIM and DVRMP interoperability over a tunnel interface.

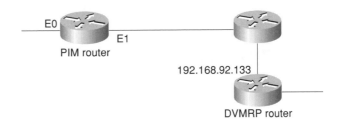

The following commands configure the PIM router:

```
ip multicast-routing
!
interface tunnel 0
ip address 192.168.47.1 255.255.255.0
ip pim dense-mode
tunnel source ethernet 1
tunnel destination 192.168.92.133
tunnel mode dvmrp
!
interface ethernet 1
ip address 192.168.23.23 255.255.255.0 secondary
ip address 192.168.243.2 255.255.255.0
ip pim dense-mode
ip dvmrp accept-filter 1
!
access-list 1 permit 192.168.48.0 0.0.0.255
access-list 1 permit 192.168.49.0 0.0.0.255
access-list 1 permit 192.168.50.0 0.0.0.255
access-list 1 deny 0.0.0.0 255.255.255.255
```

The **interface tunnel** global configuration command creates a tunnel (that is, a virtual interface). The **tunnel source** interface configuration command specifies the interface that participates in the tunnel. The **tunnel destination** interface configuration command specifies the IP address of the mrouted multicast router at the other end of the tunnel.

The **tunnel mode** interface configuration command uses the **dvmrp** keyword to configure the tunnel as a DVMRP tunnel. The **ip address** interface configuration command assigns an address to the tunnel to enable the sending of IP packets over the tunnel and to cause the router to perform DVMRP summarization. Alternatively, the **ip unnumbered** interface configuration command can be used. Either method allows IP multicast packets to flow over the tunnel. If the tunnel has a different network number than the subnet, subnets will not be advertised over the tunnel. In this case, only the network number is advertised over the tunnel.

By specifying the **dense-mode** keyword, the **ip pim** interface configuration command configures dense-mode PIM on the interface. The **ip dvmrp accept-filter** interface configuration command configures an acceptance filter for incoming DVMRP reports. Routes that match the specified access list (in this case, access list 1) are stored in the DVMRP routing table (in this case, 192.168.48.0, 192.168.49.0, and 192.168.50.0). If a Cisco router is a neighbor to router running mrouted Version 3.6, the Cisco router can be configured to advertise network 0.0.0.0 to the DVMRP neighbor by using the **ip dvmrp default-information** command and specifying the **originate** keyword.

USING APPLETALK MULTICASTING

For AppleTalk, the Simple Multicast Routing Protocol (SMRP) supports the routing of multicast packets to multicast groups, with packet replication occurring only on those interfaces that have hosts that belong to the multicast group.

Network multimedia applications, such as QuickTime Conferencing (QTC), allow two or more hosts to participate in a QuickTime Conferencing session. End-users join the multicast group for the multicast transmissions they want to receive. SMRP conserves bandwidth by routing AppleTalk packets to all members of a multipoint group without producing duplicate packets on a particular network segment. Figure 24–5 shows how SMRP works in an AppleTalk network.

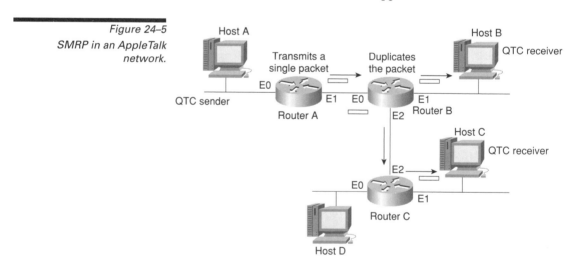

Figure 24–5
SMRP in an AppleTalk network.

Router A receives a multicast packet from Host A and sends it to Router B. Two interfaces on Router B have hosts that have registered to receive this multicast transmission, so Router B duplicates the packet and sends one packet out on Ethernet interface 1 and the other packet out on Ethernet interface 2. Only one interface on Router C has hosts that have registered to receive this multicast transmission, so Router C sends the packet out on Ethernet interface 1. The following commands configure SMRP on Router A:

```
smrp routing
!
interface ethernet 0
smrp protocol appletalk
!
interface ethernet 1
smrp protocol appletalk
```

The following commands configure SMRP on Router B:

```
smrp routing
!
interface ethernet 0
smrp protocol appletalk
!
interface ethernet 1
smrp protocol appletalk

interface ethernet 2
smrp protocol appletalk
```

The following commands configure SMRP on Router C:

```
smrp routing
!
interface ethernet 0
smrp protocol appletalk
!
interface ethernet 1
smrp protocol appletalk
!
interface ethernet 2
smrp protocol appletalk
```

The **smrp routing** global configuration command enables SMRP routing. The **smrp protocol** interface configuration command enables SMRP on the interface, and the **appletalk** keyword specifies AppleTalk as the OSI Layer 3 protocol for SMRP.

MULTICASTING OVER WAN CONNECTIONS

For the most part, users cannot detect the irregular arrival of data packets, but they can easily detect the irregular arrival of multimedia data, especially when that data includes an audio portion. Irregularly delivered video data is characterized by visible jitter and audible distortion. Smoothing jitter and distortion is especially desirable when multimedia data shares a low-bandwidth link with data traffic, as shown in Figure 24–6.

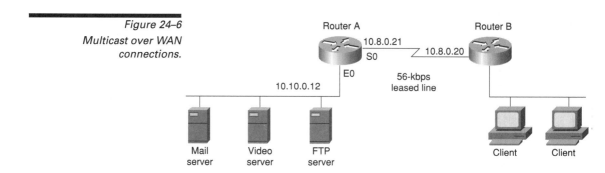

Figure 24–6
Multicast over WAN
connections.

The Cisco IOS software provides three queuing algorithms that you can use to ensure that multicast traffic arrives at its destination without jitter and distortion: weighted fair queuing, priority queuing, and custom queuing. The queuing algorithm that is best for any particular network depends on the traffic flow characteristics of that network. You might want to try all three algorithms to determine the algorithm that provides the smoothest delivery for your particular network connection.

Weighted Fair Queuing

Weighted fair queuing (introduced in Cisco IOS Software Release 11.0) is enabled by default for all interfaces that have a bandwidth less than or equal to 2048 megabits per second (Mbps) and that do not use Link Access Procedure, Balanced (LAPB), X.25, PPP, or Synchronous Data Link Control (SDLC) encapsulations. (Weighted fair queuing cannot be enabled on interfaces that use these encapsulations.) Weighted fair queuing is a traffic priority management algorithm that identifies conversations (traffic streams) and breaks them up to ensure that capacity is shared fairly. The algorithm examines fields in the packet header to identify unique conversations. For example, for AppleTalk, the algorithm uses the source network, node, and socket number; the destination network, node, and socket number; and the type. For IP, the algorithm uses the protocol, source and destination IP address; source and destination port number; and the TOS (type of service) field.

The weighted fair queuing algorithm sorts conversations into two categories: those that have high bandwidth requirements with respect to the capacity of the interface (such as FTP traffic) and those that have low bandwidth requirements (such as interactive sessions). For streams that have low-bandwidth requirements, the algorithm provides access with little or no queuing, and it shares the remaining bandwidth among other conversations. In effect, weighted fair queuing gives low-bandwidth traffic priority over high-bandwidth traffic, and high-bandwidth traffic shares the transmission service proportionally.

When weighted fair queuing is enabled on an interface, new messages for high-bandwidth conversations are discarded when the congestive-messages threshold is reached (the default congestive-messages threshold is 64 messages). To change the congestive-messages threshold, enter the following command, in which **number** is a value between 1 and 512:

```
fair-queue number
```

Priority Queuing

Priority queuing allows you to establish queuing priorities based on protocol type. When you enable priority queuing on an interface, weighted fair queuing is disabled for that interface automatically. The following commands configure priority queuing to ensure a certain quality of service level for Intel ProShare videoconferencing on Router A in Figure 24–6:

```
interface serial 0
ip address 10.8.0.21 255.0.0.0
priority-group 1
!
access-list 101 permit ip any any
!
priority-list 1 protocol IP high UDP 5715
priority-list 1 protocol IP medium TCP 25
priority-list 1 protocol IP normal TCP 20
```

The **priority-group** interface configuration command assigns priority list 1 to serial interface 0. The **priority-list protocol** global configuration commands establish a priority list that is associated with priority group 1. The priority list gives high priority to UDP packets destined for port number 5715 (the port number used by Intel ProShare), medium priority to TCP packets destined for port number 25 (SMTP mail), and normal priority to TCP packets destined for port number 20 (FTP data).

Custom Queuing

Another way to assure the timely delivery of multicast packets is to use custom queuing. With custom queuing, you can define up to 16 queues, assigning normal data to queues 1 through 15 and assigning system messages, such as keepalive messages, to queue 16. The router services each queue sequentially, transmitting a configurable percentage of traffic on each queue before transmitting packets from the next queue.

Custom queuing guarantees that mission-critical data is always assigned a certain percentage of the bandwidth, and it also assures predictable throughput for other traffic. For that reason, custom queuing is recommended for networks that need to provide a guaranteed level of service for all traffic.

When you enable custom queuing on an interface, weighted fair queuing is disabled for that interface automatically. The following commands configure custom queuing for Router A in Figure 24–6:

```
interface serial 0
ip address 10.8.0.21 255.0.0.0
custom-queue-list 1
!
access-list 101 permit ip any any
!
queue-list 1 queue 1 byte-count 57900
queue-list 1 queue 2 byte-count 19300
queue-list 1 queue 3 byte-count 19300
!
queue-list 1 protocol IP 1 UDP 5715
queue-list 1 protocol IP 2 TCP 20
queue-list 1 protocol IP 3 TCP 25
```

The **custom-queue-list** interface configuration command assigns custom queue list 1 to serial interface 0. The **queue-list queue byte-count** global configuration commands specify the size in bytes for three custom queues (in this case, 57,900, 19,300, and 19,300). Together, these **queue-list queue byte-count** commands have the effect of assigning 60 percent of the interface's bandwidth to packets in queue 1, 20 percent of the interface's bandwidth to queue 2, and 20 percent of the interface's bandwidth to queue 3.

The first **queue-list protocol** global configuration command assigns UDP packets destined for port 5715 to queue 1. The second **queue-list protocol** command assigns TCP packets destined for port 20 (SMTP mail) to queue 2, and the third **queue-list protocol** command assigns TCP packets destined for port 25 (FTP data) to queue 3.

SUMMARY

The current popularity of network multimedia applications, such as videoconferencing, is driving the development of protocols that channel the flow of multicast packets to the networks and hosts that want to receive them. As multicasting protocols are deployed, unicast and broadcast applications will be upgraded to take advantage of multicast support, and new multicast applications will be developed.

Scaling Dial-on-Demand Routing

This case study describes the design of an access network that allows a large number of remote sites to communicate with an existing central-site network. The remote sites consist of local-area networks (LANs) that support several workstations. The workstations run transaction processing software that accesses a database located at the central site. The following objectives guided the design of the access portion of the network:

- The existing network could not be modified to accommodate access by the remote sites.
- The central site must be able to connect to any remote site at any time, and any remote site must be able to connect to the central site at any time.
- When choosing between alternative technologies, choose the most cost-effective technology.
- The design must be flexible enough to accommodate additional remote sites in the future.

NETWORK DESIGN CONSIDERATIONS

The following considerations influenced the design of this network:

- Traffic Patterns
- Media Selection
- Application Protocol Requirements

Traffic Patterns

An analysis of the anticipated traffic indicated that each remote site would call the central site an average of four times an hour throughout the business day. This type of traffic pattern means that cost savings can be realized at the central site by providing one telephone line for every 2.5 remote sites (for a total of 48 telephone lines). To spread the calls evenly among the 48 lines, the remote sites connect through a hunt group. The hunt group provides an additional benefit in that all of the remote routers dial the same telephone number to access the central site, which makes the configurations of the remote site routers easier to maintain.

In order to complete a transaction initiated by a remote-site, the central site sometimes needs to call that remote site shortly after it has disconnected from the central site. To make this possible, the access network must converge rapidly. The central site also calls the remote sites periodically to update the transaction processing software on the remote workstations.

Media Selection

The designers chose asynchronous dial-up technology through the Public Switched Telephone Network (PSTN) for the following reasons:

- *Availability*—PSTN is available at all of the remote sites. Potential alternatives, such as Frame Relay and Integrated Digital Services Network (ISDN), were not available at some of the remote sites.

- *Bandwidth*—The transaction processing software causes a small amount of data to be transferred between the remote sites and the central site. For this type of low-bandwidth application, the bandwidth provided by asynchronous dial-up is acceptable. Occasionally, the central site dials the remote sites in order to maintain the transaction processing software on the remote clients. This activity will occur at night (in the absence of transaction processing activity), so the bandwidth provided by asynchronous dial-up is adequate.

- *Cost*—Given the low-bandwidth requirement, the cost of installing and operating Frame Relay or ISDN equipment could not be justified.

NOTES

Although the network described in this case study uses asynchronous dial-up technology over the PSTN, most of the concepts, such as routing strategy and addressing, also apply when scaling other circuit-switched technologies (such as ISDN).

Application Protocol Requirements

The remote workstations run transaction processing software that uses the Transmission Control Protocol /Internet Protocol (TCP/IP) to connect to a database located at the central site. The remote workstations have no need to run any other network-layer protocol. Given this requirement, the most cost-effective choice of router for the remote site is a router that provides an Ethernet interface and an asynchronous interface, and that supports the Routing Information Protocol (RIP).

THE HARDWARE SOLUTION

A Cisco AS5100 is installed at the central site to provide 48 asynchronous interfaces. The Cisco AS5100 consists of three access server cards based on the Cisco 2511 access server, making the Cisco AS5100 equivalent to three Cisco 2511 access servers. Each access server card provides 16 asynchronous lines. Each asynchronous line is equipped with a built-in U.S. Robotics Courier modem.

NOTES

For the purposes of this case study, the three Cisco AS5100 access server cards are referred to as the central-site access routers.

Each remote site is equipped with a Cisco 1020 router. The Cisco 1020 provides a single asynchronous interface and an Ethernet interface for connecting to the remote site LAN. The Cisco 1020 runs a limited set of protocols, including TCP/IP and RIP. U.S. Robotics Sportster modems provide connectivity at the remote sites. Using the same brand of modem throughout the access network simplifies chat scripts and modem definition, and makes the network more manageable.

A Cisco 4500 controls routing between the new access portion of the network and the backbone. In particular, the Cisco 4500 ensures that when hosts on the other side of the backbone need to connect to a remote site, the connection is made through the optimum central-site access router. Figure 25–1 shows the topology of the access portion of the network.

Figure 25–1
Remote access topology.

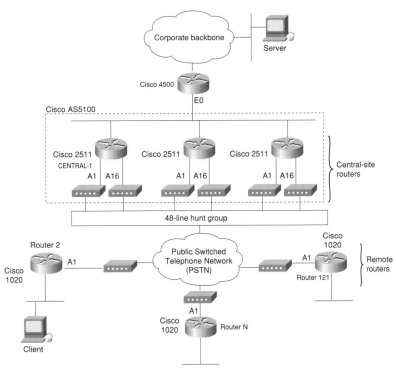

THE SOFTWARE SOLUTION

The configuration of the central-site access routers and the remote site routers must provide the following:

- Authentication
- Network Layer Addressing
- Routing Strategy

Authentication

Traffic between the remote sites and the central site includes confidential information. For that reason, authentication is a primary concern. There are two ways for sites to authenticate themselves:

- *Point-to-Point Protocol (PPP) authentication*—Either the Password Authentication Protocol (PAP) or the Challenge Handshake Authentication Protocol (CHAP) can be used.

- *Login authentication*—With login authentication, the router prompts for a host name and password when a remote router dials in. The remote router logs in and starts PPP.

In either case, the database of usernames and passwords can be stored locally or on an extended Terminal Access Controller Access System (TACACS+) server. TACACS+ provides centralized password management for all the central-site access routers and detailed accounting information about connections to and from the remote sites.

For the purposes of this network design, login authentication is used because it allows the remote sites to announce their IP addresses to the central-site access routers, as described in the section "Network Layer Addressing" later in this chapter. Alternatively, PPP could be started automatically if TACACS+ were used to support per-user IP address assignment.

Network Layer Addressing

Network layer addressing is accomplished through two strategies:

- Subnet Address Assignment
- Next Hop Address

Subnet Address Assignment

The remote routers and the central-site access routers have no need to connect to the Internet, so they use RFC 1597 addresses. The Class B address 172.16.0.0 is used for the entire access portion of the network, and Class C equivalent addresses are assigned to the remote routers. Each subnet gets one Class C equivalent (172.16.x.0 with a mask of 255.255.255.0), which makes addressing easy to manage. Network 172.16.1.0 is reserved for numbering the dialer cloud later if needed. (The dialer cloud is defined as the subnet to which all of the asynchronous interfaces are attached.)

Initially, the dialer cloud is unnumbered. If, in the future, the dialer cloud were to be numbered, the following questions must be considered:

- Can the dialer cloud use the same subnet mask as the remote sites? If not, variable length subnet mask (VLSM) support will be required. (RIP does not support VLSM.)
- Would the use of multiple subnetted Class C addresses cause discontiguous subnets at the remote sites? If so, discontiguous subnet support will be required. (RIP does not support discontiguous subnets.)

In this network, these issues are not a problem. A mask of 255.255.255.0 can be used everywhere, so there are no VLSM concerns. All subnets are from the same major Class B network, so there are no discontiguous subnet concerns. Table 25–1 summarizes the addressing for the access portion of the network.

Table 25–1 *Addressing Summary*

Site	Subnet	Mask
Central access site*	172.16.1.0	255.255.255.0
Router2	172.16.2.0	255.255.255.0
Router3	172.16.3.0	255.255.255.0
...	...	...
Router121	172.16.121.0	255.255.255.0

* Can be used for numbering the dialer cloud.

Next Hop Address

To facilitate an accurate routing table and successful IP Control Protocol (IPCP) address negotiation, all next-hop IP addressing must be accurate at all times. To accomplish this, the remote sites need to know the IP address that they will dial in to, and the central site needs to know the IP address of the remote site that has dialed in.

All central-site access routers use the same IP address on all of their asynchronous interfaces. This is accomplished by configuring the Dialer20 interface for IP unnumbered off of a loopback interface. The IP address of the loopback interface is the same on all of the central-site access routers. This way, the remote routers can be configured with the IP address of the router to which it connects, regardless of which router the remote router dials in to.

The remote router needs to announce its IP address to the central-site router when the remote router connects. This is accomplished by having the remote router start PPP on the central site using the EXEC command **ppp 172.16.x.1**. To support this, each central-site access router is configured with the **async dynamic address** interface configuration command.

NOTES

The autoselect feature allows the router to start an appropriate process, such as PPP, automatically when it receives a starting character from the router that has logged in. To use autoselect, a mechanism for supporting dynamic IP address assignment would be required, such as per-user address support in TACACS+.

Routing Strategy

The development of the routing strategy for this network is based on the following two requirements:

- When a particular remote site *is not* dialed in to the central site, that remote site must be reachable through any central-site access router by means of a static route configured in each central-site access router.

- When a particular remote site router *is* logged in to a central-site access router, that remote site must be reachable through that central-site access router by means of the dynamic route that has been established for that connection and propagated to the backbone.

To meet these requirements, the central-site access routes advertise the major network route of the remote sites to the Cisco 4500. All routes to the remote sites are equal-cost through all of the central-site access routers. Each central-site access router is configured to have a static route to each remote site. To allow the Cisco 4500 to use all of the central-site access routers for connecting to the remote sites, the **no ip route-cache** interface configuration command is configured on Ethernet interface 0 of the Cisco 4500, disabling fast switching of IP to the subnet shared with the central-site access routers. This causes the Cisco 4500 to alternate between the three access routers when initiating outbound calls. This strategy increases network reliability for those cases when one of the access routers goes down.

When a remote router logs in, it announces its IP address and sends a RIP flash. The RIP flash causes a dynamic route to the remote site to be installed immediately in the routing table of the central-site access router. The dynamic route overrides the static route for the duration of the connection.

Next, the central-site access router redistributes the RIP route into Open Shortest Path First (OSPF) and sends the route to all of its OSPF neighbors, including the Cisco 4500, which installs it in its routing table. The Cisco 4500 now has a major network route to all of the remote sites, plus a dynamic route to the specific remote site that has logged in. If a central-site host needs to communicate with a particular remote site that is currently logged in, it does so through the dynamic route.

When the remote site logs out, the dynamic route must be removed from the Cisco 4500, and the static route to the remote site must be restored on the central-site access router into which the remote router logged in.

If a central-site host requires communication with a remote site that is not logged in, it will use the major network route defined in the Cisco 4500. A central-site access router, selected in round-robin fashion, is used to initiate the call to the remote site via the static route that is defined for it in the configuration for the selected access router. As in the case of a remote site that calls the central site, once the connection is made, the remote-site router sends a RIP flash that causes a dynamic route to the remote site to be installed immediately in the routing table of the central-site access router. This dynamic route is redistributed into OSPF and is installed in the routing table of the Cisco 4500. Figure 25–2 uses a state diagram to summarize the routing strategy.

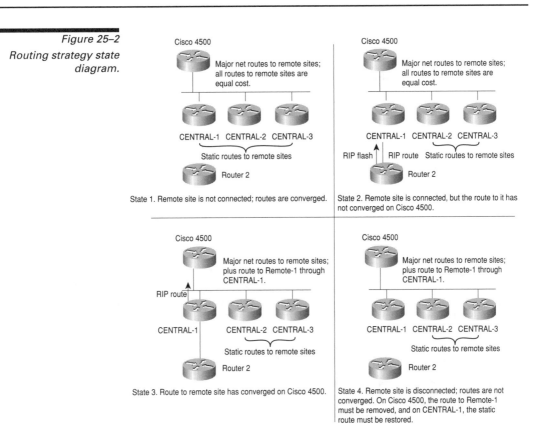

Figure 25–2

Routing strategy state diagram.

The following convergence issues pertain to the state diagram shown in Figure 25–2:

- During the time between State 2 and State 3, a host at the central site might initiate a call to the remote site. Until State 3, at which time the routes converge on the Cisco 4500, any central-site access router that dials the remote site will fail with a busy signal. In practice, only one call fails: by the time a second connection attempt is made, the routes will have converged in State 3, the dynamic route will be available for use, and there will be no need to make another call.

- When the remote site disconnects, at minimum 120 seconds will elapse before the static route is restored to the routing table of the central-site access router on which the remote site logged in. First, up to 35 seconds might elapse before RIP determines that the remote site has disconnected and is no longer sending RIP updates. Sixty seconds later, the central-site access router scans its routing table and restores one of the two static routes for the remote site, and sixty seconds after that, it scans its routing table again and restores the second of the two static routes. (For information about why there are two static routes for each remote site, see the section "Static Routing Configuration" later in this chapter.)

─ **NOTES** ──

Fast install of static routes is a new feature in Cisco IOS Software Release 11.1 that quickly converges back to the static route when a remote site disconnects.

───

If, before convergence occurs, the Cisco 4500 directs a call through CENTRAL-1 to Router 2, the call will fail and must be retried. IP fast switching is turned off on the Cisco 4500, so the Cisco 4500 (which is using equal-cost paths to each of the central-site access routers) will send the next packet through CENTRAL-2 or CENTRAL-3 (which still have a static route for Router 2) and the call will go through.

─ **NOTES** ──

When developing the routing strategy for this network, the designers considered the use of snapshot routing, which reduces connection cost by limiting the exchange of routing protocol updates. For snapshot routing to work, each remote site must connect to the same access router every time it dials into the central site. In this design, the remote routers connect to the central-site access routers through a hunt group, so there is no way to control to which central-site access router a remote router will connect for any particular connection. Therefore, snapshot routing cannot be used for this design.

───

CONFIGURING THE CENTRAL SITE ACCESS ROUTERS

This section describes how the configuration of the central-site access routers implements authentication, network layer addressing, and the routing strategy. The configuration for each central-site access router is the same with the following exceptions:

- The IP address specified for loopback interface 0
- The IP address specified for Ethernet interface 0
- The name of the router as specified by the **hostname** global configuration command

This discussion is divided among the following topics:

- Username Configuration for the Remote Sites
- Dial-Up Configuration for the Remote Sites
- Asynchronous Line Configuration
- OSPF Routing Configuration
- RIP Routing Configuration
- Static Routing Configuration
- Security Issues
- Configuration File Size

For the complete configuration see the section "CENTRAL-1 Configuration" later in this chapter.

Username Configuration for the Remote Sites

The configuration of each central-site access router includes the following **username** global configuration commands:

```
username Router2 password 7 071C2D4359
...
username Router121 password 7 0448070918
```

Each remote router can dial in to any of the three central-site access routers, so there is a **username** global configuration command for each remote router. When a remote router logs in, it specifies a name (for example, Router2) and a password (for example, outthere) that must match the values specified by a **username** command. Each remote site uses a chat script to log in and specify its host name (which must match a value specified by the **username** command) and password. (For information about the chat script that the remote sites use, see the section "Chat Script Configuration for Dialing the Central Site" later in this chapter.)

Dial-Up Configuration for the Remote Sites

The configuration of each central-site access router includes the following **chat-script** global configuration commands:

```
chat-script CALL1020 ABORT ERROR ABORT BUSY TIMEOUT 30 "" "ATDT\T" "CONNECT" \c
chat-script REM TIMEOUT 40 "name:" "CENTRAL" "word:" "secret"
chat-script USRV32BIS "" "AT&F1S0=1&d2" "OK" ""
!
interface dialer 20
dialer map ip 172.16.2.1 name Router2 modem-script CALL1020 system-script REM 5551234
...
dialer map ip 172.16.121.1 name Router2 modem-script CALL1020 system-script REM 5555678
!
line 1 16
script reset USRV32BIS
```

The three **chat-script** global configuration commands establish three scripts named CALL1020, REM, and USRV32BIS. CALL1020 and REM are invoked by the **dialer map** commands to dial and log in to the remote sites, respectively. The **script reset** command specifies that the USRV32BIS script is to be run whenever an asynchronous line is reset in order to ensure that the central-site modems are always configured correctly.

Loopback Interface Configuration

The configuration of each central-site access router includes the commands for configuring loopback interfaces. The IP address for loopback interface 0 is unique for each access router and, to satisfy the rules by which OSPF selects the router ID, must be the highest loopback IP address on the router. The IP address for loopback interface 1 is the same for each central-site access router. The commands are as follows:

```
interface loopback 0
ip address 172.16.254.3 255.255.255.255
...
interface loopback 1
ip address 172.16.1.1 255.255.255.0
```

The goal is for all three access routers to appear to have the same IP address during IPCP negotiation with the remote sites. (IPCP is the part of PPP that brings up and configures IP support.) This goal is accomplished by creating a loopback interface, assigning to it the same IP address on each central-site access router, and running the **ip unnumbered** interface configuration command using the loopback interface address. The problem with this strategy is that OSPF takes its router ID from the IP address of a loopback interface, if one is configured, which would mean that all three access routers would have the same OSPF router ID.

The solution is to create loopback interface 0 and assign to it a unique IP address (which results in a unique OSPF router ID for each router). The configuration then creates loopback interface 1 and assigns to it the same IP address on each router. Loopback interface 1 allows the **ip unnumbered** command to be applied to dialer rotary group 20 later in the configuration.

Asynchronous Line Configuration

The configuration of each central-site access router includes the following commands for configuring each asynchronous interface:

```
interface async 1
ip unnumbered loopback 1
async dynamic address
async dynamic routing
async mode interactive
dialer in-band
dialer rotary-group 20
```

For each of the 16 asynchronous interfaces provided by the access router, the configuration uses the **ip unnumbered** interface configuration command to specify that the asynchronous interface is to use the IP address of loopback interface 1 as the source address for any IP packets that the asynchronous interface generates. The IP address of loopback interface 1 is also used to determine which routing processes are sending updates over the asynchronous interface.

The **async dynamic address** interface configuration command enables dynamic addressing on the asynchronous interface. This command is required to allow each remote router to specify its IP address when it logs in. The **async dynamic routing** interface configuration command allows the interface to run a routing protocol, in this case RIP.

The **async mode interactive** interface configuration command allows a remote router to dial in and access the EXEC command interface, which allows the remote router to start PPP and specify its IP address.

The **dialer in-band** interface configuration command allows chat scripts to be used on the asynchronous interface. The chat scripts allow the access router to dial the remote sites. The **dialer rotary-group** interface configuration command assigns each asynchronous interface to dialer rotary group 20.

Dialer Interface Configuration

The configuration of each central-site access router includes the following commands for configuring dialer rotary group 20:

```
interface dialer 20
ip unnumbered loopback 1
encapsulation ppp
dialer in-band
dialer idle-timeout 60
dialer map ip 172.16.2.1 name Router2 modem-script CALL1020 system-script REM 5551234
...
dialer map ip 172.16.121.1 name Router121 modem-script CALL1020 system-script REM 5555678
dialer-group 3
dialer-list 3 list 101
access-list 101 deny udp 0.0.0.0 255.255.255.255 0.0.0.0 255.255.255.255 eq 520
access-list 101 permit ip 0.0.0.0 255.255.255.255 0.0.0.0 255.255.255.255
```

The **interface dialer** global configuration command defines dialer rotary group 20. Any interface configuration commands that are applied to a dialer rotary group apply to the physical interfaces that are its members. When the router's configuration includes multiple destinations, any of the interfaces in the dialer rotary group can be used to place outgoing calls.

The **ip unnumbered** interface configuration command specifies that the IP address of loopback interface 1 is to be used as the source address for any IP packets that dialer rotary group 20 might generate. The **dialer idle-timeout** interface configuration command causes a disconnect if 60 seconds elapses without any interesting traffic.

The configuration includes a **dialer map** interface configuration command for each remote router that the central-site access router might dial. The **ip** keyword specifies that the dialer map is to be used for IP packets, the IP address is the next-hop address of the destination that is to be called, and the **name** keyword specifies the host name of the remote router that is to be called. The **modem-script** keyword specifies that the CALL1020 chat script is to be used, and the **system-script** keyword specifies that the REM chat script is to be used. The last value specified by the **dialer map** command is the telephone number for the remote router. The dialer map commands do not specify the **broadcast** keyword, so RIP updates are not sent to the remote sites.

For the Dialer20 interface, the **dialer-group** interface configuration command defines *interesting* packets to be those packets defined by the corresponding **dial-list** command. Interesting packets cause a call to be made or cause a call to be maintained. In this case, access list 101 defines RIP as uninteresting. (RIP uses User Datagram Protocol [UDP] port 520.) All other packets are defined as interesting.

OSPF Routing Configuration

Each central-site access router uses the following commands to configure OSPF. These commands limit the routes that are redistributed into OSPF to the major Class B static route and any dynamic subnet routes that may exist for currently connected remote sites. Limiting the routes that are redistributed into OSPF simplifies the routing table on the Cisco 4500 significantly.

```
router ospf 110
redistribute static subnets route-map STATIC-TO-OSPF
redistribute rip subnets route-map RIP-TO-OSPF
passive-interface async 1
...
passive-interface async 16
```

```
network 172.19.0.0 0.0.255.255 area 0
distance 210
!
route-map RIP-TO-OSPF permit
match ip address 20
!
access-list 20 permit 172.16.0.0 0.0.255.0
!
route-map STATIC-TO-OSPF permit
match ip address 21
!
access-list 21 permit 172.16.0.0
```

The **router ospf** global configuration command enables an OSPF routing process and assigns to it a process ID of 110.

The first **redistribute** router configuration command causes static IP routes to be redistributed into OSPF. The **subnets** keyword specifies that subnets are to be redistributed, and the **route-map** keyword specifies that only those routes that successfully pass through the route map named STATIC-TO-OSPF are to be redistributed. The STATIC-TO-OSPF route map permits the redistribution of routes that match access list 21. Access list 21 permits only major network 172.16.0.0.

The second **redistribute** router configuration command causes RIP routes to be redistributed into OSPF. The **subnets** keyword specifies that subnets are to be redistributed, and the **route-map** keyword specifies that only those routes that successfully pass through the route map named RIP-TO-OSPF are to be redistributed. The RIP-TO-OSPF route map permits the redistribution of routes that match access list 20. Access list 20 permits only routes that start with 172.16 and end with .0 (the third octet is wild). In effect, the RIP-TO-OSPF route map allows only subnets that match 172.16.x.0.

For each asynchronous interface, there is a **passive-interface** router configuration command, which means that OSPF routing information is neither sent nor received through the asynchronous interfaces. The **distance** router configuration command assigns the OSPF routing process an administrative distance of 210. This allows the central-site access routers to prefer their static routes (with an administrative distance of 200) over routes learned by OSPF.

NOTES

When a remote site logs in and a dynamic route is established for it, the other access routers retain their static routes for that remote site. When a remote site logs out, the other access routers do not need to update their routing tables—their routing tables still contain the static routes that are necessary for dialing out to the remote site.

RIP Routing Configuration

Each access router uses the following commands to configure RIP:

```
router rip
timers basic 30 35 0 1
network 172.16.0.0
```

```
distribute-list 10 out Dialer20
!
access-list 10 deny 0.0.0.0 255.255.255.255
```

The **timers basic** router configuration adjusts the RIP update, invalid, holddown, and flush timers. The command specifies that RIP updates are to be sent every 30 seconds, that a route is to be declared invalid if an update for the route is not received within 35 seconds after the previous update, that the time during which better routes are to be suppressed is 0 seconds, and that one second must pass before an invalid route is removed from the routing table. These timer adjustments produce the fastest possible convergence when a remote site logs out.

The **network** router configuration command specifies that network 172.16.0.0 is to participate in the RIP routing process. There is no need to propagate RIP routes to the Cisco 1020s, so the **distribute-list out** router configuration command specifies that access list 10 is to be used to control the advertisement of networks in updates. Access list 10 prevents RIP routes from being sent to the remote site.

Static Routing Configuration

The configuration of each central-site access router includes the following commands for configuring static routes to the remote sites:

```
ip route 172.16.0.0 255.255.0.0 Dialer20
```

The first **ip route** global configuration command creates a static route for major network 172.16.0.0 and assigns it to the dialer interface 20. The route, when distributed into OSPF, tells the Cisco 4500 that this central-site access router can get to the remote sites. If the access router goes down, the Cisco 4500 learns that the route is not longer available and removes it from its routing table. This route is redistributed into OSPF by the STATIC-TO-OSPF filter. The first **ip route** command is followed by pairs of static routes, one pair for each remote site:

```
ip route 172.16.2.0 255.255.255.0 172.16.2.1 200
ip route 172.16.2.1 255.255.255.255 Dialer20
...
ip route 172.16.121.0 255.255.255.0 172.16.121.1 200
ip route 172.16.121.1 255.255.255.255 Dialer20
```

In unnumbered IP environments, two static routes are required for each remote site:

- One static route points to the next hop on the dialer map. Note that the "200" makes this route a floating static route, but that it is lower than OSPF routes (which are set to 210 by the **distance** command, earlier in the configuration). This means that a RIP route triggered by a connection to a remote site (whether the connection is initiated by the remote site or the central site) will override the static route. An OSPF update initiated by a remote site that dials in will not override a static route that points to the next hop address on the dialer map.

- One static route that defines the interface at which the next hop can be found (in this case, dialer interface 20). This static route is required for unnumbered interfaces. Note there is no need to make this a floating static route.

Security Issues

The configuration for each central-site access router includes the **login** line configuration command for each asynchronous line and specifies the **local** keyword. This command causes the access router to match the username and password specified by the **username** global configuration command against the username and password that the remote site specifies when it logs in. This security method is required to allow the remote sites to log in and specify their IP addresses.

Configuration File Size

As the number of remote sites increases, the size of the configuration file for each central-site access router might increase to a size at which it can no longer be stored in NVRAM. There are two ways to alleviate this problem:

- Compress the configuration file using the **service compress-config** global configuration command.

- Have the central-site access routers boot using configuration files stored on a Trivial File Transfer Protocol (TFTP) server.

CONFIGURING THE REMOTE SITE ROUTERS

With the exception of the host name and the IP address of the Ethernet interface of each remote site router, the configuration of each remote site router is the same. The discussion of the configuration is divided among the following topics:

- Chat Script Configuration for Dialing the Central Site
- Configuring the Asynchronous Interface
- Using the **site** Command
- Static Routing Configuration

For the complete configuration, see the section "Router2 Configuration" later in this chapter.

Chat Script Configuration for Dialing the Central Site

The configuration of each remote router includes the following **chat-script** global configuration commands:

```
chat-script CENTRALDIAL "" "ATDT 5551111" "CONNECT" "" "name:" "Router2" "word:"
"outthere" ">" "ppp 172.16.2.1"
```

The **chat-script** command defines a chat script named CENTRALDIAL that is used to place calls to the central site. The CENTRALDIAL chat script specifies the telephone number (555-1111) of the central site and the expect-send sequences that guide the modem through the dial-up process. A key feature of the chat script is that when the remote router receives the string > (the prompt indicating that the remote site router has successfully logged in to a central-site access router), the remote router sends the EXEC command **ppp 172.16.2.1**, which informs the central-site access router of the remote router's IP address.

Configuring the Asynchronous Interface

The configuration of each remote router includes the following commands that configure the asynchronous interface:

```
interface async 1
speed 38400
modem-type usr-sport-v32
dialer rotary-group 1
!
modem-def usr-sport-v32 "USR Sportster v.32bis" 38400  "" "AT&F1" "OK"
```

The **speed** line configuration command sets the baud rate to 38400 bits per second for both sending and receiving. The **modem-type** command specifies the initialization string sent to the modem when the interface is reset or when a **clear interface async** command is issued. The initialization string is defined by the **modem-def** command for usr-sport-v32. The **dialer rotary-group** interface configuration command assigns asynchronous interface 1 to dialer rotary group 1.

Using the Site Command

The configuration of each remote router includes the following **site** configuration commands:

```
site CENTRAL
dial-on demand
encapsulation ppp
ip address 172.16.1.1 255.255.255.0
routing rip broadcast
dialgroup 1
session-timeout 5
system-script CENTRALDIAL
password secret
max-ports 1
```

The **site** global configuration command defines a remote location that the router can dial in to or that can dial in to this router, or both, and names it CENTRAL. The name is used to authenticate the central site when it dials in.

The **dial-on** site configuration command uses the **demand** keyword to specify that the central site is to be dialed and a connection established only when packets are queued for the central site. The **encapsulation** site configuration command specifies that when the router establishes a connection with the central site, it is to use PPP encapsulation.

The **ip address** interface configuration command associates IP address 172.16.1.1 with the CENTRAL site. Note that IP address 172.16.1.1 is the address of the dialer 20 interface on each of the central-site access routers. The **routing rip** interface configuration command and the **broadcast** keyword specify that when the router is connected to the central site, IP routing updates are to be broadcast, but any incoming IP routing updates are to be ignored.

The **dialgroup** command specifies that dial group 1 is to be used when connecting to the central site. Earlier in the configuration, the **dialer rotary-group** command assigned asynchronous interface 1 to group 1.

The **session-timeout** site configuration command specifies that if a period of five minutes elapses during which there is no input or output traffic, the router is to close the connection. The **system-script** site configuration command specifies that the CENTRALDIAL chat script is to be used to dial the central site. The **password** site configuration command specifies that when a central-site access router logs in, its password must be the string "secret."

Static Routing Configuration

The configuration of each remote router includes the following **ip route** global configuration commands:

```
ip route 150.10.0.0 172.16.1.1 1
ip route 172.18.0.0 172.16.1.1 1
ip route 172.19.0.0 172.16.1.1 1
ip route 172.21.0.0 172.16.1.1 1
ip route 172.22.0.0 172.16.1.1 1
```

The **ip route** commands establish static IP routes for networks located at the central site, all reachable through a next-hop address of 172.16.1.1, which is the IP address shared by all of the access routers at the central site. All **ip route** commands specify an administrative distance of 1, which is the default.

THE COMPLETE CONFIGURATIONS

This section contains the complete configurations for CENTRAL-1 and Router2.

CENTRAL-1 Configuration

The complete configuration for CENTRAL-1 follows. Those portions of the configuration that must be unique to each central-site access router are highlighted in bold.

```
!
version 10.2
service timestamps debug datetime
service timestamps log datetime
service udp-small-servers
service tcp-small-servers
!
hostname CENTRAL-1
!
enable-password as5100
!
username Router2 password 7 071C2D4359
...
username Router121 password 7 0448070918
!
chat-script CALL1020 ABORT ERROR ABORT BUSY TIMEOUT 30 "" "ATDT\T" "CONNECT" \c
chat-script REM TIMEOUT 40 "name:" "CENTRAL" "word:" "secret"
chat-script USRV32BIS "" "AT&F1S0=1&d2" "OK" ""
!
interface loopback 0
ip address 172.16.254.3 255.255.255.255
```

```
!
interface loopback 1
ip address 172.16.1.1 255.255.255.0
!
interface ethernet 0
ip address 172.19.1.8 255.255.0.0
!
interface serial 0
no ip address
shutdown
!
interface async 1
ip unnumbered loopback 1
encapsulation ppp
async dynamic address
async dynamic routing
async mode interactive
dialer in-band
dialer idle-timeout 60
dialer rotary-group 20
...
interface async 16
ip unnumbered loopback 1
encapsulation ppp
async dynamic address
async dynamic routing
async mode interactive
dialer in-band
dialer idle-timeout 60
dialer rotary-group 20
!
interface dialer 20
ip unnumbered loopback 1
encapsulation ppp
dialer in-band
dialer idle-timeout 60
dialer fast-idle 60
dialer map ip 172.16.2.1 name Router2 modem-script CALL1020 system-script REM 5551234
...
dialer map ip 172.16.121.1 name Router121 modem-script CALL1020 system-script REM 5555678
dialer-group 3
!
router ospf 110
redistribute static subnets route-map STATIC-TO-OSPF
redistribute rip subnets route-map RIP-TO-OSPF
passive-interface async 1
...
passive-interface async 16
network 172.19.0.0 0.0.255.255 area 0
distance 210
!
router rip
timers basic 30 35 0 1
network 172.16.0.0
```

```
distribute-list 10 out Dialer20
!
ip default-gateway 172.19.1.10
!
ip route 172.16.0.0 255.255.0.0 Dialer20
ip route 172.16.2.0 255.255.255.0 172.16.2.1 200
ip route 172.16.2.1 255.255.255.255 Dialer20
...
ip route 172.16.121.0 255.255.255.0 172.16.121.1 200
ip route 172.16.121.1 255.255.255.255 Dialer20

access-list 10 deny 0.0.0.0 255.255.255.255
access-list 20 permit 172.16.0.0 0.0.255.0
access-list 21 permit 172.16.0.0
access-list 101 deny udp 0.0.0.0 255.255.255.255 0.0.0.0 255.255.255.255 eq 520
access-list 101 permit ip 0.0.0.0 255.255.255.255 0.0.0.0 255.255.255.255

route-map RIP-TO-OSPF permit
match ip address 20
!
route-map STATIC-TO-OSPF permit
match ip address 21
!
snmp-server community public RO
snmp-server community private RW
dialer-list 3 list 101
!
line con 0
line 1 16
login local
modem inout
script reset USRV32BIS
transport input all
rxspeed 38400
txspeed 38400
flowcontrol hardware
line aux 0
transport input all
line vty 0 4
exec-timeout 20 0
password cisco
login
!
end
```

Router2 Configuration

The complete configuration for Router2 follows. Those portions of the configuration that must be unique to each remote site router are highlighted in bold.

```
version 1.1(2)
!
hostname Router2
!
```

```
enable-password cisco-a
!
chat-script CENTRALDIAL "" "ATDT 5551111" "CONNECT" "" "name:" "Router2" "word:"
"outthere" ">" "ppp 172.16.2.1"
!
interface ethernet 0
ip address 172.16.2.1 255.255.255.0
!
interface async 1
speed 38400
modem-type usr-sport-v32
dialer rotary-group 1
!
site CENTRAL
dial-on demand
encapsulation ppp
ip address 172.16.1.1 255.255.255.0
routing rip broadcast
dialgroup 1
session-timeout 5
system-script CENTRALDIAL
password secret
max-ports 1
!
modem-def usr-sport-v32 "USR Sportster v.32bis" 38400  "" "AT&F1" "OK"
!
ip route 150.10.0.0 172.16.1.1 1
ip route 172.18.0.0 172.16.1.1 1
ip route 172.19.0.0 172.16.1.1 1
ip route 172.21.0.0 172.16.1.1 1
ip route 172.22.0.0 172.16.1.1 1
```

SUMMARY

This case study shows that it is possible to scale dial-on-demand routing to accommodate large dial-up networks. If, in the future, the number of remote sites exceeds the capacity of the 48 asynchronous interfaces, additional routers can be installed without modifying the routing strategy. Although this case study focuses on asynchronous media, many of the techniques can be applied to other dial-up technologies, such as ISDN.

PART III

Appendixes

Subnetting an IP Address Space

This appendix provides a partial listing of a Class B area intended to be divided into approximately 500 Open Shortest Path First (OSPF) areas. For the purposes of this example, the network is assumed to be a Class B network with the address 150.100.0.0.

NOTES

Although a 500-area OSPF internetwork is unrealistic, using an address space like this can help to illustrate the general methodology employed to subnet an OSPF address space.

Only the address space for two of 512 areas is shown in Table A–1. These areas are defined with the base address 150.100.2.0. Illustrating the entire address space for 150.100.0.0 would require hundreds of additional pages of addressing information. Each area would require the equivalent number of entries for each of the example areas illustrated here.

Table A–1 illustrates the assignment of 255 IP addresses that have been split between two OSPF areas. Table A–1 also illustrates the boundaries of the subnets and of the two OSPF areas shown (area 8 and area 17).

For the purposes of this discussion, consider a network that requires point-to-point serial links in each area to be assigned a subnet mask that allows two hosts per subnet. All other subnets are to be allowed 14 hosts per subnet. The use of bit-wise subnetting and variable-length subnet masks (VLSMs) permit you to customize your address space by facilitating the division of address spaces into smaller groupings than is allowed when subnetting along octet boundaries. The address layout shown in Table A–1 illustrates a structured approach to assigning addresses that uses VLSM. Table A–1 presents two subnet masks: 255.255.255.240 and of 255.255.255.252. The first mask creates subnet address spaces that are four bits wide; the second mask creates subnet address spaces that are two bits wide.

Because of the careful assignment of addresses, each area can be summarized with a single **area** router configuration command (used to define address range). The first set of addresses starting with 150.100.2.0*xxxxxxx* (last octet represented here in binary) can be summarized into the backbone with the following command:

    area 8 range 150.100.2.0 255.255.255.128

This command assigns all addresses from 150.100.2.0 to 150.100.2.127 to area 8. Similarly, the addresses from 150.100.2.128 to 150.100.2.255 for the second area can be summarized as follows:

    area 17 range 150.100.2.128 255.255.255.128

This command assigns all addresses from 150.100.2.128 to 150.100.2.255 to area 17.

Allocation of subnets allows you to decide where to draw the line between the subnet and host (using a subnet mask) within each area. Note that in this example there are only seven bits remaining to use because of the creation of the artificial area mask. The nine bits to the left of the area mask are actually part of the subnet portion of the address. By keeping these nine bits the same for all addresses in a given area, route summarization is easily achieved at area border routers, as illustrated by the scheme used in Table A–1.

Table A–1 lists individual subnets, valid IP addresses, subnet identifiers, and broadcast addresses. This method of assigning addresses for the VLSM portion of the address space guarantees that there is no address overlap. If the requirement had been different, any number of the larger subnets might be chosen and divided into smaller ranges with fewer hosts, or combined into several ranges to create subnets with more hosts.

The design approach used in this appendix allows the area mask boundary and subnet masks to be assigned to any point in the address space, which provides significant design flexibility. A change in the specification of the area mask boundary or subnet masks may be required if a network outgrows its initial address space design. In Table A–1, the area mask boundary is to the right of the most significant bit of the last octet of the address, as shown by Figure A–1.

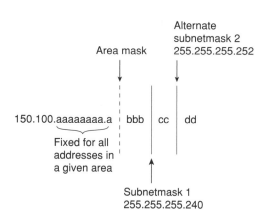

Figure A–1
Breakdown of the addresses
assigned by the example.

With a subnet mask of 255.255.255.240, the *a* and *b* bits together represent the subnet portion of the address, whereas the *c* and *d* bits together provide four-bit host identifiers. When a subnet mask of 255.255.255.252 (a typical subnet mask for point-to-point serial lines), the *a*, *b*, and *c* bits together represent the subnet portion of the address, and the *d* bits provide two-bit host identifiers. As mentioned earlier, the purpose of the area mask is to keep all of the *a* bits constant in a given OSPF area (independent of the subnet mask) so that route summarization is easy to apply.

The following steps outline the process used to allocate addresses:

Step 1 Determine the number of areas required for your OSPF network. A value of 500 is used for this example.

Step 2 Create an artificial *area mask boundary* in your address space. This example uses nine bits of subnet addressing space to identify the areas uniquely. Because $2^9 = 512$, nine bits of subnet meet our requirement of 500 areas.

Step 3 Determine the number of subnets required in each area and the maximum number of hosts required per subnet. This allows you to determine the placement of the subnet mask(s). In Table A–1, the requirement is for seven subnets with 14 hosts each and four subnets with two hosts each.

Table A–1 *Partial Example of Subnet Address Assignment Using VLSM*

IP Address (Decimal)	Subnet Portion of Last Octet (Binary)	Host Portion of Last Octet (Binary)	Subnet Number	Subnet Mask	Notes
150.100.2.0	0000	0000	150.100.2.0	255.255.255.240	Subnet identifier; area boundary; area 8 starts
150.100.2.1	0000	0001	150.100.2.0	255.255.255.240	
150.100.2.2	0000	0010	150.100.2.0	255.255.255.240	
150.100.2.3	0000	0011	150.100.2.0	255.255.255.240	
150.100.2.4	0000	0100	150.100.2.0	255.255.255.240	
150.100.2.5	0000	0101	150.100.2.0	255.255.255.240	
150.100.2.6	0000	0110	150.100.2.0	255.255.255.240	
150.100.2.7	0000	0111	150.100.2.0	255.255.255.240	
150.100.2.8	0000	1000	150.100.2.0	255.255.255.240	
150.100.2.9	0000	1001	150.100.2.0	255.255.255.240	
150.100.2.10	0000	1010	150.100.2.0	255.255.255.240	

Table A–1 *Partial Example of Subnet Address Assignment Using VLSM, Continued*

IP Address (Decimal)	Subnet Portion of Last Octet (Binary)	Host Portion of Last Octet (Binary)	Subnet Number	Subnet Mask	Notes
150.100.2.11	0000	1011	150.100.2.0	255.255.255.240	
150.100.2.12	0000	1100	150.100.2.0	255.255.255.240	
150.100.2.13	0000	1101	150.100.2.0	255.255.255.240	
150.100.2.14	0000	1110	150.100.2.0	255.255.255.240	
150.100.2.15	0000	1111	150.100.2.0	255.255.255.240	Subnet broadcast
150.100.2.16	0001	0000	150.100.2.16	255.255.255.240	Subnet identifier
150.100.2.17	0001	0001	150.100.2.16	255.255.255.240	
150.100.2.18	0001	0010	150.100.2.16	255.255.255.240	
150.100.2.19	0001	0011	150.100.2.16	255.255.255.240	
150.100.2.20	0001	0100	150.100.2.16	255.255.255.240	
150.100.2.21	0001	0101	150.100.2.16	255.255.255.240	
150.100.2.22	0001	0110	150.100.2.16	255.255.255.240	
150.100.2.23	0001	0111	150.100.2.16	255.255.255.240	
150.100.2.24	0001	1000	150.100.2.16	255.255.255.240	
150.100.2.25	0001	1001	150.100.2.16	255.255.255.240	
150.100.2.26	0001	1010	150.100.2.16	255.255.255.240	
150.100.2.27	0001	1011	150.100.2.16	255.255.255.240	
150.100.2.28	0001	1100	150.100.2.16	255.255.255.240	
150.100.2.29	0001	1101	150.100.2.16	255.255.255.240	
150.100.2.30	0001	1110	150.100.2.16	255.255.255.240	
150.100.2.31	0001	1111	150.100.2.16	255.255.255.240	Subnet broadcast
150.100.2.32	0010	0000	150.100.2.32	255.255.255.240	Subnet identifier
150.100.2.33	0010	0001	150.100.2.32	255.255.255.240	
150.100.2.34	0010	0010	150.100.2.32	255.255.255.240	
150.100.2.35	0010	0011	150.100.2.32	255.255.255.240	

Table A–1 *Partial Example of Subnet Address Assignment Using VLSM, Continued*

IP Address (Decimal)	Subnet Portion of Last Octet (Binary)	Host Portion of Last Octet (Binary)	Subnet Number	Subnet Mask	Notes
150.100.2.36	0010	0100	150.100.2.32	255.255.255.240	
150.100.2.37	0010	0101	150.100.2.32	255.255.255.240	
150.100.2.38	0010	0110	150.100.2.32	255.255.255.240	
150.100.2.39	0010	0111	150.100.2.32	255.255.255.240	
150.100.2.40	0010	1000	150.100.2.32	255.255.255.240	
150.100.2.41	0010	1001	150.100.2.32	255.255.255.240	
150.100.2.42	0010	1010	150.100.2.32	255.255.255.240	
150.100.2.43	0010	1011	150.100.2.32	255.255.255.240	
150.100.2.44	0010	1100	150.100.2.32	255.255.255.240	
150.100.2.45	0010	1101	150.100.2.32	255.255.255.240	
150.100.2.46	0010	1110	150.100.2.32	255.255.255.240	
150.100.2.47	0010	1111	150.100.2.32	255.255.255.240	Subnet broadcast
150.100.2.48	0011	0000	150.100.2.48	255.255.255.240	Subnet identifier
150.100.2.49	0011	0001	150.100.2.48	255.255.255.240	
150.100.2.50	0011	0010	150.100.2.48	255.255.255.240	
150.100.2.51	0011	0011	150.100.2.48	255.255.255.240	
150.100.2.52	0011	0100	150.100.2.48	255.255.255.240	
150.100.2.53	0011	0101	150.100.2.48	255.255.255.240	
150.100.2.54	0011	0110	150.100.2.48	255.255.255.240	
150.100.2.55	0011	0111	150.100.2.48	255.255.255.240	
150.100.2.56	0011	1000	150.100.2.48	255.255.255.240	
150.100.2.57	0011	1001	150.100.2.48	255.255.255.240	
150.100.2.58	0011	1010	150.100.2.48	255.255.255.240	
150.100.2.59	0011	1011	150.100.2.48	255.255.255.240	
150.100.2.60	0011	1100	150.100.2.48	255.255.255.240	

Table A-1 *Partial Example of Subnet Address Assignment Using VLSM, Continued*

IP Address (Decimal)	Subnet Portion of Last Octet (Binary)	Host Portion of Last Octet (Binary)	Subnet Number	Subnet Mask	Notes
150.100.2.61	0011	1101	150.100.2.48	255.255.255.240	
150.100.2.62	0011	1110	150.100.2.48	255.255.255.240	
150.100.2.63	0011	1111	150.100.2.48	255.255.255.240	Subnet broadcast
150.100.2.64	010000	00	150.100.2.64	255.255.255.252	Subnet identifier
150.100.2.65	010000	01	150.100.2.64	255.255.255.252	
150.100.2.66	010000	10	150.100.2.64	255.255.255.252	
150.100.2.67	010000	11	150.100.2.64	255.255.255.252	Subnet broadcast
150.100.2.68	010001	00	150.100.2.68	255.255.255.252	Subnet identifier
150.100.2.69	010001	01	150.100.2.68	255.255.255.252	
150.100.2.70	010001	10	150.100.2.68	255.255.255.252	
150.100.2.71	010001	11	150.100.2.68	255.255.255.252	Subnet broadcast
150.100.2.72	010010	00	150.100.2.72	255.255.255.252	Subnet identifier
150.100.2.73	010010	01	150.100.2.72	255.255.255.252	
150.100.2.74	010010	10	150.100.2.72	255.255.255.252	
150.100.2.75	010010	11	150.100.2.72	255.255.255.252	Subnet broadcast
150.100.2.76	010011	00	150.100.2.76	255.255.255.252	Subnet identifier
150.100.2.77	010011	01	150.100.2.76	255.255.255.252	
150.100.2.78	010011	10	150.100.2.76	255.255.255.252	
150.100.2.79	010011	11	150.100.2.76	255.255.255.252	Subnet broadcast
150.100.2.80	0101	0000	150.100.2.80	255.255.255.240	Subnet identifier
150.100.2.81	0101	0001	150.100.2.80	255.255.255.240	
150.100.2.82	0101	0010	150.100.2.80	255.255.255.240	
150.100.2.83	0101	0011	150.100.2.80	255.255.255.240	
150.100.2.84	0101	0100	150.100.2.80	255.255.255.240	
150.100.2.85	0101	0101	150.100.2.80	255.255.255.240	

Table A–1 *Partial Example of Subnet Address Assignment Using VLSM, Continued*

IP Address (Decimal)	Subnet Portion of Last Octet (Binary)	Host Portion of Last Octet (Binary)	Subnet Number	Subnet Mask	Notes
150.100.2.86	0101	0110	150.100.2.80	255.255.255.240	
150.100.2.87	0101	0111	150.100.2.80	255.255.255.240	
150.100.2.88	0101	1000	150.100.2.80	255.255.255.240	
150.100.2.89	0101	1001	150.100.2.80	255.255.255.240	
150.100.2.90	0101	1010	150.100.2.80	255.255.255.240	
150.100.2.91	0101	1011	150.100.2.80	255.255.255.240	
150.100.2.92	0101	1100	150.100.2.80	255.255.255.240	
150.100.2.93	0101	1101	150.100.2.80	255.255.255.240	
150.100.2.94	0101	1110	150.100.2.80	255.255.255.240	
150.100.2.95	0101	1111	150.100.2.80	255.255.255.240	Subnet broadcast
150.100.2.96	0110	0000	150.100.2.96	255.255.255.240	Subnet identifier
150.100.2.97	0110	0001	150.100.2.96	255.255.255.240	
150.100.2.98	0110	0010	150.100.2.96	255.255.255.240	
150.100.2.99	0110	0011	150.100.2.96	255.255.255.240	
150.100.2.100	0110	0100	150.100.2.96	255.255.255.240	
150.100.2.101	0110	0101	150.100.2.96	255.255.255.240	
150.100.2.102	0110	0110	150.100.2.96	255.255.255.240	
150.100.2.103	0110	0111	150.100.2.96	255.255.255.240	
150.100.2.104	0110	1000	150.100.2.96	255.255.255.240	
150.100.2.105	0110	1001	150.100.2.96	255.255.255.240	
150.100.2.106	0110	1010	150.100.2.96	255.255.255.240	
150.100.2.107	0110	1011	150.100.2.96	255.255.255.240	
150.100.2.108	0110	1100	150.100.2.96	255.255.255.240	
150.100.2.109	0110	1101	150.100.2.96	255.255.255.240	
150.100.2.110	0110	1110	150.100.2.96	255.255.255.240	

Table A–1　*Partial Example of Subnet Address Assignment Using VLSM, Continued*

IP Address (Decimal)	Subnet Portion of Last Octet (Binary)	Host Portion of Last Octet (Binary)	Subnet Number	Subnet Mask	Notes
150.100.2.111	0110	1111	150.100.2.96	255.255.255.240	Subnet broadcast
150.100.2.112	0111	0000	150.100.2.112	255.255.255.240	Subnet identifier
150.100.2.113	0111	0001	150.100.2.112	255.255.255.240	
150.100.2.114	0111	0010	150.100.2.112	255.255.255.240	
150.100.2.115	0111	0011	150.100.2.112	255.255.255.240	
150.100.2.116	0111	0100	150.100.2.112	255.255.255.240	
150.100.2.117	0111	0101	150.100.2.112	255.255.255.240	
150.100.2.118	0111	0110	150.100.2.112	255.255.255.240	
150.100.2.119	0111	0111	150.100.2.112	255.255.255.240	
150.100.2.120	0111	1000	150.100.2.112	255.255.255.240	
150.100.2.121	0111	1001	150.100.2.112	255.255.255.240	
150.100.2.122	0111	1010	150.100.2.112	255.255.255.240	
150.100.2.123	0111	1011	150.100.2.112	255.255.255.240	
150.100.2.124	0111	1100	150.100.2.112	255.255.255.240	
150.100.2.125	0111	1101	150.100.2.112	255.255.255.240	
150.100.2.126	0111	1110	150.100.2.112	255.255.255.240	
150.100.2.127	0111	1111	150.100.2.112	255.255.255.240	Subnet broadcast; area boundary; area 8 ends
150.100.2.128	1000	0000	150.100.2.128	255.255.255.240	Subnet identifier; area boundary; area 17 starts
150.100.2.129	1000	0001	150.100.2.128	255.255.255.240	
150.100.2.130	1000	0010	150.100.2.128	255.255.255.240	
150.100.2.131	1000	0011	150.100.2.128	255.255.255.240	
150.100.2.132	1000	0100	150.100.2.128	255.255.255.240	

Table A–1 *Partial Example of Subnet Address Assignment Using VLSM, Continued*

IP Address (Decimal)	Subnet Portion of Last Octet (Binary)	Host Portion of Last Octet (Binary)	Subnet Number	Subnet Mask	Notes
150.100.2.133	1000	0101	150.100.2.128	255.255.255.240	
150.100.2.134	1000	0110	150.100.2.128	255.255.255.240	
150.100.2.135	1000	0111	150.100.2.128	255.255.255.240	
150.100.2.136	1000	1000	150.100.2.128	255.255.255.240	
150.100.2.137	1000	1001	150.100.2.128	255.255.255.240	
150.100.2.138	1000	1010	150.100.2.128	255.255.255.240	
150.100.2.139	1000	1011	150.100.2.128	255.255.255.240	
150.100.2.140	1000	1100	150.100.2.128	255.255.255.240	
150.100.2.141	1000	1101	150.100.2.128	255.255.255.240	
150.100.2.142	1000	1110	150.100.2.128	255.255.255.240	
150.100.2.143	1000	1111	150.100.2.128	255.255.255.240	Subnet broadcast
150.100.2.144	1001	0000	150.100.2.144	255.255.255.240	Subnet identifier
150.100.2.145	1001	0001	150.100.2.144	255.255.255.240	
150.100.2.146	1001	0010	150.100.2.144	255.255.255.240	
150.100.2.147	1001	0011	150.100.2.144	255.255.255.240	
150.100.2.148	1001	0100	150.100.2.144	255.255.255.240	
150.100.2.149	1001	0101	150.100.2.144	255.255.255.240	
150.100.2.150	1001	0110	150.100.2.144	255.255.255.240	
150.100.2.151	1001	0111	150.100.2.144	255.255.255.240	
150.100.2.152	1001	1000	150.100.2.144	255.255.255.240	
150.100.2.153	1001	1001	150.100.2.144	255.255.255.240	
150.100.2.154	1001	1010	150.100.2.144	255.255.255.240	
150.100.2.155	1001	1011	150.100.2.144	255.255.255.240	
150.100.2.156	1001	1100	150.100.2.144	255.255.255.240	
150.100.2.157	1001	1101	150.100.2.144	255.255.255.240	

Table A–1 *Partial Example of Subnet Address Assignment Using VLSM, Continued*

IP Address (Decimal)	Subnet Portion of Last Octet (Binary)	Host Portion of Last Octet (Binary)	Subnet Number	Subnet Mask	Notes
150.100.2.158	1001	1110	150.100.2.144	255.255.255.240	
150.100.2.159	1001	1111	150.100.2.144	255.255.255.240	Subnet broadcast
150.100.2.160	1010	0000	150.100.2.160	255.255.255.240	Subnet identifier
150.100.2.161	1010	0001	150.100.2.160	255.255.255.240	
150.100.2.162	1010	0010	150.100.2.160	255.255.255.240	
150.100.2.163	1010	0011	150.100.2.160	255.255.255.240	
150.100.2.164	1010	0100	150.100.2.160	255.255.255.240	
150.100.2.165	1010	0101	150.100.2.160	255.255.255.240	
150.100.2.166	1010	0110	150.100.2.160	255.255.255.240	
150.100.2.167	1010	0111	150.100.2.160	255.255.255.240	
150.100.2.168	1010	1000	150.100.2.160	255.255.255.240	
150.100.2.169	1010	1001	150.100.2.160	255.255.255.240	
150.100.2.170	1010	1010	150.100.2.160	255.255.255.240	
150.100.2.171	1010	1011	150.100.2.160	255.255.255.240	
150.100.2.172	1010	1100	150.100.2.160	255.255.255.240	
150.100.2.173	1010	1101	150.100.2.160	255.255.255.240	
150.100.2.174	1010	1110	150.100.2.160	255.255.255.240	
150.100.2.175	1010	1111	150.100.2.160	255.255.255.240	Subnet broadcast
150.100.2.176	101100	00	150.100.2.176	255.255.255.252	Subnet identifier
150.100.2.177	101100	01	150.100.2.176	255.255.255.252	
150.100.2.178	101100	10	150.100.2.176	255.255.255.252	
150.100.2.179	101100	11	150.100.2.176	255.255.255.252	Subnet broadcast
150.100.2.180	101101	00	150.100.2.180	255.255.255.252	Subnet identifier
150.100.2.181	101101	01	150.100.2.180	255.255.255.252	
150.100.2.182	101101	10	150.100.2.180	255.255.255.252	

Table A–1 *Partial Example of Subnet Address Assignment Using VLSM, Continued*

IP Address (Decimal)	Subnet Portion of Last Octet (Binary)	Host Portion of Last Octet (Binary)	Subnet Number	Subnet Mask	Notes
150.100.2.183	101101	11	150.100.2.180	255.255.255.252	Subnet broadcast
150.100.2.184	101110	00	150.100.2.184	255.255.255.252	Subnet identifier
150.100.2.185	101110	01	150.100.2.184	255.255.255.252	
150.100.2.186	101110	10	150.100.2.184	255.255.255.252	
150.100.2.187	101110	11	150.100.2.184	255.255.255.252	Subnet broadcast
150.100.2.188	101111	00	150.100.2.188	255.255.255.252	Subnet identifier
150.100.2.189	101111	01	150.100.2.188	255.255.255.252	
150.100.2.190	101111	10	150.100.2.188	255.255.255.252	
150.100.2.191	101111	11	150.100.2.188	255.255.255.252	Subnet broadcast
150.100.2.192	1100	0000	150.100.2.192	255.255.255.240	Subnet identifier
150.100.2.193	1100	0001	150.100.2.192	255.255.255.240	
150.100.2.194	1100	0010	150.100.2.192	255.255.255.240	
150.100.2.195	1100	0011	150.100.2.192	255.255.255.240	
150.100.2.196	1100	0100	150.100.2.192	255.255.255.240	
150.100.2.197	1100	0101	150.100.2.192	255.255.255.240	
150.100.2.198	1100	0110	150.100.2.192	255.255.255.240	
150.100.2.199	1100	0111	150.100.2.192	255.255.255.240	
150.100.2.200	1100	1000	150.100.2.192	255.255.255.240	
150.100.2.201	1100	1001	150.100.2.192	255.255.255.240	
150.100.2.202	1100	1010	150.100.2.192	255.255.255.240	
150.100.2.203	1100	1011	150.100.2.192	255.255.255.240	
150.100.2.204	1100	1100	150.100.2.192	255.255.255.240	
150.100.2.205	1100	1101	150.100.2.192	255.255.255.240	
150.100.2.206	1100	1110	150.100.2.192	255.255.255.240	
150.100.2.207	1100	1111	150.100.2.192	255.255.255.240	Subnet broadcast

Table A–1 *Partial Example of Subnet Address Assignment Using VLSM, Continued*

IP Address (Decimal)	Subnet Portion of Last Octet (Binary)	Host Portion of Last Octet (Binary)	Subnet Number	Subnet Mask	Notes
150.100.2.208	1101	0000	150.100.2.208	255.255.255.240	Subnet identifier
150.100.2.209	1101	0001	150.100.2.208	255.255.255.240	
150.100.2.210	1101	0010	150.100.2.208	255.255.255.240	
150.100.2.211	1101	0011	150.100.2.208	255.255.255.240	
150.100.2.212	1101	0100	150.100.2.208	255.255.255.240	
150.100.2.213	1101	0101	150.100.2.208	255.255.255.240	
150.100.2.214	1101	0110	150.100.2.208	255.255.255.240	
150.100.2.215	1101	0111	150.100.2.208	255.255.255.240	
150.100.2.216	1101	1000	150.100.2.208	255.255.255.240	
150.100.2.217	1101	1001	150.100.2.208	255.255.255.240	
150.100.2.218	1101	1010	150.100.2.208	255.255.255.240	
150.100.2.219	1101	1011	150.100.2.208	255.255.255.240	
150.100.2.220	1101	1100	150.100.2.208	255.255.255.240	
150.100.2.221	1101	1101	150.100.2.208	255.255.255.240	
150.100.2.222	1101	1110	150.100.2.208	255.255.255.240	
150.100.2.223	1101	1111	150.100.2.208	255.255.255.240	Subnet broadcast
150.100.2.224	1110	0000	150.100.2.224	255.255.255.240	Subnet identifier
150.100.2.225	1110	0001	150.100.2.224	255.255.255.240	
150.100.2.226	1110	0010	150.100.2.224	255.255.255.240	
150.100.2.227	1110	0011	150.100.2.224	255.255.255.240	
150.100.2.228	1110	0100	150.100.2.224	255.255.255.240	
150.100.2.229	1110	0101	150.100.2.224	255.255.255.240	
150.100.2.230	1110	0110	150.100.2.224	255.255.255.240	
150.100.2.231	1110	0111	150.100.2.224	255.255.255.240	
150.100.2.232	1110	1000	150.100.2.224	255.255.255.240	

Table A–1 *Partial Example of Subnet Address Assignment Using VLSM, Continued*

IP Address (Decimal)	Subnet Portion of Last Octet (Binary)	Host Portion of Last Octet (Binary)	Subnet Number	Subnet Mask	Notes
150.100.2.233	1110	1001	150.100.2.224	255.255.255.240	
150.100.2.234	1110	1010	150.100.2.224	255.255.255.240	
150.100.2.235	1110	1011	150.100.2.224	255.255.255.240	
150.100.2.236	1110	1100	150.100.2.224	255.255.255.240	
150.100.2.237	1110	1101	150.100.2.224	255.255.255.240	
150.100.2.238	1110	1110	150.100.2.224	255.255.255.240	
150.100.2.239	1110	1111	150.100.2.224	255.255.255.240	Subnet broadcast
150.100.2.240	1111	0000	150.100.2.240	255.255.255.240	Subnet identifier
150.100.2.241	1111	0001	150.100.2.240	255.255.255.240	
150.100.2.242	1111	0010	150.100.2.240	255.255.255.240	
150.100.2.243	1111	0011	150.100.2.240	255.255.255.240	
150.100.2.244	1111	0100	150.100.2.240	255.255.255.240	
150.100.2.245	1111	0101	150.100.2.240	255.255.255.240	
150.100.2.246	1111	0110	150.100.2.240	255.255.255.240	
150.100.2.247	1111	0111	150.100.2.240	255.255.255.240	
150.100.2.248	1111	1000	150.100.2.240	255.255.255.240	
150.100.2.249	1111	1001	150.100.2.240	255.255.255.240	
150.100.2.250	1111	1010	150.100.2.240	255.255.255.240	
150.100.2.251	1111	1011	150.100.2.240	255.255.255.240	
150.100.2.252	1111	1100	150.100.2.240	255.255.255.240	
150.100.2.253	1111	1101	150.100.2.240	255.255.255.240	
150.100.2.254	1111	1110	150.100.2.240	255.255.255.240	
150.100.2.255	1111	1111	150.100.2.240	255.255.255.240	Subnet broadcast; area boundary; area 17 ends

IBM Serial Link Implementation Notes

The following discussions clarify some common misconceptions and points of confusion associated with half-duplex, full-duplex, and multipoint connections.

COMPARING HALF DUPLEX AND FULL DUPLEX

Half-duplex and full-duplex serial links can often be confusing. One reason for the confusion is that there are several different contexts in which these two terms are used. These contexts include asynchronous line implementations, IBM Systems Network Architecture (SNA)-specific implementations, and data communications equipment (DCE) implementations. Each is addressed in the discussions that follow.

Asynchronous Line Definitions

Duplex, as seen on asynchronous communication lines (and in terminal emulation software parameters), implies *full duplex* as it applies to the echoing of transmitted characters by a host back to a terminal. This is also referred to as *echoplex* mode. In this context, half-duplex mode involves no character echo. Some common misconfigurations of terminals and hosts follow:

- Full duplex specified on a terminal when the host is set for half duplex results in typing blind at the terminal.

- Half duplex specified on a terminal when the host is set for full duplex results in double characters on the terminal. This is because the terminal displays entered characters if the terminal's configuration indicates that the host will not echo characters.

NOTES

This interpretation of duplex does not apply in a router context.

IBM SNA-Specific Definitions

IBM's master glossary for VTAM, NCP, and NetView terms defines *duplex*, *full duplex*, and *half duplex* as follows:

- *Duplex*—In data communications, pertaining to a simultaneous two-way independent transmission in both directions; synonymous with full duplex; contrast with half duplex.

- *Half duplex*—In data communications, pertaining to an alternate, one-way-at-a-time, independent transmission; contrast with duplex.

These definitions can be applied in two contexts that are the main source of duplex definition confusion:

- First, there is *full-duplex* and *half-duplex data transfer*. This typically applies to the capability or inability of data terminal equipment (DTE) to support simultaneous, two-way data flow. SNA PU 4 devices (front-end processors such as 3705, 3720, 3725, and 3745 devices) are capable of full-duplex data transfer. Each such device employs a separate data and control path into the control program's transmit and receive buffers.

- Some PU 2.1 devices are also capable of *full duplex data mode*, which is negotiable in the XID-3 format frame—unless the NCP PU definition statement DATMODE=FULL is specified. If FULL is specified, full-duplex mode is forced. PU 2s and PU 1s operate in *half-duplex data mode*.

DCE Definitions

Finally, there is *full duplex* and *half duplex* as it applies to the communication facility, or DCE. This is where most of the technological advancement has been achieved with respect to half and full duplex. DCE installations primarily consist of channel service units (CSUs), data service units (DSUs), or modem devices, and a communications line. The modem can be synchronous or asynchronous and can be analog or digital. The communications line can be two-wire or four-wire and can be leased or switched (that is, dial-up).

Older modems are capable of transmitting or receiving only at a given time. When a DTE wants to transmit data using an older modem, the DTE asserts the Request To Send (RTS) signal to the modem. If the modem *is not* in receive mode, the modem enables its carrier signal in preparation for transmitting data and asserts Clear To Send (CTS). If the modem *is* in receive mode, its Data Carrier Detect (DCD) signal (that is, the carrier signal from the remote modem) is in the active state. The modem does not activate the CTS signal, and the DTE does not transmit, because DCD is in the active state.

Contemporary modems are capable of transmitting and receiving simultaneously over two-wire or four-wire and leased or switched lines. One method uses multiple carrier signals at different frequencies, so that the local modem's transmit and receive signals, as well as the remote modem's transmit and receive signals, each have their own carrier frequency.

DTE equipment in an SDLC environment have configuration options that specify which mode of operation is supported by DCE equipment. The default parameters for most PU 2 devices are set for half duplex, although they can also support full-duplex operation. If the facility is capable of full duplex, RTS can be asserted at all times. If the facility supports half duplex or is operating in a *multipoint* environment using modem-sharing devices (as opposed to multipoint provided by a Postal Telephone and Telegraph [PTT] or by a telephone company), RTS must only be asserted when transmitting. A full-duplex-capable communication facility that connects a PU 4 to a PU 2 device or to a PU 1 device (with each PU device specifying full-duplex DCE capability) experiences improved response time because of reduced turnaround delays.

Older PU 2 and PU 1 devices cannot be configured for full-duplex DCE mode. Also, because older PU 2 and PU 1 devices can only support half-duplex data transfer, transmit and receive data cannot be on the line at the same time (in contrast to a PU 4-to-PU 4 full-duplex exchange).

UNDERSTANDING MULTIPOINT CONNECTIONS

Multipoint operation is a method of sharing a communication facility with multiple locations. The telephone company or PTT communications authorities offer two-wire and four-wire multipoint configurations for analog service (modem attachment) or four-wire for digital service (CSU/DSU attachment). Most implementations are master-polling, multiple-slave drop implementations. The master only connects to one drop at a time. The switching takes place at a designated local exchange in proximity to the master DTE site. Some service providers offer analog multipoint services that support two-way simultaneous communication, which allows DTEs to be configured for permanent RTS.

Modem-sharing devices and line-sharing devices also provide multipoint capability. These implementations allow a single point-to-point link to be shared by multiple devices. Some of these devices have configurable ports for DTE or DCE operation, which allow for configurations that can accommodate multiple sites (called *cascaded configurations*). The main restriction of these devices is that when RTS is active, other users are locked out. You cannot configure DTEs for permanent RTS and you must accept the turnaround delays associated with this mode of operation.

SNA Host Configuration for SRB Networks

When designing source-route bridging (SRB) internetworks featuring routers and IBM Systems Network Architecture (SNA) entities, you must carefully consider the configuration of SNA nodes as well as routing nodes. This appendix provides examples that focus on three specific SNA devices:

- Front-end processors (FEPs)
- Virtual Telecommunications Access Method (VTAM)-switched major nodes
- 3174 cluster controllers

Figure C–1 illustrates a typical environment. Tables C–1 through C–6 present the definition parameters for the devices shown in Figure C–1.

NOTES

This material provides host-related configuration information pertinent to design material provided in Chapter 4, "Designing SRB Internetworks."

Figure C–1
Typical SNA host environment.

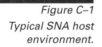
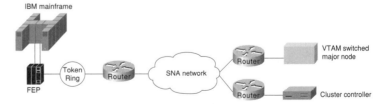

FEP CONFIGURATION

The parameters listed in Tables C–1 through C–6 illustrate input to the Network Control Program (NCP) system generation process that runs in the host processor using the Network Definition Facility

(NDF). The NDF is part of the ACF/NCP/System Support Program utility. The output produced by the generation process is a *load module* that runs in an FEP. Its typical size can be slightly under one MB to more than three MB. The ACF/NCP/System Support Program utility is also used for loading and dumping an FEP.

The following tables outline relevant parameters for generating Token Ring resources.

Table C–1 *BUILD Definition Parameters*

Parameter	Example, Parameter Value, or Range	Parameter Description and Implementation Notes
LOCALTO	1.5	Local ring acknowledgment timer (seconds).
REMOTTO	2.5	Remote ring acknowledgment timer (seconds).
MAXSESS	5000	Maximum amount of sessions for all attached resources.
MXRLINE	None	Maximum number of NTRI physical connections (Version 5.2.1 and earlier only).
MXVLINE	None	Maximum number of NTRI logical connections (Version 5.2.1 and earlier only).
T2TIMER	(*localt2, remott2, N3*)	(Version 5.R4 and later only.) Parameters specify a receiver acknowledgement/timer(T2) for local and remote Token Rings whether from peripheral or subarea nodes. Acceptable values: *localt2* range is 0 to 2.0 seconds; *remott2* range is 0 to 2.0 seconds; *N3* range is 1 to 127 (default is 2). The values for *localt2* and *remott2* should be 10.0 percent of the value of the adjacent stations's T1 timer. *N3* specifies the maximum number of I-frames received without sending an acknowledgment for subarea connections.

The LUDRPOOL definition shown in Table C–2 specifies the number of peripheral resources required for the correct amount of control block storage to be reserved for new connections.

Table C–2 *LUDRPOOL Definition Parameters*

Parameter	Example, Parameter Value, or Range	Parameter Description and Implementation Notes
NUMTYP2	None	Maximum is 16,000.
NUMILU	None	Required for LU Type 2.1 devices (independent LUs).

The GROUP definition shown in Table C–3 specifies group definition parameters.

Table C–3 *GROUP Definition Parameters*

Parameter	Example, Parameter Value, or Range	Parameter Description and Implementation Notes
AUTOGEN	*Number*	Specifies the number of LINE/PU pairs for this group.
COMPOWN	Y	Twin FEP backup capable resource.
COMPSWP	Y	TIC portswap capable (hot backup).
COMPTAD	Y	TIC capable of IPL loading FEP.
DIAL	YES or NO	Applies to ECLTYPE parameter specifications. YES required for (LOGICAL,PERIPHERAL); NO required for all other combinations indicated in ECLTYPE specification.
ECLTYPE	(PHYSICAL,ANY)	Allows PU 4 and PU 2 devices to attach.
	(PHYSICAL, PERIPHERAL)	Allows PU 2 devices only.
	(PHYSICAL, SUBAREA)	Allows PU 4 devices only.
	(LOGICAL, PERIPHERAL)	Defines devices attaching as PU 2.
	(LOGICAL, SUBAREA)	Defines devices attaching as PU 4.
LNCTL	SDLC	Required for NCP processing compatibility.
PHYPORT	None	Required for ECLTYPE LOGICAL only; links this to a ECLTYPE PHYSICAL.
TIMER	error, ras, stap, or lstap	Entry points for NTRI timer routines.

The LINE definition shown in Table C–4 specifies line definition parameters.

Table C–4 *LINE Definition Parameters*

Parameter	Example, Parameter Value, or Range	Parameter Description and Implementation Notes
ADAPTER	TIC1	4-MB Token Ring interface
	TIC2	4- or 16-MB Token Ring interface

Table C–4   *LINE Definition Parameters, Continued*

Parameter	Example, Parameter Value, or Range	Parameter Description and Implementation Notes
ADDRESS	1088 to1095	Range of valid addresses for TICs; only one specified per LINE definition
BEACTO	52	Time in seconds the ring can beacon before TIC considers it down; maximum is 600
LOCADD	4000*abbbbbbb*	Locally administered TIC address, where *a* is any value from 0 to 7; and *b* is any integer value from 0 to 9
LOCALTO	1.5	V5R4; same as in BUILD, but only for PU 4 (LOGICAL, SUBAREA) devices; allows granularity for individual TICs for SUBAREA connections
REMOTTO	2.5	V5R4 parameter; same as LOCALTO; see BUILD parameters in Table C–1
T2TIMER	*localt2, remott2, N3*	V5.4 parameter; see BUILD parameters in Table C–1; can be defined in LINE definition only if a subarea node was defined in GROUP definition
MAXTSL	2044 to 16732	Specifies maximum data in bytes that NTRI can transmit; TIC1 maximum is 2044; TIC2 maximum at TRSPEED16 is 16732
PORTADD	*Number*	For association of physical to logical ECLTYPEs; matches physical or logical ECLTYPE specification
RETRIES	*m, t, n, ml*	Where *m* = number of retries for remote ring sessions, *t* = pause between retry sequence, *n* = number of retry sequences, and *ml* = number of retries in a sequence for local ring sessions
TRSPEED	4 or 16	TIC speed

Table C–5 specifies physical unit (PU) definition parameters.

Table C–5   *FEP Physical Unit (PU) Definition Parameters*

Parameter	Example, Parameter Value, or Range	Parameter Description and Implementation Notes
ADDR	*aa*4000*bccccccc*	Destination service access point (DSAP) and MAC address for the PU of the Token Ring device in the FEP, where *aa* = the DSAP and is a nonzero hexadecimal multiple of 4; *b* = 0 to 7;

Table C–5 *FEP Physical Unit (PU) Definition Parameters, Continued*

Parameter	Example, Parameter Value, or Range	Parameter Description and Implementation Notes
		$c = 0$ to 9; enter 4000 as shown; only specified if ECLTYPE defined in GROUP definition is one of the following: (LOG,SUB), (PHY,SUB), (PHY,ANY)
PUTYPE	1, 2, or 4	Depends on ECLTYPE: • For NTRI LOGICAL resources, only PUTYPE=2 is valid; for NTRI PHYSICAL resources, only PUTYPE=1 is valid • For NTRI PHYSICAL/SUBAREA LINES and PHYSICAL PERIPHERAL LINES, only PUTYPE=1 is valid. For NTRI LOGICAL PERIPHERAL LINES, only PUTYPE=2 is valid
XID	YES or NO	Defines the capability of a PU to receive and respond to an XID while in normal disconnected mode; for NTRI LOGICAL LINES, only YES is valid; for NTRI PHYSICAL LINES, only NO is valid

Table C–6 specifies logical unit (LU) definition parameters.

Table C–6 *FEP Logical Unit (LU) Definition Parameter*

Parameter	Example, Parameter Value, or Range	Parameter Description and Implementation Notes
LOCADDR	0	Specify this response only

VTAM-SWITCHED MAJOR NODE DEFINITIONS

Devices that are attached to Token Ring and communicate with an IBM host application must be defined via the VTAM access method associated with the host. These devices are seen as dial-in resources from the host side and are defined in a configuration component named *Switched Major Node*. Some common definitions used in network configurations are outlined in Table C–7 through Table C–9.

Table C–7 *VBUILD Definition Parameter*

Parameter	Example, Parameter Value, or Range	Parameter Description and Implementation Notes
TYPE	SWNET	Specifies a type of resource for VTAM; SWNET indicates switched major node type

Table C-8 *VTAM PU Definition Parameters*

Parameter	Example, Parameter Value, or Range	Parameter Description and Implementation Notes
IDBLK	017	Typical values: • 017 = 3X74 • 05D = PC-base VTAM PU • 0E2 = Cisco SDLLC (registered with IBM)
IDNUM	xxxxx	Unique number identifying a device
MAXOUT	1 to 7	Number of I-frames sent before acknowledgment is required
MAXDATA	265	Indicates maximum number of bytes a PU 2 device can receive; ignored for PU 2.1, as this value is negotiable Default for 3174 is 521
PUTYPE	2	Only valid value
XID	YES or NO	YES should be used for PU 2.1 devices NO should be specified for any other device

Table C-9 *VTAM LU Definition Parameter*

Parameter	Example, Parameter Value, or Range	Parameter Description and Implementation Notes
LOCADDR	2 through FF	Logical unit (LU) addresses attached to a PU

3174 CLUSTER CONTROLLER CONFIGURATION EXAMPLE

The following configuration was taken from 3174-13R cluster controller serial number 45362 connected to a Token Ring. These entries were used with a specific 3174 running on a 4-Mbps Token Ring. The configuration of this 3174-13R involved three specific configuration screens. Tables C-10 through C-12 list the configuration line numbers, entries used, and descriptions of the configuration line. When applicable, extended descriptions are included for configuration entries that are relevant to the requirements of the routed internetwork.

NOTES

Of particular interest when configuring 3174 devices for a router-based SRB environment are configuration line items 106, 107, and 384 in configuration screen 2 (refer to Table C–9). These specify the required addresses and relevant Token Ring type for the cluster controller.

Table C–10 *3174-13R Screen 1 Configuration Details*

Configuration Line Number	Sample Value	Parameter Description and Implementation Notes
98		Online test password
99	TKNRNG	Description field
100	13R	Model number
101	7	Host attachment type

Table C–11 *3174-13R Screen 2 Configuration Details*

Configuration Line Number	Sample Value	Parameter Description and Implementation Notes
106	4000 2222 4444 04	The first 12 hexadecimal digits form the source MAC address of the cluster controller (4000 2222 4444); the last two digits are the source SAP (SSAP) for LLC2 (0x04 = SNA).
107	4000 0037 4501 04	The first 12 hexadecimal digits form the destination MAC address of the FEP (4000 0037 4501); the last two digits are the DSAP for LLC2 (0x04 for SNA).
108	0045362	Serial number of the cluster controller
110	0	MLT storage support
116	0	Individual port assignment
121	01	Keyboard language
123	0	Country extended code page support
125	00000000	Miscellaneous options (A)
126	00000000	Miscellaneous options (B)
127	0 0	RTM definition
132	0000	Alternate base keyboard selection
136	0000	Standard keyboard layout

Table C–11 *3174-13R Screen 2 Configuration Details, Continued*

Configuration Line Number	Sample Value	Parameter Description and Implementation Notes
137	0000	Modified keyboard layout
138	0	Standard keypad layout
141	A	Magnetic character set
165	0	Compressed program symbols
166	A	Attribute select keypad
168	0	Additional extension; mode key definition
173	0000	DFT options
175	000000	DFT password
179	000	Local format storage
213	0	Between bracket printer sharing
215	45362	PU identification
222	0	Support for command retry
382	0521	Maximum ring I-frame size; range of values is 265 to 2057.
383	2	Maximum number of I-frames 3174 will transmit before awaiting an acknowledgment (transmit window size).
384	0	Ring speed of the Token Ring network: • 0 = 4 Mbps • 1 = 16 Mbps normal token release • 2 = 16 Mbps early token release

Table C–12 *3174-13R Screen 3 Configuration Details*

Configuration Line Number	Sample Value	Parameter Description and Implementation Notes
500	0	CSCM unique
501	TOSFNID	Network identifier
503	TOSFCTLR	LU name

SNA end stations implement Logical Link Control type 2 (LLC2) when attached to a local-area network (LAN). LLC2 implements the following:

- Timers
- Sequencing
- Error recovery
- Windowing
- Guaranteed delivery
- Guaranteed connection

Figure C–2 illustrates how the T1 reply timer and error recovery operates for a 3174. Assume that the link between the two routers just failed. The following sequence characterizes the error recovery process illustrated in :

1. The 3174 sends a data frame and starts its T1 timer.
2. The T1 timer expires after 1.6 seconds.
3. The 3174 goes into error recovery.
4. The 3174 sends an LLC request (a receiver ready with the poll bit on), which requests the 3745 to immediately acknowledge this frame.
5. The 3174 starts its T1 timer.
6. The T1 timer expires after 1.6 seconds.

This operation is retried a total of seven times. The total elapsed time to disconnect the session is calculated as follows:

- The first attempt plus seven retries multiplied by 1.6 seconds:

  = 8 x 1.6 seconds

  = 12.8 seconds

Figure C–2
T1 timer and error recovery process for 3174.

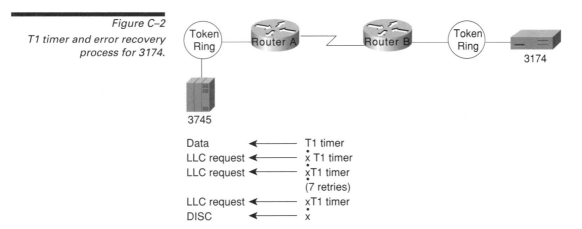

SNA Host Configuration for SDLC Networks

This appendix outlines router implementation information related to the following topics:

- Front-end processor (FEP) configuration for SDLC links
- 3174 SDLC configuration worksheet example

Table D–1 outlines 3x74 SDLC point-to-point connection support for AGS+, MGS, and CGS DCE appliques.

Table D–1 *3x74 SDLC Point-to-Point Connection Support for AGS+, MGS, and CGS DCE Appliques*

Controller Type	RS-232 DCE	RS-232 NRZI/DCE
3274 1st Generation		
• 3274-1C	Supported	Supported
3274 2nd Generation		
• 3274-21C	Not tested	Supported
3274 3rd Generation		
• 3274-31C	Supported	Not tested
• 3274-51C	Supported	Not tested
3274 4th Generation		
• 3274-41C	Need to tie DSR and DTR together on CU side, break DSR to router	Not tested
• 3274-61C	Same as 3274-41C	Supported
• Telex 274	Supported	Not tested
• Telex 1274	Supported	Not tested

Table D–1 *3x74 SDLC Point-to-Point Connection Support for AGS+, MGS, and CGS DCE Appliques, Continued*

Controller Type	RS-232 DCE	RS-232 NRZI/DCE
DCA/IRMA 3274 emulation for DOS workstations	Not tested	Supported
DEC SNA gateway	Not tested	Supported
RS 6000 multiprotocol adapter	Not tested	Supported
3174 Subsystem CUs		
• 3174-01R	Not tested	3174 ties pin 11 low, (-11VDC) which forces the applique into DTE mode (DCE mode is set when pin 11 is set high)
• 3174-03R	Same as 3174-01R	Same as 3174-01R
• 3174-51R	Same as 3174-01R	Same as 3174-01R
3174 Establishment CUs		
• 3174-11R	Not tested	Supported
• 3174-13R	Same as 3174-11R	Not tested
• 3174-61R	Same as 3174-11R	Not tested
• 3174-91R	Same as 3174-11R	Supported
• Telex 1174	Supported	Not tested

FEP CONFIGURATION FOR SDLC LINKS

Table D–2 through Table D–5 present relevant parameter definitions for an FEP configured to operate within a router-based environment. These parameters are configured as part of the system generation process associated with the Network Control Program (NCP) on an IBM host.

Table D–2 *FEP SDLC Configuration Sample GROUP Parameter Listing and Definitions*

Parameter	Sample Value	Description and Implementation Notes
LNCTL	SDLC	Line control parameter that specifies link protocol.
REPLYTO	2	T1 timer; this timer specifies the reply timeout value for LINEs in this GROUP.

Table D–3 *FEP SDLC Configuration Sample LINE Parameter Listing and Definitions*

Parameter	Sample Value	Description and Implementation Notes
ADDRESS	(001,HALF)	The value 001 is the physical LINE interface address of the FEP. The second parameter specifies whether half- or full-duplex data transfer within the FEP is used. It also effects the DUPLEX parameter: If FULL is specified here, DUPLEX defaults to FULL and attempts to modify this characteristic are ignored.
DUPLEX	HALF	This parameter specifies whether the communication line and modem constitute a half-duplex or full-duplex facility. If HALF is specified, the RTS modem signal is activated only when sending data. If FULL is specified, RTS always remains active. Refer to the ADDRESS parameter in this table.
NRZI	YES	Encoding for this line; options are NRZ or NRZI.
RETRIES	(6,5,3)	Number of retries when REPLYTO expires. Entry options: (m, t, n) where m = number of retries, t = pause in seconds between retry cycles, and n = number of retry cycles to repeat. This example would retry six times—pausing the value of the REPLYTO between each RETRY (two seconds per Table D–2), pause five seconds, and repeat this sequence three times for a total of 63 seconds. At the end of this period, the session is terminated.
PAUSE	2	The delay time in milliseconds between poll cycles. The cycle extends from the time NCP polls the first entry in the service order table to the moment polling next begins at the same entry. During this pause, any data available to send to the end station is sent. If end stations have data to send when polled and the time to send the data extends beyond the PAUSE parameter, the next poll cycle begins immediately.

Table D–4 *FEP SDLC Configuration Sample PU Parameter Listing and Definitions*

Parameter	Sample Value	Description and Implementation Notes
ADDR	C1	SDLC address of secondary end station.
MAXDATA	265	Maximum amount of data in bytes (including headers) that the UP can receive in one data transfer; that is, one entire PIU or a PIU segment.
MAXOUT	7	Maximum number of unacknowledged frames that NCP can have outstanding before requesting a response from the end station.

Table D–4   *FEP SDLC Configuration Sample PU Parameter Listing and Definitions, Continued*

Parameter	Sample Value	Description and Implementation Notes
PASSLIM	7	Maximum number of consecutive PIU or PIU segments that NCP sends at one time to the end station represented by this PU definition.
PUTYPE	2	Specifies PU type; PU type 2 and 2.1 are both specified as PUTYPE=2.

Table D–5   *FEP SDLC Configuration Sample LU Parameter Listing and Definitions*

Parameter	Sample Value	Description and Implementation Notes
LOCADDR	2	LU address of devices connected to the end station PU.

3174 SDLC CONFIGURATION WORKSHEET

Table D–6 through Table D–8 present a configuration taken from an SDLC-connected 3174-91R cluster controller. The configuration of this 3174-91R involved three specific configuration screens. Table D–6 through Table D–8 list the configuration line numbers, entries used, and descriptions of the configuration lines for each screen. Where applicable, extended descriptions are included for configuration entries that are relevant to the requirements of the routed internetwork.

Table D–6   *3174-91R Screen 1 Configuration Details*

Configuration Line Number	Sample Value	Parameter Description and Implementation Notes
98		Online test password
99	TKNRNG	Description field
100	91R	Model number
101	2	Host attachment type: • 2 = SDLC • 5 = SNA (channel-attached) • 7 = Token Ring network

---

NOTES

Configuration line items 104, 313, 317, and 340 in Configuration screen 2 (refer to Table D–7) are of particular interest when configuring 3174 devices for a router-based SDLC environment. These lines specify the required SDLC address and relevant SDLC options for the cluster controller.

Table D–7 *3174-91R Screen 2 Configuration Details*

Configuration Line Number	Sample Value	Parameter Description and Implementation Notes
104	C2	Specifies the cluster controller SDLC address. It is the same address that you configure on the router's serial line interface. It also represents the PU address of the controller. In multipoint environments, multiple SDLC addresses may be specified on a single serial interface.
108	0045448	Serial number of the cluster controller
110	0	MLT storage support
116	0	Individual port assignment
121	01	Keyboard language
123	0	Country extended code page support
125	00000000	Miscellaneous options (A)
126	00000000	Miscellaneous options (B)
127	00	RTM definition
132	0000	Alternate base keyboard selection
136	0000	Standard keyboard layout
137	0000	Modified keyboard layout
138	0	Standard keypad layout
141	A	Magnetic character set
150	0	Token Ring network gateway controller
165	0	Compressed program symbols
166	A	Attribute select keypad
168	0	Additional extension; mode key definition
173	0000	DFT options
175	000000	DFT password
179	000	Local format storage
213	0	Between-bracket printer sharing
215	45448	PU identification

Table D–7   *3174-91R Screen 2 Configuration Details, Continued*

Configuration Line Number	Sample Value	Parameter Description and Implementation Notes
220	0	Alert function
310	0	Connect dataset to line operation
313	0	NRZ = 0; NRZI = 1
317	0	Telecommunications facility: • 0 = Nonswitched • 1 = Switched (dial-up)
318	0	Full/half speed transmission; 0 = full speed, 1 = half speed. Controls speed of modem; can be used in areas where line conditions are poor
340	0	RTS control options: • 0 = Controlled RTS (for LSD/MSD operation) • 1 = Permanent RTS (improves performance) • 2 = BSC (not valid for SDLC operation)
365	0	X.21 switched-host DTE connection
370	0	Maximum inbound I-frame size: • 0 = 265 bytes • 1 = 521 bytes (recommended for better performance)

Table D–8   *3174-91R Screen 3 Configuration Details*

Configuration Line Number	Sample Value	Parameter Description and Implementation Notes
500	0	Central Site Change Management (CSCM) unique
501	xxxxxxxx	Network identifier
503	xxxxxxxx	LU name (for CSCM)

Broadcasts in Switched LAN Internetworks

To communicate with all or part of the network, protocols use broadcast and multicast datagrams at Layer 2 of the Open Systems Interconnection (OSI) model. When a node needs to communicate with all of the network, it sends a datagram to MAC address 0xFFFFFFFF (a *broadcast*), which is an address to which the network interface card (NIC) of every host must respond. When a host needs to communicate with part of the network, it sends a datagram to address 0xFFFFFFFF with the leading bit of the vendor ID set to 1 (a *multicast*). Most NICs with that vendor ID respond to a multicast by processing the multicast to its group address.

Because switches work like bridges, they must flood all broadcast and multicast traffic. The accumulation of broadcast and multicast traffic from each device in the network is referred to as *broadcast radiation*.

Because the NIC must interrupt the CPU to process each broadcast or multicast, broadcast radiation affects the performance of hosts in the network. Most often, the host does not benefit from processing the broadcast or multicast—that is, the host is not the destination being sought, it doesn't care about the service that is being advertised, or it already knows about the service. High levels of broadcast radiation can noticeably degrade host performance.

The following sections describe how the desktop protocols—IP, Novell, and AppleTalk—use broadcast and multicast packets to locate hosts and advertise services, and how broadcast and multicast traffic affects the CPU performance of hosts on the network.

USING BROADCASTS WITH IP NETWORKS

There are three sources of broadcasts and multicasts in IP networks:

- *Workstations*—An IP workstation broadcasts an Address Resolution Protocol (ARP) request every time it needs to locate a new IP address on the network. For example, the command **telnet mumble.com** translates into an IP address through a Domain Name System (DNS) search, and then an ARP request is broadcast to find the actual station. Generally,

IP workstations cache 10 to 100 addresses for about two hours. The ARP rate for a typical workstation might be about 50 addresses every two hours or 0.007 ARPs per second. Thus, 2000 IP end stations produce about 14 ARPs per second.

- *Routers*—An IP router is any router or workstation that runs RIP. Some administrators configure all workstations to run RIP as a redundancy and reachability policy. Every 30 seconds, RIP uses broadcasts to retransmit the entire RIP routing table to other RIP routers. If 2000 workstations were configured to run RIP and if 50 packets were required to retransmit the routing table, the workstations would generate 3333 broadcasts per second. Most network administrators configure a small number of routers, usually five to 10, to run RIP. For a routing table that requires 50 packets to hold it, 10 RIP routers would generate about 16 broadcasts per second.

- *Multicast applications*—IP multicast applications can adversely affect the performance of large, scaled, switched networks. Although multicasting is an efficient way to send a stream of multimedia (video data) to many users on a shared-media hub, it affects every user on a flat switched network. A particular packet video application can generate a seven-mega-byte (MB) stream of multicast data that, in a switched network, would be sent to every segment, resulting in severe congestion.

Figure E–1 shows the results of tests that Cisco conducted on the effect of broadcast radiation on a Sun SPARCstation 2 with a standard built-in Ethernet card. The SPARCstation was running SunOS version 4.1.3 without IP multicast enabled. If IP multicast had been enabled, for example, by running Solaris 2.*x*, multicast packets would have affected CPU performance.

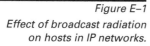

Figure E–1

Effect of broadcast radiation on hosts in IP networks.

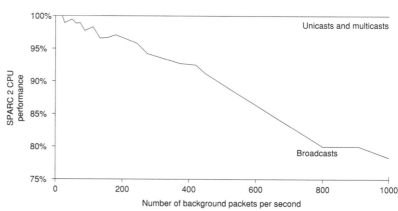

As indicated by the results shown in Figure E–1, an IP workstation can be effectively shut down by broadcasts flooding the network. Although extreme, broadcast peaks of thousands of broadcasts per second have been observed during "broadcast storms." Testing in a controlled environment with a range of broadcasts and multicasts on the network shows measurable system degradation with as few as 100 broadcasts or multicasts per second. Table E–1 shows the average and peak number of broadcasts and multicasts for IP networks ranging from 100 to 10,000 hosts per network.

Table E–1 *Average Number of Broadcasts and Multicasts for IP Networks*

Number of Hosts	Average Percentage of CPU Loss per Host
100	.14
1000	.96
10,000	9.15

Although the numbers in Table E–1 might appear low, they represent an average, well-designed IP network that is not running RIP. When broadcast and multicast traffic peak due to "storm" behavior, peak CPU loss can be orders of magnitude greater than average. Broadcast "storms" can be caused by a device requesting information from a network that has grown too large. So many responses are sent to the original request that the device cannot process them, or the first request triggers similar requests from other devices that effectively block normal traffic flow on the network.

USING BROADCASTS WITH NOVELL NETWORKS

Many PC-based LANs use Novell's Network Operating System (NOS) and NetWare servers. Novell technology poses the following unique scaling problems:

- NetWare servers use broadcast packets to identify themselves and to advertise their services and routes to other networks.

- NetWare clients use broadcasts to find NetWare servers.

- Version 4.0 of Novell's SNMP-based network management applications, such as NetExplorer, periodically broadcast packets to discover changes in the network.

An idle network with a single server with one shared volume and no print services generates one broadcast packet every four seconds. A large LAN with high-end servers might have up to 150 users per PC server. If the LAN has 900 users with a reasonably even distribution, it would have six or seven servers. In an idle state with multiple shared volumes and printers, this might average out to four broadcasts per second, uniformly distributed. In a busy network with route and service requests made frequently, the rate would peak at 15 to 20 broadcasts per second.

Figure E–2 shows the results of tests that Cisco conducted on the effect of broadcast radiation on the performance of an 80386 CPU running at 25 MHz. Performance was measured with the Norton Utilities System Information utility. Background traffic was generated with a Network General Sniffer and consisted of a broadcast destination packet and a multicast destination packet, with data of all zeroes. CPU performance was measurably affected by as few as 30 broadcast or multicast packets per second. Multicast packets had a slightly worse effect than broadcast packets.

Figure E–2

Effect of broadcast radiation on hosts in Novell networks.

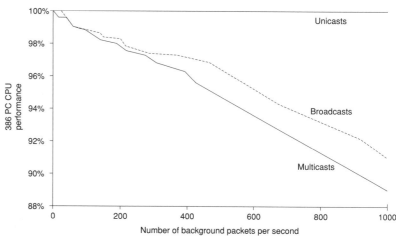

Table E–2 shows the average and peak number of broadcasts and multicasts for Novell networks ranging from 100 to 10,000 hosts per network.

Table E–2   *Average Number of Broadcasts and Multicasts for Novell Networks*

Number of Hosts	Average Percentage of CPU Loss per Host
100	.12
1000	.22
10,000	3.15

The results listed in Table E–2 represent multihour, average operation. Peak traffic load and CPU loss per workstation can be orders of magnitude greater than with average traffic loads. A common scenario is that at 9 a.m. on Monday, everyone starts their computers. Normally, in circumstances with an average level of utilization or demand, the network can handle a reasonable number of stations. However, in circumstances in which everyone requires service at once (a demand peak), the available network capacity can support a much lower number of stations. In determining network capacity requirements, peak demand levels and duration can be more important than average serviceability requirements.

USING BROADCASTS WITH APPLETALK NETWORKS

AppleTalk uses multicasting extensively to advertise services, request services, and resolve addresses. On startup, an AppleTalk host transmits a series of at least 20 packets aimed at resolving its network address (a Layer 3 AppleTalk node number) and obtaining local "zone" information.

Except for the first packet, which is addressed to itself, these functions are resolved through Apple-Talk multicasts.

In terms of overall network traffic, the AppleTalk Chooser is particularly broadcast intensive. The Chooser is the software interface that allows the user to select shared network services. It uses AppleTalk multicasts to find file servers, printers, and other services. When the user opens the Chooser and selects a type of service (for example, a printer), the Chooser transmits 45 multicasts at a rate of one packet per second. If left open, the Chooser sends a five-packet burst with a progressively longer delay. If left open for several minutes, the Chooser reaches its maximum delay and transmits a five-packet burst every 270 seconds. By itself, this does not pose a problem, but in a large network, these packets add to the total amount of broadcast radiation that each host must interpret and then discard.

Other AppleTalk protocols, such as the Name Binding Protocol, which is used to bind a client to a server, and the Router Discovery Protocol, a RIP implementation that is transmitted by all routers and listened to by each station, are broadcast intensive. The system in it called AutoRemounter (part of the Macintosh operating system) is also broadcast intensive.

NOTES

The AppleTalk stack is more efficient than the Novell stack because the AppleTalk stack discards non-AppleTalk broadcasts earlier than the Novell stack discards non-Novell broadcasts.

Figure E–3 shows the results of tests that Cisco conducted on the effect of broadcast radiation on the performance of a Power Macintosh 8100 and a Macintosh IIci. Both CPUs were measurably affected by as few as 15 broadcast or multicast frames per second.

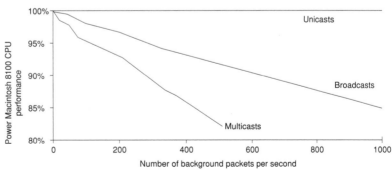

Figure E–3

Effect of broadcast radiation on hosts in AppleTalk networks.

Table E–3 shows the average and peak number of broadcasts and multicasts for AppleTalk networks ranging from 100 to 10,000 hosts per network.

Table E–3   *Average Number of Broadcasts and Multicasts for AppleTalk Networks*

Number of Hosts	Average Percentage of CPU Loss per Host	Peak Percentage of CPU Loss per Host
100	.28	6.00
1,000	2.10	58.00
10,000	16.94	100.00

Slow LocalTalk-to-Ethernet connection devices are a major problem in large-scale AppleTalk networks. These devices fail in large AppleTalk networks because they have limited ARP caches and can process only a few broadcasts per second. Major broadcast storms arise when these devices lose their capability to receive Routing Table Maintenance Protocol (RTMP) updates. After this occurs, these devices send ARP requests for all known devices, thereby accelerating the network degradation because they cause their neighbor devices to fail and send their own ARP requests.

USING BROADCASTS WITH MULTIPROTOCOL NETWORKS

The following can be said about the interaction of AppleTalk, IPX, and IP:

- AppleTalk stacks ignore any other Layer 3 protocol.
- AppleTalk and IP broadcast and multicast packets affect the operation of IP and IPX stacks. AppleTalk and IP packets enter the stack and then are discarded, which consumes CPU resources.

These findings show that AppleTalk has a cumulative effect on IPX and IP networks.

APPENDIX F

References and Recommended Reading

BOOKS AND PERIODICALS

Apple Computer, Inc. *AppleTalk Network System Overview.* Reading, Massachusetts: Addison-Wesley Publishing Company, Inc.; 1989.

Apple Computer, Inc. *Planning and Managing AppleTalk Networks.* Reading, Massachusetts: Addison-Wesley Publishing Company, Inc.; 1991.

Black, U. *Data Networks: Concepts, Theory and Practice.* Englewood Cliffs, New Jersey: Prentice Hall; 1989.

Black, U. *Physical Level Interfaces and Protocols.* Los Alamitos, California: IEEE Computer Society Press; 1988.

Case, J.D., J.R. Davins, M.S. Fedor, and M.L. Schoffstall. "Network Management and the Design of SNMP." *ConneXions: The Interoperability Report,* Vol. 3: March 1989.

Case, J.D., J.R. Davins, M.S. Fedor, and M.L. Schoffstall. "Introduction to the Simple Gateway Monitoring Protocol." *IEEE Network:* March 1988.

Clark, W. "SNA Internetworking." *ConneXions: The Interoperability Report*, Vol. 6, No. 3: March 1992.

Coltun, R. "OSPF: An Internet Routing Protocol." *ConneXions: The Interoperability Report*, Vol. 3, No. 8: August 1989.

Comer, D.E. *Internetworking with TCP/IP: Principles, Protocols, and Architecture*, Vol. I, 2nd ed. Englewood Cliffs, New Jersey: Prentice Hall; 1991.

Davidson, J. *An Introduction to TCP/IP.* New York, New York: Springer-Verlag; 1992.

Ferrari, D. *Computer Systems Performance Evaluation.* Englewood Cliffs, New Jersey: Prentice Hall; 1978.

Garcia-Luna-Aceves, J.J. "Loop-Free Routing Using Diffusing Computations." *IEEE/ACM Transactions on Networking*, Vol. 1, No. 1, 1993.

Green, J.K. *Telecommunications*, 2nd ed. Homewood, Illinois: Business One Irwin; 1992.

Hagans, R. "Components of OSI: ES-IS Routing." *ConneXions: The Interoperability Report*, Vol. 3, No. 8: August 1989.

Hares, S. "Components of OSI: Inter-Domain Routing Protocol (IDRP)." *ConneXions: The Interoperability Report*, Vol. 6, No. 5: May 1992.

Jones, N.E.H. and D. Kosiur. *Macworld Networking Handbook*. San Mateo, California: IDG Books Worldwide, Inc.; 1992.

Joyce, S.T. and J.Q. Walker II. "Advanced Peer-to-Peer Networking (APPN): An Overview." *ConneXions: The Interoperability Report*, Vol. 6, No. 10: October 1992.

Kousky, K. "Bridging the Network Gap." *LAN Technology*, Vol. 6, No. 1: January 1990.

LaQuey, Tracy. *The Internet Companion: A Beginner's Guide to Global Networking*, Reading, Massachusetts: Addison-Wesley Publishing Company, Inc.; 1994.

Leinwand, A. and K. Fang. *Network Management: A Practical Perspective*. Reading, Massachusetts: Addison-Wesley Publishing Company, Inc.; 1993.

Lippis, N. "The Internetwork Decade." *Data Communications*, Vol. 20, No. 14: October 1991.

McNamara, J.E. *Local Area Networks*. Digital Press, Educational Services, Digital Equipment Corporation, 12 Crosby Drive, Bedford, MA 01730.

Malamud, C. *Analyzing DECnet/OSI Phase V*. New York, New York: Van Nostrand Reinhold; 1991.

Malamud, C. *Analyzing Novell Networks*. New York, New York: Van Nostrand Reinhold; 1991.

Malamud, C. *Analyzing Sun Networks*. New York, New York: Van Nostrand Reinhold; 1991.

Martin, J. *SNA: IBM's Networking Solution*. Englewood Cliffs, New Jersey: Prentice Hall; 1987.

Martin, J., with K.K. Chapman and the ARBEN Group, Inc. *Local Area Networks. Architectures and Implementations*. Englewood Cliffs, New Jersey: Prentice Hall; 1989.

Medin, M. "The Great IGP Debate—Part Two: The Open Shortest Path First (OSPF) Routing Protocol." *ConneXions: The Interoperability Report*, Vol. 5, No. 10: October 1991.

Meijer, A. *Systems Network Architecture: A tutorial*. New York, New York: John Wiley & Sons, Inc.; 1987.

Miller, M.A. *LAN Protocol Handbook*. San Mateo, California: M&T Books; 1990.

Miller, M.A. *LAN Troubleshooting Handbook*. San Mateo, California: M&T Books; 1989.

O'Reilly, T. and G. Todino. *Managing UUCP and Usenet*, 10th ed. Sebastopol, California: O'Reilly & Associates, Inc.; 1992.

Perlman, R. *Interconnections: Bridges and Routers*. Reading, Massachusetts: Addison-Wesley Publishing Company, Inc.; 1992.

Perlman, R. and R. Callon. "The Great IGP Debate—Part One: IS-IS and Integrated Routing." *ConneXions: The Interoperability Report*, Vol. 5, No. 10: October 1991.

Rose, M.T. *The Open Book: A Practical Perspective on OSI*. Englewood Cliffs, New Jersey: Prentice Hall; 1990.

Rose, M.T. *The Simple Book: An Introduction to Management of TCP/IP-based Internets*. Englewood Cliffs, New Jersey: Prentice Hall; 1991.

Ross, F.E. "FDDI—A Tutorial." *IEEE Communications Magazine*, Vol. 24, No. 5: May 1986.

Schlar, S.K. *Inside X.25: A Manager's Guide*. New York, New York: McGraw-Hill, Inc.; 1990.

Schwartz, M. *Telecommunications Networks: Protocols, Modeling, and Analysis*. Reading, Massachusetts: Addison-Wesley Publishing Company, Inc.; 1987.

Sherman, K. *Data Communications: A User's Guide*. Englewood Cliffs, New Jersey: Prentice Hall; 1990.

Sidhu, G.S., R.F. Andrews, and A.B. Oppenheimer. *Inside AppleTalk*, 2nd ed. Reading, Massachusetts: Addison-Wesley Publishing Company, Inc.; 1990.

Spragins, J.D. et al. *Telecommunications Protocols and Design*. Reading, Massachusetts: Addison-Wesley Publishing Company, Inc.; 1991.

Stallings, W. *Data and Computer Communications*. New York, New York: Macmillan Publishing Company; 1991.

Stallings, W. *Handbook of Computer-Communications Standards*, Vols. 1–3. Carmel, Indiana: Howard W. Sams, Inc.; 1990.

Stallings, W. *Local Networks*, 3rd ed. New York, New York: Macmillan Publishing Company; 1990.

Sunshine, C.A. (ed.). *Computer Network Architectures and Protocols*, 2nd ed. New York, New York: Plenum Press; 1989.

Tannenbaum, A.S. *Computer Networks*, 2nd ed. Englewood Cliffs, New Jersey: Prentice Hall; 1988.

Terplan, K. *Communication Networks Management*. Englewood Cliffs, New Jersey: Prentice Hall; 1992.

Tsuchiya, P. "Components of OSI: IS-IS Intra-Domain Routing." *ConneXions: The Interoperability Report*, Vol. 3, No. 8: August 1989.

Tsuchiya, P. "Components of OSI: Routing (An Overview)." *ConneXions: The Interoperability Report*, Vol. 3, No. 8: August 1989.

Zimmerman, H. "OSI Reference Model—The ISO Model of Architecture for Open Systems Interconnection." *IEEE Transactions on Communications* COM-28, No. 4: April 1980.

TECHNICAL PUBLICATIONS AND STANDARDS

Advanced Micro Devices. *The Supernet Family for FDDI.* Technical Manual Number 09779A. Sunnyvale, California; 1989.

———— *The Supernet Family for FDDI.* 1989 Data Book Number 09734C. Sunnyvale, California; 1989.

American National Standards Institute X3T9.5 Committee. *FDDI Station Management (SMT).* Rev. 6.1; March 15, 1990.

————. Revised Text of ISO/DIS 8802/2 for the Second DIS Ballot, "Information Processing Systems—Local Area Networks." Part 2: Logical Link Control. 1987-01-14.

———— T1.606. Integrated Services Digital Network (ISDN)—Architectural Framework and Service Description for Frame-Relaying Bearer Service. 1990.

———— T1.617. Integrated Services Digital Network (ISDN)—Signaling Specification for Frame Relay Bearer Service for Digital Subscriber Signaling System Number 1 (DSS1). 1991.

———— T1.618. Integrated Services Digital Network (ISDN)—Core Aspects of Frame Protocol for Use with Frame Relay Bearer Service. 1991.

ATM Data Exchange Interface (DXI) Specification, Version 1.0. Document ATM_FORUM/93-590R1; August 4,1993.

Banyan Systems, Inc. *VINES Protocol Definition.* DA254-00, Rev. 1.0. Westboro, Massachusetts; February 1990.

Bellcore. *Generic System Requirements in Support of a Switched Multi-Megabit Data Service.* Technical Advisory, TA-TSY-000772; October 1989.

————. *Local Access System Generic Requirements, Objectives, and Interface Support of Switched Multi-Megabit Data Service.* Technical Advisory TA-TSY-000773, Issue 1; December 1985.

————. *Switched Multi-Megabit Data Service (SMDS) Operations Technology Network Element Generic Requirements.* Technical Advisory TA-TSY-000774.

Chapman, J.T. and M. Halabi. *HSSI: High-Speed Serial Interface Design Specification.* Menlo Park, California and Santa Clara, California: Cisco Systems and T3Plus Networking, Inc.; 1990.

Consultative Committee for International Telegraph and Telephone. *CCITT Data Communications Networks—Services and Facilities, Terminal Equipment and Interfaces, Recommendations X.1–X.29.* Yellow Book, Vol. VIII, Fascicle VIII.2; 1980.

————. *CCITT Data Communications Networks—Interfaces, Recommendations X.20–X.32.* Red Book, Vol. VIII, Fascicle VIII.3; 1984.

DDN Protocol Handbook. Four volumes; 1989.

Defense Communications Agency. *Defense Data Network X.25 Host Interface Specification.* Order number AD A137 427; December 1983.

Digital Equipment Corporation. *DECnet/OSI Phase V: Making the Transition from Phase IV.* EK-PVTRN-BR; 1989.

———. *DECserver 200 Local Area Transport (LAT) Network Concepts.* AA-LD84A-TK; June 1988.

———. *DIGITAL Network Architecture (Phase V).* EK-DNAPV-GD-001; September 1987.

Digital Equipment Corporation, Intel Corporation, Xerox Corporation. *The Ethernet, A Local-Area Network, Data Link Layer and Physical Layer Specifications.* Ver. 2.0; November 1982.

Feinler, E.J., et al. *DDN Protocol Handbook*, Vols. 1–4, NIC 50004, 50005, 50006, 50007. Defense Communications Agency. Alexandria, Virginia; December 1985.

Garcia-Luna-Aceves, J.J. "A Unified Approach to Loop-Free Routing Using Distance Vectors or Link States." ACM 089791-332-9/89/0009/0212, pp. 212–223; September 1989.

Hemrick, C. and L. Lang. "Introduction to Switched Multi-megabit Data Service (SMDS), an Early Broadband Service." *Proceedings of the XIII International Switching Symposium* (ISS 90), May 27–June 1, 1990.

Hewlett-Packard Company. X.25: The PSN Connection; An Explanation of Recommendation X.25. 5958-3402; October 1985.

IEEE 802.2—*Local Area Networks Standard, 802.2 Logical Link Control.* ANSI/IEEE Standard; October 1985.

IEEE 802.3—*Local Area Networks Standard, 802.3 Carrier Sense Multiple Access.* ANSI/IEEE Standard; October 1985.

IEEE 802.5—*Local Area Networks Standard, 802.5 Token Ring Access Method.* ANSI/IEEE Standard; October 1985.

IEEE 802.6—*Local & Metropolitan Area Networks Standard, 802.6 Distributed Queue Dual Bus (DQDB) Subnetwork of a Metropolitan Area Network (MAN).* ANSI/IEEE Standard; December 1990.

International Business Machines Corporation. ACF/NCP/VS network control program, system support programs: general information. GC30-3058.

———. *Advanced Communications Function for VTAM (ACF/VTAM), general information: introduction. GS27-0462.*

———. *Advanced Communications Function for VTAM, general information: concepts. GS27-0463.*

———. *Dictionary of Computing. SC20-1699-7; 1987.*

———. *Local Area Network Technical Reference. SC30-3883.*

———. *Network Problem Determination Application: general information. GC34-2010.*

———. *Synchronous Data Link Control: general information. GA27-3093.*

———. *Systems Network Architecture: concepts and products. GC30-3072.*

————. *Systems Network Architecture: technical overview.* GC30-3073-1; 1985.

————. *Token-Ring Network Architecture Reference.* SC30-3374.

————. *Token-Ring Problem Determination Guide.* SX27-3710-04; 1990.

International Organization for Standardization. *Information Processing System—Open System Interconnection; Specification of Abstract Syntax Notation One (ASN.1).* International Standard 8824; December 1987.

McGraw-Hill/Data Communications. *McGraw-Hill's Compilation of Data Communications Standards.* Edition III; 1986.

National Security Agency. *Blacker Interface Control Document.* March 21, 1989.

Novell, Inc. IPX Router Specification, Version 1.10. Part Number 107-000029-001. October 16, 1992.

————. NetWare Link Services Protocol (NLSP) Specification, Revision 0.9. Part Number 100-001708-001. March 1993.

StrataCom. *Frame Relay Specification with Extensions.* 001-208966, Rev.1.0; September 18, 1990.

Xerox Corporation. *Internet Transport Protocols.* XNSS 029101; January 1991.

K

L

CISCO CERTIFIED INTERNETWORK EXPERT

Cisco's CCIE certification programs set the professional benchmark for internetworking expertise. CCIEs are recognized throughout the internetworking industry as being the most highly qualified of technical professionals. And, because the CCIE programs certify individuals—not companies—employers are guaranteed any CCIE with whom they work has met the same stringent qualifications as every other CCIE in the industry.

To ensure network performance and reliability in today's dynamic information systems arena, companies need internetworking professionals who have knowledge of both established and newer technologies. Acknowledging this need for specific expertise, Cisco has introduced three CCIE certification programs:

WAN Switching

ISP/Dial

Routing & Switching

CCIE certification requires a solid background in internetworking. The first step in obtaining CCIE certification is to pass a two-hour Qualification exam administered by Sylvan-Prometric. The final step in CCIE certification is a two-day, hands-on lab exam that pits the candidate against difficult build, break, and restore scenarios.

Just as training and instructional programs exist to help individuals prepare for the written exam, Cisco is pleased to announce its first CCIE Preparation Lab. The CCIE Preparation Lab is located at Wichita State University in Wichita Kansas, and is available to help prepare you for the final step toward CCIE status.

Cisco designed the CCIE Preparation Lab to assist CCIE candidates with the lab portion of the actual CCIE lab exam. The Preparation Lab at WSU emulates the conditions under which CCIE candidates are tested for their two-day CCIE Lab Examination. As almost any CCIE will corroborate, the lab exam is the most difficult element to pass for CCIE certification.

Registering for the lab is easy. Simply complete and fax the form located on the reverse side of this letter to WSU. For more information, please visit the WSU Web page at www.engr.twsu.edu/cisco/ or Cisco's Web page at www.cisco.com.

CISCO CCIE PREPARATION LAB

REGISTRATION FORM

Please attach a business card or print the following information:

Name/Title: _____

Company: _____

Company Address: _____

City/State/Zip: _____

Country Code (_____) Area Code (_____) Daytime Phone Number _____

Country Code (_____) Area Code (_____) Evening Phone Number _____

Country Code (_____) Area Code (_____) Fax Number _____

E-mail Address: _____

Circle the number of days you want to reserve lab: 1   2   3   4   5

Week and/or date(s) preferred (3 choices):

_____

_____

_____

Have you taken and passed the written CCIE exam?   Yes   No

List any CISCO courses you have attended:

Registration fee: _____ $500 per day × _____ day(s) = Total _____

Check Enclosed (Payable to WSU Conference Office)

Charge to: _____   MasterCard or Visa exp. Date _____

CC# _____

Name on Card _____

Cardholder Signature _____

Refunds/Cancellations: The full registration fee will be refunded if your cancellation is received at least 15 days prior to the first scheduled lab day.

Wichita State University
University Conferences
1845 Fairmount
Wichita, KS 67260
Attn: Kimberly Moore
Tel: 800-550-1306
Fax: 316-686-6520